George Watt

Economic Products of India Exhibited in the Economic Court, Calcutta International Exhibition 1883 - 84

Part VI

George Watt

Economic Products of India Exhibited in the Economic Court, Calcutta International Exhibition 1883 - 84
Part VI

ISBN/EAN: 9783741118029

Manufactured in Europe, USA, Canada, Australia, Japa

Cover: Foto ©Lupo / pixelio.de

Manufactured and distributed by brebook publishing software (www.brebook.com)

George Watt

Economic Products of India Exhibited in the Economic Court, Calcutta International Exhibition 1883 - 84

ECONOMIC PRODUCTS OF INDIA

EXHIBITED IN THE ECONOMIC COURT,

Calcutta International Exhibition, 1883-84.

BY

GEORGE WATT, M.B., C.M., F.L.S.,

BENGAL EDUCATIONAL SERVICE.

In charge of the Economic Court and of the Central Office, Calcutta International Exhibition of 1883-84.

ASSISTED BY

L. LEOTARD,

IMPERIAL REVENUE AND AGRICULTURAL DEPARTMENT.

PART VI.

FOODS, FOOD-STUFFS, AND FODDERS.

CALCUTTA:

PRINTED BY THE SUPERINTENDENT OF GOVERNMENT PRINTING, INDIA.

1883.

ECONOMIC PRODUCTS OF INDIA

EXHIBITED AT THE

Calcutta International Exhibition, 1883-84.

PART VI.—Foods, Food-stuffs, and Fodders.

ABIES.

Abies Webbiana, *Lindl.*, CONIFERÆ. 1

THE HIMALAYAN SILVER FIR.

Vern.—*Bádar*, KASHMIR; *Rag, re, tosh, spun, rewari, pun, palúdar, búdar*, HIMALAYAN NAMES; *Gobria sulah*, NEPAL; *Ragha*, KUMAUN; *Dumohing*, BHUTIA.

Found in the Himalaya, from the Indus to Bhutan; in the North-Western Himalaya, between 7,000 and 12,000 feet; in the inner ranges of Sikkim and Bhutan, between 9,000 and 13,000 feet; in the outer ranges it does not descend below 10,000 feet.

In tracts near the Jhelum the twigs and leaves are cut and stored for winter use as fodder and litter for cattle. (*Brandis.*)

ABROMA.

Abroma augusta, *Linn.*, STERCULIACEÆ. 2

Vern.—*Ulatkambal*, BENG.

A small bush, widely spread, native or cultivated, throughout the hotter parts of India.

Flowers most profusely during the rains, and the seeds ripen in the cold season. The fruits are five-celled, with many seeds in each cell.

ABRUS.

Abrus precatorius, *Linn.*, LEGUMINOSÆ. 3

INDIAN OR WILD LIQUORICE ROOT, *Eng.*; LIANE À REGLISSE, *Fr.*

Vern.—*Gunchi, rati, chirmiti*, HIND; *Gunja, ghungachi*, BOM.; *Maspati*, NEPAL; *Kunch, gunch, chun-hati*, BENG.; *Gunja, krish, nala, kaka chinchi*, SANS.; *Aainudek*, ARAB.; *Chashme-khuros*, PERS.; *Gundumani*, TAM.; *Ghurie-ghénsá*, TEL.

A beautiful climber, met with all along the Himalayas, ascending to 3,000 feet, and spreading through the plains of India to Ceylon and Siam.

There are three principal varieties described by **Roxburgh**—

1st.—With rose-coloured flowers, red seed and black eye.
2nd.—With dark-coloured flowers, black seed and white eye.
3rd.—With white flowers and white seed.

ACACIA.

The seeds, known vulgarly as crab's eyes, are said to be used in Egypt as food when boiled; if eaten in any quantity they produce violent headache. When injected hypodermically they are poisonous.

ACACIA.

4 **Acacia arabica,** *Willd.*, LEGUMINOSÆ.

INDIAN GUM ARABIC.

Vern.—*Babúl, babla, kikar,* HIND., BENG., and DEC.; *Vabbúla, barbara,* SANS.; *Ammughilan,* ARAB.; *Kari-mughilan,* PERS.; *Babboa,* SIND.; *Karúvelum,* TAM.; *Nella tuma,* TEL.; *Babhúla, kali-kiker, ráma-kúti,* BOM.; *Gobli,* KAN.

Wild in Sind, Rajputana, Guzerat, and the Northern Deccan; common everywhere throughout the plains of India.

The green pods with tender shoots and leaves are given as fodder for cattle, sheep, goats, and camels; and are specially valuable for this purpose during a season of drought when other fodder fails.

The Gum is highly nutritious, and to a limited extent forms an article of food, largely so in times of scarcity; in fact, there are few trees more valuable to the cultivator than the babul. It yields his most valuable timber, luxuriating on the poorest waste lands, and even in seasons of drought it is ever-green. Its bark forms a useful domestic medicine, and along with the leaves and pods it is also used in dyeing and tanning. The leaves are a never-failing source of fodder, and the gum an article of food; each tree yielding about 2 lbs. The young, thorny twigs are universally used for dry fences to protect certain crops; tied into bundles, they form decoys for fishermen.

5 **A. Catechu,** *Willd.*

CATECHU, *Eng.*; CUCHORE, *Fr.*; CATECHU, *Germ.*

Vern.—*Khair, katha,* HIND.; *Khayer,* BENG.; *Khaderi, khaira,* BOM.; *Katthah,* DEC.; *Khoira, koir,* ASS.; *Khadir,* SANS.; *Khoiru,* URIYA; *Karangalli, búga, kasku kutti, wodalior,* TAM.; *Kanchu, podala-manu,* TEL.; *Rat-kihiri,* CINGH.; *Sha,* BURM.

A moderate-sized, gregarious, thorny, deciduous tree, common in most parts of India and Burma, extending in the sub-Himalayan tract westward to the Indus. (*Gamble.*)

The chief product of this tree is *kath* and cutch, obtained by boiling down a decoction from the chopped wood, say for 20 hours continuously; twigs are then placed in it. On these twigs the *kath* crystallises. Both *kath* and cutch are known commercially as Catechu, but the former is regarded as purer than the latter, and is largely used as an ingredient in the prepared *pán* or betel-leaf which the natives of India are so fond of chewing. The *kath* is reduced to a fine powder, a little of which is smeared on the *pán* leaf, together with some white lime and crushed betel-nuts. It is the *kath* in combination with the lime which gives the teeth and lips the red colour so characteristic of Hindus. Cutch is made by boiling down the decoction until it forms a hard extract; it is used as a tan and a medicine—the true Catechu of European commerce.

6 **A. concinna,** *DC.*

Vern.—*Rithá, kochi,* HIND.; *Ban-rithá,* BENG.; *Aila, rassaul,* OUDH; *Sikekai, shika,* BOM., DEC.; *Shika,* TAM.; *Chikaya, gogu,* TEL.; *Ken bwon, soopwotnway,* BURM.; *Sigé,* KAN.

A climbing shrub found in South India, Bengal, Assam, and Burma. Ainslie first described the properties of the pods. Under the name of

'soap-pods' they are largely used instead of soap as a detergent, especially in washing the hair; they are also deobstruent and expectorant.
The acid leaves are eaten.

Acacia Jacquemontii, *Benth.* 7

Vern.—*Hansa*, AFG.; *Kikar, babul, bamul, babbil*, PB.; *Ratabauli*, GUZ.

A small, bushy, thorny shrub met with on the east flank of the Sulaiman Range, ascending to 2,500 and at times to 3,200 feet; on the outer Himalaya near the Jhelum to about the same elevation; on the Punjab plains, in Sindh, and on the banks of the Nerbudda. Common in ravines and dry water-courses in Rájputana and North Guzerat. (*Brandis.*)
The bark of the root is used in the distillation of spirits; the branches are cut, and the leaves, thrashed out with sticks, are used as fodder.

A. leucophlæa, *Willd.* 8

Vern.—*Safed kikar, rerú, raunj, karir, ringa, rinj*, HIND.; *Sharab-kikar*, DEC.; *Hevúr, pándharyá*, BOM.; *Ve-velam*, TAM.; *Tellatúma*, TEL.; *Aring*, RAJ.; *Tanoung*, BURM.

Found on the plains of the Punjab, from Lahore to Delhi, and in the forests of Central and South India and Burma.
The young pods and seeds are eaten, and even the bark in times of scarcity. The latter is used in preparing spirits from sugar and palm-juice, to precipitate, by the tannin which it contains, the albuminous substances in the juice. The fruit is largely collected for fodder in the Punjab.

A. modesta, *Wall.* 9

Vern.—*Palosa*, AFG.; *Phulahi*, PB.

Found on the Sulaiman and Salt Ranges, the sub-Himalayan tract, between the Indus and the Sutlej, and the northern part of the Punjab plains.
This is one of the characteristic trees of the Punjab. The leaves and fallen blossoms are collected for fodder.

ACER.

Acer cæsium, *Wall* SAPINDACEÆ. 10

A. pictum, *Thunb.* 11

Syn.—A. CULTRATUM, *Wall.*

Vern.—(Of the former) *Mandar, trekhan, tilpattar*, PB.; *Kilu*, KUMAUN. (Of the latter) *Kilpattar, trekhan, kakru, kanzal* or *hanzal, kanjar, jerimu, laur*, PB.; *Kancheli*, N. W. P.; *Dhadonjra, jerimu*, SIMLA.

Large, deciduous trees common on the North-West Himalaya from the Indus to Nepal, ascending to 11,000 feet.
The branches are lopped for fodder.

A. villosum, *Wall.* 12

Vern.—*Karendera*, SIMLA.

A large, handsome tree of the temperate Himalaya, from Kashmir to Nepal, altitude 7,000 to 9,000 feet.
Leaves lopped for fodder.

ADHATO-DA.

ACORUS.

13 **Acorus Calamus,** *Linn.*, AROIDEÆ.

THE SWEET-FLAG.

Vern.—*Bach, ghorbach,* HIND.; *Vakhanda,* BOM.; *Vacha,* SANS.; *Vaj,* ARAB.; *Agre turki,* PERS.; *Bach,* BENG; *Bari boj,* PB.; *Vashambu,* TAM.; *Vadaja,* TEL.; *Linhe,* BURM.

A semi-aquatic perennial, with indefinitely branched rhizomes, from which rise sword-shaped leaves 2 to 3 feet in length; a native of Europe and North America; cultivated in damp, marshy places in India and Burma, altitude 3,000 to 6,000 feet; exceedingly common in Manipur and the Naga hills, often on the cultivated fields, spreading apparently from the division walls. The whole plant has a strong, sweet, aromatic smell.

Occasional in the Punjab Himalaya from 3,000 to 6,000 feet. (*Dr. Stewart.*)

The leaves of the American species are said never to be eaten by cattle.

ADANSONIA.

14 **Adansonia digitata,** *Linn.*, MALVACEÆ.

THE BAOBAB TREE, SOUR GOURD OF MONKEY BREAD TREE OF AFRICA.

Vern.—*Gourkh amli,* HIND.; *Hathi-khatyan,* DEC.; *Anai-puliya-roy,* TAM.; *Hujed,* ARAB.; *Gorakh chints churi chints,* BOM.

A native of Africa, growing to the height of 40 feet only, with a diameter of some 30 feet, an old Baobab being more like a forest than a single tree. Cultivated in some parts of India to a small extent. It deserves to be extended.

The fruit, which is of the size of a lemon, resembles a gourd, contains many black seeds, is somewhat acid, and makes a cooling and refreshing drink. It is also eaten by the natives. **Major Pedley**, in his expedition in search of Mungo Park, lived almost exclusively on it for twelve days. In Guzerat, the fishermen along the sea coast use the fruit as a float for their nets, eat the leaves with their food, and consider them cooling. In Senegal the negroes use the bark and leaves powdered as a condiment.

Adenanthera aculeata, *Roxb. See* **Prosopis spicigera,** *Linn.*, LEGUMINOSÆ.

ADHATODA.

15 **Adhatoda Vasica,** *Nees,* ACANTHACEÆ.

Vern.—*Arusha,* HIND.; *Bakas, vásaka,* BENG.; *Bhekkar, basúti, torabujja, bashang arús,* HIMALAYAN NAMES; *Arus, vasaka,* SANS.; *Adha, dodé,* TAM.; *Adasara,* TEL.

A small shrub common in the sub-Himalayan tract from Nepal westward, throughout the plains of India up to 4,000 feet. A small, much-branched, gregarious bush in the Naga hills, grown as a hedge plant to cover the passages leading to the villages.

Not browsed by any animals except goats, and even these crop only a few leaves.

ÆGLE.

Ægle Marmelos, *Correa*, RUTACEÆ. 16

THE BAEL FRUIT.

Vern.—*Bel*, HIND., BENG.; *Bela, bila, bilva*, BOM.; *Sriphal*, SANS. (the *Bilva, Mabura* or *Matura* of the ancients); *Vilva*, TAM.; *Maredu*, TEL.; *Okshit*, BURM. (**Roxburgh** says a small variety is called *Shriphula* in Bengal).

A tree of the sub-Himalayan forest from the Jhelum eastward, and South India and Burma.

Flowers in the hot season, and bears its hard-shelled fruit, which is ripe after the rains in Southern India, and in the early spring in Lower Bengal and the Upper Provinces.

The fruit when ripe is sweetish, wholesome, nutritious and very palatable, and much esteemed and eaten by all classes. The ripe fruit, diluted with water, forms, with the addition of a small quantity of tamarind and sugar, a delicious and cooling drink.

ÆSCULUS. 17

Æsculus indica, *Colebr.*, SAPINDACEÆ.

THE INDIAN HORSE CHESTNUT.

Vern.—*Bankhor, gún, kanor*, HIND., PB.

A native of the Western Himalayas, ranging from 4,000 to 10,000 feet in altitude, and spreading from the Indus to Nepal. It grows on any soil, and produces annually an abundant crop of nuts and thick foliage.

The nuts are variously utilised; in Turkey the nuts of the European species are ground with other food and given to horses, hence the name; in France they are employed in the manufacture of starch; in Ireland they are macerated in water, and being saponaceous are used to whiten linen; in the Himalayas they are eaten greedily by cattle, and in times of drought and scarcity by men after being steeped in water, and sometimes mixed with flour. The leaves are lopped for cattle fodder.

AGARICUS.

Agaricus campestris, *Linn.*, FUNGI. 18

THE MUSHROOM.

Vern.—*Alombe, khumbah*, BOM.; *Mánskhel*, KASHMIR; *Moksha*, CHAMBA; *Khúmbah, khámbúr, chattri*, AFG. BAZAR NAMES; *Kúmbh samarogh (Stewart), Herar (Poisonous forms).*

There are several species, used indiscriminately, but as these have not as yet been accurately determined by botanists, it is preferable to refer to all under the common name which in English they would doubtlessly receive, *viz.*, The Mushroom.

The common mushroom, says **Dr. Stewart**, is abundant in cattle fields in many parts of the Central Punjab after the rains, and also abounds in the desert tracts of Central and Southern Punjab. It is largely eaten by the natives, and is described as excellent and equal to the English mushroom by those Europeans who have eaten it. It is also extensively dried for future consumption, and is said to preserve its flavour tolerably well. Mushrooms are largely used in the manufacture of ketchup.

AGAVE.

19 **Agave americana,** *Linn.*, AMARYLLIDEÆ.

AMERICAN ALOE; VEGETABLE SILK.

Vern.—*Pita, bakas-puttah, bans keora, anink-katrashai, peetha-kalabantha,* TAM.

A large, succulent-leaved plant which may be 40 or 50 years old before flowering. The flower stem grows often six inches a day attaining the height of 20 or 30 feet.

Originally a native of America, it is now wild in many parts of India.

In Mexico a fermented liquor called *Pulque* is made from the stem by incision, and from this an ardent spirit of disagreeable odour is distilled.

AGLAIA.

20 **Aglaia edulis,** *A. Gray*, MELIACEÆ.

Vern.—*Late mahwa,* NEPAL; *Sinakadang,* LEPCHA; *Gumi,* GARROW HILLS and SYLHET.

A middling size tree of Eastern Bengal, as also the Garrow Hills and Sylhet; flowers in June-July; fruit ripens two or three months later.

Fruit is eaten by the natives.

AGROSTIS.

21 **Agrostis alba,** *Linn.*, GRAMINEÆ.

FIORIN OR WHITE BENT GRASS.

Syn.—A. STOLONIFERA, *Savi*; A. SYLVATICA, *Host*.

Inhabits Northern India, and ascends the Himalaya up to 13,000 feet. Grows in all kinds of soils; delights in one that is rich and moist. A most valuable fodder grass.

AJOWAN.

Ajowan. *See* Carum copticum, *Benth.*, UMBELLIFERÆ

ALANGIUM.

22 **Alangium Lamarckii,** *Thwaites*, CORNACEÆ.

Syn.—A. HEXAPETALUM, *Lamk.* (*Roxb., Fl. In.*); A. DECAPETALUM, *Lamk.*

Vern—*Akola, thaila,* HIND., DEC.; *Ankola, kalá-akolá,* BOM.; *Akarkanta, baghankara,* BENG.; *Alangi, ashinji,* TAM.; *Amkolam-chettu,* TEL.; *Ankola,* GOND; *Ankola,* SANS.; *Dhalákura,* BENG. (in *U. C. Dutt's Mat. Med.*)

A deciduous shrub or small tree of the sub-Himalayan tract from the Ganges eastward to Oudh and Bengal; also of Central and South India.

The fruit, a fleshy one-seeded drupe, is edible but not palatable. The Malays believe it to be a hydragogue purgative.

ALBIZZIA.

Albizzia Lebbek, *Benth.*, LEGUMINOSÆ. 23

Vern.—*Siris, siras, sirin, sirai, tantai, garso,* HIND.; *Siris, sirisha,* BENG.; *Vaghe,* TAM.; *Dirasan, darshana,* TEL.; *Kal baghi, bengha,* KAN., *Kokoh,* BURM.; *Beymadá, gachoolá,* AND.

A large, spreading tree, found wild or cultivated in most parts of India.

The leaves are used for camel fodder.

A. odoratissima, *Benth.* 24

Vern.—*Siris, bhandir, bersa, bansa,* HIND.; *Jati-koroi,* ASS.; *Lasrin, karambru, polach,* PB.; *Siras,* BOM.; *Kal-thuringi, kar vaghe, bilwara,* TAM; *Shinduga,* TEL.; *Thitmagyi,* BURM.

A large, deciduous tree of the sub-Himalayan tract from the Indus eastward, ascending to 3,000 feet; of Bengal, Burma, Central and South India.

The leaves are used for fodder.

A. stipulata, *Boivin.* 25

Vern.—*Oi, oö, shirsha,* PB.; *Siran, samsundra,* HIND.; *Chakua, amluki,* BENG.; *Kat turanji,* TAM.; *Kal baghi,* KAN.; *Kabal,* CINGH.; *Boomaisa,* BURM.

Met with in the sub-Himalayan tract, Oudh, Bengal, South India, and Burma.

The branches are lopped for cattle fodder. (*Gamble*).

ALEURITES.

Aleurites moluccana, *Willd.*, EUPHORBIACEÆ. 26

THE BELGAUM OR INDIAN WALNUT.

Syn.—A. TRILOBA, *Forst.*

Vern.—*Akrot,* BENG., HIND.; *Jangli akhrota, japhala,* BOM.

A handsome tree, introduced from the Malay Archipelago, and now found in cultivation or running wild in many parts of South India.

It is cultivated for the sake of its fruit, 2 inches in diameter, with the wallnut flavour; hence the name.

Algaroba. *See* **Prosopis grandulosa**, *Torr.*, LEGUMINOSÆ.

ALHAGI.

Alhagi maurorum, *Desv.*, LEGUMINOSÆ. 27

THE CAMEL THORN; THE HEBREW MANNA PLANT.

Syn.—HEDYSARUM ALHAGI, *Willd. in Roxb. Fl. Ind., C. B. C. Ed.* (*p.* 574.)

Vern.—*Juwása* or *junvásá* or *yavásá,* HIND., BOM.; *Dulallabhá,* BENG.; *Duralabha, girikarnika, yavása,* SANS.; *Shutarkhor,* PERS.; *Alhaju,* ARAB.

A widely-spread shrub of the Ganges Valley and the arid and northern zones; a native of South Africa, the deserts of Egypt, Arabia,

ALLIUM.

Asia Minor, Beluchistan, and Central India. Abounds in many of the arid parts of the Punjab plains; very common near Delhi.

In the hot season when almost all the smaller plants die, this puts forth its leaves and flowers which are used as fodder for camel. Just about this time the leaves and branches exude a gummy-looking liquid which soon thickens into solid grains; these are gathered by shaking the branches and constitute the eatable substance known as manna. This secretion, however, is apparently not found on the Indian plant, but is apparently found on the plant at Kandahar and Herat, whence small quantities of the manna are imported into Peshawar.

ALLIUM.

28 **Allium ascalonicum,** *Linn.*, LILIACEÆ.

THE SHALLET.

Vern.—*Gandhan*, PB.; *Gandana*, AFG.; *Shallot* (*Stewart*).

A hardy, bulbous perennial, native of Ascalon in Palestine.

The bulbs separate into what are termed cloves like those of garlic; and are used for culinary purposes, being of milder flavour than onions. They also make excellent pickle. It is cultivated apparently in Afghanistan for the sake of the leaves, which may be cut two or three times a year for 25 or 30 years.

29 **A. Cepa,** *Linn.*

ONION, *Eng.*; OGNON, *Fr.*; ZWIEBEL, *Ger.*

Vern.—*Pelándu*, SANS.; *Piyáj*, BENG.; *Piyás*, HIND.; *Vella-vengayam*, TAM.; *Nirelli*, TEL.; *Ky-et-thwon-ni*, *kesun-ni*, BURM.

Onions, leeks and garlic were cultivated in Egypt in the time of Moses, but it is stated that £428,800 were paid for the onions and garlic eaten by the workmen of the great pyramid.

The onion is cultivated very widely all over India, especially in the neighbourhood of large towns, and is consumed both by Europeans and natives. Its cultivation takes place during the dry months from October to February. The Mussulmans of India never cook curry without onions, but the strict Hindus of Bengal regard them as objectionable, and rarely if ever eat them. The Patna onion is of a superior kind, and is much sold in the Calcutta markets. The onions of the Northern Provinces are larger and more succulent than those of Bengal and the Southern Provinces.

When pressure of work or any other cause prevents the cooking of curry, the natives frequently eat onions with their daily meal, which, in the case of the poorer Bengalis, may be stale rice and water with salt, and with the natives of Upper India is coarse bread only: the onion in these cases is eaten raw, for the purpose apparently of flavouring the meal. (*Mr. L. Liotard.*)

30 **A. Rubelium,** *Bieb.*

Vern.—*Jangli pias*, *barani pias*, *chiri piasi*, HIND.

Slender-leaved species, common in North-Western India, and extending into Lahoul.

In most places the root is eaten raw or cooked. (*Stewart.*)

Allium sativum, *Linn.* 31

GARLIC.

Vern.—*Mahaushadha, lasuna,* SANS.; *Sir,* PERS.; *Rasun,* BENG.; *Lasan,* HIND.; *Vallai-pandu,* TAM.; *Vellulli, tella-gadda,* TEL.; *Kyet-thwon pen, kesún-phiu,* BURM.

It is cultivated all over India.
Used as a condiment in native curries throughout the country.

A. sphærocephalum, *Linn.* 32

Grows wild in Lahoul.
The root and dried leaves are eaten (*Stewart*).

Almond. *See* **Terminalia Catappa**, *Linn.*, COMBRETACEÆ.

ALNUS.

Alnus nitada, *Endl.*, CUPULIFERÆ. 33

ALDER.

Vern.—*Shrol, sawali, champ, kúnsh, gira,* PB.

Found on the Punjab hills and plains.
Leaves sometimes used as fodder.

ALOE.

Aloe vera, *Linn.*, LILIACEÆ. 34

INDIAN ALOE, *Eng.*; ALOES, *Fr.*; ALOE, *Ger.*

Syn.— A. BARBADENSIS, *Miller;* A. PERFOLIATA, *Roxb.*; A. VULGARIS, (*Bauhin*), *Lam.*

Vern.—*Ghikuwári, kumári,* HIND.; *Ghirta-kunmári, girta-kanvár,* BENG.; *Ghirta-kumári, kanyá,* SANS.; *Sibr,* ARAB.; *Sibr, bole-siyah,* PERS.; *Eliya* (resin), *Kora-kand* (the plant), *kumári,* DEC.; *Kanvaár, kora kanda, kora-phad,* SIND.; *Kariya-polam, kattáli,* TAM.; *Musham báram,* TEL.; *Mok,* BURM.

Var. officinalis, sp., *Forsk.* 35

Syn.—A. RUBESCENS, *DC.*; A. INDICA, *Royle.*

Vern.—*Kumari,* HIND.; *Ghikawár,* N. W. P.; *Ghirta-kanvár,* BENG.; *Sirrúghá, kuttalay,* TAM. (*see Ainslie*); *Nabatussibr, áúlsi,* ARAB.; *Dura-khte-sibr,* PERS.

This is the form met with in a semi-wild condition in Bengal and the North-West Provinces. It has beautiful reddish and orange flowers, with the bases of the leaves purple-coloured and so dilated as to have in all probability suggested the name **A. perfoliata.**

The pulp of the leaves is eaten by poorer people in times of famine, when the seeds also are eaten.

ALOPECURUS.

Alopecurus agrestis, *Linn.*, GRAMINEÆ. 36

SLENDER FOX-TAIL GRASS.

Found in the Punjab in cultivated ground.

Duthie, quoting **Parlatore**, says the latter describes it as a good fodder grass, fresh or dry.

AMARYL-LIS.

37 **Alopecurus geniculatus,** *Linn.*

FOX TAIL GRASS.

Syn.—A. FULVUS, *Sm.*

Inhabits the plains of Northern India, and ascends the Himalaya in Kumaun and Kashmir valley.

Mueller describes it as a good fodder grass for swampy land. A variety, **pumila**, was found by **Royle** on the banks of the Jumna.

38 **A. pratensis,** *Linn.*

MEADOW FOX-TAIL GRASS.

Inhabits the North-West Himalayas, 5,000 to 8,000 feet, and ascends in Lahoul up to 13,000 feet; also found in Kashmir and on the Punjab plains.

A perennial pasture grass, considered one of the best of its class. Sheep thrive well on it. **Loudon** mentions it as an excellent fodder grass in England.

ALTHÆA.

39 **Althæa officinalis,** *L.*, MALVACEÆ.

MARSH MALLOW.

Found in Kashmir and Afghanistan.

Is used as a green vegetable.

AMARANTUS.

40 **Amarantus Anardana,** *Hamilt.*, AMARANTACEÆ.

Vern.—*Ganhar, tawal, chaulai, sil* (seed), PB.; *Ság*, BENG.

Cultivated and wild in Bengal and the Upper Provinces.

The leaves are eaten as a pot-herb. The seeds, after being parched, are used in some places as a food-grain, and are considered heating.

41 **A. frumentaceus,** *Buch.*

Vern.—*Kiery*, SOUTH INDIA.

Cultivated by the natives in Southern India for the seed, which they make into flour and use as food.

42 **A. mangostanus,** *L.*

Vern.—*Chaulai, ganhar*, UPPER INDIA; *Sag*, BENG.

Occasionally cultivated in the plains.

The leaves are used as a pot-herb.

AMARYLLIS.

43 **Amaryllis grandiflora,** AMARYLLIDEÆ.

The Amaryllis is chiefly a native of Brazil, but cultivated largely in England.

No information as to its cultivation in India.

AMOMUM.

Amomum aromaticum, *Roxb.*, SCITAMINEÆ. 44

CARDAMOM PLANT.

Vern.—*Morung, elachi,* BENG.; *Eelachi,* HIND., DEC.; *Aila cheddi,* TAM.; *Yaslakulu,* TEL.; *Yalum,* MAL.

During **Roxburgh's** time this was most probably the plant which yielded the greater Cardamom. It is met with in the mountains of Eastern Bengal. Apparently it is not now used, or there was some mistake on the part of **Dr. Roxburgh** as to this being the greater Cardamom of Bengal.

A. dealbatum, *Roxb.* 45

A native of Eastern Bengal and the adjoining frontier; a stately species flowering in March and April and ripening its seed in September and October.

A. subulatum, *Roxb.* 46

THE GREATER CARDAMOM; THE GRAINS OF PARADISE.

Vern.—*Bara-elachi,* BENG., HIND.; *Yelarsi,* TAM.; *Yelakulu,* TEL.; *Ben,* BURM.

A native of the Eastern Archipelago.

Dr. King clearly proved that this is the greater Cardamom of the present day, which is obtained from Nepal and largely used in Bengal as a condiment.

A. maximum, *Roxb.* 47

This was stated by **Dr. Pareira** to be the Greater Cardamom of Bengal, but erroneously. **Dr. Roxburgh** says it was introduced from the Malay Islands by the late **Colonel Kyd.**

The flowering time is the hot season, and the seeds ripen three or four months afterwards; they possess a warm pungent taste somewhat like that of the Cardamoms, but by no means so grateful.

AMORPHOPHALLUS.

Amorphophallus campanulatus, *Blume.*, AROIDEÆ. 48

Syn.—ARUM CAMPANULATUM, *Roxb.*

Vern.—*Ole,* BENG., HIND.; *Zaminkand,* NORTH INDIA; *Kunda, kulla,* SANS.; *Karuna,* TAM., MAL.; *Munchá kunda,* TEL.

A stemless plant annually sending up a large compoundly dissected leaf, with beautiful variegated petiole, common in Bengal, and throughout the plains of India.

Much cultivated throughout India,—in some places more commonly than in others,—for the sake of the corms or solid bulbs, which are considered nutritious and wholesome when cooked, and are accordingly in common use as an article of food. They are boiled like potatoes and eaten with mustard; they are cooked in curries; they are cut into slices, boiled with tamarind leaves, and made into pickles; and they are also cooked in syrup and made into preserves.

The larger corms have small tuberosities, which are separated and form cuttings for propagatoin. These are planted immediately after the first rains (say in May and June) in loose, rich soil, repeatedly ploughed. In twelve months they are fit to be taken up for use. If cultivated under favorable circumstances, each corm will weigh from 4 to 8lbs.; which may be preserved if kept dry. The average out-turn is about 200 to 400 maunds per bigha, and the price is about a rupee a maund.

ANABASIS.

49 **Anabasis multiflora,** *Moq.*, CHENOPODIACEÆ.

Vern.—*Ghalme, goraline, dana*, PB.

Is found in the Punjab.

Camels are fond of the plant.

ANACARDIUM.

50 **Anacardium occidentale,** *Linn.*, ANACARDIACEÆ.

CASHEW NUT.

Vern.—*Hijli bádám*, BENG.; *Kajú*, HIND.; *Mundiri, kottai*, TAM.; *Jidi mamidi*, TEL.; *Thee-noh thayet*, BURM.; *Kempu girus*, KAN.

Now established in the coast forests of Chittagong, Tenasserim, the Andaman Islands, and South India, near the sea; naturalised from the West Indies, America, Ceylon, &c.

Produces a small fruit, within which is the nut known as the Cashew nut commonly eaten roasted, a process which improves the flavour.

ANANASSA.

51 **Ananassa sativa,** *Linn.*, BROMELIACEÆ.

THE PINE-APPLE.

Vern.—*Anánas*, HIND. (DEC.); *Anánash* (vulgarly *anáras*), BENG.; *Ana-ras*, GUZ.; *Anáshap-pazhane*, TAM.; *Anása-pandu*, TEL.; *Kaita-chakka* MAL.; *Aainunnás*, ARAB & PERS.; *Annasi*, CINGH.; *Nanna-si*, BURM.

A perennial universally cultivated in all tropical and sub-tropical countries. The entire natural order to which this much-prized fruit belongs are natives of America, and were unknown to Europe, Africa and Asia prior to discovery of the Western Continent. The Pine-Apple is apparently a native of Brazil and it was first made known to Europe by **Goncallo Hernandez** in 1513; it was introduced by the Portuguese into Bengal in 1594. "Its introduction is expressly mentioned by Indian authors such as **Abul Fuzl** in the *Ayeen Akbari*, and again by the author of *Dhara Shekoih* (*Royle.*) The rapidity with which it spread through Europe, Asia and Africa is unparalleled in the history of any other fruit. It seems to have met with universal acceptance, hence, apparently, the purity with which its American name *Anasi* or *Nanas* has passed through so many languages. The Asiatic recipient of a living plant seems to have carried off and adopted as his own the name by which so valuable a treasure was made known to him. The first pine-apples which appear to have reached England were those presented to Cromwell. The next notice is of the "Queen pine" presented to Charles II on the 19th July 1688, having been sent from Barbados, and the first pine-apple grown in England seems to have been reared from the rejected crowns of these. It was first systematically cultivated in Europe by **M. Le Cour,** a Dutch Merchant near Leyden. It was first fruited in England in the year 1712; since then its cultivation may be said to have become universal all over Southern Europe; the largest pine on record was reared in England, and it weighed over 14 lbs.

In India the fresh juice of the leaves is regarded as a powerful anthelmintic, and that of the fruit an antiscorbutic. A friend informs me that the natives regard the fresh juice of the fruit as poisonous if hypodermically injected.

In the Malabar coast near Mahé, and in British Burma, near Myanoung, the pine-apple is remarkably abundant. In the former tract the natives have a prejudice against eating the fruit from an idea that it is poisonous, and they consequently destroy the fruit, or give it away. In Myanoung, **Monsieur d'Avera** is trying to make use of the large quantities that grow there to manufacture champagne. I am in correspondence with him on the subject, and he seems hopeful of success. Should the experiment succeed, it could be repeated on the Malabar coast. (*Mr. L. Liotard.*)

ANDROPOGON.

Andropogon Bladhii, *Retz.*, GRAMINEÆ. 52

Syn.—LEPEOCERCIS BLADHII, *Nees.*

Vern.—*Loari*, Beng.; *Donda, nilon*, N. W. P.

Described by **Roxburgh** as a native of hedges and road-sides, but chiefly of old pasture grounds. **Duthie** says it inhabits the plains of the North-Western Provinces and Punjab.

A. citratus. 53

THE LEMON GRASS.

Vern.—*Olá cháhá, gandhat rince*, BOM.

A large, coarse grass, found under cultivation in various islands of the Eastern Archipelago, and growing wild on extensive tracts of land in India and Ceylon; it rarely or never bears flowers. It is grown especially for its odoriferous oil in Ceylon and Singapore.

A. contortus, *Linn.* 54

Vern.—*Yeddi*, TEL.

Grows on pasture grounds. *See* **Heteropogon contortus**, *R. & S.*

A. laniger, *Desf.* 55

(The **Herbba Schœnanthi** or **Juncus Odoratus** of Pharmacists.)

Syn.—A IWARANCUSA, *Roxb.*

Vern.—*Khawi, panni, solára, san*, PB.; *Ibharankusha, kurankusha*, BENG., HIND.

Native of the Lower Himalayan tract, extending through the plains of the North West Provinces and Punjab to Sindh.

Roxburgh says it grows in large tufts, each tuft composed of a number of plants adhering together by their roots. The roots are aromatic. Cattle are said to be very fond of the grass.

ANDRO-
POGON.

56 **Andropogon miliaceus,** *Roxb.*

HILL GRASS.

Syn.—A. MILIFORMIS, *Stend.*

A grass, erect, from 6 to 10 feet in height, inhabiting the mountains north of Oudh.

Roxburgh writes:—"The seeds of this most beautiful stately grass were sent me from Lucknow by the late **Gen. Claude Martin,** under the name of Hill Grass. * * * It blossoms during the latter part of the rains."

57 **A. muricatus,** *Retz.*

CUSCUS, KHUS-KHUS or KOOSA.

Syn.—A. SQUARROSUS, *Linn.*; PHALARIS ZIZANOIDES, *Linn.*; ANATHERUM MURICATUM, *Retz.*

Vern.—*Bena* (the plant), *khas-khas* (the root), BENG., HIND.; *Virunung*, SANS.; *Wœtiwear*, TAM.

A perennial tufted grass very common on every part of the Coast, and in Bengal, where it meets with a low, moist, rich soil, especially on the banks of water-courses, &c. (*Roxb.*) Inhabits the plains of the Punjab and North West Provinces, and ascends into Kumaun, 1,000 to 2,000 feet in altitude (*Duthie*).

The roots, well known in India as the *khas-khas*, have a fragrant odour, especially when moistened, and are much used for the manufacture of screens or blinds which, applied to doors and windows during the hot weather and moistened, give out a fragrant odour and cool the apartment. The grass itself when young affords good fodder.

58 **A. pertusus,** *Willd.*

Syn.—A. PUNCTALUS, *Roxb.*; HOLEUS PERTUSUS, *Linn.*; A. ANNULATUS, *Forsk.*

Vern.—*Pulwal, pulréah, rukar*, N. W. P.; *Pulwan, miniyar*, PB.

Found on old pasture ground generally shaded by trees, in the plains of the Punjab and North West Provinces, and at lower elevations of the Himalaya.

Dr. Stewart, writing under **A. annulatus,** says: "It is considered excellent fodder for bullocks, &c., and for horses, when green." In Australia it is regarded as one of the best grasses to withstand long droughts, while it will bear any amount of feeding. (*Baron von Mueller.*)

59 **A. scandens,** *Roxb.*

Found in the Punjab, in Kashmir and Bundelkhand. It is a coarse grass growing commonly in hedges. It flowers during the rains.

Cattle are apparently not fond of it.

60 **A. Schœnanthus,** *Linn.*

LEMON GRASS.

Syn.—A. MARTINI, *Roxb.*

Vern.—*Mirchia-gard*, SIWALIKS; *Ageea-ghas*, HIND.; *Gundha-bena*, BENG.; *Malatrinukung, bhoostrinung*, SANS.

Inhabits the hilly districts of the Punjab, North West Provinces, the Siwaliks, and is grown under cultivation in most gardens.

It is the **Juncus Odoratus** of the *Materia Medica*; and yields the famous *rusa-ka-tel* or grass oil of Nimar. Its roots are used in cases of intermittent fever in Northern India.

The fresh leaves are much used as a substitute for tea, and the white succulent centre of the leaf-bearing culms is often put into curries to give them an agreeable flavour.

Duthie writes: "The grass is a favourite fodder for cattle, and **Mr. Millar** tells me that at Banda (North West Provinces) it is grown in meadows kept for the purpose and sold in the bazar."

General Martin collected seeds of this grass in the high-lands of Balaghat while there with the army during the war with Tippoo Sultan, and after growing it in Lucknow sent specimens to **Dr. Roxburgh**, with the remark that he had noticed the cattle were voraciously fond of it, and that it had so strong an aromatic and pungent taste that the flesh of the animals, as also the milk and butter, had a very strong scent of it.

Anethum Sowa, *Roxb.* *See* **Peucedanum graveolens,** *Benth.*, UMBELLIFERÆ.

ANGELICA.

Angelica glauca, *Edgw.*, UMBELLIFERÆ. 61

Vern.—*Chúra*, PB.

Common on the Himalaya from Kashmir to Sikkim.

Its aromatic root is added to food to give it a flavour like that of celery.

ANONA.

Anona reticulata, *Linn.*, ANONACEÆ. 62

BULLOCK'S HEART.

Vern.—*Nona*, BENG.; *Rawsita*, TAM.

A small tree, common everywhere; wild apparently in some districts, but chiefly met with in cultivation.

The fruit, which resembles a bullock's heart, ripens during the latter part of the rainy season, and is eaten by the natives, and rarely by the Europeans.

A. squamosa, *Linn.* 63

THE CUSTARD APPLE OR SWEET SOP.

Vern.—*Ata*, BENG.; *Saripha, sitaphal*, HIND.; *Sita*, TAM.; *Atta*, MAL.; *Ausa*, BURM.

A small tree, the Sweet-sop of the West Indies; naturalised in Bengal and the North West Provinces.

It is cultivated throughout India in gardens. The fruit ripens in summer, is of a more delicate flavor than the fruit of **A. reticulata**, and is eaten with relish by both the natives and the Europeans.

ANTHOCEPHALUS.

Anthocephalus Cadamba, *Miq.*, RUBIACEÆ. 64

Syn.—NAUCLEA CADAMBA, *Roxb.*

Vern.—*Kaddam, raram*, HIND.; *Kadam*, BENG.; *Kadamba*, SANS.; *Pandúr*, LEPCHA; *Roghu*, ASS.; *Vella, cadamba*, TAM.; *Kadambe*, TEL.; *Kadam*, MAR.; *Kadamba, nhyú*, BOM.; *Maoo, maookadoom*, BURM.

A large tree with spreading branches and thick foliage; wild or cultivated in gardens and alleys, from the Himalayas to Ceylon.

The fruit is eaten, and the foliage is sometimes used as fodder for cattle.

ANTIDESMA.

65 **Antidesma diandrum,** *Tulasne.*, EUPHORBIACEÆ.

Vern.—*Amli, amári, sarshoti,* HIND.; *Mutta,* BENG.; *Patimil,* NEPAL.; *Kantjer,* LEPCHA.; *Pella-gumudu, masúr bauri,* GOND.; *Kimpa-lin,* BURM.

A small tree, with smooth, grey bark, met with in Garhwal, Kumaun, Oudh, Bengal, South India, and Burma.

"The leaves are acid, and are eaten. They resemble sorrel, and are made into chatni; the fruit is eaten." (*Gamble.*)

66 **A. Ghæsembilla,** *Gærtn.*

Vern.—*Khádi jamb, limtoá,* BENG.; *Pulsur, polari, pollai,* TEL.; *Jondri,* MAR.; *Byait-sin,* BURM.; *Boo-ambilla,* CINGH.

A small, deciduous tree of Nepal, Oudh, Bengal, Burma, Chanda District, and South India.

The leaves are eaten in Bengal.

67 **A. Menasu,** *Mull. Arg.*

Vern.—*Kumbyáng, tungcher,* LEPCHA; *Kin-pa-lin,* BURM.

A small tree of Sikkim, Khásia Hills, Burma, and the Andaman Islands. Fruit is eaten.

APIUM.

68 **Apium graveolens,** *Linn.*, UMBELLIFERÆ.

CELERY.

Vern.—*Ajmod, karafsh* (roots), HIND.; *Chanu,* BENG.; *Karafsh,* ARAB.; *Kursab,* PERS.

A native of England and other parts of Europe. Cultivated in different parts of India during the cold weather, chiefly as garden cultivation in the vicinity of towns, for the use of the European population by whom it is eaten as a salad and pot-herb, or made into soup. It is also cultivated sometimes in Bengal for its seed, and in the Punjab for its root.

The seed is used by the natives in diet and medicine; the root is regarded as medicinal.

Aplotaxis auriculata, *DC.* *See* **Saussbrea hypoleuca** *Spreng.*, COMPOSITÆ.

A. gossypina, *DC.* *See* **Saussurea gossypifera,** *Don.*, COMPOSITÆ.

APLUDA.

69 **Apluda aristata,** *Linn.*, GRAMINEÆ.

Syn.—A. ROSTRATA.

Vern.—*Bhanjuri, bhanjra, send,* BUNDELKHAND; *Goroma,* BENG.; *Put-strangali,* TEL.

A creeping, perennial grass, commonly found in hedges, or other shady places, the plains of Northern India, and in Himalaya ascending to 7,000 feet in altitude.

Used for fodder.

APONOGETON.

Aponogeton monostachyum, *Linn.*, NAIADACEÆ. 70

Vern.—*Ghechu*, HIND.; *Kakangi*, SANS.; *Nama*, TEL.

"A native of shallow, standing, sweet water; in Bengal appearing during the rains.

The natives are fond of the roots, which are nearly as good as potatoes. (*Roxb.*)

Apple. *See* **Pyrus Malus**, *Linn.*, ROSACEÆ.

Apricot. *See* **Prunus armeniaca**, *Linn.*, ROSACEÆ.

ARACHIS.

Arachis hypogæa, *Linn.*, LEGUMINOSÆ. 71

THE GROUND NUT OF EARTH NUT.

Vern.—*Buchanaka*, SANS.; *Mát-kalai, chiner-bádám*, BENG.; *Mungphali*, HIND.; *Viláyeti-múng*, DEC.; *Bhuimúga, bhuisenga, viláyatimúga*, BOM.; *Vérk-kadalai*, TAM.; *Verushanaga-káya*, TEL.; *Mibé*, BURM.

An annual of South America, now generally cultivated in South India and some parts of Bengal and Upper India.

Produces the well-known ground nut, so called because the pod attains maturity under ground.

In India the nuts are sold in the bazars or by the street hawkers either parched, with the shell on and put up in paper packets, or shelled and roasted in oil. They are eaten by natives of all classes and even by Europeans. In Bombay they are a favorite food of the Hindus during certain fasts.

ARALIA.

Aralia achemirica, *Dcne.*, ARALIACEÆ. 72

Vern.—*Banakhor, churial*, PB.

A plant growing rank in the basins of the Jhelum and the Chenab. Eaten by goats.

ARECA.

Areca Catechu, *Linn.*, PALMÆ. 73

THE ARECA NUT, OR BETEL PALM.

Vern.—*Supári*, HIND.; *Supári, gud*, BENG.; *Gubak*, SANS.; *Kottai pakka*, TAM.; *Poka-vakka*, TEL.; *Kwyun*, BURM.; *Adiki*, KAN.; *Kwam-thee-beng*, BURM.

A native of Cochin China, Malayan Peninsula and Islands; it is cultivated throughout Tropical India.

The nut is one of the indispensable ingredients which enter into the preparation of the *pán* or betel-leaf chewed so universally by natives of all classes. It is often chewed by itself in small pieces, and is sold in every bazar throughout India. It is said to stimulate digestion.

A. Dicksonii, *Roxb.* 74

A native of the Malabar hills; flowers and fruits in spring.

The nut is used by the poorer classes as a substitute for the Areca Nut (*supari*).

ARENARIA.

75 **Arenaria holosteoides,** *Edgw.*, CARYOPHYLLEÆ.

Vern.—*Kakua, gandial*, PB.; *Chiki*, LADAK.

An herb found in the Punjab Himalayas.

Used as a vegetable in Chumba and Ladak.

ARENGA.

76 **Arenga sacchrifera,** *Labill.*, PALMÆ.

Syn.—SAGUERUS RUMPHII, *Roxb.* (*Fl. Ind., iii, 626.*)

Vern.—*Toung-ong*, BURM.

A Malayan tree generally cultivated in India, but said by Kurz to be wild in Burma.

"The heart of the stem contains large quantities of sago, and the cut flower stalks yield a sugary sap made into sugar and palm wine." (*Gamble*).

ARGANIA.

77 **Argania Sideroxylon,** *R.S.*, SAPOTACEÆ.

Is the Argan tree of Morocco, which is found growing gregariously in forests in the Atlas mountains.

The fruit, of the size of a small plum, is used for feeding cattle, the skin and pulp being much relished.

ARISTIDA.

78 **Aristida depressa,** *Retz.*, GRAMINEÆ.

Vern.—*Spin-khalak, spin-wege, jandar lamba*, PB.; *Nali-putiki*, TEL.

Inhabits the plains in Northern India; also found in the Southern Provinces. Grows in a dry, barren, binding soil.

Roxburgh did not find that it was put to any use; but **Stewart** says it is a favorite food for cattle in Northern India.

79 **A. setacea,** *Retz.*

Vern.—*Shipur-gadi*, TEL.; *Thodapga-pulla*, TAM.

Common in dry parts of the Punjab and North-West Provinces; also in Southern India where it grows in dry, barren, binding soil.

Roxburgh writes: "Cattle do not eat it, yet it is very useful. The Telinga paper-makers construct their frames of the culms; it also serves to make brooms and tooth-picks. It is employed in preference to other grasses for making the screens called *tatties;* for this purpose it is spread thin on bamboo frames and tied down: these placed on the weather side of the house during the hot land winds and kept constantly watered during the heat of the day renders the temperature of the air in the house exceedingly pleasant, compared to what it is without." It is used in fact like the *khas-khas* roots in Northern India. As to the remark that cattle do not eat this grass, **Roxburgh** was apparently mistaken, for **Bidie** says it is eaten by bullocks.

Arrowroot. *See* **Maranta arundinacea,** *Linn.*, SCITAMINEÆ.

ARTEMISIA.

80 **Artemisia parviflora,** *Roxb.*, COMPOSITÆ.

Vern.—*Kanyúrts*, PB.; *Burmar*, LADAK.

Common in the higher regions of North-West Himalaya, in Lahoul and Ladak.

Browsed by goats and sheep.

Artemisia sacrorum, *Ledeb.* 81

Vern.—*Tatwen, burmach,* LADAK.

Grows in the drier tracts of Northern Punjab and ascends the Himalaya.

Browsed by cattle and sheep.

ARTOCARPUS.

Artocarpus hirsuta, *Lamk.,* URTICACEÆ. 82

Vern.—*Anjeli,* TAM.; *Ayeni, ansjeli,* MAL.

A large tree, native of the Malabar forests, and extends into Travancore.

Produces a fruit, the size of a large orange, which contains a pulpy substance much relished by the natives.

A. incisa, *Linn.* 83

It has been long introduced into Bengal, but the winters are too rigorous for its growth. In Bombay it succeeds better, and a tree in the garden attached to the Albert and Victoria Museum was in bearing when I saw it in March 1879.

A. integrifolia, *Linn.* 84

THE JACK FREE.

Vern.—*Panas,* HIND.; *Kanthal,* BENG.; *Panasa,* SANS.; *Palah,* TAM.; *Peingnai,* BURM.

A large tree of the Bread fruit family, has a dense dome of deep dark foliage, with immense fruits clustered around the stem; one of the most characteristic associates of the Indian rural village.

The fruit, 12 to 18 inches in length and 6 to 8 inches in diameter, ripens during the rains and has then a strong odour; it is stocked with luscious flakes, each flake containing a seed. It is much relished by the natives of all classes, but seldom or never eaten by Europeans.

The seeds or nuts of the ripe fruit are eaten either roasted or cooked in curry.

The fruit when unripe is cut into small pieces and cooked into curry with shrimps. The seeds of the ripe fruit, when roasted in hot ashes, are very palatable and nutritious, and resemble somewhat Spanish chestnuts in taste. (*Mr. L. Liotard.*)

A. Lakoocha, *Roxb.* 85

Vern.—*Barhal,* HIND.; *Dephal,* BENG.; *Lakucha,* SANS.; *Lowi,* DEC.; *Tiún,* PB.; *Kammaregu,* TEL.; *Myouklouk,* BURM.

Grows on the outer hills of Kumaun, Sikkim, Eastern Bengal, and Burma.

A middling size tree common all over Bengal; flowers in March, and produces a fruit which is eaten by the natives. The male spadix is used by the natives in curry. Mann says the bark is chewed in Assam. The male flower-heads are picked, and the fruit eaten." (*Gamble.*)

A. nobiles, *Thw.* 86

Vern.—*Del, aludel,* CINGH.

A large tree met with in Ceylon.

The seeds are roasted and eaten by the Cinghalese.

ARUM.

Arum campanulatum. *See* **Amorphophallus campanulatus,** *Blume.*, AROIDEÆ.

A. Colocasia, *Willd.* *See* **Colocasia antiquorum,** *Schott.*, AROIDEÆ.

ARUNDINARIA.

87 **Arundinaria Hookeriana,** *Munro,* GRAMINEÆ.

BAMBOO.

Vern.—*Praong, prong,* LEPCHA; *Singhani,* NEPAL.

A bamboo, with stems 12 to 15 feet in height, common about Dumsong. Grows in Sikkim at 4,000 to 7,000 feet in altitude. (*Gamble.*)

The seeds are edible.

88 **A. racemosa,** *Munro.*

Vern.—*Pummoon,* LEPCHA; *Pathioo,* NEPAL; *Myooma,* BHUTIA.

Very common all over the Siwalik hills above 7,000 feet.

Extensively used for fodder.

ASPARAGUS.

89 **Asparagus officinalis,** *Willd.*, LILIACEÆ.

ASPARAGUS.

Vern.—*Nak-doun, hillooa,* HIND., PERS.; *Hilyoon,* BENG.

There are several wild Indian species used by the hill people of Eastern India. Indian species have climbing or trailing stems, often spinose.

The species eaten by Europeans is the cultivated one, and this is grown as a rule in private gardens or by the natives near the neighbourhood of towns.

ASPHODELUS.

90 **Asphodelus fistulosus,** *Linn.*, LILIACEÆ.

Vern.—*Piazi, bokat, binghar bij* (seed), PB.

A field weed, abundant in the Punjab plains.

Eaten as a vegetable in times of scarcity.

Asteracantha longifolia, *Nees.* *See* **Hygrophila spinosa,** *T. And.*, ACANTHACEÆ.

ASTRAGALUS.

91 **Astragalus multiceps,** *Wall.*, LEGUMINOSÆ.

Vern.—*Kandiara kandei, katar-kanda, sarmul,* PB.; *Tinani, diddani,* AFG.

A spinous plant of the temperate zone, the West Himalayas, up to 12,000 feet.

At times browsed by cattle. The calyces, which have a sweetish pleasant taste, are said to be eaten in the Salt Range by the natives.

ATRIPLEX.

92 **Atriplex hortensis,** *L.*, and **A. laciniata,** *L.*, CHENOPODIACEÆ.

Vern.—*Korake, suraka,* PB.

Inhabit the Western Himalayas in the temperate zone, also submontane tracts in the Punjab, and in Afghanistan.

A. hortensis is said to be a favorite vegetable in the Peshawar valley. Is this the "mallows" of Job XXX, 4?

AVENA.

Avena fatua, *Linn.*, GRAMINEÆ. 93

THE WILD OAT?

Vern.—*Kuljud, gandal, jai*, HIND.

Inhabits the plains and hills of Northern India; common as a field weed in cereal crops throughout the plains; ascends the Himalaya up to 9,500 and 11,500 feet. The awn is long and rigid and sensitive to the changes of the atmosphere, as regards moisture.

Stewart says that in almost all the places where it grows it is gathered for fodder.

A. pratensis, *Linn.* 94

MEADOW OAT GRASS.

Syn.—A. BROMOIDES, *Kunth.*

Found in Lahoul. **Duthie** quotes **Baron von Mueller**, who says it thrives well on dry, clayey soil, produces a sweet fodder, and is recommended for arid ground, particularly such as contains some lime, being thus as valuable as **Festuca ovina.**

A. pubescens, *L.* 95

DOWNY OAT GRASS.

Syn.—TRISETUM PUBESCENS, *R. & S.*

Royle found it at Simla.

It is a sweet, nutritious, prolific, perennial grass, requiring dry but good soil containing lime.

A. sativa, *Linn.* 96

OATS.

Vern.—*Jai, wilayati-jau*, HIND.

Of recent introduction into Indian agriculture; it was first grown in Northern India under English auspices round cantonments and stud depôts for the supply of horses.

The cultivation of oats, although it has found its way among the native ryots, has not gained much extension. It is still confined to Northern India, where it is restricted chiefly to districts where horse-breeding is carried on, *viz.*, in the Meerut and Rohilkhand Divisions of the North-West Provinces, and in the Hissar and Karnal districts of the Punjab. In the Meerut Division the area annually under oats is 5,000 acres and in Rohilkhand 3,000 acres. The total area under the crop in the 30 temporarily-settled districts of the North-West Provinces and Oudh, including of course the two divisions just mentioned, is returned at 9,781 acres.

In the Punjab it is grown chiefly in connection with the Government cattle and stud farms at Hissar and Karnal.

Oats are grown as a rule on the better class of soils near village sites. **Messrs. Duthie** and **Fuller** write: "With a copious supply of water it has been found that oats are an invaluable green fodder crop for the cold season, yielding as many as three cuttings, and then making sufficient growth to bear a thin crop of grain. A large area under oats is most successfully treated in this way each year at the Hissar Government cattle farm. When grown in this manner they class rather as a green fodder than as a grain crop."

When grown for grain the outturn is (in Northern India) 18 maunds on irrigated and 10 maunds on unirrigated land, per acre.

AVICENNIA.

The figures in the following table will show the quantity and value of exports of oats made in the year 1882-83 from Bengal and Bombay to other countries:—

Exported from.	Quantity in cwts.	Value in rupees.	Countries to which exported.	Quantity in cwts.	Value in rupees.
Bengal . .	57,782	1,96,853	Mauritius .	55,285	1,86,522
			Arabia . .	6,594	15,847
			United Kingdom	2,253	5,514
Bombay . .	8,924	21,625	Australia . .	1,778	7,500
			Other countries .	796	3,095
TOTAL .	66,706	2,18,478	TOTAL .	66,706	2,18,478

The produce probably comes from the northern parts of the Punjab and the North-West Provinces.

AVERRHOA.

97 **Averrhoa Bilimbi,** *Linn.*, GERANIACEÆ.

BILIMBI TREE.

Vern.—*Bilimbi*, BENG., HIND.

Cultivated in gardens on the plains of India. It flowers in the beginning of summer and ripens in about two or three months after. The fruit is cylindrical, about two inches long, and pulpy, and is very sour when green but loses some of its acidity when ripe.

The fruit is generally used in pickle and in curry. The flowers are made into preserves.

98 **A. Carambola,** *Linn.*

Vern.—*Karmal*, HIND.; *Kámrángá*, BENG.; *Karmurunga*, SANS.; *Khamaraka, karamara*, BOM.; *Khamrak*, DEC.; *Tamarta*, TAM.; *Karomonga*, TEL.

A small tree with sensitive leaflets, 15 to 20 feet in height, a native of Ceylon and the Moluccas, but now common in gardens almost throughout the plains of India.

It blossoms in the rainy season, and the fruit, which ripens in December and January, is about three inches long, and is eaten raw to a small extent by the natives. The flesh is soft, juicy and refreshing. It is sometimes stewed in syrup with a little cinnamon and is then very pleasant; it is also made into an agreeable jelly.

AVICENNIA.

99 **Avicennia officinalis,** *Linn.*, VERBENACEÆ.

THE WHITE MANGROVE.

Vern.—*Bina (Bani in Gamble)*, BENG.; *Mada, nalla-mada*, TEL.; *Tivara*, SIND.; *Oepata*, MAL.; *Thamé*, BURM.

A small tree or shrub of the salt marshes and the tidal forests of India and Burma, found also in Andaman Islands. **Roxburgh** says it is common near the mouths of rivers, where the spring tides rise; also is found everywhere in the Sunderbans, often becoming a tree of considerable size, but on the Coromandel Coast it is only bush.

The kernels are bitter but edible.

A remarkable feature of the Mangrove is the germinating of its seeds in the fruit, while still hanging on the tree, and producing a root, 3 or 4 feet long, which ultimately falls into the mud and forms a new centre.

BACCAUREA.

Baccaurea sapida, *Mull.-Arg.*, EUPHORBIACEÆ. 100

RAMLEH.

Vern.—*Lutco*, HIND.; *Kala bogoti*, NEPAL; *Latecku*, ASS.; *Koli, kuki*, KAN.; *Kanaso*, BURM.

A small tree, met with in Bengal, Burma and the Andaman Islands.

It produces a fruit of the size of a large gooseberry, yellow and smooth, with seeds embedded in a pulpy aril. It is acid and pleasant. The natives esteem it. In the Rangoon market it is generally plentiful.

BALANITES.

Balanites Roxburghii, *Planch.*, SIMARUBEÆ. 101

Syn.—B. ÆGYPTIACA, *Delile.*

Vern.—*Hingu, ingua, hingol, hingola*, HIND.; *Garrah*, GOND; *Gari, ringri*, TEL.; *Nanjunda*, TAM.; *Hingan*, MAR.

A small tree growing in the drier parts of India and Burma.

The young twigs and the leaves are browsed by cattle.

BALLOTA.

Ballota limbata, *Benth.*, LABIATÆ. 102

Vern.—*Bui, phútkonda, lana, aghzan, awani-buti*, PB.

A small, prickly shrub with yellow flowers: occurs in the north-western parts of the Punjab plains.

Browsed by goats.

BAMBUSA.

Bambusa arundinacea, *Retz.*, and other species, GRAMINEÆ. 103

THE BAMBOO.

Vern.—*Bans*, BENG.; *Bans, kattang, magar bans, nal bans*, HIND.; *Mandgay*, BOM.; *Vansa*, SANS.; *Mangil*, TAM.; *Mulhas*, TEL.; *Kyakatwa*, BURM.

The common bamboo of Central and South India and Burma. Cultivated in many places in North West India.

Mr. Duthie writes:—"The simultaneous flowering and subsequent dying of almost every individual plant of this species in certain districts and at certain stated times has been an interesting subject for observation. There seems to be no particular age at which the flowering takes place; the event is probably to a great extent influenced by the nature of the season." An abnormally dry season seems to promote the flowering and subsequent seeding. The plant does not seem to be able to survive the seeding.

The seed resembles unhusked rice, and is eaten by the poorer classes like that cereal. As it appears at the very season when drought occurs and other crops fail, it is of some advantage to the poor. The young shoots of some species are cut when tender, and eaten like asparagus.

BASSIA.

The leaves and twigs form an important fodder, this species being largely consumed by elephants.

104 **Bambusa spinosa,** *Roxb.*

Vern.—*Bur, behor báns* (*Duthie.*)

Inhabits South India, and is cultivated in North West India.

Closely allied to the preceding, with which Dr. Brandis seemed inclined to unite it.

Banana or **plantain.** *See* Musa.

Barley. *See* Hordeum vulgare.

BASELLA.

105 **Basella alba,** *L.*, CHENOPODIACEÆ.

INDIAN SPINACH.

Vern.—*Poi* (cultivated), *bon-poi* (wild), BENG., HIND.; *Matto-batsala*, TEL.

A succulent climber met with, wild and cultivated, in many parts of the damper regions of India. There are three other species, *viz.*, **B. rubra, B. cordifolia, B. lucida,** commonly cultivated by the natives near their homesteads and in vegetable gardens, and sold in nearly every market place.

The succulent leaves and stems used as a pot-herb (made into curry) by natives of all classes.

BASSIA.

106 **Bassia butyracea,** *Roxb.*, SAPOTACEÆ.

Vern.—*Chiura, chaiura, phulel*, KUMAUN; *Cheuli*, OUDH; *Phalwara*, HIND; *Churi*, NEPAL; *Yel, yelpote*, LEPCHA.

A deciduous tree of the sub-Himalayan tract, from Kumaun to Bhutan, between 1,500 and 4,500 feet.

The pulp of the fruit is eaten. The juice of the flowers is made into sugar.

107 **B. latifolia,** *Roxb.*

THE BUTTER OR MAHWA TREE.

Vern.—*Mahúa, mahwa, mowa*, HIND.; *Mahwa, mahúla, maul*, BENG.; *Mowd, mahuá*, BOM.; *Katillipi, illupi, elupa*, TAM.; *Ippi, yeppa*, TEL.; *Madhuka*, SANS.; *Irúp, irrip*, GONDI.; *Honge*, KAN.; *Bonam*, MAL.; *Moho*, MAR.

The well-known *Mahua* tree, indigenous to the forests of Central India, cultivated and self-sown throughout the warmer regions of India. Very gregarious and often associated with the *Sál*.

In the *Linnæan Society's Journal* there appeared an admirable report of the uses of the Mahua from the pen of Mr. Lockwood, formerly Magistrate and Collector of Monghyr, in which he urged the importance of its introduction into Europe as a food for cattle.

The tree is of great economic importance to a very large number of the poorer natives, and has, of late, been the subject of a legislative measure in the Bombay Presidency. Mr. L. Liotard instituted certain special enquiries with regard to its economic uses, and embodied the results of his investigation in a Note, dated the 13th July 1882, published by the Government of India. As it is of importance in connection with the study of the question of the resources of the people, the following summary of Mr. Liotard's Note may be reproduced here:—

Punjab.—Sub-Himalayan tracts, not particularly abundant, except in parts of Kangra.

North-Western Provinces.—(1) Sub-Himalayan tracts; (2) south of Jumna tracts, on the skirts of the Vindhya plateau, abundant.

Oudh.—Fairly abundant, especially in Sub-Himalayan tracts.

Bundelkhand.—Native States common.

Bengal.—Common on the strip of country along the Satpura range, *i. e.*, on the edge of the Central Indian plateau; and there is a fair sprinkling of the tree along the Sub-Himalayan tracts of Behar. It gradually disappears towards Calcutta and occurs only sparsely in the Madras Presidency, where it is succeeded by an allied species called **B. longifolia**, which stands in every way similar in its economic uses to **B. latifolia**.

Central Provinces.—Abundant in every district, especially on the Satpura Range.

Bombay Presidency.—Very common in Guzerat and on the west of the ghâts.

The tree thrives on dry, stony ground, and is seldom cultivated. It sheds its leaves gradually from February to April. The cream-coloured corolla, clustering near the ends of branches, appear in March and April, and are soon followed by the new leaf-buds. The fruits are green when unripe, and reddish yellow or orange when ripe, fleshy, one to two inches in length, with one to four seeds, which ripen about three months after the flowers have fallen.

The tree is valued for its flowers, its fruit, and the kernel of its seed; and is of considerable economic importance to a large proportion of the poorer classes of natives.

The flowers.—When the buds appear, the natives clear away the grasses and jungle from beneath the trees; and when the flowers fall, women and children, and sometimes men, may be seen busily occupied in the early mornings gathering in baskets large quantities of flowers. It is reckoned that each tree during the season gives from 6 to 8 maunds of flowers, varying according to the size of the tree and the nature of the season. This produce is used in two ways: (1) as an article of food, and (2) as a material for the manufacture of a spirituous liquor.

As an article of food it possesses, when fresh, a peculiar luscious taste, with an odour somewhat suggestive of mice. When dried the flavour has some resemblance to that of inferior kinds of figs, and they form an important addition to the food-supply of the poorer classes of parts of the country in which the tree grows in abundance. Under the Mahratta rule it is said to have been a common practice to cut down the mahua trees in the Bhil country so as to afflict the lawless hill tribes and reduce them to straits. This shows how greatly the hill tribes of the Central Provinces depended on the produce of these trees for food.

The flowers are used either freshly gathered, or after being sun-dried. They are eaten cooked or uncooked, often with parched grain or with the seeds of the *sál* tree, or with leaves of other plants. Jackals, bears, wild pigs and deer are very fond of Mahua.

For the manufacture of spirits, the flowers when dried are sold by the hill people at various rates either to the village distillers or to the baniahs, by whom they are exported. The dried flowers are immersed in water for four days; they are then fermented, and thereafter distilled. The liquor produced from a single distillation is extremely weak, ranging from 60° to 90° under proof. But a second distillation is sometimes resorted to, especially where still-head duty is levied irrespective of strength, and in this case a spirit averaging 25° below proof is obtained. The distillation is practised in the Punjab to a small extent; in Rajputana every village apparently has its spirit shop for the sale of the distilled liquor; in the North-West Provinces and Oudh the liquor is made in the eastern and southern districts and is of common use among certain classes; in the western districts of Bengal it is abundantly distilled; so also in the Central Provinces, and in parts of the Bombay Presidency, especially in the northern and southern divisions.

The fruit.—The fruit is sometimes eaten. In the western tracts of Bengal it is dried in the sun and eaten in times of scarcity.

The seed.—The seed is chiefly used for the sake of the oil it contains. The kernels are taken out for this purpose from the smooth, chestnut-coloured pericarp by being bruised, rubbed and subjected to a moderate pressure. They are then ground and the oil obtained by cold expression. In the Central Provinces, the kernels are pounded and boiled and then wrapped up in two or three folds of cloth and the oil thereafter expressed. In the western tracts of Bengal and in the Central Provinces, besides being used for lighting, it forms a very inexpensive substitute for ghi. In the Rewa Kantha State of Guzerat some local trade is carried on in

BAUHINIA.

the *mahua* oil; and in the Ahmedabad district of Bombay it is used locally and also for export to neighbouring places.

The export of the *mahua* to England has lately been made the subject of experiment. It is said to be an excellent food for pigs; but the trade, however, is not yet established, although hopes exist that it will be.

108 **Bassia longifolia,** *Willd.*

Vern.—*Kat illupi, elupa,* TAM.; *Ippi, yeppa, pinna,* TEL.; *Hippe,* KAN.; *Mu,* CINGH.; *Kan zan,* BURM.

An evergreen tree of South India, on the Coromandel and Malabar coasts.

The economic uses of this tree in Southern India are similar to those of **B. latifolia** in the central regions of the country.

Bassorine. *See* **Orchis mascula,** ORCHIDEÆ.

Batatas edulis, *Chois.* *See* **Ipomœa Batatas,** *Lamk.*, CONVOLVULACEÆ.

BAUHINIA.

109 **Bauhinia malabarica,** *Roxb.*, LEGUMINOSÆ.

Vern.—*Amli, amlosa,* HIND.; *Karmai,* BENG.; *Kattra,* ASS.; *Pulla dondur,* TEL.; *Cheppura,* KAN.; *Bwaygyin,* BURM.

Found in the sub-Himalayan tract, from the Ganges to Assam, Bengal, Burma, and South India.

The leaves are very acrid; but are eaten by people in Burma (*Brandis*).

110 **B. purpurea,** *Linn.*

Vern.—*Rakta-kanchan,* BENG.; *Kaliar,* HIND.; *Kachnar,* PB.; *Pedda-are,* TAM.; *Mahalay-kani,* BURM.; *Sarul,* KAN.

An ornamental tree, 20 to 30 feet in height, met with chiefly in Bengal, Burma, North-West Provinces, and South India.

Dr. Stewart says that the flowers are used as a pot-herb in curries and that they are also made into pickles; the leaves are given to cattle as fodder.

111 **B. racemosa,** *Lam.*

Syn.—B. PARVIFLORA, *Vahl.*

Vern.—*Kachnál, gúriál, ashta, makkúna, thaur, dhorára,* HIND.; *Banraj,* BENG.; *Kosúndra, taur,* PP.; *Dhondri, bosha,* GOND.; *Jhinja,* AJMERE; *Ambhola,* URIYA; *Ari, arro,* TEL.; *Ati, areka,* TAM.; *Hpalan,* BURM.

Met with in the sub-Himalayan tract, from the Ravi eastward, Oudh, Bengal, Burma, Central and South India.

In parts of Northern India the leaves are eaten by buffaloes. The seeds are eaten by the people in some parts of the country.

112 **B. Vahlii,** *W. & A.*

Vern.—*Maljan, malghán, malu, maurain, jallur,* HIND.; *Chehur,* BENG.; *Shioli,* URIYA; *Sungung rik,* LEPCHA; *Chanbuli,* DEC.; *Adda,* TAM.

Found in the sub-Himalayan tract, North and Central India, and Tenasserim.

The seeds are eaten raw, when ripe, tasting like cashew-nut. (*Drury.*)

The leaves form plates, umbrellas, hats, bellows; the young pods are cooked and eaten by the hill tribes, and the stems form natural ropes, used in the construction of their huts.

BERBERIS.

Bauhinia variegata, *Linn.* 113

Vern.—*Kachnár, koliár, bariál, kurál, kaniár, kándan, khairwál,* HIND.; *Rakta kánchan,* BENG.; *Borara,* URIYA; *Rha,* LEPCHA; *Taki,* NEPAL; *Segapumunthari,* TAM.; *Kanchivalo-do,* KAN.; *Bwaycheng,* BURM.

A small tree met with on the Himalayas from the Indus eastward and in the forests of India and Burma.

It flowers in February-March; the seeds ripen two months later. The buds are eaten as vegetables when prepared with animal food (*Drury*).

Beet and Beet-root. *See* **Beta vulgaris,** *Moq.*, CHENOPODIACEÆ.

BEGONIA.

Begonia Rex, *Puiz.*, and other species, BEGONIACEÆ. 114

Many species of this herbaceous plant, having succulent stems, are used as a pot-herb, and when fresh have a pleasant, acid taste.

Beleric myrobalan. *See* **Terminalia belerica,** *Roxb.*, COMBRETACEÆ.

BENINCASA.

Benincasa cerifera, *Savi.*, CUCURBITACEÆ. 115

THE WHITE MELON.

Syn.—CUCURBITA PEPO, *Roxb.*, includes this plant as well as C. PEPO, *DC.*

Vern.—*Kumrá,* BENG.; *Kumra, pethá, bhúttuá,* HIND.; *Kumbuli,* TAM.; *Budidi gummadi,* TEL.; *Kushmánda,* SANS.

A climbing plant, cultivated all over India, frequently upon the roofs of huts. Supposed to be originally a Native of Japan and Java.

To distinguish it from **Cucurbita Pepo,** *DC.*, the following characters may be given:—*Male,* flowers large, solitary, *petals* 5, early free, *stamens* 3, inserted near the mouth of the tube, *anthers* free, exserted; *fruit* 1 to 1½ feet, cylindric, without ribs, hairy when young, and bright green, ultimately becoming smooth and covered with a bluish white, waxy bloom, flesh white.

The white gourd melon is used in the following ways: (*a*) as a vegetable, (*b*) as a curry, and (*c*) as a sweetmeat called *heshmi.*

BERBERIS.

Berberis aristata, *DC.*, and **B. Lycium,** *Royle,* BERBERIDEÆ. 116

THE BARBERRY.

Vern.—*Chitra, chotra, dar-haldi, rasaut, kashmal,* HIND.; *Súmlú, simlú, kasmal,* PB.; *Chitra,* NEPAL; *Chitra, sirishk,* PERS.

Thorny shrubs, with small, simple, spiny leaves, met with throughoue the Himalaya. The former is found from the Sutlej to Bhutan, altitudt 6,000 to 10,000 feet to the western ghats; the latter seems to be confined to the North-Western Himalaya. It is a native of Nepal.

The fruit, oblong, purplish or pinkish and wrinkled, is eaten and is very palatable. The berries are dried in the sun like raisins.

B. asiatica, *Roxb.* 117

Vern.—*Kilmara,* KUMAUN; *Mâte, kissi, chitra,* NEPAL.

Dry valleys of the Himalaya, altitude 3,000 to 7,500 feet; from Bhutan to Garhwal, Behar, or hill Parasnath, altitude 3,500 feet.

The fruit is used just as that of **B. aristata,** *DC.* and **B. Lycium** *Royle.*

118 **Berberis vulgaris,** *Linn.*

Vern.—*Zeirishk, kashmal, chochar,* PB.

In the western half of the Himalayan range and in Afghanistan.

The dried fruits, under the name of *sirish-tursh* (sour currants) are imported from Cabul, Herat and Kandadar into the Punjab. The fruit forms a pleasant acid preserve; and the unripe ones are pickled as a substitute for capers.

Bergera Kœnigii, *Linn.* *See* **Murraya Kœnigii,** *Spr.*, RUTACEÆ.

BETA.

119 **Beta vulgaris,** *Moq.*, CHENOPODIACEÆ.

COUNTRY SPINACH.

Vern.—*Palak,* BENG., HIND.

Cultivated by natives to a certain extent over most parts of the country. Used as a pot-herb.

Betel leaf. *See* **Piper Betle,** *Linn.*, PIPERACEÆ.

Betel nut. *See* **Areca Catechu,** *Linn.*, PALMÆ.

BETULA.

120 **Betula Bhojpattra,** *Wall.*, CUPULIFERÆ.

INDIAN PAPER BIRCH.

Vern. *Burj, bursal, bhuj,* PB.; *Shákpád, phatak, takpa,* HIMALAYAN NAMES; *Bhujpattra,* HIND.; *Phuspat,* NEPAL

A moderate-sized, deciduous tree, on the higher ranges of the Himalaya, forming the upper edge of arborescent vegetation.

The leaves are lopped for cattle fodder.

Birch. *See* **Betula Bhojpattra,** *Wall,* CUPULIFERÆ.

BŒHMERIA.

121 **Bœhmeria Salicifolia,** *D. Don,* URTICACEÆ.

Vern.—*Amrer, chenjul, sansaru, thana, siaru, pincho, shakei,* PB.

A shrub generally near water in the outer Himalayan tracts of the Punjab, also in Eastern Punjab and in North West Provinces.

Browsed by sheep. The aggregated small berries yield an edible fruit. (*Royle.*)

BOMBAX.

122 **Bombax malabaricum,** *DC.*, MALVACEÆ.

Syn. B. HEPTAPHYLLA, *Cav.*

Vern.—*Semul, shembal, semur, pagun, somr,* HIND., BENG.; *Simbal, sharlan,* HIMALAYAN NAMES; *Bouro,* URIYA; *Bolchú,* GARO; *Búrga, búrgú, buraga,* TEL.; *Illavam, puld,* TAM.; *Katu-imbúl,* CINGH. *Letfan,* BURM.; *Salmali,* SANS.

Throughout India and Burma, ascending the Himalayas to 4,000 feet in altitude; chiefly met with in the hotter forests of East India.

The leaves and twigs are lopped probably for fodder. The flower-buds are eaten as a pot-herb.

BORASSUS.

Borassus flabelliformis, *Linn.*, PALMÆ. 123

THE PALMYRA PALM.

Vern.—*Tál, tála, tár,* HIND.; *Tál,* BENG.; *Potu tádi* (the male tree), *Penti tadi* (the female), TEL.; *Panam, pannie,* TAM.; *Tád,* GUZ.; *Htan,* BURM.

Occurring in abundance along the sea coast tracts of Southern India, also about the Dinapore Division in Bengal; elsewhere less numerous, but still common.

Cultivated throughout tropical India, and beyond the tropics in Bengal, and the southern part of the North West Provinces.

Under the head of food the following uses may be mentioned:—

(1) The tree on being tapped yields juice which, before sunrise, is sweet and agreeable to the taste, and is then either drunk or made into sugar by boiling down and drying by exposure. In the Madras Presidency the quantity of jaggery sugar made from the juice of the palmyra palm is very considerable. After sunrise the juice rapidly ferments, and is then converted into toddy, and used as an intoxicating drink.

(2) The tree flowers in the beginning of the hot season, and produces in bunches large fruits about 3 inches in diameter,—which are green when unripe, and black on the outside when ripe. They contain three hard seeds. "The fruit, when young and green, is carefully plucked and cut open, and the immature seeds are cut out of the fleshy part of the fruit with a sharp *dao*. Each seed then forms a thin soft, pulpy shell filled with juice. They are taken to the bazars for sale or sold by street hawkers, and are much relished by natives of all classes. They are known as *talsans* in Bengal. They are cool and refreshing. They are sometimes cut into small pieces, sugared adnt flavoured with rose water. Prepared in this way they form one of the most refreshing and pleasant delicacies for the hot season.

"A certain number of the fruit ripens on the trees. Their seeds then become hard and are of no use except for reproduction; the pulp inside the hard shell is the part then eaten. It has a peculiar odour, and is sweetish; it is either eaten raw, or is mashed and strained with a little flour and sugar, completely mixed up to form a mass which is then made into small flat cakes and fried in ghi or mustard oil; the cakes are known as *peetahs*."

"The young plant is used as a vegetable, and is made into curry or preserve or pickle, but not commonly."

BOUCEROSIA.

Boucerosia edulis, *Edge.*, ASCLEPIADEÆ. *See* **Caralluma edulis,** *Benth.*

BOUEA.

Bouea burmanica, *Griff.*, ANACARDIACEÆ. 124

Vern.—*Meriam, mayan,* BURM.

A moderate-sized, evergreen tree of Burma and Andaman Islands. The tree has an edible fruit for which it is often cultivated.

BRASSICA.

Brassica, a genus of **Cruciferæ,** exceedingly important to man. There are about 80 species known, and nearly all are now almost entirely in a

BRAS-
SICA.

state of cultivation. They are antiscorbutic, and, it may be stated that no plant with a four-merous condition of the corolla, and with four long and two short stamens, is known to be poisonous. These are the eye-marks of the **Cruciferæ**, a family which yields the majority of the vegetables used by the inhabitants of temperate countries. Of the cruciferous genera, **Brassica** is the most important. To it belongs the mustard, the cabbage, the cauliflower, the broccoli, the borecole, the radish and the turnip, with their innumerable varieties. The following are the important Indian wild or cultivated species, with their principal culinary forms.

125 1. **Brassica alba,** *H. f. & T. T.*

THE WHITE MUSTARD.

Vern.—*Siddhartha*, SANS.

This is the plant which yields the so-called White Mustard. It is by no means a common plant, but may be recognised by its spreading pods, few seeded, with a long empty beak. *See* **B. Nigra.**

Properties and Uses.

The leaves, eaten when young.
The seeds, large and white.
The flour, rarely used alone.
The oil, little known.

The plant is also used as salad, the seeds being sown thickly, and the young seedling plants being cut when about 2 inches high. The cake much used in Europe, to feed sheep. The white mustard oil cake is regarded as fattening for sheep. The black oil cake is not considered so good for this purpose.

126 2. **B. campestris,** *Linn.*

To this species belong the Turnip and a group of plants closely related to the Mustard. These are generally known as Rape, Coleseed, Colza, Sarson, &c. It may be as well to refer the cultivated series of forms belonging to this species to their respective botanical varieties.
See **Rape.**

127 **Var. 1, campestris** *proper*, (**var. dichotoma,** *Duthie and Fuller.*)

THE COLZA, WILD NEVEW, NAVATTEE; THE SWEDISH TURNIP, and SARSON, *Eng.*; CHOU DESCHAMPS, NAVETTEE, *Fr.*

Syn.—SINAPIS DICHOTOMA, *Roxb*; S. BRASSICATA, *Roxb.*

Vern.—*Kali sarson* or *serson, sursi, jariya, lahsta, laita, jadiya*, HIND.; *Surshi* or *sursi, sanchi, kali-sarson, sada-rai*, BENG.; *Sarshapa*, SANS.

Properties and Uses.

Leaves used for culinary purposes, the ground ones being more or less hairy.

Seeds, small, smooth, light brown, form oil cake for feeding cattle.

Colza Oil is used by the natives of India chiefly to anoint the body and for illuminating purposes.

This includes the Swedish Turnip, the Colza or Wild Nevew and many other forms, amongst which may be mentioned the *Sarson* or the plant to which **Roxburgh** gave the name of **Sinapis dichotoma.** This may be called the Swedish Turnip and Colza series.

See **Colza** under **Rape.**

BRAS-
SICA.
128

Var. 2, Napus.

RAPESEED, NEVEW, or COLESEED, *Eng.*; CHOU-NAVET, *Fr.*; DER RUBEN, KOHLRAPSANT, *Ger.*

Sub-var.—GLAUCA *(var. Duthie and Fuller.)*

Syn.—*SINAPIS* GLAUCA, *Roxb.*

Vern.—*Sarson, sarson-sard, bang-sarson, pila-sarson, rara-rada, rara-sarson*, HIND.; *Shwet-rai*, BENG.; *Rajika*, SANS.

Properties and Uses.

The leaves are used for culinary purposes, the ground ones being quite glabrous.

Pods very thick, ½ to ⅓ inch length, seeds round, smooth and white, occasionally coloured.

The oil is superior to the preceding and much used in diet and in anointing the body before the daily ablutions by the natives.

The various forms of what may be called *sarson* are generally cultivated as mixed crops. This, which is a convenient or commercial section, practically includes the forms which we have referred to **Campestris** *proper* as well as sub-variety **glauca**.

In the North-Western Provinces and Oudh, *sarson* is very seldom grown alone, but is sown in greater or less quantity in nearly every field of wheat and barley, chiefly in the Doab districts lying between Meerut and Allahabad, but the exact area cannot be stated; the outturn of seed is from 1½ to 2 mds. per acre.

Sub-var. toria *(var. Duthie and Fuller).*

Syn.—SINAPIS GLAUCA, *Royle.*

Vern.—*Tori, toriya, khetiya,* **also** *dain,* **and** *dain-lai*, HIND.; *Tuverica*, SANS.

Properties and Uses.

The leaves, used for culinary purposes, the whole plant glabrous.

Pods rather slender 1½ to 1¾ long; seeds small, roundish or semi-compressed, reddish brown.

The oil, not known.

This plant is as a rule grown alone; it is produced in the greatest abundance in the districts which border on the Himalayan Terai; and in the North-Western Provinces and Oudh, occupies annually about 35,000 acres in the 30 temporarily-settled districts, yielding 4 to 6 maunds of seed per acre.

General Account.

Roxburgh's three species (**S. dichotoma, glauca, brassicata**), and **S. glauca**, *Royle*, referred by Hooker's *Flora of British India* to **Brassica campestris**, represent individually agricultural products of the greatest importance to India. They would seem sufficiently distinct to have justified their retention at least as varieties, very much corresponding to the original species. The natives display a highly-developed power of observation in this direction; they have long become perfectly familiar with these plants, and can as a rule name them with unerring certainty.

Since writing this account we have, through the kindness of the authors of the *Field and Garden Crops of the North-Western Provinces and Oudh*, seen the proof sheets of Part II of that work, and find that they write that "from an agricultural point of view the varieties of **B. campestris** may be classed under two heads, one including all those known as *sarson*, and the other including the variety known as *lahi* or *toria*. These are distinguished very sharply in their method of cultivation."

Whether or not it be correct botanically to sub-divide the Indian forms of **B. campestris** into two sections resembling Rape and Colza, and to identify these sections with the corresponding European forms, it

BRASSICA.

cannot be doubted that such a classification will serve a commercial purpose. It will separate the oil which in Indian commerce is called Rape Oil, from that which should receive the name of Colza, as well as both these from Mustard Oil, and the other oils obtained from the remaining members of this genus. It will be enough, however, to suggest this separation; subsequent research may reveal further corrections and sub-divisions, for there are many points which it is difficult to settle definitely in the present state of information. Perhaps the only botanical character that could be cited in support of the proposed separation is the glabrous nature of the ground leaves of the forms above referred to as *Navet* (Rape), and the more or less hairy ground leaves of **S. dichotoma,** corresponding with those of *Navette* (Colza). The seeds in the former are smooth and white, in the latter smooth or rough, but dark coloured. Rape Oil (**S. glauca**) is regarded as better in quality than (Colza Oil) the oil from **S. dichotoma,** the latter being used chiefly to anoint the body, while the former is largely used in cookery and is exported to Europe for illuminating purposes, and in the India rubber manufactory. It is probable that in the trade returns of the exportation of Rape Oil and Seed from India, both the above are included as different qualities of Rape, if not also the oil expressed from **B. juncea** and **Eruca sativa.**

In his *Punjab Products,* **Mr. Baden-Powell** has apparently mistaken these plants; he identifies *Sarson* or *Rape* with **Sinapis juncea,** *Mustard* with **S. campestris,** of which he apparently views **S. alba** and **nigra** as varieties. Regarding **Mr. Atkinson** as correct, I have in substance followed his admirable division. *See* MUSTARD.

In European commerce Rape and Colza oils are synonymous or nearly so, and the separation here recommended of the probable corresponding Indian forms has been deemed advisable chiefly with a view to more clearly identifying the Indian oils allied to Mustard. **Simmonds** in his *Tropical Agriculture* (1877) remarks of Indian so-called Rape Seed, that "the prices in the London market in the beginning of 1877 were, for Calcutta brown, 59*s.* 6*d.* to 60*s.* per quarter, and for Ferozepore, 59*s.*" Under Mustard he seems to include **S. chinensis, S. dichotoma, S. pekinensis, S. ramosa, S. glauca** and **S. juncea** as the mustard-yielding species of Asia. The majority of these plants are those which yield the so-called Rape Seed as exported from India, **Brassica (Sinapis) juncea** alone falling within those pronounced to be Mustard. In fact it is probable that the bulk of the seed exported as Mustard is obtained from **B. juncea** and not from **B. alba** and **nigra,** the true Mustards.

"In India Rape Seed is very commonly sown mixed with Mustard Seed, and almost as an auxiliary with grain crops. It prefers loams, and does not thrive on clay soils. The sowing takes place in October, and the harvest in the following February, the plants being cut somewhat prematurely, otherwise the pods would burst, and much of the seed be lost. The latter is ripened by exposure to the sun for 3 or 4 days on the threshing-floor, and is then easily dislodged." "The Indian seed known as 'Guzerat Rape' largely crushed at Dantzic, is found to yield 3½ per cent. more oil than European seed, and leaves a cake richer in fatty matter and albuminoids; it is shipped from Bombay and brings the highest price of any." (*Spons' Encycl.*)

The North-Western Provinces export a large quantity of Rape Seed, and the trade centres at Cawnpore. The following figures show the railway-borne traffic in Rape Seed in 1881-82:

	Mds.
Exports to Calcutta	11,75,463
,, other places	6,13,882
Total exports	17,89,345
,, imports	14,958

BRASSICA.

When fodder gets scarce the Rape crop is sometimes cut green and given to cattle.

The following table will show the Exports of Rape Seed to other countries by *Sea* during the six years ending 1881-82 :—

Years.	Quantity in Cwts.	Value in Rupees.
1877-78	3,193,488	1,91,84,378
1878-79	2,165,475	1,36,67,869
1879-80	1,380,572	85,37,717
1880-81	1,255,580	67,10,338
1881-82	1,935,621	1,03,19,272
1882-83	2,821,420	1,57,05,233

The following analysis of the exports of Rape Seed for the year 1882-83 shows the Presidencies or Provinces whence exported and the countries to which consigned :—

Presidency or province.	Quantity in Cwts.	Value in Rupees.	Country to which exported.	Quantity in Cwts.	Value in Rupees.
Bengal .	1,529,889	74,63,415	United Kingdom	1,392,628	69,18,218
Bombay .	779,052	49,47,430	Belgium . .	478,580	30,06,442
Sind . .	480,362	31,43,780	France . .	810,199	49,74,926
Madras .	32,117	1,50,608	Germany . .	1,932	10,626
			Holland . .	3,001	18,560
			Italy . .	3,610	22,854
			Spain . .	2,668	17,679
			Egypt . .	128,783	7,35,800
			Other Countries .	19	128
TOTAL .	2,821,420	1,57,05,233	TOTAL .	2,821,420	1,57,05,233

The foregoing remarks will show that it is impossible to determine at present how far the exports of the so-called Indian Rape Seed correspond to exports of the forms of **B, campestris** alone (the true Rape), or include **B. juncea** (Indian Mustard) or even **Eruca sativa,** and that it is next to impossible to know what is meant by Mustard, and what by Rape, in our trade returns.

Var. 3, Rapa. 129

THE TURNIP.

Vern.—*Shalgam*, HIND., BENG.

Properties and Uses.

The young leaves, used as food.

The root, largely used as food.

The seeds are used for reproduction.

The common cultivated Turnip may almost be said to be acclimatised in India, and to have gained great favour with the natives as a vegetable. The Brahmans and Baniyas have a prejudice against it from a suspicion of its relation or resemblance to beef or animal matter.

BRASSICA.

130 **3. Brassica juncea,** *H. f. & T. T.*

THE RAI OR INDIAN MUSTARD.

Syn.—SINAPIS RAMOSA, *Roxb.*; S. CUNCIFOLIA, *Roxb.*; S. RUGOSA, *Roxb.*; S. NUNCEA, *Linn.*

Vern.—*Rai, sarson, sarson-lahi, gohna-sarson, bari-rai, barlái, bádshahi-lae, shahsada-rai and khas-rai,* HIND.; *Rajika,* SANS.

Properties and Uses.

The leaves are used as a vegetable.

The seeds, small, round, dark, may be called Indian Mustard seed.

The seeds ground into flour are used largely as an adulterant with the true Mustard.

The oil, clear, not rancid, are largely eaten by the natives with their curries, &c. **Roxburgh** apparently regarded this oil as inferior to Rape Oil.

General Account.

This plant may be called Indian Mustard; in point of structure it is perhaps more nearly allied to the true Mustard than to any other member of the genus. Its properties seem also very similar, and in fact it is largely used to adulterate, or as a substitute for, Mustard in the preparation of the flour. The oil is of a much purer kind than that from **B. campestris**; it has not the peculiar rancid smell characteristic of Rape and Colza; it is clearer in colour and used almost entirely as an article of food, being the oil most generally used in the plains of India for that purpose. The seeds are small, round, dark brown and pitted or rugose. About 15 to 20 occur in each cell of the pod, and in these respects **B. juncea** seems recognisable from the other members of the genus, most of which have large light-coloured or yellow seeds, generally smooth, with rarely more than half the number of seeds in the pod. The seeds, whole or broken, are often used to flavour curries.

In the North-West Provinces and Oudh generally grown in borders of fields of wheat, barley or peas, sometimes broadcast at the rate of about 3 lbs. per acre, when its outturn is 3 to 4 maunds of seed to the acre. The oil yielded is one-fourth the weight of the seed.

In Kumaun the plant is cultivated chiefly for its leaves which are eaten as a vegetable (*Atkinson*).

When the supply of fodder happens to run short in January or February, the Mustard crop is cut green and given to cattle.

131 **4. B. nigra,** *Koch.*

THE BLACK OR TRUE MUSTARD, *Eng.*; MOUTARDE NOIRE, *Fr.*; MUSTERT, SEUFSAMEN, *Ger.*; SENAPA, *It.*; MOSTARDA, *Por.*

Syn.—SINAPIS ERYSIMOIDES, *Roxb.*; SINAPIS NIGRA, *Linn.*

Vern.—*Rai, kali rai, lahi, benarsi, jagrai, asl-rai, ghor-rai, makara-rai, &c.,* HIND.; *Rai sarisha,* BENG.; *Kadagho,* TAM.; *Avalo,* TEL.; *Ganaba,* CINGH.; *Kiditsai,* CHINESE; *Rajika, sarshap,* SANS.; *Sirshaf* (the name by which it is known in Indian hospitals), PERS.; *Khirdal,* ARAB.

This may be distinguished from **B. alba** by its stem clasping or adpressed and nearly glabrous short pods.

Properties and Uses.

The leaves, petioled and lyrate. They are used for culinary purposes.

The seeds, large, oblong, and dark-coloured.

A bland oil, expressed from the seeds, used for various economic purposes; also used by native doctors medicinally.

BRASSICA.

The flour, used medicinally as a poultice and counter-irritant. In Japan and China it is regarded as of great importance.

An essential oil, obtained through the action of water.

General Account.

The majority of the plants, to which Europeans in India give the name of Mustard, should be transferred bodily to Rape and its associates, to which they are certainly much more nearly allied. The true Mustard is very scarce in India, and seems to have been introduced. **Ainslie** fixes its introduction within the present century, and the first time **Roxburgh** saw the plant was when raised from seeds sent him from the Wynaad in South India. It is nowhere extensively cultivated, but is met with chiefly on the hills, and it is more than probable that it existed on the Himalayas from remote times, although unknown to the fathers of Indian botanical science It is quite likely that the ancient Sanskrit writers had not seen the true black and white Mustard, and that the word *rajika* may have originally denoted a form of **Brassica juncea** and the word *siddhartha* a form of **B. campestris.** Now-a-days these names are chiefly applied to the true black and white Mustard **B. nigra** and **B. alba** respectively.

The leaves are eaten green as a cress. The seeds are ground into what is known as Mustard Flour. The French Mustard Flour is much darker in colour than the English, because the seeds are not first husked. It is much more acrid and pungent, for the husk contains the principal store of pungency. Mustard Flour is never prepared in India, or, at all events, never used as a condiment, except in making pickles from green mangoes and other sub-acid fruits. The seeds are ground and used as a poultice, and the expressed oil is also used medicinally. In Japan and China, Mustard is regarded as a medicine of great importance. The ancient Hindus do not appear to have known the Essential Oil of Mustard. This oil does not exist in the seeds originally, but is chemically produced by the action of water, as, for example, when a seed or a little of the flour is put into the mouth. Chemically, mustard seeds consist of a bland fixed oil (obtained by pressure) and a peculiar inodorous substance called Myroncic acid, together with a third substance which has been called Myrosyne. By the action of water upon these substances the Essential Oil is produced, which is known chemically as Pyrosyne.

White Mustard is much inferior commercially, but is generally mixed with the black Mustard. It is said to be cultivated at Ferozpur but is scarcely known in India. The white oil cake is a valued food for sheep.

In the preparation of Mustard Flour the relative quantities of black and white mustard used are commonly two parts of black to three of white, but the proportions vary. In Russia **B. juncea** is ground into Mustard Flour, and so may most of the other Indian species; but they yield an inferior article to the true Mustard Flour of commerce, and, as already indicated, their true position is with the Rape and Colza of Europe. It is much to be regretted that the true Mustard Oil, **B. nigra** and **B. alba**, the Rape Oil (**B. napus** or in India **B. glauca**), the Colza Oil, **B. campestris**, *proper*, or in India **B. dichotoma**, and the oil from **B. juncea**, if not also the oil from **Eruca sativa**, have become so hopelessly confused in our trade reports under the common name of Rape Oil or Rape Seed. A considerable injury has thereby been done, and a check given to the development of foreign trade in these oils and seeds. It will require time and careful observation to remove this fully and to identify and distinguish the commercial products.

The quantity of pure Mustard produced in India cannot at present

BRASSICA.

be very great; from the confusion referred to above, it is impossible to arrive at any very definite information, as it is impossible to determine how far the term "Mustard" may be confined to the products of **Brassica alba** and **nigra.** It is chiefly cultivated in the hills and used in medicine or for culinary purposes. In the official catalogue of the Paris Exhibition of 1867, it is stated that 3,000 tons of flour, equal to 2,000,000 francs worth, were annually produced in France.

The annual Statement of the Trade and Navigation of British India with Foreign Countries gives the following figures as the exports from India for the past five years under the head of "Mustard":—

Exportation of Mustard.

Years.	Quantity in Cwts.	Value in Rupees.
1877-78	7,782	49,777
1878-79	5,016	33,876
1879-80	2,369	15,181
1880-81	17,448	1,03,240
1881 82	24,346	1,44,508

The following analysis of the exports of Mustard for the year 1881-82 is interesting as showing the relative quantities produced in these provinces, and the more important foreign countries to which it was exported:—

Presidency from which exported.	Quantity in Cwts.	Value in Rupees.	Country to which exported.	Quantity in Cwts.	Value. in Rupees.
			United Kingdom .	13,230	80,883
Bengal .	1,287	7,067	France . .	6,778	38,819
Bombay .	21,792	1,29,970	Mauritius . .	1,449	8,032
Sindh .	920	5,497	United States .	2,401	14,197
Madras .	347	1,974	Straits . .	223	1,196
			Other Countries .	265	1,381
TOTAL .	24,346	1,44,,508	TOTAL . .	24,346	1,44,508

132 5. **Brassica oleracea,** *Linn.*

THE CABBAGE.

To this species belong the Cabbage and all its associates, supposed to have been produced by cultivating the European Wild Colewort or Wild Cabbage.

The following are the principal cultivated forms:—

B. (oleracea) **sylvestris**—The Wild Colewort.
B. (oleracea) **acephala**—The Green Kale or Borecole.
B. (oleracea) **bulleata**—The Savoy Cabbage.
B. (oleracea) **gemmifera**—The Brussels Sprout.
B. (oleracea) **capitata**—The Red and White Cabbage.
B. (oleracea) **caulo-rapa**—The Turnip-stemmed Cabbage or *Kobh Rabi*.
B. (oleracea) **botrytis**—The Cauliflower and Broccoli.

For fuller details *see* CABBAGE.

6. B. quadrivalvis, *H. f. & T. T.* *See* **B. trilocularis,** *H. f. & T. T.* 133
The seeds.

7. B. tournefortu, *Gouan.* 134
Is said to be cultivated between Ajmir and Delhi, but is unknown commercially. The flowers are pale yellow, and the seeds large and compressed.

8. B. trilocularis, *H. f. & T. T.* and **B. quadrivalvis,** *H. f. & T. T.* 135
Seeds.

Will probably prove to be cultivated forms of **B. campestris,** nearly allied to **S. glauca,** *Roxb.* The seeds are large and white. An interesting series of specimens have been placed in the Calcutta Botanic Gardens prepared by **Mr. Duthie,** Superintendent of the Botanic Gardens, Saharanpur. These seem to prove that the number of the valves in the fruit is of little or no importance, and depends more upon treatment than upon specific peculiarities.

Bran. 136
A coarse product of wheat, separated from the latter in the milling process. *See* **Triticum sativum.**

Bread fruit tree. *See* **Artocarpus incisa,** *Linn.*, URTICACEÆ.

BRIEDELIA.

Briedelia montana, *Willd.*, EUPHORBIACEÆ. 137

Vern.—*Kargnalia, khaja, geia, kusi,* HIND.; *Geio,* NEPAL; *Kaisho,* ASS.; *Patenga,* TEL.

A moderate-sized, deciduous tree of the sub-Himalyan tract from the Jhelum eastward, ascending to 4,000 feet, Oudh, and Bengal.
The leaves are lopped for cattle fodder.

B. retusa, *Spreng.* 138

Syn.—B. SPINOSA, *Willd.*

Vern.—*Pathor, mark,* PB.; *Khaja, kassi,* HIND.; *Lamkana, angnera,* RAJPUTANA; *Kosi,* URIYA; *Muluvengay, kamanji,* TAM.; *Tsichyee,* BURM.

A large, deciduous tree of the sub-Himalayan tract, from the Chenab eastward, ascending to 3,600 feet, Oudh, Bengal, Central and South India, Burma, especially in Assam, the Circars and Travancore.
The fruit is eaten, and the leaves cut to feed cattle.

Brinjal. *See* **Solanum melongena,** *Linn.*

BROMUS.

Bromus asper, *Linn.*, GRAMINEÆ. 139

HAIRY-STALKED BROME GRASS.

A perennial grass found in North West Himalaya.
A good fodder grass for tracts sheltered by woods.

BUPLEU-RUM.

140 **Bromus schaderi,** *Kunth.*

PRAIRIE GRASS OF AUSTRALIA.

Syn.—CEROTOCHLOA PEDULA, *Schrad.*

Recently introduced for trial cultivation in the Botanical Gardens at Saharunpur and elsewhere. Mr. Duthie notes: "Mueller describes this as one of the richest of all grasses, growing continuously and spreading readily from seeds, particularly on fertile and somewhat humid soil."

Brocoli. *See* **Cabbage.**

Brussels sprout. *See* **Cabbage.**

BRYONIA.

141 **Bryonia laciniosa,** *Linn.*, CUCURBITACEÆ.

BRYONY.

Vern.—*Gargu-naru,* HIND.; *Mala,* BENG.; *Nehoe-maka,* MAL.

Throughout India from the Himalaya to Ceylon.

The leaves are boiled and eaten as greens.

B. umbellata, *Wall.* *See* **Trichosanthes cucumerina,** *Linn.*

BUCHANANIA.

142 **Buchanania latifolia,** *Roxb.*, ANACARDIACEÆ.

Vern.—*Chirauli,* PB.; *Achar, char, chironji,* C. P.; *Piál, payála,* GARHWAL; *Piár,* OUDH; *Charwari,* HYDERABAD; *Kat maá, aima,* TAM.; *Chara, morli,* TEL.; *Pyal, chároli,* BOM.; *Lamboben, lonepho, mda,* BURM.

A small tree of the lower mountains of India and the outer Himalaya, ascending to an altitude of 3,000 feet.

The kernels are a common substitute for almonds amongst the natives. The fruit is eaten by the hill tribes of Central India. The kernels are largely used in sweetmeats.

Buck-wheat or **Brauk.** *See* **Fagopyrum esculentum. ?**

Buffalo Grass or **Gama Grass.** *See* **Tripsacum dactyloides. ?**

Bullock's Heart. *See* **Anona reticulata. ?**

BUPLEURUM.

143 **Bupleurum falcatum,** *Linn.*, **var. marginata,** *Wall.*, UMBELLIFERÆ.

Vern.—*Kali sewar, sipil,* PB.

Met with in the mountainous tracts of Northern India.

The root is said to be eaten in some places.

BUTEA.

Butea frondosa, *Roxb.*, LEGUMINOSÆ. 144

Vern.—*Dhák, palás, kankrei, chichra,* HIND.; *Palás,* BENG.; *Kinsuka,* SANS.; *Porásu,* URIYA; *Palási, bulyeltra,* NEPAL; *Lahoking,* LEPCHA; *Porasan,* TAM.; *Modugu,* TEL.; *Muttugá, thorás,* KAN.; *Parás,* MAR.; *Pouk, pin,* BURM.

Found throughout India and Burma, extending in the North-Western Himalaya as far as the Jhelum. Its bright, orange-red flowers are produced before the leaves.

The leaves are used as fodder for buffaloes and elephants.

Cabbage.—See under **Brassica (oleracea) capitata.** 145

The Cabbage was introduced into India by the Europeans at an early date of their occupation.

It is now cultivated throughout the country, during the cold weather in the plains, and in spring and summer in the hills. In the plains it is very largely grown in the vicinity of towns.

The natives commonly make curry with it.

Cacao. *See* **Theobroma Cacao,** *Linn.*, STERCULIACEÆ.

Caden. *See* **Phœnix sylvestris,** *Roxb.*, PALMÆ.

CAJANUS.

Cajanus indicus, *Spreng.*, LEGUMINOSÆ. 146

PIGEON, NO-EYE, OF CONGO PEA, OF DHAL.

Syn.—C. FLAVUS, *DC.*; C. BICOLOR, *DC.*

Vern.—*Arhar, thor, thur, dal,* N. W. P. and OUDH; *Arhuku,* SANS.

Native apparently of equatorial Africa (*DeCandolle*). Cultivated in most parts of India, and wherever cultivated, forms an important article of food.

There are two chief varieties: **C. flavus,** with the pea plain yellow and known in the vernacular as *thor,* and **C. bicolor,** with the pea veined with purple and known as *arhar.* The latter is the one most commonly cultivated in the North West Provinces and Oudh, while in the Central Provinces and the Deccan *thor* takes the place of *arhar.* In the North West Provinces and Oudh, *arhar* is grown mostly as a subordinate crop along with *juar, bajra* and cotton, and also singly to a comparatively much smaller extent. Hence, when it is grown along with other crop the soil on which it is grown requires to be chosen and prepared in a way answering the purpose of the other principal crop. When sown with *juar* it requires the heaviest, and when with *bajra* the lightest, of the soils in the Provinces; but a light, moist soil is generally favorable for its growth, for then it can strike its roots freely into it. About 6 seers of seed are required for an acre if sown singly, and 2 seers when along with other crops. It is sown at the commencement of the rains, and is reaped in March or April, with an average outturn of 7 maunds of grain and 16 maunds of *bhusa* per acre off land on which *arhar* is the only crop, and of 1 to 5 maunds when grown along with other crops.

The leaves are considered to be an excellent fodder; the stalks are used for roofing, basket-making, and the tubular wicker-work fascines (*bira* or *ajar*) used to line wells to prevent the earth from falling in.

CALO-
PHYL-
LUM.

CALAMUS.

147 **Calamus Rotang,** *Linn.*, PALMÆ.

THE RATTAN CANE.

Vern.—*Bed*, PERS.; *Bet*, BENG., HIND.; *Perambu*, TAM.; *Beta mu*, TEL.

Met with in Bengal, Assam, South India, and Burma. It delights in rich, moist soil where there are bushes and trees for it to climb on. (*Roxb.*)

Flowers during the rains, and the fruit, which ripens in the cold season, consists of a fleshy substance which surrounds the seeds. The fleshy substance is eaten by the natives, who also eat the young tender shoots as a delicacy.

CALENDULA.

148 **Calendula officinalis,** *Linn.*, COMPOSITÆ.

MARIGOLD.

Vern.—*Aklel-ul-mulk.*

Found in the fields of the Punjab and Sind, scarcely indigenous; Peshawar. (*Aitchison*). Stewart says it is called *sergul* in the Trans-Indus tracts where it is "common wild in some parts."

Bellew mentions the belief that when browsed by cows it increases their milk. An extract of the flowers is used for coloring butter and cheese.

CALLICARPA.

149 **Callicarpa lanata,** *Wall.*, VERBENACEÆ.

Vern.—*Bastra*, HIND; *Coat comul*, TAM.; *Tondi teregam*, MAL.

A shrub of Southern India, and the Circars.

"The bark, which is sub-aromatic and slightly bitter to taste, is chewed by the Cingalese instead of betel leaves." (*Drury.*)

CALLIGONUM.

450 **Calligonum polygonoides,** *Linn.*, POLYGONACEÆ.

Vern.—*Balanja, phok, phogalli* (flowers), PB.

A shrub of the southern and south-western Punjab, and Sind. It has a pleasing appearance with its leafless branches and small pink flowers, which in May are succeeded by small fruit.

The shoots are relished by goats and camels. The flowers, when fallen, are gathered and used as food by the natives. The abortive flowers are eaten either made into bread or cooked with ghee.

CALOPHYLLUM.

151 **Calophyllum Wightianum,** *Wall.*, GUTTIFERÆ.

Syn.—C. SPURIUM, *Chois.*

Vern.—*Cheroo-pinnay*, TAM.; *Tsiron-panna*, MAL.

Found in the mountains of the western coast of the western peninsula from the Konkan to Travancore.

The fruit, when ripe, is red and sweet. It is eaten by the natives. (*Drury.*)

Caltrops. *See* **Trapa bispinosa,** *Roxb.* ONAGRACEÆ

CAMELLIA.

Camellia theifera, *Griff.*, TERNSTRŒMIACEÆ. 152

THE CHINA TEA PLANT.

Syn.—THEA CHINENSIS, *Linn.*; T. ASSAMICA, *Mast.*

Vern.—*Cha.*

A shrub with thin, grey bark, cultivated in many districts in India, especially in Kangra, Kúlu, Dehra Dun, Kumaun, Darjeeling, the Western Dúars, Assam, Cachar, Chittagong, and Hazaribagh in Northern India, as well as in the Nilgiri Hills and Ceylon.

The leaves are eaten, and a decoction of them used as a common drink.

CANNA.

Canna indica, *Linn.*, SCITAMINEÆ. 153

INDIAN SHOT.

Vern.—*Surbo-jaya*, BENG.; *Kullvalei-mani*, TAM.; *Krishna-tamarah*, TEL.; *Katoo-bala*, MAL.; *U'kilbar-ki-munker*, DEC.

Several varieties common all over India, chiefly in gardens, as ornamental and flowering plants. Flower all the year.

Drury says "nearly all the species contain starch in the root-stock which renders them fit to be used as food after being cooked. From the root of one kind, **C. edulis,** a nutritious aliment is prepared; this is peculiarly fitted for invalids, not being liable to turn acid."

CANNABIS.

Cannabis sativa, *Linn.*, URTICACEÆ. 154

HEMP.

Vern.—*Gánjé-ká-pér*, HIND.; *Ganjá, bháng*, BENG.; *Ganja-chedi*, TAM.; *Gánjari-chettu* TEL.; *Bhánbin*, BURM.; *Gulu (seeds), Chel (fibre).*

The systematic cultivation of the hemp plant in Northern India is restricted to the Himalaya and the belt of country lying immediately beneath it, where it grows wild. It is generally cultivated for its fibre and the intoxicating drugs, *ganjá*, obtained from the immature female flowers and floral envelopes, and smoked like tobacco, and *bhang* from the leaves, which is macerated in water and made into a drink. *Bhang* also is intoxicating.

Messrs. **Duthie and Fuller,** writing about the Himalayan tracts within the North-Western Provinces, say that the seed is not uncommonly roasted and eaten by the hill-men, and that occasionally oil is expressed from it, and the oil cake given to their cattle. **Dr. Stewart** writes that on the Sutlej the seeds are roasted and eaten in small quantities with wheat.

CANARIUM.

Canarium commune, *Linn.*, BURSERACEÆ. 155

JAVA ALMOND TREE.

Vern.—*Jungli badam*, HIND.

Found in the Peninsula and Malabar. Introduced into Bengal, where it was found not to thrive well owing to the rigour of winter.

CAPSICUM.

Cultivated in the Moluccas for its fruit which is a three-sided drupe, containing generally only one perfect seed, tasting somewhat like an almond. An oil expressed from the nuts, when fresh, is mixed with food in Java. Bread is also made from the nuts in the island of Celebes. If eaten fresh or too frequently they may produce diarrhœa. (*Drury.*)

CANAVALIA.

156 **Canavalia ensiformis,** *D.C,* LEGUMINOSÆ.

SWORD BEAN.

Syn.—C. GLADIATA, *DC.*

Vern.—*Makham shim,* BENG.; *Suffed* or *lal kudsumbal,* HIND.; *Segapu,* TAM.; *Tellay tumbetten kasa,* TEL.

Extends along the eastern part of India from the Himalaya to Ceylon, wild or cultivated.

The young, tender, half-grown pods are used as French beans at the tables of Europeans. Natives also eat them commonly in curry.

CAPPARIS.

157 **Capparis aphylla,** *Roth.,* CAPPARIDEÆ.

Vern.—*Kirra, kerin, karil, tenti, delha, pinju,* PB.

A dense, branching shrub of the Punjab and Western India, chiefly in arid tracts. Flowers in spring and fruits in April.

Dr. Stewart says the bud is cooked fresh as a pot-herb, and the fruit is very largely consumed by the natives, "great numbers of whom go out for the purpose of collecting it both when green and after it is ripe. In the former state it is generally steeped for 15 days in salt and water, being put in the sun to ferment till it becomes acid, pepper and oil being then added. * * * It is eaten to an ounce or two at a time usually with bread. The ripe fruit is generally made into pickle with mustard or other oil, to be taken with bread." The young flower-buds are preserved as pickle.

158 **C. horrida,** *Linn.*

Vern.—*Hiun-garna, karoila,* PB.; *Karralura,* OUDH; *Atanday,* TAM.; *Adonda,* TEL.; *Katerni,* GOND.; *Gitoran,* AJMERE.

Inhabits the Punjab plains.

In the southern Punjab and Sind the fruit is made into pickle.

159 **C. spinosa,** *Linn.*

CAPER BUSH.

Vern.—*Kabra,* LADAK; *Kaur, kiari, bauri, ber, bandar, bassar,* PB.

This is the plant which in Europe produces the Caper. In India it occurs in the central and northern parts of the Punjab.

The ripe fruit is either eaten raw or made into pickle by the natives. Mr. Edgeworth found the buds (prepared in the style of 'Capers') to answer very well as a substitute for its European congener.

CAPSICUM.

160 **Capsicum frutescens,** *Linn.,* SOLANACEÆ.

SPURPEPPER, CAYENNE PEPPER AND CHILLIES.

Vern.—*Lal gách marich, lal lonka morich,* BENG.; *Lal gách mirich,* HIND.

This is the most common species. It is grown on light, sandy soil in most parts of India, and very extensively so in parts of Bengal,

Orissa, and Madras, during the cold weather. When ripe it is generally of a bright red colour: it is then picked off the plant, laid out on mats in the sun to dry.

Every bazar has its store of these chillies, for it is one of the indispensable ingredients in native curries.

Capsicum minimum, *Roxb.* 161

Vern.—*Dhan-morich*, BENG.; *Dhan-mirich*, HIND.

A very small "chilly," grown to a limited extent, and very hot. It is rarely used by natives, but by Europeans it is steeped in vinegar, mixed with salt, and used as a seasoning in stews, chops, &c.

C. grossum, *Willd.* 162

BELL PEPPER.

Vern.—*Kafri-morich*, BENG., HIND.

The thick, fleshy skin of this species is less hot than that of the others.

Cultivated to a limited extent in gardens, chiefly for Europeans, who either use them in stews or have them opened, stuffed with certain spices, and pickled in vinegar.

CARAGANA.

Caragana pygmæa, *DC.*, LEGUMINOSÆ. 163

Vern.—*Tama, dama*, LADAK.

A low shrub inhabiting the dry high lands of the West Himalaya.

It is browsed by goats.

CARALLUMA.

164

Caralluma edulis, *Benth.*, ASCLEPIADEÆ.

Vern.—*Chung, pippa*, PB.

Grows in the arid tracts of the Punjab and Sind.

The stems have a semi-acid or bitterish taste, and are eaten by the poorer class of natives as a relish to their food.

Carambola. *See* **Averrhoa Carambola,** *Linn.*, GERANIACEÆ,

CARDAMINE.

Cardamine hirsuta, *Linn.*, CRUCIFERÆ. 165

Found in all temperate regions of India. In Bengal it is a cold weather weed.

Eaten as water cress.

CARDUUS.

Carduus nutans, *Linn.*, COMPOSITÆ. 166

THISTLE.

Vern.—*Kanchari, tiso*, PB.

Found in the Western Himalaya, Western Tibet; Nubra, altitude 13,000 feet.

Eaten by camels greedily. When bruised to destroy the prickles the thistles are given to cattle. They are also used as fodder in dry seasons.

CAREYA.

167 **Careya arborea,** *Roxb.*, MYRTACEÆ.

Vern.—*Kumbi, khumbi,* HIND.; *Gummar,* GOND; *Boktok,* LEPCHA; *Dambel,* GARO; *Ayma, pailæpoota-tammi,* TAM.; *Buda-durmi, dudippi,* TEL.; *Gavuldu,* MYSORE; *Bambway,* BURM.

The genus called after the Rev. Dr. Carey, the Serampore Missionary.

Found in the sub-Himalayan tract, from the Jumna eastward to Bengal, and Burma, and in Central and South India.

Blossoms during the hot season, and the seed ripens about three or four months after. (*Roxb.*) Fruit called *khuni* is eaten in the Punjab. The fleshy calyx leaves are used in Sindh for the cure of colds.

CARICA.

168 **Carica Papaya,** *L.*, PASSIFLOREÆ.

THE PAPAW OR PAPAYA TREE.

Vern.—*Painpai,* BENG.; *Papaya,* HIND.; *Arand-kharbusa,* PB.

Commonly cultivated in most gardens throughout India, from Delhi to Ceylon. It fruits all the year round, but the fruit is most luscious during the summer.

When ripe the interior is soft, yellow and sweetish; eaten by all classes and esteemed innocent and wholesome. When green it is used by natives in curry, also pickled. A few drops of the milk of the papaw renders any meat tender.

The green fruit, when peeled, boiled, cut into small pieces, and served with sweet oil, vinegar, salt and pepper, serves as a very palatable vegetable, and is very similar to squash in taste. (*Mr. L. Liotard.*)

CARISSA.

179 **Carissa Carandas,** *Linn.*, APOCYNACEÆ.

Vern.—*Karenja,* BENG.; *Karaunda,* HIND.; *Kalaaha,* TAM.; *Waaka,* TEL.

A small, gnarled tree found throughout India and Burma, often in gardens, and more commonly in dry, uncultivated parts. It flowers in February-April, and produces a small fruit which is grape green when young, white and pink when approaching maturity, and nearly black when ripe. The fruit ripens in July-August.

The fruit is made into pickle just before it is ripe, or employed in tarts. When ripe it makes a very good jelly, for which it is cultivated in gardens owned by Europeans. The natives universally eat it raw.

Carob tree. *See* **Ceratonia siliqua,** *Linn.*, LEGUMINOSÆ.

Carrot. *See* **Daucus Carota,** *Linn.*, UMBELLIFERÆ.

CAROXYLON.

170 **Caroxylon Griffithii,** *Moq.*, CHENOPODIACEÆ.

Vern.—*Laghme, khar,* PB.

Grows in parts of the Punjab, where it is a favourite food of camels:

large quantities of this shrub are said by **Edgeworth** to be taken into Multan for this purpose.

CARTHAMUS.

Carthamus oxyacantha, *Bieb.*, COMPOSITÆ. 171

Vern.—*Kantiari, kandiara, poli, kharesa,* PB.

Found in the North-West Provinces and Punjab, most common in the more arid tracts.

The seeds are sometimes eaten by the natives parched, alone or with wheat.

C. tinctorius, *Linn.*

THE SAFFLOWER OF BASTARD SAFFRON. 172

Vern.—*Kamalottara,* SANS.; *Kusum,* BENG., HIND., DEC.; *Sendurgam, kashumba,* TAM.; *Agnisikha,* TEL.; *Hshoo,* BURM.

An annual, grown extensively all over India.

"Poultry fatten on the seeds. An oil of a light yellow colour is procured from the seeds. It is used for lamps and for culinary purposes." (*Drury.*)

CARUM.

Carum Carui, *Linn.*, UMBELLIFERÆ. 173

CARAWAY. SEED.

Vern.—*Jira,* BENG.; *Zira,* HIND.; *Shimai-shombu,* TAM.; *Shimai-sapu,* TEL.

The plant is cultivated for its seeds as a cold season crop on the plains; also frequent on the hills.

The seed is used parched and powdered, or raw and entire. In the former case it is used to flavour curries; in the latter it is put in cakes. It is also used in confectionery and in flavouring drinks.

C. copticum, *Benth.* 174

TRUE BISHOP'S WEED; LOVAGE.

Syn.—PTYCHOTIS AJOWAN, *DC.*

Vern.—*Jowan,* BENG.; *Ajowan,* HIND.; *Oman,* TAM.; *Omamu,* TEL.

Cultivated in many parts of India for its seeds.

The seeds are aromatic, and form an ingredient of the preparation known as *pán.*

C. Roxburghianum, *Benth.* 175

Vern.—*Chanu,* BENG.; *Ajmúd,* HIND.; *Rundhani,* BENG.; *Asham tagam,* TAM.; *Ajumóda-vomaru,* TEL.

Often raised in gardens during the cold season for the seed which is used in flavouring curry.

CARYOTA.

Caryota urens, *Willd.*, PALMÆ. 176

Vern.—*Rungbong,* LEPCHA; *Bara flawar,* ASS.; *Salopa,* URIYA; *Condapanna,* TAM.; *Jirugu,* TEL.; *Minbo,* BURM.

This graceful palm inhabits the mountainous regions of India; and flowers in summer. **Roxburgh** writes:—"This tree is highly valuable to the natives of the countries where it grows in plenty. It yields them, during the hot season, an immense quantity of toddy or palm wine. I

CASSIA.

have been informed that the best trees will yield at the rate of 100 pints in the 24 hours.

"The pith or farinaceous part of the trunk of old trees is said to be equal to the best sago; the natives make it into bread, and boil it into thick gruel; these form a great part of the diet of these people; and during the late famine (1830?), they suffered little while those trees lasted. I have reason to believe this substance to be highly nutritious."

The sap in some cases continues to flow for about a month. When fresh the toddy is a pleasant drink, but it soon ferments; and when distilled becomes arrack, the gin of India. The sugar called jaggery is obtained by boiling the toddy.

CARYOPHYLLUS.

177 **Caryophyllus aromaticus,** *Linn.*, MYRTACEÆ.

CLOVES.

Vern.—*Lavanga*, BENG.; *Long*, HIND.; *Kirambar*, TAM.; *Lavangalu*, TEL.

It is indigenous in the Moluccas. Cultivated in parts of Southern India.

The unexpanded dried flowers of this Myrtle tree is, under the name of Cloves, used to a limited extent as a hot spice throughout India.

The Dutch tried to restrict its cultivation to the island of Amboyna, but in the course of time it got introduced to India and other places.

Cashew-nut. *See* **Anacardium occidentale.** *Linn.*, ANACARDIACEÆ.

Cassareep. *See* **Manihot utilitissima,** EUPHORBIACEÆ.

Cassava Bread, Tapioca. *See* **Manihot utilitissima,** EUPHORBIACEÆ.

Cassia Buds. *See* **Cinnamomum Tamala,** *Nees.*, LAURINEÆ.

CASSIA.

178 **Cassia Fistula,** *Linn.*, LEGUMINOSÆ.

THE INDIAN LABURNUM OF PUDDING PIPE.

Syn.—CATHARTOCARPUS FISTULA, *Pers.*

Vern.—*Amaltás*, HIND.; *Alash, karangal, kiár, ali*, PB.; *Bahava, giramálá*, BOM. and SIND; *Gurmala*, GUZ.; *Sundali, bandarlati*, BENG.; *Suvarnak*, SANS.; *Sandari*, URIYA; *Raj birij*, NEPAL; *Sonalú*, GARO; *Sunaru*, ASS.; *Bandolat*, CACHAR; *Kitwáli, kitoli, shimarra, sim, warga*, N. W. P.; *Bhawa*, DEC.; *Warga*, OUDH; *Gaggarwah, aila, karachu*, C. P.; *Kone, sirikone, koki*, TAM.; *Reylu*, TEL.; *Gnooshway*, BURM.

Grows in the sub-Himalayan regions and throughout India and Burma.

Leaves parched are eaten for medicinal purposes.

C. lignea. *See* **Cinnamomum Tamala,** *Nees.*, LAURINEÆ.

179 **C. Tora,** *Linn.*

THE FŒTID CASSIA.

Vern.—*Chakunda*, HIND. and BENG.; *Tánkalá, kovariya*, BOM.; *Tarota*, DEC.; *Ushit-tagari*, TAM.; *Tagarisha chettu*, TEL.; *Dan-ky-wai*, BURM.; *Prabanatha*, SANS.

A gregarious under-shrub, from 1 to 2 feet in height, found everywhere in Bengal, widely spread and abundant throughout India.

An annual weed, producing a small seed eaten in times of scarcity. Recently this seed was brought to notice in British Burma as worthy of use as a substitute for coffee when roasted and grounded.

CASTANEA.

Castanea vulgaris, *Lam.*, CUPULIFERÆ. 180

THE SWEET CHESTNUT OF SPANISH CHESTNUTS.

"Introduced in the Himalaya, and grown in various localities, and especially in a large nnmber of places in the Punjab and the hills of the North West Provinces, in Darjeeling and the Khásia Hills." (*Gamble.*)

The nuts are eaten. When ground into meal they form an important article of food for the poor.

CASTANOPSIS.

Castanopsis indica, *A. DC.*, CUPULIFERÆ. 181

Vern.—*Banj katús*, NEPAL; *Kashiorón*, LEPCHA; *Serang*, ASS.; *Charang*, GARO; *Tailo*, CACHAR; *Nikari*, SYLHET.

A moderate-sized, evergreen tree of Nepal, East Bengal, Assam, and Chittagong, ascending to 5,000 feet.

The fruit is eaten; it much resembles the filbert both in shape and in flavour.

C. rufescens, *Hook f. & Th.* 182

Vern.—*Dalnd katús*, NEPAL; *Sirikishu*, LEPCHA; *Hingore*, ASS.

A very large, evergreen tree of the Sikhim Himalaya, from 6,000 to 9,000 feet.

The fruit is small, but edible and of good flavour.

C. tribuloides, *A. DC.* 183

Vern.—*Túmari, kutonj*, KUMAUN; *Musré katús, kotúr*, NEPAL; *Bar hingori*, ASS.; *Kyansa*, BURM.

An evergreen tree met with in south-east Kumaun, Nepal, East Bengal, ascending from the plains to 6,000 feet. Also found in Chittagong and hills of Burma above 3,000 feet.

The fruit is eaten.

Cauliflower. *See under* **Brassica B. (oleracea) botrytis.** 184

The cauliflower was introduced by Europeans into India.

It is now widely cultivated during the cold weather, and is eaten by Europeans boiled as a vegetable, and by natives cooked as curry.

CEDRELA.

Cedrela Toona, *Roxb.*, MELIACEÆ. 185

THE TOON OF INDIAN MAHOGANY TREE.

Syn.—C. SERRATA, *Royle*.

Vern.—*Tún*, HIND., BENG.; *Drawi*, PB.; *Túpa, kudaka*, BOM.; *Poma*, ASS.; *Simal*, LEPCHA; *Tunamarum*, TAM.; *Nandi*, TEL.; *Tundú*, KAN.; *Thitkado*, BURM.

A tree about 50 to 60 feet in height, growing in the plains of India and lower mountains.

The seeds are used to feed cattle.

CEDRUS.

186 **Cedrus Deodara,** *Loudon,* CONIFERÆ.

DEODAR; HIMALAYAN CEDAR.

Vern.—*Nakhtar,* AFG.; *Diár, deodár, dadár,* KASHMIR, GARHWAL, KUMAUN; *Kelu, keoli, kilar,* HIMALAYAN NAMES; *Giam,* TIBET.

Grows in the North-Western Himalaya.

It yields a true resin, and, by destructive distillation, an oil, dark-coloured, and resembling turpentine.

The young shoots and plants are eagerly browsed by goats, &c.

CELASTRUS.

187 **Celastrus senegalensis,** *Lam.,* CELASTRINEÆ.

Syn.—C. MONTANA, *Roxb.*; GYMNOSPORIA MONTANA, *Lawson.*

Vern.—*Sherawane,* TRANS-INDUS; *Talkar, dajkar, kharái,* PB.; *Baikal gajachinni,* C. P.; *Mál kangoni,* BOM.; *Danti, pedda chintu,* TEL.

A tall, spinescent shrub of the northern dry and intermediate zones, North West India, ascending to 4,000 feet, Central India, and the drier parts of the Peninsula.

The leaves are used for fodder.

Celery. *See* Apium graveolens, *Linn.,* UMBELLIFERÆ.

CELOSIA.

188 **Celosia argentea,** *Linn.,* AMARANTACEÆ.

Vern.—*Sarwali,* PB.

A weed occurring in abundance in fields in the Punjab.

Used as a pot-herb in times of scarcity.

CELTIS.

189 **Celtis australis,** *Linn.,* URTICACEÆ.

Vern.—*Kharak,* SIMLA; *Tagho,* AFG.

A moderate-sized, deciduous tree of Sulaiman and Salt Ranges, Himalaya, from the Indus to Bhutan, ascending to 8,500 feet, Khásia Hills.

The tree is largely planted for fodder.

190 **C. caucasica,** *Willd.*

Vern.—*Batkar, brumij, kanghol mirch (the fruit),* PB.

A fine tree growing in the Punjab Himalayas.

The fruit, a small drupe, is eaten by the natives, who regard it as sweetish, but it has almost no flesh. (*Roxb.*)

CENCHRUS.

191 **Cenchrus echinatus,** *Linn.,* GRAMINEÆ.

Vern.—*Dhaman, agana,* N. W. P.; *Basla, leá, lapta,* PB.

This grass is met with in arid ground in the plains of the North West Provinces and the Punjab.

Eaten by cattle in the hot weather; nutritious shoots are given out during the hottest season (*Crooke quoted by Duthie*). By some it is considered excellent fodder, by others only middling. The seeds are used in times of scarcity. (*Stewart.*)

CEPHALOSTACLYON.

Cephalostaclyon capitatum, *Munro*, GRAMINEÆ. 192

Vern.—*Gobia, gopi*, NEPAL; *Sili, sullea*, KHASIA.

This "bamboo has stems 12 to 30 feet, thin, yellow, semi-scandent strong, with long internodes of about 2½ feet, used for bows and arrows by the Lepchas. It is often gregarious. It flowered in Sikkim in 1874." (*Gamble.*)

This bamboo, when it flowers, produces, like those common in India, a rice-like grain eaten by the natives in times of scarcity. The leaves are good for fodder.

CERATONIA.

Ceratonia Siliqua, *L.*, LEGUMINOSÆ.

THE CAROB TREE, ST. JOHN'S BEAN, OF BREAD OR LOCUST TREE. 193

Vern.—*Kharnub-nubti*, PB.

A native of the Mediterranean coast, supposed by some to have furnished the "locusts" of St. John. Introduced into India with some degree of success.

The pods, full of sweet, nutricious pulp, are a common article of food in the Mediteranean for man, horses, pig and cattle, and are imported into the Punjab under the name of *Kharnub-nubti*. (*Brandis.*) They form an important constituent in the patent cattle-foods. They are supposed to be the "husks" of the Prodigal son, and the Locusts of John the Baptist.

CEROPEGIA.

Ceropegia bulbosa, *Roxb.*, var. esculenta, *Edge.*, ASCLEPIADEÆ. 194

Met with in the Punjab.

Tubers and leaves used as pot vegetables in Multan and Sind.

Ceylon Moss. *See* **Gracilaria lichenoides,** *Greville*, ALGÆ.

Chanay Kelengu. *See* **Tacca pinnatifida.** ?

CHENOPODIUM.

Chenopodium album, *L.*, CHENOPODIACEÆ. 195

Vern.—*Betu-sag*, BENG.; *Irr, em, bathua, lunak*, PB.

A weed common in parts of Northern India and Bengal, ascending the Punjab Himalayas.

Used by the natives sometimes as a pot-herb.

Cherry. *See* **Prunus.** ?

Chestnut, Horse. *See* **Æsculus indicus.** ?

Chestnut, Sweet. *See* **Castanea vulgaris.** ?

Chestnut, Water. *See* **Trapa nutans.** ?

Chicory. *See* **Cichorium Intybus,** *Linn.*, COMPOSITÆ.

CHLORIS.

196 **Chloris barbata,** *Swartz.*, GRAMINEÆ.

Syn.—ANDROPOGON BARBATUS, *Linn.*

Vern.—*Gandi, gavung, pulooah,* N. W. P.; *Konda-pulla,* SOUTH INDIA.

Very common in Northern India and Sind; grows in large tufts on pasture ground.

Cattle eat it till in flower, after which they do not seem to touch it.

Chocolate nut or **Bean.** *See* **Theobroma Cacao.**

Chowlee. *See* **Dolichos sinensis.**

CHRYSOPHYLLUM.

197 **Chrysophyllum Roxburghii,** *G. Don,* SAPOTACEÆ.

THE STAR APPLE.

Vern.—*Petakara,* BENG.; *Pithogarkh,* ASS.; *Hali,* KAN.; *Farsi,* MAR.; *Lawúlú,* CINGH.; *Thankya,* BURM.

An evergreen tree of Bengal, Burma, Western Ghâts, and Ceylon. Fruit edible.

CHRYSOPOGON.

198 **Chrysopogon acicularis.,** *Retz.*, GRAMINEÆ.

Syn.—ANDROPOGON ACICULATUS, *Roxb.*; C. ACICULATUS.

Vern.—*Chore-kanta,* BENG.; *Shunkhini, chore pushpi, keshini,* SANS.; *Kudira-pullu,* MAL.

A small, coarse grass, grows on barren, moist, pasture ground throughout Bengal, also in the North West Provinces and Central Provinces.

Cattle do not seem to like it. Its thin, straight culms, 1 to 2 feet high, flower, and the small sharp-pointed seeds which follow are troublesome to those who walk through the grass, as they stick to the stockings and produce a pricking and itching sensation until removed.

299 **C. gryllus,** *Trin.*

Syn.—C. ROYLEANUM, *Nees.*; ANDROPOGON GRYLLUS, *Linn.*

Inhabits the plains and hills in the Punjab and North-West Provinces.

Mueller says it is a useful fodder grass.

Cicca disticha, *Linn.* *See* **Phyllanthus distichus,** *Mull. Arg.*, EUPHORBIACEÆ.

CICER.

200 **Cicer arietinum,** *Linn.*, LEGUMINOSÆ.

THE COMMON GRAM OF CHICKEN PEA.

Vern.—*Cholá, bút,* BENG.; *Chaná, chenna,* HIND.; *Chenuka,* SANS.; *Kadalay,* TAM.; *Sunagalu,* TEL.; *Kudoly,* KAN.; *Hims,* ARAB.; *Nakhud,* PERS.

Cultivated for its seed throughout India on any soil, from the heaviest clay to the lightest loam; but on heavy clays it is said to give the largest

CICER.

produce. It is generally sown alone, or along with wheat, or barley, or mustard. The sowing is carried on in September and October, in the different parts of the country, the rate being from 80 to 100 lbs. of seed per acre; scarcely any irrigation is required; the harvest takes place in March and April, a fortnight or so after the wheat, or barley, or mustard, with which it is sown is reaped.

In the North West Provinces and Oudh there are two varieties of grain: one a large, reddish grain, the other a small light, brown one. A very large white-grained kind known as *Cabuli* is also grown, but more as a curiosity than in ordinary cultivation. The area under gram in the 30 temporarily-settled districts of the North West Provinces is given by **Messrs. Duthie** and **Fuller** at about 4,270,000 acres; it is grown more in the districts west of Allahabad than in those east of it. The cost of cultivation, including rent, is stated by the authors just mentioned to be Rs. 12-13-0, and they give the figures of out-turn to be—

	MAUNDS OF GRAM PER ACRE.	
	On unirrigated land.	On irrigated land.
For gram alone	5 to 8	12
" " and barley	6 " 9	14
" " and wheat	6 " 9	13

The exports of gram by sea to other countries have been as follows during the last five years:—

	Quantity in Cwts.	Value in Rs.
1878-79	288,506	13,86,314
1879-80	285,956	13,34,443
1880-81	284,095	10,14,873
1881-82	365,690	9,99,336
1882-83	312,953	8,28,647

Analysis of exportation of gram from British India for the year 1882-83:—

Provinces from which exported.	Quantity in Cwts.	Countries to which exported.	Quantity in Cwts.
Bengal	142,403	Mauritius	164,969
Bombay	31,354	Ceylon	56,521
Sindh	826	Straits Settlements	29,784
Madras	108,267	Réunion	29,094
British Burma	30,103	Australia	25,890
		Other countries	6,695
TOTAL	312,953		312,953

201 **Cicer soongaricum,** *Steph.*

Vern.—*Tishu, jawani,* PB.

Met with in the Western Himalayas, temperate and alpine region, altitude 9,000 to 15,000 feet; Piti, Lahoul, Kumaun, Tibet.

Said to fatten cattle quickly, and to be used as a pot-herb. The peas are eaten both raw and cooked by the people.

CICHORIUM.

202 **Cichorium Intybus,** *Linn.*, COMPOSITÆ.

CHICORY.

Vern.—*Kasni,* HIND., PERS.; *Kindyba,* ARAB.; *Kashini-virai,* TAM.; *Hand, gul, suchal, kasni,* PB.

North-West India, Kumaun, probably an escape from cultivation.

"The young plant is in some places used as a vegetable." (*Roxb.*)

It is used as a salad, the young leaves being blanched like endine. Its roots are roasted, ground, and mixed with coffee to flavour it.

CINNAMOMUM.

203 **Cinnamomum obtusifolium,** *Nees,* LAURINEÆ.

Vern.—*Tezpat,* BENG.; *Bora singoli,* NEPAL; *Looleng-kyaw,* BURM.

A large tree of the outer North-West Himalaya, ascending to altitude 7,000 feet; Eastern Bengal, Burma, and the Andaman Islands.

Leaves are aromatic; used in curry.

204 **C. Tamala,** *Nees.*

CASSIA LIGNEA or CINNAMON.

Vern.—*Dalchini, kirkiria,* HIND.; *Tamálá,* BOM.; *Chota,* NEPAL; *Dopatti* ASS.

The leaves are known as *Tejpat,* and the bark as *Taj.*

A moderate-sized, evergreen tree, occasionally met with on the Himalaya, from the Indus to the Sutlej, altitude 3,000 to 7,000 feet, becoming common eastward to Bengal, Khásia hills and Burma. (*Gamble.*)

The bark and the dried leaves are used to flavour dishes. It is much used to adulterate true cinnamon.

205 **C. zeylanicum,** *Breyn.*

TRUE CINNAMON.

Vern.—*Dalchini,* HIND.; *Karruwa,* TAM.; *Sanalinga,* TEL.; *Rassu, kurundu,* CINGH.; *Loolengkyau,* BURM.

It is a native of the Ceylon forests, but now cultivated on the western coast of that island.

It is chiefly used as a condiment and for flavouring confectionery; also used in curry, and enters into the preparation known as *pán.*

CISSUS.

206 **Cissus carnosa,** *Lam.*, AMPELIDEÆ.

Vern.—*Karik, girdardak,* PB.

A climber found in valleys at the foot of the Punjab Himalaya and in Kashmir.

It is eaten by camels.

CITRULLUS.

CITRULLUS.

Citrullus Colocynthis, *Schrad.*, CUCURBITACEÆ. 207

ENGLISH COLOCYNTH.

Vern.—*Indrayan*, HIND.; *Makhal*, BENG.; *Indra-varuni, vishala*, SANS.; *Paycoomuti*, TAM.; *Putsa kaya*, TEL.; *Indrawan*, DEC.; *Sheti-putsa*, CINGH.

An annual found wild in waste tracts of North-West, Central and South India. It is the wild gourd of the Book of Kings.

The spongy seed-bearing portion of the fruit is used as a medicine; it is intensely bitter and acts as a purgative.

The seeds, which are wholesome, are deprived of their poisonous skin and pulp, made into a paste, and eaten with dates. The young fruits are also eaten.

C. vulgaris, *Schrad.* 208

THE WATER-MELON.

Vern.—*Tarbusa, kalinda, hindwana*, N. W. P.; *Samanka*, HIND.; *Chayapula*, SANS.

Cultivated very generally for its cool, refreshing fruit, especially in Upper and Northern India, and appreciated by Natives as well as Europeans. It is supposed to be the Melon of Egypt, the loss of which the Israelites regretted so much.

The fruit is large, ovoid, green, and smooth; the flesh is whitish yellow, or red.

The seeds are compressed and variable in shape and colour; they are sometimes dried and the kernels eaten.

It is usually sown in January and February, and the fruit ripens in April and May.

In the North West Provinces and Oudh, it is largely cultivated, but statistics of the areas are wanting; the only districts for which figures are available are Bulandshahr, Jalaun and Meerut, and these show respectively 56, 48 and 26 acres annually.

var. fistulosus. 209

In the *Flora of British India* **C. fistulosus** has been given as a synonym to **C. vulgaris**, *Schrad*, but **Duthie** makes it a variety.

Vern.—*Tendus, tensi*, N. W. P.; *Tinda*, PB.; *Meho, trindus, dilpasand, tinda, alvinda*, SIND.

"Cultivated in Sindh from April to September, generally in the same plot of ground with common melons, gourds and cucumbers. The fruit is picked when about two-thirds grown, the size and shape of a common field turnip * * * It is pared, cut in quarters, the seeds extracted, well boiled in water, and finally boiled in a little milk, with salt, black-pepper and nutmeg. Musalmans generally cut it into dice, and cook it together with meat in stews or curries. Hindus fry it in *ghi* with split gram-peas (**Cicer arietinum**) and a curry powder of black-pepper, cinnamon, cloves, cardamoms, dried cocoanut, turmeric, salt and asafœtida. It is sometimes made into a preserve in the usual manner. It is sometimes picked when small, cooked without scraping out the seeds, and regarded a greater delicacy than when more advanced." (*Dr. Stocks in Hooker's Journal of Botany, quoted by Duthie and Fuller.*)

In the North West Provinces and Oudh the *tensi* is cultivated in the western districts before the rains in well-manured land, either as a sole crop or with other vegetables, and is eaten during the rainy season.

CITRUS.

CITRUS.

210 **Citrus Aurantium,** *Linn.*, RUTACEÆ.

THE ORANGE.

Vern.—*Narangi, naringi*, HIND.; *Kamla nibu*, BENG.; *Suntala*, NEPAL; *Santra*, PB.; *Kitchli*, TAM.; *Kittali*, TEL.

Found wild in Western and Upper India.

Cultivated in most parts of India, especially in Sikkim and Sylhet, Punjab and Nagpur.

Sir J. Hooker, in his *Flora of British India*, gives three varieties under the above species, *viz.* :—

1. **Aurantium,** *proper*, which he calls the sweet orange.
2. **Bigaradia,** which he says does not seem to be cultivated in India, except in gardens, and calls it the bitter or Seville orange.
3. **Bergamia,** which he says is rarely cultivated in India, and calls it the Bergamot Orange whence is got the Bergamot Oil.

The variety most common and cultivated largely in the above-mentioned tracts is the **Aurantium,** *proper*. From Sylhet it is largely imported into and distributed over Bengal, the largest quantity finding its way into the Calcutta markets. The fruit has a thin rind, and is sweet and juicy.

The orange grown in and about Delhi is on the average larger, but more spongy and thick-peeled than the preceding. The Nagpur orange is compact, sweet and excellent.

Orange trees attain great age—upwards of 600 years,—and some have been known to produce as many as 6,000 fruits in a year, and to grow to a height of 50 feet, with a trunk 12 feet in circumference.

"The Nagpur oranges are distributed over parts of the Central Provinces, and find their way as far as Allahabad. They are excellent, and will, it may be anticipated, compete with the Sylhet orange if Nagpur be connected with Calcutta by railway lines." (*Mr. L. Liotard.*)

211 **C. decumana,** *Willd.*

THE SHADDOCK, OR POMELO, OR FORBIDDEN FRUIT.

Vern.—*Batavi nebu, mahá nibu, chakotra.*

Introduced into India from Java and into the West Indies by Captain Shaddock, hence its name. It is cultivated in most tropical countries in India, chiefly in gardens throughout the plains. It is more perfect and more common in Bengal and Southern India than in the North West Provinces.

There are two varieties: one with whitish, and the other with reddish, pulp. Besides, the individual fruits differ from one another in size, reaching 2 feet in circumference and quality according to the soil, climate and situation.

In appearance it resembles the orange. The larger ones are known as Pomeloes, the smaller as Forbidden Fruit.

212 **C. medica,** *Linn.*

THE CITRON, LEMON, LIME.

Vern.—*Beg-pura, horna-nebu*, BENG.; *Jambira*, SANS.; *Limbu, kutla, nimbu, limu*, HIND.; *Bijapúra, mahálunga, bijori*, BOM.; *Elumich-champasham*, TAM.; *Nimma-pandu*, TEL.; *Nimbe hannu*, KAN.; *Limu*, ARAB. and PERS.; *Thanba-ya*, BURM.

Wild in Burma, Chittagong, 'Sitakund Hill,' Khási, foot of the

Himalaya ascending to 4,000 feet; in the hot valleys of Sikkim, ascending to 4,000 feet.

Sir J. Hooker, in his *Flora of British India*, classes the different kinds of Lime into four varieties :—

Var. 1.—medica proper.

This, the Citron, he describes as having "flowers usually numerous, fruit large, oblong, or obovoid, rind thick, tender, aromatic, pulp scanty, sub-acid."

Var. 2.—Limonum.

The Lemon he describes as having "fruit middle-sized, ovoid, yellow, rind thin, pulp abundant, acid."

Var. 3.—acida.

The Sour Lime of India has "flowers small, fruit usually small, globose or ovoid, with a thick or thin rind, pulp pale, sharply acid."

Var. 4.—Limetta.

"Leaves and flowers as in **var. acida**; fruit globose, 3 to 5 inches in diameter, rind thin, smooth; juice abundant, sweet, not aromatic." This is the Sweet Lime of India.

All the four varieties are cultivated, to a limited extent, throughout India, chiefly in gardens; and are sold in almost every bazar.

Cloves. *See* **Caryophyllus aromaticus,** *Linn.*, MYRTACEÆ.

Clover. *See* **Trifolium pratense,** *Linn.*, LEGUMINOSÆ.

CEPHALANDRA.

Cephalandra indica, *Naud.*, CUCURBITACEÆ. 213

Syn.—COCCINIA INDICA, *W. & A.*

Vern.—*Kanduri, ghol, kundru*, PB.

Common throughout India.

The fruit is of the size of a pigeon's egg, and of a purple color.

Dr. Stewart says that in the Punjab it is wild in the plains, and that its fruit is eaten, generally raw.

CLERODENDRON.

Clerodendron Colebrookianum, *Walp.*, VERBENACEÆ. 214

Vern.—*Kadungbi*, LEPCHA.

A small, ever-green tree of Sikkim and Khásia Hills, 3,000 to 6,000 feet.

The young leaves are eaten by the Lepchas.

COCCULUS.

Cocculus Leæba, *DC.*, MENISPERMACEÆ. 215

Vern.—*Hlar, vallúr, vehri, parwatti, perkhatúna*, PB.

An extensive climber of the drier zones, especially of West India.

On the Trans-Indus, Stewart says, it is browsed by goats but by no other animals.

COCOS.

216 **Cocos nucifera**, *Linn.*, PALMÆ.

THE COCOA-NUT TREE.

Vern.—*Narikel*, BENG.; *Nariel*, HIND.; *Tenna*, TAM.; *Narikadam*, TEL.; *Ong*, BURM.

Cultivated throughout the outer regions of India, *i. e.*, those near the sea coast. On the eastern and western coasts it is very abundant. There are several varieties. All flower in the hot season, and the nuts ripen in from September to November.

Under the head of food products, we must note the following:—

Cocoanut cabbage.—This is the terminal bud at the summit of the tree. It is used as a vegetable and also makes an excellent pickle.

Young cocoanut (VERN. *dab*).—This is the tender fruit, plucked off the tree for the cooling, sweetish, clear water, and the soft, creamlike pulp it contains. The water is drunk and the pulp eaten by natives of all classes.

Mature cocoanut (VERN. *jhoona narkel*).—This is the fruit in its mature state with its outer thick fibrous covering completely dried. It contains less water, but has a thicker and harder albumenous layer than the tender fruit. This is eaten with parched rice, or rasped and put into curries. It is also made into sweet-meats. An oil is extracted from it which is employed for various culinary uses, and is also exported to a certain extent. The cocoanut also yields wine and sugar. The quantity and value of cocoanut oil exported from India is given as follows during the past five years:—

Official years.	Quantity in Gallons.	Value in Rupees.
1878-79	725,852	10,07,492
1879-80	1,221,875	14,94,670
1880-81	1,888,122	20,90,797
1881-82	1,064,575	10,78,418
1882-83	856,527	9,49,608

Analysis of exportation of cocoanut oil from British India for the year 1882-83:—

Provinces from which exported.	Quantity in Gallons.	Countries to which exported.	Quantity in Gallons.
Madras	845,739	United Kingdom	510,038
Bombay	8,667	Germany	188,342
Bengal	1,902	Austria	72,095
Sindh	169	France	69,620
British Burma	50	Aden	6,208
		United States	5,734
		Italy	4,214
TOTAL	856,527	TOTAL	856,527

CODONOPSIS.

Codonopsis ovata, *Benth.*, CAMPANULACEÆ. 217

Vern.—*Ludut*, PB.

Inhabits Western Himalaya.

Its large tap-root is ground into flour and eaten in Lahoul.

COFFEA.

Coffea, *Linn.*, RUBIACEÆ. 218

COFFEE.

A small, much-branched tree, 20 feet in height, with whitish bark and white orange-like flowers that perfume the air, a native of Abyssinia.

The young fruit, which is red on ripening, is about the size of a small cherry, each containing two seeds, closely united. These, on being separated, constitute the Coffee berries of Commerce; and on being ground and roasted, the coffee of the shops.

In India, in the southern regions, **Coffea arabica,** the coffee plant, is largely cultivated. The other cultivated species are mentioned below since described in *Flora of British India*:—

C. bengalensis, *Roxb.*, occurring from Kumaun to Mishmi, also in Bengal, Assam, Sylhet, Chittagong, and Tenasserim. Fruit ovoid-oblong.

C. Wightiana, *W. & A.*, of the Western Peninsula; in arid places from Coorg to Travancore. Fruit much broader than long, with a deep furrow.

C. travancorensis, *W. & A.*, occurring in Travancore. Fruit broader than long.

C. fragrans, *Korth.*, of Sylhet and Tenasserim. Fruit much like the two last.

C. khasiana, *Hook, f.*, of Khási and Jaintia. Fruit ½ inch in diameter, smooth; seeds ventrally concave.

C. Jenkinsii, *Hook. f.*, of Khási Mountains. Fruit and seeds different from the last, being ellipsoid.

These species are not, however, of any special economic importance; and very little coffee is grown in the tracts in which they are said to be found. The coffee-cultivating region is Southern India, and the enterprise there has gained much importance. It at present not only supplies most of the coffee consumed in India, but exports large quantities to other countries, as the following figures (which are those of the last five years) will show:—

Official years.	Quantities in Cwts.	Value in Rs.
1878-79	341,186	1,54,36,427
1879-80	359,313	1,62,67,465
1880-81	369,357	1,59,96,688
1881-82	346,364	1,44,74,650
1882-83	353,324	1,39,22,040

COLOCASIA.

Analysis of exportation of Coffee from British India for the year 1882-83 :—

Provinces from which exported.	Quantities in Cwts.	Countries to which exported.	Quantities in Cwts.
Madras	308,576	United Kingdom . .	216,861
		France	89,826
Bombay . . .	44,711	Persia	11,698
		Egypt	11,659
Bengal	21	Arabia	10,828
		Turkey in Asia . .	7,727
Sindh	16		...
TOTAL .	353,324		353,324

The Coffee crops of Southern India and Ceylon have suffered much of late years from a disease called the Coffee Blight, which is caused by a fungus (*Hemileia vastatrix*) spreading over the leaves, whose functions it completely destroys, resulting in a failure of the Coffee crops. No cure has as yet been discovered.

COIX.

219 **Coix lachryma,** *Linn.*, GRAMINEÆ.

JOB'S TEARS.

Syn.—C. ARUNDINACEA, *Lamk.*; LITHAGROSTIS LACRYMA JOBI, *Gærtn.*

Vern.—*Sankroo,* HIND.; *Gurgur* or *kunch,* BENG.; *Kassaibija,* BOM.; *Kudhiá, thiá* (black variety), *sótsá* (white variety), *Re-see* (collective name), NAGA HILLS.

Met with in the plains of the Punjab, the North West Provinces and the warm hill-sides and valleys of the Himalayas. In Bengal it is common on the rice grounds as a weed of cultivation and in ditches; it grows to the height of from 4 to 6 feet. In the Naga hills it occurs at 5,000 feet near Kohima.

Throughout Assam and the Eastern frontier of India this coarse cereal constitutes an important article of food with the hill tribes, to a large extent taking the place of the Millets used by the hill tribes of North and South India. In Burma the seeds are eaten parched like maize; it is also largely eaten by Hill Tribes in India; in South China it is used as a material for matting. The tears or grains of this and several wild or less frequently cultivated species are used like beads in the construction of earrings and other ornaments worn by the hill tribes, especially the Angami Nagas.

COLOCASIA.

220 **Colocasia antiquorum,** *Schott.*, AROIDEÆ.

TARO, EDDOES or SCRATCH-COCO

Vern.—*Kachú, gori-kachú, ashú-kachú,* HIND., BENG.; *Ghuiya, auri,* N.W.P.; *Alu,* BOM.; *Dsü,* NAGA.

Met with at Kohima, in Manipur, altitude from 3,000 to 5,000 feet. Cultivated on high ground around the Naga villages throughout Manipur and the Naga hills.

The plant has large heart-shaped leaves, borne on long foot-stalks, rising from a short farinaceous corm. This corm forms an important article of food to the natives throughout India, being largely cultivated, but rarely if ever eaten from the wild state of the plant which occurs every where as a weed of damp places. The wild condition of the plant is by the Angami Nagas called *Kirth.*

Colocasia indica, *Schott.* 221

Syn.—ARUM INDICUM, *Lour.*

Vern.—*Man-kochoo,* BENG.

Much cultivated in Bengal, especially near the huts of the natives, in much the same way as the *Ol* (**Amorphophalus**).

Roxburgh says of this plant: "Much cultivated about the huts of the natives for its esculent stems and small pendulous bulbs or tubers, these being very generally eaten by people of all ranks in their curries."

There are two varieties of this plant, one with darker stems; both are propagated by the viviparous bulbules, fertile seeds being rarely if ever produced.

COMMELINA.

Commelina bengalensis, *L.,* COMMELINACEÆ. 222

Vern.—*Kanchura, kanuraka,* BENG.; *Chura, kanna,* PB.

In the Northern Punjab plains and hills.

Leaves eaten by the poor people as a pot-herb, especially in times of scarcity. The fleshy rhizomes of some of the species of this genus contain much starch, mixed with mucilage, and are therefore wholesome food when cooked.

Conocarpus latifolia, *Roxb.* *See* **Anogeissus latifolia,** *Wall.,* COMBRETACEÆ.

CORCHORUS.

Corchorus olitorius, *Linn.,* TILIACEÆ. 223

Vern.—*Pat,* BENG.

Indigenous in many parts of India.

The leaves and tender shoots are eaten by the natives.

CORDIA.

Cordia Myxa, *Linn.,* BORAGINEÆ. 224

SEBESTENS.

Vern.—*Lasora, bhokar, gondi,* HIND.; *Laswara,* PB.; *Lesuri,* SIND. *Borla,* KUMAUN; *Bohari, buhal,* BENG.; *Vidi, verasu,* TAM.; *Thanat,* BURM.; *Nimat,* LEPCHA.

A moderate-sized tree of the Salt Range, the Sub-Himalayan tract from the Chenab to Assam, Khási Hills, Bengal, Burma, and Central and South India.

The fruit grows in clusters and consists of a drupe, the pulp of which is soft and clammy.

"The fruit when ripe is eaten by the natives and also pickled * * the smell of the nuts when cut is heavy and disagreeable: the taste of the kernels is like that of filberts." (*Drury.*)

C. **Latifolia** is the larger variety, and it also is eaten by the natives.

CORNUS.

225 **Cordia Rothii**, *Rom. & Sch.*

Syn.—C. ANGUSTIFOLIA, *Roxb.*

Vern.—*Gondi, gundui, gundi,* HIND.; *Liar,* SIND; *Narvilli,* TAM.

A small tree in the dry zones of North West and South India.

The pulp of the fruit is eaten. (*Gamble.*)

226 **C. vestita**, *H. f. & T.*

Vern.—*Kumbi, karuk,* PB.

Common in parts of North India.

The fruit is eaten by the natives, and is said to be sweet. It is preferred to that of **C. Myxa.**

CORIANDRUM.

227 **Coriandrum sativum**, *Linn.*, UMBELLIFERÆ.

THE CORIANDER.

Vern.—*Dhanyaka,* SANS.; *Dhania,* BENG., HIND.; *Kotamalli,* TAM.; *Danyalu,* TEL.; *Nan nan,* BURM.

This plant is cultivated all over India.

Eaten by the natives as a vegetable. The seeds are universally used as a condiment, and forms one of the ingredients in curry.

They are also used in confectionery, and for flavouring spirits.

CORIARIA.

228 **Coriaria nepalensis**, *Wall.*, CORIARIEÆ.

Vern.—*Guch, balel.*

Native of Nepal, where its fruit is said to be eaten.

A small, straggling shrub of many places in the Himalaya; 2,500 to 7,500 feet in altitude.

"The branches are browsed by sheep. The fruit is very insipid but is eaten, although at times it is said to cause thirst and colic." (*Dr. Stewart.*)

CORNUS.

229 **Cornus capitata**, *Wall.*, CORNACEÆ.

Var.—BENTHAMIA FRAGIFERA, *Lindl.*

Vern.—*Tharwar, thesi,* PB.

A small tree met with from the Punjab Himalaya to Bhutan.

Dr. Stewart says that the ripe fruit is sweetish, and is made apparently into a preserve and eaten by the natives. The fruit resembles a strawberry.

230 **C. macrophylla**, *Wall.*

Vern.—*Kasir, kachir, haleo, allian, haddú, naug, kaksh, kachúr, ruchia,* HIND.; *Patmoro,* NEPAL; *Kandar, kasir, haddu,* PB.

A doubtfully distinct species from Dogwood, **Cornus sanguinea**; common in the Punjab Himalaya. I found it in the Naga hills and Manipur.

Goats feed on its leaves, and the natives eat the fruit.

CORYLUS.

Corylus colurna, *Linn.*, CUPULIFERÆ. 231

THE INDIAN HAZEL NUT.

Syn.—C. LACERA, *Wall.*; C. JACQUEMONTII, *Dcne.*

Vern.—*Curri*, NEPAL; *Langura*, BHUTIA; *Urni, winri, thangi, jangi, shúrli, banpálu, kapasi, bhotia badam*, HIMALAYAN NAMES. *Findák*, the PB. name for the nuts.

A moderate-sized tree of the North-West Himalaya, between altitude 5,500 and 10,000 feet.

The nuts are smaller than the European variety, but are fairly as good, and are largely eaten by the natives, and brought into the various hill stations in the Himalaya.

C. Ferox, *Wall.* 232

Vern.—*Curri*, NEPAL; *Langura*, BHUTIA.

A small tree of Nepal, Sikkim, 8,000 to 10,000 feet. The fruit is covered with a prickly cup; the kernel is edible.

CORYPHA.

Corypha umbraculifera, *Linn.*, PALMÆ. 233

THE TALIPAT PALM.

Vern.—*Conda-pani*, TAM.; *Bind*, KAN.; *Tala*, CINGH.; *Pebeng*, BURM.

A tall tree of Ceylon and the Malabar coast. Cultivated in Bengal and Burma.

A kind of sago is yielded by the pith. (*Gamble.*)

COSTUS.

Costus speciosus, *Sm.*, SCITAMINEÆ. 234

Vern.—*Kúst, keú*, BENG., HIND.; *Gudúrichákánda, kemuka*, BOM.; *Bomma kachika*, TEL.; *Tsjana-kua*, MAL.; *Kemúka*, SANS.

One of the most elegant plants of this family; its spirally-twisted stem carries its glossy leaves and white flowers above the brushwood in our tropical jungles. It is common everywhere throughout India, especially so in Bengal, frequenting moist, shady places.

The rhizomes are made into a preserve, eaten by the natives. **Piesse** says of it: "I have made some experiments with a sample of *kusht*; it appears to be scarcely as odorous as Orris Root. The tincture has an agreeable smell, and would be useful, but no quantity has as yet been seen in our markets." An unlimited quantity might easily enough be exported from Bengal were some effort made to bring this root before the perfumers of Europe.

The root is cooked in syrup and made into preserve in some parts of India. The natives consider it wholesome.

COUSINIA.

Cousinia minutu, *Boiss.*, COMPOSITÆ. 235

Syn.—C. CALCITRAPIFORMIS, *Jaub & Spach.*

Vern.—*Lakhtei, kandieri*, PB.

Occurs in a wild state in some parts of the Western Punjab plains. The young plant is used as a vegetable.

CROTALARIA.

236 **Crotalaria juncea,** *Linn.*, LEGUMINOSÆ.

FALSE HEMP, SAN HEMP, TAG HEMP.

Vern.—*Sanai san, sani, phulsan, arjha san*, N. IND.

The False Hemp is cultivated to a certain extent in the plains of Northern India, chiefly for its fibre. In the North West Provinces and Oudh, it is mostly cultivated in the Rohilkhand, Allahabad and Agra divisions.

It is sown at the commencement of the rains in light, sandy soils, and cut in September and October, the chief object of the cultivation being the fibre. The cost of cultivation, including rent, is paid at Rs. 15-6 per acre, and the average out-turn of clean fibre is about 8 maunds or 640 lbs. to the acre. It is the belief that the fibre is in its best condition when the plants are flowering. Consequently when the flowers appear the plants are cut.

Under the head of food it may be noted that the tops are cut off and given to cattle, and the fibre is extracted from the stalks.

CTENOLEPIS.

237 **Ctenolepis Garcini,** *Naud.*, CUCURBITACEÆ.

Vern.—*Zudi muralu*, TEL.

An annual climber of Bundelkhand and the Deccan. Grows on rubbish and hedges.

CUCUMIS.

238 **Cucumis Melo.,** *Linn*, CUCURBITACEÆ.

THE SWEET-MELON.

Vern.—*Kharmuj*, BENG.; *Kharbúja, khurbúj*, HIND.; *Kharabúja, chibáda*, BOM.; *Gidhro*, SIND.; *Vellari-verai*, TAM.; *Mulampandu*, TEL.; *Re-mó*, NAGA.

Extensively cultivated in the North West Provinces, in the sandy basins of the rivers, on account of its fruit. Native of North West India, Beluchistan, and perhaps West tropical Africa (*DC.*) including numerous varieties which present differences both in shape and use of the fruit.

In the North West Provinces and Oudh it is grown commonly on sandy stretches in river beds. "So soon as the sand-banks are exposed by the falling of the river, operations commence by enclosing small plots with grass fences in order to protect them from the inroad of drifting sand. A plentiful stock of manure is then carried to the spot, and large holes dug at regular intervals throughout the plot, into which the manure is distributed. The melons are sown over the manure in the holes, which act therefore in the same manner as forcing beds. This is the practice in growing melons in the beds of rivers such as the Ganges and Jumna, which consist wholly of white sand. Where the river deposit is of richer quality and contains a mixture of organic matter, a much less amount of manure is required, and it is reported that occasionally manure is altogether dispensed with. The melon beds commence fruiting in April and continue yielding until they are overwhelmed by the rise of the rivers in June." (*Duthie and Fuller.*) The area under melons in the North West Provinces may be estimated at 23,000 acres annually.

In Manipur it is cultivated by the Nagas and is of a spherical form with ten segments.

The flesh of the fruit is usually sweetish and pleasant, and eaten by Europeans as well as natives.

Cucumis Melo, *Linn.*, **var. Momordica** *(sp. Roxb.)* 239

Vern.—*Phuti*, BENG.; *Phut, túti, kachra* (unripe), HIND.; *Kakari-kai*, TAM.; *Pedda-kai, pedda dosray*, TEL.

There are two varieties, one appearing in the rains and the other in the hot season.

One of the more marked varieties of **C. Melo**, differing only in the form and nature of the fruit, which is cylindrical, quite smooth, 1 to 2 feet long, 3 to 6 inches diameter, when ripe bursts spontaneously, and has seeds rather smaller than those of the common melon. (*Duthie and Fuller.*)

In the North West Provinces and Oudh, the area under *phut* ranges from 7 acres in Mainpuri to 183 in Allahabad, and 212 in Bijnor.

"The fruit is much eaten both by natives and Europeans; when young they are a good substitute for the common cucumber, and when ripe (after bursting spontaneously) with the addition of a little sugar they are little inferior to the melon, and reckoned very wholesome." (*Roxb. Fl. Ind. l. c.*)

C. Melo, *Linn.*, **var. utilissimus** *(sp. Roxb.)* 240

Syn.—C. UTILLISSIMUS, *Roxb.*

Vern.—*Kankri*, HIND.; *Kán kur*, BENG.; *Dosray*, TEL.; *Kákadi*, BOM.

Cultivated in Upper Bengal, the North West Provinces and Punjab during the hot weather and the rains. "The fruit varies from short oval or cylindrical to elongate, and is either straight or curved like some varieties of cucumber. It varies in colour from dark green to nearly white, usually changing to a bright orange colour when ripe." (*Duthie and Fuller.*)

Kakri is an important article of food with the poorer classes during the hot weather months. **Roxburgh** gives the following account of the fruit:—

"This appears to me to be by far the most useful species of **Cucumis** that I know; when little more than one half grown, they are oblong, and a little downy; in this state they are pickled; when ripe they are about as large as an ostrich's egg, smooth and yellow; when cut they have much the flavour of the melon, and will keep good for several months, if carefully gathered without being bruised aud hung up; they are also in this stage eaten raw, and much used in curries, by the natives.

"The seeds, like those of the other cucurbitaceous fruits, contain much farinaceous matter, blended with a large portion of mild oil; the natives dry and grind them into a meal, which they employ as an article of diet; they also express a mild oil from them, which they use in food and to burn in their lamps. Experience, as well as analogy, prove these seeds to be highly nourishing, and well deserving of a more extensive culture than is bestowed on them at present."

C. sativus, *Linn.* 241

THE CUCUMBER.

Vern.—*Sasa*, BENG.; *Khira*, HIND.; *Kákadi, khira*, BOM.; *Sukasa*, SANS.; *Muluvelari*, TAM.; *Dorga-kaia*, TEL.; *Khyar*, PERS.

A native of Northern India, but cultivated in Egypt in the time of Moses, where it forms a great part of the food of the people.

"There are two forms of this plant, one a creeping plant cultivated in the fields during the hot season, and the other a climber cultivated in homesteads in the rains." (*Amsterd. Cat.*) The hot weather kind has

CUCURBITA.

small egg-shaped fruits, and is sown in February and March in any soil, preferably in a rich one, in drills. The rainy season varieties have much larger fruits, one of a dark green, and the other a creamy-white; both when full-grown change their colour to a rusty brown. The area under this variety in the North West Provinces ranges from 15 acres in Meerut to 153 in Budaun and 183 in Allahabad. Another variety (**C. Hardwickii**, *Royle*, grows wild in the Himalaya and is called *air alu* in Kumaun, and *pahari indrayan* in the tracts bordering the foot of those mountains. (*Duthie.*)

The rainy season varieties are the most common, and are universally eaten by natives of all classes as well as by Europeans. The other varieties are also used as food, the small hot weather kind, and those gathered in a young state, and known as Ghirkins, are made into pickles. The cucumber is also eaten in curry by the natives.

CUCURBITA.

242 **Cucurbita maxima,** *Duchesne*, CUCURBITACEÆ.

SQUASH GOURD.

Vern.—*Kadu*, HIND.; *Pushini-kaia*, TAM.; *Gummaddikaia*, TEL.; *Shawep-ha-yung*, BURM.

Cultivated all over India for its fruit.

This plant produces the largest known fruit, some weighing as much as 240 lbs., and measuring nearly 8 feet in circumference. The fruit is wholesome, and when young used as a vegetable.

This gourd is sweetish and yellow. When mature it will keep for many months if hung up in an airy place. It is largely used by natives of all classes in curry.

When very young and tender it may be used as a pleasant vegetable for the European table, by being boiled, pressed down to extract the water, and served warm, with butter, salt, and pepper (*Mr. L. Liotard*).

243 **C. moschata,** *Duchesne.*

THE MUSK MELON.

Syn.—C. MELOPEPO, *Roxb.*

Vern.—*Kharbúj, sitaphal, saphari kumhra, kumra, kaddú, mitha-kaddú*, N. W. P.

Includes the forms of Squash, Pumpkin, and Vegetable Marrow. The true Vegetable Marrow does not seem to be cultivated in India, **C. moschata** is the species of **Cucurbita** cultivated to any extent in the North West Provinces; statistics of the area are not available except for Farukhabad and Cawnpore, which show 138 and 20 acres respectively.

244 **C. Pepo,** *DC.*

THE PUMPKIN.

Syn.—C. PEPO, *Roxb.*, included this plant (the Pumpkin), as well as **Benincasa cerefera**, *Savi*, the white melon.

Vern.—*Kumra, safed kaddu, lanka, konda kúmara, kadimah*, BENG., HIND.

Cultivated for its fruit almost throughout India. Grown in vegetable gardens, and near the huts of the natives, often allowed to spread over their roof.

CUMINUM.

Cuminum Cyminum, *Linn.*, UMBELLIFERÆ. 245

CUMMIN.

Vern.—*Jiraka*, SANS.; *Jira*, BENG.; *Zira*, HIND.; *Siragam*, TAM.; *Jiraka*, TEL.

An annual of the Carrot family, extensively cultivated in Rajputana and other parts of Upper India.

It has seeds like Celery, of an aromatic, but somewhat bitter flavour, used by the natives to flavour their curry.

CURCUMA.

Curcuma angustifolia, *Roxb.*, SCITAMINEÆ. 246

WILD OR EAST INDIAN ARROWROOT.

Vern.—*Tikhur*, HIND.; *Ararut-ke-gadde*, DEC.; *Ararút-kishangu*, TAM.; *Ararút-gaddalu*, TEL.

An excellent kind of arrowroot is prepared from the tubers of this species, especially in Travancore, where the plant grows in abundance. **Roxburgh** observes that a sort of *starch* or arrowroot-like fecula is prepared, which is sold in the markets of Benares, and is eaten by the natives. The flour, when boiled in milk, forms an excellent diet for patients or children. It is largely used for cakes, puddings, &c., though it is often complained to produce constipation. (*Drury; Roxb.*)

C. longa, *Roxb.* 247

TURMERIC.

Vern.—*Haldi*, HIND.; *Halud*, BENG.; *Halada*, BOM.; *Haridra*, SANS.; *Manjal*, TAM.; *Pasupu*, TEL.

A perennial herb of the Ginger family, in general circulation throughout the whole of the Eastern Tropics, cultivated all over India. **Roxburgh** gives the following account of its cultivation:—

"The ground must be rich, friable, and so high as not to be overflowed during the rainy season, such as the Bengalis about Calcutta call *danga*. It is often planted on land where sugar-cane grew the preceding year, and is deemed a meliorating crop. The soil must be well ploughed and cleared of weeds, &c. It is then raised in April and May, according as the rains begin to fall, into ridges, nine or ten inches high, and eighteen or twenty broad, with intervening trenches nine or ten inches broad. The cuttings or sets, *viz.*, small portions of the fresh root, are planted on the tops of the ridges, at about eighteen inches or two feet asunder. One acre requires about nine hundred such sets, and yields in December and January, about two thousand pounds weight of the fresh root."

Turmeric forms one of the indispensable ingredients in curries, and is used for coloring confections, &c.

CYAMOPSIS.

Cyamopsis psoralioides, *DC.*, LEGUMINOSÆ. 248

Vern.—*Gudr, davarhi, kuwára, kauri, syansundari, phaligawar, kachhur, khurti, khulti*, N. W. P. and OUDH.

Cultivated in many parts from the Himalayas to the Western Peninsula as a vegetable for human consumption, and as a pulse for horses and cattle. For the former purpose it is grown on well-manured land near villages and has a luxuriant growth. The part eaten by natives is the pod while green, but its cultivation for this purpose is not very common. As a cattle fodder it is grown for its grain, and its cultivation is of considerable importance in the western districts of the North-West Provinces, where it is sown on light, sandy soil, side by side, and often mixed, with *bajra*. The time for sowing *guar* is the commencement of the rains, and the harvest is gathered in October. The average produce of dry pulse is about 10 maunds per acre.

CYCAS.

249 **Cycas pectinata,** *Griff.*, CYCADACEÆ.

Vern.—*Shakul*, NEPAL.

An evergreen, palm-like tree of Sikkim, East Bengal, and Burma, often found in sál or eng or pine forests.

Yields a coarse sago, which, with the fruits, is eaten by the hill-people in Sikkim. (*Gamble.*)

250 **C. Rumphii,** *Miq.*

Syn.—C. CIRCINALIS, *Willd.*

Vern.—*Wara-gudu*, TEL.; *Todda-maram*, MAL.

A plant abundant in the Malabar and Cochin forests.

A kind of sago is prepared from the pith, which is much used by the poorer natives and the forest tribes; the nutty seeds are used as food.

CYDONIA.

251 **Cydonia vulgaris,** *Tourn.*, ROSACEÆ.

THE QUINCE.

Vern.—*Bihi*, HIND.; *Bamtsunt, bamsutu*, KASHMIR.

Cultivated in Afghanistan and the North-West Himalayas up to 5,500 feet.

When ripe the fruit is eaten; it is sweet, slightly juicy and astringent. It is also made into preserve, and, as having a powerful odour, is often used to flavour marmalade and other preserves. Wine is sometimes made from it. It is supposed to have been the Golden Fruit of the Hesperides.

CYNARA.

252 **Cynara Scolymus,** *Linn.*, COMPOSITÆ.

ARTICHOKE.

Vern.—*Hati-choke*, BENG., HIND.

Cultivated to a limited extent over most parts of India by or for Europeans only, who eat it boiled.

The lower parts of the thick imbricated scales of the flower-heads are called artichoke bottoms, and being thick and fleshy are eaten as a vegetable.

CYNODON.

Cynodon Dactylon, *Pers.*, GRAMINEÆ. 253

CREEPING PANIC GRASS OR DOORWA.

Syn.—C. STELLATUS, *Willd.*; PANICUM DACTYLON, *Linn.*; PASPALUM DACTYLON, *DC.*

Vern.—*Dúb, daurva, kabbar*, PB.; *Chibbur*, SIND; *Dub, durba*, BENG.; *Durva, ourooha*, SANS.; *Arugam-pilla*, TAM.; *Ghericha*, TEL.

A perennial, creeping grass; grows everywhere abundantly throughout India, except perhaps in the sandy parts of Western Punjab, where it is rare. In winter it appears scanty. It abounds in the Sunderbuns.

It is the most common and useful grass in India, and its roots form a large proportion of the food of horses and cows. **Mr. Duthie** says it varies considerably both in habit and nutritive qualities, according to the nature of the soil or climate. **Roxburgh** mentions that "it is by the Brahmans of the coasts held sacred to Ganesha under the name of *Doorwall.*" A cooling drink is also said to be made from the roots.

CYNOSURUS.

Cynosurus cristatus, *Linn.*, GRAMINEÆ. 254

Syn.—PHLEUM CRISTATUM, *Scop.*

Found in the Himalaya, 12,000 to 14,000 feet in altitude. **Mr. Duthie** writes: **Baron von Mueller** remarks that this grass is particularly valuable for its power to withstand drought, the roots penetrating to considerable depths.

It is cultivated for hay or fodder.

CYPERUS.

Cyperus bulbosus, *Vahl.*, CYPERACEÆ. 255

Vern.—*Shilandi*, TAM.; *Pura-gadi*, TEL.

Grows in sandy situations on the Coromandel coast.

"The roots are used as flour in times of scarcity and eaten roasted or boiled." When roasted they have the taste of potatoes, and would be valuable for food, but that they are so small.

C. rotundus, *Linn.* 256

Syn.—C. HEXASTACHYOS, *Roxb.*

Vern.—*Muthá*, BENG.; *Mustá*, SANS.; *Koray*, TAM.; *Shaka tunga*, TEL.; *Mustá, kachará*, BOM.; *Kore-ke-jhár*, DEC.

The root or tubers of this grass is more frequently used in lower Bengal than of **C. bulbosus**, being more plentiful; but it does not seem to be used as food, except by hogs.

Cattle eat the plant.

DACTYLIS.

Dactylis glomerata, *Linn.*, GRAMINEÆ. 257

COCK'S FOOT GRASS.

Syn.—D. HISPANICA, *Roth.*; D. GLAUCESCENS, *Willd.*

A tall, perennial grass, common in the Himalaya of the North-West Provinces and the Punjab. It receives its English name from the fancied resemblance its flowers bear to a fowl's foot.

Highly valued in Europe as a fodder grass for cattle. It forms a portion of most good pasture, especially in chalky or loamy soil.

Dactyloctenium ægyptiacum, *Willd.*, GRAMINEÆ. *See* **Eleusine ægyptiaca,** *Pers.*

DÆMIA.

258 **Dæmia extensa,** *R. Br.*, ASCLEPIADEÆ.

Vern.—*Utran, jutuk,* HIND., DEC.; *Chhágul-báti,* BENG.; *Karial, siali,* PB.; *Vélip-parutti, uttámani,* TAM.; *Jittupáku, gurti-chettu,* TEL.; *Hála-koratige,* KAN.

A twining, shrubby plant, found wild in Bengal and in the Himalaya from Darjeeling to Nepal; it is also one of the commonest weeds in the Deccan.

Browsed by goats.

DALBERGIA.

259 **Dalbergia Sissoo,** *Roxb.*, LEGUMINOSÆ.

THE SISSOO.

Vern.—*Shisham, sissu, sissai,* HIND.; *Táli, safedar, shisham,* PB.; *Sissdi,* OUDH; *Sasam, sasem,* ARAB.; *Yette, nukku-kattái,* TAM.; *Sissu, karra,* TEL.

A large, deciduous tree of the sub-Himalayan tract, from the Indus to Assam, ascending to 3,000 feet. It is now largely cultivated throughout the plains of India as an ornamental tree along roads, &c.

The young trees are liable to be browsed by cattle, goats and camels (*Stewart*); but the forest conservation arrangements prevent this as much as practicable.

DAPHNE.

260 **Daphne mucronata,** *Royle,* THYMELÆACEÆ.

Vern.—*Pech,* SIND; *Kútilál, kanthan, gandalún,* PB; *Laghúne,* AFG.

A small, evergreen shrub, met with in the Sulaiman Range, from 3,000 to 7,000 feet, Himalaya from 2,300 to 9,000 feet.

The berries are eaten, but are said to cause nausea and vomiting; on the Sutlej a spirit is distilled from them (*Brandis*).

DAUCUS.

261 **Daucus Carota,** *Linn.*, UMBELLIFERÆ.

THE CARROT.

Vern.—*Gájar,* BENG., HIND.; *Garjara,* SANS.; *Jazar,* ARAB; *Zardak,* PERS.; *Gájjara kelangu, manjal-mutlangi,* TAM.; *Gajjara gadda, pita-kanda,* TEL.

Cultivated in many parts of India. A hardy, acclimatised form, with almost green roots, is extensively cultivated in India, and is rapidly finding its way into the vegetable gardens of the natives. It is an exceedingly coarse form, but quite hardy in Behar, growing right through the hot season.

Still, the common or yellow carrot is widely cultivated and is eaten by Europeans and Natives.

In the drought and consequent scarcity which occurred in 1878-79 in parts of the North-West Provinces and Oudh, the cultivators thought it expedient to cultivate carrot to an extent larger than usual around their wells, and succeeded in obtaining by this means a supply of food which, in spite of the absence of their usual field cereals, sufficiently answered their purpose. It is useful as food to man and beast, and its juice is sometimes used to colour butter and cheese.

DECAISNEA.

Decaisnea insignis, *Hook. f. & Th.*, BERBERIDEÆ. 262

Vern.—*Nomorchi*, LEPCHA; *Lúdúma*, BHUTIA.

Inhabits the eastern parts of the Himalaya, in Bhutan and Sikkim, at a height of 6,000 to 10,000 feet.

Produces a very palatable fruit, which ripens in October; and which is eaten by the Lepchas of Sikkim.

DENDROCALAMUS.

Dendrocalamus Hamiltonii, *Nees & Arn.*, GRAMINEÆ. 263

Vern.—*Tama*, NEPAL; *Pao*, LEPCHA; *Pa-shing*, BHUTIA; *Kokwa*, BENG.; *Wab*, MECHI; *Wahnok*, GARO.

Inhabits the lower Himalayan region from Kumaun to Assam.

The young shoots are boiled and eaten in Sikkim, Bhutan, and Assam.

D. strictus, *Nees.* 264

THE MALE BAMBOO.

Syn.—BAMBUSA STRICTUS, *Roxb.*

Vern.—*Bans, bans kaban, kopar*, HIND.; *Karail*, BENG.; *Bas, udha*, BOM.; *Kanka*, TEL.; *Myinwa*, BURM.

Plains and lower hills in Northern India and Central Provinces. This bamboo has often deciduous leaves; the stems, attaining a height of 100 feet or more, are strong, elastic, and nearly solid.

"Generally known to Europeans in India as the male bamboo, and is universally used for spear staffs. Extremely variable in forage." (*Duthie.*) The leaves are used sometimes as fodder.

D. Tulda, *Nees.* *See* **Bambusa Tulda,** *Roxb.*

DIGERA.

Digera arvensis, *Forsk.*, AMARANTACEÆ. 265

Syn.—D. MURICATA, *Mart.*

Vern.—*Tartara, tandala, leswa*, PB.

A weed common in the Punjab fields and lower hills.

Serves often as a pot-herb. Leaves and tender tops are used by the natives in their curries (*Voigt*).

DILLENIA.

Dillenia indica, *Linn.*, DILLENIACEÆ. 266

Vern.—*Cháltá*, BENG., HIND.; *Phamsikol*, LEPCHA; *Olengah*, ASS.; *Rai*, URIYA; *Uva*, TAM., TEL.; *Syalita*, MAL.; *Thabyoo*, BURM.

A large tree of Bengal, Central and South India, and Burma. Flowers in summer, and its fruit ripens in February.

DIOSCO-REA.

The fruit is large, about 3 inches in diameter, and is surrounded by fleshy accrescent calyces which, when the fruit is full grown, have an agreeably acid taste, and are eaten by the natives, either raw or cooked—chiefly cooked in curries. They are also made into a pleasant jelly. The acid juice sweetened with sugar forms a cooling drink.

267 **Dillenia pentagyna,** *Roxb.*

Vern.—*Karkotta*, BENG.; *Aggai*, OUDH; *Shukni*, LEPCHA; *Akshi*, ASS.; *Kallai*, C. P.; *Rai*, URIYA, TAM.; *Rawadan*, TEL.; *Malé-geru*, KURG; *Zimbryun*, BURM.

This tree, with leaves sometimes 2 feet long, inhabits the same regions as **D. indica**, and extends into Oudh. It flowers in March and April.

The flowers, buds, and fruit when green are eaten by the natives.

DIOSCOREA.

268 **Dioscorea aculeata,** *Roxb.*, DIOSCOREACEÆ.

PRICKLY-STEMMED YAM OR GOA POTATOE.

Vern.—*Mou-alu*, BENG., HIND.; *Kantu-kelangu*, TAM.; *Kata-kelenga*, TEL.

A native of Bengal, Western and Southern India. The roots are oblong, pendulous, delicately white, and generally about two pounds in weight. They are dug up in the forest during the cold season, and are sold in market places.

They make a good vegetable, and are commonly eaten by the natives cooked in curry.

269 **D. alata,** *Linn.*

YAM, OR WING-STALKED YAM.

Vern.—*Kham-alu*, BENG., HIND.; *Yams-kalung*, TAM.; *Niluvu-pendalum*, TEL.

This species is much cultivated in various parts of India. (*Roxb.*)

The tubers are oblong, white, and are a favourite vegetable with the natives.

270 **D. bulbifera,** *Linn.*

BULB-BEARING YAM.

Vern.—*Zaminkand*, HIND.; *Karukarinda*, DEC.; *Malay-kaya-pendalam*, TEL.; *Katu-katsjil*, MAL.

Cultivated in the Konkan.

The bulb on the stem and the roots are used as vegetables (*Birdwood*). The latter are bitter, but are rendered eatable by being covered with ashes and steeped in cold water.

Dr. Stewart, under the name of **D. deltoides**, *Wall*, with the vernacular names, *kniss tar*, *kithi*, *tardi*, *gun.;ru*, *kaspat*, mentions a plant which grows abundantly in many parts of the Punjab Himalaya, and of which the root (several pounds weight) is largely eaten, cooked, by various classes in parts of the Siwaliks and outer hills, *after steeping it in ashes and water to remove acridity.* This may probably be the same as the **D. bulbifera.**

271 **D. fasciculata,** *Roxb.*

Vern.—*Susni-alu*, BENG.

"Cultivated to a considerable extent in the vicinity of Calcutta." (*Roxb.*)

DIOSPY-ROS.

The root consists of several small, smooth, light-coloured tubers, which are used by the natives for food and for the manufacture of starch. (*Roxb.*)

Dioscorea globosa, *Roxb.* 272

YAM.

Vern.—*Chúpri-alú*, BENG., HIND.

This species is largely cultivated, especially in parts of Bengal. The tubers are roundish, sometimes very large, inside very white.

They are the most esteemed of the tuberous roots eaten by the natives, and are also much liked by Europeans in India. The former eat them in curries, and also boiled.

D. pentaphylla, *Willd.* 273

Vern.—*Kanta-alu*, BENG.; *Nureni-kelangu*, MAL.

Common in jungles, on low hills in Bengal and Southern India.

The tubers are oblong, large, and white, considered wholesome and palatable. The natives dig up the tubers whenever required by them for food.

D. purpurea, *Roxb.* 274

Vern.—*Lal-gurania-alu*, BENG.

Cultivated in parts of Bengal.

"The root is oblong, throughout of a lighter or darker purple, but always considerably deep in the tinge." (*Roxb.*)

It is reckoned by the natives as the third best among the yams, the **D. globosa** being considered as the first and **D. alata** as the second best.

D. rubella, *Roxb.* 275

Vern.—*Guraniya-alu*, BENG.

Much cultivated in parts of Lower Bengal, especially about Calcutta. Tubers oblong, sometimes three feet long, deeply tinged with red under the scarf skin.

Held fourth in estimation by Bengalis, and used by them as food.

D. sativa, *Willd.* 276

COMMON YAM.

Vern.—*Rátalu*, HIND.; *Yamskollung*, TAM.

Cultivated all over India for its roots.

The roots or tubers are eaten cooked, and are a common article of food.

D. versicolor, *Wall.* 277

Vern.—*Genthi, gajir, ganjira*, HIND.

A kind of yam found wild in the Kumaun Himalayas.

DIOSPYROS.

Diospyros Embryopteris, *Pers.*, EBENACEÆ. 278

GAUB or GAB.

Syn.—D. GLUTINOSA, *Roxb.*

Vern.—*Gáb, makur-kendi*, BENG., HIND.; *Tinduka*, SANS.; *Kendu*, ASS.; *Tumbika, panichika*, TAM.; *Tumik*, TEL.; *Timboree*, BOM.

A small tree or evergreen shrub, forming a dense dome of foliage; met with throughout India and Burma.

Produces a round fruit as big as a middle-sized apple, green when unripe, rusty yellow when ripe; and in the latter stage contains a somewhat astringent pulp in which the seeds are embedded.

The fruit when green is commonly used in caulking the bottom of boats; when ripe it is eaten by the natives, but is not very palatable. The leaves are also eaten as a vegetable.

279 **Diospyros Lotus,** *Linn.*

THE EUROPEAN DATE PLUM.

Vern.—*Ambuk, maluk, bissarhi,* PB.

A middle-sized tree of the northern parts of the Punjab, ascending the Himalaya, and extending into Kashmir, Afghanistan, and Beluchistan.

The fruit, when ripe, is sweetish, and is eaten, either fresh or dried, by Afghans and other tribes. The former bring quantities of it to the Peshawar bazars. It is sometimes also used in *sherbat.*

This small fruit is supposed by some to be one of those eaten by the people called Lotophagi. In Southern France it is eaten when half-rotten like the Medlar. (*Gamble.*)

280 **D. melanoxylon,** *Roxb.*

Vern.—*Tendu, kendu, abnú,* HIND.; *Kend, kyou,* BENG.; *Tumri, tummer, tumki,* GOND.; *Tumbi, tumbali,* TAM.; *Tumi, tumki,* TEL.; *Balai,* KAN.

Found throughout India, but not in Burma. It is a moderate-sized tree, and produces an ebony wood, though not the true ebony of commerce.

Flowers in April and May, and produces a fruit which, when ripe, is eaten by the natives. It has an astringent taste, and is not very palatable.

281 **D. pyrrhocarpa,** *Miq.*

Vern.—*Tay,* BURM.

A tree of the Andaman islands.

The fruit is said to be eaten by the Burmese.

282 **D. tomentosa,** *Roxb.*

Vern.—*Kyou,* BENG; *Tumal,* HIND.; *Kakindu,* SANS.; *Kinnee, kendu,* PB.

Found in the northern parts of Bengal, also in the Siwalik tracts of the Punjab. It produces whitish flowers in April, and small berries, which ripen in June.

When ripe the berries are yellowish, and are filled with a soft, yellow, sweetish, astringent pulp, eaten by the natives.

DOCYNIA.

283 **Docynia indica,** *Dcne.,* ROSACEÆ.

Vern.—*Mehul, possy,* NEPAL; *Lihung,* LEPCHA; *Sopho,* KHÁSIA.

A small tree of the Himalaya in Sikkim, Bhutan and Assam, also of the Khásia Hills, and Burma.

Produces a fruit which is yellow green with orange patch, is 1 to 1½ inches in diameter, and rounded at the base. When ripe the fruit has a slight quince flavour, and it is eaten when half ripe by the hill tribes.

DOLICHOS.

Dolichos biflorus, *Linn.*, LEGUMINOSÆ. 284

HORSE GRAM OR KOOLTEE

Syn.—D. UNIFLORUS, *Lam.*; GLYCINE UNIFLORUS, *Lam.*

Vern.—*Kurti-kalai*, BENG.; *Kulthi gahat*, HIND.; *Koolutha*, SANS.; *Kallat, kúlat, kult, kolt, barát, gulatti*, PB.; *Kollu*, TAM.; *Wulawalli*, TEL.; *Kulitba gaglip*, SIND.

An erect annual (*forma uniflora*) or twining (*forma biflora*), met with chiefly in a state of cultivation as a pulse crop on the tropical and sub-tropical Himalaya, to Burma and Ceylon. It is extensively cultivated on the coast. It is sown either singly, or along with other grains. The sowing is made in October and November, generally in dry, light, rich soils; and the crop is reaped in February.

The grain is eaten by the poorer classes of natives, and by horses and cattle. The straw is given to cattle as fodder. The pods are flat and curved like a sickle, and used for feeding cattle.

D. Lablab, *Linn.* 285

Vern.—*Shim, makhan-sim, borboti, gheea-sim, pauch-sim*, BENG.; *Sim, makhan-sim, lobia, borboti*, HIND.; *Shimbi*, SANS.; *Kechu*, NAGA; *Alsanda, boberlu, tella-chikurkai*, TEL.

Wild and cultivated throughout India; ascends to 6,000—7,000 feet on the Himalaya. The climbers may be seen commonly grown along the borders of tall crops, twining round the plants on the margin of the fields. In some parts of the country the castor oil plant is a favourite support. They are also grown commonly in little patches round houses, and allowed to climb on the walls and roof.

There are several varieties of this bean. **Roxburgh** describes thirteen cultivated. They are all known by the vernacular names given above; and are, most of them, eaten cooked as curry by the natives. For Europeans a few of them, when young and tender, are good substitutes for the common **Phaseolus** known as French beans.

D. sinensis. 286

Syn.—VIGNA SINENSIS.

It is cultivated in India for its pods, two feet long, which contain pea-like seeds, forming a considerable article of food.

DRACOCEPHALUM.

Dracocephalum heterophyllum, *Benth.*, LABIATÆ. 287

Vern.—*Zanda, shanku, karamm*, N. PB. and LADAK.

Grows in the Punjab Himalaya and Ladak from 13,000 to 17,000 feet.

The plant is browsed by goats and sheep, and its root appears to be used as a vegetable (*Dr. Stewart*).

DURIO.

Durio Zibethinus, *DC.*, MALVACEÆ. 288

DURIAN, OR CIVET-CAT FRUIT TREE.

Vern.—*Duyin*, BURM.; *Durian*, MALAY.

A large tree of the Malay Islands, wild in South Tenasserim, and cultivated as far north as Moulmein.

ELÆAGNUS.

Produces a large fruit, 10 inches by 7, called the *durian*, or civet-cat fruit, whose cream-coloured fleshy aril or pulp enveloping the seed, like that of the Jack, is the part eaten. It is well known and much prized and eaten by the natives, but it has a rather strong odour, considered by Europeans as highly offensive, resembling that of putrid animal matter or rotten onions. The fruit is, however, highly prized even by Europeans. Natives regard it as extremedy luscious, and it forms a great part of their food. The roasted seeds and the boiled unripe fruit are also eaten as vegetables.

EDWARDSIA.

289 **Edwardsia Hydaspica,** *Edge.*, LEGUMINOSÆ.

Vern.—*Kun, kohen, malan,* PB.

A shrub of the Salt Range and Trans-Indus regions of the Punjab.

Occasionally browsed by goats, but said to be injurious to other animals.

EHRETIA.

290 **Ehretia acuminata,** *Br.*, BORAGINEÆ.

Syn.—E. SERRATA, *Roxb.*

Vern.—*Pányan, kurkuna, arján,* HIND.; *Nalshuna,* NEPAL; *Bual,* ASS.; *Kula-aja,* BENG.; *Narra,* GARHWAL; *Pursan, kalthaun,* PB.

Native of Bhutan and eastern parts of Bengal, introduced elsewhere in Bengal.

Has oblong, serrated, smooth leaves, and fragrant flowers, which appear in the hot season. It also produces a fruit which is described by Dr. Glass as delicious.

291 **E. lævis,** *Roxb.*

Vern.—*Chamrúr, koda,* HIND.; *Mosonea,* URIYA; *Dotti,* GOND.; *Paldatam, seregad,* TEL.

A tree of the Sulaiman Range, Punjab, sub-Himalayan tract, Oudh, Bengal, Central and South India, and Burma (*Gamble*).

Produces a fruit which is eaten by the natives, who, in times of famine, also eat the inner bark.

ELÆAGNUS.

292 **Elæagnus hortensis,** *M. Beib.*, ELÆAGNEÆ.

OLEASTER.

Syn.—E. ANGUSTIFOLIA and E. ORIENTALIS.

Vern.—*Sanjit,* AFG.; *Sirshing,* TIBET; *Shiúlik,* N. W. P.

A small tree of Ladák, Baltistan and Afghanistan.

Produces small, yellow leaves which perfume the air to a great distance, and a fruit which is eaten; from the latter a spirit is distilled in Yarkand.

The berries, called Trebizond dates, are dried by the Arabs and made into cakes.

293 **E. latifolia,** *Linn.*

Syn.—E. CONFERTA, *Roxb.*

Vern.—*Ghiwain, mijhanla,* KUMAUN; *Jarila,* NEPAL; *Guara,* BENG.; *Kamboong,* MAGH.

A straggling, evergreen shrub of the Himalaya, from Kumaun to Bhutan, Khási hills, Eastern Bengal and South India.

Produces an acid fruit which is eaten.

Elæagnus umbellata, *Thunb.* 294

Vern.—*Ghiwain, ghain, kankoli, bammewa*, PB.

A thorny, deciduous shrub on the Himalaya, from near the Indus to Bhutan, between 3,000 and 10,000 feet.

The fruit of this is eaten by the natives. The fruits of these different species of **Elæagnus** are also used in curries, or pickled like olives.

ELÆOCARPUS.

Elæocarpus lanceæfolius, *Roxb.*, TILIACEÆ. 295

Vern.—*Sufed-pai*, SYLHET; *Bhadras*, NEPAL; *Shephyew*, LEPCHA; *Sakalang*, ASS.

A large tree, inhabiting Eastern Himalaya and Khásia Hills, and extends into Sylhet and Tenasserim. The plant flowers in the beginning of the rains, and the fruit ripens in September and October.

The fruit is eaten by the natives.

E. serratus, *Linn.* 296

Vern.—*Jalpai*, BENG.; *Perinkara*, KAN.

A tree found in the north-east regions of the Himalaya, in Bengal and on the western coast.

Produces numerous small, white flowers in the hot season, and a fruit which is very hard, oblong-shaped and smooth. The fruit is dried and used in curries by the natives; and also pickled.

E. Varunua, *Ham.* 297

Vern.—*Tultealy, saulkuri*, ASS.

A tree met with in the Himalaya from Kumaun to Sikkim; also in Assam and Chittagong.

Like the other species this also produces a fruit which is edible.

ELEONURUS.

Eleonurus hirsutus, *Vahl.*, GRAMINEÆ. 298

Vern.—*Bhanjuri*, N. W. P.

Grows in light soil in Sindh, and extends to the Punjab as far as the Salt Range and to the North West Provinces in Bundelkhand.

Used as fodder to a small extent.

ELETTARIA.

Elettaria Cardamomun, *Maton*, SCITAMINEÆ. 299

THE LESSER CARDAMOM.

Vern.—*Chota-eláchi*, BENG., HIND.; *Ellakay*, TAM., TEL.; *Panlat*, BURM.

A native of India with perennial, reed-like stems, producing fruit for several years. Extensively cultivated in the hilly districts of South India. This is the lesser or white Cardamom of South India, and exported to Europe.

ELEU-SINE.

Used by the natives in flavouring sweetmeats and certain cooked dishes; also as a spice, and sometimes chewed in the betel-leaf *pán*.

ELEUSINE.

300 **Eleusine ægyptiaca,** *Pers.*, GRAMINEÆ.

Syn.—CYNOSURUS ÆGYPTIACUS, *Linn.;* DACTYLOCTENIUM ÆGYPTIACUM, *Willd.*

Vern.—*Makra-jali,* BENG., HIND.; *Makra, makri, ghurchua,* NORTH INDIA; *Madana, chimbari, chubrei,* PB.; *Cavara-pullu,* MAL.

Grows wild in pasture ground, and by the roads ides in the plains of the Punjab and North-West Provinces. Allied to **E coracana**, and bearing the same vernacular name; occurs commonly throughout Upper India, and presents on a superficial examination hardly any points of difference from the cultivated plant. .

"Its seeds are occasionally eaten in times of scarcity, and it is reckoned good as a fattening and milk-producing pasture." (*Dr. Stewart.*)

It is a good fodder grass, and cattle are very fond of it (*Duthie.*) The seed of the wild plant is collected by the poorer classes as an unpalatable though often very serviceable food (*Duthie and Fuller*).

301 **E. corocana,** *Gaertn.*

MILLET, NATCHNEE OT RAGEE.

Vern.—*Mandua, marua, makra, rolka,* N. W. P. and OUDH; *Mandal, chalodra,* PB.; *Koda,* HIMALAYAN NAME; *Marua,* BENG.; *Rajika,* SANS.; *Raji,* DEC. and SOUTHERN INDIA; *Kayur,* TAM.; *Ponassa, pedda, tamidalu,* TEL.

A decumbent grass, native of India, widely cultivated as a rain weather crop in the northern and southern provinces in light soils; it yields very profitable returns. In the North West Provinces, it is cultivated to the extent of about 43,169 acres in light soils; the rate of seed sown is 10 lbs. to the acre. It suffers greatly from heavy rain. The average yield ranges from 12 to 14 maunds of grain to the acre where carefully cultivated, to 5 or 6 maunds in the hills.

The grain is not considered very wholesome, but is made into hand-bread or *chapathis* and eaten by the poor. The stalks are given to cattle as fodder. (*See Roxb.*, Vol I, page 343, under **E. Coracana** and **E. stricta.**)

In Abyssinia it is called *Tocussa*; on the Coromandel Coast, *Natchnee.* The Mahomedans call it *Raggee.* A fermented liquor is prepared from the seeds called *Bojah* in the Mahratta country. It is the staple grain of the Mysore country, where it is stored up in pits, keeping sound for many years. (*W. Elliot.*)

302 **E. flagellifera,** *Nees.*

Syn.—E. ARABICA, *Hochst.*

Vern.—*Gurdub,* N. W. INDIA.

A small, creeping, perennial grass, found in arid parts of the Punjab. Affords very good fodder for cattle.

303 **E. indica,** *Gærtn.*

Syn.—CYNOSURUS INDICUS, *Linn.*

Vern.—*Gudha, jhinjhor,* N. W. INDIA.

A coarse grass inhabiting Northern India in the plains, and ascending the hills.

Not liked by cattle.

ENTADA.

Entada scandens, *Bth.*, LEGUMINOSÆ. 304

Syn.—E. PURSÆTHA, *DC.*; MIMOSA SCANDENS, *Linn.*

Vern.—*Gilla*, BENG.; *Geredi*, URIYA; *Pangra*, NEPAL; *Gardal*, BOM.; *Kongnyin-nway*, BURM.

A large climber of the forests of East Bengal, South India, Burma, the Andaman Islands and Ceylon, ascending on the Himalaya to 4,000 feet. Flowers in March and April, and produces broad flat pods, from 2 to 4 feet long, which ripen towards the close of the year.

The pods contain large, flat, hard, polished, chestnut-coloured seeds, or rather nuts, which are, after being steeped in water and roasted, sometimes eaten by the natives.

EPHEDRA.

Ephedra Gerardiana, *Wall.*, GNETACEÆ. 305

Vern.—*Asmánia, bútshúr, búdshúr, chewa, khanna*, PB. Brandis gives these Vern. names under E. vulgaris, *Rich.*; but E. Gerardiana is the name given by Dr. Stewart.

A small shrub of the inner arid north-west Himalaya; at places on the Sutlej and Chenab, and in the Jhelam basin, at from 7,800 to 11,200 feet, and in Ladak to 15,000 feet.

The plant is browsed by goats. It produces pretty red berries, which, Dr. Stewart says, have a not unpleasant, mawkish, sweet taste, and are sometimes eaten by the natives. They are not unwholesome.

EQUISETUM.

Equisetum debile, *Roxb.*, EQUISETACEÆ. 306

THE HORSE TAIL.

Vern.—*Matti, skinung, bandukei, nari, trotak, búki*, PB.

Found in Dindigal, Burma, Bengal, Sylhet, North Doab, Dehra Dun, and Manipur; also in wet places throughout the Punjab Plains, where, Dr. Stewart thinks, it is at times given to cattle as fodder.

ERAGROSTIS.

Eragrostis Brownei, *Nees.*, GRAMINEÆ. 307

Syn.—POA BROWNEI, *Kunth.*

Vern.—*Bharree*, Aligarh. (in *Duthie.*)

A perennial grass.

"At Aligarh it grows on barren, wet soil, and is eaten by cattle and horses." (*Lang quoted by Duthie.*) Baron von Mueller describes it as a valuable species, keeping green in the driest Australian summer even on poor soil.

E. cynosuroides, *Retz.* 308

Syn.—POA CYNOSUROIDES, *Retz.*; BRIZA BIPINNATA, *Linn.*

Vern.—*Dab, daboi*, N. W. P.; *Dib, kusa*, PB.; *Kusha*, BENG.; *Kusha, kutha, durbha*, SANS.; *Durbha, dubha, durpa*, TEL.

A strong, coarse grass, common in dry, barren ground, and sandy soil on the plains of the North-West Provinces, the Punjab, and Sindh. The

ERIOBO-TRYA.

culms are straight, round and smooth, one to three feet in height; leaves long and numerous. Its long roots keep it fresh throughout the year. Mr. Wilson (quoted by *Mr. Duthie*), however, says, "it will not grow on the worst type of *usar* land on which the *kar usara* grass (**Sporobols tenacissimus**) appears to thrive."

Mr. Duthie says: "Cattle do not eat it as a rule, though it is liked by buffaloes when young; it produces an excellent rope fibre; paper is also made from it, and the upper part of the stem is used for making sieves."

Roxburgh writes:—"It is employed by the Brahmans in their religious ceremonies. Can this be **Gramen capillaceum**? *Cusa* or *Cusha*, the Sanskrit name of this much-venerated grass, was given to it at a very early period, by the Hindu philosophers, and believed by **Sir Wilson Jones**, to have been consecrated to the memory of *Cush*, one of the sons of Ram;" but the name is much older than that of Ram or his son.

309 **Eragrostis flexuosa**, *Roxb.*

Syn.—POA FLEXUOSA, *Roxb.*

Found in the plains of the North West Provinces and the Punjab. **Roxburgh** says it is a pretty large species growing in tufts on old walls so exactly resembling **P. unioloides** as to be easily mistaken for it.

310 **E. nutans**, *Retz.*

Syn.—POA NUTANS, *Roxb.*

Grows in the North West Provinces and the Punjab, but frequents banks of water-courses, borders of rice fields and other rich, moist soil.

Cattle are not fond of it.

311 **E. plumosa**, *Link.*

Syn.—POA TENELLA, *Linn.*; P. PLUMOSA, *Retz.*

Vern.—*Phularwa, bhurbhuri, galgala, jhusa*, N. W. P. *(Duthie.)*

Inhabits the plains of the North-West Provinces, Oudh and the Punjab, where it grows in tufts on pasture ground.

Eaten by cattle and horses.

EREMURUS.

312 **Eremurus spectabilis**, *Bieb.*, LILIACEÆ.

Vern.—*Shili, bre, prau*, PB.

A plant with close spikes of white flowers, and linear radial leaves it is common in the north of the Punjab.

"The leaves when young are much eaten, both fresh and dry, cooked as vegetables." (*Dr. Stewart.*)

ERIOBOTRYA.

313 **Eriobotrya japonica**, *Lindl.*, ROSACEÆ.

LOQUAT OR JAPAN MEDLAR.

Vern.—*Loquat*, BENG., HIND.

A tree of the apple family, cultivated in Japan, China, Australia, and Southern Europe, for its fruit, which has the apple flavour.

Introduced from China into Bengal, thence extended to other Provinces, and now cultivated in many parts of India, chiefly on account of its fruit.

The *loquat* fruit, which grows in clusters, is now well known. It is a small yellow fruit, 1 to 1½ inches long, with a thin skin, luscious pulp, and brown seeds. It improves in its quality in the plains of Northern India, than in those of the Lower Provinces; and it is esteemed by Europeans as well as natives.

ERIODENDRON.

Eriodendron anfractuosum, *DC.*, MALVACEÆ. 314

SILK COTTON TREE, or WHITE COTTON TREE.

Syn.—BOMBAX PENTANDRUM, *Roxb.*

Vern.—*Shwet-simúl*, BENG.; *Hatian, senibal, kuntan, safed simal, katan*, HIND.; *Elava, ilavan, maram*, TAM.; *Pur, kadami*, TEL.

A tall, deciduous tree, common throughout the hotter parts of India and Ceylon.

On the Coromandel Coast the Tamuls plant them about their temples.

There are apparently three closely allied species, one of which was probably introduced from the West Indies.

ERUCA.

Eruca sativa, *Lam.*, CRUCIFERÆ. 315

Syn.—BRASSICA ERUCA, *Linn*; B. ERUCOIDES, *Roxb.*

Vern.—*Duan, sahwan, tira, tara, taramira, dua, chara*, N. W. P. and OUDH; *Suffed-shorshi*, BENG.; *Siddartha*, SANS.; *Tara, assu usan*, PB.

A native of South Europe and North Africa. Cultivated in places in North and Central India, Western Himalaya, ascending to 10,000 feet, also met with in the Upper Gangetic valley. (*Hooker f. & T. And.*) Generally raised as a cold weather crop and reaped in spring. In the Punjab it is more commonly cultivated in the arid parts.

In the North-West Provinces and Oudh its cultivation is most general in the western portions, it being commonly grown mixed with gram or barley, occasionally alone on dry lands and frequently in cotton fields; the total area is not known, but is probably over 40,000 acres; sowing takes place at any time between the beginning of September and the end of November, and the crop ripens in March to May. When grown alone or with cotton its produce of seed per acre varies from 4 to 12 maunds.

The seed is consumed to a great extent as human food, and is also used for expressing the oil which serves for lighting purposes and for anointing the hair. The dry leaves and stalks are not made use of; but the crop is sometimes cut green and given to cattle when fodder runs short. It is used in Southern Europe as salad.

ERVUM.

Ervum Lens, *Linn.*, LEGUMINOSÆ.

LENTIL. 316

Vern.—*Masuri*, BENG.; *Masur*, HIND.; *Misurpurpur*, TAM.; *Misur-pappu*, TEL.

A weak, pea-like, wing-leaved annual and a valuable pulse, a native of west temperate Asia, Greece and Italy, spread through Egypt to Europe and India (*DeCandolle*). It is the Lentil of Scriptures of which Esau's pottage was made.

In India it is largely grown as a winter crop, and it is universally eaten cooked, both by natives and Europeans. In the Punjab, excluding perhaps the more arid tracts, it is grown everywhere in the plains and hills, and up to 10,000 or 11,000 feet in the Himalaya. In the North-West Provinces and Oudh it is sown in all kinds of soils, but chiefly in low land (1 maund of seeds to the acre), and produces on an average 6½ to 8 maunds grain per acre from unirrigated, and from 10 to 12 maunds from irrigated, land. The average area covered with the crop in the 30 temporarily-settled districts, North-West Provinces, is about 114,225 acres. In Bengal and the Central Provinces also it is cultivated to some considerable extent.

A trade is carried on in this pulse, but as the trade returns do not mention it separately it is not possible to give any figures regarding it.

The meal of Lentil, which is regarded as wholesome, is sold in England under the names of Evalenta or Revalenta, as food for invalids.

EUCHLÆNA.

317 **Euchlæna luxurians,** *Téosinté*, GRAMINEÆ.

Syn.—REANA LUXURIANS.

A native of Guatemala. Attempts have recently been made to introduce this grass into the North-West Provinces and the Punjab.

The grass is described as a most excellent fodder for cattle, a prolific seed-bearer, with vigorous growth, attaining a height of from 14 to 15 feet in rich soil, but requiring constant irrigation The attempts hitherto made to introduce this grass have not had any definite results, for, while in some places it has been favourably reported on, in others it has failed, and the general opinion is that it could never compete with the existing fodder plants of India, such as *juar*, &c., as its cultivation on a large scale would be too expensive owing to its requiring rich soil and constant irrigation.

EUGENIA.

318 **Eugenia aquea,** *Burm.*, MYRTACEÆ.

Vern.—*Jambo-ayer.*

A native of the Moluccas, introduced into Bengal. Blossoms in March, and ripens in May and June. The fruit is "about the size of a large *medlar* (*loquat*), with both ends flattened, surface smooth and polished, but uneven." (*Roxb.*)

There are two varieties: in one the fruit has a most beautiful, pale rose-colour and aromatic taste; in the other it is perfectly white.

319 **E. claviflora,** *Roxb.*

A tree of Sikkim and Khasia mountains, altitude 2,000 to 4,000 feet, of Sylhet, Chittagong and Pegu, Nicobar and Andaman Islands, Tenasserim, Singapore and Penang.

The fruit is eaten by the natives.

320 **E. formosa,** *Wall.*

Vern.—*Bara-jaman*, NEPAL; *Bunkonkri*, MECHI; *Bolsobak*, GARO; *Famsikol*, LEPCHA.

A moderate-sized tree of the Eastern Himalaya and sub-Himalayan tract, near streams; also of Chittagong and Tenasserim. (*Gamble.*) Blossoms in April, and the fruit ripens in June and July.

The fruit is of the size of a walnut, and is eaten by the natives.

Eugenia Jambolana, *Lam.* 321

Vern. *Jáman, jám, jamoon,* HIND. and BENG.; *Chambu,* GARO; *Jamu,* ASS.; *Naval, naga,* TAM.; *Nasedu, nairuri,* TEL.; *Jambool,* BOM.; *Thabyai-pyoo,* BURM.

A moderate-sized tree, found wild or in cultivation all over India, from the Indus eastward, ascending to 5,000 feet. It flowers in the beginning of the hot season, and the fruit ripens in July and August.

The fruit, is of the size of a pigeon's egg and is eaten by all classes of people: it is purple, sub-acid and rather astringent, and is improved in taste by being pricked and rubbed with a little salt, and allowed to stand an hour.

E. Jambos, *Linn.* 322

ROSE APPLE.

Syn.—JAMBOSA VULGARIS, *DC.*

Vern.—*Golab-jam,* BENG., HIND.

A small-sized tree, native of the East Indies, which eminently combines the beauty of flower, fruit and foliage. The fruit, which is of the size of a hen's egg, is specially lovely.

Common in gardens in most parts of India and its islands; it flowers in February, and its fruit ripens in April to May.

The fruit is small, yellowish, rather wanting in juice, hollow, with two brown seeds, and is eaten by all classes. A preserve is sometimes made from the fruit.

E. Javanica, *Lamk.* 323

Syn.—E. ALBA, *Roxb.*

Vern.—*Jamrool,* BENG., HIND.

A tree of Malacca, Andaman and Nicobar Islands. Introduced into Bengal, where it is now common, chiefly in gardens. Produces abundantly, in the hot and rainy seasons, a fruit which, grape green when young, and pure white when ripe, shining, "peelless," watery and refreshing, but almost tasteless.

The fruit is eaten by all classes of people.

E. malaccensis, *Linn.* 324

MALAY APPLE or the KAVIKA TREE.

Vern.—*Malacca jamrool,* BENG., HIND.; *Thabyoo-thabyay,* BURM.

A handsome tree, with a profusion of either white or scarlet flowers, followed by an abundance of fruit of the size of a small apple. It is a native of the Malay Islands, and is now cultivated in Bengal and Burma, chiefly in gardens.

Produces at different periods of the year a large, juicy fruit, which is very commonly eaten, though rather insipid. (*Roxb.*) The pulp of the fruit is said to be wholesome and agreeable.

In the Malay's eye, the 'kavika' tree represents all that is lovely and beautiful. The Indian species, as shown by the contradictory accounts given of the fruit, seems to be different from the Malayan.

E. obovata, *Wall.* 325

Vern.—*Kiamoni,* NEPAL; *Jung-song,* LEPCHA; *Boda-jam,* MECHI.

An evergreen tree found in the Bengal and Burma forests.

Produces a fruit which is eaten by the natives.

326 **Eugenia operculata,** *Roxb.*

Vern.—*Rai-jaman, dugdugia,* HIND.; *Yethabyay,* BURM.

Met with along the sub-Himalayan tract, also in Chittagong, Burma, and Western Ghâts. It blossoms in March and April, and its fruit ripens two months later.

The fruit is eaten.

327 **E. Pimenta,** *DC.*

THE PIMENTO TREE

Introduced from America.

The leaves are sweetly aromatic, astringent, and often used in sauce. The berries are used for culinary purposes.

EULOPHIA.

328 **Eulophia campestris,** *Lindl.,* ORCHIDEÆ.

Vern.—*Sálib misri,* PB.

An orchid found in Oudh and Rohilkhand, and in the Siwaliks of the Gangetic Doab.

The tubers are collected and used by the natives chiefly as a tonic and aphrodisiac, and a small trade is carried on in the commodity. The Europeans in Northern India and some of the Himalayan and Nilgiri Hill stations collect the roots of this and some other allied species and use it for family consumption as salep, as it is an easily digestible kind of farinaceous food.

329 **E. vera,** *Royle.*

The remarks under **E. Campestris** apply here also.

EUONYMUS.

330 **Euonymus fimbriatus,** *Wall.,* CELASTRINEÆ.

THE SPINDLE TREE.

Vern.—*Siki, wattal, banchor, karun, sidhera,* PB.

A small tree found in the Himalaya, Kumaun to Sikkim.

The leaves are eaten by goats.

EURYALE.

331 **Euryale ferox,** *Salisb.,* NYMPHÆACEÆ.

THE GORGON PLANT.

Syn.—ANNESLEA SPINOSA, *R.*

Vern.—*Makhana,* BENG., HIND.; *Jewar,* PB.

A plant of the Water Lily family, a native of India.

A stemless, aquatic plant of the sweet-water lakes and ponds of East Bengal, Oudh and Kashmir. Its circular leaves, 2 to 3 feet in diameter, float full flat on the surface of the water. Has long flowers of a lovely blue violet or bright red with green on the outside, and produces round prickly berries of the size of an orange which swell out in various places by the growth of the seeds within.

The seeds, which are black in color and of the size of peas, are farinaceous, sold in the public bazars, and much liked by the natives, by whom they are much eaten after being roasted in hot sand and husked.

EXCÆCARIA.

Excæcaria baccata, *Müll.*; EUPHORBIACEÆ. 332

Vern.—*Lal-kainjal,* NEPAL; *Adamsali,* ASS.; *Billa,* SYLHET; *Linhlin,* BURM.

A large tree of North and East Bengal and Burma.

The bark is chewed by the natives of Assam.

FAGOPYRUM.

Fagopyrum emarginatum, *Meisn.*, POLYGONACEÆ. 333

Vern.—*Phapar,* KUMAUN; *Bhe,* BHUTIA; *Daran, phulan,* PB.

Grows at elevations 7,000 to 12,000 feet. Has a white or yellow flower; ripens in September and October. The seeds are oval, acute, nearly triangular, with acute, smooth, brilliant angles. (*Atkinson*).

The leaves are used as pot-herb.

F. esculentum, *Mœnch.* 334

THE BUCKWHEAT OR BRANK.

Syn.—POLYGONUM FAGOPYRUM.

Vern.—*Chin, trumba, katu, phaphra, kaspat,* PB.

Cultivated to a certain extent in Upper India.

Used by the poorer classes of natives as food. Its seeds are ground into meal and made into thin cakes. Its seeds are used to feed pheasants. While ranking higher than rice as a nutritious food for men, it is greatly inferior to wheat.

FERONIA.

Feronia Elephantum, *Correa,* RUTACEÆ. 335

THE WOOD-APPLE.

Vern.—*Bilin, kapittha,* SANS.; *Kat-bel,* HIND.; *Kait, kath-bel,* BENG.; *Kavatha, katori,* SIND.; *Vallanga, vela, hairt,* TAM.; *Velagá, yellanga,* TEL.; *Hman,* BURM.

Found in the sub-Himalayan forests from the Ravi eastward, in Bengal, South India, and the Chanda district of the Central Provinces. It is indeed common throughout India, Ceylon and Burma. Produces a round, hard-shelled fruit, of the size of a large apple, and of strong odour when ripe, and very acrid. It tastes like the Bengal quince.

Natives sometimes eat the raw fruit with sugar. A jelly, much resembling black-currant jelly, is prepared from it, which, however, has a very astringent taste.

FERULA.

Ferula Narthex, *Boiss.*, UMBELLIFERÆ. 336

ASAFŒTIDA.

Vern.—*Hing,* BENG., HIND.; *Hingu,* SANS.; *Perungayam,* TAM.; *Inguva,* TEL.; *Angusa,* AFG.

A perennial plant of the Carrot family; it is a native of Persia, Afghanistan and the region of the Oxus.

In Afghanistan the leaves are used as a vegetable, and the succulent part of the young stem, after being roasted, is eaten with salt and butter. The stinking juice of its root, known to commerce as the drug Asafœtida, is used for seasoning curries and other food.

FESTUCA.

337 **Festuca duriuscula,** *Linn.*, GRAMINEÆ.

HARD FESCUE GRASS.

Syn.—F. OVINA, *Linn.*

This fodder grass inhabits the Himalaya, and extends into Kashmir and Western Tibet.

A good sheep fodder.

338 **F. elatior,** *Linn.*

Met with in Kumaun.

Mueller writes: "It is well adapted for permanent pastures, has tender leaves, produces excellent hay, and is early out in the season"; and he adds that it is superior to rye grass in produce.

339 **F. gigantea,** *Vill.*

Syn.—F. TRIFLORA, *Sm.*; BRORNUS GIGANTEUS, *Linn.*; B. TRIFLORUS, *Linn.*

A good forest grass of the north-western tracts of the Himalaya.

340 **F. ovina,** *Linn.*

SHEEP'S FESCUE.

Met with in the North-West Himalaya and Kashmir.

This is a short, wiry grass on which sheep feed.

341 **F. rubra,** *Linn.*

PURPLE FESCUE.

Occurs in Mussouree hills.

Royle says, that this grass, from its greater produce, is more valued than **F. ovina.**

FICUS.

342 **Ficus bengalensis,** *Linn.*, URTICACEÆ.

THE BANYAN TREE.

Syn.—F. INDICA, *Roxb.*

Vern.—*Bor, bar, ber, bargat,* HIND.; *Bur, but,* BENG.; *Boru,* URIYA; *Borar,* NEPAL; *Kangji,* LEPCHA; *Banket,* GARO; *Bot,* ASS.; *Ala,* TAM.; *Mári, peddi-mari,* TEL.; *Ahlada,* KAN.; *War, vada,* MAR.; *Pyee-nyoung,* BURM.

A large tree, wild in the lower regions of the East Himalayan tracts, Bengal and Central India, and planted throughout India.

Under the head of food the only use that can be mentioned is that the small, reddish, yellow fruit is sometimes eaten by the poorer natives.

343 **F. Carica,** *Linn.*

THE COMMON FIG.

Vern.—*Anjir,* HIND.; *Kimri, fagu, fagúri, fagari,* PB.; *Anjira,* BOM.

Cultivated in the North-Western Provinces, the Punjab, and the Western Himalayas.

The so-called fruit of the Fig is not a true fruit, but a fleshy receptacle, in the interior of which are found the true flowers and seeds. From Afghanistan, figs of a better quality than those grown in India are imported into the Punjab in certain quantities annually.

The fruit is not uncommon, and is eaten to a certain extent chiefly by the natives. It is inferior to the fig of Western Asia.

Ficus cordifolia, *Roxb.* 344

Vern.—*Gai aswat,* BENG.; *Rumbal, badha,* PB.; *Kabar, gajna, pipul,* HIND.; *Pakar,* NEPAL; *Pakri,* ASS.; *Prab,* GARO; *Nyoungpyoo,* BURM.

A large tree of the outer Himalaya, Bengal, Central India and Burma. Produces a fruit which is perfectly round, and when ripe has the size and appearance of a black cherry.

The fruit is eaten by the natives. The leaves and branches are used for cattle fodder.

F. Cunia, *Buch.* 345

Vern.—*Khewnau, khurhur,* HIND.; *Kunia,* KUMAUN; *Kanhya,* NEPAL; *Dumbur, yajya-domur,* BENG.

A moderate-sized tree of the sub-Himalayan tract from the Chenab eastward, ascending to 4,000 feet. It is also found in Bengal and Burma.

The fruit is eaten and is good, though somewhat insipid.

F. glomerata, *Roxb.* 346

Vern.—*Gúlar, paroa, umar,* HIND.; *Jagya, doomoor,* BENG.; *Dumri,* NEPAL; *Tchongtay,* LEPCHA; *Kathgular, krumbal, dadhuri,* PB.; *Atti,* TAM.; *Moydi,* TEL.; *Ye-tha-pan,* BURM.

A large tree of the Salt Range, sub-Himalayan tract, Bengal, Central and South India, and Burma.

The fruit is very inferior, but is occasionally, says **Dr. Stewart,** eaten raw and in curries by the poor. **Gamble** says that the ripe fruit is eaten, and is good either raw or stewed.

F. hispida, *Linn. f.* 347

Syn.—F. OPPOSITIFOLIA, *Roxb.*; F. DÆMONA, *Konig.*

Vern.—*Kako-doomoor,* BENG.; *Daduri, degar,* PB.; *Konea-doombur, kagsha, gobla, totmila,* HIND.; *Khoskadu-mar,* ASS.; *Boda-mamadi,* TEL.; *Kadot,* BURM.

A moderate-sized tree of the outer Himalaya from the Chenab eastward, ascending to 3,500 feet; found also in Bengal, Central and South India, Burma, and the Andaman Islands.

The fruit, which is small and covered with much short white hair, is not often eaten. The leaves are lopped for cattle fodder.

F. infectoria, *Wall.* 348

Vern.—*Pakur,* HIND., BENG.; *Jangli-pipli, war,* PB.; *Safed-kabra,* NEPAL; *Pepre, kurku,* TAM.; *Nyoungchin,* BURM.

A large tree extending from the Sulaiman and Salt Ranges, along the outer Himalaya, to Bengal, Central India, and Burma.

The young shoots are said to be eaten in curries by the natives. The leaves make good elephant fodder. (*Gamble.*)

F. nemoralis, *Wall.* 349

A moderate-sized tree of the outer Himalaya from Jhelum to Sikkim. The leaves are lopped for cattle fodder (*Gamble*).

FLACOURTIA.

350 **Ficus religiosa,** *Linn.*

THE SACRED FIG OR PEEPUL TREE.

Vern.—*Pipal,* HIND.; *Ashathwa, aswat, asúd,* BENG.; *Arasa,* TAM.; *Rái, ragi, ravi,* TEL.; *Nyoungbandi,* BURM.

A large tree, sacred to Hindus and Buddhists, is commonly cultivated along roadsides throughout India, and grows wild in the sub-Himalayan tract, in Bengal and Central India.

The small, smooth, elliptical leaves and branches are good elephant fodder. The young leaf buds are eaten in Central India in famine times. (*Gamble.*)

351 **F. Roxburghii,** *Wall.*

Syn.—F. MACROPHYLLA, *Roxb.*

Vern.—*Doomoor,* BENG.; *Timal,* HIND.; *Kasrekan,* NEPAL; *Kundoung,* LEPCHA; *Sin-tha-hpan,* BURM.

A native of the outer Himalaya from the Indus eastward, also of Sylhet, Chittagong and Burma.

The fruit is eaten in curries. The leaves are used as fodder.

352 **F. virgata,** *Roxb.*

Syn.—F. CARICOIDES, *Roxb.*

Vern.—*Gular, khabar, anjiri, beru,* HIND.; *Fagara, thapur* (plains), *fagu, dudhi, kak* (hills), PB.; *Anjir,* AFG.

A moderate-sized tree, found on the Sulaiman and Salt Ranges, and in the outer Himalaya eastward to Nepal (*Gamble*).

The fruit is eaten by the natives in the Punjab hills, but is generally poor fruit. The leaves are given to cattle as fodder.

FLACOURTIA.

353 **Flacourtia inermis,** *Roxb.*, BIXINEÆ.

Vern.—*Tomi-tomi,* MAL.; *Ubbolu,* KAN.

Probably introduced from the Moluccas. At present found in Sylhet, South India and Martaban. The tree blossoms during the dry season, and ripens its fruit towards the close of the rains.

The fruit, says **Roxburgh,** is too sour to be eaten raw; but makes very good tarts. In the Moluccas it is eaten.

354 **F. Ramontchi,** *L'Herit.*, **var. sapida.**

THE INDIAN PLUM.

Vern.—*Bincha,* BENG.; *Suadoo-huntuka,* SANS.; *Kundayee, bunj, bowchee,* HIND., DEC.; *Kúkai, kangú, kukoa, kandei,* PB.; *Bávache,* SIND.; *Peda-kanru,* TEL.; *Na-yuwai,* BURM.

A large shrub or small tree, which is found along the lower hills, sometimes to 3,500 feet, in the Salt Range, on the skirts of the Sulaiman Range and the Western Gháts; also in Prome.

The fruit and the leaves are eaten. The fruit is of the size of the plum, and of a sharp but sweetish taste.

355 **F. sepiaria,** *Roxb.*

Vern.—*Kondai,* HIND.; *Sherawane, sargal, dajkar, jidkar, khatdi, kingaro,* PB.; *Atrúna,* BOM.; *Kanru,* TEL.

A small, stiff, spiny shrub, found in dry jungles throughout Bengal, the Western Peninsula, and Ceylon. It occurs about Delhi, in the Salt Range, and on the skirts of the Sulaiman Range, and is extensively used as hedges.

The fruit is said to be eaten by the natives in the Punjab tracts where it is found, but it is small, hard and insipid; it is however by others described as "pleasant, refreshing and sub-acid." The leaves are thrashed out for cattle fodder.

FLEMINGIA.

Flemingia congesta, *Roxb.*, LEGUMINOSÆ. 356

Vern.—*Bara-salpan (as in Roxb.), bhalia (as in Gamble),* BENG. and HIND.; *Batwasi,* NEPAL; *Mipitmúk,* LEPCHA. Roxburgh also gives for **var. nana** the vernacular names of *Supta, cusunt,* HIND.

An erect, woody shrub of the pea family, common in the thickets and forests of the warmer parts of India.

The *Flora of British India* reduces to this species the following forms described by Roxburgh as distinct (*see Ed. C. B. C., pp. 571-72*):—

F. procumbens, F. prostrata, F. nana, F. congesta and **F. semialata** forming four varieties:—

Var. 1.—**semialata**—Central Himalaya, ascending to 5,000 feet.
Var. 2.—**latifolia**—Khási Hills, altitude 2,000 to 3,000 feet.
Var. 3.—**Wightiana**—Nilgiris, Bhutan, Ava.
Var. 4.—**nana**—Central and Eastern Himalaya and the Konkan.

The legumes produced by this species are probably eaten by the natives.

F. vestita, *Benth.* 357

Cultivated in many parts of the North-West Provinces for the sake of its edible tuberous roots, which are nearly elliptical and about an inch long. (*Lindley and Moore's Treasury.*)

FŒNICULUM.

Fœniculum vulgare, *Gærtn.*, UMBELLIFERÆ. 358

FENNEL.

Syn.—F. PANMORIUM, *DC.*; F. OFFICINALE, *Allion*; ANETHUM FŒNICULUM, *Linn.*

Vern.—*Saunf,* HIND.; *Mauri,* BENG.; *Sohikire,* TAM.; *Wariaree,* GUZ.; *Pedda-jila-kurra,* TEL., *Bari-shopha,* BOM.

This perennial of the Carrot family attains a height of 5 to 6 feet, and is commonly cultivated throughout India in all altitudes up to 6,000 feet; sometimes wild.

The fennel seeds produced by this plant are well known. The plant itself is frequently cultivated as a pot-herb in the plains. Its leaves are strongly aromatic and are used in fish sauces. Fennel oil is got from its roots. Roxburgh says:—"This plant is cultivated in various parts of Bengal during the cold season for the seed, which the natives eat with their betle, and also use in their curries. Seed time—the close of the rains, about the end of October. Harvest in March, when the plants perish.

FRAGARIA.

359

Fragaria indica, *Andr.*, ROSACEÆ.

INDIAN STRAWBERRY.

Grows in the Himalayas from east to west, altitude 7,500 to 8,000 feet; also in Khásia hills and Nilgiris.

The fruit is spongy and insipid.

360 **Fragaria vesca,** *Linn.*, var ?

STRAWBERRY.

Vern.—*Kansars, ingrach, bunun, tawai,* PB.

Found wild in the temperate Himalaya from Murree and Kashmir, altitude 5,000 to 10,000 feet, to Sikkim, altitude 6,000 to 13,000 feet. (*Hooker.*)

Dr. Stewart says this is excellent when gathered dry, and improves by cultivation in a garden. It is one of the most wholesome of fruits.

FRAXINUS.

361 **Fraxinus xanthoxyloides,** *Wall.*, OLEACEÆ.

THE ASH.

Vern.—*Hanuz, nuch, shilli, chuj, thum, shangal,* PB.; *Shang,* AFG.; *Auga, gaha,* N. W. P.

A small tree of Afghanistan, the Trans-Indus and the North-West Provinces from the Jhelum to Kumaun. (*Gamble*)

Dr. Stewart says its leaves are used as fodder.

GARCINIA.

362 **Garcinia Cambogia,** *Desr.*, GUTTIFERÆ.

Vern.—*Aradal,* KAN.; *Heela,* BURGHERS.

A small, evergreen tree on the Western Coast, and met with in Ceylon.

The acid rinds of the ripe fruit are eaten, and in Ceylon are dried and eaten as a condiment in curries.

363 **G. indica,** *Choisy.*, GUTTIFERÆ.

Vern.—*Brindall,* GOA.; *Amsool, kokum,* BOM.

Common in the Western Gháts, in Konkans and Kanara.

Produces a purple fruit of the size of a small orange, with an agreeable acid flavour. A syrup is made from it.

364 **G. Mangostana,** *Linn.*

THE MANGOSTEEN.

Vern.—*Mengkop,* BURM.

An evergreen tree, native of the Straits; cultivated in British Burma on account of its fruit, which is pronounced the most delicious of all known fruits.

The fruit is of about the size of a small apple, of a reddish brown colour when ripe. Inside its thick, succulent, astringent rind is a juicy white pulp of a delicate, refreshing, sweet flavour.

Repeated attempts at introducing the tree into India in various parts have failed. The steamers from the Straits bring up large quantities annually to Calcutta. The fruit is much esteemed both by Europeans and Natives.

365 **G. Morella,** *Desr.*

THE GAMBOGE TREE.

Syn.—G. PICTORIA, *Roxb.*

Vern.—*Aradal, punar puli,* KAN.; *Gokatú, kanagoraku,* CINGH.; *Makki,* TAM.

An evergreen tree met with in the forests of the Khásia Hills, East Bengal, Western Coast, and Ceylon.

A concrete oil is obtained from the seeds, which is chiefly used as a lamp-oil by the better classes of natives, and by the poor as a substitute for ghee.

Garcinia pedunculata, *Roxb.* 366

Vern.—*Tikul, tikur,* BENG. ; *Borthekra,* ASS.

A tall tree, native of Rangpur, Goalpara, and Sylhet. Flowers from January to March, and its fruit ripens from that time to June. The fruit is large, round, smooth and yellow when ripe.

Roxburgh writes:—"The fleshy part of the fruit which covers the seeds and their proper juicy envelope, or aril, is, in large quantity, of a firm texture and of a very sharp, pleasant, acid taste. It is used by the natives in their curries and for acidulating water. If cut into slices and dried it retains its qualities for years, and might be most advantageously employed during long sea voyages as a succedaneum for lemons or limes, to put into various messes, where salt meat is employed, &c."

G. stipulata, *T. And.* 367

Vern.—*Sama-kadan,* LEPCHA.

Found in Sikkim and Bhutan, up to 4,000 feet.

The fruit produced by this species is yellow, and is sometimes eaten by the Lepchas.

GARUGA.

Garuga pinnata, *Roxb.*, BURSERACEÆ. 368

Vern.—*Ghogar, kaikar,* HIND.; *Júm, kharpat,* BENG. ; *Gendeli poma,* ASS. ; *Dabdabbi,* NEPAL ; *Gia,* MECHI ; *Chitompa,* GARO ; *Kharpat, kilmira, sarota,* PB. ; *Kukar, kaikra,* C. P. ; *Garuga, gár-gá,* TEL. ; *Karre vembu,* TAM. ; *Mohi,* URIYA.

A large tree of the sub-Himalaya, Central and South India, and Burma. Flowers in the hot season, and produces a fruit which is eaten by the natives, both raw and cooked. In the Punjab, and perhaps elsewhere, the leaves are used as fodder especially for elephants.

GLYCERIA.

Glyceria fluitans, *R. Br.*, GRAMINEÆ. 369

MANNA GRASS.

Syn.—FESTUCA FLUITANS, *Linn.* ; POA FLUITANS, *Scop.*

Met with in Baspa Valley, 9,000 feet in altitude. (*Brandis.*)

A perennial grass with tender foliage ; delights in stagnant water, ditches, pools, ponds, and slow flowing streams, covering their surface.

The seeds are sweet and tender, and are in many countries used for porridge.

GLYCINE.

Glycine Soja, *Sieb. & Zucc.*, LEGUMINOSÆ. 370

THE SOY BEAN.

Syn.—DOLICHOS SOJA, *Linn.* ; SOJA HISPIDA.

Vern.—*Gari-kulay,* BENG. ; *Bhat, bhatwan,* HIND. ; *Tsu dza,* NAGA.

A pulse (densely clothed with fine, ferruginous hairs) sub-erect met with in tropical regions and outer Himalaya, from Kumaun to Sikkim, the Khási and the Naga Hills to Upper Burma. Dr. Stewart mentions a field of *Bhat*

GOSSYPIUM.

having been observed in Bissahir in the Punjab, altitude 6,000 feet. It is chiefly met with in a state of cultivation. **Dr. Roxburgh** first saw the plant from seed received from the Moluccas in 1798.

The pulse is an important food article in Tibet. It is made in India into a sauce called Soy.

The advisability of extending its cultivation in Himalayan tracts was pressed on the Government of India in 1882, by **Professor Kinch**, and the attention of local officials also was called to it.

GLYCOSMIS.

371 **Glycosmis pentaphylla,** *Correa.*, RUTACEÆ.

Vern.—*Ban-nimbu, potali, girgitti,* HIND.; *Kirmira,* BOM.; *Taushouk,* BURM.

Throughout tropical and sub-tropical Himalaya, Upper Assam, and southwards to Travancore and Ceylon.

One of the commonest plants in India, *if* (**Sir J. Hooker** writes) the shrubby **G. pentaphylla** and arboreous **G. arborea** are the same species.

Both produce a white edible berry usually of the size of a large pea.

GMELINA.

372 **Gmelina arborea,** *Roxb.*, VERBENACEÆ.

Vern.—*Gumar,* BENG., HIND.; *Gambari,* NEPAL, URIYA; *Gomari,* ASS.; *Bolkobak,* GARO.; *Guniadi, cummi,* TAM.; *Gumartek, tagumudu,* TEL.; *Shewney,* KAN.; *Shewan,* MAR.; *Chimman,* BHIL.; *Kurse,* GOND.; *Yamaney,* BURM.

A large timber tree of the sub-Himalayan tract from the Chenab eastwards, and throughout India, Burma and the Andaman Islands.

Flowers in the beginning of the hot season, and produces a fruit which is eaten by Gonds and other wild hill tribes. The leaves are used as fodder, and deer are very fond of them.

GNETUM.

373 **Gnetum scandens,** *Roxb.*, GNETACEÆ.

Syn.—G. EDULE, *Bl.*

Vern.—*Nanu-witi,* SYLHET; *Kumbal, umbli,* BOM.; *Gyootnway,* BURM.

A large, climbing shrub of Sikkim, Khásia Hills, East Bengal, Western Gháts, Burma and the Andamans. Flowers in March and April, and its fruit ripens in September and October.

The fruit is rather larger than the largest olive, and, when ripe, it becomes smooth, orange-coloured. The outer succulent coat or pulp is commonly eaten by the natives, and the seeds are roasted and eaten.

GOSSYPIUM.

374 **Gossypium herbaceum,** *Linn.*, MALVACEÆ.

THE COMMON INDIAN COTTON.

Vern.—*Rui,* HIND., PB.; *Kapas,* BENG., DEC.; *Vun-paratie,* TAM.; *Pauttie,* TEL.; *Karpasi,* SANS.; *Pambah,* PERS.; *Kurtam ussul,* ARAB.

A small specimen was exhibited in Madras in 1855. This may be a mistake for **G. arboreum,** if not for **Bombax malabaricum.**

The cotton plant of all species grown in India may be included under the head of "food," because the seeds of all are to a small extent given as food to cattle. The seeds, which are of about the size of small peas, contain a large quantity of oil, and are said, when crushed and made into cakes, to be nourishing to cattle, and might be more generally used for such a purpose.

GREWIA.

Grewia asiatica, *Linn.*, TILIACEÆ. 375

Vern.—*Phálsa, pharoah,* HIND., SIND., PB.; *Dhami,* AJMIR; *Phálase,* BOM.; *Shukri,* BENG.; *Phutiki* or *Putiki,* TEL.

A small, hazel-like tree wild in Central India and Rajputana; cultivated more or less commonly throughout India; and said to be indigenous in the Salt Range, Poona, Oudh and Ceylon. It flowers about the end of the cold season, and its little fruit ripens in April and May.

The fruit has a pleasant, acid taste, and is commonly eaten. It is also as commonly distilled, and a syrup is made from it which is refreshing and pleasant in the hot months. It is also used for flavouring sherbets.

Var. vestita, *Wall.* 376

Vern.—*Pharsia, dhamun, bimla,* HIND.; *Farri, phalwa,* PB.; *Poto-dhamun,* PALAMOW; *Kunsung,* LEPCHA; *Pintayan,* BURM.

Met with in the sub-Himalayan tract, Bengal, Central India, and Burma.

The branches are lopped for fodder.

G. excelsa, *Vahl.* 377

Syn.—G. ROTHII, *DC.*; G. SALVIFOLIA, *Roxb.*

A shrub of East Bengal, Assam, and Coromandel; found also in Sikkim and Bundelkhand.

Flowers in the hot season, and its fruit ripens a few months later. The fruit is small, agreeable to the taste, and eaten by the natives.

G. oppositifolia, *Roxb.* 378

Vern.—*Dhamman, pharwa,* PB.; *Biul, biung, bahul, bhengal, bhenwa, bhimal,* HIND.; *Pastuwanne,* AFG.

A small tree of the North West Himalaya, from the Indus to Nepal, both wild and cultivated. Flowers during the summer, and its fruit ripens in autumn.

The leaves are commonly used for fodder during the winter. The berries have a pleasant, acid taste, and are used for making *sherbet.*

G. populifolia, *Vahl.* 379

Syn.—G. BETULÆFOLIA, *Juss.*

Vern.—*Ganger,* PB.; *Gango,* SIND.; *Gangerun,* RAJPUTANA.

A small shrub of the arid tracts of the Punjab, Sindh, Rajputana, and Western Peninsula down to the Nilgiris.

Produces a small, orange-red, acid fruit, which is eaten by the natives.

G. salvifolia, *Heyne.* 380

Vern.—*Bather, nikki-bekkar, gargas,* PB.; *Saras,* AJMERE; *Jara,* CIRCARS.

A small tree met with in the Punjab, Sind and Central Provinces, and South India.

Fruit small, but edible.

HARD-WICKIA.

381 **Grewia scabrophylla,** *Roxb.*

Vern.—*Pharsia*, KUMAUN.

A small shrub of the tropical Himalaya, Assam and Chittagong.

Flowers in April, and its fruit ripens in October. The fruit is of the size of a large gooseberry, nearly round, brownish grey when ripe; its pulp is glutinous, and of a pale yellow colour, eaten by the natives.

382 **G. tiliæfolia,** *Vahl.*

Vern.—*Pharsa, dhamin*, HIND.; *Khesla*, GOND; *Charachi*, TEL.; *Dhamono*, URIYA; *Dhamnah*, BHIL; *Sadachu*, MAL.

A moderate-sized tree of the tracts under the Himalaya from the Jumna to Nepal, also of the hot, dry forests in Western, Central and South India.

It flowers in the hot season, and the fruit is eaten by the natives.

383 **G. villosa,** *Willd.*

Vern.—*Inzarra, pas, tuwanne*, PB.; *Dhohan*, AJMERE; *Jalidar, kaskúsri, thamther*, SALT RANGE.

Found in Western and Southern India, extending from Punjab and Sindh to Travancore.

The fruit is sometimes eaten by the natives, but is poor.

GUAZUMA.

384 **Guazuma tomentosa,** *Kunth*, STERCULIACEÆ.

Vern.—*Thainpuche*, TAM.; *Rudraksha*, TEL.

Generally distributed and frequently cultivated, in the warmer parts of India and Ceylon, but perhaps only introduced.

The fruit is filled with mucilage, which is very agreeable to the taste.

GYNANDROPSIS.

385 **Gynandropsis pentaphylla,** *DC.*, CAPPARIDEÆ.

Syn.—CLEOME PENTAPHYLLA, *Linn.*

Vern.—*Kanala*, BENG.; *Hulhul, bugra, gandhuli*, PB.; *Nai-kadughu, nai-vaila*, TAM.; *Caat-kododu*, MAL; *Wominta*, TEL.

A small, annual plant, flowers in July and August.

Abundant throughout the warmer parts of India and all tropical countries (*Hook. f. & Thomas*).

The leaves are eaten by natives in curries.

HARDWICKIA.

386 **Hardwickia binata,** *Roxb.*, LEGUMINOSÆ.

Vern.—*Anjan*, HIND., MAR.; *Acha, alti*, TAM.; *Naryepi, yapa*, TEL.; *Kamrá*, KAN.; *Parsid*, SINGROWLI.

A large tree found in the dry forests of South and Central India, as far north as the Banda district of the North-West Provinces, also in Behar.

The leaves are given as fodder to cattle.

HEDERA.

Hedera Helix, *Linn.*, ARALIACEÆ. 387

THE IVY.

Vern.—*Halbambar, kuri, harur, dakari, karbara, banda,* PB.; *Dudela,* NEPAL.

A large, woody climber common in places throughout the Himalaya, at 6,000 to 10,000 feet extending into the Khási Hills.

Dr. Stewart writes: "It is stated to be a favourite food of goats, and in Kulu the leaves are said to be added to the beer of the country to make it strong." Its berries afford abundance of food to birds.

HELIANTHUS.

Helianthus tuberosus, *Linn.*, COMPOSITÆ. 388

THE JERUSALEM ARTICHOKE.

Stated to be originally a native of Brazil, extensively cultivated as a vegetable for its roots which are similar to small potatoes. They are regarded as more wholesome and nutritious than potatoes, and may be eaten by invalids when required to abstain from vegetable food. They must not be confounded with the true Artichoke. The name Jerusalem Artichoke is a corruption of the Italian *Gerasoli Articocco* or Sun-flower Artichoke.

HEMARTHRIA.

Hemarthria compressa, *R. Br.*, GRAMINEÆ. 389

Syn.—ROTTBŒLLIA COMPRESSA, *Linn.*; R. GLABRA, *Roxb.*

Vern.—*Ranshероо, buksha,* BENG.; *Shervoo,* TEL.

A perennial grass of Bengal, inhabiting also the plains and hills of the Punjab and North West Provinces. Roxburgh says that it is found on the borders of lakes, amongst other roots of long grass and brushwood; and he mentions the variety **R. glabra** as growing on pasture lands, the borders of rice-fields and other moist places.

Cattle are fond of it; and graziers in Gyppsland, says **Mueller**, highly esteem it for moist pasture.

HERACLEUM.

Heracleum, Sp., UMBELLIFERÆ. 390

Vern.—*Padali, poral,* PB.

Common in parts of the Punjab Himalaya, from 8,500 to 11,000 feet in altitude.

Dr. Stewart says that in Bissahir and Chumba it is collected for winter fodder, and quotes **Cleghorn**, who mentions that it is believed to increase the milk of goats fed with it.

HETEROPOGON.

Heteropogon contortus, *R. & S.*, GRAMINEÆ. 391

THE SPEAR GRASS.

Syn.—ANDROPOGON CONTORTUS, *Linn.*

Vern.—*Parba, banda, sarwar, musel, lap,* N. W. P.; *Suriala, surari,* PB.; *Yeddi,* TEL.

Grows in tufts on rich pasture ground. **Duthie** writes: "Common both

HIBISCUS.

in the plains and on the hills of the Punjab and North West Provinces. It grows in light soil about Banda, attaining a height of about 3 feet; in soil mixed with kunkur (*rakar*) it reaches 5 feet in height (*Miller.*) It is common on the rock tablelands of the hilly country south of Allahabad (*Benson*). Abundant also on the warm lower slopes of the Himalayas, and up to an elevation of 7,000 feet in some parts.

"Cattle eat it when fresh; it makes good hay when the seeds fall off; it is the main fodder grain of Bandelkhand" (*Crooke*).

HIBISCUS.

392 **Hibiscus Abelmoschus,** *Linn.*, MALVACEÆ.

THE MUSK MALLOW.

Syn.—ABELMOSCHUS MOSCHATUS, *Mœnch.*

Vern.—*Kasturi, kalla kasturi, bhenda,* HIND., BOM.; *Mushakdana, kala-kasturi,* BENG.; *Mushk-bhendi-ke-binj,* DEC.; *Kastura benda, kathe kasturi,* TAM.; *Kasturi-bendavittulu,* TEL.; *Hub-ul-mushk,* ARAB.; *Mushk-dana,* PERS.

A herbaceous bush, springing up with the rains and flowering in the cold season. Leaves of various shapes; the lower, broad, ovate, cordate; the upper, narrow, hastate, very hairy. Common throughout the hotter parts of India, now met with in most other tropical countries.

393 **H. cannabinus,** *Linn.*

INDIAN OR DECCANI HEMP; ROSELLE HEMP; HEMP-LEAVED HIBISCUS; BASTARD JUTE.

Vern.—*Mesta-pát, nalki, pulua,* BENG.; *Patsan, pitwa, san, lattia-san,* HIND.; *Gakró,* NAGA HILLS; *Ambádá,* BOM.; *Ambdri, sankukla, pat-san, suni,* DEC., HIND.; *Palungú,* TAM.; *Goukura,* TEL.; *Garnikura,* SANS.

A small, herbaceous shrub, with prickly stems apparently wild east of the Northern Gháts; and cultivated, in the North West Provinces, Oudh, and the Punjab, northern portion of Bengal, and met with in the Naga Hills. Stewart says it grows at Ghuzni, altitude 7,000 feet, and is not uncommon on the North-Western Himalaya at 3,000 feet.

No details of the area cultivated are available. It is, however, rarely cultivated as the only crop, but as a border to fields of cotton, indigo and sugar-cane.

The chief object of the cultivation is the fibre, which, although extracted in the most primitive system by submerging the stalks in water for a number of days and pulling off the bark by hand, is soft, white and silky.

The young foliage of the crop is eaten as a vegetable by the natives of the tracts where it is grown; and the seeds are roasted and also eaten by them.

394 **H. esculentus,** *Linn.*

THE EDIBLE HIBISCUS; OCHRO OF WEST INDIES; GOMBO, *Fr.*

Vern.—*Bhindi, ranturi,* HIND.; *Dhenras,* BENG.; *Vendi* (or *bhendi*), *vendaik-kay,* TAM.; *Venda-kaya,* TEL.; *Bamya,* ARAB., PERS.

A herbaceous, annual bush, naturalised in all tropical countries; only met with in a cultivated state; probably a native of both India and the West Indies.

The unripe fruit is a favourite vegetable and medicine. When young and tender the fruits, being very mucilaginous, are commonly eaten boiled or in soup by Europeans. Natives eat it more matured chiefly in curries.

Hibiscus ficulneus, *Linn.* 395

Vern.—*Ban-dhenras,* BENG.; *Dula,* PB.; *Parupu benda,* TAM.

Grows in the hotter parts of India.

The seeds are often put in sweetmeats, and are employed in Arabia for giving perfume to coffee.

H. Sabdariffa, *Linn.* 396

THE ROZELLE FIBRE.

Vern.—*Mesta,* BENG.; *Lal-ambari, patwa,* DEC., HIND.; *Lala ambádi,* SIND.; *Sivappu-kashuruk-kai,* TAM.; *Erra-gom kaya,* TEL.

A small bush, cultivated in many parts of India on account of the succulent and acrid calyx.

The fleshy calyx and capsule are largely made into jam and other preserves, and in the fresh state are very acrid but refreshing. A decoction of them sweetened and fermented is commonly called in the West Indies Sorrel drink. The leaves are used in salads.

HIPPOPHÆ.

Hippophæ rhamnoides, *Linn.*, ELÆAGNEÆ. 397

Vern.—*Tsarap, sirma, tsuk, tarru, niechak,* NORTH PB., LADAK to LAHOUL.

A shrub in moist, gravelly stream-beds of the Punjab Himalaya, from 5,000 to 10,000 feet in altitude.

Produces a small, sour fruit, which makes a good jelly, and is sometimes eaten.

Smith, in his *Economic Dictionary*, says the fruit is acrid and poisonous.

HOLARRHENA.

Holarrhena antidysenterica, *Wall.*, APOCYNACEÆ. 398

Syn.—H. PUBESCENS, *Wall.*; H. CODAGA, *Don*; ECHITES ANTIDYSENTERICA, *Roxb.*; CHONEMORPHA ANTIDYSENTERICA, *Don.*

Vern.—*Inderjau, dudhu-ki-lakri,* HIND.; *Vepali, veppaula, veppalay,* TAM.; *Kodoga-pala, pala-chettu,* TEL.

A plant of the sub-Himalayan tract, Oudh, Bengal, Central and South India.

The seed is largely used as a medicine, being antidysenteric, in small doses tonic, eaten for this purpose. The leaves appear to be used as fodder. (or litter?) (*Stewart.*)

HOLBŒLLIA.

Holbœllia latifolia, *Wall.*, BERBERIDEÆ. 399

Vern.—*Gophla,* KUMAUN; *Bagul,* NEPAL; *Pronchadik,* LEPCHA; *Domhyem,* BHUTIA.

A climber found in the Himalaya, altitude 4,000 to 9,000 feet, from Kumaun eastward also in the Khásia Hills, and Upper Assam.

Produces a large, edible fruit.

HORDEUM.

400 **Hordeum vulgare,** *Linn.*, GRAMINEÆ.

BARLEY.

Syn.—H. HEXASTICHON, H. DISTICHON, *Linn.*; H. CŒLESTE, *Viborg.* *(beardless Barley).*

Vern.—*Jub*, BENG.; *Jao*, HIND.; *Tosa*, NEPAL; *She-eer*, ARAB.; *Yuva*, SANS.; *Satoo*, DEC.; *Barli-arisi*, TAM.; *Java*, TEL.; *Mu-yan*, BURM.

Native of Western Temperate Asia (*DeCandolle*). Cultivated from remote ages.

There are two chief varieties, the ears of one of which contain two rows of grain (**H. distichon**); and the other six rows (**H. hexastichon**). The latter is the one ordinarily cultivated in this country. The former is commonly grown in England, but is rare here. The average area under barley in the 30 temporarily-settled districts of the North West Provinces is given by **Messrs. Duthie** and **Fuller** at 4,728,344 acres.* "It forms an important crop in every portion of the Provinces, being most commonly grown alone in the districts of the Benares Division, mixed with wheat in Rohilkhand, and mixed with gram in Agra and Allahabad."

A curious sub-variety of two-rowed barley (**H. gymnodistichon**) resembling wheat and known in the vernacular as *rasuli* is grown largely in Tibet and Kotgarh. In 1879 some of the seed was obtained and grown on the Cawnpore Farm, and the yield, upon manuring and irrigation to a certain extent, was 21¼ maunds of grain per acre.

The sowing is done in October; generally in light, sandy, not highly-manured soils; the quantity of seed sown is from 100 to 150 lbs. per acre. It requires very little irrigation.

The average out-turn of barley per acre on irrigated land in the North West Provinces and Oudh is given by **Messrs. Duthie and Fuller** at 16 maunds of grain when only barley is sown; at 15 maunds when wheat is sown with the barley, and at 14 maunds when the barley is sown with gram. For unirrigated land the out-turn is estimaed at from 7 to 11, 6 to 10, and 6 to 9 maunds per acre, respectively, in the three cases mentioned.

Barley constitutes about ⅗ths of the total produce when grown with either wheat or gram. The weight of straw is ascertained by **Messrs. Duthie** and **Fuller** to be 1½ times that of the grain.

Barley undergoes a process to form malt of which ale is made. It is put to this use to a certain extent by the Himalayan breweries. Pearl and Scotch barley are formed by the removal of the thin, hard integuments, the grain being hardened by drying.

HOVENIA.

401 **Hovenia dulcis,** *Thunb.*, RHAMNEÆ.

Ver.—*Chambun*, PB.

A tree found throughout the Himalaya, 3,000 to 6,500 feet in altitude, commonly cultivated.

Produces a fruit which is a capsule with three seeds, and rests on an enlarged peduncle which is soft, fleshy, and contains a sweet juice. The peduncle tastes like a Bergamot pear, and is commonly eaten.

* No reliable figures are available of the area in the five remaining districts and in Oudh.

HUMU-LUS.

HUMULUS.

Humulus Lupulus, *L.*, URTICACEÆ. 403

HOPS.

The female flowers consist of leafy conelike catkins (*strobili*) of a light colour, which are called Hops. In England the finest hops are produced in Kent, and in that county the plant is extensively cultivated.

Dr. Stewart gives the following account of the hop cultivation in Kashmir and other places :—

"**Lowther** states that he had heard of the hop plant being seen in Kashmir (as others have done elsewhere in the Himalaya), but it is nowhere indigenous. In 1851 he proposed its introduction into Kashmir. It has been successfully cultivated in Dehra Dun for many years, so far as mere growth is concerned, but heavy rain at the flowering period prevents the flower from reaching perfection. As to quantity and quality of the powder, on which its value depends, the results have, on the whole, been unsatisfactory. Within the last few years, the plant has been tried at Kyelang and Kilar in the arid tract on the Upper Chenab, and it has flourished. But unfortunately it appears to have been found out, after several years' care, that the sets, introduced at the latter place, were those of male plants, so that the experiment has still to get a fair trial there. At Kyelang female flowers are sparingly produced. At the Murree Brewery, however, where the rain-fall is much lighter than further east, a considerable number of hop plants have been grown for some years with fair success as to quantity and strength of hops actually got. And it may be hoped that still better results will by-and-bye be obtained."

Since the above was written attempts have been made with success in introducing the hop-plant into Kashmir, and certain quantities of hops are now annually produced in that State. In June 1883, about 15,000 lbs. of hops were purchased from Kashmir by one of the Himalayan breweries; and next year the produce will probably be greater. The plant has also been successfully introduced into the Chamba State of the Punjab, and samples of the hops obtained there were reported upon favorably by the Himalayan breweries to which they were sent by the Government of India.

Mr. L. Liotard, in a note published in April 1883, says:—

"Beer-making industry in India has on the whole progressed very satisfactorily, and it now reckons 24 breweries actually at work,—in Murree, at Kasauli, at Solon, at Mussourie, and at Naini Tal, in the Nilgiris, in Mysore and in Rangoon."

The quantity of beer brewed in the last four years is given by him as—

	Gallons.
1879	1,569,026
1880	1,974,578
1881	2,448,711
1882	......

Of this the quantity brewed in the Punjab Himalaya alone amounts to over one million of gallons, and in the North West Provinces over 600,000 gallons. Of the total out-turn the Commissariat Department alone takes 1¼ million gallons for the troops.

The Indian breweries depend upon Europe for their supplies of hops, and the following figures represent the value of the importations of hops

HYOSCYAMUS.

into this country during the last five years and the countries whence the supplies come :—

OFFICIAL YEARS.	Value in Rs.	FIGURES FOR 1882-83.	
		Country whence imported.	Value in Rs.
1877-78	1,69,715	United Kingdom . .	2,30,691
1878-79	1,28,863	Italy	1,89,379
1879-80	4,16,413	China	9,759
1880-81	2,32,754		
1881-82	2,67,654		
1882-83	4,29,829		4,29,829

HYDROCOTYLE.

404 **Hydrocotyle asiatica,** *Linn.*, UMBELLIFERÆ.

Vern.—*Thul-kura*, BENG.; *Vularei*, TAM.; *Babassa*, TEL.; *Codagam*, MAL.

A creeping shrub, common in moist, shady places throughout India, from the Himalaya to Ceylon, in all altitudes up to 2,000 feet. Appears with most luxuriance during the rains.

The leaves are sometimes made into a soup which serves more as a medicine than as a food.

HYMENODICTYON.

405 **Hymenodictyon excelsum,** *Wall.*, RUBIACEÆ.

Syn.—CINCHONA EXCELSA, *Roxb., Fl. Ind.*, i. 529.

Vern.—*Bhaulan, bhalena, bhamina, dhauli, kúkúrkat, bhúrkúr, phaldu, bhohár, patur*, HIND.; *Bartu, baxthoa*, PB.; *Kaldkadú*, BOM.; *Sagapu*, TAM.; *Dudiyetta, chetippa, bandara*, TEL.

A deciduous tree, 30 to 40 feet high, with smooth bark, met with on the dry hills at the base of the Western Himalayas, from Garhwal to Nepal, ascending to 2,500 feet; throughout the Deccan and Central India to the Annamalays. Also in Tenasserim and Chittagong. (*Hooker.*)

The leaves are used as cattle fodder.

HYOSCYAMUS.

406 **Hyoscyamus niger,** *Linn.*, SOLANACEÆ.

HENBANE.

Vern.—*Basrul, khorasani ajowan*, BENG., HIND.; *Kurashani-yomam*, TAM.; *Kurasani-vaman*, TEL.; *Dandura, datura*, PB.

A herbaceous plant of the temperate Western Himalaya, altitude 8,000 to 11,000 feet, common from Kashmir to Garhwal.

It is frequent in waste ground near houses, and is said to be eaten by cattle.

ILEX.

Ilex dipyrena, *Wall.*, ILICINEÆ. 407

Vern.—*Shangala, kalucho, diwsa,* PB.; *Kaula,* NEPAL; *Kadera,* SIMLA.

A small tree of the Himalaya from the Indus to Bhutan.

The leaves are occasionally given as fodder for sheep.

ILLICIUM.

Illicium anisatum, *Linn.*, MAGNOLIACEÆ. 408

THE STAR ANISE of China and Japan.

Syn.—I. RELIGIOSUM.

Vern.—*Bádiánkhatái* (fruit), BOM.

The sacred Star Anise tree is not met with in India, but we have two if not three allied species, chiefly on the Khási and Naga Hills. One species I found, a giant of the forest of North Manipur and the Naga Hills, altitude 8,000 feet.

Being highly aromatic, it is in great repute in China and other Eastern countries in the manufacture of condiments and flavouring of spirits.

IMPATIENS.

Impatiens Balsamina, *Linn.*, GERANIACEÆ. 409

GARDEN BALSAM.

Vern.—*Bantil, trual, halu,* PB.

A native of India, introduced into England in 1596.

The seeds are eaten in Chumba, and the oil expressed is eaten and burned.

I. sulcata, *Wall.* 410

A gigantic annual, often 15 feet in height, frequent on the temperate Himalaya, altitude 7,000 to 12,000 feet.

In Lahoul the husks of the seeds are eaten raw.

IMPERATA.

Imperata arundinacea, *Cyrill*, GRAMINEÆ. 411

Syn.—SACCHARUM CYLINDRICUM, *Linn.*; LAGURES CYLINDRICUS, *Linn.*

Vern.—*Ulu,* BENG.; *Usirh, sir sil, bharwi,* UPPER IND.; *Barumbiss,* TEL.

A small grass inhabiting the plains and hills of Bengal, the North-West Provinces, the Punjab and Sindh, in moist, stiff, pasture ground. It is particularly common over Bengal and Lower Himalaya, altitude 7,500 feet. The fields are white with its silky heads when in flower, after the first rains.

The grass is much used by Bengalis for thatching. The Telingas use it in their marriage ceremonies. It is not of much use as fodder, because cattle refuse it except when it is quite young, or when no other forage can be got.

INDIGOFERA.

412 **Indigofera Dosua,** *Ham.*, LEGUMINOSÆ.

Syn.—I. HETERANTHA, *Wall.*

Vern.—*Khenti, shagali, mattu, kaskei,* PB.; *Theot,* SIMLA.

A shrub of the North-West Himalaya up to 8,000 feet in altitude.

The flowers are said to be eaten in Kangra as a pot-herb.

413 **I. pulchella,** *Roxb.*

Vern.—*Sakena, hakna,* HIND.; *Baroli,* MAR.; *Togri,* BHIL; *Hikpi,* LEPCHA; *Tau maiyain,* BURM.

A large shrub of the sub-Himalayan tract, South India, and Burma.

Produces pink flowers which are sometimes eaten in Central India by the natives as a vegetable.

IPOMÆA.

414 **Ipomæa aquatica,** *Forsk.*, CONVOLVULACEÆ.

Vern.—*Kalmi-sak,* BENG.; *Kalambi,* SANS.; *Ganthiam, nari,* PB.

An aquatic plant common throughout India, and abundant in the Bengal plain.

Commonly eaten by the poorer classes as a vegetable. The roots also are said to be eaten.

415 **I. Batatas,** *Lamk.*

SWEET POTATOE.

Syn.—BATATAS EDULIS, *Chois.*

Vern.—*Ranga-aloo, lal-aloo, shakarkand* BENG.; *Meeta-aloo, shakarkand,* HIND.; *Chilagada,* TEL.; *Kapa-kalenga,* MAL.; *Kaswan,* BURM.

Cultivated in almost all parts of India to a small extent; requires very little care, and grows in almost any soil, is planted like potatoes, and is dug up in the cold weather.

There are two kinds: the one with red tubers, the other with white. The red is the more common and is considered the better. Both are sweet and very palatable when roasted under hot ashes or boiled in water.

The sweet potato is eaten by all classes of the natives, either in curry or simply roasted as just stated, or cut in half, lengthwise, and fried. Another way of preparing it is to boil it, cut it in slices, and add rasped cocoanut, milk and sugar. In this way it becomes a good Indian dessert. It is also boiled, mashed, and made into pudding in the usual European style with sugar, egg, and milk. (*L. Liotard.*)

416 **I. eriocarpa,** *Br.*

Syn.—I. SESSILIFLORA, *Roth.*

Vern.—*Bhanwar,* PB.

Throughont India, altitude 0—4,000 feet; common in Ceylon.

This plant is eaten in times of famine.

IRIS.

417 **Iris kumaonensis,** *Wall.*, IRIDEÆ.

Vern.—*Pias, karkar,* PB.

Common in parts of the Punjab Himalaya, at altitudes from 5,000 to 12,000 feet; also in Ladak.

In Ladak the leaves are said to be used as fodder.

JUGLANS.

Juglans regia, *Linn.*, JUGLANDEÆ. 418

THE WALNUT.

Vern.—*Akhrot*, HIND.; *Akrut*, BENG.; *Charmaghz*, PERS.; *Akhor*, KASHMIR; *Tagashing*, BHUTIA; *Kowal*, LEPCHA.

A large tree wild in the North West Provinces and the Sikkim Himalaya, and largely cultivated throughout the hills.

The edible portions of the walnut are the two seed lobes which are crumpled up within the shell. One tree has been known to produce as many as 25,000 nuts in one year. The fruit ripens in July-September, and several varieties of it are met with, the best being the thin-shelled or *Kaghazi-akhrot.*

Walnuts are largely eaten by the hill tribes both rich and poor, and there is scarcely any village in the Himalayas of the North West and the Punjab which has not its own supply of walnuts. They are also traded in largely, and are brought down far into the plains from Afghanistan and the Himalaya by the natives, Afghans and others. An oil is expressed from the kernels of the fruit which is used both for burning and culinary purposes. The twigs and leaves are used for fodder. The wild tree has a thick shell and small kernel, and is rarely eaten.

JUNIPERUS.

Juniperus communis, *Linn.*, CONIFERÆ. 419

THE JUNIPER.

Vern.—*Nách, pethra, bentha, betar, lang shúr, chichia,* HIMALAYAN NAMES.

A large shrub found in uncultivated rocky places, in the North West Himalayas, ascending to 14,000 feet, extending eastward to Kumaun.

The fruit, or berry, is sweet and aromatic, and is used as medicine. Dr. Stewart, quoting Madden, says that from the berries, with barley meal, a spirit is distilled. The berries are also used for flavouring gin.

J. excelsa, *M. Bieb.* 420

HIMALAYAN PENCIL CEDAR.

Vern.—*Apúrs,* BELUCHISTAN; *Chalai, shúkpa, luir, shúrbuta,* HIMALAYAN NAMES; *Dhúp, padám,* N. W. P.; *Dhúpi,* NEPAL.

Arid tract of the North West Himalaya and Western Tibet, extending eastward to Nepal, and in the mountains of Afghanistan and Beluchistan.

KŒLERIA.

Kœleria cristata, *Pers.*, GRAMINEÆ. 421

Syn.—ARIA CRISTATA, *Linn.*

This is a beautiful perennial grass; inhabits the Himalaya at moderate elevations; found on dry, sandy soil.

Possesses fairly nutritious properties. May be used as fodder.

LACTUCA.

Lactuca scariola, *Linn.*, **var. sativa,** *Linn.*, COMPOSITÆ. 422

LETTUCE.

Vern.—*Sálád,* BENG.; *Kahu,* HIND., PB.

Commonly cultivated during the cold season, from October to Febru-

LATHYRUS.

ary, throughout the plains of India. Also in the sub-Himalayan tracts near, or below, the hill stations.

It is somewhat narcotic, and is rarely, if ever, eaten by the natives; cultivated chiefly for the European population.

LAGENARIA.

423 **Lagenaria vulgaris,** *Seringe.*, CUCURBITACEÆ.

THE BOTTLE GOURD.

Vern.—*Kaddu, lauki, al-kaddu, tumba, toombe, kathiphal, gol-kadu, kabuli,* also *tumri* (a small variety), HIND.; *Kodu, lau,* BENG.; *Kaddu, kabuli, lauki, tumba,* PB.; *Soriai-kai,* TAM.; *Sorakaya, kundanuga,* TEL.; *Me-kuri,* NAGA.

This climbing plant is found wild in India, Moluccas, and Abyssinia; at present cultivated in warm parts of America, Australia, and China, and extensively so in many places in India.

In the North West Provinces and Oudh it occupies annually from 30 to 200 acres in each district. It is cultivated also throughout the Naga hills. It thrives in any land, but best in richly-manured, sandy soil; the sowing is done in from February to July, and the gourd is ready for use three months after.

The gourd is used by Europeans and natives; by the former it is boiled when young and used as vegetable marrow; by the latter it is sliced and cooked as a curry. The young shoots and leaves are also eaten by all classes. Its fruit, which is sometimes nearly 6 feet long, is shaped like a bottle, and beggars and others use it when dried and empty as a bottle The small variety called *tumri* is used for making the stringed instrument called *sitar*. The Nagas use the fruit for water a d "Zoo" bottles.

LATHYRUS.

424 **Lathyrus Aphaca,** *Linn.*, LEGUMINOSÆ.

Vern.—*Jangli-matar,* BENG.; *Rawan rawari,* HIND., PB.

A much-branched herb, or field weed, found throughout the plains of Bengal, North West Provinces, Oudh, and Punjab till Hazara, Kumaun, and Kashmir.

The leaves of this annual have no real leaflets, but are reduced to a tendril between two large leaf-like stipules. It is found as a weed of cultivation in the plains, appearing in the cold season.

It is often pulled up and collected, and given to cattle for fodder. Ripe seeds are narcotic when eaten abundantly, but when young perfectly harmless. *(Voigt.)*

425 **L. imphalensis,** *Watt., MS.*

Vern.—?

Found at Myang-khong, in Manipur, 4,000 feet in altitude.

Largely used as a fodder, allowed to cover the fields as a weed after removal of the crops.

426 **L. sativus,** *Linn.*

JAROSSE OR GESSE.

Vern.—*Khesari,* BENG.; *Kasóri, kassar, tiura, tiuri, latri,* N. W. P.

Common in the Northern Provinces of India, from the plains of Bengal to Kumaun where it reaches 4,000 feet in altitude,. often cultivated.

and in some places wild. When cultivated, it is sown about the close of the rains (October) in heavy clay soils and on land hardened after submersion during the rains, and occasionally in rice fields before the rice is cut. Its cultivation in the North West Provinces and Oudh is commonest in the eastern districts, and in parts of Allahabad and Azimgarh. No reliable statistics of its area are forthcoming.

The pulse is chiefly used as a green fodder for cattle, and seems to spring more as a weed of other crops. The seeds are very irregular in form, generally wedge-shaped, gray-coloured, and minutely spotted. They enjoy in Europe the reputation of causing paralysis of the lower extremities, but this curious property would appear to have escaped the notice of the natives of India, except in Allahabad, where it seems to be known. It is extensively used in some parts of the country as a substitute for *dál*, and bread is made from the flour. Pigs fed upon it are said to lose the use of their limbs, but fatten well. It would be exceedingly interesting to have this curious property verified by authentic experiment, for, if there be any truth in it, this might perhaps account for the prevalence of paralysis in some districts of India. Were the curious property to be proved true with the lower animals, it would seem desirable to discourage the cultivation of this plant as a food-crop. In most parts of India it can scarcely be called a food-crop, although the split pea must be largely used to adulterate *dál*, from which it can scarcely be distinguished when sold in the split form. It is used to a certain extent by the poorer classes as a substitute for other pulses, but is hard and indigestible.

LEEA.

Leea aspera, *Wall.*, AMPELIDEÆ. 427

Vern.—*Holma*, PB.

Found in the southern regions of the Western Himalaya from Jamu to Nepal, ascending to 6,000 feet in altitude and descending into Oudh; also met with in Western India from Kandesh to the Konkan.

Produces a small fruit which is black and succulent, and is eaten by the natives.

LEPIDIUM.

Lepidium sativum, *Linn.*, CRUCIFERÆ. 428

THE GARDEN CRESS.

Vern.—*Aleverie, haleem*, BENG., HIND.; *Adala-vitala*, TEL.; *Haleem*, DEC.; *Ahreo*, SIND.

Cultivated throughout India and Western Tibet, but is not known in an indigenous state.

Cultivated in the cold weather in vegetable gardens, chiefly for its leaves, which are cut young for the consumption of the European population. It is often cultivated with mustard, both being used as salad.

The leaves when full grown are used for garnishing dishes like those of parsley.

Leptadenia viminea, *Bth.* *See* **Orthanthera viminia,** *W. & A.*, ASCLEPIADEÆ.

LEMONIA.

429 **Lemonia acidissima,** *Linn.*, RUTACEÆ.

Syn.—L. CRENULATA, *Roxb.*

Vern.—*Beli*, HIND.; *Tor-elaya*, TEL.; *Kawat*, MAR.; *Thee-haya-sa*, BURM.

A shrub of dry hills in various parts of India, *e.g.*, Simla, Kumaun, Monghyr, Assam, Western Ghâts, Coromandel, Malabar.

Flowers in the hot season, and produces a round berry, which, though very acid, is sometimes eaten by the natives.

LOLIUM.

430 **Lolium perenne,** *Linn.*, GRAMINEÆ.

PERENNIAL RAY OR RYE-GRASS OR HAY.

Met with in Western Tibet at 15,000 feet in altitude.

In Europe it is extensively grown along with clover (*Duthie*). In Australia it is considered one of the most important of all fodder grasses, and stands the dry heat very well (*Mueller*).

431 **L. temulentum,** *Linn.*

DARNEL.

Syn.—L. ARVENSE, *With.*

Vern.—?

Inhabits the plains and hills of Northern India.

Mr. Duthie writes: "The seeds of this grass have for a long time been supposed to possess poisonous properties, and numerous instances have been given as to the ill effects after eating flour or bread into which the grains of this grass have been purposely or accidentally introduced. Recent experiments, however, rather indicate that healthy darnel grain is perfectly innocuous, the evil effects being produced by ergotized or otherwise diseased grains. As darnel is often a common weed in corn-fields, the grains are very liable to be ground up with those of wheat."

LONICERA.

432 **Lonicera angustifolia,** *Wall.*, CAPRIFOLIACEÆ.

Vern.—*Geang, pilru, philku*, PB.

A small Himalayan shrub found from the Indus and Kashmir to Sikkim and Kumaun at altitudes from 6,000 to 10,000 feet.

Produces fruits which are eaten.

433 **L. hypoleuca,** *Dne.*

Vern.—*Kharmo, shido, rapesho*, PB.

A small shrub of the arid tracts of the Punjab Himalaya, at altitudes from 8,400 to 11,000 feet, also of Garhwal.

Goats eat the leaves, and are said to fatten on them.

434 **L. quinquelocularis,** *Hardwicke.*

Vern.—*Jarlangei, phut, bakru, khum, dendra, kraunti*, PB.; *Bhat-kukra*, KUMAUN; *Tita-bateri*, KASHMIR.

A shrub of the western Himalaya, from Kashmir to Kumaun, at altitudes from 4,000 to 12,000 feet; also common in Bhutan and on he Sulaiman Range.

Cattle are fed on the leaves, or are allowed to browse on them.

LUFFA.

Luffa acutangula, *Roxb.*, CUCURBITACEÆ. 435

Vern.—*Torooi, jinga, turi,* HIND.; *Káli-taroi, satpatiya,* BUNDALKHAND; *Jhinga, jinga,* BENG.; *Peekun-kai,* TAM.; *Burkai, bira-kaya,* TEL.; *Peechenggah,* MAL.; *Turai, sirola,* BOM.; *Turi,* SIND.

Met with in the North West Himalaya to Sikkim, Assam, East Bengal, and Ceylon. Cultivated in most parts of India.

No information of a trustworthy nature can be given as to the area occupied by the crop, but it is regularly cultivated every year, especially in the plains, where it is common. The sowing is done from March to the beginning of June in lines at short distances; the fruits are ready in three months, and the plant continues to bear for a couple of months.

Natives value the fruit highly and eat it in curry. **Roxburgh** says that the half-grown fruit, when boiled and dressed with butter, pepper, and salt, are little inferior to green peas. Cut in round slices, and made into *fricasse*, it is an exceedingly nice vegetable dish. (*Mr. L. Liotard.*)

L. ægyptiaca, *Mill, ex Hook. f.* 436

Syn.—L. PENTANDRA, *Roxb.*

Vern.—*Dhundul,* BENG.; *Tarod, ghiya-taroi, turai, dhandhal,* KUMAUN; *Nuni-beerd,* TEL.; *Ghosali, parosi,* BOM.

A native of India, cultivated or naturalised in most of the hot countries of the world. In India it is common everywhere, and is often cultivated especially in the plains. The seeds are sown from March to June, and the fruit ripens from June to October. The North West Provinces show an area which ranges from 29 acres in Jalaun and 65 in Cawnpore, to 199 acres in Meerut and 256 in Allahabad; but complete figures are not available.

The fruit is commonly used by the natives in curry.

LYCIUM.

Lycium europæum, *Linn.*, SOLANACEÆ. 437

Vern.—*Ganger, kangu, niral, chirchitta,* PB.

A thorny shrub of the drier plains of the Punjab, Sindh, and Guzerat.

The berries are eaten by the natives in some places. The plant is browsed by camels and goats, and the young shoots are used as a vegetable.

LYCOPERSICUM.

Lycopersicum esculentum, *Miller,* SOLANACEÆ. 438

LOVE-APPLE, or TOMATO.

Syn.—SOLANUM LYCOPERSICUM, *Linn.*

Vern.—*Gur-begun, teemoti, tamati,* BENG., HIND.

A trailing plant introduced from South America. At present cultivated in many parts of India for its large red or sometimes yellow fruits which are used for culinary purposes. In the plains the seed is sown in autumn, and the fruit ripens during the winter and spring seasons. In the hills the plant grows more luxuriously than in the plains, and bears fruits throughout the summer and autumn months.

The natives are beginning to appreciate the fruit, but the plant is chiefly cultivated for the European population. The Bengalis use it in their sour curries.

LYSIMACHIA.

439 **Lysimachia candida,** *Lindl.*, PRIMULACEÆ.

Syn.—L. SAMOLINA, *Hance.*

Found in Manipur valley in rice fields at 2,000 to 3,000 feet in altitude. Eaten by the Manipuris as a pot-herb along with fish.

MABA.

440 **Maba buxifolia,** *Pers.*, EBENACEÆ.

Syn.—FERREOLA BUXIFOLIA, *Roxb.*

Vern.—*Irambali, eruvali, humbili,* TAM.; *Nela-madi, pishina,* TEL.; *Me-pyoung,* BURM.

A small tree of South India, the Circar mountains, and Tenasserim; common in Ceylon.

Flowers during the hot season, and produces berries which, when ripe, are generally eaten by the natives, and are said to taste well.

MÆSA.

441 **Mæsa argentea,** *Wall.*, MYRSINEÆ.

Vern.—*Phusera, gogsa,* HIND.

A large shrub of the outer Himalaya, found from Garhwal and Kumaun to East Nipal, at altitudes from 3,000 to 7,000 feet.

Produces fruits which are larger than those of the other Indian species, and are probably eaten by the natives, but there is no information as to this.

Mahonia nepalensis, *DC.* *See* **Berberis nepalensis,** *Spreng.* (*in Hook. & St.*)

MALVA.

442 **Malva parviflora,** *Linn.*, MALVACEÆ.

Vern.—*Narr, panirak, supra, sonchal, gogi-sag,* PB. & SIND.

A small, spreading herb in Upper Bengal, North-West Himalaya (low altitudes), the Punjab, and Sindh.

Frequently eaten as a pot-herb by the natives, specially in times of scarcity.

MANGIFERA.

443 **Mangifera fœtida,** *Lour.*, ANACARDIACEÆ.

Vern.—*Lamote,* BURM.; *Bachang,* MALAY.

A large tree cultivated in Southern Tenasserim.

Produces pink or dark red flowers, and a coarse-flavoured fruit which is eaten by the natives, and for which the tree is cultivated.

444 **M. indica,** *Linn.*

THE MANGO TREE.

Vern.—*Amb,* BENG.; *Am,* HIND.; *Ghariam,* ASS.; *Amra,* SANS.; *Mda, mangas,* TAM.; *Mamadi, mamid,* TEL.; *Ambá, áma,* BOM.; *Thayet,* BURM.

A large, evergreen tree, of the Cashew Nut family, is wild on the Western Gháts, and cultivated all over India. It is really *the* apple of India.

It blossoms, according to situation, from February to April, and the fruit ripens from May to July, and continues for two months. It is a favorite fruit among both natives and Europeans, and is very largely eaten throughout the country. The fruit is of many varieties, differing in size, shape, color, and flavour; for example, some are as heavy as a pound in weight, others not four ounces; while some are (1) large and pale yellow, (2) middle-sized bright yellow, (3) middle-sized tinged with red, and others are (4) of different sizes with a greenish colour even when ripe; and each of these varieties possesses a different flavour. The first, known as Malda mango, is generally juicy but wanting in sweetness; the second is either sweet and delicious, or of a turpentine taste, or stringy, or acid, some so stringy and terebinthaceous as to have been compared to a mouthful of tow soaked in turpentine. Yet this is the mango most common in India. The third is either sweet and juicy or sour; while the fourth is generally of an exquisite flavour, sweet and juicy, and known as the Bombay mango. It is cultivated with great care in gardens in many parts of the country. Malda and the Bombay varieties are generally eaten by the well-to-do.

The fruit serves as an important addition in many parts of the country to the marginal resources of a large section of the native population who own the trees.

Fine, luscious fruits, weighing ½ lb. each, were, a few years ago, produced on an old tree in the Kew Gardens, London.

"Besides being eaten as a ripe fruit, the mango is used as follows:

"*When green*, the stone is extracted, the fruit cut into halves or slices, and (*a*) put into curries, (*b*) made into pickle with salt, mustard oil, chillies, and other ingredients, (*c*) made into preserves and jellies by being boiled and cooked in syrup, (*d*) boiled, strained, and with milk and sugar made into a custard known as *ma go phool*, (*e*) dried and made into the native 'amb-choor,' used for adding acidity to certain curries, (*f*) when very young cut into small pieces, mixed with a little salt, and sliced chillies and milk added, it forms a 'tasty' salad.

When ripe (*a*) it is made into curry which has a sweet-acid not unpleasant taste; (*b*) it is cut into small pieces, and made into salad with vinegar and chillies (the sour fruit is sometimes used thus); (*c*) the juice is squeezed out, spread on plates and allowed to dry, and forms the thin cakes known as *amb-sath*" (*Mr. L. Liotard*).

Preserves, tarts, and pickles are made from the mango fruit and largely exported to England and elsewhere.

There seems to be little truth in the charge brought frequently against the mango. that it is a fruitful cause of boils. The blue stain produced on the cutting knife results from the presence of gallic acid in the pulp, which likewise contains citric acid and gum.

Mangifera sylvatica, *Roxb.* 445

Vern.—*Bun-am*, ASS.; *Lakshmi-am*, SYLHET; *Chuchi am*, NEPAL; *Katur*, LEPCHA; *Hseng neng thayet*, BURM.

A wild mango tree of Nepal, Eastern Bengal, and the Andamans, also occasionally met with in Burma.

The fruit is sometimes eaten fresh or dried.

MANIHOT.

Manihot utilissima, *Pohl.*, EUPHORBIACEÆ.

BITTER CASSAVA; TAPIOCA. 446

Syn.—JANIPHA MANIHOT, *Kth.*

Vern —*Maravuli*, TAM.; *Marachini*, MAL.; *Pulu pinan myouk*, BURM.

A slender, erect-stemmed shrub of tropical America, introduced and

MEDICAGO.

cultivated in Travancore, parts of adjoining British districts, and Burma. Requires little or no cultivation, thrives on any waste lands, and bears a most profitable out-turn. In Travancore, for instance, the cultivator merely clears away the low brushwood, puts the root under ground, and then it grows luxuriantly on the most exposed situations near the sea coast or inland, needing little care except to preserve it from the depredations of cattle. But sometimes it is given to the cattle as food.

The object of the cultivation of the plant is the large, fleshy roots which, under the following preparation, yield the Tapioca of commerce and the Cassava flour, both very nourishing articles of food. About the preparation of Tapioca, **Ainslie** gives the following account :—

"An amylum or starch is first to be obtained from the fresh roots, which starch, to form it into Tapioca, must be sprinkled with a little water and then boiled in steam; it is in this way converted into viscid, irregular masses, which must be dried in the sun till they have become quite hard, and then they may be broken into small grains for use." As the roots contain a juice of a highly poisonous character, the edible meal is obtained by grating them to a pulp. From this pulp the poisonous juice is expelled by pressure and washing, and subsequently by heat. What remains is formed into the Cassava flour or bread, or Tapioca of commerce.

Well-boiled it is eaten with fish curry by the natives.

A large proportion of the poorer classes of Travancore and the adjoining districts live on the flour in the months of July, August and September, and it becomes especially serviceable in exceptional years when rice is scarce and consequently dear.

The produce has been estimated at 10 tons of green roots per acre yielding about 2,800 lbs. of tapioca flour. There is abundant room for improvement in the manufacture of the prepared article, as it is found cheaper to bring the manufactured article from England by the Europeans than buy it on the spot where it grows.

MARLEA.

447 **Marlea begoniæfolia,** *Roxb.*, CORNACEÆ.

Vern.—*Marlea* or *marlisa*, SYLHET; *Garkum, budhal, tumbri*, N.W.P.; *Sialu, tilpatra, kurkui*, PB.; *Timil, palet*, NEPAL; *Tapuay*, BURM.

A tree commonly met with throughout Northern India, at altitudes from 1,000 to 6,000 feet, also in Burma. Flowers in April, and ripens its seed in July.

Cattle are sometimes fed on its leaves.

MARSILEA.

448 **Marsilea quadrifolia,** *Linn.*, MARSILEACEÆ.

Vern.—*Paflu, tripattra*, PB.

A plant growing abundantly in water in the Punjab plains and in the hills up to 5,000 feet.

It is said to be eaten as a pot-herb by the natives.

MEDICAGO.

449 **Medicago denticulata,** *Willd.*, LEGUMINOSÆ,

Syn.—M. POLYMORPHA, *Roxb.*

Vern.—*Maina*, PB.

A field weed in the plains and low hills of Bengal, North West Provinces, Oudh, the Punjab, and Sindh.

It is largely gathered for cattle fodder, as it is considered good for milch cows.

Medicago falcata, *Linn.*, 450

THE PURPLE MEDICK OR LUCERNE.

Syn.—M. SATIVA, *Wall.*

Vern.—*Rishka, hol,* AFG., LAHOUL.

M. falcata is found wild or cultivated for fodder in Kashmir, Ladak, and other highland places in and over the Himalaya.

M. Sativa is probably a cultivated variety of it, and is not uncommonly grown for forage in South India, Bengal, and parts of the North West Provinces. It is a tall, slender, clover-like plant, regarded as a native of England but rarely found wild there Its herbage is green and succulent, and yields two rather abundant green crops of green food in the year.

M. lupulina, *Linn.* 451

THE HOP OF BLACK MEDICK OF NON-SUCH.

"Tropical and temperate tracts of the north-west, ascending from the Indus valley and Gangetic plain to 10,000 or 12,000 feet in altitude." (*Baker in Fl. Br. Ind.*)

A common weed, collected frequently for fodder. Its flowers resemble hop cones, hence its English name.

It mixes well with grasses and clovers for artificial pastures.

MELIA.

Melia Azadirachta, *Linn.*, MELIACEÆ. 452

THE NEEM TREE OF MARGOSA TREE.

Syn.—AZADIRACHTA INDICA, *Adr. Juss.*

Vern.—*Nim, nimb,* HIND., BENG.; *Nimba,* SANS.; *Belain,* KUMAUN; *Kohumba,* GUZ.; *Veypam, veypale,* TAM.; *Yapa, vepa,* TEL.; *Aria-bepon,* MAL.; *Thimbaubhempu,* or *thimbau-ta-ma-kha,* BURM.

A middle-sized, sometimes large, tree with small, luxuriant foliage; common everywhere in India from the Jhelum to Assam and Ceylon.

The leaves are cooked in curry, or are simply parched and eaten. The natives are very fond of them on account of the slightly bitter taste of the curry cooked with those leaves. They are also used for camel fodder. By tapping the tree a kind of toddy is obtained, which the Hindus regard as stomachic.

M. Azedarach, *Linn.* 453

THE PERSIAN LILAC, THE PRIDE OF INDIA, BASTARD CEDAR OR BEAD TREE.

Vern.— *akayan, betain, drek, bakain,* HIND.; *Ghora nim,* BENG.; *Gori nim,* BOM.; *Chein, kachein,* SUTLEJ; *Maha-limbo, malla, nim,* C. P.; *Bakainú,* NEPAL; *Mallai vembu, malai veppam,* TAM.; *Taruka vepu, makanim,*TEL.; *Tam-a-kha,* BURM.; *Mahanimba,* SANS.

A tree with smooth, grey bark, commonly cultivated throughout India, and believed to be indigenous in the outer Himalaya, Siwalik tract, and the hills of Beluchistan.

There are different opinions as to the wholesomeness of the pulp of the berry, some regarding it as edible, others treating it as poisonous. The fruit is greedily eaten by goats and sheep." (*Aitchison.*)

MELILOTUS.

454 **Melilotus parviflora,** *Desf.*, LEGUMINOSÆ.

Syn.—TRIFOLIUM INDICUM, *Linn.*

Vern.—*Bon-methi*, BENG.; *Sinji*, PB.

Met with in the Bombay Presidency, Bengal, North-West Provinces, and the Punjab.

Used for fodder in parts of the above tracts, and considered good for milk.

MELOCANNA.

455 **Melocanna bambusoides,** *Tærin.*, GRAMINEÆ.

Vern.—*Máli, metunga, bish*, BENG.; *Kayoung-wa*, MAGH.

The common gregarious bambu of the Chittagong hills.

The fruit is large, pears-haped, 3 to 5 inches long, and edible (*Gamble*).

MEMECYLON.

456 **Memecylon edule,** *Roxb.*, MELASTROMACEÆ.

THE IRON-WOOD TREE.

Vern.—*Anjan, kurpa*, BOM.; *Casau-chetty*, TAM.; *Alli*, TEL.

A small tree or shrub of South India (on the Eastern Gháts), also of Tenasserim and the Andamans.

Flowers in the beginning of the hot season, and produces astringent, pulpy berries, which, when ripe, are eaten by the natives.

MENTHA.

457 **Mentha arvensis,** *Linn.*, LABIATÆ.

THE MARSH MINT.

Syn.—M. SATIVA, *Linn.*

Vern.—*Pudina*, BENG., HIND., DEC.

This plant is grown for culinary purposes, and for its oil. It is frequent in the gardens of Europeans in India; it grows freely and easily in Behar and the North West Provinces, but does not flower in the plains of India.

The leaves are used in food.

458 **M. piperita,** *Linn.*

PEPPERMINT.

A herbaceous plant of the temperate regions.

It is cultivated to a limited extent in most gardens, and is used for culinary and confectionery purposes. From it is made the cordial called Peppermint water.

459 **M. viridis,** *Linn.*

THE SPEARMINT OF MINT.

Vern.—*Pahari pudina*, HIND.; *Nagbó, shah-sufiam*, PERS.

This plant is common in the plains in a state of cultivation, and is known in Bengal as *Púndia*.

This is more largely used for culinary purposes under the name of mint than peppermint, as its flavour is preferable.

MESUA.

Mesua ferrea, *Linn.*, GUTTIFERÆ. 460

THE INDIAN IRON-WOOD.

Vern.—*Naghas* or *Nagesar*, HIND., BENG.; *Nangal*, TAM.; *Ganjan*, BURM.; *Nahar*, ASS.

A middle-sized, glabrous-barked tree, of the Gamboge family, met with in the mountains of Eastern Bengal, East Himalaya, and the Eastern and Western Peninsula, and the Andaman Islands. A very variable tree, the under-surface of whose leaves is often quite destitute of the waxy meal. Flowers in April and May, and produces a fruit which is reddish and wrinkled when ripe, and has a rind like that of the chesnut.

It is like the chesnut in size, shape, and taste, and is eaten by the natives.

MICHELIA.

Michelia Champaca, *Linn.*, MAGNOLIACEÆ. 461

Vern.—*Champa*, HIND.; *Champa, champaka*, BENG.; *Pivald chápha*, BOM.; *Titsappa*, ASS.; *Shimbu, sempangam*, TAM.; *Tsaga*, BURM.

A large, handsome tree, with deep-yellow, sweetly-scented flowers; cultivated throughout India, wild in Bengal, Nepal, and Assam. The Hindus regard the tree as sacred to Vishnu, to whose image they offer its strong-scented flower. Its little straw-coloured fruit, which is said to be edible, ripens in the cold season.

Mimosa dulcis, *Roxb.* *See* **Pithecolobium dulce**, *Benth.* LEGUMINOSÆ.

M. scandens, *Linn.* *See* **Entada scandens**, *Bth.* LEGUMINOSÆ.

MIMUSOPS.

Mimusops Elengi, *Linn.*, SAPOTACEÆ. 462

Vern.—*Bokul, bohl*, BENG.; *Mulsári, maulser*, HIND.; *Bakuli, ovali*, BOM.; *Magadam*, TAM.; *Pogada*, TEL.; *Bokal, bohlu*, KAN.; *Elengi*, MAL.; *Vavoli*, MAR.; *Khaya*, BURM.

A large, evergreen tree, wild on the Western Gháts as far north as Khandalla, in the Northern Circars, Burma, the Andaman Islands, and Ceylon. (*Gamble.*) Grown throughout India, chiefly in gardens for shade or ornament.

Produces during the hot season small fragrant flowers in abundance which fall in showers. These are succeeded by small, oval berries, which are yellowish when ripe, and have a small quantity of sweetish pulp, sometimes eaten by the poorer natives. The berries also afford an abundance of oil, and the highly fragrant flowers yield their perfume to water.

M. hexandra, *Roxb.* 463

Syn.—M. INDICA, *A. DC.*

Vern.—*Khir, khirni*, HIND.; *Rain*, MEYWAR; *Palla, kannu-palle*, TAM.; *Palle panlo*, TEL.; *Palu*, CINGH.

Found on the mountains of South India, extending in Central India to the sandstone hills of Pachmari, north of the Godavari.

Flowers in April to June, and produces an olive-shaped, yellow berry, which is eaten.

464 **Mimusops Kauki,** *Linn.*

Vern.—*Booa-sow*, MALAY; ? *Adoma*, GOA.

A large tree of Burma (Amherst) and the Malayan Peninsula.

Flowers during the hot season, and produces a fruit which is eaten by the natives.

MOMORDICA.

465 **Momordica Balsamina,** *Linn.*, CUCURBITACEÆ.

A climber of Northern India, Sindh, and Punjab.

Produces a fruit 1 to 4 in. long, orange or red, usually quite smooth, which belies its generic name, given (from *mordeo*, I bite) because of the very jagged or bitten appearance of the seeds. The fruit is mentioned by **Atkinson** as a food.

466 **M. Charantia,** *Linn.*

Syn.—M. MARICATA, *DC.*

Vern.—*Karela, kareli, karola*, HIND.; *Karalá*, BENG.; *Susuvi*, SANS.

Cultivated all over India on the plains. There are practically two kinds, one grown in the rainy season, which has smaller fruit and is more esteemed; the other grown in hot weather is more bitter: it is sown in rich soil in February and March, and fruit is ready for use from April.

The fruit, which is of a bright orange-yellow colour, 1 to 6 inches long, is eaten cooked in curries, or sliced and fried; but a special treatment in hot water is necessary previous to cooking or frying to take away a portion of the bitterness. When sliced and dried, it remains good for many months.

467 **M. dioica,** *Roxb.*

Vern.—*Dhár, karela, kirara*, PB.; *Kurtoli*, BOM.; *Palúpaghel-kalung*, TAM.; *Puagakara* (male plants), *agakara* (female plants), TEL.

Found throughout India at different altitudes, up to 5,000 feet, generally in thickets, on banks of rivers, &c.

Flowers during the wet and cold seasons, and produces a fruit which, when green and tender, is eaten in curries by the natives. The tuberous roots of the female plant are also eaten, and they are larger than those of the male.

MORCHELLA.

468 **Morchella semilibera,** *L.*, FUNGI.

MORELL.

Syn.—M. ESCULENTA, *Linn.*

Vern.—*Kana kach, girchhatra* (hills), *khumb* (plains), PB.

This fleshy fungus is found in and near Kashmir abundant, also near Chumba, and in parts of North Punjab.

Commonly eaten, both fresh and dry, by natives, and preferred to the mushroom. **Dr. Stewart** says that "it is considered a great dainty by natives, and relished by those Europeans who have tasted it."

Of a pale brown or grey colour, and marked all over with deep pits; it is used to give flavour to dishes similar to those of mushroom ketchup.

MORINDA.

Morinda citrifolia, *Linn.*, RUBIACEÆ. 469

Sometimes called the INDIAN MULBERRY and MORINDA BARK TREE.

Vern.—*Al*, HIND.; *Ach, aich or achhu*, BENG.; *Ald, bartondi*, BOM.; *Munja-pavattary*, TAM.; *Yai-ya*, BURM.; *Suranji*, a trade name.

A small tree, cultivated or wild (?) throughout the hotter parts of India, Burma, and Ceylon. Supposed to be truly wild in Malacca. *Fruit*, of many drupes, coalescent into a fleshy, globose head, one inch in diameter.

The fruits are eatable but insipid.

M. tinctoria, *Roxb.* 470

Vern.—*Ach*, BENG.; *Al*, HIND.; *Achchhuka*, SANS.

Found throughout India from the Sutlej eastward, and southward to Ceylon and Malacca.

"The green fruits are picked by the Hindus, and eaten with their curries." (*Roxb.*)

MORINGA.

Moringa concanensis, *Nimmo*, MORINGEÆ. 471

Vern.—*Sainjna*, RAJPUTANA.

A tree of Rajputana, Sind, and the Konkan.

The fruit of this species is half an inch long, and is eaten when unripe in curries by the natives.

M. pterygosperma, *Gærtn.* 472

THE HORSE RADISH OR BEN NUT TREE.

Vern.—*Saina, sujana*, BENG.; *Soanjna, sanjna*, HIND.; *Segata, segava*, BOM.; *Morunga*, TAM.; *Daintha*, BURM.

Wild in the sub-Himalayan tract from the Chenab to Oudh; commonly cultivated in India and Burma. It is most easily raised from seed and cuttings. It flowers in February, and fruits in March and April. The fruit is a long whip-like bean. In Bengal and Southern India especially, there is scarcely any native homestead without its *sajna* or *morunga* tree.

The leaves, the flowers, and the beans are very commonly eaten in curries by natives of all classes. After the beans are taken off the tree, the branches are universally lopped off and the leaves are then given to cattle as fodder. The root has a strong flavour of horse radish, and besides being used in medicine as a vesicant, is also eaten by the natives sometimes like radish.

MORUS.

Morus.

The genus **Morus** contains numerous forms developed probably from difference in soil and climate and long periods of cultivation. It contains six species, which are all referred to one, **M. Alba**, by Bureau, in *DC. Prodr., Vol. XVII.* Here we have adopted **Gamble's** classification of this genus as found in his *Manual of Indian Timbers.*

473 **Morus alba,** *Linn.*, URTICACEÆ.

THE WHITE MULBERRY.

Vern.—*Tút, túl, túlklu, chinni, chún,* HIND.

Cultivated in Afghanistan, Kashmir, and the plains and hills of the Punjab, chiefly for feeding the silkworm with its leaves, and for its fruit, which is eaten, either fresh or dried, by the people who regard it as delicious eating. The fruit is white or pale red.

474 **M. atropurpurea,** *Roxb.*

Introduced from China and now cultivated in many parts of India.

475 **M. cuspidata,** *Wall.*

Vern.—*Bola,* ASS.; *Singtok,* BHUTIA; *Nambyong,* LEPCHA; *Kimbu,* NEPAL.

A tall tree of the valleys of the outer Eastern Himalaya, from Sikkim to Assam.

476 **M. indica,** *Linn.*

Vern.—*Tút,* BENG.; *Tutri,* HIND.; *Nuni,* ASS.; *Mekrap,* LEPCHA.; *Chota kimbu,* NEPAL; *Shahtút,* KUMAUN; *Túl,* PB.; *Posa,* BURM.

A moderate-sized, deciduous tree, cultivated throughout North India, ascending in the Sikkim valleys up to 4,000 feet in altitude, and in the sub-Himalayan tract to 5,000 feet.

Cultivated chiefly for its leaves, which are used to feed silkworms.

477 **M. lœvigata,** *Wall.*

Vern.—*Tut,* HIND.; *Malaing,* BURM.

Wild and cultivated in the Himalaya from the Indus to Assam up to 4,000 feet, also in Bengal and Assam.

The fruit is long, cylindrical, sweet, but insipid.

478 **M. serrata,** *Roxb.*

Vern.—*Kimu, himu,* HIND.; *Karún, tút, kaúra, soá, án, shta, chimu,* PB.

A large, deciduous tree of the North-West Himalaya, ranging from 4,000 to 9,000 feet.

Under one or other of the six above the following may perhaps be included:

M. Multicaulis.
M. Nigra.
M. Parviflora.

M. Nigra, or Black Mulberry, has been largely superseded in Europe by **M. Alba** or white Mulberry, for the feeding of silkworms, and is now chiefly cultivated for its fruit.

MUCUNA.

479 **Mucuna monosperma,** *DC.*, LEGUMINOSÆ.

NEGRO BEAN.

A plant of the East Himalayas and Khásia Hills, and met with in Assam, Chittagong, Pegu, Tavoy, and the Hills of West Peninsula and Ceylon up to 3,000 feet.

Is a favourite vegetable.

480 **M. nivea,** *DC.*

Perhaps a cultivated race of **M. Pruriens.** (*Alkushi,* BENG.)

The tender, fleshy pods when skinned make an excellent vegetable for the table, scarcely inferior to the Garden Bean of Europe.

MUKIA.

Mukia scabrella, *Arn.*, CUCURBITACEÆ. 481

Vern.—*Chiráti, bellari,* SIND.

A climber common throughout India in the plains and hills as far as tropical warmth extends.

Atkinson mentions this amongst his foods.

MULGEDIUM.

Mulgedium tartaricum, *DC.*, COMPOSITÆ. 482

Vern.—*Khawe.*

Common in Ladak from 11,000 to 14,500 feet.

Dr. Stewart says the plant is occasionally browsed by sheep.

MURRAYA.

Murraya Kœnigii, *Spr.*, RUTACEÆ. 483

CURRY-LEAF or LIMBLEE OIL TREE.

Syn.—BERGERA KŒNIGII, *Linn.*

Vern.—*Gandla, gandi, bowla,* PB.; *Harri, Karay-paak, karea-phul, katnim,* HIND.; *Karea-phul, barsanga,* BENG.; *Chanangi,* HYDERABAD; *Karepak, karivepa,* TEL.; *Kammepila,* TAM.; *Karea-pela,* MAL.

A small tree of the outer Himalaya, ascending to altitude 5,000 feet, from the Ravi to Assam, Bengal, South India, and Burma.

Largely cultivated on the plains on account of its leaves, which are used, either fresh or dry, to flavour curries; they have an aromatic smell when rubbed.

MUSA.

Musa paradisiaca, *Linn.*, SCITAMMEÆ. 484

THE PLANTAIN.

M. sapientum, *Linn.* 485

BANANA.

Vern.—*Kadali,* SANS.; *Kala,* BENG.; *Kela,* HIND., BOM.; *Vaxhaip pazham,* TAM.

A perennial herb of 8 to 15 feet in height, extensively cultivated throughout India, nearer the coast tracts than inland, chiefly for its fruit, which is a very common article of diet among both Europeans and natives, especially the latter.

When we consider its great size, the beauty and breadth of its leaves, the quality and abundance of its fruit, and the number of months it is in season, and the beauty of its flowers, the plantain may well be regarded as the king of vegetables. The fruit is produced in the form of a gigantic bunch weighing from 40 to 80 lbs., from the top of the sheathing stem. As a food-plant the plantain or banana is cultivated with very little labour throughout the tropics in both hemispheres; and far even into cooler latitudes. It has been calculated that the same area of soil which would yield 33 lbs. of wheat, or 99 lbs. of potatoes, would yield 4,400 lbs. of plantains, but though highly nutritious, it is not so much so as either

MUSA.

potatoes or wheat. Still it serves as the staple food of a large proportion of the human race. It is the household god of many a labourer's cottage in many parts of the world, being to many what rice is to the Hindu, loaf-bread to the Englishman, potato to the Irishman, and what the oatcake used to be to the Scotchman. In India, it grows from the extreme south of the Peninsula to 30° north at a height of 4,590 feet above the sea-level.

The Plantain stem, laden with fruit, is very suggestively employed by Hindus at their marriage feasts as emblematic of plenty and fruitfulness. A bunch of Plantains contains as many as 100 fruits, each from 4 to 9 inches long and 3 to 5 inches in circumference. The horse plantain grows in India, fruits a foot in length filled with hard, black seeds, which are fried in ghi and eaten. In Madagascar there are plantains as large as a man's fore-arm; and in the mountains of the Philippines a single fruit or two are said to be a load for a man. The edible part is soft and more or less mawkish and pulpy and of agreeable flavour. When dry and powdered it forms a very useful meal, nearly allied to that of rice. In South America the flour is baked into biscuits. But here in India no means are taken to preserve the plantain as meal or otherwise. But in other dry countries it is preserved for any number of years. There are 20 varieties of plantain in Tenasserim, 10 in Ceylon, and 30 in Burma, and as many as 17,000 acres are under plantain cultivation in the Madras Presidency, chiefly in Tinnevelly. Shoots or suckers from the parent plant are put into the ground shortly before the rains, and ten months thereafter the fruit is ripe, and as they renew themselves with off-shoots at different degrees of development, ripe fruit, blossoms and young off-sets are met with in the same garden at one and the same time, and as a consequence ripe fruit may be obtained with little or no labour the whole year round; and it requires to be renewed in good soil only once in 40 years.

"In Bengal there are several kinds of plantain, known commonly as the *table plantain*, the *champa*, the *daccai*, the *kantali*, and the *kanch kolla*.

"The first is the most tasty, being creamy, farinaceous and sweet, but can be had only during the rains in any quantity, and is eaten commonly by Europeans and well-to-do natives. In the cold season the few procurable are very inferior.

"The *champa* is the next best, and, like the preceding, the best specimens are available during the rains; it is more largely eaten by the poorer people, and the better qualities of it often find a place on the tables of Europeans.

"The *Daccai* plantain, native of Dacca, is rather longer (9 inches) than either of the first two. It has a light pink, soft flesh, and is not found in abundance except in the east of Bengal.

"The *kantali* is slightly glutinous and has often seeds in it. It is eaten only by natives, more commonly by the poorer classes.

"The *kanch-kolla* is hardly ever allowed to ripen; it is a coarse, rather astringent, variety, and is mostly used when unripe, being cooked in curries.

Besides the fruit, the purple flower stock and the tender heart or pith of the plant are also eaten very commonly by the natives, curries being made of them. They contain much starch. The use of these parts do not affect the production of the fruit, because they are taken, when the fruit attains its proper development, by cutting down the tree.

"The plant itself (excepting the heart) is chopped up and given very commonly to cattle, especially to cows, as fodder, but the nutritive element contained in it is very small." (*Mr. L. Liotard.*)

The fruit is served either raw, stewed, fried, or as curries. Sometimes they are roasted in the ashes and used as bread or boiled and eaten as potatoes with salt meat, or pounded and made into puddings. American Indians manufacture an intoxicating liquor from the plantain and call it "rum." The plantain meal is regarded as more digestive and strengthening than arrowroot, and thus more suitable for children and invalids. Its flavour is also preferable. Vinegar is easily and cheaply manufactured from the fruit, when it is in danger of rotting from its superabundance as food.

MUSSÆNDA.

Mussænda frondosa, *Linn.*, RUBIACEÆ. 486

Vern.—*Asari*, NEPAL; *Tumberch*, LEPCHA; *Maa-senda*, CINGH.; *Bhúta-kesa, lándachúta*, BOM.

A handsome shrub; North-East Himalaya, Bengal, South India, and Burma. It is often cultivated in gardens, and is conspicuous by its yellow flowers and large white calycine leaf.

MYRICA.

Myrica Integrifolia, MYRICACEÆ. 487

SOPHEE.

A shrub of the Candleberry family.

Its fruit is eaten by the natives.

M. Nagi. 488

THE YANGMÆ OF CHINA.

Native of China, a bushy shrub or tree 15 to 20 feet high, bearing a dark-red or yellowish fruit somewhat like, but larger than, the fruit of the strawberry tree, or **Arbutus.** It is known in Western India, but very inferior to that of China.

M. sapida, *Wall.* 489

Vern.—*Kaphal, kaiphal*, N. W. P.; *Kayaphala*, BOM.; *Kobusi*, NEPAL; *Dingsolir*, KHASIA.

A moderate-sized tree of the outer Himalaya, altitude 3,000 to 6,000 feet; extending to the Khási hills and Burma.

Produces a fruit which, although wanting in a fair supply of flesh, has a pleasant sweet-sour taste, and is very commonly eaten by the hill people. It is also sometimes eaten by Europeans; and is used in *sherbats*.

MYRICARIA.

Myricaria elegans, *Royle*, TAMARISCINEÆ. 490

Vern.—*Humbu*, PB., LADAK.

A small bush of the inner western Himalayan regions, extending into Tibet.

The twigs are browsed by sheep and goats.

M. germanica, *Desv.* 491

Vern.—*Ombu*, LAHOUL; *Bis, shalakat kathi*, PB.

A shrub of the inner Himalayan regions from Punjab to Sikkim.

The branches are used to feed sheep and goats.

MYRISTICA.

492 **Myristica moschata**, *Willd.*, MYRISTICEÆ.

THE NUTMEG; MACE.

Syn.—M. OFFICINALIS, *Linn. f.*

Vern.—*Jatiphala*, SANS; *Jaephal, juephal*, HIND.; *Jaia-phula*, BENG.; *Jadicai*, TAM.; *Jajikaia*, TEL.; *Sadikka, jatipullum*, CINGH; *Jaipal* (Nutmeg), *jati, jauntari* (Mace), HIND.

This tree of 20 to 25 feet in height, with aromatic leaves and peach-like fruit, is cultivated in many parts of India, though at one time the culture of nutmegs was almost entirely in the hands of the Dutch, who tried to monopolise its trade and cultivation.

The kernel of the seed is the spice known as the Nutmeg and Mace of commerce.

NASTURTIUM.

493 **Nasturtium indicum**, *DC.*, CRUCIFERÆ.

Common throughout India, chiefly in damp places. **N. Bengalense**, *DC.*, seems a variety of this.

The stems and leaves of the various species possess more or less of an acrid flavour, causing when eaten "a convulsed nose," *nasus tortus*, hence the name.

494 **N. officinale**, *Br.*

THE COMMON WATER-CRESS.

Vern.—*Halim*, BENG., HIND.

Found in the Punjab, Rohilkhand, and near all the hill stations. Cultivated in gardens in Bengal during the cold weather, to be used by the European population as salad.

Atkinson mentions this among his foods.

495 **N. montanum**, *Wall.*

Found along the outer and warmer Himalayan regions, also in Khási hills and Burma.

496 **N. palustre**, *DC.*

Abundant in the temperate Himalayas and North-West India; met with in Bengal and Assam, but rare.

Nauclea Cadamba, *Roxb.* *See* **Anthocephalus Cadamba**, *Miq.*, RUBIACEÆ.

NELUMBIUM.

497 **Nelumbium speciosum**, *Willd.*, NYMPHÆACEÆ.

SACRED, PYTHAGOREAN or EGYPTIAN BEAN or LOTUS.

Vern.—*Kanwal, kanval*, HIND.; *Padma*, BENG.; *Kanwal, pamposh, kanwal, kakri*, PB.; *Ambal*, TAM.

A large, broad-leaved herb of the Water Lily family, found throughout the plains of India and in Kashmir, in tanks and sweet water lakes. Produces large, magnificent flowers, bright magenta or white, during the hot season, and ripens its seed about the close of the rains.

The tender farinaceous roots or rhizomes between the joints are eaten by the natives. In Kashmir and parts of the Punjab, **Dr. Stewart** says, the roots are dug out in October when the leaves dry up, are then sliced and used cooked or pickled. The stalks are eaten as a vegetable. The seeds, which consist of oblong nuts twice the size of peas, are, when perfectly ripe, so hard as to require a hammer to break them, and are eaten by the natives either raw, roasted, or boiled.

Herodotus (B. C. 413) says that its kernels were eaten on the banks of the Nile, "either tender or dried." It was then regarded as sacred in Egypt, and it is still so regarded in India. Its fibres are used as wicks to burn at idol worship, and its leaves as plates on which the offerings are placed. Of all flowers the Hindus and Buddhists regard the "wasp-nest" like flower of the Sacred Lotus, as Herodotus described it, the most beautiful, and they never tire of its praise.

NEPHELIUM.

Nephelium Litchi, *Camb.*, SAPINDACEÆ.

THE LITCHI. 498

Vern.—*Lichi*, BENG., HIND.

A tree introduced from South China into Bengal, now common in this province and north-westwards in Behar, and other parts of India, chiefly in gardens.

Cultivated for its delicious, round, red or chocolate brown fruit, with its thin brittle shell, and wart-like protuberances, filled with its sweet, white, almost transparent, jelly-like pulp, which encloses a large, shining brown seed.

The edible pulp has a delicious sub-acid flavour when fresh. In its preserved state it is exported from China and sold in the London shops. In Bengal it ripens in the hot season, and is eaten by all classes, both Native and European.

N. Longana, *Camb.* 499

THE LONGAN.

Vern.—*Ashphal*, BENG.; *Poovati*, TAM.; *Puné*, COURTALLUM; *Wumb*, BOM.; *Mul ahcotá*, KAN.; *Kyetmouk*, BURM.; *Morre*, CINGH.

A moderate-sized, evergreen tree of Mysore, Western Gháts, and Burma. It is also found in China, where it is called *Longan*.

The fruit of this species is smaller than that of the above, being only about half an inch to an inch in diameter, while **N. Litchi** is an inch and a half. Its pulp, which is also edible, resembles that of the *Litchi* in flavour.

NEPHRODIUM.

Nephrodium eriocarpum, FILICES. 500

Grows in the Punjab Himalaya.

Commonly eaten in spring by the natives of Kumaun.

NIGELLA.

Nigella sativa, *Linn*, RANUNCULACEÆ. 501

BLACK CUMIN SEED.

Vern.—*Kálejira, kálongi*, BOM., HIND.; *Kalajira, mugrela*, BENG.; *Carinsiragum*, TAM.; *Nulla-gilakara*, TEL.

This is supposed to be the Fitches of Isaiah, and is a native of South

Europe, the Levant, &c. It is an annual, growing a foot or more in height, with white or light blue flowers, and a five-celled capsule containing numerous black seeds.

Extensively cultivated. The seeds have a strong, pungent, fennel-like odour, and an aromatic, acrid, oily taste. Hence they are used as a spice in curries and other Indian dishes; much liked by natives, commonly used in cooking meat, and spread over cakes like comfits. Placed among linen they are supposed, by the natives, to keep away insects.

NIPA.

502 **Nipa fruticans,** *Wurmb.*, PALMÆ.

Vern.—*Gólgá, gabna*, BENG.; *Da-ne*, BURM.; *Poothadah*, AND.; *Golphal* (fruits), BENG.

A soboliferous palm of the river estuaries and tidal forests of the Sundarbans, Chittagong, Burma, and the Andamans.

The inside of the large fruit is, when young, edible; a toddy is obtained from the spathe. (*Gamble.*)

NUSSIESSYA.

Nussiessya hypoleuca, *Wedd.* *See* **Bœhmeria Salicifolia,** *D. Don.*, URTICACEÆ.

NYMPHÆA.

503 **Nymphæa alba,** *Linn.*, NYMPHÆACEÆ.

THE LOTUS, OR WHITE WATER LILY.

Vern.—*Nilofar, brim-posh, kamud-bij* (seeds), PB., KASHMIR.

A large herb of the Kashmir lake.

The root and seeds are eaten in times of scarcity.

The root-stocks contain a large quantity of starch, and are used in France in the preparation of a kind of beer.

504 **N. Lotus,** *Linn.*

THE WHITE OTUS OF THE NILE.

Syn.—N. EDULIS, *DC.*; N. RUBRA, *Roxb.*

Vern.—*Sháluk*, BENG.; *Koi*, HIND.; *Kumuda*, SANS.; *Tella-kalwa*, TEL.

This plant has white flowers tinted with pink and strongly-toothed leaves; and is common throughout the plains of India, in pools, &c., of fresh water. This is the herb of which Moore in his 'Paradise and the Peri' sings:—

Those virgin lilies, all the night
  Bathing their beauties in the lake
That they may rise more fresh and bright
  When their beloved sun's awake.

The roots are collected in the dry season, and are made into curries and other dishes. The seeds are also edible. (*Amsterd. Cat.*)

Nymphæa stellata, *Willd.* 505

Var.—CYANEA, *H. f. & T. l.c.*; PARVIFLORA., *H. f. & T. l.c.*; VERSICOLOR, *H. f. & T. l.c.*

Vern.—*Nilsáphalá*, BENG.; *Nilotpala*, SANS.

Common throughout the warmer parts of India.

The roots and seeds are sometimes eaten by the people, especially in times of scarcity.

OCHROCARPUS.

Ochrocarpus Longifolius, *Benth. & Hook.*, GUTTIFERÆ. 506

Syn.—CALYSACCION LONGIFOLIUM, *Wight.*, CALOPHYLLUM LONGIFOLIUM, *Wall.*

Vern.—*Suringi*, MAR.; *Sara-ponna*, TEL.; *Serraya*, MAL.

Found in the forests of the Western Peninsula from Kanara to the Konkan.

The fruit is delicious to the taste. (*Drury.*)

OCIMUM.

Ocimum Basilicum, *Linn.*, LABIATÆ. 507

THE SWEET OR COMMON BASIL.

Syn.—O. PILOSUM, *Willd.*

Vern.—*Babui tulsi*, BENG., HIND.; *Salsat*, DEC.; *Tirunitrup-pattri*, TAM.; *Vibudi-patri*, TEL.

This small, herbaceous shrub of the Mint family is found in almost all parts of India, Java, &c. It is of erect growth, and of about a foot in height, much branched and furnished with very small flowers arranged in clustered whorls.

The seeds are cooling and said to be very nourishing. They are sometimes steeped in water and eaten. The plant has a strong, aromatic flavour, like that of cloves, and is often used for culinary purposes, for seasoning of soups, stews, sauces, &c.

O. sanctum, *Linn.*

Birdwood makes mention of this in his list of *Condiments and Spices*, but says nothing about its use.

There are two forms of this plant, which will be recognisable as met with in cultivation, owing chiefly to the difference in colour of leaf; they scarcely deserve to be regarded as varieties :—

Var. *1st*—**sanctum proper.** 508

THE SACRED TULSI OR TULASI OF THE HINDUS.

Vern.—*Kala* or *krishna túlsi*, HIND., BENG., and TEL.; *Tulasa*, BOM.; *Babúri*, PB.

This, the most sacred plant of the Hindus, is found in or near almost every Hindu house throughout the country. Its cultivation and worship are most intimately associated with the worship of Vishnu, the second person in the Hindu triad. It is a hairy-stemmed plant, nearly two feet in height, with small flowers of a purplish hue. It is profusely branched; and the *branches* also clothed with dark purple hairs; *leaves* about 1½ inches long and 1 inch broad, dark-coloured; *bracts* cordate. It is generally cultivated in pots or broken *jallahs*, or in brick or earthen pillars, hollow at the top, in which earth is deposited, and the plant grows.

509 **Var. 2nd—villosum, Sp.**, *Roxb.*

Vern.—*Túlsi* or *túlasi*, HIND. & BENG.

A small herb, clothed with white or pale green hairs; *leaves* ovate, oblong, crenate, serrate, obtuse; from 1 to 2 inches long; *bracts* reniform.

These varieties of **O. Sanctum**, like **O. Basilicum**, are also used for culinary purposes, as having the same aromatic flavour.

ODINA.

510 **Odina Wodier**, *Roxb.*, ANACARDIACEÆ.

Vern.—*Kiamil, kimál, kamlai, jhingan, mowen, mohin, ginyan*, HIND.; *Jiyal, lohar-bhadi*, BENG.; *Simati, moya*, BOM.; *Jhingan, jiban. sindan, haralla*, N. W. P.; *Wodier*, TAM.; *Kiakra*, GOND.; *Gumpini, dumpini*, TEL.; *Púnil, shimli*, KAN.; *Nabhay*, BURM.

A moderately sized or large, deciduous tree of the sub-Himalayan tract, from the Indus eastward, ascending to 4,000 feet; found also in the forests of India and Burma.

"The tree is pollarded for fodder especially for elephants." (*Gamble.*)

OLAX.

511 **Olax scandens**, *Roxb.*, OLACINEÆ.

Vern.—*Dheniani*, HIND.; *Koko-aru*, BENG.; *Kurpodur*, TEL.; *Harduli*, MAR.; *Lailoo*, BURM.

A large, rambling shrub, sometimes a climber, of the sub-Himalayan tract, in Kumaun, Behar, Central and South India, Burma.

The fruit is used in Hazaribagh for making sherbet. (*Gamble.*)

OLEA.

512 **Olea Cuspidata**, *Royle*, OLEACEÆ.

Syn.—O. FERRUGINEA, *Royle.*

Vern.—*Kau*, HIND.; *Khwan, shwan*, TRANS-INDUS; *Zaitún*, AFG.; *Ko, kohú, kao, kau*, PB.; *Khau*, SIND.

A moderately sized, deciduous tree of the Sind, Sulaiman and Salt Ranges, and North West Himalaya, extending as far as the Jumna eastward, and ascending to 6,000 feet. (*Gamble.*)

The fruit ripens in October, and is sometimes eaten by the natives. The leaves are given to goats as fodder.

513 **O. europœa**, *Linn.*

THE OLIVE.

This valuable plant, the cream and butter of those countries in which it is pressed, has been introduced on the Himalaya and the Nilgiris. It has more recently been cultivated with some success in the Bhadgaon farm in Khandesh.

It only requires to be better known to be largely appreciated and cultivated by the people of India; and, though called **Europæa**, it is well-known to be a native of Western Asia.

The small, white flowers of the plant are succeeded by an oblong, berry-like fruit of a bluish-black color. The valuable oil known as Olive oil, Salad or Florence oil, is obtained by pressing the pulp of this fruit. This is the "pure oil" of which king Solomon gave "twenty measures" to Hiram, King of Tyre; and this is the tree which gave its name to the well-known "Mount of Olives." The oil is principally used as food. The Olive groves of Persia are said to yield 100,000 cwts. of fruit a year.

OPLISMENUS.

Oplismenus Burmanni, *Linn.*, GRAMINEÆ. 514

Syn.—O. BROMOIDES, *Boj.*; PANICUM BURMANNI, *Retz.*; P. HIRTELLUM, *Burm.*

This grass extends from Oudh and Banda to Saharunpore and the Jhelum valley.

Occurs on pasture ground under the shade of large trees.

O. colonus, *Kunth. See* **Panicum colonum,** *Linn.*

O. compositus, *R. & S.* 515

Syn.—PANICUM COMPOSITUM, *Linn.*; P. SYLVATICUM, *Lam.*

Found in the Himalaya at Simla, Kumaun, Mussourie, and at Dehra Dun at the foot of the Mussourie Hills.

Roxburgh, under **Panicum lanceolatum,** describes this grass, and says that it grows under the shade of trees.

O. frumentaceus, *Roxb. See* **Panicum frumentaceum,** *Roxb.*

ORIGANUM.

Origanum heracleoticum, LABIATÆ. 516

WINTER MARJORAM.

This plant, of the genus **Origanum,** so called from the *gay* (*ganos*, joy) appearance of the *hills* (*Oros*, mountain) on which it grows, is a native of Northern India.

It is cultivated as a pot-herb.

O. Marjorana, *Linn.* 517

SWEET MARJORAM.

Vern.—*Murwa*, DEC., SIND.; *Murroo*, TAM.; *Misunjoosh, mardakusch*, ARAB.

A common, wild plant in Kumaun, cultivated in gardens throughout India, especially in South India, for its seeds.

It is a seasoning herb. **Birdwood** mentions it in the list of *Condiments and Spices.*

O. normale, *Don.* 518

Vern.—*Mirsanjosh*, PB.

Common in the Punjab Himalaya at altitudes between 2,500 and 10,500 feet.

In Lahoul it is eaten as a pot-herb.

ORTHANTHERA.

Orthanthera viminea, *Wight.*, ASCLEPIADEÆ. 519

Syn.—APOCYNEA VIMINEA, *Wall.*; LEPTADENIA VIMINEA, *Bth.*, *Hook.* In the *Genera Plantarum* the genus **Orthanthera** has been reduced to **Leptadenia,** but **J. D. Hooker,** in the *Flora of British India*, takes a different view of the subject, and says "the long sepals and salver-shaped corolla are such strong generic characters that I do not follow the *Genera Plantarum* in uniting this genus with **Leptadenia.**"

Vern.—*Mowa, lancbar*, TRANS-INDUS; *Matti*, BEAS; *Khip*, DELHI; *Kip*, SIND.; *Chaphia*, KUMAUN; *Mahur*, HIND.

A glabrous shrub of the arid and northern dry region from Sind to Oudh.

The flower buds are eaten as a vegetable by the natives.

ORYZA.

ORYZA.

520 **Oryza sativa**, *Linn.*, GRAMINEÆ.

THE RICE, *Eng.*; ORUZA, *Greek*; AROZ, *Lat.*, *Por.*, and *Sp.*; RIZ, *Fr.*; REIZ, *Ger.*; RYST, *Dutch*.

Vern.—*Dhan* (unhusked), *chāwal* (husked), *bhat* (boiled), HIND., BENG.; *Baranj*, PERS.; *Arus*, ARAB.; *Vrihi*, SANS.; *Arisi*, TAM.; *Bras, padi*, MALAY; *Motsj*, JAPAN; *Tan*. CHIN.

The rice has developed into numerous varieties throughout the many countries in which its cultivation has extended. In India alone there are supposed to be over 5,000 varieties and sub-varieties; but they do not possess any very marked peculiarities, except such as are due to difference in climate, soil, and mode of cultivation. Curiously enough some of the forms possess two and others three grains within the pericarp, thus showing a tendency to revert to what must be presumed the ancestral type.

The total area under rice cultivation in India may be estimated at about 60,000,000 acres, of which Bengal owns about 37½ million acres, Madras 6¼ millions, North-Western Provinces and Oudh 4¾ millions, Central Provinces 4½ millions, British Burma 2½ millions, Bombay a little over 2 millions; in the other Provinces (Punjab, Assam, Berar) and in the Native States of Mysore and Hyderabad the area is less, aggregating somewhat less than 3 million acres.

The weight of straw is from ⅓ to ½ as much again as that of the grain; the straw is used for thatching, for cattle fodder, and more recently for paper-making.

The times for sowing and harvesting are many: the sowing being carried on in all months from January to July. The suitable soil is a stiff clay. The seed is sown either broad-cast or in nurseries and transplanted; as a rule the finer kinds of rice are raised according to the latter method. A good deal of moisture is in any case necessary. The harvest takes place in the period from May to November.

Rice is eaten chiefly boiled and sometimes parched by the natives. They also prepare cakes of several kinds from the rice-flour.

The out-turn of rice per acre varies according to natural climatic conditions and method of cultivation, and ranges, according to **Mr. Liotard**, between 25 maunds in the best rice tracts of the Sundarbans and British Burma and about 20 maunds in average districts of Bengal, and about 14 maunds in the Central Provinces; while in the North-Western Provinces and Oudh, **Mr. Fuller** estimates the yield at from 10 to 12 and 16 maunds. These out-turns are of *unhusked* rice, and must be reduced by about 25 per cent. to arrive at the weight of husked grain.

The following table shows the exports of rice from India during the last five years:—

	1878-79.	1879-80.	1880-81.	1881-82.	1882-83.
	Cwts.	Cwts.	Cwts.	Cwts.	Cwts.
Unhusked rice . . .	615,521	257,720	496,696	368,999	228,567
Husked rice . . .	20,621,712	21,908,045	26,769,344	28,519,422	31,029,721
Rice-flour . . .	2,554	1,478	6,140	500	1,579

The exports are subject to a duty of 3 annas per Indian maund.

Analysis of the exportation of unhusked rice from British India for the year 1882-83:—

Whence exported.	Quantity in Cwts.	Value in Rs.	To what countries exported	Quantity in Cwts.	Value in Rs.
Bengal . .	7,837,818	221,36,834	United Kingdom	12,381,486	321,13,987
Bombay . .	552,525	20,94,047	Straits Settlements	4,092,521	121,01,949
Sindh . .	71,473	1,93,862	Ceylon . .	2,883,534	80,81,726
Madras . .	1,318,967	37,77,317	Egypt . .	2,973,703	78,54,124
British Burma .	21,248,938	561,98,849	Malta . .	2,732,442	67,51,080
			Arabia . .	832,574	26,49,924
			South America .	786,557	24,47,338
			Mauritius . .	1,227,671	31,78,668
			France . .	605,735	14,02,839
			Réunion . .	521,563	15,95,607
TOTAL .	31,029,721	844,00,909	TOTAL .	31,029,721	844,00,909

OSMANTHUS.

Osmanthus fragrans, *Lour.*, OLEACEÆ. 521

Vern.—*Shilling, silang*, KUMAUN; *Tungrung*, LEPCHA.

A small tree of the Himalaya, from Kumaun to Bhutan, sometimes gregarious, but more often planted for the sake of its sweet-scented flowers. The flowers are used in China to flavour tea. (*Gamble*).

Osphromenus olfax. 522

OSTRYA.

Ostrya edulis. 523

THE HOP HORNBEAM.

The fruit is a small-bearded, one-seeded nut.

OUGEINIA.

Ougeinia dalbergioides, *Benth.*, LEGUMINOSÆ. 524

Vern.—*Sándan, asainda, tinnas*, HIND.; *Shánjan, pánan*, OUDH; *Bandhona*, URIYA; *Dargu, tella, motku*, TEL.; *Telus*, KHANDESH.

Grows in the sub-Himalayan tract, from the Sutlej to the Teesta, in Central India, and on the West Coast.

The leaves appear after the blossoms, and are in summer given as fodder to cattle, for which purpose the branches are lopped off.

OVIS.

Ovis aries. 525

OXALIS.

526 **Oxalis corniculata,** *Linn.*, GERANIACEÆ.

Vern.—*Amrool,* HIND.; *Surchi, khatta-mitha, chukha,* PB.; *Pooliarai,* TAM.; *Pulichinta,* TEL.; *Umbuti,* DUK.

A weed abundant in cultivated places throughout the warmer regions of India and Ceylon, and up to 7,000 feet in the Himalaya.

In some parts of the country it is eaten raw and cooked as a pot-herb.

OXYBAPHUS.

527 **Oxybaphus Himalaicus,** *Edge.*, NYCTAGINEÆ.

Vern.—*Pumae, baus,* PB.

A scrambling herbaceous plant, with a large carrot-like root, was found by **Edgeworth** and subsequently by **Dr. Stewart** in the northern tracts of the Punjab.

It is collected by the natives for winter fodder.

OXYRIA.

528 **Oxyria reniformis,** *Hook.*, POLYGONACEÆ.

Vern.—*Amlu,* PB.

This small, acid plant is common in the higher regions of the Punjab Himalaya, and in Tibet.

Sometimes eaten raw and in *chatni,* in Chamba for instance; and is said to have a pleasant sorrel taste.

OXYSTELMA.

529 **Oxystelma esculentum,** *Br.*, ASCLEPIADEÆ.

Syn.—PERIPLOCA ESCULENTA, *Linn.*; ASCLEPIAS ROSEA, *Roxb.*

Vern.—*Kirui, doodhi, doodh-luta,* BENG.; *Dooghdika,* SANS.; *Doodi-palla,* or *ourū palay,* TEL.; *Gharot, gani,* PB.

A slender, glabrous climber, is met with throughout the plains and lower hills of India,—**Roxburgh** says in hedges and bushes on the banks of water courses, pools, &c.; **Dr. Stewart** says in arid tracts.

It produces a fruit which is eaten in some parts of the country. Cattle eat the plant.

OXYTROPIS.

530 **Oxytropis microphylla,** *DC.*, LEGUMINOSÆ.

A stemless herb of Sikkim and also of the West Himalaya, at altitudes between 11,000 and 16,000 feet.

Browsed by sheep.

PACHYRHIZUS.

531 **Pachyrhizus angulatus,** *Rich.*, LEGUMINOSÆ.

YAKA OR WAYAKA.

Syn.—DOLICHOS BULBOSUS, *Linn.*

A wide, climbing herb, cultivated in many parts of India for its large, tuberous root, or rather underground stem, which is 6 to 8 feet in length, and as thick as a man's thigh, and which resembles a turnip in taste and consistence, and is eaten both raw and boiled. In its cooked state it has a dirty white colour and insipid flavour; but palatable enough in times of scarcity.

PANDANUS.

Pandanus odoratissimus, *Willd.*, PANDANEÆ. 532

Vern.—*Keura,* HIND.; *Keá,* BENG.; *Ketaki,* SANS.; *Thalay, talum,* TAM.; *Mugalik,* TEL.; *Kaida, thala,* MAL.; *Mudu-kaiyeya,* CINGH.; *Tsat-tha-pu,* BURM.

A common, much-branched shrub, frequently planted on account of the powerful fragrance of the flowers, but wild on the coasts of North India, Burma, and the Andamans.

The floral leaves are eaten either raw or boiled. The lower pulpy part of the drupes is eaten by the natives in times of scarcity. The flowers together, with catechu and certain spices, form a substance known as *Keá Khoir,* which is used in *pán.*

PANICUM.

Panicum antidotale, *Retz.*, GRAMINEÆ. 533

Syn.—P. ULIGINOSUM, *Roxb.* ?

Vern.—*Gamur, ghamor,* N. W. P.; *Garm, girui, mangrur,* PB.

A tall grass, common in the Gangetic plain, also on the plains of the Punjab, in the Salt Range, and in Sindh.

Some think this good forage for cattle, others consider it bitter and not liked by cattle. **Mr. Duthie,** however, notes that at Aligarh and at Muttra is eaten by cattle.

P. brizoides, *Linn.* 534

Syn.—P. FLAVIDUM, *Linn.*; P. FLACIDUM.

Vern.—*Oda, udu-gadi,* TEL.

A grass common in every soil and situation. Grows in tufts; parts of it are often tinged with purple.

P. colonum, *Linn.* 535

Syn.—OPLISMENUS COLONUS, *Kunth.*; ECHINOCHLOA COLONNA, *Kunth.*

Vern.—*Shama,* BENG.; *Sarwak, jangli sawank, shamak,* N. W. P.

Abundant throughout the plains, especially in cultivated soil (*Messrs. Duthie and Fuller*) and rich pasture grounds.

One of the best grasses for forage (*Stewart*); cattle are fond of it.

P. crus-galli, *Linn.* 536

Syn.—P. STAGNINUM, *Linn.*; P. HISPIDULUM, *Roxb.*; P. TOMENTOSUM, *Roxb.*

Vern.—*Dhand, jal-sawank,* N. W. P.

Found on the plains, and ascends to 6,000 feet in the Himalaya.

It is a coarse species of grass which grows wild; cattle are not fond of it. The seeds are collected by the poorer classes of natives who use them as an article of diet.

P. fimbriatum, *Kunth.* 537

Syn.—DIGITARIA FIMBRIATA, *Link.*; CORODOCHLOA FIMBRIATA, *Nees.*; PASPALUM DISTANS, *Nees.*

Found in Moradabad and the Punjab (*Duthie quoting T. T. & Jacq.*).

PANICUM.

538 **Panicum fluitans,** *Roxb.*

Found in the Punjab and Sindh on banks of water-courses, borders of rice-fields, and other moist, rich soil.

539 **P. frumentaceum,** *Roxb.*

SHAMOOLA.

Syn.—OPLISMENUS FRUMENTACEUS, *Link.*

Vern.—*Damra-shama,* BENG.; *Sawan, sanwan, sawan-bhadeka, sama* or *samei,* N. W. P. and OUDH.; *Mandira, jhangora,* KUMAUN and GARHWAL; *Karni,* KASHMIR; *Shyamaka,* SANS.; *Bonta-shama, shamaloo* (the seed), TELING.

The quickest growing of all the millets. It has a special utility to the poorer classes in affording, by its early ripening, a supply of cheap grain before the main autumn food crop is harvested. It is, however, liable to damage from excessive rain and blight. The soil best suited to it is described by **Roxburgh** as light, tolerably dry and rich. The grain is wholesome and nourishing, and is a favourite one for home consumption amongst the poorer classes.

In the North West Provinces it is sown in light soils in the middle of June, usually with juar; the quantity of seed sown is 10 lbs. to the acre; the area covered is about 76,000 acres; the crop is cut at the end of August, and the yield ranges from 4 maunds of grain per acre on poor soils, to from 8 to 10 maunds in fairly good soil. The stalks are used as fodder for cattle.

" In a season of drought, when the usual summer rains fail, the cultivation of the *Sawan,* or *shama,* on a larger scale than usual, should be resorted to (in the same way as carrots were tried with success in the North-West Provinces in 1878), as it will, with little irrigation on any light soil, afford a harvest within six weeks from the date of sowing. (*Mr. L. Liotard.*)

540 **P. helopus,** *Trin.*

Syn.—P. JOWANICUM, *Poir.*; P. KOENIGII, *Spreng.*; UROCHLOA PUBESCENS, *Kunth.*

Vern.—*Basaunta,* N. W. P.

Found on the plains and the Himalaya up to 5,500 feet in Kumaun.

Considered a good fodder grass in Dehra Dun. (*J. F. D. quoted by Duthie.*)

541 **Var.—hirsutum, sp.,** *Koen.*

Syn.—P. SETIZERUM, *Royle.*

Vern.—*Kuni, kuru,* or *chirkal,* N. W. P.

Found in parts of the North West Provinces and the Punjab close to the Himalaya.

Considered by **Muller** and **Royle** to be a good fodder grass, and said by the latter to produce a grain which is eaten.

542 **P. hydaspicum,** *Edgew.*

Found in the Punjab.

The seeds are said to be eaten by the poor people in Multan.

P. italicum, *Linn.* *See* **Setaria italica,** *Beauv.*

543 **P. jumentosum,** *Pers.*

GUINEA GRASS.

Syn.—P. MAXIMUM, *Jacq.*

A perennial grass, native of tropical Africa. Needs very little care

PANICUM.

after being once planted, and is an excellent fodder grass. It has been highly recommended for cultivation in parts of India.

Panicum miliaceum, *Linn.* 544

VERAGOO, WARREE, CHENA OF INDIAN MILLET.

Syn.—P. MILIUM, *Pers.*; P. ASPERRIMUM, *Lag.*

Vern.—*Cheena*, HIND., BENG.; *Chehna, chinwa, chirwa, sawan-chaltwa, sawan-jethwa, kuri, phikar, rali, bansi*, N. W. P.; *Chinan, arsan*, PB.; *Dukhun*, ARAB.; *Arsan*, PERS.; *Unoo, vreehib-heda*, SANS.; *Varagu*, S. IND.; *Worga, worglo* (the grain), TELING.

Considered a native of Egypt or Arabia (*DC.*), introduced at a very early period into India (*Duthie*); and now extensively cultivated in India, generally on elevated, light, rich soil. In the Himalaya it ascends 10,000 feet in altitude. It is, however, inferior to **P. italicum**, and fetches a lower price in the bazars. Besides, it is slow growing, thus occupying the soil for a long time. In some places the grain is consumed mostly unground.

The season for cultivation is stated by **Roxburgh** to be immediately after the rains; this would take the crop into the cold weather, and coincides with **Dr. Royle**, who says it is grown in winter. **Messrs. Duthie** and **Fuller**, however, say it is grown in the North West Provinces in April to May under irrigation from wells, and that it is a precarious crop liable to damage from the hot winds. The area thus cultivated in the North West Provinces is reported to be about 12,400 acres; the quantity of seed sown is 10 lbs. to the acre, and the average yield is given at from 6 to 8 maunds of grain per acre.

In the Deccan it is sown by hand in June or July and is sometimes transplanted, weeded in August-September, and reaped in November-December.

In the Punjab the crop is grown mostly in the northern districts.

The straw is of no use as fodder, and is thrown on the manure heap, or used as bedding.

P. miliare, *Lamb.* 545

SHAMAY.

Vern.—*Kutki*, HIND.; *Nella-shama, nella-shamaloo* (the grain).

Known usually in Bengal as the little millet; is a native of India, but is not extensively cultivated. Cultivated in the Punjab up to the Kheree Pass, also in Nepal and Central India.

"One of the sorts of dry or small grain which is generally cultivated on an elevated, light, rich soil. The seed is an article of diet with those Hindus who inhabit the higher lands. Cattle are fond of the straw." (*Roxb.*)

P. neurodes, *Schult.* 546

Syn.—P. NERVOSUM, *Roxb.*; P. NEPALENSE, *Spreng.*

Found in the Jumna valley in wet ground; also in Saharunpore. (*J. F. D. and Royle, quoted by Duthie.*)

P. paludosum, *Roxb.* 547

Syn.—P. NATANS, *Koen.*

Vern.—*Barethi, kalasnar*, BENG.

Found in western parts of the North West Provinces; bears a resemblance to **P. uliginosum** (*Roxb.*).

It is a coarse grass; cattle are not fond of it; and it becomes much smaller on dry ground. (*Roxb.*)

548 **Panicum plicatum**, *Roxb.*

Syn.—P. NERVOSUM, *Roxb.*; P. NEPALENSE, *Spreng.*; P. ASPERATUM, *Kunth.*

Found in Nepal and sub-Himalayan tract of the North West Provinces.

It is of too coarse a nature for cattle, but its foliage makes it ornamental. (*Roxb.*)

549 **P. prostratum**, *Lamb.*

Syn.—P. PROCUMBENS, *Nees.*; P. SETIGERUM, *Retz.*; P. REPENS, *Burm.*; P. CÆSPITORUM, *Swartz.*

Inhabits the plains of the Punjab and the North West Provinces.

Mueller recommends it for pasture.

550 **P. psilopodium**, *Trin.*

Syn.—P. ROYLEANUM, *Nees.*

Vern.—*Kutki, mijhri*, N. W. P.

A millet found in Central and Northern India, ascending the Himalaya to 6,000 feet, towards Kumaun and Mussourie.

Common in the Central Provinces, and is grown there in very poor soil. In the North West Provinces also it is grown on the poorest village lands, but the cultivation is very limited. In Bundelkhand the area cultivated with *kutki* is reported to be 16,849 acres. The season for cultivation is from June to October.

551 **P. repens**, *Linn.*

Syn.—P. ISCHÆMOIDES, *Retz.*

Found in Oudh and the Punjab.

A pretty, perennial grass on river banks and in swampy places.

Cattle are fond of it, and the Cinghalese regard it as a good fodder grass.

552 **P. sanguinale**, *Linn.*

Syn.—PASPALUM SANGUINALE, *DC.*; SYNTHERISMA VULGARE, *Schrad.*

Vern.—*Mothi-kabbal, takri*, and *farw*, PB.; *Kewai*, N. W. P.

Mr. Duthie says this grss is very common on the plains, and on the hills. Dr. Stewart considers it to be one of the best fodder grasses.

553 Var. **ciliare**, *Retz.* sp.

Syn.—PASPALUM CILIARE, *DC.*

Vern.—*Makur-jali, thakhriya, tikhria, kewai*, N. W. P.

Found on the plains of the North West Provinces and the Punjab, also in Nepal; delights most in newly laid-down pasture ground.

Cattle are very fond of this grass.

554 **P. semialatum**, *R.Br.*

A superior tall grass of easy dispersion in warm, humid localities. (*Mueller.*) Inhabits the Himalaya in Kumaun from 3,000 to 6,000 feet, also in Nepal.

PAPAVER.

555 **Papaver somniferum**, *Linn.*, PAPAVERACEÆ.

THE WHITE POPPY; OPIUM.

Vern.—*Post, apim, aphing*, BENG., HIND.; *Khash-khash-ka-post*, DEC.; *Gasa-gasa-tol*, TAM.; *Gasa-gasa-tolu*, TEL.

Extensively cultivated in North and Central India.

The seeds are, in Upper India, sometimes put into sweet cakes which are eaten by the higher ranks of Hindus at their festivals. Mr. Bingham says that "the seed has no narcotic qualities, but has a sweet taste, and is used parched by the lower class of natives as a food;" and that "it is also much used by the sweetmeat makers as an addition in their wares." After the oil is extracted, "the cake is sold as a food to the poorer classes." The oil is used as Salad oil for cooking purposes. The seed is the *maw* seed given to cage-birds.

Paritium tiliaceum. *W. & A. See* **Hibiscus tiliaceus.** *Linn.*, MALVACEÆ.

PARKINSONIA.

Parkinsonia aculeata, *Linn.*, LEGUMINOSÆ. 556

THE JERUSALEM THORN.

Vern.—*Vilaiati kikkar*, PB.

An introduced shrub, or small tree, now almost naturalised in India, especially in the arid zones, where it is grown as a hedge plant. (*Gamble.*)

In the Punjab it is lopped of its smaller branches which are given to goats as fodder.

PASPALUM.

Paspalum scrobiculatum, *Linn.*, GRAMINEÆ. 557

MILLET KHODA.

Vern.—*Koda-ka-choul*, HIND.; *Kodon, koda, kodram, marsi*, N. W. P. and OUDH; *Kodon, kodra*, PB.; *Koda*, BENG.; *Korudoosha, kodruva*, SANS.; *Arugu*, TELING.

A native of India. Cultivated by the natives in many parts of India. It delights in a light, dry, loose soil, but will grow in a very barren one; time of cultivation being the rainy season.

In the North West Provinces it is grown chiefly by the lower classes on inferior outlying land; and its cultivation is far more extensive than that of any of the other minor millets, owing to the readiness with which it grows in the poorest soil: the area under *kodon* in the thirty temporarily-settled districts of these provinces is reported to be 213,000 acres: the sowing takes place at the commencement of the rains, at the rate of from 12 and 20 lbs. of seeds per acre, and the crop is cut in October, with a yield of from 10 to 12 maunds of grain per acre, including the chaff, which is of large proportion and difficult of separation.

This common and cheap grain is an article of diet with the poorer classes, particularly those who inhabit the mountains and the more barren parts of the country, but it is not considered wholesome, as it produces diarrhœa. Being a comparatively unprofitable crop, it is not sown where more valuable crops will grow. "A curious fact connected with the grain is its liability to produce a sort of intoxication, which is vouched for by many authorities." (*Duthie.*)

The straw is given as fodder to cattle, and is readily eaten by them, whether green or dry.

Var.—fluitans, *Duthie.* 558

Syn.—P. KORA, *Linn.*

Vern.—*Kodu*, HIND.; *Neer-aruga*, TELING.

This grass is found near water edges, and is considered by Mr. Duthie to be probably the wild state of **P. scrobiculatum.** Roxburgh placed it as a distinct species under **Paspalum.**

Cattle are fond of it, whether green or dry.

Pavia indica. *See* **Æsculus indica,** *Colebr.*, **Sapindaceæ.**

PENTA-TROPIS.

Penicillaria spicata. *See* **Pennisetum typhoideum,** *Rich*, GRAMINEÆ.

PENNISETUM.

559 **Pennisetum cenchroides,** *Rich*, GRAMINEÆ.

Syn.—P. RUFESCENS, *Spreng.*; CENCHRUS CILIARIS, *Linn.*; C. ECHINOIDES' *Wight.*

Vern.—*Angan, dhaman, kurkan,* PB.; *Kusa, charwa,* N. W. P.

Common in the Punjab and North West Provinces on the plains and lower hills.

Described by Dr. Stewart as one of the best of all the wild grasses for forage for cows and horses. In the dry parts round Multan the seeds are used by the natives as food.

560 **P. typhoideum,** *Rich.*

THE BULRUSH, CUMBOO, OF SPIKED MILLET; DEKKELÉ, *Fr.*

Syn.—HOLCUS SPICATUS, *Linn.*; PANICUM SPICATUM, *Roxb.*; PENICILLARIA SPICATA, *Lindl.*; P. CYLINDRICA, *R. & B.*

Vern.—*Bajra, bajri, lahra,* HIND.; *Pedda-ganti* (plant), *gantiloo* (grain), TEL.; *Chambu,* TAM.

A native of tropical Asia, Nubia and Egypt. Cultivated to a large extent in Northern and Southern India during the rainy season: seed sown in June and July brodcast at the rate of 2½ to 3 seers per acre, reaped in September and October and November; and yields about 668 lbs of seed and 3 tons of straw per acre. The grain is used chiefly by the lower classes of natives. It is eaten most in the cold weather as flour and made into *roties* (hand-bread), and occasionally with butter milk. With the usual adjuncts of a little milk, &c., it forms the staple food of many. It is considered heating. But it is more nutritious than rice.

There are two well-marked varieties, one (*bajra*) with greenish, coloured grain, and the other (*bajri*) with reddish grain. (*Duthie.*)

The green chopped stalks and leaves are used as fodder for cattle.

It is much cultivated in the higher lands on the Coromandel Coast.

In the North West Provinces and Oudh the area grown with *bajra* and *bajra-arhar* in the thirty temporarily-settled districts is 1,965,471 acres. It is grown on poor light-soiled outlying land. The cost of cultivation including rent is Rs. 9½ per acre; the out-turn is from 5½ to 7 maunds of grain to the acre, with about 30 maunds of dry fodder. (*Messrs. Duthie and Fuller.*) By the addition of hops a pleasant beer may be made of the decorticated pith.

An export trade exists in this millet to other countries by sea, but the trade returns do not give the figures separately for it but put it under *Juar*, which see.

The fruit spike is thicker than a man's thumb and 6 to 9 inches long in India, being twice as long as that of the African species.

Except Sorghum this is the most cultivated grain in India.

PENTATROPIS.

561 **Pentatropis microphylla,** *Wight & Arn.*, ASCLEPIADEÆ.

This shrub is much like the following in habit and character; inhabits the Sundarbans, the Deccan southwards, and Pegu.

Pentatropis spiralis, *Dcne.* 562

Vern.—*Ambarvel, van-veri,* PB.

A twining, slender shrub found from the Punjab and Sind to the Jumna river eastwards, and to Afghanistan westwards.

In the Punjab the small tubers which grow on its roots in spring are peeled and eaten, and are said to be sweet and filling. (*Dr. Stewart*).

PERILLA.

Perilla ocimoides, *Linn.,* LABIATÆ. 563

Vern.—*Kenia,* NAGA.

Native of Nepal, introduced into parts of Bengal. Also found wild and cultivated in Manipur, where the leaves and seeds are used as articles of food.

PERIPLOCA.

Periploca aphylla, *Decaisne,* ASCLEPIADEÆ. 564

Syn.—CAMPELEPIS VIMINEA, *Falc.*

Vern.—*Buraye,* SIND.; *Barrarra, bane,* TRANS-INDUS; *Battia,* JHELUM and CHENAB.

A shrub of the arid, dry zones of the Punjab and Sind.

In various places in these tracts the buds are eaten by the natives, raw or cooked, as a vegetable: they are said to taste like raisins.

The plant is eaten by goats.

PETROSELINUM.

Petroselinum sativum, *Hoff & Koch,* UMBELLIFERÆ. 565

PARSLEY.

Vern.—*Pitar-saleri,* PB.

A native of Sardinia, wild in many parts of England, and cultivated for the sake of its finely-cut leaves, which are largely used for flavouring dishes.

Dr. Stewart says it is cultivated on the plains of India, but probably only for the European residents.

PEUCEDANUM.

Peucedanum graveolens, *Benth.,* UMBELLIFERÆ. 566

SOWA.

Syn.—ANETHUM SOWA, *R.*

Vern.—*Sulpha,* BENG.; *Sowa,* HIND.

Found throughout tropical and sub-tropical India; often cultivated. (*C. B. Clarke in Fl. Br. Ind.*)

The time of culture is the cold season, and the object of the cultivation is the carminative seed, which is used for culinary and medicinal purposes, and is met with in every market. It is from this seed that the useful Bishop's weed oil is obtained.

The natives commonly use the seed in their curries.

"The leaves also are used in a similar way, in vegetable as well as in meat curries, and give a peculiar flavour to the curry. (*Mr. L. Liotard.*)

PHASEO-LUS.

PHASEOLUS.

567 **Phaseolus aconitifolius,** *Jacq.*, LEGUMINOSÆ.

Vern.—*Moth, mothi,* HIND.; *Mokushtha,* SANS.

Found from the "Himalayas to Ceylon, tropical regions up to 4,000 feet in the North-West." (*Baker in Fl. Br. Ind.*) Closely related to **P. trilobus,** and agreeing with it in flowers and general habits. Cultivated as a hot weather crop in the plains in dry, light, sandy soil.

In the North West Provinces and Oudh it is grown as a sole crop and also among millets; the area under Moth *as a sole crop* is returned at 211,906 acres in the thirty temporarily-settled districts; the seed is sown broad-cast at the rate of 4 seers to the acre; the average out-turn is 8 maunds of grain to the acre, with rather less than double this amount of fodder. (*Messrs. Duthie and Fuller.*)

The grain is used as food by the natives, and is said to cure flatulency, but is not considered wholesome. It is also used as cattle-food, and is considered a fattening diet. The leaves and stalks are also given to cattle.

568 **P. calcaratus,** *Roxb.*

Closely allied to P. MUNGO; P. TOROSUS, *Roxb.*, is probably a cultivated form.

Inhabits all parts of the tropical zone from the Himalayas to Ceylon, and appears both cultivated and wild.

569 **P. lunatus,** *Linn.*

Syn.—P. LUNATUS, *Willd.*; P. VULGARIS, *Wall.*

A tall, biennial plant; legume 2 to 3 inches long, scimitar-shaped, seeds large, variable in colour; like the 'French Bean' in general aspect, but with smaller and more numerous flowers. Its pod is flat and broad with only two or three seeds. Everywhere cultivated.

For cultivated varieties, *see Fl. Br. Ind. II.*, *200.*

570 **P. Mungo,** *Linn.*

Syn.—P. MAX, *Roxb.*; P. AURENS, *Ham.*; P. HIRTUS, *Rets.*

Vern.—*Mug,* BENG.; *Mung,* HIND.; *Mudga,* SANS.; *Pucha-payaroo,* TAM.; *Pessaloo,* TEL.

Cultivated throughout the plains, and ascends to 6,000 feet in the outer ranges of the North West Himalaya. Requires a strong, rich, dry soil; seldom grown alone, but generally as a subordinate crop in fields of millet or cotton; the seeds, at the rate of 12 seers per acre, are sown at the commencement of the rains; and the crop is reaped in October, a fortnight before the millets. The out-turn of grain is stated by **Roxburgh** to be thirty-fold, and by **Messrs. Duthie** and **Fuller** about 5 maunds to the acre (nine-fold): the latter is probably nearer the mark.

The ripe grain has a good taste, is wholesome and nutritious, is much esteemed, and commands a comparatively high price. The crushe dstalks and leaves are prized as fodder for cattle.

It is not, however, possible to give even an approximately correct estimate of the area covered by the crop, owing to the almost invariable practice just noted of growing it as a subordinate crop.

Mr. Fuller writes: "It is in some respects remarkable that it is not more frequently grown alone, since its grain commands a far higher price than that of millet, but this is no doubt partly explained by the precariousness of its growth; heavy and continuous rain, especially in September (when it is in flower) often causing absolute ruin. But as a counterpoise to this it bears, and justly, the reputation of being able to withstand a great deal of drought, and in a season of scanty rainfall, when millets have utterly failed, it, with *urd*, *lobia* and *moth*, forms a most valuable food resource, the so-called 'subordinate' crop becoming in this case of first-rate importance. Another advantage which these pulses share with *arhar* is that of not impoverishing the soil, or at all events not to the extent of gramineous crops such as the millets."

Var. radiatus. *Linn.* 571

Syn.—P. ROXBURGHII, *W. & A.*

Vern.—*Mash-kolai*, BENG.; *Urd, mash*, HIND.; *Masha*, SANS.; *Mimumulee*, TEL.

This variety differs from **P. Mungo** in having longer and more trailing stems, in the plant being much more hairy, the reddish brown pubescens giving the foliage a lighter tint; in the seeds being fewer, larger and longer, and usually of a dark-brown colour (*Duthie and Fuller*).

Urd itself (**radiatus**) has two distinct sub-varieties, one with large black seeds ripening in August and September, and the other with smaller green seeds ripening in October and November. Both are, however, sown at the commencement of the rains: the soils which suit the crop are of the heavier classes.

It is cultivated in most parts of the plains. In the North West Provinces and Oudh it is grown everywhere, generally as a subordinate crop with millet or cotton, but sometimes by itself; the area covered annually by *urd* alone is returned at about 258,495 acres in the 30 temporarily-settled districts, and if the area be added in which it is sown as a subordinate crop, the total would be twelve times as large as this for the 30 districts. The rate of seed sown is 4 to 6 seers per acre when grown alone; and the out-turn in this case is estimated at 5 maunds of grain to the acre, with three times this weight of straw; when grown with other crops the out-turn varies considerably, owing to the absence of any definite proportion (*Duthie and Fuller*).

Phaseolus trilobus, *Ait.* 572

Syn.—DOLICHOS TRILOBATUS, *Linn.*

Vern.—*Mugani*, BENG.

Ranges throughout India, wild and commonly cultivated; ascends in the North West to 7,000 feet.

Seeds gathered and eaten by the poor.

Affords good fodder. (*Voigt.*)

P. vulgaris, *Linn.* 573

KIDNEY OR FRENCH BEANS, OR HARICOT.

Syn.—P. VULGARIS, *Willd.*; P. NANUS, *Linn.*

Cultivated, for the sake of its young pods, in all parts of India, chiefly in gardens. The green pod and its immature beans are cut up into slices, boiled, and eaten.

Stems low or suberect, twining; legumes 4 to 6 inches long.

Drs. Birch and Russel, in the *Indian Review*, strongly recommend as a tropical food "French Beans," being equally nutritive with meat while costing only one-fifth of the price, and add:—"These when suitably dressed are more readily assimilated than flesh, and the eater feels lighter and less oppressed than after a meal of the latter." As dried beans they might be largely utilised by the *shikari* and the soldier in the field.

PHLEUM.

574 **Phleum pratense,** *Linn.*, GRAMINEÆ.

TIMOTHY OR MEADOW CAT'S-TAIL GRASS.

Syn.—P. NODOSUM, *Linn.*

This perennial meadow and hay grass, the family badge of the Sutherlands, is one of the most valuable fodder grasses, especially for heavy, moist soils, as it is one of the earliest and most productive.

PHŒBE.

575 **Phœbe attenuata,** *Nees.*, LAURINEÆ.

Vern.—*Dudri*, NEPAL; *Lepcha-phal*, DARJEELING; *Phani*, LEPCHA.

A large, evergreen tree of Sikkim and Bhutan, from 4,000 to 8,000 feet, hills of East Bengal.

The fruit is large, of the size of green walnut, when ripe; it is eaten by the Lepchas. (*Gamble.*)

PHŒNIX.

576 **Phœnix acaulis,** *Roxb.*, PALMÆ.

Vern.—*Khajuri, pind-khajur, jangli-khajur*, HIND.; *Schap*, LEPCHA; *Boichind*, MAR.; *Chindi*, GOND.; *Thinboung*, BURM.

A low, stemless palm of the sub-Himalayan tract from the Jumna eastward to Behar, and southwards to Central India; it is also found in Burma. Flowers in the cold season, ripens its fruit in April and May.

The fruit is small, but is eaten by the natives. The natives of Chutia Nagpur make a kind of sago from the pith of the tree which they eat.

577 **P. dactylifera,** *Linn.*

DATE PALM.

Vern.—*Khajur, khaji*, HIND. In the Punjab the fruit is *pind, chirwi, bagri*, the cabbage of leaves *gadda, galli*.

This wing-leaved palm, which attains a height of 50 feet or more, is cultivated and self-sown in South Punjab and adjoining parts of Sind. It does not thrive well in Lower Bengal. It produces, in bunches of 20 to 30 or more, the true Date fruit which, for some part of the year in the tracts just mentioned, forms a large proportion of the food of the natives.

This palm has from 2 or 6 to 12 or 14 spadices, sometimes so numerous as to måke it necessary for the preservation of the tree to remove some. As much as 4 cwt. of dates have been gathered from one tree in Egypt. To attain to such fertility it must be frequently irrigated. The best trees are those produced, not from seeds, but from a slip taken from the root of the step of an adult tree, planted, and watered daily for six weeks, and frequently thereafter. In this way a crop of 14,400 lbs. of dates will be obtained per hectare of 2½ acres. The most refreshing way to use them is to eat them as paste mixed with barley.

The yellow dates are the smallest, and the black generally the largest, each ripening separately, and thus making room for others. The crushed dates sold in mass in the foreign markets are the inferior and damaged sorts.

Edgeworth, when Commissioner of Multan, tried to make sugar from the juice of the Date: he employed for this purpose experienced persons, natives of Jessore (Bengal), and found, after some trials, that the male tree produces but little juice, that the female yields more, but that its fruit is much more valuable than the sugar was likely to be.

When trees are cut down, the terminal bunch or heart of young leaves is taken by the natives, and eaten by them both raw and cooked. It is excellent, and makes a good curry.

The hard kernels of the fruit are ground and serve as food for camels, goats, sheep, horses, and other animals. Roasted they are sometimes sold as Date Coffee. From the sap is made a fermented wine which is drunk as an intoxicating beverage. This is supposed to be the Date tree whose branches are mentioned by St. John (xii. 13).

Phœnix farinifera, *Willd.* 578

Vern.—*Chilta-eita*, TEL.; *Ichal*, KAN.

A small, almost stemless, palm of sandy lands, near the sea at Coringa. Flowers in January and February, and its fruit ripens in May.

The fruit has a small quantity of pulp, but it is sweet and mealy, and is eaten by the natives.

The trunk of the tree yields a farinaceous substance which is eaten by the natives. The account given of it by **Dr. Roxburgh** seems worthy of notice :—

"The small trunk, when divested of its leaves, and the strong, brown fibrous web that surrounds it at their insertions, is generally about fifteen or eighteen inches long, and six in diameter at the thickest part; its exterior or woody part consists of white fibres matted together; these envelope a large quantity of farinaceous substance which the natives use for food in times of scarcity. To procure this meal, the small trunk is split into six or eight pieces, dried, and beat in wooden mortars, till the farinaceous part is detached from the fibres; it is then sifted to separate them; the meal is then fit for use. The only further preparation it undergoes is the boiling it into a thick gruel, or as it is called in India, *Kangi*; it seems to possess less nourishment than the common sago, and is less palatable, being considerably bitter when boiled; probably a little care in the preparation and varying the mode might improve it; however, it certainly deserves attention, for during the end of the last, and beginning of this year, and even again at this present time, May 1792, it has saved many lives. Rice was too dear, and at times not to be had, which forced many of the poor to have recourse to these sorts of food. Fortunately it is one of the most common plants on this part of the coast, particularly near the sea."

P. rupicola, *T. And.* 579

Vern.—*Schiap*, LEPCHA.

"A beautiful palm of the lower hills of Darjeeling and Bhutan." (*Gamble.*)

It is commonly seen growing on rocks, and is sometimes cut down by Lepchas for the interior of the stem, which they eat.

P. sylvestris, *Roxb.* 580

WILD DATE OR CADEN.

Vern.—*Khejoor*, BENG.; *Khajur, khaji, salma, thakil*, HIND.; *Pedda eita*, TEL.; *Periaeetcham*, TAM.; *Seindi*, BERAR.

Wild and cultivated throughout India.

Appears in all soils and situations, flowers at the beginning of the hot season, and produces in summer inferior yellowish or reddish fruit, eaten by native boys and the poorer classes.

The trees are, however, useful in yielding the "*Khejjur rus*" (Date juice) from which "Tari" or Palm-wine and sugar are made. The juice is extracted as follows :—

The lower leaves and their sheaths are removed, a notch is cut into the pith of the tree close to the remaining leaf sheaths, and a thin channelled

PHYL-
LANTHUS.

slip of wood or piece of the date or palmyra leaf is inserted into the notch. The juice issues from the notch, is conducted by the channel and falls into an earthen pot which is tied on to receive it. In the cold season, *i. e.*, from the end of October to February, the trees are thus tapped in the evening, and the juice is taken before sunrise. It is used in two ways: (*a*) in its unfermented fresh state, (*b*) in its fermented state. In its fresh state it is used in two ways. In a smaller proportion it is sold in the early mornings as *Khejjur-rus*: it is then the sweet juice and is drank by the natives as such. In a larger proportion, also in the early morning, the sweet juice is collected, generally under some shady bamboo grove or tamarind tree, in large, open earthen vessels and boiled over wood-fire until the juice becomes thick. It is then taken off the fire, and dried by exposure. The substance obtained is Jageri or Goor, or raw Date sugar. The quantity of raw sugar thus made in Bengal, Orissa, and the southern regions every year is large.

A small proportion of the juice, instead of being used in the two ways above described, is exposed to the sun's influence and soon ferments, and is then known as *Toddy* (English) or *Tari* (Beng., Hind,). In the making of *Toddy* the tapping of the trees is not confined to the cold season only, but is practised throughout the year. Toddy is used for two purposes—(1) as an intoxicating drink, (2) as yeast in making bread.

PHRAGMITES.

581 **Phragmites communis,** *Trin.*, GRAMINEÆ.

COMMON REED.

Syn.—ARUNDO PHRAGMITES, *Linn.*

Vern.—*Dila*, PB.

Inhabits the highlands of western Tibet, Lahoul and Ladak up to 14,000 feet, and through Kashmir, Jhelum valley, and Garhwal, down to Lahore and Ferozepur.

In Ladak eaten by cattle, in Lahoul used for roofing. Sandals are made from its stems.

PHYLLANTHUS.

582 **Phyllanthus distichus,** *Mull. Arg.*, EUPHORBIACEÆ.

Syn.—P. LONGIFOLIA, *Jacq.*

Vern.—*Loda, nori*, BENG.; *Harfaruri, chalmeri*, HIND.; *Russa-usareki*, TEL.; *Arunilli*, TAM.; *Kirneli*, MYSORE; *Thin-bo-si-pyoo*, BURM.

An elegant, small tree common in gardens in South India, Burma, and the Andaman Islands.

Produces at the beginning of the hot season numerous small reddish flowers, which are succeeded by small, fleshy fruits not unlike gooseberries. The fruits are much used as an article of food, either raw or dressed in various fashions, or pickled, or made into preserves.

583 **P. Emblica,** *Linn.*

Vern.—*Ambal, ámbli*, PB.; *Daula, ámla, aonla, ámlita, aura*, HIND.; *Amla, ambolati, amulati, ald thanda*, BENG.; *Anvala*, BOM.; *Ambari*, GARO.; *Amluki*, ASS.; *Nelli, nellekai*, TAM.; *Osirka, usri, aserski*, TEL.; *Nelli*, KAN.; *Shabjee, tasha*, BURM.

A moderate-sized tree in the dry forests of India and Burma.

The acid fruit of this species, which is of the size of a small gooseberry, with a fleshy outer covering, and a hard three-celled nut, containing six seeds, is the Emblic Myrabolan. It is used, among other purposes, for food and preserves by the natives. It is made into a sweetmeat with sugar, or eaten raw as a condiment. It is also used as a pickle or preserved in sugar. Branches of the tree are sometimes placed in wells with the view of imparting a pleasant flavout to the water.

PHYSALIS.

Physalis minima, *Linn.*, SOLANACEÆ. 584

Vern.—*Bun-tepoori*, BENG.; *Tulati-pati*, HIND.

An herb common in places throughout the tropical regions of India.

Produces berries which are smaller than the following and are eaten by natives.

P. peruviana, *Linn.* 585

CAPE GOOSEBERRY.

Syn.—P. EDULIS.

Vern.—*Tepoori*, BENG.; *Tepari*, HIND.

A native of tropical America. A weak, sub-erect plant cultivated to a limited extent, and here and there, throughout India for its fine-flavoured, luscious fruit.

The berries are large, yellowish, and palatable; and are eaten raw by all classes. Europeans eat them raw, as well as in preserve.

Physochlaina præalta, *Hook f.*, SOLANACEÆ. 586

Vern.—*Sholar, bajar-bang, nandru, dandarna*, PB.; *Lang bang*, LADAK.

Met with in North Kashmir and Western Tibet, altitude 12,000 to 15,000 feet.

The leaves are used medicinally, and are said to be poisonous. At Lahoul, however, they are browsed by cattle.

PHYTOLACCA.

Phytolacca acinosa, *Roxb.*, VERBENACEÆ. 587

Vern.—*Lubar, burgee, rinsag, jirka, matasor, sarunga*, PB.

An herbaceous, erect plant in the Himalaya, from the Punjab to Nepal, at altitudes of 3,500 to 8,000 feet.

The fruit and perhaps the leaves are said to produce delirium when eaten. The leaves are, however, eaten by the natives in Nepal and elsewhere in curries.

PICEA.

Picea Webbiana, *Lamb.*, CONIFERÆ. 588

Vern.—*Paludar, badar, rag, dhunnu, spun, bajur*, PB.

A large tree in many parts of the Punjab Himalaya from 1,500 to 5,500 feet.

The twigs and leaves are much used as fodder in parts of the Jhelum basin.

PICRASMA.

Picrasma quassioides, *Benn.*, SIMARUBEÆ. 589

A large, scrambling shrub or plant of sub-tropical Himalaya, met with from Jamu to Nepal and Bhutan.

Produces green flowers and small red fruit or drupes. The fruit is eaten in some parts of the above tracts by natives. The shrub is browsed by goats and sheep.

PIMPINELLA.

590 **Pimpinella Anisum,** *Linn.*, UMBELLIFERÆ.

THE ANISE SEED.

Vern.—*Belati-radhúni.*

This annual of the Carrot family is a native of Europe.

Sometimes met with in cultivation in gardens during the cold season; introduced from Europe.

In the Peshawar valley the plant is said to be used as a vegetable, and perhaps it is so used in some other parts also. But it is cultivated chiefly for its seeds which are officinal and is used in confectionery. From them is made the well-known cordial called Aniseed.

PINUS.

591 **Pinus Gerardiana,** *Wall.*, CONIFERÆ.

THE NEOSA PINE.

Vern.—*Chilghosa, jalghosa,* AFG.; *Chiri, pritu, mirri, galgoja,* CHENAB; *Kashti,* RAVI; *Chilgoja,* SIMLA.

A moderate-sized tree with very thin grey bark; found in the inner dry and arid parts of the North-West and Punjab Himalaya, in isolated areas of no great extent, generally between 6,000 and 10,000 feet; also on the mountains of North Afghanistan and Kafiristan. The tree is valued on account of the cylinder-shaped, almond-like seeds contained in the cones. The latter ripen towards the end of October, and the seeds are extracted from the unopened cones by heating.

They are largely eaten by the natives, are stored for winter use, and are also sold, in considerable quantities, in the Himalayan and sub-Himalayan tracts, and exported partly to the plains. Besides the local supplies, large quantities are imported into the Punjab from Afghanistan

No statistics are available of the probable annual produce, but the following furnishes some data: a full-sized cone yields more than a hundred seed; each tree produces from 15 to 25 cones; the seed is sold in the Simla bazars at from 6 to 8 seers per rupee.

592 **P. longifolia,** *Roxb.*

Vern.—*Nakhtar,* AFG.; *Chil, chir, dráb chir,* PB.; *Anander,* JHELUM; *Dhúp,* OUDH; *Dhúp, sala dhúp,* NEPAL.

A large tree of Afghanistan, outer North-West Himalaya, ascending to 7,500 feet; Sikkim, and Bhutan, ascending to 4,000 feet, though scarce above 3,000 feet.

Dr. Stewart writes: "In parts of the Jhelum basin, the turpentiny seed is at times eaten when food is scarce, but it cannot be a pleasant, and is probably not a nutritious, food."

PIPER.

593 **Piper Betle,** *Linn.*, PIPERACEÆ

Syn.—CHAVICA BETLE, *Miq.*

Vern.—*Pán,* HIND., BENG.; *Támbula,* SANS.; *Vettilee,* TAM.; *Tamal-pakoo,* TEL., *Pána, nagavela,* BOM.

Cultivated throughout India for its leaves.

The leaves of this plant, together with lime, catechu, and betelnut, and also certain spices, such as cardamoms, nutmegs, and cloves, are made into little packets called *pán*, generally chewed by the natives of India, especially after meals.

Piper nigrum, *Linn.* 594

BLACK PEPPER.

Vern.—*Kala-marich, gole-marich*, BENG., HIND.; *Choka*, DEC.; *Milagu*, TAM.; *Miriyalu*, TEL.

A climber, extensively cultivated for the sake of its currant-like berries in South India.

These berries are at first green, then red, but on being gathered and dried become black, and as Black Pepper are very commonly used both by Natives and Europeans in food, and to a small extent medicinally.

White Pepper is the same berry, but divested of its skin by maceration in water and subsequent rubbing; made whiter by chlorine. The highest esteemed Pepper comes from the Malabar coast. When left to itself the Pepper-vine attains a height of upwards of 20 feet, but it is found convenient to keep it down to 12 feet. They attach themselves to rough-bark trees and bear their berries from the time they are 3 till they are 7 or 8 years old.

A large export trade is carried on in Pepper by sea to foreign countries. The following table will show the extent of the trade during the last five years:—

Official years.	Quantity in lbs.	Value in Rs.
1878-79	7,149,323	12,17,365
1879-80	3,315,901	6,42,853
1880-81	4,917,548	10,32,771
1881-82	3,617,634	8,01,463
1882-83	9,265,411	23,06,721

Analysis of exportation of Black Pepper from India for the year 1882-83:—

Provinces from which exported.	Quantity in lbs.	Countries to which exported.	Quantity in lbs.
Madras	7,509,919	France	6,742,901
Bombay	1,748,328	United Kingdom	854,075
Bengal	6,244	Persia	461,551
Sindh	920	Turkey in Asia	461,151
		Arabia	371,648
		Aden	217,952
		Egypt	126,800
		Other countries	299,333
TOTAL	9,265,411	TOTAL	9,265,411

P. sylvaticum, *Roxb.* 595

Vern.—*Pahari-peepul*, N. W. BENGAL.

Met with in the mountains on the north-west border of Bengal. The natives use this pepper, both green and ripe, in their dishes.

PISTACIA.

696 **Pistacia integerrima,** *J. L. Stewart,* ANACARDIACEÆ.

Vern.—*Kaka, kakkar, kangar, tunga,* PB.; *Kakrasinghi,* BENG.

A tree with rough bark, met with on the Sulaiman Range, the outer North-West Himalaya, extending eastward to Kumaun, altitude 6,000 feet.

"The leaves are lopped for fodder for buffaloes and camels." (*Gamble.*)

597 **P. vera,** *Linn.*

THE PISTACHIO NUT.

Vern.—*Pista,* BENG., HIND., & BOM.

A small tree of Western Asia and Afghanistan.

Produces the pistachio nut which is oval-shaped and sometimes an inch long, but generally not more than half-an-inch. It has a brittle shell enclosing the eatable part which is of a greenish color and an agreeable flavour. It is eaten by all the well-to-do classes. Large quantities are imported from Afghanistan into many parts of India as far down as Calcutta. It is simply dried like almonds or made into articles of confectionery.

The exact quantity cannot be ascertained, as the trade returns do not specify the nut, but lump it under the head of "fruits, nuts and vegetables."

They are supposed to be the nuts sent by Jacab into Egypt.

PISUM.

598 **Pisum arvense,** *Linn.,* LEGUMINOSÆ.

THE GREY OF FIELD PEA.

Vern.—*Desi-mattar, chota mattar,* HIND., BENG.; also *kalon, kulai batana* in parts of N. W. P.

Native of Greece and the Levant, and probably the parent of **P. Sativum.** Cultivated in many parts of India during the cold weather.

Produces small, round, compressed, greenish and marbled grains; and is by Roxburgh considered to be a variety of the common grass field pea, and by Baker in *Fl. Br. Ind.* to be a sub-species. It may be a sub-species of the next (**P. sativum**).

It must be, however, carefully distinguished from the *Kesari,* **Lathyrus sativus**, which is a different species, but to which it bears some resemblance both in appearance of the grain and the mode of cultivation. *See* **Lathyrus sativus**, also the next.

Field peas are often, in England, drilled with horse-beans, the mixture being known as Poults, a corruption of Pulse. Pease straw is highly esteemed as fodder.

599 **P. sativum,** *Linn.*

THE COMMON PEA.

Vern.—*Mattar, gol-mattar,* N. W. P.; *Harenso,* SANS.

An annual tendril climber, a native of the South of Europe. Cultivated in many parts of India during the cold weather. It includes the white peas known as *Cabli* and *Patnai* according as they are large or small. **P. sativum** is more valuable and prolific than **P. arvense**.

Peas are sown in the North West Provinces and Oudh from the end of September to the middle of October on heavy soil at the rate of 1½ maunds per acre if of the fine and at 1 maund if of the coarse kind; the cost of production per acre is about Rs. 12-13 for the latter and Rs. 17-13 for the former kinds, assuming that the soil is twice watered during the whole season. The crop suffers from frost and the ravages of caterpillar; the average area sown annually in the thirty temporarily-settled districts of the North West Provinces is reported to be about 379,852 acres. The average out-turn is from 10 to 16 maunds per irrigated and from 7 to 8 maunds per unirrigated acre. The out-turn of chaff (bhusa) is about equal to that of grain.

This, one of the oldest and most valuable of cultivated legumes, when dried and split, is used for soups, or ground into meal for puddings, &c. It contains upwards of one-seventh more of nourishing matter than is found in the same weight of wheaten bread. But it is when young and green that it is chiefly used by Europeans, and more especially when in the beginning of the season it is scarce and regarded as a vegetable delicacy.

PITHECOLOBIUM.

Pithecolobium dulce, *Benth.*, LEGUMINOSÆ. 600

MANILLA TAMARINDS.

Syn.—MIMOSA DULCIS, *Roxb.*; INGA DULCIS, *Willd.*

Vern.—*Dakhani-babul*, HIND.; *Karkapili*, TAM.; *Sime hunase*, KAN.; *Kwaytanyeng*, BURM.

A large tree introduced from Mexico and now cultivated throughout India and in large numbers along the railway lines in the Madras Presidency.

Flowers during the cold season in this country, and produces annually in abundance pods 4 to 5 inches in length and ½ inch in breadth with six to eight seeds.

The seeds are half enveloped in a sweet, wholesome and edible, whitish pulp contained in a cylindrical, irregularly-swollen pod, curled at the top.

POA.

Poa annua, *Linn.*, GRAMINEÆ. 601

Syn.—P. SUPINA, *Schrad.*

Vern.—*Chirua*, N. W. P.

A very common grass in Europe where it is considered good for early pasturage. In India it inhabits the plains and Himalaya within the limits of the Punjab and North-West Provinces. (*Duthie.*)

P. plumosa, *Retz.* *See* **Fragrostis pulmosa,** *Link.*

P. pratensis, *Linn.* 602

SMOOTH-STALKED MEADOW GRASS.

Syn.—P. ANGUSTIFOLIA, *Linn.*

Found in Tibet, Kashmir, and the Himalaya.

Mr. Duthie writes:—"In England it is considered to be a good fodder grass, and valuable for early hay. In America it is known by the name of 'Kentucky blue grass,' and is much prized for pastures and lawns."

This and the following are regarded as specially valuable for agricultural purposes.

PONGA-
MIA.

603 **Poa trivialis,** *Linn.*

ROUGH MEADOW GRASS.

Met with in the highlands of Western Tibet, 12,000 to 14,000 feet in altitude.

Thrives well in moist and rich soil, and considered a valuable grass in such soils.

PODOPHYLLUM.

604 **Podophyllum emodi,** *Wall.*, BERBERIDÆ.

Vern.—*Papri, ban-kakri, chijakri, gul-kakru*, PB.

A stout, erect herb of the inner Himalaya from Sikkim to Hazara and Kashmir, at 9,000 to 14,000 and 6,000 feet.

Produces handsome red fruits which ripen in September and October and are eaten by natives in most parts. Europeans consider the fruit insipid.

POLLINIA.

605 **Pollinia eriopoda,** *Hance*, GRAMINEÆ.

BANKASS.

Syn.—SPODIODOGON ANGUSTIFOLIUS, *Trin.*; ANDROPOGON NOTOPOGON *Nees.*

Vern.—*Bhabar, bankas, munji*, HIND.

Inhabits the plains of the Punjab and North-West Provinces, common also along the Terai, and at low elevations on the hills. (*Duthie.*)

Much used for cordage in the Gorakhpur district, also for the construction of swing bridges in the hills. (*Duthie*) Used as a cattle fodder.

POLYGONUM.

606 **Polygonum molle,** *Don.*, POLYGONACEÆ.

Vern.—*Totnye, patu-swa*, NEPAL.

A straggling shrub extremely common in the hills of Sikkim and Bhutan, from 5,000 to 8,000 feet in altitude.

The young shoots are pleasantly acid and are eaten like rhubarb.

607 **P. polystachyum,** *Wall.*

Vern.—*Amhdandi, chuchi, tror*, PB.

A tall tree of the Punjab Himalaya, from 6,000 to 12,000 feet in altitude.

The young leaves are eaten by the natives as a pot-herb. The stalks are eaten raw in some places after being peeled. When stewed they are a good imitation of rhubarb.

PONGAMIA.

608 **Pongamia glabra,** *Vent.*, LEGUMINOSÆ.

Vern.—*Karanj, papar*, HIND.; *Dalkaramcha, karanja*, BENG.; *Ponga*, TAM., *Kanga*, TEL.; *Thenwian*, BURM.

An erect tree or climber in the lower Himalayan tract and plains, from the Ravi eastward, also in Bengal, Central and South India, and Burma. Produces during the hot season flowers of a beautiful mixture of blue, white, and purple, and legumes which ripen during the close of the year. From the seed is obtained Poonga Oil

Cattle are fond of the leaves.

POPULUS.

Populus balsamifera, *Linn.*, SALICINEÆ. 609

THE TACAMAHAC.

Vern.—*Phalsh, makhal,* PB.; *Berfa, changma,* W. TIBET.

A large tree of the inner arid Himalaya and Tibet, 8,000 to 14,000 feet, is remarkable for its fine foliage and the pleasant balsamic odour of its leaves and buds.

The branches are lopped for cattle fodder.

P. ciliata, *Wall.* 610

Vern.—*Safeda, phalja, dud-phras, pahari-pipal,* PB.; *Garpipal,* KUMAUN; *Chalun,* SIMLA.

A large tree in the Himalaya from the Indus to Bhutan.

The leaves are used as fodder for goats.

P. euphratica, *Olivier.* 611

HIMALAYAN POPLAR.

Vern.—*Bahan,* SIND., PB.; *Hodung,* LADAK.

A large tree on the banks of the Indus in Sindh and Punjab, ascending into Tibet, supposed to be the willow of Psalm 137.

The leaves are used as fodder for goats and cattle.

PORTULACA.

Portulaca oleracea, *Linn.*, PORTULACEÆ. 612

THE COMMON PURSLANE.

Vern.—*Loonia, nooniya-shág,* BENG., HIND.

This low, succulent, annual herb is found throughout India, and up to 5,000 feet in the Himalaya.

Often eaten as a pot-herb by the natives, especially in times of scarcity. Its young shoots make an excellent salad, and the older ones pot-herb or pickle.

There are three varieties, the Common Green, the Golden, and the large-leaved Golden, grown in gardens.

P. quadrifida, *Linn.* 613

Syn.—P. MERIDIONA, *Linn.*

Vern.—*Nooniya,* BENG.; *Lunak-haksha,* PB.; *Pail-kura,* TEL.

An annual, diffuse herb found in the warmer parts of India and on the lower Himalaya; common in gardens, chiefly as a weed.

Used as a vegetable by natives, and considered cooling.

POTAMOGETON.

Potamogeton crispus, *Linn.*, NAIADACEÆ. 614

Vern.—*Sawál,* PB.; *Chúsbal,* LADAK.

Found on the Punjab plains and up to Ladak; common in the latter.

Used as fodder and for refining sugar.

PRINSE-PIA.

615 **Potamogeton gramineus,** *L.*

Vern.—*Jála, simbil, phus,* PB., LADAK.

Also found on parts of the Punjab plains, and ascends into Ladak. Used for fodder, also in refining sugar.

616 **P. lucens,** *L.*

Vern.—?

Common in Kashmir, where large quantities are used as fodder.

POTENTILLA.

617 **Potentilla fruticosa,** *Linn.*, ROSACEÆ.

Vern.—*Spang-jho, merino,* PB.; *Pinjung, penma,* LADAK.

A shrub, with pinnate leaves and yellow flowers, is found growing in bushy places in the temperate and sub-alpine Himalaya from Kashmir eastward to Sikkim, at 8,000 to 16,000 feet altitude. Appears in various forms, *viz.*, much-branched, robust, erect, or prostrate, leafy, low or tall.

Its fragrant leaves are in the higher parts of the Chenab basin used as a substitute for tea. (*Stewart* quoting *Aitch.* and *Long.*) It is browsed by sheep.

618 **P. Salessovii,** *Steph.*

Vern.—*Shour,* LADAK.

A shrub in Lahoul, Spiti, Ladak, and Northern Kashmir. Browsed by sheep.

PREMNA.

619 **Premna integrifolia,** *Linn.*, VERBENACEÆ.

Syn.—P. SERRATIFOLIA, *Linn.* as in *Roxb. Fl. Ind. III* 77; [SPINOSA, *Roxb.*

Vern.—*Arni,* HIND.; *Bhut-bhiravi,* BENG.; *Ganiari,* OUDH; *Bakarcha,* GARWAHL; *Gineri,* NEPAL; *Munnay,* TAM.; *Ghebu-nelli,* TEL.; *Chamari,* MAR.

A small tree in Northern India, from Oudh eastward, also in South India, Tenasserim, and the Andaman Islands.

In parts of India the leaves are used for feeding cattle.

620 **P. latifolia,** *Roxb.*

Vern.—*Gineri,* NEPAL; *Michapgong,* LEPCHA; *Gondhona,* URIYA; *Pedda-nella-kura,* TEL.

A small tree in the sub-Himalayan tract from Kumaun eastwards, and Southern India.

The leaves have a pretty strong, not unpleasant smell, and are eaten by the natives in curries, especially in South India. They are also sometimes given as fodder to cattle.

PRINSEPIA.

621 **Prinsepia utilis,** *Royle,* ROSACEÆ.

Vern.—*Bhekal, bekkra, karanga,* HIND.; *Gurinda,* HAZARA; *Tatua, phulwara, jinti,* CHENAB; *Bekling,* KANAWAR.

A thorny shrub, from Hazara to Bhutan, between 2,000 and 9,000 feet, also in Khási hills.

The oil yielded by the fruit is used in food and for burning.

PROSOPIS.

Prosopis dulcis, LEGUMINOSÆ. 622

ALGAROBA of PARAY.

Vern.—*Algoraba.*

Introduced from America into Madras, where they are now known as 'Tamarinds,' and planted along railway lines.

Its sweetish, succulent pods, from 20 to 24 inches long, enclosing black seeds embedded in white pulp, are largely used for feeding cattle,

P. glandulosa, *Torr.* 623

THE "MESQUIT OR ALGORABA OF TEXAS."

A native of the mountain regions of western Texas. Produces pods the interior of which is filled with a sweet pulp.

The sweet mucilage of the pod, by fermentation and boiling, makes a not unpleasant drink. The seeds or beans, powdered and mixed with water, forms a paste, which, on being dried in the sun, makes an article of food, and keeps for a considerable time.

P. pubescens, *Bth.* 624

SCREW BEAN, OR SCREW MESQUIT OF the TORNILLO.

This produces the true Mesquit bean of the Texas, and is being experimentally cultivated in the Royal Botanic Gardens, Calcutta. It is a native of Texas and New Mexico.

The beans or pods are screw-shaped, and borne in abundance; they ripen at all times of the year, and contain much saccharine and nutritious matter. From this matter molasses is made by boiling.

The screw-like form of its pods gives it its name Tornillo or Screw Bean.

The pods form an important article of food to the natives, and are largely devoured by cattle. Great caution is required in their use as fodder for horses.

P. spicigera, *Linn.* 625

Syn.—ADENANTHERA ACULEATA, *Roxb.*

Vern.—*Jhand, khar,* PB.; *Kandi, samada, sami,* SIND; *Khijra,* RAJPUTANA; *Semru, hamra,* GUZ.; *Shami,* BENG.; *Perumbe, jambu,* TAM.

A moderate-sized tree in the north and south dry zones of India; the Punjab, Sind, Rajputana, Guzerat, Bundelkhand, and Dekkan.

The pods ripen before and during the rains, and contain, when scarcely ripe, a considerable quantity of a sweetish, farinaceous substance, which has the flavour of that of the carob tree, and is largely consumed as food in the Punjab, Guzerat, and the Deccan; in some parts by all classes, in others only by the poor and in times of scarcity.

It is eaten in different ways: green or dry; raw and alone; boiled with salt, onions and ghi and eaten with bread, or mixed with *dahi*. The pods are also sometimes used as fodder for camels, cattle, and goats.

PRUNUS.

Prunus amygdalus, *Baillon.,* ROSACEÆ. 626

THE ALMOND TREE.

Syn.—AMYGDALUS COMMUNIS, *Willd.*

Vern.—*Badám.*

Cultivated in Afghanistan, Persia, Kashmir, and the Punjab.

PRUNUS.

The almond tree seldom exceeds 15 feet in height, but by being grafted on the plum, it attains to a height of 20 to 30 feet, with a trunk from 8 to 10 inches in diameter.

Sweet almonds are largley used as dessert and in confectionery, and are also eaten by the well-to-do natives. The part eaten are the two seed lobes or kernel, which is nutty and sweet. Bitter almonds, a distinct variety, yield prussic acid and an oil.

Considerable quantities of almond are imported from Afghanistan into India, and reach so far down as Calcutta.

627 **Prunus armeniaca,** *Linn.*

THE APRICOT, MISHMUSH or 'MOON OF THE FAITHFUL'.

Vern. –*Jard-aru kari, gardalu, shirán, kush,* PB.; *Khubani, chúari, sard álu,* HIND.

A moderately sized tree, wild and cultivated in the Himalaya of the Punjab and North-West Provinces.

The fruit is largely eaten by all classes, fresh or dried, but chiefly fresh, and sometimes in preserve by Europeans.

Sometime they are pressed together and rolled out into thin sheets or 'moons', 2 or 3 feet in diameter, like to a Blacksmith's apron.

From Afghanistan large cuantities of the dried fruit are imported into India, and distributed by trade far into the plains till Calcutta.

They are believed to be the "Apples" of the English Bible.

628 **P. Avium,** *Linn.*

SWEET CHERRY.

Vern.—*Gilás.*

Cultivated in the N. W. Himalaya up to 8,000 feet, and almost naturalised.

Flowers in April-May, and the fruit ripens in June. The European varieties introduced have not succeeded in these hills owing to the effect of the heavy rain on the young fruit. (*Atkinson.*)

629 **P. Cerasus,** *Linn.*

WILD CHERRY.

Vern.—*Alu-balu,* PERS.; *Kerasya,* ARAB.

Cultivated in the Himalaya of the Punjab and North-West Provinces up to 8,000 feet in altitude.

The fruit is eaten by all classes; those of the wild variety being used only by the poorer class of natives.

630 **P. communis,** *Huds.*

THE PLUM.

Var. domestica.

Vern.—*Alucha, olchi, shaft álu,* PB., *Bhotiya badám, Laddkhi badam,* ALMORA.

Cultivated from Garhwal to Kashmir in the Western Himalaya.

The fruit when ripe is large, yellow, sweet, and juicy. Eaten by all classes and much esteemed.

631 **Var. Insititia.**

THE BOKHARA PLUM,

Vern.—*Alu-Bokhárá,* HIND., BOM., PERS.; *Alpo-gadda-pasham,* TAM.

Found in the western temperate Himalaya; cultivated or indigenous from Garhwal to Kashmir, altitude 5,000 to 7,000 feet.

The Bokhara plum is met with in a dry state in the Indian bazars.

A *chatni* is generally prepared from it and much relished by the natives.

Prunus Padus, *Linn.* 632

THE BIRD CHERRY.

Vern.—*Jamana*, HIND.; *Likh-arm*, NEPAL; *Páras, kalakat, sambu, dudla*, PB.; *Hlo sa klot-kúng*, LEPCHA.

A moderate-sized tree in the Himalaya, from the Indus to Sikkim. Produces an acid fruit, or drupe, of the size of a large pea.

P. persica, *Benth. & Hook.* 633

THE PEACH.

Syn.—AMYGDALUS PERSICA, *Linn.*

Vern.—*Aru, aor*, PB.; *Ghwareshtai*, AFG.; *Shúftalú*, PERS.

Commonly cultivated everywhere throughout the Himalaya and in Upper Burma.

Eaten by all classes. The *nectarine* is a form of this.

P. prostrata, *Labill.* 634

A small shrub in the arid parts of the western temperate Himalaya from the Sutlej westwards.

Produces a small berry, red-purple flesh, scarcely eatable, though juicy.

P. Puddum, *Roxb.* 635

Vern.—*Paddam*, HIND.; *Chamiári, amalgach*, PB.; *Kongki*, LEPCHA.

Wild in the Himalaya, from the Indus to Assam and Khásia hills. Produces an oblong berry with scanty yellow or reddish acid pulp.

PSIDIUM.

Psidium Guyava, *Raddi*, MYRTACEÆ.

THE GUAVA TREE. 636

Vern.—*Amrút, amrúd*, HIND. & N. W. P.; *Péyara, geciabu*, BENG.; *Peru*, BOM.; *Amuk*, NEPAL; *Modhuriam*, ASS.; *Segapu*, TAM.; *Jama, coya*, TEL.; *Malaka beng*, BURM.

A small, evergreen tree, of 15 to 20 feet in height; introduced from America, now widely cultivated, from the eastern tracts of the Punjab to Bengal, Central and Southern India, and in some parts semi-wild.

There are two varieties: one, **pyriferum,** *Linn*, is pear-shaped; the other **pomiferum,** *Linn.*, is round or ovoid. The latter is generally pink inside, and the former white, but the colour is not constant, both being sometimes irrespectively white or pink. The better cultivated trees produce excellent fruit, with a thin bright yellow rind, filled with a pulpy yellowish, creamlike or red flesh, which has a pleasantly acid-sweet flavour.

The fruit is very common, and is universally eaten by all classes. The natives generally eat it in its natural ripe state. Europeans eat it so, as well as made into stew or the well-known "Guava jelly" or "Guava cheese."

PSORALEA.

Psoralea plicata, *Delile*, LEGUMINOSÆ.

Vern.—*Bakhtmal*, PB. 637

A low, much-branched shrub in the arid plains of the Punjab. Camels are fond of it.

PTERIS.

638 **Pteris equilina**, *Linn.*, GRAMINEÆ.

BRAKE or BRACKEN.

Vern.—*Kakhash, kakei, lungar, dio,* PB.

A fern, abundant in the Punjab Himalaya.

The underground running stems rhizome produce numerous winged herbaceous stems called "fronds," varying in height from 3 to 6 feet. The underground stems contain a quantity of mucilage and starch, which, on being prepared by washing and pounding and mixed with meal, make bread in times of scarcity. Even in England attempts have been made to use it as food. **Dr. Clark** considered it a wholesome table vegetable when young and blanched like asparagus, but it is rather astringent. The fronds, in quite a young state, are eaten at times cooked as a pot-herb, and are juicy, though rather insipid.

PTEROCARPUS.

639 **Pterocarpus Marsupium**, *Roxb.*, LEGUMINOSÆ.

GUM KINO.

Vern.—*Bija, bijasar,* HIND.; *Vengai,* TAM.; *Peddagi,* TEL.; *Beebla, asán,* BOM.

A large tree of Central and South India, found in the forests of Ceylon and all parts of the Madras Peninsula, extending north to the Rajmehal hills in Behar. Often cultivated in gardens.

The leaves are the favorite food of cattle and goats, and are much in demand.

Ptychotis Ajowan, *DC.*; also **P. coptica**, *DC.* *See* **Carum copticum**; *Benth.*, UMBELLIFERÆ.

PUERARIA.

640 **Pueraria tuberosa**, *DC.*, LEGUMINOSÆ.

Syn.—HEDYSARUM TUBEROSUM, *Roxb.*

Vern.—*Siali, badar, billi, pona,* HIND.; *Dari, gumodi,* TEL.

A climber in the tropical zone of the Western Himalaya, in the Western Gháts, and in Orissa. Produces during the hot season bright blue flowers, and pendulous, pointed, compressed legumes.

The roots are very large and tuberous. They are eaten, said to be sweet, and are exported to the plains. (*Stewart.*)

PUNICA.

641 **Punica Granatum**, *Linn.*, LYTHRACEÆ.

THE POMEGRANATE; GRENADES, *Fr.*; GRANATS, *Ger.*

Vern.—*Anar, darim,* HIND.; *Dalim,* BENG., KUMAUN; *Anar-kajhur,* DEC., *Mad-alaich-chedi,* TAM.; *Danimma-chettu,* TEL.; *Shajratur-rumman* ARAB.; *Darakhte-nar,* PERS.; *Thalé,* BURM.

A small tree cultivated in most parts of India and Burma; wild in the north-western regions of the Himalaya and Sulaiman Range.

The fruit is peculiar, in its being composed of two whorls of carpels, one placed above the other, the lower consisting of 3 or 4 and the upper of from 5 to 10 carpels. The seeds also have a pellucid, pulpy coating. The fruit is universally eaten and is much esteemed. It is of different qualities; and in the Lower Provinces of Bengal it is inferior to its congener of the North-West and hilly regions. The best kinds are produced still further west in Afghanistan, and large quantities of it are imported thence into most parts of India. The fruit, usually about as large as a full-sized apple, with a hard rind of a brown yellowish color, keeps for a long time. A pleasant cooling *sherbet* is made from the pulp, which is appreciated by all who have drank it, and is highly esteemed by certain classes of natives.

PUTRANJIVA.

Putranjiva Roxburghii, *Wall.*, EUPHORBIACEÆ. 642

Syn.—NAGEIA PUTRANJIVA, *Roxb.*

Vern.—*Putájan*, PB.; *Jia puta, joti-juti, pútra-jiva*, HIND.; *Karupale*, TAM.; *Kadrajuvi*, TEL.; *Toukyap*, BURM.

A moderate-sized, evergreen tree, with pendant branches; found in the sub-Himalayan tract from the Chenab eastward, in Oudh, Bengal, Burma, and South India; and chiefly distinguished by the fruit which is always one seeded.

The leaves are lopped for fodder.

PYRULARIA.

Pyrularia edulis, *A. DC.*, SANTALACEÆ. 643

Vern.—*Amphi*, NEPAL; *Saphyi*, LEPCHA.

A small, thorny tree of Nepal, Sikkim and the Khásia hills.

The fruit is eaten by the natives.

PYRUS.

Pyrus baccata, *Linn.*, ROSACEÆ. 644

Vern.—*Ban-mehal, gwálam*, HIND.; *Lin, liwar, lhijo*, PB. HIMALAYA.

A small tree found in the Himalaya from the Indus to Bhutan, 6,000 to 10,000 feet in altitude, and on the Khásia hills 6,000 feet. Produces a small, very sour fruit, of a red or scarlet colour, with the true apple flavour.

Eaten by the natives of the tracts where it grows.

P. communis, *Linn.* 645

THE COMMON PEAR.

Vern.—*Naspati, nak*, PB.; *Tang, nak, sunkeint, naspate*, PB. HILLS; *Amrud*, KASHMIR.

A small, thorny tree wild in Kashmir, and cultivated in the Himalaya.

The fruit, which is the common pear, is generally hard, but not unpleasant to the taste, and is largely eaten, especially by the natives. Europeans generally make it into preserve or stew.

The liquor, known as Perry, is the fermented juice of pears.

P. kumaoni, *Dcne.* 646

Vern.—*Doda, chitana, mahaul, ban-pala, gun, palos*, PB.

Confined to the western regions of the Himalaya, from Kashmir to Kumaun.

Produces a small fruit of very indifferent taste. Eaten generally half rotten by the poorer natives.

647 **Pyrus lanata**, *Don.*

Vern.—*Doda, maila, morphal,* PB.; *Galion, mauli,* HIND.

A moderate-sized tree in the Himalaya, from the Indus to Bhutan. Produces a large fruit, which is eaten half rotten by the natives.

648 **P. Malus,** *Linn.*

APPLE.

Vern.—*Seo,* HIND.; *Shu, chunt, palu, seo,* PB.; *Kushu,* LADAK; *Shewa,* AFG.

A tree apparently wild in the North-West and Punjab Himalaya and Western Tibet; cultivated in the Lower Himalaya, Punjab, Sind, and Central India. Produces a fruit which is indifferent in the plains, but improves in the Himalaya, and is very pleasant, especially when cultivated, though still inferior to the English and American Apple.

In Tibet and Afghanistan the fruit is really good, and large quantities are imported from the latter country into various parts of the Punjab. Recently attempts have been made with considerable success in introducing the English apple tree into parts of the Himalaya, such as Mussourie, Ranikhet, Simla, &c., and already the supply of fruit from this source is rapidly increasing in those parts.

The Maharaja of Kashmir some years ago made attempts at making cyder in his territories, but no marked results were apparently obtained.

649 **P. Pashia,** *Ham.*

Syn.—P. VARIOLOSA, *Wall.*

Vern.—*Mehal, mol,* HIND.; *Passi,* NEPAL; *Lee,* LEPCHA; *Tang, keint, thindar, shegul,* PB.

A moderate-sized tree of the outer Himalaya, from Kashmir to Bhutan, also in the Khásia hills.

Sometimes cultivated in the Himalaya. The fruit is dark yellow-brown, scurfy, covered with raised white spots. It is eatable when over-ripe, and natives eat it in this state and when half rotten.

650 **P. vestita,** *Wall.*

Vern.—*Maylull, gáhor,* NEPAL; *Singha,* BHUTIA.

A deciduous tree of the Eastern Himalaya, between 8,000 and 10,000 feet.

Fruit is edible.

QUERCUS.

651 **Quercus dilitata,** *Lindl.*, CUPULIFERÆ.

Vern.—*Ban, barachar, parungi, chora, maru, karsh,* PB.; *Moru, kilonj, timsha,* N. W. P.

A large tree in the Sulaiman Range and north-west regions of the Himalaya, at 7,000 to 9,000 feet in altitude.

The leaves are severely lopped for fodder for sheep and goats.

652 **Q. Ilex,** *Linn.*

THE HOLLY-LEAVED OAK; THE EVERGREEN OR HOLM OAK.

Vern.—*Charrei, serei, balút,* AFG.; *Chár, kharsu, dú, yúru, heru, ban,* PB.

A middle-sized tree or large bush, met with in Europe and on the Himalaya, and discovered by Dr. Watt as far east as Manipur.

The leaves without prickles are used for winter fodder, for which purpose they are stored. The acorns are eaten in France.

Quercus incana, *Roxb.* 653

Vern.—*Vari, rhin, rinj, ban,* PB.

A large tree of the lower Himalayan ranges from the Indus to Nepal, the commonest of all the North West Himalayan Oaks.

The acorns are eaten by monkeys and bears.

Q. lanuginosa, *Don.* 654

Vern.—*Ranj, rai-banj,* KUMAUN; *Banga,* NEPAL.

A large tree apparently limited in its area of growth to Naini Tal and a few other places in Kumaun.

The leaves are used as fodder.

Q. semicarpifolia, *Smith.* 655

Vern.—*Barchar, kreu, karshu, sauj,* PB.; *Ghesi, kasru,* NEPAL.

A large tree of Afghanistan and the Himalaya from the North-West; to Nepal and Bhutan.

The leaves of this are used as fodder, for which purpose they are also stored in winter.

RANDIA.

Randia dumetorum, *Lam.*, RUBIACEÆ. 656

Vern.—*Mainphal, manyúl, karhar, arar,* HIND.; *Mindla, mandkolla,* PB.; *Maidal, amuki,* NEPAL; *Panji,* LEPCHA; *Pativa,* URIYA; *Madu-karray,* TAM.; *Manda,* TEL.; *Kare,* KAN.

A small, thorny shrub, common on the Himalaya, from the Chenab, eastward. Produces, like other species of this genus, highly fragrant flowers, and round, smooth berries, which when ripe are yellow, and contain a large quantity of a firm, fleshy pulp.

The fruit or berry is roasted and eaten by the natives.

R. uliginosa, *DC.*, RUBIACEÆ. 657

Syn.—POSOQUERIA ULIGINOSA, *Roxb.*

Vern.—*Piralo,* BENG.; *Pindalu, panar, paniah, katul,* HIND.; *Maidal,* NEPAL; *Pendra,* URIYA; *Katil, pender,* GOND; *Kaurio,* PANCH MEHALS; *Nalaika,* TEL.; *Wagata,* TAM.; *Karé,* KAN.; *Panelra, pindra,* MAR.; *Mhaniben,* BURM.

A small tree of the sub-Himalayan tracts, Oudh, Bengal, Central and South India, and Burma. Common in moist places; produces large, white, fragrant flowers generally in the beginning of the hot season.

The fruit, of the size and shape of a hen's egg, and olive-grey in colour, contains a large quantity of hard, dry pulp, which is eaten by the natives.

RANUNCULUS.

Ranunculus sceleratus, *Linn.*, RANUNCULACEÆ. 658

An herbaceous annual found on river banks in Bengal and Northern India, in marshes of Peshawar, and warm valleys of the Himalaya. It appears in the cold season and remains till the rains.

The inhabitants of Wallachia use it as a vegetable when boiled, a remarkable fact, when it is remembered that it is poisonous, and a powerful vesicant when uncooked.

REPTONIA.

RAPHANUS.

659 **Raphanus sativus,** *Linn.*, CRUCIFERÆ.

THE RADISH.

Vern.—*Mula*, BENG.; *Muli*, HIND.; *Mooluka*, SANS.

An annual herb of the cabbage family, unknown in its wild state, but is cultivated, here and there, throughout the plains of India and in the hills up to 16,000 feet in the Himalaya. It is a cold weather crop in the plains, and grows nearly all the year round in the hills and mountains. There are several varieties grown in India: the large, long, pale-pink; the small, longish, pale-pink; and the small, round, bright red. The last is raised generally in gardens with selected seeds.

The two first are the more common and are universally eaten by all classes of natives, either in their natural state or cooked in curry. The second, when young and tender, and the last, are eaten by Europeans.

The plump and still young and green pods are used for pickling, alone or with other vegetables, and are regarded a fair substitute for capers.

There seems some difference of opinion as to the origin of this cultivated plant. **Bentham** thinks it may possibly have come from the British wild plant **R. Raphanistrum,** *Linn.;* others that its home is in China and India. The English radish is so utterly different from the coarse plant met with in India that it would seem as if the most natural explanation would be that the European Radish had been derived from **R. Raphanistrum** and the Indian species from an Indian and Chinese indigenous wild plant now apparently lost. The Indian radish is almost warm, temperate or tropical in its habit instead of temperate. It is often perennial and may be transplanted from one field to another, yielding its seed in the second year. The root grows to an enormous size, sometimes as large as a man's leg, rising partly above ground like a stem. It is pale red or white coloured without the pleasant pungency of the English plant. It is eaten cooked or raw, and the seeds yield an oil used in cooking.

660 **Var.—Caudatus.**

Vern.—*Mugra.*

This extraordinary form is cultivated in the Punjab and in Northern and Western India on account of its pods, which are used as a vegetable. The younger Linnæus is said to have obtained this plant from Java, but the vernacular name given by him "Mongri" so closely corresponds with the Hindustani name "Mugra," and this again with the other Indian names for the Radish proper as to point forcibly to the idea that if obtained from Java it was most probably originally an importation into Java from India. Mr. Baden-Powell in his *Punjab Products*, page 260, states that the seeds sell in the Punjab for Rs. 2 per seer, a price which shows how highly the plant is prized. He adds: "The natives have an idea that this plant is only **R. sativus,** subjected to a peculiar treatment, *viz.*, by being taken up and having all its roots cut close round and then replanted." There seems little doubt of the origin of this plant from the same stock as the ordinary Indian radish, but the habit of removing the tap root as a vegetable and replanting the stock for the production of seed is quite common with the poorer classes. The rat-tail-like pods of **Caudatus** are eaten either boiled or pickled.

REPTONIA.

661 **Reptonia buxifolia,** *A. DC.*, MYRSINEÆ.

Vern.—*Gurgura*, PB.; *Garar*, AFG.

The only species known of this genus is a small tree in the Salt Range and on the Trans-Indus hills.

The rounded, black edible drupes, of the size of marbles, are collected in April and eaten by the natives; but are very poor to European taste. The fruit is mainly occupied by the seed, which is not eaten.

RHAMNUS.

Rhamnus persicus, *Boiss.*, RHAMNEÆ.

BUCKTHORN.

Vern.—*Kukai, jalidar, kuchni*, PB.

A shrub common in the Salt Range and the Trans-Indus tracts and in the temperate Himalaya.

Produces small, black fruit, said to be sweet, but to affect the head if eaten in excess. (*Dr. Stewart.*)

RHAZYA.

Rhazya stricta, *Dcne.*, APOCYNACEÆ.

Vern.—*Sunwar*, HIND.; *Vena, gandera*, PB.; *Sehur, sewur*, SIND.

A small shrub, abundant in the Trans-Indus tracts, and sparse in the Salt Range.

Its leaves, which are very bitter, are used for fodder for goats after steeping for some days. (*Dr. Stewart.*) In Sind the natives use them in the preparation of cool drinks in the hot weather.

RHEUM.

Rheum Emodi, *Wall.*, POLYGONACEÆ.

TURKEY RHUBARB.

Vern.—*Renchini*, BENG.; *Dolu*, HIND.; *Chutial, pambash, atsu, artso, chukri, rawâsh*, names in the Punjab Himalaya and in Afghanistan.

A shrub frequent in parts of the Punjab Himalaya.

The stalks are eaten by the natives either boiled with water, or in their natural state pounded and mixed with salt and pepper; they are also dried, stored and eaten with other food, and sometimes they are made into preserves.

A poisonous principle of greater or lesser intensity is said to pervade the whole of the germs, and many cattle—goats—are said to die yearly in Sikkim from eating the leaves of **R. Cinabarinum.** As bearing on food, it may be mentioned that the leaves of **R. Arboreum.** yield such a quantity of honey that the ground becomes wet under the plants.

RHIZOPHORA.

Rhizophora mucronata, *Lamk.*, RHIZOPHOREÆ.

THE MANGROVE TREE.

Syn.—R. MANGLE, *Linn.*

Vern.—*Bhara*, BENG.; *Kámo*, SIND; *Upoo-poma*, TEL.; *Byu*, BURM.; *Bairada*, AND.

A large shrub or tree generally met with in the tidal shores and creeks of rivers in India, Burma, and the Andaman Islands.

The fruit is said to be sweet and edible, and the juice to be made into a kind of light-wine. Salt is also extracted from its aerial roots.

RHODODENDRON.

666 **Rhododendron arboreum,** *Sm.*, ERICACEÆ.

Syn.—R. PUNICEUM, *Roxb.*

Vern.—*Chán, ardáwal, mandál, chiu, bras, burans,* PB.; *Brus,* KUMAUN; *Bhorans, lal-guras,* NEPAL; *Etok,* BHUTIA, LEPCHA; *Billi, poomaram,* NILGIRIS.

A tree, 25 feet high, of Nepal and the outer Himalaya, at 3,000 to 11,000 feet in altitude; the hills of Southern India, of Karenni in Burma, and Ceylon.

The flowers have a sweetish-sour taste, are commonly eaten by the hill tribes, and are made into preserve by the higher classes and Europeans.

667 **R. Nobile.**

Vern.—*Chuka.*

Dr. Hooker, describes this plant as upwards of a yard high and forming conical towors of the most delicate straw-colored, shining, semi-transparent, concave imbricating bracts, the large, bright, glossy, shining, green radical leaves with red.

The natives eat the pleasantly acid stems.

RHODOMYRTUS.

668 **Rhodomyrtus tomentosa,** *Wight.*, MYRTACEÆ.

HILL GOOSEBERRY.

Syn.—MYRTUS TOMENTOSA, *Ait.*

Vern.—?

A shrub much resembling the common myrtle, found in the higher mountains of South India.

Produces small, dark-purple berries which have fleshy, sweet, aromatic pulps, and are eaten when ripe either raw or made into a jam called "thaontz."

RHUS.

669 **Rhus semi-alata,** *Murray*, ANACARDIACEÆ.

Syn.—R. BUCKIAMELA, *Roxb.*; R. JAVANICA, *Linn.*; R. AMELA, *Don.*

Vern.—*Tatri, titri, chechar, arkhar, arkol, kakri, dúdla, wánsh, hulashing,* PB.; *Rashtu,* SUTLEJ; *Dakhmila, daswila,* N. W. P.; *Bakkiamela, bhagmili,* NEPAL; *Tukhril,* LEPCHA.

A small tree met with in the outer Himalaya from the Indus to Assam (up to 7,000 feet in altitude) and the Khási hills (up to 5,000 feet). Produces numerous, pale yellowish green flowers, and small drupes (the size of a pea) of a greenish white color or red when ripe.

The drupes, or berries, are covered with a small quantity of pulp which has a sharp, acid taste, and is eaten by the Nepalese and the Lepchas; and from it is prepared a wax called *Omlu* in Nepal. (*Gamble.*)

RIBES.

670 **Ribes glaciale,** *Wall.*, SAXIFRAGACEÆ.

Vern.—*Robhay,* BHUTIA., *Kukuluya, kalakalaya,* HIND.

A small shrub in the Himalaya, from Kashmir to Bhutan.

Yields a sour unpalatable fruit of no value. H. Strachey found it near Nabhi in Byáns where it is very abundant, and yields a fruit described by him "as small and insipid." The flowers appear in May, and the fruit ripens in September-October. (*Atkinson.*)

Ribes Grossularia, *Linn.* 671

THE ROUGH OF HAIRY GOOSEBERRY.

Vern.—*Pilsa, kansi, teila,* LAHOUL.

A wild shrub frequently met with in the higher altitudes of the Himalaya, from Kumaun to Kashmir.

Produces a small, very sour fruit, hardly ever eaten even by the natives.

The gooseberries cultivated in the plains of India are very palatable, and are largely grown for consumption either raw or in preserves.

H. Strachey records having found it at Tala kuwa in Byáns in September, and pronounces it worthless. The European cultivated varieties have been introduced, but do not thrive nor bear freely." (*Atkinson.*)

R. nigrum, *Linn.* 672

BLACK CURRANT.

Vern.—*Papar,* KUMAUN; *Muradh, nabar, mandri, beli, shdhtekas,* PB.

Confined to the Himalayan tracts from Kunawar to Kashmir.

The fruit is very like the cultivated black currant, and very fair eating. (*Dr. Stewart.*) The flowers appear in July and the fruit ripens in August-September. **Major Garstin** states that the fruit is quite as large and as palatable as the cultivated variety. (*Atkinson.*)

By cultivation the fruit has been greatly improved; and is largely used as a cooling desert fruit as well as for tarts, preserves, wines, &c.

R. rubrum, *Linn.* 673

RED CURRANT.

Vern.—*Niangha,* LAHOUL; *Dak, rade, aus, hadar, wara, wane,* PB.

Met with in the Himalaya from Kumaun to Kashmir, at 8,000 to 12,000 feet in altitude.

The fruit, according to **Stewart,** is acid and nearly worthless, but **Aitchison** calls it a sweetish acid. It might by cultivation be made as useful as the above, as it is in Europe.

RICINUS.

Ricinus communis, *Linn.*, EUPHORBIACEÆ. 674

CASTOR-OIL OF PALMA CHRISTI.

Vern.—*Arend, rendi, reri, bhatreri,* HIND.; *Reri bherenda,* BENG.; *Eranda,* SANS.; *Amadum,* TEL; *Kyetsu,* BURM.

Grown almost everywhere in India, usually as a field border, commonly on the border of cotton and sugarcane fields, sometimes on isolated patches of a few square yards near dwelling-houses and used as a support for the creeping bean known as *sím.* But the areas are not as a rule large in any one province.

The oil expressed from the seeds is in certain places used for culinary purposes. The seeds are also put into curries. Its leaves are relished by cattle, and is said to be coming into repute as food for a species of silkworm.

See OILS AND OILSEEDS.

RODETIA.

675 **Rodetia Amherstiana,** *Moq.*, AMARANTACEÆ.

Vern.—*Bilga*, KOTI.

A large, straggling shrub of the north-west regions of the Himalaya, also in Burma.

Produces bright crimson berries which are eaten by the natives. The natives also eat the young shoots fried in ghee.

ROSA.

676 **Rosa macrophylla,** *Lindl.*, ROSACEÆ.

Vern.—*Gulab, ban-gulab*, HIND.; *Tikjik, akhiari, breri*, PB.

A thorny, pink-flowered shrub, common in the Himalaya from the Indus to Sikkim.

The fruit is said to be eaten.

NOTE.—Rose water is largely drunk by the natives of Calcutta in ordinary water and also in ærated water, made in large qualities from other species chiefly as perfumery.

677 **R. Webbiana,** *Wall.*

Vern.—*Kantian, shawali*, PB.; *Chua*, LAHOUL; *Sia*, LADAK, SPITI.

An erect, pink-flowered shrub of the arid tracts of the inner Himalaya.

The fruit is eaten.

ROSMARINUS.

678 **Rosmarinus officinalis,** *Linn*, LABIATEÆ.

ROSEMARY

Vern.—*Ukleel-ul-jilbul, hasalban-achnr*, ARAB.

A native of South Europe and of Asia Minor.

Cultivated chiefly as a perfume; it is also used as a conserve, and liqueur is made from it. Mentioned by Birdwood in the list of Spices and Condiments.

RUBIA.

679 **Rubia tinctorum,** *Linn.*, RUBIACEÆ.

THE EUROPEAN MADDER.

Diagnostic characters.—*Leaves* subsessile, 4 to 6 in a whorl, elliptic or lanceolate, *penni-nerved*; 2-4 by 1-1½ in., acuminate, margins and nerves beneath prickly.

Cultivated in Kashmir, Sind (*Flora of British India*), and distributed wild or cultivated to Afghanistan and westward to Spain.

This plant will be found noticed more fully in the section relating to "DYES." Here it may be noted that the leaves and herbage are used in some parts of Sind as fodder for camels and other animals.

RUBUS.

680 **Rubus biflorus,** *Ham.*, ROSACEÆ.

Vern.—*Akhreri, kantauch, harer, akhe, dher*, PB.

A strong, rambling shrub of the temperate Himalaya, from Sirmur to Bhutan, in altitude 7,000 to 9,000 feet.

Produces white flowers, and roundish, succulent fruit of a golden yellow colour.

Rubus ellipticus, *Smith.* 681

Syn.—R. FLAVUS, *Ham.*; R. ROTUNDIFOLIUS, *Wall.*

Vern.—*Akhi, kunachi, guracha, pukana*, PB.; *Esar, hisalu*, KUMAUN; *Escali*, NEPAL; *Kashgem*, LEPCHA.

A tall bush of temperate and sub-tropical Himalaya, from Sirmur, altitude 2,000 to 7,000 feet, to Sikkim, altitude 4,000 to 7,000 feet, and Bhutan; also in Khásia Hills, altitude 4,000 to 5,000 feet, Burma, Western Gháts and Ceylon.

"The fruit is yellow and with the flavour of the raspberry; it is commonly eaten and made into preserves in the Himalaya, and is certainly one of the best of the wild fruits of India." (*Gamble.*)

R. fruticosus, *Linn.* 682

THE BLACKBERRY OF BRAMBLE.

Vern.—*Ankri, alish, kanachi, chench, pakhána*, PB.

A shrub with arched stems, in the temperate regions of the Himalaya from Murree to Jamu.

Produces pink flowers, and many small, black, fleshy fruits. They are edible.

R. Idæus. 683

THE RASPBERRY.

This cane-stemmed shrub of the Rose family is a native of Britain and most parts of temperate Europe, and is also found in the Sikkim Himalaya,

The natives eat the fruit in its wild state; and Europeans cultivate it in gardens as a dessert fruit and for jams, jellies, cooling drink and raspberry vinegar. The fruit thus used consists of numerous little achenia embedded in pulp and forming a compound fruit.

R. lasiocarpus, *Smith.* 684

Vern.—*Gunacha, tulouch, stin, galka*, PB.; *Kalawar, kala-hisalu*, KUMAUN; *Kandiari, kharmuch*, KASHMIR; *Kala, aselu*, NEPAL; *Kajutalam*, LEPCHA.

A large, rambling, very variable plant in the Himalaya (temperate zone) from Murree to Sikkim, also in the Khási Hills, southern tracts of the Western Gháts (high zone), and Burma. Comprises several varieties.

The flowers are generally deep pink; the fruits are numerous, dry or fleshy, of a red or orange colour. Gamble says that the fruit has a glaucous, blue-black color, is small, and of good flavour.

R. lineatus, *Reinw.* 685

Var. 1.—**Angustifolia.**

" 2.—**Glabrior.**

Vern.—*Gempe aselu*, NEPAL.

A strong, sub-erect herb of the Sikkim Himalaya.

Fruit red and edible.

R. moluccanus, *Linn.* 686

Vern.—*Bipemkanta*, NEPAL.; *Sufok-ji*, LEPCHA.

A wide-spreading plant common in many parts in the north-east Himalaya, Assam and Khási Hills, South India and Burma.

Produces red edible fruits.

687 **Rubus niveus,** *Wall.*

Vern.—*Kalga*, SUTLEJ.

A large, rambling bush along the Himalaya in the temperate Himalaya, from Kashmir to Bhutan at elevation of 6,000 to 10,000 feet in the west and 5,000 to 11,500 feet in the east. There are apparently many varieties.

Fruit large or small, roundish, dry or fleshy.

688 **R. nutans,** *Wall.*

Vern.—?

A thin bush met with in Garhwal and Kumaun, at 8,000 to 10,000 feet in altitude.

Produces fruit of few scarlet drupes.

689 **R. paniculatus,** *Smith.*

Syn.—R. TILIACEUS, *Sm.*

Vern.—*Kala-akhi*, KANGRA; *Anchu, kala hisalu*, HIND.; *Numing rik*, LEPCHA.

A very rambling climber common in the temperate Himalaya from Rajaori to Sikkim, also in the Khásia Hills.

Produces white flowers, and many large, round, black drupes. Stewart says the fruit is not much prized.

690 **R. purpureus,** *Bunge.*

Found in the western temperate zone of the Himalaya and the Tibetan region.

Produces round red fruit.

691 **R. rosæfolius,** *Smith.*

A small shrub found in the Himalaya from Kumaun to Sikkim, in the Khásia Hills and in the hills of Burma.

Has a large, red, edible fruit, which is sold in the bazar in Darjeeling.

RUMEX.

692 **Rumex hastatus,** *Don.*, POLYGONACEÆ.

Vern.—*Khatimal, ami, amla, amlora*, PB.

A shrub or under-shrub, common in the north-western regions of the Himalayan tracts, 2,500 to 9,000 feet in altitude.

The leaves have a pleasant acid taste, and are eaten raw as Sorrel.

693 **R. vesicarius,** *Linn.*

SORREL.

Vern.—*Chúka pálak, chuka-palang*, N. W. P.; *Kata-mita, saluni, triwaka*, PB.

Common in the Trans-Indus and Salt Range tracts of the Punjab, up to 3,000 feet in altitude.

It has a more pleasant taste than the last, and is eaten raw and also as a pot-herb.

SACCHA-RUM.

Rumex Wallichii, *Meisn.* 694

Syn.—R. ACUTUS, *Roxb.*

Vern.—*Bun-palung,* BENG.; *Jool-palum,* HIND.; *Jungli-palak, sagukei obul, kula,* PB.

Common in many places throughout North India on the plains, and in the hills up to 12,000 feet in altitude.

The leaves are used as a pot-herb, and are reckoned cooling.

SACCHARUM.

Saccharum canaliculatum, *Roxb.*, GRAMINEÆ. 695

Vern.—*Kans,* HIND., BENG.

A perennial, stately grass from 8 to 12 feet in height; the culms are about as thick as a common ratan, filled with pith; the leaves are from 5 to 7 feet long, semi-cylindric, not thicker than a pack-thread. Found in Bengal, North-West Provinces and Oudh, and in the Himalayas. In Bengal Roxburgh says it is found in most thickets where the soil is rich, and flowers in August and September.

As a material for paper-making it deserves attention.

Browsed by cattle (?)

S. fuscum, *Roxb.* 696

Syn.—ERIOCHRYS S FUSCA, *Trin.*

Vern.—*Kilut* or *tilluk,* HIND.; *Khuri* or *patee-khori,* BENG.

This is smaller than the preceding grass, being 5 to 8 feet high, as thick as the little finger; the leaves are about 3 or 4 feet long and 2 inches broad. Inhabits damp places over Bengal, stretches along the banks of the Ganges, and is met within Kashmir up to 3,000 feet. In Bengal it flowers during the rainy season.

The natives make their pens of the culms of this and other species, and use it for screens and light fences. (*Roxb.*)

Browsed by cattle when young and tender (?)

S. officinarum, *Linn.* 697

THE SUGARCANE.

Vern. *Ikh, ikhari, ukh, ukhari,* N. W. P. and OUDH; *Nai-shakar,* PERS.; *Ik, ák, ak, kúshiar,* also *poori* and *kullooa* (the pale varieties), *kajooli* (the red), BENG.; *Ikshu, rusala* (the pale), *poondra, kanguruku* (the red), SANS.; *Cherukoo-bodi,* TEL.

A strong cane-stemmed grass from 8 to 12 feet high producing a large feathery plume of flowers, found wild and cultivated throughout tropical and sub-tropical Asia, and the Islands of the Indian and Pacific Oceans. It is cultivated for its sugar, which is its expressed juice and which by boiling by other processes and becomes crystalised as brown sugar. On being refined it is frequently moulded into loaf or lump sugar. The uncrystalised is call gurh, treacle, or molasses. From the scum and rough portions of the latter, rum is manufactured by distillation. The sugar is probably the sweet cane of Jeremiah, VI. 20.

There are several varieties of sugarcane cultivated in India, some being grown entirely for the manufacture of sugar, others for eating raw. The latter are, as a rule, thicker, softer, and more juicy than the former.

SACCHARUM.

The total area under sugarcane in India is estimated to be approximately acres, of which the Punjab owns acres, the North-West Provinces and Oudh 950,000 acres, Bengal acres, Central Provinces acres, the remaining provinces (Madras, Bombay, Berar, Assam) aggregating acres.

It has been estimated that in 1876 about 2,140,000 tons of sugar had been manufactured from the sugar-cane all over the world. As the cultivation of the cane extends westwards from India and China, its native place, the exports from India naturally diminishes, as represented by the figures £948,582 in 1854, £716,857 in 1864, and £281,743 in 1874.

The sugar-cane season comprises nearly a twelvemonth. The land chosen is usually a good loam or light clay, manured. The leafy ends of the preceding season's canes are cut off or the whole cane is chopped into pieces so as in any case to include two nodes or joints, and these, to the number of about 20,000 per acre, are planted in furrows in January and February. The land is irrigated occasionally from this time to the commencement of the rains. The harvest begins in the beginning of December, and the cutting and crushing of the canes and boiling of the juice are carried on till January and February. Excepting the few mills under European management the crushing and boiling are performed by primitive and therefore rude processes. The average outturn per cent of cane in the North-West Provinces is stated by Messrs. Duthie and Fuller to be as follows: 100 of canes=50 of juice=18·0 of gurh + 17·5 of shukr, + 19·5 of *rab*; the *rab* gives 13 *putri* +6·5 shira; the shira gives 6·5 chini +6·5 shira.

The average cost of growing an acre of cane in the North-West Provinces is stated to be Rs. 62-13; the average outturn of gurh per acre is about 30 maunds and costs Rs. 1-6 per maund.

The following statistics of the trade in sugar are taken from the Reports on the inland trade of the different provinces and on the trade by sea.

The Punjab received from other Indian Provinces in 1881-82, refined sugar 2,29,355 maunds and unrefined 10,18,158 maunds. The supplies came chiefly from the North-West Provinces and Oudh (refined 1,98,001 maunds, unrefined 967,791 maunds) and in smaller quantities from Sindh. The Punjab exported to other Indian Provinces, refined sugar 22,161 maunds and unrefined 2,53,990 maunds; the bulk of the exports went to Rajputana and a small proportion to Sindh.

The North-West Provinces and Oudh received of refined sugar 1,85,522 maunds and of unrefined 2,20,026 maunds in 1882-83; the bulk of the supplies came from Bengal exclusive of Calcutta (refined 1,63,474 maunds, unrefined 1,93,324 maunds), with small quantities from various other parts, in the case of refined sugar chiefly from Bombay port (10,696 maunds) and of unrefined from Calcutta (11,124 maunds). The North-West Provinces and Oudh exported of refined sugar 268,726 maunds and of unrefined 23,78,081 maunds. The exports went chiefly—

	Refined, in Mds.	Unrefined, in Mds.
To Rajputana	1,09,501	9,76,385
„ Punjab (including Delhi City) . .	71,444	9,86,082
„ Central Provinces	24,401	2,12,145
„ Southern India	41,649	1,94,362

with much smaller quantities to Bengal, to Calcutta and to Bombay port.

SACCHARUM.

Bengal receives* very little sugar from other provinces, the total of refined in 1881-82 being only 8,576 maunds and of unrefined 4,378 maunds, and these came almost wholly from the North-West Provinces. The exports of sugar from Bengal on the other hand were considerable, thus—

	Refined, in Mds.	Unrefined, in Mds.	Of which from Calcutta, refined and unrefined, in Mds.
To North-West Provinces and Oudh .	1,60,914	85,911	12,618
" Central Provinces	33,206	98,341	402
" Bombay	4,977	1,08,651	72
" Rajputana	12,455	89,514	6,510
" Punjab	10,321	12,357	5,535
" Assam	11,272	2,643	...
	2,33,145	3,97,417	25,137

For the other provinces trustworthy figures of the inland trade are not available.

By sea to other countries, India exports the following quantities of sugar :—

Presidency from which exported.	Refined or crystallised sugar, Cwts.	Unrefined sugar, *viz.*, molasses or gur, Cwts.
Bengal	85,952	79,445
Bombay	11,992	6,356
Sindh	26	463
Madras	13,290	1,119,930
British Burma	14	1,230
TOTAL . . .	111,274	1,207,424
TOTAL VALUE, Rs.. .	13,01,331	67,86,428

The exports have largely increased during the past five years as the following figures for 1878-79 will show :—

	Cwts.	Rs.
Refined sugar	51,043	6,96,792
Unrefined sugar	228,713	13,46,808

* Figures are those of 1881-82, hence probably discrepancy in exports to North-West Provinces and Oudh, as compared with the imports into those Provinces from Bengal.

SACCHARUM.

The exports proceed to the following countries (the figures are those of 1882-83):—

Country to which exported.	Refined sugar, Cwts.	Unrefined sugar, Cwts.
United Kingdom	78,724	1,053,276
Egypt	...	132,692
Ceylon	14,827	9,210
Arabia	10,264	6,884
Other countries (Australia, France, Persia, the Straits, Aden, Siam, Turkey in Asia, &c.)	7,459	5,362
TOTAL . .	111,274	1,207,424

693 **Saccharum procerum,** *Roxb.*

Vern.—*Teng,* BENG.

A perennial grass from 10 to 20 feet high, erect; culms straight filled with insipid pith; leaves 3 to 5 feet long, tapering to a long fine point; sheaths bearded round the mouth. Native of Bengal, also found in Kangra and Kheree Pass.

Roxburgh says it is by far the most beautiful of the genus he met with, and that it comes nearest in appearance to **S. officinarum,** but is taller and much more elegant. "The seeds or culms," he adds, "are long, strong and straight, and employed by the natives for screens, and various other economical purposes."

699 **S. Sara,** *Roxb.*

Vern.—*Sara, shur,* BENG.; *Sarpat, sara, munj sarkar, shur,* HIND.; *Gundra, shura,* TEL. and SANS.

A grass common in the plains of the North-West Provinces and Punjab 8 to 12 feet high; leaves flat, narrow, 4 to 8 feet long; culms perennial, erect, from 6 to 16 feet high, thick as the little finger, strong; sheaths from 12 to 18 inches long; flowers late in the rainy season.

It is stated that the tops, just before flowering, form a good fodder for milk, and that in South Punjab the delicate pith contained in the upper part of the stem is eaten by the poor.

700 **S. spontaneum,** *Linn.*

Vern.—*Kash,* BENG.; *Kans, kagara, kosa, kus,* HIND.; *Rellu-gaddi,* TEL.; *Khan, kahu,* SIND.; *Kahi, kans,* PB.; *Kásha,* SANS.

Common in Bengal, the sub-Himalayan tract and Bundelkhand.

Roxburgh says this grass "grows on the banks of rivers, in hedges, moist, uncultivated land; in a good soil it is frequently from 10 to 15 feet and on high, in a poorer soil from 5 to 10." **Duthie** describes it as "a troublesome grass and difficult to eradicate on account of its deeply penetrating roots." The culms are annual, erect, leafy, round; leaves sheathing, remarkably long and narrow but firm.

This grass is so coarse that cattle do not eat it; it is, however, given when young as fodder to buffaloes. It is used for thatching and matting; the culms serve to make the native pens.

In Bundelkhand it has encroached upon large areas of arable land, and persistent efforts have recently been made with some success by the Provincial Department of Agriculture to eradicate it and reclaim the land.

SACCOPETALUM.

Saccopetalum tomentosum, *Hook. f. & T. T.*, ANONACEÆ. 701

Syn.—UVARIA TOMENTOSA, *Willd.*

Vern.—*Karna, karri*, HIND.; *Hoom*, BOM.; *Chilkadudu*, TEL.; *Thoska*, GOND.

A large tree in Oudh and Gorakhpur, Behar, Central India and the Western Ghâts. Blossoms during the hot season and produces oval berries.

The leaves are used as fodder.

SAGERETIA.

Sageretia Brandrethiana, *Aitch.*, RHAMNEÆ. 702

Vern.—*Ganger, goher*, PB.; *Maimuna*, AFG.

A scrubby shrub abundant in the Sulaiman and Salt Ranges, and occurs in the extreme north-west parts of the Himalaya.

Produces a small black fruit, of the size of a small pea, sweet, and pleasant eating when fresh; it is well known in the bazars of Peshawar and Afghanistan, and is much eaten by Afghans and by the natives of the frontier districts.

S. oppositifolia, *Brongn.* 703

Vern.—*Kanak, gidardak, drange, girthan*, PB.; *Aglaia*, KUMAUN.

A large shrub in the north-western parts of the Himalaya, from Peshawar to Nepal, also in Southern India from Konkan southwards.

Produces a small, black, succulent, sweetish fruit, which is eaten by the natives.

S. theezans, *Brongn.*

THE TIA OF THE CHINESE.

Vern.—*Drangie, ankol, karur, phomphli, kanda, brinkol, katrain, thum*, PB.; *Dargola*, SIMLA. 704

A shrub of the Salt and Sulaiman Ranges (altitude 2,000 to 8,000 feet) and of Western Himalaya from Kashmir to Simla (altitude 3,000 to 8,000 feet).

The fruit is small, round, dark-brown, sweet and succulent, and is extensively eaten. The leaves are said to be used as a substitute for tea.

SALIX.

Salix alba, *Linn.*, SALICINEÆ.

THE WHITE OR HUNTINGDON WILLOW.

Vern.—*Bis, yúr, changma, málchang, kharwala*, PB. 705

A large tree cultivated in the Western Himalaya. Useful timber from which cricket bats are made.

The branches are severely lopped, and used as fodder. The young shoots and bark of the larger trees are removed by hand and used as fodder.

S. daphnoides, *Vill.* 706

Vern.—*Bed, biddi, betsa, bashal*, PB.; *Yúr*, KASHMIR; *Changma*, WEST TIBET; *Richang*, LAHOUL.

A shrub of the North-West Himalaya, both on the outer ranges and in the inner arid tract. (*Gamble.*)

The branches and leaves are used for cattle fodder.

SALVADORA.

707 **Salix elegans,** *Wall, Koch.*

THE WEEPING WILLOW.

Syn.—S. BABYLONICA.

Vern.—*Bail, bhains,* SIMLA.

A small shrub of the Himalaya from Lahoul to Nepal, in altitudes ranging from 1,500 to 7,000 feet.

The leaves and twigs are used for fodder for cattle and goats.

708 **S. tetrasperma,** *Roxb.*

Vern.—*Pani-jama,* BENG.; *Baishi, bed, bent,* HIND.; *Burun,* SANS.; *Laila, bains, bilsa,* N. W. P. and OUDH; *Bis, bitsa, bidu, bakshel, safedar, badha,* PB.; *Bhi,* ASS.; *Bhesh,* GARO; *Walunj, bacha,* BOM.; *Niranji,* KAN.; *Momakha,* BURM.

A middle-sized tree on river banks and moist places throughout India, ascending the Himalayan valleys up to 6,000 feet.

The leaves are lopped and given to cattle as fodder.

SALSOLA.

Salsola indica, *Willd.* *See* **Sueda indica,** *Moq.*, CHENOPODACEÆ.

SALVADORA.

709 **Salvadora oleoides,** *Linn.*, SALVADORACEÆ.

Vern.—*Kabbar, jhar, diar, jal, vani jhal, ughai, koku,* HIND., PB., TAM.; *Pilu,* MAR.

A large, evergreen shrub of the Punjab and Sindh, often forming the greater part of the vegetation of the desert, and ascending the Trans-Indus hills and Salt Range to 3,000 to 24,000 feet in altitude. Flowers in April and its fruit ripens at the beginning of the hot weather. The fruit "is sweetish and is largely eaten by the natives, large numbers of whom go out to collect it in the season; and so much do they depend on it that **Coldstream** states that a bad crop is reckoned as a calamity * * * and that in Mozaffurgarh the fruit is often dried for future use, and has then much the appearance and flavour of currants." (*Dr. Stewart.*)

The leaves serve as fodder for camels.

710 **S. persica,** *Garcin.*

Syn.—S. INDICA, *Wight*; S. WIGHTIANA, *Planch.*; CISSUS ARBOREA, *Forsk.*; EMBELIA GROSSULARIA, *Rets.*

Vern.—*Jit, kauri van, kaurijal, choti van,* PB.; *Jal,* N. W. P.; *Kabar, khoridjhar,* SIND.; *Pedda-warago-wenki,* TEL.; *Opa, ughai,* TAM.

A small thick-stemmed, soft, wooded tree, wild in many of the drier parts of India, *e.g.*, Punjab, Sind, Rajputana, North-Western Provinces, Guzerat, Konkan, and the Circars. Produces flowers and very small black red juicy currant-like berries, having a strong aromatic smell, and pungent taste like mustard or garden cresses.

The shoots and leaves are pungent, and are eaten as salad and given as fodder to camels.

SALVIA.

Salvia Moorcroftiana, *Wall.*, LABIATÆ. 711

Vern.—*Káli jarri, sholri, thut, halu, gurgumna, laphra, papra,* PB.

Common in the North-west Punjab plains Salt Range, and Himalaya up to 9,000 feet.

The stalks are in some parts peeled and eaten, and have a mawkish sweet taste.

S. pumila, *Benth.* 712

Vern.—*Tukhm malanga,* PB.

A small plant common in western Punjab.

Browsed by goats and sheep.

SAPINDUS.

Sapindus attenuatus, *Wall*, SAPINDACEÆ. 713

Vern.—*Lal koi-pura,* SYLHET; *Sir-hutungchir,* LEPCHA; *Achatta,* NEPAL.

A shrub of Eastern Himalaya and Assam, extending to Eastern Bengal. Produces small red flowers, and red or dark purple fruit of the size of an olive.

The fruit is eaten by the natives in Sylhet.

S. Mukorrossi, *Gaertn.* 714

Vern.—*Ritha, dodan, kanmar,* HIND.; *Ritha,* BENG.

Cultivated throughout North-West India and Bengal.

The only part of this saponaceous tree which can be noted under the section of "Food" are the leaves, which are given to cattle as fodder.

SAURAUJA.

Saurauja napaulensis, *DC.*, TERNSTRŒMIACEÆ. 715

Vern.—*Gogina, gogonda,* HIND.; *Gogen,* NEPAL; *Kasur,* LEPCHA.

A moderate-sized tree of the Himalaya from Bhutan to Garhwal, also in the temperate Khásia Hills. Produces pink flowers, and green, mealy inside, sweet, edible fruit.

The leaves are lopped for cattle fodder.

SCHLEICHERA.

Schleichera trijuga, *Willd*, SAPINDACEÆ.

THE LAC TREE OF KOOSUMBIA. 716

Vern.—*Kosum, gausam,* HIND.; *Kásinb,* BOM.; *Rusam,* URIYA; *Pává, pú, púlachi, aolim-buriki,* TAM.; *Pusku, may, roatanga,* TEL.; *Gyoben,* BURM.; *Cong, conghas,* CINGH.

A large, deciduous tree of the sub-Himalayan tract, from the Sutlej eastward, Central and South India, and Burma. Flowers in February and ripens its fruit in May,

The fruit contains a whitish pulp which is of a pleasant sub-acid taste, is much liked during the hot, dry weather, and is often eaten by the natives.

SCIRPUS.

717 **Scirpus Kysoor,** *Roxb.*, CYPERACEÆ.

Vern.—*Kasurio*, HIND.; *Kesur, kesuri*, BENG.; *Kaseruka*, SANS.; *Kaseru, dila*, PB.

A weed common on the borders of lakes and ponds of fresh water in Bengal; grows in Northern India.

The tuberous roots are eaten raw by the natives. Dr. Stewart, in his *Punjab Plants*, mentions S. maritimus, *Linn*, as common in marshes and when fresh a fair forage.

SCOPOLIA.

Scopolia præalta, *Dunal*, *See* Physochlaina præalta, *Hook. f.* SOLANACEÆ.

SCUTELLARIA.

718 **Scutellaria linearis,** *Benth.*, LABIATÆ.

Vern.—*Mastiara*, PB.

Not uncommon in the Salt Range and Jhelam basin to 4,000 feet.

In the Salt Range the plant is eaten, although very bitter.

SECURINEGA.

Securinega Leucopyrus, *Müll-Arg.*, EUPHORBIACEÆ.

719 **Vern.**—*Partho, aindha*, N.-W. P.; *Kakun, rethei*, PB.; *Pera pastawane*, AFG.; *Kiran*, SIND.; *Challa mantu*, C. P.; *Achal*, NEPAL.

A large shrub or small tree of the outer Himalaya, ascending to 5,000 feet throughout India and Burma.

The fruit is eaten.

720 **S. obovata,** *Müll.*

Syn.—PHYLLANTHUS RETUSUS & VIROSUS, *Roxb.*; CICCA OBOVATA, *Kurz.*

Vern.—*Dalme, dhani, ghari, gwala, darim*, HIND.; *Iktibi*, LEPCHA; *Kodarsi* MAR.; *Korchi*, GOND; *Yae-chinya*, BURM.

A small tree of the Sulaiman range and outer and sub-Himalayan tracts, extending to Eastern Bengal, Central and South India, and Burma.

Produces small round, pure white, smooth, succulent berries in abundance.

Edible?

SEMECARPUS.

721 **Semecarpus Anacardium,** *Linn. f.*, ANACARDIACEÆ.

THE MARKING-NUT TREE.

Vern.—*Bhála bhilawa, bheyla*, HIND.; *Bhela, bhelatuki*, BENG.; *Shaing*, TAM.; *Jiri, nela-jedi*, TEL.; *Chyai beng*, BURM.

Sub-Himalayan tract from the Sutlej eastward to Assam and Chittagong, but not to Burma; ascending 3,500 feet. Produces dull greenish yellow flowers from May to August, and ripens in January and February.

The yellow fleshy cup which surrounds the seed is roasted in ashes, and eaten by the natives.

The seeds, called Malacca-beans or Marsh-nuts, are also eaten. They are supposed to stimulate the mental powers and especially the memory.

SESBANIA.

SESAMUM.

Sesamum indicum, *Linn.*, PEDALINEÆ. 722

GINGELLY OF SESAME OIL; BENNE OIL, HUILE DE SESAME, *Fr*; SESAMOL, *Ger*.

Vern.—*Mithá tél, krishna-tél*, HIND.; *Tél, tili*, BENG.; *Tila*, SANS.; *Róghane kunjad*, PERS.; *Duhn*, ARAB.; *Gingili*, SOUTH IND.; *Nal lenney, yelloo cheddie*, TAM.; *Manchi-núne noovooloo*, TEL.; *Bárik-tél*, DEC.; *Hnan* BURM.

This annual herb is commonly cultivated in India (where it is indigenous) in nearly every tropical country.

"There are two varieties, the black-seeded and the white-seeded; the former being generally known as *til*, and the latter as *tili*. *Til* ripens rather later than *tili*, and is more commonly grown mixed with high crops such as *juar*, while *tili* does best when mixed with cotton. *Tili* oil is preferred of the two for human consumption." (*Messrs. Duthie* and *Fuller*.)

The oil is extracted by simple pressure in a wooden mill of a very primitive kind, worked by a bullock which is driven by a man or boy seated on the revolving beam.

Tili oil is not only used for human consumption as other oil, but is also employed in sweetmeat making and in adulterating *ghi*, also occasionally for lighting, and for anointing the body. For this last purpose it is sometimes scented by keeping the seeds between alternate layers of strong-scented flowers, before the oil is pressed out: in its scented state the oil is called *phulel* and fetches Rs. 160 per maund. The seeds are also made into sweetmeats which are eaten by the natives.

The oil bears a strong resemblance to olive oil; and for it it is frequently substituted, and with it it is frequently adulterated.

The oil cake (or residue remaining after the oil is extracted) is used as cattle food, and in some parts of the country it is much prized as such. In times of drought and scarcity it is even used as human food by the poorer classes.

The figures available for the areas under *til* and *tili* cultivation are very incomplete, and no distinction is made in the returns between the two varieties, both being reported under the name of *til* in North, and *gingelly* in South India.

In the North-Western Provinces *til* is grown as a sole crop in the districts lying under the Himalayas, where its area is annually about 6,310 acres, and in the districts of Bundelkhand where the area is 148,100 acres. In the other parts of the Provinces it is almost universally grown to a greater or less extent in fields of juar, bajra and cotton, more in the western than in eastern parts.

The sowing is performed at the commencement of the rains, generally in light soil (in Bundelkhand the light yellowish soil); the seed is sown broadcast when mixed with other crops, otherwise in parallel lines. The crop is liable to damages from ill-timed rain; the outturn in the North-Western Provinces varies from 25 to 60 seers of seed to the acre when the crop is sown with juar or cotton, to 4 to 6 maunds when grown alone.

The dry stocks, after the harvest, are used for fuel.

SESBANIA.

Sesbania ægyptiaca, *Pers.*, LEGUMINOSÆ. 723

Syn.—ÆSCHYNOMENE SESBAN, *Linn.*

Vern.—*Jait, jhinjan, janjhan*, HIND.; *Jayanti*, BENG.; *Saori*, BERAR; *Shewar*, DEC.; *Suiminta*, TEL.; *Yaythagyee*, BURM.

A soft-wooded shrub of short duration cultivated in many parts of the plains of India from the Himalayas to Ceylon, and in Burma. Produces pale yellow flowers, more or less tinged with deep-red, and long, weak legumes or pods.

The leaves and branches are lopped for cattle fodder.

724 **Sesbania grandiflora,** *Pers.*

Syn.—ÆSCHYNOMENE GRANDIFLORA, *Roxb.*; AGATI GRANDIFLORA, *Desv.*

Vern.—*Basna*, HIND.; *Buka, bak*, BENG.; *Agati*, TAM.; *Avisi*, TEL.; *Poukpan*, BURM.

A short-lived, soft-wooded tree, cultivated in South India, Burma, and in the Ganges Doab (*Gamble*), generally near villages. Produces large, handsome, pink, or white flowers, tinged with red, and long narrow pods.

The leaves, flowers, and tender pods are eaten in curry by all classes of natives. Cattle also eat the leaves and tender parts.

SETARIA.

725 **Setaria glauca,** *Beauv.*, GRAMINEÆ.

Syn.—PANICUM GLAUCUM, *Linn.*

Vern.—*Bhandra, bhandri, dissi*, N. W. P. & PB.

Very common both in the plains and on the hills. Very variable as to the size of the spikes and their colour; a small variety is common on dry ground.

726 **S. italica,** *Kunth.*

GERMAN OR ITALIAN MILLET.

Syn.—PANICUM ITALICUM, *Linn.*

Vern.—*Kakun, kangri, kauni, tangan, kukni*, N. W. P. and OUDH; *Kungu*, SANS.

China, Japan, and the Indian Archipelago are mentioned as probably the countries in which this plant originated and whence it spread. (*De-Candolle.*) Duthie says it is supposed to have originated in India and New Holland.

It *alias* millet is extensively cultivated in India both in the plains and on the hills up to 6,500 feet. It is sown in the North-Western Provinces and Oudh on good village lands at the commencement of the rains to an extent which is reported to be over 14,000 acres, and is reaped in September with an outturn of 3½ to 5 maunds of seed per acre. A second crop may be had from the same ground between September and the end of January. It is, however, more commonly grown as a subordinate crop than by itself. When thus understood the above-stated area is much below the truth. In the Punjab it is found wild or cultivated in parts of the Himalayan region.

There are two varieties—one straw yellow and the other reddish yellow.

The grain is much esteemed as an article of human food in some parts of the country and is eaten in the form of cakes and porridge in the North-West Provinces. In the Madras Presidency it is valued as an excellent material for making pastry. At Chenab the leaves are used as a pot-herb. Boiled with milk, it forms a light and pleasant meal for invalids. The Brahmins specially esteem it. It is also grown as food for cage birds, and for feeding poultry in the Punjab and North-West Provinces.

When ripe the ears only are plucked, the straw being afterwards cut for fodder. As fodder the straw is not very nourishing: it is given to goats in parts of the Punjab Himalaya.

Setaria verticillata, *Beauv.* 727

Syn.—PANICUM VERTICILLATA, *Linn.*

Vern.—*Kootta chirchitta, burdunni,* N. W. P.; *Dora-byara,* HIND.; *Chick-lenta,* TEL.

Found on the plains and hills of the Punjab and North-West Provinces, and ascends the Himalaya up to 6,500 feet in Naini Tal; also found in Nepal. Delights in a rich soil in out of the way corners where there is rubbish. (*Roxburgh.*)

Cattle eat it when young, that is, before the flower spikes are formed; the seeds are eaten by small birds. (*Duthie.*)

SHOREA.

Shorea robusta, *Gærtn.,* DIPTEROCARPEÆ. 728

THE SAL TREE.

Vern.—*Sál, súla, sálwa, sákhu,* HIND.; *Sakwa,* NEPAL; *Teturl,* LEPCHA; *Bolsal,* GARO; *Koroh,* OUDH; *Sarei, rinjal,* C. P.; *Gugál,* TEL.

A tall, sparsely-branched, deciduous tree, often so crowded and gregarious as to have long, straight stems, growing to a height of 100 feet, with only a terminal tuft of branches. One of the most valuable timber trees of India.

The seed ripens at the commencement of the rains, and is the means of reproduction. Sonthals, however, especially in times of scarcity, collect the seed and eat it, by roasting it and mixing it with the flowers of the *Mahua* tree (**Bassia latifolia**); which see.

SIDEROXYLON.

Sideroxylon tomentosum, *Roxb.,* SAPOTACEÆ. 729

Syn.—S. ELONGGIDES, *Bedd.*

Vern.—*Pala,* TAM.

A tree common in the Western Ghâts from the Konkan southwards. The fruit is made into pickles and curries.

Sinapis juncea, *Linn.* *See* **Brassica juncea,** *H. F. & T.,* CRUCIFERÆ.

Sinapis ramosa, *Roxb.* *See* **Brassica juncea.**

SIZYGIUM.

Sizygium jambolanum, *DC.,* MYRTACEÆ. 730

Vern.—*Jaman, jam, jámun,* HIND; *Káldjam,* BENG.; *Chambu,* GARO.; *Jamu,* ASS.; *Uaval, naya,* TAM.; *Nasodu, nairuri,* TEL.; *Jambool,* BOM.; *Thab-gai-pyoo,* BURM.

A tree found wild or in cultivation all over India.

The fruit is astringent, but is eaten by the natives, who also eat the kernels in times of famine.

SKIMMIA.

Skimmia Laureola, *Hook. f.,* RUTACEÆ. 731

Vern.—*Ner, baru,* PB.; *Nehar, gurl pata,* KUMAUN; *Chumlani,* NEPAL; *Timburnyok,* LEPCHA.

An aromatic shrub of the Himalaya from the west to Bhutan,

SOLANUM.

5,000 to 11,000 feet in altitude, also in the Khásia Hills, in altitude 5,000 to 6,000 feet.

The leaves are eaten in curries by the hill people.

732 **Soja hispida,** *Mœnch.*, LEGUMINOSÆ.

Cultivated in India for its seeds or beans which are made into sauce called soy, used both in Asia and Europe for flavouring dishes, specially beef, and believed to help digestion.

SOLANUM.

733 **Solanum coagulans,** *Forsk.*, SOLANACEÆ.

Syn.—S. SANCTUM, *Linn.*

Vern.—*Maraghúne, bari manhári, tingi,* PB.

A plant resembling **M. Melongena**, met with in the Punjab and Sindh.

The fruit is, in some places, eaten by the natives, either fresh or in pickles.

734 **S. gracilipes,** *Dcne.*

Vern.—*Howa, marghi-pal, kandiari, pilak, valur,* PB.

A thorny under-shrub of Western India, in Punjab and Sindh.

It produces a small fruit which is eaten by the natives.

It is not known wild in India. **A. DC.** says it is a native of Asia, not America, and **Sendtner**, *l. c.*, fixes its origin in Arabia. As an escape from cultivation it becomes often intensely prickly. (*Fl. Br. Ind.*)

735 **S. melongena,** *Linn.*

EGG-PLANT OF BRINJAL.

Syn.—S. INCANUM, *Linn.*; S. ESCULENTUM, *Dunal*; S. ZEILANICUM, *Scop.*; S. LONGUM, *Roxb.*

Vern.—*Begoon, kooli-begoon,* BENG.; *Baigun,* HIND.; *Wang-kai,* TEL.

More or less common throughout India, generally in cultivation.

There are many varieties distinguishable by the colour of the fruit: thus—deep purple, white, &c. The white ones are more rare and are supposed to be more tender and pulpy, but this is probably a mere idea.

Brinjals are much eaten in curry by all classes of natives, and are sold in every bazar.

"They are used in different ways: (*a*) made into curries, either with potatoes, or shrimps, or both; (*b*) roasted under hot ashes and made into a *bhartha* by being mashed and seasoned with salt, onions, chillies and lime-juice or mustard oil; (*c*) cut into slices and fried in oil; (*d*) when young and tender they are pickled with mustard oil, chillies, salt, &c." (*Mr. L. Liotard.*)

736 **S. nigrum,** *Linn.*

Syn.—S. RUBRUM, *Miller.*

Vern.—*Kambei, kachmach, mako,* PB.; *Gurkhi,* BENG.

A common herbaceous plant found throughout India and Ceylon, altitude 0—7,000 feet.

Produces a small, round berry, red or black (hence its name), sometimes yellow, eaten by the natives; also by the soldiers in British Kaffraria.

Its leaves possess slight narcotic properties, and are eaten in place of spinach in Bourbon and the Mauritius.

Solanum tuberosum, *Linn.* 737

POTATO.

Vern.—*Alu,* HIND., BENG.; *Alú,* PB.; *Wallarai kilangoo,* TAM.; *Ootalay gudda,* TEL.; *Batata,* BOM.; *Rata innala,* CINGH.

Native of Peru and Chili, introduced into Spain in the beginning of the 16th century, whence it was introduced into India. The under-ground stem or tuber is in common use as an esculent. Coarse tasting brandy is also made from the potato.

The potato is now cultivated in all parts of India in the plains and in the hills up to 9,000 feet.

Potato is eaten by almost all classes.

It enters largely into the manufacture of wheaten bread.

S. verbascifolium, *Linn.* 738

Vern.—*Kala-mewa, tiari, ola, kharawune,* PB.

A shrub common throughout India in the tropical and sub-tropical zones.

Produces small, round, yellow fruit or berries, which in Southern India are used in curries.

S. xanthocarpum, *Schrad. & Wendl.* 739

Syn.—S. JACQUINI, *Willd.*

Vern.—*Kateli, katai,* HIND; *Kantakári,* BENG.; *Warumba, choti mauhari, harnauli,* PB.

A prickly, diffuse herb, commonly met with from the Punjab to Assam and Ceylon. In blossom and fruit most part of the year.

In some places the seeds are eaten.

SONCHUS.

Sonchus oleraceus, *Linn.*, COMPOSITÆ. 740

MILK THISTLE.

Vern.—*Dodak,* PB.; *Ratrinta,* TEL.

A weed with hollow milky stems, yellow flowers and glossy leaves, more or less common throughout India in fields and cultivated places, and up to 8,000 feet in the Himalaya.

Kashmiris use it as a vegetable. Cattle are fond of it.

SONNERATIA.

Sonneratia acida, *Linn. f.*, LYTHRACEÆ. 741

Syn.—S. APETALA.

Vern.—*Orcha, archaká,* BENG.; *Tapu, tamu,* BURM.

A small, evergreen tree of the tidal creeks and littoral forests of India, Burma and the Andamans. (*Gamble.*)

Flowers during the hot and rainy seasons, and produces a slightly acid bitter fruit which is eaten in the Sundarbuns. It is also eaten by the Malays as a condiment. A kind of silk-worm feeds upon its leaves.

SORGHUM.

Sorghum bicolor, *Willd,* GRAMINEÆ. 742

Vern.—*Killo-debdhaor, dedhún,* BENG.

Cultivated in India.

Grain much used for food.

SOR-GHUM.

743 **Sorghum halepense,** *Pers.*

Syn.—HOLCUS HALEPENSIS, *Linn.*

Vern.—*Barua, braham,* PB.; *Bajra, bara,* BUNDELKHAND.

Common in parts of the Siwalik tracts, also on the plains and hills of the Punjab and North-West Provinces; described by **Mueller** as a rich, perennial grass.

This is a fodder grass when young, and **Stewart** says it is at times browsed by cattle, but, he adds: "I was told in Hazara that after eating it cattle sometimes have fatal head affections."

744 **S. saccharatum,** *Pers.*

BROOM CORN or CHINESE SUGARCANE.

Syn.—ANDROPOGON SACCHARATUS.

The seeds of this annual grass, sugar producing millet or sweet cane were obtained by the Government of India . . . . . and distributed to the different Provincial Governments for experimental cultivation.

This grass is cultivated in Northern India.

This plant might be advantageously utilised for preparing treacle; as the saccharine sap would amount to from 100 to 300 gallons per acre.

The grass is used as a valuable fodder for cattle.

745 **S. vulgare,** *Pers.*

THE INDIAN or GREAT MILLET or GUINEA CORN.

Syn.—HOLCUS SORGHUM, *Linn.*; ANDROPOGON SORGHUM, *Brot.*

Vern.—*Juar, junri, choti juar, bajra-jhupanwa,* N. W. P. and OUDH; *Juar, kurbi* and *chari* (stalks), BENG., HIND.; *Zoorna,* SANS.; *Talla, jonna, bonda-janu* (the plant), *tella-janular* (the grain), TEL.; *Cholum,* TAM., *Chavela,* MAL.

An annual cane-like corn grass, similar to Indian-corn, producing a dense head of spikelets, bearing numerous small corn grains, which are very valuable as food. The stalk of this plant was most probably the 'reed' of Matthew, and its spikelets the 'hyssop' of St. John.

This is one of the most important of the rainy season food crops in India, and with rice and wheat form the chief staple food of the country. From it are made bread, porridge and other food preparations; occupying the same place to many natives that oats do to many of the inhabitants of Scotland. Its small yellow seed when crushed makes also a good auxiliary food for cattle horses, swine, poultry, and sheep. It contains 2½ per cent. of flesh-forming matters and about 11 per cent. of fat or heat-producing matters. It is sometimes known as Durra.

There are numerous varieties of juar (or cholum) as might be expected from the large extent to which it is cultivated. (*Duthie* and *Fuller.*)

The area under this crop in the different Provinces of India may be given approximately as follows:—

	Acres.
Punjab	
North-Western Provinces and Oudh .	3,690,000
Bengal (chiefly Behar)	
Central Provinces	
Bombay Presidency	
Berar	
Madras Presidency	
Total .	

SPOUDIAS.

For the Rajputana and Central India States, the Nizam's Territories and Mysore no figures are available.

In Madras in 1870 there were devoted to food grains of the millet species.

	Acres.
Cholum (**Sorghum Vulgare**) . .	4,855,000
Raggy (**Elensine corocana**) . .	1,611,000
Veragu (**Panicum miliaceum**) .	1,605,000
Cumboo (**Pencilliaria spicata**) .	3,197,000
Corraloo (**Panicum italicum**) .	1,018,000
Millet of various kinds . .	614,000
Total . .	12,900,000

The seed (at the rate of 3 to 6 seers per acre) is sown broadcast at the commencement of the rains in rather elevated soil, chiefly of the loamy or clayey kind, sometimes with other minor crops of pulses; irrigation is seldom used; the pulses are first harvested, and the juar harvest begins a fortnight later, *i. e.*, in November.

The cost of cultivation, including rent, in the North-Western Provinces and Oudh is given by **Messrs. Duthie and Fuller** at Rs. 13-13-0 per acre; and the outturn they estimate at about 10 maunds of grain, and 60 maunds of dry fodder on irrigated, and 8 maunds of grain and 45 maunds of dry fodder on unirrigated land; in addition to the outturn of the subordinate crops—arhar 5 maunds, other pulses 2 maunds, til ½ maund.

The dry stalks and leaves are chopped to form the ordinary cattle fodder of the country for some months of the season. Occasionally, in parts of the North-West Provinces and Oudh and the Punjab, juar is grown solely for cattle fodder, in which case the stalks are cut while green before the seed matures. In this case it is usually sown in the hot weather before the rains, requires irrigation, and is cut early enough to be succeeded by one of the cold weather crops. The outturn per acre is on irrigated land 300 maunds of green fodder (known as *chari*), equal to 100 maunds of dry fodder; and on unirrigated land 280 maunds equal to 90 maunds of dry fodder.

SPINACIA.

746

Spinacia oleracea, *Mill.*, CHENOPODIACEÆ.

GARDEN SPINACH.

Vern.—***Paluk, sag-paluk***, HIND.; ***Palung***, BENG., ***Bij-palak***, PB.; ***Ispanaj, is-panaj***, ARAB., PERS.; ***Vusayley-keeray***, TAM.

This plant is cultivated in some parts of India, chiefly under garden cultivation; both kinds, the one with smooth, the other with prickly seeds.

Its large fleshy insipid but wholesome leaves are used as a favourite pot-herb in the early spring and summer months. When properly dressed and deprived of moisture, mashed with butter and a few sorrel leaves, they make an excellent dish which may be eaten with any kind of meat.

SPONDIAS.

Spondias dulas. 747

OTAHEITE APPLE OR VI.

Vern.—*Amara.*

A tree of from 50 to 60 feet high, a native of the Polynesian Islands.

STERCULIA.

introduced into many parts of the tropics; has golden apples sometimes weighing 1 lb. 2 ozs. and measuring a foot in circumference. The rind tastes of turpentine, but the pulp has a fine apple-like smell and an agreeable flavour.

748 **Spondias mangifera,** *Pers.*, ANACARDIACEÆ.

THE HOG-PLUM.

Syn.—S. AMARA, *Lamk.*

Vern.—*Amra*, BENG.; *Amra, ambodha*, HIND.; *Amara*, NEPAL, ASS.; *Ronchiling*, LEPCHA; *Tongrong*, GARO; *Hamara*, GOND; *Ambera*, KURKU; *Kat-mara*, TAM.; *Aravi-mamadi*, TEL.; *Kat ambolam*, MAL.; *Amb*, MAR.; *Amte*, KAN.; *Gway*, BURM.

A deciduous tree, wild and cultivated, more or less common throughout India, *e. g.*, Sub-Himalayan tract from the Indus to Eastern Bengal, very common in Bengal, rare in Central India, frequent in South India, and Burma. Blossoms at the beginning of the hot season, the leaves follow immediately, and the fruit ripens in winter when the leaves fall off, leaving the fruit in bunches.

The fruit is eaten raw when ripe, and while green it is pickled or put in curries.

In Bengal, at least, there are two varieties of the *Amara*, or hog-plum; one is larger, pleasantly sweetish-acid, and has more pulp over the nut—it is probably the **Spondias dulcis**, *Willd.*, said to be introduced from the South Sea Islands; the other is smaller, disagreeable to the taste and has less pulp. The former is known by the natives as *bilaiti-amra* [European apple], is rare and is cultivated in gardens; the latter is known as *desi-amra* [country apple], and is more common and wild in parts of the country.

The *bilaiti-amra* is often eaten in its natural state when ripe, and is rarely put in curries. The *desi-amra* is rarely eaten in its natural state except by the poorer natives, and is more commonly put in fish or vegetable curries, or in lentil, to give these dishes an acid taste much liked by natives, or it is made into pickle with mustard oil, salt, chillies, &c. (*L. Liotard.*)

SPOROBOLUS.

749 **Sporobolus tenacissimus,** *Beauv.*, GRAMINEÆ.

Syn.—S. ORIENTALIS, *Kunth.*; AGROSTIS TENACISSIMA, *Linn.*

Vern.—*Usar-ki-ghas, khar-usara-ghas, kalusra*, N. W. P.; *Tama-gerika*, TEL.

Grows on dry, barren ground on the plains of the North-West Provinces, the Punjab and Sindh, and on old, poor, stiff pasture ground in Madras, where it forms extensive plants of tenacious turf.

Mr. Duthie says it is a good fodder grass, that it grows remarkably well on barren *usar* land, and that it has very long roots, which deeply penetrate into the soil in search of moisture.

STERCULIA.

750 **Sterculia balanghas,** *Linn.*, STERCULIACEÆ.

Vern.—*Cavalum*, MAL.

A tree found throughout the hotter parts of India and Ceylon. The seeds are wholesome, and when roasted are nearly as palatable as chestnuts. (*Roxb.*).

Sterculia fœtida, *Linn.* 751

Vern.—*Jangli-badam*, HIND.; *Pindri*, TAM.; *Gurapu-badam*, TEL. *Hlyanpyoo, letkop*, BURM.

A large, evergreen tree in Konkan, Malabar, and Burma. Produces large flowers of a dull crimson and orange colour, variously blended, and fruit or rather capsules of the size of a man's fist, pretty, smooth, and fibrous. These contain each from 10 to 15 seeds, of the size of filberts, oblong, hard and smooth.

The seeds are roasted and eaten like chestnuts, but are not much esteemed.

S. urens, *Roxb.* 752

Vern.—*Gúhú, kúlú, gúlar tabsi, karrai*, HIND.; *Odla*, ASS.; *Hittum*, GOND; *Takli*, KURKU; *Talbsu*, TEL.; *Vellay pútali*, TAM.; *Kalru*, AJMIR.

A large, deciduous tree, with five-lobed hand-shaped leaves, found in the sub-Himalayan tract from the Ganges eastward to Assam, common in forests in Behar, South India and Burma. Produces, during the cold season, small, numerous yellow flowers; and the leaves appear with the fruit about the beginning of the hot season. The fruit, or rather capsules which are clothed with stiff bristly stinging hairs, are in bunches of five united in the form of a star.

They contain each from 3 to 5 seeds, which are oblong, chestnut-coloured, and are roasted and eaten by the poorer tribes of natives, such as the Gonds and Kurkis of the Central Provinces. A kind of coffee may be made from the seeds.

STRYCHNOS.

Strychnos potatorum, *Linn. fil.*, LOGANIACEÆ. 753

THE CLEARING NUT TREE.

Vern.—*Nirmali, nelmal*, HIND.; *Kotaku*, URIYA; *Ustumri*, GOND; *Tetrankottai*, TAM.; *Chilla, induga, katakamee*, TEL.; *Nirmali*, MAR.; *Tetam-parel*, MAL.; *Chilu*, KAN.

A moderately-sized tree of Bengal, Central and South India.

Flowers during the hot season, and produces a black fruit of the size of a cherry, with one seed, the pulp of which when ripe is eaten by the natives.

It receives its name because of its singular power of clearing muddy water by its being rubbed round the vessel containing the water.

SUŒDA.

Suœda indica, *Moq.*, CHENOPODACEÆ. 754

Vern.—*Ella-kura*, TEL.

A plant on and near salt, moist ground near the sea. Flowers during most part of the year; the leaves are scattered round every part of the branchlets, and are fleshy, smooth, half inch long, green in young plants, coloured in older ones.

Dr. Roxburgh wrote :—

"The green leaves of this species are universally eaten by all classes of natives who live near the sea, where it is to be had; it is reckoned very wholesome, and must be so, as during times of scarcity and famine it is a very essential article of the food of the poor natives; they dress it in their curries, &c. The leaves of this plant alone, the natives say, saved many thousand lives during the late famine of 1791-2-3; for, while the plant lasted, most of the poorer classes who lived near the sea had little else to eat."

TANACETUM.

SYRINGA.

755 **Syringa Emodi,** *Wall.*, OLEACEÆ.

Vern.—*Bán-phúnt, banchir, rasli, rangkrun, lolti, sháfri, dud en,* PB. *Ghia,* KUMAUN.

A large shrub of the Himalaya, from the north-west regions to Kumaun, ascending to 11,000 feet.

The leaves are eaten by goats.

TACCA.

756 **Tacca pinnatifida,** *Forsk.*, TACCACEÆ.

SOUTH-SEA ARROWROOT, CHÁNAY KÉLÉNGU or PI.

Vern.—*Carachunal,* TAM.; *Cunda,* TEL.

Found in the Concan southwards, also on the Parell hills near Bombay.

Has a large, round, tuberous root, which yields a large quantity of white nutritious fecula, resembling arrowroot, much eaten by the natives, specially in Travancore, where it forms an important article of trade.

It is equal to the best arrow-root. The tubers are dug up after the leaves have died away; and are rasped and macerated for four or five days in water when the fecala separates in the same manner as sago does. It is a favorite ingredient for puddings and cakes in the South Seas.*

TAMARINDUS.

757 **Tamarindus indica,** *Linn.*, LEGUMINOSÆ.

THE TAMARIND.

Vern.—*Amli, ambli, imli,* HIND.; *Tintri, tintil,* BENG.; *Titri,* NEPAL; *Tintuli,* URIYA; *Púli,* TAM.; *Chinta,* TEL.; *Karangi, kamal, asam,* MYSORE; *Magyee,* BURM.

A large, evergreen tree, growing to a height of 80 feet and a circumference of 25 feet, cultivated throughout India and Burma as far north as the Jhelum. Produces abundantly long, narrow pods with exceedingly sour pulp.

Its large flat pods, 4 to 6 inches in length, when ripe are sold in every bazar; in the way of food the pulp being put into curries to give an acid flavour. It makes a pleasant, cooling drink when a small quantity is diluted in water and sweetened with sugar. The tender leaves are also made into curries by the poorer classes. The pods pressed in syrup or sugar form the preserved 'Tamarinds' of English shops.

In Western India they are used in preserving or pickling fish, which under the name of tamarind-fish is regarded a delicacy.

TANACETUM.

758 **Tanacetum senecionis,** *Gay in DC.*, COMPOSITÆ.

Syn.—T. TOMENTOSUM, *DC.*

Vern.—*Purkar,* LADAK.

A plant of the Western Himalaya, Lahoul, Kunawar, and Garhwal. Altitude 11,000 to 14,000 feet.

Browsed by goats.

* "It possesses a considerable degree of acrimony, and requires frequent washing in cold water previous to being dressed. In Travancore, where the root grows to a large size, it is much eaten by the natives, who mix certain agreeable acids with it to subdue its natural pungency." (*Drury.*)

Tanacetum tenuifolium, *Jacq.* 759

Vern.—?

Inhabits Kumaun and Western Tibet, and closely resembles T. tibeticum, *Hook f. & Tho.*

Used for flavouring puddings.

TARAXACUM.

Taraxacum officinale, *Wigg.*, COMPOSITÆ. 760

DANDELION.

Vern.—*Dudal, baran, kanphúl, radam, shamukei, dudh-bathal,* PB.

A common weed found throughout the Himalaya and Western Tibet, at 1,000 to 18,000 feet; comprises several forms.

The young plant is eaten as a vegetable. The leaves are bitter and tonic and used as a salad like endive, but too bitter to be agreeable. They are eaten by cattle with advantage, as also by rabbits.

Its roots are also used by some with coffee instead of chicory.

TAXUS.

Taxus baccata, *Linn.*, CONIFERÆ. 761

THE YEW.

Vern.—*Saráp, badar,* AFG.; *Birmi, barma, túng, thúnu, chatung,* KASHMIR; *Thúner, geli, gullu, lust,* N. W. P.; *Pung-chu,* LADAK.

A large tree, met with all along the Himalaya, from the Indus to Bhutan, between 6,000 and 10,000 feet. Common in the forests of Manipur.

The bark is used in Kunawar as a substitute for tea or mixed with it. (*Dr. Stewart.*) The berries are eaten by the poorer natives, although in Europe they are regarded as poisonous. The leaves are eaten by goats and sheep.

The seeds are regarded by some as poisonous, and the branches and leaves highly poisonous to horses and horned cattle. But the red succulent cups, in which the seeds are seated, are frequently eaten because of their sweet mawkish taste. Birds feed largely on them in winter, so also do wasps and caterpillars.

Tea. *See* **Camellia theifera,** *Griff.*, TERNSTRŒMIACEÆ.

TECOMA.

Tecoma undulata, *G. Don.*, BIGNONIACEÆ. 762

Syn.—BIGNONIA UNDULATA, *Roxb.*

Vern.—*Reodana, rebdan, lahura, rahira,* PB.; *Lohuri,* SIND.; *Roira,* MHAIR.; *Rakt-reora,* MAR.

An evergreen shrub common in the Sulaiman and Salt Ranges, and Western India till Guzerat. Produces gorgeous orange-coloured blossoms in April.

The foliage is used as cattle fodder.

THEA.

TERMINALIA.

763 **Terminalia belerica,** *Roxb.*, COMBRETACEÆ.

MYROBALANS.

Vern.—*Bhaira, baherá,* HIND.; *Bohera,* BENG.; *Thara,* URIYA; *Bherda,* MAR.; *Balra, batra, balda,* DEC.; *Babela,* PERS.; *Kanom,* LEPCHA; *Chiroræ,* GARO; *Hulluch,* ASS.; *Tani, kattu, elupay,* TAM.; *Tani, tandi,* TEL.; *Thitsein,* BURM.; *Bulu,* CINGH.

A deciduous tree, attaining a height of 60 to 80 feet, having narrow lance-like leaves, growing in tufts at the tops of the branches; common in the plains and lower hills throughout India (except in the desert regions of West India).

The oval pentagonal fruit, the size of a nutmeg, is one of the Myrabolans of commerce, and is eaten, when fresh, by goats, sheep, cattle, deer and monkeys. The kernels of the fruit are also eaten, but produce intoxication when taken in excess.

In Kangra the leaves are considered the best fodder for milch cows.

764 **T. Catappa,** *Linn.*

ALMOND.

Vern.—*Badam,* BENG.; *Taru,* KAN.; *Natvadum,* TAM.; *Vedam,* TEL.; *Catappa,* MALAY.

A large, exceedingly handsome tree, widely cultivated throughout the tropical parts of India; wild in the Malay, and perhaps also in the Andaman Islands. It assumes an autumnal tint in the cold season, and the leaves fall off in the beginning of the hot season.

The kernels are cylindrical having the taste of almonds as also their shape and whiteness but not their peculiar flavour, and commonly eaten by natives and to a small extent by Europeans also, but by the latter as a dessert.

765 **T. chebula,** *Retz.*

Vern.—*Jangli-badam,* HIND.; *Herra, har, harara,* HIND.; *Hilikha,* ASS.; *Haritaki,* BENG.; *Silim,* LEPCHA; *Harla, harla,* DEC.; *Karka, harra,* GOND.; *Kadakai,* TAM., *Karak,* TEL.; *Pangah,* BURM.

A large tree, attaining the height of 80 to 100 feet, abundant in North India from Kumaun to Bengal, and southward to the Deccan table-lands; and to Ceylon, Burma, and the Malayan Peninsula. The fruit is one of the myrabolans of commerce.

The fruit is smooth and oval about an inch and a half long and an inch in diamater, having a considerable quantity of pulp. Its leaves are eaten by cattle, the kernels are also eaten and taste like filberts; but in large quantities produce intoxication.

766 **T. tomentosa,** *W. & A.*

Syn.—PANTAPTERA TOMENTOSA, *Roxb.* (*Fl. Ind., Ed. C. B. C.,* 383.)

Vern.—*Saj, sein, asan, assaim, asna, sadri,* HIND.; *Piasal, usan,* BENG.; *Sahāju,* URIYA; *Amari,* ASS.; *Taksor,* LEPCHA; *Kara marda, anemui,* TAM.; *Maddi, nella-madu,* TEL.; *Karkaya, sadora,* HYDERABAD; *Ain, madat,* MAR.; *Toukkyan,* BURM; *Kúmbúk,* CINGH.

A large tree of the sub-Himalaya from the Ravi eastward ascending to altitude 4,000 feet; Bengal, Central and South India and Burma.

The ashes of the bark give a kind of lime which, Gamble says, is eaten by the natives with betel leaf (*pán*).

Thea chinensis, *Linn.*; **T. assamica** *Masters.* *See* **Camellia theifera,** *Griff.*, TERNSTRŒMIACEÆ.

THEOBROMA.

Theobroma Cacao, *Linn.*, STERCULIACEÆ. 767

THE CACAO OR CHOCOLATE PLANT.

This small tree, 16 to 18 feet high, bears a pod-like fruit 6 to 10 inches long, and 3 to 5 in girth, containing 50 or more seeds. The ripe seeds, covered with mucilage are taken from the fruit and allowed to ferment. They are then dried in the sun, and thus become the brown chocolate bean or nut of commerce. Roasted and split or broken they become the cocoa nibs of the shops. The cocoa powder is simply the ground nibs, which formed into cakes, &c., flavoured with vanilla and sugar, make the chocolate of the shops.

The tree has been grown in some parts of India and Ceylon, where it is cultivated to a certain extent on the Malabar Coast by the Roman Catholic missionaries, who make small quantities of cacao regularly for their own use and for sale to Europeans of those parts. "The Cacao-seeds were made use of by the Mexicans previous to the arrival of the Spaniards boiled with maize and roughly bruised between two stones, and eaten, seasoned with capsicum and honey." (*Drury.*)

TODDALIA.

Toddalia aculeata, *Pers.*, RUTACEÆ. 768

TODDALIA.

Syn.—SCOPOLIA ACULEATA, *Sm.*

Vern.—*Kanj*, HIND.; *Dahan, lahan*, RAJPUTANA; *Meinkara*, NEPAL; *Saphijirik*, LEPCHA; *Milkaranai*, TAM.; *Konda-cahinda*, TEL.

A bushy shrub, or extensive climber, in the outer Himalaya from Kumaun eastwards, Khásia hills and Western Ghâts. (*Gamble.*)

The fresh leaves are eaten raw, and the ripe berries are pickled by the natives of the Coromandel coast; both the leaves and berries have a strong pungent taste.

On the Malabar Coast it is known as *Kaka Toddali*; hence the botanical name.

Tomato. *See* **Lycopersicum esculentum,** *Miller*, SOLANACEÆ.

TRAPA.

Trapa bispinosa, *Roxb.*, ONAGRACEÆ. 769

Vern.—*Pani-phal*, BENG.; *Singhara*, HIND.; *Sringata*, SANS.; *Gaunri*, KASHMIR.

A floating herb found on tanks and pools throughout India.

Flowers during the rainy season, and produces small, dark brown triangular nuts, sold in the markets when in season.

The kernel of the nut is white, sweetish and farinaceous, is much esteemed and very commonly eaten, both raw and cooked, by the natives, especially by the Hindus. Cakes are prepared from the kernel.

Dr. Stewart mentions (quoting from Moorcroft) that in the Kashmir valley it furnishes almost the only food of at least 30,000 people for five months of the year; and referring to a "good authority" he adds that the Maharajah draws more than a lakh of rupees annually from duty on the nut taken from the Wular lake. In some parts of India the food supplied by the nut, especially to the poorer classes, must be of consider-

TRICHO-SANTHES.

able importance. In Guzerat it forms an important article of diet, and in Manipur the immense lakes to the south of the valley afford food for a few months for a large community.

TRIANTHEMA.

770 **Trianthema crystallina,** *Vahl.*, FICOIDEÆ.

Vern.—*Alethi,* PB.; *Kuka-pal-kura,* TEL.

A prostrate-branched herb met with throughout India, from the Punjab to Ceylon, excepting Bengal.

In the Punjab it is very common, and near Multan its seeds are swept up in times of famine and used as food. (*Dr. Stewart.*)

771 **T. monogyna,** *Linn.*

Syn.—T. OBCORDATA, *Roxb.*; T. PENTANDRA, B. OBCORDATA, *DC.*

Vern.—*Swet-sabuni, lal-sabuni,* HIND.; *Yurra-galjeror, bodo-pel-kura,* TEL.

Common throughout India and Ceylon.

The leaves and tender tops are eaten by the natives in curries.

772 **T. pentandra,** *Linn.*

Syn.—T. OBCORDATA, *Wall.*

Common as a weed in waste grounds on the plains of the Punjab, Sindh and the North-West Provinces.

The tender tops of this plant, together with its leaves, are eaten as a pot-herb.

TRIBULUS.

773 **Tribulus alatus,** *Delile,* ZYGOPHYLLEÆ.

Vern.—*Lotak, bakhra, gokhrudesi,* PB.; *Krunda,* SIND.

A prostrate herb of Sind and the Punjab.

"The young plant is in some places eaten as a pot-herb; and the seeds are used as food, especially in times of scarcity."

774 **T. cistoides,** *Linn.*

The *Flora of British India* gives Bengal, in the vicinity of Calcutta, as a locality for this plant, a doubtfully distinct species from the following. This I regard as a mistake, for, during ten years' study of the Bengal plants, I have only once come across a specimen of Tribulus, and that I regarded as an escape.

775 **T. terrestris,** *Linn.*

This low trailing annual plant is common throughout India, ascending to 10,000 feet, rarer in Lower Bengal, and absent from the vicinity of Calcutta, abundant in Behar and everywhere in the Madras Presidency and the North-Western Provinces and Oudh.

The small spiny fruits of this plant is said to have constituted the chief food of the people during the Madras famine. They are supposed to be the thistles of St. Matthew.

TRICHOSANTHES.

776 **Trichosanthes anguina,** *Linn.*, CUCURBITACEÆ.

SNAKE-GOURD.

Vern.—*Chachinga,* HIND.; *Chichingá,* BENG.; *Jalar-tor pandol, chichinda,* PB.

A native either of India or the Indian Archipelago, believed by Mr. C. B. Clarke, to be a cultivated state of T. cucumerina.

TRIFOLIUM.

Sown in April and May throughout the plains and grown as a rain crop. Its pendulous, cylindrical, snake-like gourd, 3 feet long, is eaten cooked in curry, and is a common article of food.

Trichosanthes cucumerina, *Linn.* 777

THE DOOMMAALA.

Vern.—*Ban-patol*, BENG.; *Jangli-chachinda*, HIND.; *Gwal kakri, mohakri*, PB.; *Pipudel, pudel*, TAM.; *Chyad-potta*, TEL.

A pretty extensive climbing annual, found throughout India.

The fruit is oblong, 1 to 4 inches long, striated with white and green when unripe, and red when ripe. It contains a red pulp, which is eaten unripe, generally in curries, but is very bitter.

T. dioica, *Roxb.* 778

Vern.—*Potal*, BENG.; *Palbal* or *palwal*, HIND.; *Putulika*, SANS.

Cultivated during the rains throughout the plains of Northern India, from the Punjab to Bengal Proper and Assam.

The fruit is oblong, smooth, about 2 to 4 inches long, green when unripe, and yellow or orange when ripe.

It is eaten when unripe and always cooked, and is a much esteemed vegetable. Natives generally make it into curry.

It is also eaten in other ways, chiefly by Europeans: (*a*) cut in halves, boiled and served as a vegetable with butter, salt, and pepper; (*b*) cut in halves and fried; (*c*) cut in slices and stewed in sauce; (*d*) cut in halves and preserved in syrup with cinnamon or vanille. (*Mr. L. Liotard.*)

T. lobata, *Roxb,* 779

Vern.—*Bun-chichinga*, BENG.

Found in hedges and among bushes in the Deccan Peninsula (*Fl. Br. Ind.*) Flowers during the rains and produces an oblong, acute fruit, which, however, is not apparently eaten.

TRIFOLIUM.

Trifolium fragiferum, *Linn.*, LEGUMINOSÆ. 780

STRAWBERRY-HEADED CLOVER.

Vern.—*Chit-batto*, KASHMIR.

Confined to Kashmir, and much like **T. repens.**

Eaten by cattle. It receives its English name from the fruit-like aspect of its Calyces, which expand and take on a reddish colour after the flowers fade.

T. pratense, *Linn.* 781

RED or BROAD-LEAVED CLOVER or COW GRASS.

Vern.—*Trepatra*, PB.

Extends from Kashmir to Garhwal, at 4,000 to 8,000 feet in altitude and is not uucommon. Not well adapted for light soil.

Browsed by cattle. It is regarded as a good cropper where the commoner clover had failed.

TRITICUM.

782 **Trifolium repens,** *Linn.*

WHITE or DUTCH CLOVER or the SHAMROCK of IRELAND.

Vern.—*Shaftal, shotul,* PB.

A slender, wide creeping herb, common in many parts of the Himalaya, in the temperate zone, and up to 20,000 feet; also in the Nilgiris.

Browsed by cattle; a valuable feeding plant in dry and thin soils. Should be freely employed in laying down permanent pastures.

TRIGONELLA.

783 **Trigonella Fœnum-grœcum,** *Linn.,* LEGUMINOSÆ.

THE FENUGREEK or FENUGÆC.

Vern.—*Methi,* HIND., BENG.; *Vendayam,* TAM.; *Mentulu,* TEL.; *Ventagam,* MAL., *Men, thya,* KAN.; *Méthi,* MAHR., GUZ.; *Punantosi,* BURM.

A small, herbaceous plant, cultivated in parts of India, particularly in the higher inland provnces.

The seeds are commonly used as a condiment, chiefly in curries, and give a peculiar smell offensive to European taste.

Containing the principle called Coumarin, which imparts the pleasant smell to hay, they are employed to give false importance to or render palatable damaged hay, and to flavour the so-called concentrated cattle foods. It is also used as a substitute for coffee.

TRITICUM.

784 **Triticum sativum,** *Lam.,* GRAMINEÆ.

COMMON WHEAT.

Syn.—T. VULGARE, *Vill.;* T. ÆSTIVUM, *Linn.*

Vern.—*Gam,* BENG.; *Genhu, gohun,* HIND.; *Gandum,* PERS.; *Burr,* ARAB.; *Gudhuma, soomuna,* SANS.; *Godumai,* TAM., *Gódu muhi,* TEL.; *Kótanpan,* MAL.; *Gódhi,* KAN.; *Gahung* MAR; *Gujon saba,* BURM.

A native of the Euphrates region. (*DeCandolle.*) Cultivated from great antiquity: hence the present numerous varieties. In India it is cultivated in North-Western India, Central Provinces, and Bombay.

The variations are classed chiefly according to the consistency of the grain; thus, hard or soft wheat. The soft wheats are in most demand for the United Kingdom, while the hard ones go to the Mediterranean ports and are also preferred by the natives of India as the more wholesome. Each of these two classes may be grouped according to the colour of the grain in being white or red; and these again may be further sub-divided according to the presence or absence of bristles, which makes them known as bearded or beardless.

In India wheat is cultivated more or less in every Province, most largely in those of the north; and all the different kinds just mentioned are grown. They in many cases are cultivated with barley, gram, rape, and linseed as secondary crops.

TRITICUM.

The areas in each Province under wheat are estimated to be as follows :—

	Areas in Acres, 1880-81.
Punjab	6,509,225
North-West Provinces and Oudh	7,200,000
Central Provinces	3,391,441
Bengal	1,000,000
Bombay	1,352,474
Berar	774,870
Sindh	227,487
Madras	19,058
Mysore	21,058
Assam	11,475
Ajmere	8,683
TOTAL .	20,515,771

In the North-West Provinces and Oudh (**Messrs. Duthie** and **Fuller** write) "the cultivation of wheat grown alone reaches its maximum in the Meerut and Rohilkhand divisions, where winter rains may be safely reckoned upon, and it is in these divisions that the finest varieties have their home. In the drier districts of the Agra and Allahabad divisions and Bundelkhand wheat is rarely grown by itself, and is generally sown with either barley or gram, which by their superior hardiness continue to eke out a crop in cases where the wheat would fail from insufficient moisture."

The sowing of wheat is done in October and November in the different parts of the country. A rather heavy loam is considered best suited to its cultivation, but the cereal is grown also in almost any soil excepting the very light sand. The land is ploughed at the very commencement of the rains, and is allowed to remain open throughout their continuance. The seed is sown in October and November in the different provinces, at the rate of from 100 to 140 lbs. per acre. Irrigation is resorted to where available or necessary.

For the North-West Provinces and Oudh **Messrs. Duthie** and **Fuller** estimate on the best authorities that the total cost of cultivation (including rent and irrigation) is about Rs. 31-7 per acre; and that the outturn on irrigated land may be taken at 15 maunds of grain for wheat with barley, and 13 maunds for wheat with gram; on unirrigated land at from 6 to 10, and 7 to 9 maunds respectively in the first two and the third cases.

The chaff or chopped straw (bhusa) affords valuable fodder for cattle.

Indian wheats were not much known or appreciated in the European markets previous to the year 1871-72. From that year some attention was given to this Indian product; and the Government of India, following up the movement, abolished in January 1873 the duty of 3 annas per maund to which Indian wheat was subject on export. The result has been that

TRITI-CUM.

from that year the export rose suddenly, and it has since steadily been increasing as will be seen from the following figures :—

Exports of Wheat from India by Sea to other Countries.

Official years.	Quantity in Cwt.	Value in Rs.
1871-72	637,099	23,56,445
1872-73	394,010	16,76,900
1873-74	1,755,954	82,76,064
1874-75	1,069,076	49,04,352
1875-76	2,498,185	90,10,255
1876-77	5,583,336	195,63,325
1877-78	6,340,150	285,69,899
1878-79	1,044,709	51,37,785
1879-80	2,195,550	112,10,148
1880-81	7,444,375	327,79,416
1881-82	19,863,520	860,40,815
1882-83	14,144,407	606,89,341

The exports proceed to the following countries (the figures are those of 1882-83) :—

Country to which exported.	Quantity in Cwts.
United Kingdom	6,575,160
France	3,567,712
Belgium	1,458,898
Egypt	799,550
Holland	578,246
Gibraltar	494,098
Italy	176,063
Malta	163,358
Aden	140,132
TOTAL	14,144,407

The proportion in which the exports are shared by each of the five Maritime Provinces is given in the next table, and it will be seen from the figures of 1871-72, 1879-80, and 1881-82, which are given by way of comparison, that in Cwts. the increase has taken place chiefly in the exports from Bengal, Bombay, and Sind :—

Official years.	Bengal.	Bombay.	Sind.	Madras.	British Burma.
1871-72	346,979	127,945	152,359	3,836	5,980
1879-80	1,586,473	333,189	274,764	1,030	94
1881-82	6,668,047	11,328,585	1,852,334	10,996	3,558
1882-83	4,439,405	6,957,752	2,732,275	6,599	8,376

The exports from Bengal, Bombay, and Sind, besides including the produce of those Provinces, also comprise that of the North-West Provinces and Oudh, of the Punjab and of the Central Provinces, to the following quantities (the figures are those of 1881-82) :—

EXPORTED FROM	EXPORTED TO		
	Calcutta port.	Bombay port.	Karachi.
	Mds.	Cwts.	Cwts.
North-West Provinces and Oudh . .	40,73,456	22,851	......
Punjab	4,50,728	78,501	1,660,955
Central Provinces	58,146	7,571,217	......

TRIUMFETTA.

Triumfetta annua, *Linn.*, TILIACEÆ. 785

Vern.—*Aadai-otti*, TAM.; *Chikti*, HIND.

A herbaceous shrub common in tropical Himalaya, from Simla to Sikkim, the Khásia Mountains, Assam, Konkan, Ava, and Andaman Islands.

Produces orange-coloured flowers, and fruit of the size of a large pea.

Green paroquets feed on their ripe fruits or burrs, hence in Jamaica, these plants are known as Paroquet Burr.

T. pilosa, *Roth.* 786

Found throughout the tropical parts of India from the Himalaya to Travancore and Ceylon.

Produces yellow flowers and small fruit of the size of a cherry.

The remark made of the fruits of the above is here equally applicable.

T. rhomboidea, *Jacq.* 787

Syn.—T. BARTRAMIA, *Roxb.*; T. TRILOCULARIS, *Roxb.*; T. ANGULATA, *Lam.*

An herbaceous plant met with throughout tropical and sub-tropical India, and up to 4,000 feet in the Himalaya.

Eaten as a pot-herb in times of scarcity.

TULIPA.

Tulipa stellata, *Hook.*, LILIACEÆ. 788

Vern.—*Shandai-gul, bhumphor, chamui, paduna, jal kukar, chamoti*, PB.

Common in Western Punjab, the Salt Range, the Siwaliks and the outer Himalaya to Kumaun.

The bulbs are frequently eaten by the natives, and are for that purpose sold in some of the bazars in Peshawar. They are also in some parts eaten by animals.

TURPINIA.

Turpinia pomifera, *DC.*, SAPINDACEÆ. 789

Vern.—*Thali*, NEPAL; *Murgtu*, LEPCHA; *Nila*, NILGIRIS.

A moderately-sized deciduous tree of the Terai from the Nepal frontier eastward to Assam, Eastern Bengal, and Burma.

The leaves are given as fodder to cattle.

The fruit of some of the Turpinias is edible.

VACCINIUM.

TYPHA.

790 **Typha angustifolia,** *Linn.*, TYPHACEÆ.

THE REED MACE OR THE LESSER CAT'S TAIL.

Vern.—*Dib, kundar, lukh, boj,* PB.; *Pits, yira,* KASHMIR.

A kind of bulrush common in marshes in the Punjab and Kashmir.

In Kashmir the roots are eaten.

The flowers are of separate sexes, the male containing a quantity of pollen of which a kind of bread is made.

791 **T. elephantina,** *Roxb.*

ELEPHANT-GRASS.

Vern.—*Hogla,* BENG.; *Pan,* PB.; *Emiga-junum,* TEL.

Grows in fresh-water tanks, brooks, and slow-stream rivers.

Elephants are fond of it.

ULMUS.

792 **Ulmus campestris,** *Linn.*, URTICACEÆ.

THE ELM.

Vern.—*Kain, brari, brankul, marash, maral, hembar, imbir,* PB.

A large tree of the Punjab Himalaya at altitudes of from 3,500 to 9,500 feet.

The leaves, says Dr. Stewart, are a favorite fodder, and the trees are often very severely lopped on this account.

793 **U. integrifolia,** *Roxb.*

Vern.—*Papri, khulen, arján, rajáin,* PB.; *Papar, kanju,* KUMAUN; *Papri, dhamna, kánj, karanji, chilbil,* HIND.; *Aya,* TAM.; *Namli, peddanolwli, eragu,* TEL.; *Myoukseit,* BURM.

A large, deciduous tree of the sub-Himalayan tract from the Beas eastward, Central and South India, Burma.

The leaves are lopped for cattle fodder.

794 **U. Wallichiana,** *Planch.*

Vern.—*Kain, bren, amrai, marari,* PB.; *Mored, pabuna,* HIND.

A large, deciduous tree of the North-West Himalaya, from the Indus to Nepal, between 3,500 and 10,000 feet.

The leaves of this species also are lopped for cattle fodder.

URTICA.

795 **Urtica parviflora,** *Roxb.*, URTICACEÆ.

No information under food.

VACCINIUM.

796 **Vaccinium Leschenaultii,** *Wight.*, VACCINIACEÆ.

Vern.—*Andúvan,* NILGIRIS.

A tree of the mountains of Southern India and Ceylon, common at altitudes from 4,000 to 8,000 feet.

Produces an edible fruit.

VANGUERIA.

Vangueria edulis, *Vahl.*, RUBIACEÆ. 797

THE VOA-VANGA OF VOA-VANGUER OF MADAGASCAR.

Vern.—*Voa-vanga.*

A small tree, native of Madagascar, resembling **V. spinosa**, but unarmed, is cultivated in India for the sake of its edible fruit. (*Fl. Br. Ind.*)

Its fruits are also eaten by the people of Madagascar, from whose vernacular name the botanical name of the genus has been got.

V. spinosa, *Roxb.* 798

Vern.—*Hsaymakyee*, BURM.; *Muyna*, BENG.

A thorny, large shrub of Bengal, Burma, Pegu, and Tenasserim; flowers in the beginning of the hot season, and its fruit ripens in three or four months thereafter.

The fruit is round, size of a cherry, smooth, yellow when ripe, and succulent; and is eaten by the natives.

VERNONIA.

Vernonia anthelmintica, *Willd.*, COMPOSITÆ. 799

Syn.—SERRATULA ANTHELMINTICA, *Roxb.*; CONYZA ANTHELMINTICA, *Linn.*

Vern.—*Buckche, kalieseorie*, HIND.; *Somraj*, BENG.; *Neernoochie, caat-siragum*, TAM.; *Neela-vayalie, aduvie-sula-kuru*, TEL.; *Kali-zeerie*, DEC.; *Sanni-nayan*, CINGH; *Kalee-jeeree*, BOM.

A plant met with in parts of India, especially on the Himalaya.

"Common on high, dry, uncultivated ground and rubbish. It flowers during the cold season." (*Roxb.*)

Its seeds by pressure yield a valuable solid green oil.

VIBURNUM.

Viburnum coriaceum, *Bl.*, CAPRIFOLIACÆ. 800

Vern.—*Kala titmaliya*, KUMAUN; *Bara gorakuri*, NEPAL.

A large shrub, common on the Himalaya from the Punjab to Bhutan, altitude 4,000 to 8,000 feet, Khási hills, Nilgiris and Ceylon.

The oil extracted by the Nepalese from the seeds is used by them for food and for burning.

V. cotinifolium, *Don.* 801

Vern.—*Mar-ghalawa, bankúnch, bathor, papat-kalam, katonda, jawa, tus-tus*, PB.; *Richabi, gúch*, KASHMIR; *Gwia*, KAMAUN.

A large shrub of the Sulaiman Range, North-West Himalaya, from 4,000 to 11,000 feet in altitude.

Produces a fruit which, when ripe, is sweetish and eaten in many places by the natives.

V. fœtens, *Decaisne.* 802

Vern.—*Gúch, úklu, telhanj, pulmu, tandei, tunani, thilkain*, PB.; *Guya*, KUMAUN; *Kilmich, guch, kulara, jamara*, KASHMIR.

A large shrub of the North-West Himalaya, from 5,000 to 11,000 feet in altitude.

The fruit is sweetish, when ripe, and is eaten by the natives.

803 **Viburnum nervosum,** *Don.*

Vern.—*Ambre, ari, ris, dab, thilkain,* PB.

A shrub of the Himalaya, met with from Kumaun to Sikkim. It produces a pretty red fruit which is eaten.

804 **V. stellulatum,** *Wall.*

Syn.—V. MULLAH, *Ham.*

Vern.—*Jal-bagu, eri, era,* PB.; *Amliacha, phulsel,* KASHMIR; *Lal-titmaliya,* KUMAUN.

A shrub of the North-West Himalaya, in altitude 6,000 to 10,000 feet. The fruit is eaten by the natives.

VICIA.

805 **Vicia Faba,** *Linn.*, LEGUMINOSÆ.

THE FIELD BEAN.

Found in a cultivated state in Nepal, Kashmir, and Tibet, introduced into Purnea (Bengal) and probably into some European gardens on the plains; at present cultivated commonly in the North-West Provinces.

The pod is tumid, leathery, spongy. At its base, on the lower side, there is a small hole, through which the internal water evaporates, so that the seeds become dry before the dehiscing of the pod. In England the ripe seeds or beans are extensively used for feeding horses. In an unripe condition Europeans eat them at their tables as vegetables. Sometimes the beans are ground into flour for food; and are also sometimes given to cattle.

806 **V. hirsuta,** *Koch.*

THE HAIRY TARE.

Syn.—ERVUM HIRSUTUM, *Linn.*

Vern.—*Jhunjhuni-ankari,* HIND.

An herb of the North-West Provinces, Punjab, and Nepal, up to 6,000 feet, and also of the Nilgiris. **Roxburgh** says it is a native of Bengal. Frequently met with in cultivated grounds during the cold season.

In the inland provinces it is sometimes cultivated for fodder.

VIGNA.

807 **Vigna Catiang,** *Endl.*, LEGUMINOSÆ.

THE CHOWLEE OF INDIA and TOW COK OF CHINA.

Syn.—DOLICHOS CATIANG, *Linn.*; D. SINENSIS, *Linn.*; VIGNA SINENSIS, *Endl.*

Vern.—*Barbati,* BENG.; *Boberloo,* TEL.; *Lobia, rawás, rausa, sonta,* N. W. P. and OUDH.

Universally cultivated in India in the tropical zone, as a rule for its grain, which forms one of the summer millets, ripening in October and November.

The pod is two feet in length and contains a number of pea-like seeds which form a considerable article of food. In Bengal the young green entire pods are cooked in curry.

In the North-West Provinces and Oudh its grain is not much valued, being difficult of digestion. The leaves and stems are used as cattle fodder. This bean is not often grown as a sole crop except in Rohilkhand, where it covers 5,000 acres; but it forms portions of the undergrowth in a large proportion of millet and cotton fields, with which it is sown at the commencement of the rains, and yields a produce of about the same quantity as that of *urd*. (*Duthie* and *Fuller*.)

Vigna pilosa, *Baker*. 888

Syn.—DOLICHOS PILOSUS, *Roxb.*

Vern.—*Jhikrái, kalái*, BENG.

Cultivated in Bengal, Western Peninsula, Orissa, and Prome. The grain is eaten as dál by the natives. Cattle eat the straw of this plant.

VILLARSIA.

Villarsia nymphoides, *Vent.*, GENTIANIACEÆ. 809

Vern.—*Kuru, phair-posh*, KASHMIR.

Common in Kashmir about the lakes.
Very largely used for fodder.

VITEX.

Vitex leucoxylon, *Linn. f.*, VERBENACEÆ. 810

Vern.—*Goda, horina, ashwal*, BENG.; *Luki, neva-ledi*, TEL.; *Sengeni*, KAN.; *Longarbi-thiras*, MAR.; *Htouksha*, BURM.

A very large tree of South-East Bengal, South India, Burma and the Andamans.

Flowers in April, and produces a small, black fruit containing very soft pulp.

The fruit is eaten by the Burmese.

VITIS.

Vitis.

THE GRAPE VINE.

There are several species of this genus, which, in the *Flora of British India*, are reduced to the following :—

Vitis indica, *Linn.*, AMPELIDEÆ. 811

Confined to the western parts of the Peninsula, from the Konkan southwards.

The fruit is round, the size of a large currant.

V. lanata, *Roxb.* 812

"A very variable plant in the size, shape and vestiture of the leaves." Met with in the Himalaya at altitudes from 1,000 to 7,000 feet, also in the hills of Eastern Bengal, the Circars, and Burma.

The fruit is round, purple, the size of a large pea.

V. vinifera, *Linn.* 813

THE VINE.

Vern.—*Angur, dakh*, HIND.; *Angúr-phal, kismis, manakká*, BENG.; *Draksha*, SANS.; *Kodi mun-dirippa-sham*, TAM.; *Drakshapondu*, TEL.; *Draksha*, MAHR.; *Sabi-si*, BURM.; *Lanang*, KANAWAR.

Supposed to have been originally a native of the region of the Caspian, but very early cultivated in Western Asia. The fruit is a berry growing

WITHANIA.

in bunches called grapes. It thrives best on the sunny side of hills between 32° and 50° of Latitude.

The most important uses to which the vine is put are the fresh grapes; wine (fermented and unfermented) vinegar, currants and raisins, both of which are the dried fruits.

The vine accommodates easily to artificial treatment, so that it can be cultivated in almost all climates by much care and trouble.

Cultivated, here and there, in North-West India, and probably wild in the Himalaya of those parts; rare in the Southern Provinces.

The fruit is eaten raw; largely exported into India from Afghanistan during the winter season. It is kept in wooden, round boxes, arranged in layers. In India it is generally eaten by the well-to-do. In Afghanistan Bellew states that a grape wine is prepared which is consumed by the rich Mussulmans, and a raisin wine for the Hindus. Attempts have been made to manufacture wine in the Punjab on European principles with some success.

WALDHEIMIA.

814 **Waldheimia Tridactylites,** *Kartskir*, COMPOSITÆ.

Vern.—*Pallo*, LADAK.

"A small plant with a pretty lilac flour, common in Lahoul and Ladak. * * *

"It is browsed by goats and sheep when under stress of hunger." (*Dr. Stewart.*)

WENDLANDIA.

815 **Wendlandia exserta,** *DC.*, RUBIACEÆ.

Vern.—*Chaulai, chila, tila, tilki*, HIND.; *Kangi, tilki*, NEPAL; *Kursi*, SEONI; *Marria*, GOND; *Filliah*, MANDLA.

A small tree in found the dry forests of the sub-Himalayas, Oudh, Orissa, Central and parts of Southern India.

The leaves are given as fodder to cattle in some parts.

WITHANIA.

816 **Withania coagulans,** *Dun*, SOLANACEÆ.

Vern.—*Punirke-bif*, HIND.; *Ashvagadha*, BENG.; *Anukhurd-virai*, TAM.; *Kaknag*, BOM.; *Spin-bajja, panir, khanijira*, PB.; *Panir-bad*, PERS.

A small shrub common in the Punjab and Sindh, Afghanistan, and Beluchistan.

Produces small berries used by the natives in curdling milk to make cheese.

817 **W. Somnifera,** *Dun.*

BURR-WOOD.

Vern.—*Ak, sin, aksan*, PB.

A plant of the drier, sub-tropical parts of India, common westward and inland, rare in Lower Bengal.

Browsed by goats.

XANTHIUM.

Xanthium strumarium, *Linn.*, COMPOSITÆ. 818

BUR-WEED ; LAMPOURD, *Fr.* ; SPITZKLETTE, *Ger.*

Syn.—X. INDICUM, *Kon.* (*in Roxb., Fl. Ind., Ed. C. B. C., 660*) ; X. ORIENTALE, *L.*

Vern.—*Bun-okra*, BENG. ; *Isur, chirru, sungtu*, PB. ; *Shankeshvara*, BOM. ; *Marlumulta*, TAM. ; *Veri-tel-nep*, TEL. ; *Aristha*, SANS.

A rank weed-like plant, met with everywhere throughout the plains of India, and a source of great annoyance to the cultivator. Common in waste places, river banks, and especially so in the vicinity of villages.

In the United States this plant, in its young state, is often eaten by cattle. It is said to paralyse the heart inducing torpur without pain or struggle.

Xanthochymus pictorius, *Roxb.* *See* **Garcinia Xanthochymus,** *Hook. f.*, GUTTIFERÆ.

XIMENIA.

Ximenia americana, *Willd.*, OLACINEÆ. 819

TALSE SANDAL WOOD.

Vern.—*Uranechra*, TEL. ; *Pinlaytsee*, BURM.

A straggling shrub of South India, the Circars, Tenasserim, and Andamans.

Produces about the beginning of the hot weather small dull white fragrant flowers, smelling of cloves. These are followed by small oval red or yellow pulpy fruit, an inch long, of an acid-sweet aromatic taste, with some degree of austerity. When ripe, it is eaten by the natives. The kernels (says Roxburgh) are also eaten and taste much like filberts.

ZANTHOXYLUM.

Zanthoxylum Rhetsa, *DC.*, RUTACEÆ. 820

Syn.—FAGARA RHETSA, *R.*

Vern.—*Rhetsa maum*, TEL. ; *Sessal*, MAR.

A large tree of the Western and Eastern Ghâts in South India.

Produces very small yellow flowers in the beginning of the hot season, and small round berries which, when unripe, are "aromatic and taste like the skin of a fresh orange." (*Roxb.*)

"The ripe seeds taste exactly like black pepper, but weaker." (*Roxb.*)

ZEA.

Zea Mays, *Linn.*, GRAMINEÆ. 821

MAIZE OF INDIAN-CORN.

Vern.—*Janar, bhutta*, BENG. ; *Bhutta, makka, makai, junri, bara-juar, kukri*, HIND. ; *Makha-jowari*, DEC. ; *Makka, cholam*, TAM. ; *Makka, sonalu*, TEL.

This beautiful, annual, cane-like grass, from 4 to 5 in height, bears a dense head of closely packed grains, the size of peas, enclosed in a sheath called the cob.

A native of South America, which since the discovery of America has been introduced into and cultivated in all tropical and sub-tropical countries and forming in many of them a staple article of food. No other cereal except rice is so extensively cultivated. Though preferring moist

ZINGI-BER.

and rich soils, it can be raised in tropical climates, at upwards of 9,000 feet above sea-level. It is produced from the warmest climates of the torrid zone to the short summers of Canada. Besides it ripens at a time when most other grains are harvested, thus affording to the husbandman employment, when otherwise there would be little to do. It stands third in nutritiveness, but some place it second only to wheat.

Largely cultivated in Upper India and the Himalayas.

The seed is sown at the commencement of the rains in manured land, generally in rows, with cucumber or the lesser millets between the rows. The crop requires a moderate but constant supply of moisture, and has consequently to be irrigated when the rains are deficient.

The cobs are either pulled while green and sold as vegetables to be roasted and the grains eaten; or they are allowed to ripen. In the latter case the grain is threshed out and either parched and eaten, or made into flour and converted into bread. A fine flour called maizena and corn-flour is made from this grain and extensively used as an article of diet for custards, light puddings, &c. But whether as a vegetable, or as a cereal, the maize is a common article of food of a very large section of the population of Northern, Central and Himalayan tracts of India; and it is more in use as a cereal than as a vegetable.

The stalks, which are still green and fresh, serve as cattle fodder; in the former, the stalks are so hard as to be almost useless for any purpose but thatching or perhaps fuel.

In the North-West Provinces the total area under maize is about 718,000 acres in the thirty temporarily-settled districts. No statistics are available as regards the remaining five districts and Oudh, but the cultivation is extended over the whole area. About 6 seers of seed are used to the acre, and the average outturn of grain to the acre may be taken at from 10 maunds in unirrigated to 14 maunds in irrigated land.

A variety called *Cusco maize* with very large grains was imported from the Andes in 1875 by the Government of India and largely distributed throughout the country for experimental cultivation. There were many failures and some success, which was especially in Northern India and Ajmere. **Mr. Duthie** reports that it was successfully cultivated in the Government Garden near Mussoorie, that a hybrid between this latter and the ordinary kind has also been produced, and that the distribution of the hybridised will, no doubt, be the means of improving the quality of the crops in the sub-Himalayan districts.

ZEUXINE.

822 **Zeuxine sulcata,** *Lindl.*, ORCHIDEÆ.

Vern.—*Shwet-huli*, BENG.

Dr. Stewart writes:—"This small orchid is common at places throughout the Punjab plains, as elsewhere in India. It generally grows in turfy ground in low parts. I have once been told that its tubers are locally used as *Salep* by natives."

ZINGIBER.

823 **Zingiber officinale,** *Roscoe*, SCITAMINEÆ.

GINGER.

Vern.—*Ada, adroke*, BENG.; *Adrak*, HIND.; *Adrukum*, SANS.; *Ingie*, TAM.; *Allam*, TEL.; *Ischi*, MAL.

This plant is cultivated in all parts of India, including the outer Himalayan tracts.

ZIZYPHUS.

The object of the cultivation is the tuberous rhizome, lobed or fingered, known as ginger or 'races of ginger.' From these underground stems proceed reed-like stems clothed with grass-like foliage. In cultivation the cuttings from the preceding year's rhizomes are planted in May and June in a carefully prepared and manured soil of a red heavy nature.

Ginger is sold in every market-place throughout India. Its chief use is as a condiment in curries. It is also pickled; and an excellent preserve is made by cooking the fresh younger roots in syrup.

An infusion of ginger, under the name of ginger-tea, is sold in military cantonments; it is also used largely in the manufacture of an ærated water called gingerade, and in the beer known as gingerbeer.

In this form it constitutes an ingredient in the famous Chinese chow-chow, which the natives of Delhi and other towns have recently taken to imitate in pretty considerable quantities.

The following figures, which are those of the last five years, show that the export trade in ginger has fallen off:—

Official years.	Quantity in lbs.	Value in Rs.
1878-79	9,190,945	13,05,246
1879-80	6,960,006	9,94,149
1880-81	4,979,196	6,28,822
1881-82	3,804,879	5,31,172
1882-83	3,948,622	6,55,542

The following analysis of the exports shows the countries to which exported, the figures being those of 1882-83:—

Province whence exported.	Quantity in lbs.	Country to which exported.	Quantity in lbs.
Bombay . . .	1,926,483	United Kingdom .	1,842,230
Madras . . .	1,772,369	Aden . . .	823,154
Bengal . . .	249,770	Arabia . . .	706,549
		Persia . . .	142,561
		Ceylon . . .	128,810
		Other countries . .	305,318
TOTAL .	3,948,622	TOTAL .	3,948,622

ZIZYPHUS.

Zizyphus Jujuba, *Lam.*, RHAMNEÆ. 824

JUJUBE, OR CHINESE DATES.

Vern.—*Kúl, ber,* HIND., BENG.; *Bhor,* MAR.; *Elandap-pazham, yallande,* TAM.; *Rengha, regi,* TEL.; *Ziben,* BURM.; *Yelchi,* KAN.

A small, stiff-branched, hooked, thorny tree, common throughout India and Burma, wild and cultivated.

The fruit is ovate, with a central stone surrounded by a fleshy edible layer. It is the Indian plum of most authors, and is eaten by all classes of people, and also largely preserved in chutney.

It yields an excellent dessert fruit, of which many varieties are cultivated, especially in China.

ZYGO-PHILLUM.

825 **Zizyphus nummularia,** *W. & A.*

Vern.—*Karbanna,* AFG.; *Malla, bér, jhari, kanta,* N. W. P.; *Gangè, jangra,* SIND.; *Parpalli,* KAN.

Drier parts of the Punjab, Guzerat, Deccan and Konkan.

The fruit is small, round and very inferior to the preceding. It is eaten by the poorer people, especially in seasons of scarcity. In parts of the Punjab and Deccan, where fodder is scarce, the leaves are beaten off the branches and given as fodder to cattle.

826 **Z. Œnoplia,** *Mill.*

Vern.—*Shyakul,* BENG.; *Makai,* HIND.; *Barokoli,* URIYA; *Irun,* C. P.; *Parami,* TEL.; *Tauseenway,* BURM.

A straggling shrub met with throughout the hotter parts of India, from the Punjab to Assam and Ceylon.

The fruit of this species is also eaten.

827 **Z. rugosa,** *Lamk.*

Syn.—Z. LATIFOLIA, *Roxb.*

Vern.—*Dhaura,* OUDH; *Suran,* C. P.; *Rukh baer,* NEPAL.

A large, scrambling shrub of the sub-Himalayan tract, met with from the Ganges eastward to Assam, Sylhet, to Burma, Central and South India.

The fruit is eaten by the natives.

828 **Z. vulgaris,** *Lamk.*

Syn.—Z. FLEXUOSA, *Wall.*

Vern.—*Sinjli, simli, ban,* HIND.

A stiff-branched, hooked, spiny shrub or small tree of the Punjab extending to Bengal, and ascending in the North-Western Himalaya to 6,000 feet. It occurs wild and cultivated.

The fruit is eaten by the natives, acid when fresh, but dried, this and Z. Jujuba form the jujubes of the shops and as such eaten in large quantities by Europeans. The lozenges known as jujubes were either manufactured from or flavoured with them. They are taken to allay cough.

This is supposed to be the thorn from which Christ's "Crown of Thorns" was made. It is cultivated in gardens.

829 **Z. xylopyra,** *Will.*

Vern.—*Katber, beri, goti, chittania, sitaber, ghont,* HIND.; *Goti,* TEL.; *Bhor-goti,* MAR.

A large, scrambling shrub found in the sub-Himalayan tract and in Central and South India.

The fruit is not eatable. The kernels, according to Roxburgh, taste like filberts, and are eaten by natives. The shoots and leaves are eaten by cattle.

ZYGOPHILLUM.

830 **Zygophillum simplex,** *Linn.,* ZYGOPHYLLEÆ.

Vern.—*Alethi,* PB.

A prostrate, much-branched herb of the arid, sandy tracts in Sind and the Punjab.

The seeds are swept up from the ground by the nomad tribes and used as food under the above name.

The smell is so detestable that no animal will eat the foliage.

ECONOMIC PRODUCTS OF INDIA.

Index to Foods, Food-stuffs, and Fodders.

A

Aadal-otti, *Tam.*, Triumfetta annua, *Linn.*, TILIACEÆ.
Foods .
Aalnudek, *Arab.*, Abrus precatorius, *Linn.*, LEGUMINOSÆ.
Foods .
Aainunnás, *Arab. & Pers.*, Ananassa sativa, *Linn.*, BROMELIACEÆ.
Foods .
Abe-balu, *Pers.*, Prunus Cerasus, *Linn.*, ROSACEÆ.
Foods .
Abnú, *Hind.*, Diospyros melanoxylon, *Roxb.*, EBANACEÆ.
Foods .
Ach, *Beng.*, Morinda citrifolia, *Linn.*, RUBIACEÆ.
Foods .
Ach, *Beng.*, Morinda tinctoria, *Roxb.*, RUBIACEÆ.
Foods .
Acha, *Tam.*, Hardwickia binata, *Roxb.*, LEGUMINOSÆ.
Foods .
Achal, *Nep.*, Securinega Leucopyrus, *Müll.-Arg.*, EUPHORBIACEÆ.
Foods .
Achar, *C. P.*, Buchanania latifolia, *Roxb.*, ANACARDIACEÆ.
Foods .
Achatta, *Nep.*, Sapindus attenuatus, *Wall.*, SAPINDACEÆ.
Foods .
Achchhuka, *Sans.*, Morinda tinctoria, *Roxb.*, RUBIACEÆ.
Foods .
Ada, *Beng.*, Zingiber officinale, *Roscoe*, SCITAMINEÆ.
Foods .
Adad, *Gujaráti*, Phaseolus Mungo, *Linn.*, LEGUMINOSÆ.
Foods .
Adala-vitala, *Tel.*, Lepidium sativum, *Linn.*, CRUCIFERÆ.
Foods .
Adamsali, *Ass.*, Excæcaria baccata, *Müll.*, EUPHORBIACEÆ.
Foods .
Adasara, *Tel.*, Adhatoda Vasica, *Nees.*, ACANTHACEÆ.
Foods .
Adavie-zula-kuru, *Tel.*, Vernonia anthelmintica, *Willd.*, COMPOSITÆ.
Foods .
Adda, *Tam.*, Bauhinia Vahlii, *W. & A.*, LEGUMINOSÆ.
Foods .
Adha, *Tam.*, Adhatoda Vasica, *Nees.*, ACANTHACEÆ.
Foods .
Adiki, *Kan.*, Areca Catechu, *Linn.*, PALMÆ.
Foods .
Adoma, *Goa.*, Mimusops Kauki, *Linn.*, SAPOTACEÆ.
Foods .
Adonda, *Tel.*, Capparis horrida, *Linn.*, CAPPARIDEÆ.
Foods .
Adrak, *Hind.*, Zingiber officinale, *Roscoe*, SCITAMINEÆ.
Foods .

o

Adroke, *Beng.*, Zingiber officinale, *Roscoe*, SCITAMINEÆ.
Foods .
Adrakum, *Sans.*, Zingiber officinale, *Roscoe*, SCITAMINEÆ.
Foods .
Agakara (female plants), *Tel.*, Momordica dioica, *Roxb.*, CUCURBITACEÆ.
Foods .
Agana, *N.-W. P.*, Cenchrus echinatus, *Linn.*, GRAMINEÆ.
Foods .
Agati, *Tam.*, Sesbania grandiflora, *Pers.*, LEGUMINOSÆ.
Foods .
Ageea-ghas, *Hind.*, Andropogon Schœnanthus, *Linn.*, GRAMINEÆ.
Foods .
Aggai, *Oudh*, Dillenia pentagyna, *Roxb.*, DILLENIACEÆ.
Foods .
Aghzan, *Pb.*, Ballota limbata, *Benth.*, LABIATÆ.
Foods .
Aglaia, *Kumaun*, Sageretia oppositifolia, *Brongn.*, RHAMNEÆ.
Foods .
Agnisikha, *Tel.*, Carthamus tinctorius, *Linn.*, COMPOSITÆ.
Foods .
Agre turki, *Pers.*, Acorus Calamus, *Linn.*, AROIDEÆ.
Foods .
Ahlada, *Kan.*, Ficus bengalensis, *Linn.*, URTICACEÆ.
Foods .
Ahreo, *Sind*, Lepidium sativum, *Linn.*, CRUCIFERÆ.
Foods .
Aich or achhu, *Beng.*, Morinda citrifolia, *Linn.*, RUBIACEÆ.
Foods .
Aila, *C. P.*, Cassia Fistula, *Linn.*, LEGUMINOSÆ.
Foods .
Aila, *Oudh*, Acacia concinna, *DC.*, LEGUMINOSÆ.
Foods .
Aila-cheddi, *Tam.*, Amomum aromaticum, *Roxb.*, SCITAMINEÆ.
Foods .
Aima, *Tam.*, Buchanania latifolia, *Roxb.*, ANACARDIACEÆ.
Foods .
Ain, *Mar.*, Terminalia tomentosa, *W. & A.*, COMBRETACEÆ.
Foods .
Aindha, *N.-W. P.*, Securinega Leucopyrus, *Müll.-Arg.*, EUPHORBIACEÆ.
Foods .
Ajmod, *Hind.*, Apium graveolens, *Linn.*, UMBELLIFERÆ.
Foods .
Ajmúd, *Hind.*, Carum Roxburghianum, *Benth.*, UMBELLIFERÆ.
Foods .
Ajowan, *Hind.*, Carum copticum, *Benth.*, UMBELLIFERÆ.
Foods .
Ajowan, Khorasani, *Beng.*, *Hind.*, Hyoscyamus niger, *Linn.*, SOLANACEÆ.
Foods .
Ajumóda-vomaru, Carum Roxburghianum, *Benth.*, UMBELLIFERÆ.
Foods .
Ak, *Beng.*, Saccharum officinarum, *Linn.*, GRAMINEÆ.
Foods .
Ak, *Pb.*, Withania Somnifera, *Dun.*, SOLANACEÆ.
Foods .
Akarkanta, *Beng.*, Alangium Lamarckü, *Thwaites*, CORNACEÆ.
Foods .
Akayan, *Hind.*, Melia Azedarach, *Linn.*, MELIACEÆ.
Foods .
Akhe, *Pb.*, Rubus biflorus, *Ham.*, ROSACEÆ.
Foods .
Akhi, *Pb.*, Rubus ellipticus, *Smith*, ROSACEÆ.
Foods .

Akhiari, *Pb.*, Rosa macrophylla, *Lindl.*, ROSACEÆ.
Foods .
Akhor, *Kashmir*, Juglans regia, *Linn.*, JUGLANDEÆ.
Foods .
Akhreri, *Pb.*, Rubus biflorus, *Ham.*, ROSACEÆ.
Foods .
Akhrot, *Hind.*, Juglans regia, *Linn.*, JUGLANDEÆ.
Foods .
Akhrota, Jangli, *Bom.*, Aleurites moluccana, *Willd.*, EUPHORBICEÆ.
Foods .
Aklel-ul-mulk, Calendula officinalis, *Linn.*, COMPOSITÆ.
Foods .
Akola, *Hind.*, *Dec.*, Alangium Lamarckü, *Thwaites*, CORNACEÆ.
Foods .
Akrot, *Beng.*, *Hind.*, Aleurites moluccana, *Willd.*, EUPHORBIACEÆ.
Foods .
Akrut, *Beng.*, Juglans regia, *Linn.*, JUGLANDEÆ.
Foods .
Aksan, *Pb.*, Withania Somnifera, *Dun.*, SOLANACEÆ.
Foods .
Akshi, *Ass.*, Dillenia pentagyna, *Roxb.*, DILLENIACEÆ.
Foods .
Alá thanda, *Beng.*, Phyllanthus Emblica, *Linn.*, EUPHORBIACEÆ.
Foods .
Alash, *Pb.*, Cassia Fistula, *Linn.*, LEGUMINOSÆ.
Foods .
Alangi, *Tam.*, Alangium Lamarckü, *Thwaites*, CORNACEÆ.
Foods .
Ala, *Tam.*, Ficus bengalensis, *Linn.*, URTICACEÆ.
Foods .
Alá, *Bom.*, Morinda citrifolia, *Linn.*, RUBIACEÆ.
Foods .
Al, *Hind.*, Morinda tinctoria, *Roxb.*, RUBIACEÆ.
Foods .
Al, *Hind.*, Morinda citrifolia, *Linn.*, RUBIACEÆ.
Foods .
Alder, *Eng.*, Alnus nitada, *Endl.*, CUPULIFERÆ.
Foods .
Alethi, *Pb.*, Trianthema crystallina, *Vahl.*, FICOIDEÆ.
Foods .
Alethi, *Pb.*, Zygophillum simplex, *Linn.*, ZYGOPHYLLEÆ.
Foods .
Aleverie, *Beng.*, *Hind.*, Lepidium sativum, *Linn.*, CRUCIFERÆ.
Foods .
Algaroba of Parry, *Eng.*, Prosopis dulcis, LEGUMINOSÆ.
Foods .
Algoraba, Prosopis dulcis, LEGUMINOSÆ.
Foods .
Algoraba of Texas, *Eng.*, Prosopis glandulosa, *Torr.*, LEGUMINOSÆ.
Foods .
Alhaju, *Arab.*, Alhagi maurorum, *Desv.*, LEGUMINOSÆ.
Foods .
Ali, *Pb.*, Cassia Fistula, *Linn.*, LEGUMINOSÆ.
Foods .
Alish, *Pb.*, Rubus fruticosus, *Linn.*, ROSACEÆ.
Foods .
Al-kaddu, *Hind.*, Lagenaria vulgaris, *Seringe.*, CUCURBITACEÆ.
Foods .
Allam, *Tel.*, Zingiber officinale, *Rosce*, SCITAMINEÆ.
Foods .
Alli, *Tam.*, Hardwickia binata, *Roxb.*, LEGUMINOSÆ.
Foods

Alli, *Tel.*, Memecylon edule, *Roxb.*, MELASTROMACEÆ.
Foods .
Allian, *Hind.*, Cornus macrophylla, *Wall.*, CORNACEÆ.
Foods .
Almond, *Eng.*, Terminalia Catappa, *Linn.*, COMBRETACEÆ.
Foods .
Almond Tree, *Eng.*, Prunus amygdalus, *Baillon.*, ROSACEÆ.
Foods .
Almond Tree, Java, *Eng.*, Canarium commune, *Linn.*, BURSERACEÆ.
Foods .
Aloe, *Ger.*, Aloe vera, *Linn.*, LILIACEÆ.
Foods .
Aloe, American, *Eng.*, Agave americana, *Linn.*, AMARYLLIDEÆ.
Foods .
Aloe, Indian, *Eng.*, Aloe vera, *Linn.*, LILIACEÆ.
Foods .
Aloes, *Fr.*, Aloe vera, *Linn.*, LILIACEÆ.
Foods .
Alombe, *Bom.*, Agaricus campestris, *Linn.*, FUNGI.
Foods .
Aloo, Meeta, *Hind.*, Ipomæa Batatas, *Lamk.*, CONVOLVULACEÆ.
Foods .
Alpo-gadda-pazham, *Tam.*, Prunus communis, *Huds.*, var. Insititia, ROSACEÆ. Foods .
Alsanda, *Tel.*, Dolichos Lablab, *Linn.*, LEGUMINOSÆ.
Foods .
Alu, *Hind.*, *Beng.*, Solanum tuberosum, *Linn.*, SOLANACEÆ.
Foods .
Alu, *Bom.*, Colocasia antiquorum, *Schott.*, AROIDEÆ.
Foods .
Alú, *Pb.*, Solamum tuberosum, *Linn.*, SOLANACEÆ.
Foods .
Alu Bokhárá, *Hind.*, *Bom.*, *Pers.*, Prunus communis, *Huds.*, var. Insititia, ROSACEÆ. Foods .
Alucha, *Pb.*, Prunus communis, *Huds.*, var. domestico, ROSACEÆ.
Foods .
Alu Chupri, *Beng.*, *Hind.*, Dioscorea globosa, *Roxb.*, DIOSCOREACEÆ.
Foods .
Aludel, *Cingh.*, Artocarpus nobilis, *Thw.*, URTICACEÆ.
Foods .
Alu Guraniya, *Beng.*, Dioscorea rubella, *Roxb.*, DIOSCOREACEÆ.
Foods .
Alu Kanta, *Beng.*, Dioscorea pentaphylla, *Willd.*, DIOSCOREACEÆ.
Foods .
Alu Kham, *Beng.*, *Hind.*, Dioscorea alata, *Linn.*, DIOSCOREACEÆ·
Foods .
Alu Lal-guraniya, *Beng.*, Dioscorea purpurea, *Roxb.*, DIOSCOREACEÆ.
Foods .
Alu Susni, *Beng.*, Diascorea fasciculata, *Roxb.*, DIOSCOREACEÆ.
Foods .
Alvinda, *Sind*, Citrullas vulgaris, *Schrad.*, var. fistulosus, CUCURBITACEÆ.
Foods .
Am, *Hind.*, Mangifera indica, *Linn.*, ANACARDIACEÆ.
Foods .
Amá, *Bom.*, Mangifera indica, *Linn.*, ANACARDIACEÆ.
Foods .
Amadum, *Tel.*, Ricinus communis, *Linn.*, EUPHORBIACEÆ.
Foods .
Amalgach, *Pb.*, Prunus Paddum, *Roxb.*, ROSACEÆ.
Foods .
Amaltás, *Hind.*, Cassia Fistula, *Linn.*, LEGUMINOSÆ.
Foods .

Amlita, *Hind.*, Phyllanthus Emblica, *Linn.*, EUPHORBIACEÆ.
Foods .
Amlora, *Pb.*, Rumex hastatus, *Don.*, POLYGONACEÆ.
Foods .
Amlosa, *Hind.*, Bauhinia malabarica, *Roxb.*, LEGUMINOSÆ.
Foods .
Amlu, *Pb.*, Oxyria reniformis, *Hook.*, POLYGONACEÆ.
Foods .
Amluki, *Beng.*, Albizzia stipulata, *Boivin.*, LEGUMINOSÆ.
Foods .
Ammughilan, *Arab.*, Acacia arabica, *Willd.*, LEGUMINOSÆ.
Foods .
Amphi, *Nep.*, Pyrularia edulis, *A. DC.*, SANTALACEÆ.
Foods .
Amra, *Sans.*, Mangifera indica, *Linn.*, ANACARDIACEÆ.
Foods .
Amra, *Hind.*, Spondias mangifera, *Pers.*, ANACARDIACEÆ.
Foods .
Amra, *Beng.*, Spondias magnifera, *Pers.*, ANACARDIACEÆ.
Foods .
Amrai, *Pb.*, Ulmus Willichiana, *Planch.*, URTICACEÆ.
Foods .
Amrer, *Pb.*, Bœhmeria salicifolia, *D. Don.*, URTICACEÆ.
Foods .
Amrool, *Hind.*, Oxalis corniculata, *Linn.*, GERANIACEÆ.
Foods .
Amrúd, *Hind. & N.-W. P.*, Psidium Guyava, *Raddi.*, MYRTACEÆ.
Foods .
Amrút, *Hind. & N.-W. P.*, Psidium Guyava, *Raddi.*, MYRTACEÆ.
Foods .
Amsool, *Bom.*, Garcinia indica, *Choisy.*, GUTTIFERÆ.
Foods .
Amte, *Kan.*, Spondias mangifera, *Pers.*, ANACARDIACEÆ.
Foods .
Amuk, *Nep.*, Psidium Guyava, *Raddi.*, MYRTACEÆ.
Foods .
Amuki, *Nep.*, Randia dumetorum, *Lam.*, RUBIACEÆ.
Foods .
Amulati, *Beng.*, Phyllanthus Emblica, *Linn.*, EUPHORBIACEÆ.
Foods .
An, *Pb.*, Morus serrata, *Roxb.*, URTICACEÆ.
Foods .
Anai-puliya-roy, *Tam.*, Adansonia digitata, *Linn.*, MALVACEÆ.
Foods .
Anánas, *Hind.* (*Dec.*), Ananassa sativa, *Linn.*, BROMELIACEÆ.
Foods .
Anánash (*vulgarly* **anáras**), *Beng.*, Ananassa sativa, *Linn.*, BROMELIACEÆ.
Foods .
Anander, *Jhelum*, Pinus longifolia, *Roxb.*, CONIFERÆ.
Foods .
Anar, *Hind.*, Punica Granatum, *Linn.*, LYTHRACEÆ.
Foods .
Anaras, *Guz.*, Ananassa sativa, *Linn.*, BROMELIACEÆ.
Foods .
Anar-kajhur, *Dec.*, Punica Granatum, *Linn.*, LYTHRACEÆ.
Foods .
Anása-pandu, *Tel.*, Ananassa sativa, *Linn.*, BROMELIACEÆ.
Foods .
Anázhap-pazhane, *Tam.*, Ananassa sativa, *Linn.*, BROMELIACEÆ.
Foods .
Anchu, *Hind.*, Rubus paniculatus, *Smith*, ROSACEÆ.
Foods .

Andfivan, *Nilgiris,* Vaccinium Leschenaultii, *Wight,* VACCINIACEÆ.
Foods .
Anemul, *Tam.,* Terminalia tomentosa, *W. & A.,* COMBRETACEÆ.
Foods .
Angan, *Pb.,* Pennisetum cenchroides, *Rich.,* GRAMINEÆ.
Foods .
Angnera, *Rajputana,* Briedelia retusa, *Spreng.,* EUPHORBIACEÆ.
Foods .
Angur, *Hind.,* Vitis vinifera, *Linn.,* AMPELIDEÆ.
Foods .
Angúr-phal, *Beng.,* Vitis vinifera *Linn.,* AMPELIDEÆ.
Foods .
Anguza, *Afg.,* Ferula Narthex, *Boiss.,* UMBELLIFERÆ.
Foods .
Anink-katrazhai, *Tam.,* Agave americana, *Linn.,* AMARYLLIDEÆ.
Foods .
Anise seed, *Eng.,* Pimpinella Anisum, *Linn.,* UMBELLIFERÆ.
Foods .
Anjan, *Hind. Mar.,* Hardwickia binata, *Roxb.,* LEGUMINOSÆ.
Foods .
Anjan, *Bom.,* Memecylon edule, *Roxb.,* MELASTROMACEÆ.
Foods .
Anjeli, *Tam.,* Artocarpus hirsuta, *Lamk.,* URTICACEÆ.
Foods .
Anjir, *Afg.,* Ficus virgata, *Roxb.,* URTICACEÆ.
Foods .
Anjír, *Hind.,* Ficus carica, *Linn.,* URTICACEÆ.
Foods .
Anjíra, *Bom.,* Ficus carica, *Linn.,* URTICACEÆ.
Foods .
Anjiri, *Hind.,* Ficus virgata, *Roxb.,* URTICACEÆ.
Foods .
Ankol, *Pb.,* Sageretia theezans, *Brongn.,* RHAMNEÆ.
Foods .
Ankola, *Bom.,* Alangium Lamarckii, *Thwaites,* CORNACEÆ.
Foods .
Ankola, *Gond.,* *Sans.,* Alangium Lamarckii, *Thwaites,* CORNACEÆ.
Foods .
Ankri, *Pb.,* Rubus fruticosus, *Linn.,* ROSACEÆ.
Foods .
Annasi, *Cingh.,* Ananassa sativa, *Linn.,* BROMELIACEÆ.
Foods .
Ansjeli, *Mal.,* Artocarpus hirsuta, *Lamk.,* URTICACEÆ.
Foods .
Anukhurá-virai, *Sans.,* Withania coagulans, *Dun.,* SOLANACEÆ.
Foods .
Anvala, *Bom.,* Phyllanthus Emblica, *Linn.,* EUPHORBIACEÆ.
Foods .
Aonla, *Hind.,* Phyllanthus Emblica, *Linn.,* EUPHORBIACEÆ.
Foods .
Aor, *Pb.,* Prunus persica, *Benth. & Hook.,* ROSACEÆ.
Foods .
Aphing, *Beng.,* *Hind.,* Papaver somniferum, *Linn.,* PAPAVERACEÆ.
Foods .
Apim, *Beng.,* *Hind.,* Papaver somniferum, *Linn.,* PAPAVERACEÆ.
Foods .
Apple, *Eng.,* Pyrus Malus, *Linn.,* ROSACEÆ.
Foods .
Apple, custard, *Eng.,* Anona squamosa, *Linn.,* ANONACEÆ.
Foods .
Apple, Malay, *Eng.,* Eugenia malaccensis, *Linn.,* MYRTACEÆ.
Foods .

Apple, Otaheite, *Eng.*, Spondias dulas, , ANACARDIACEÆ.
Foods .
Apple Rose, *Eng.*, Eugenia Jambos, *Linn.*, MYRTACEÆ.
Foods .
Apricot, *Eng.*, Prunus armeniaca, *Linn.*, ROSACEÆ.
Foods .
Apúra, *Beluchistan*, Juniperus excelsa, *M. Bieb.*, CONIFERÆ.
Foods .
Aradal, *Kan.*, Garcinia Cambogia, *Desr.*, GUTTIFERÆ.
Foods .
Aradal, *Kan.*, Garcinia Morella, *Desr.*, GUTTIFERÆ.
Foods .
Arand-kharbuza, *Pb.*, Carica Papaya, *L.*, PASSIFLOREÆ.
Foods .
Arar, *Hind.*, Randia dumetorum, *Lam.*, RUBIACEÆ.
Foods .
Ararút gaddalu, *Tel.*, Curcuma angustifolia, *Roxb.*, SCITAMINEÆ.
Foods .
Ararut-ke-gadde, *Dec.*, Curcuma angustifolia, *Roxb.*, SCITAMINEÆ.
Foods .
Ararút-kishangu, *Tam.*, Curcuma angustifolia, *Roxb.*, SCITAMINEÆ.
Foods .
Arasa, *Tam.*, Ficus religiosa, *Linn.*, URTICACEÆ.
Foods .
Aravi-mamadi, *Tel.*, Spondias mangifera, *Pers.*, ANACARDIACEÆ.
Foods .
Archaká, *Beng.*, Sonneratia acida, *Linn.*, LYTHRACEÆ.
Foods .
Ardáwal, *Pb.*, Rhododendron arboreum, *Sm.*, ERICACEÆ.
Foods .
Areka, *Tam.*, Bauhinia racemosa, *Lam.*, LEGUMINOSÆ.
Foods .
Arend, *Hind.*, Ricinus communis, *Linn.*, EUPHORBIACEÆ.
Foods .
Arhar, *N.-W. P. & Oudh.*, Cajanus indicus, *Spreng.*, LEGUMINOSÆ.
Foods .
Arhuku, *Sans.*, Cajanus indicus, *Spreng.*, LEGUMINOSÆ.
Foods .
Ari, *Pb.*, Viburnum nervosum, *Don.*, CAPRIFOLIACEÆ.
Foods .
Ari, *Tel.*, Bauhinia racemosa, *Lam.*, LEGUMINOSÆ.
Foods .
Ariabepon, *Mal.*, Melia Azadirachta, *Linn.*, MELIACEÆ.
Foods .
Aring, *Raj.*, Acacia leucophlæa, *Willd.*, LEGUMINOSÆ.
Foods .
Arisi, *Tam.*, Oryza sativa, *Linn.*, GRAMINEÆ.
Foods .
Aristha, *Sans.*, Xanthium strumarium, *Linn.*, COMPOSITÆ.
Foods .
Arjan, *Pb.*, Ulmus integrifolia, *Roxb.*, URTICACEÆ.
Foods .
Arjha, *San.*, *N. Ind.*, Crotalaria juncea, *Linn.*, LEGUMINOSÆ.
Foods .
Arjún, *Hind.*, Ehretia acuminata, *Br.*, BORAGINEÆ.
Foods .
Arkhar, *Pb.*, Rhus semi-alata, *Murray*, ANACARDIACEÆ.
Foods .
Arkol, *Pb.*, Rhus semi-alata, *Murray*, ANACARDIACEÆ.
Foods .
Arni, *Hind.*, Premna integrifolia, *Linn.*, VERBENACEÆ.
Foods .

Aroz, *Lat., Por. and Sp.*, Oryza sativa, *Linn.*, GRAMINEÆ.
Foods .
Arro, *Tel.*, Bauhinia racemosa, *Lam.*, LEGUMINOSÆ.
Foods .
Arrowroot, South Sea, *Eng.*, Tacca pinnatifida, *Forsk.*, TACCACEÆ.
Foods .
Arrowroot, Wild or East Indian, *Eng.*, Curcuma angustifolia, *Roxb.*, SCITAMINEÆ. Foods .
Artichoke, *Eng.*, Cynara Scolymus, *Linn.*, COMPOSITÆ.
Foods .
Artichoke, Jerusalem, *Eng.*, Helianthus tuberosus, *Linn.*, COMPOSITÆ.
Foods .
Artso, *Pb.*, *Himalaya & Afg.*, Rheum Emodi, *Wall.*, POLYGONACEÆ.
Foods .
Aru, *Pb.*, Prunus persica, *Benth. & Hook.*, ROSACEÆ.
Foods .
Arugam-pilla, *Tam.*, Cynodon Dactylon, *Pers.*, GRAMINEÆ.
Foods .
Arugu, *Tel.*, Paspalum scrobiculatum, *Linn.*, GRAMINEÆ.
Foods .
Arunilli, *Tam.*, Phyllanthus distichus, *Müll.,-Arg.*, EUPHORBIACEÆ.
Foods .
Arus, *Sans.*, Adhatoda Vasica, *Nees*, ACANTHACEÆ.
Foods .
Arusha, *Hind.*, Adhatoda Vasica, *Nees.*, ACANTHACEÆ.
Foods .
Aruz, *Arab.*, Oriza sativa, *Linn.*, GRAMINEÆ.
Foods .
Arzan, *Pb.*, *Pers.*, Panicum miliaceum, *Linn.*, GRAMINEÆ.
Foods .
Asafœtida, *Eng.*, Ferula Narthex, *Boiss.*, UMBELLIFERÆ.
Foods .
Asainda, *Hind.*, Ougeinia dalbergioides, *Benth.*, LEGUMINOSÆ.
Foods .
Asam, *Mysore.*, Tamarindus indica, *Linn.*, LEGUMINOSÆ.
Foods .
Asán, *Bom.*, Pterocarpus Marsupium, *Roxb.*, LEGUMINOSÆ.
Foods .
Asan, *Hind.*, Terminalia tomentosa, *W. & A.*, COMBRETACEÆ.
Foods .
Asari, *Nep.*, Mussœnda frondosa, *Linn.*, RUBIACEÆ.
Foods .
Aselu, *Nep.*, Rubus lasiocarpus, *Smith*, ROSACEÆ.
Foods .
Aselu, *Nep.*, Rubus lineatus, *Reinw.*, ROSACEÆ.
Foods .
Aserekí, *Tel.*, Phyllanthus emblica, *Linn.*, EUPHORBIACEÆ.
Foods .
Ash, *Eng.*, Fraxinus Xanthoxyloides, *Wall.*, OLEACEÆ.
Foods .
Asham lagam, *Tam.*, Carum Roxburghianum, *Benth.*, UMBELLIFERÆ.
Foods .
Ashathwa, *Beng.*, Ficus religiosa, *Linn.*, URTICACEÆ.
Foods .
Ashta, *Hind.*, Bauhinia racemosa, *Lam.*, LEGUMINOSÆ.
Foods .
Ashú-kachú, *Hind.*, *Beng.*, Colocasia antiquorum, *Schott.*, AROIDEÆ.
Foods .
Ashvagadha, *Beng.*, Withania coagulans, *Dun.*, SOLANACEÆ.
Foods .
Ashwal, *Beng.*, Vitex leucoxylon, *Linn.*, VERBENACEÆ.
Foods .

Asmánia, *Pb.*, Ephedra Gerardiana, *Wall.*, GNETACEÆ.
Foods .
Asna, *Hind.*, Terminalia tomentosa, *W. & A.*, COMBRETACEÆ.
Foods .
Asphal, *Beng.*, Nephelium Longana, *Camb.*, SAPINDACEÆ.
Foods .
Asparagus, *Eng.*, Asparagus officinalis, *Willd.*, LILIACEÆ.
Foods .
Assain, *Hind.*, Terminalia tomentosa, *W. & A.*, COMBRETACEÆ.
Foods .
Assu, *Pb.*, Eruca sativa, *Lam.*, CRUCIFERÆ.
Foods .
Asúd, *Beng.*, Ficus religiosa, *Linn.*, URTICACEÆ.
Foods .
Aswat, *Beng.*, Ficus religiosa, *Linn.*, URTICACEÆ.
Foods .
Ata, *Beng.*, Anona squamosa, *Linn.*, ANONACEÆ.
Foods .
Atanday, *Tam.*, Capparis horrida, *Linn.*, CAPPARIDEÆ.
Foods .
Ati, *Tam.*, Bauhinia racemosa, *Lam.*, LEGUMINOSÆ.
Foods .
Atrúna, *Bom.*, Flacourtia sepiaria, *Roxb.*, BIXINEÆ.
Foods .
Atsu, *Pb.*, *Himalaya & Afg.*, Rheum Emodi, *Wall.*, POLYGONACEÆ.
Foods .
Atta, *Mal.*, Anona squamosa, *Linn.*, ANONACEÆ.
Foods .
Atti, *Tam.*, Ficus glomerata, *Roxb.*, URTICACEÆ.
Foods .
Auga, *N.-W. P.*, Fraxinus xanthoxyloides, *Wall.*, OLEACEÆ.
Foods .
Aúlsi, *Arab.*, Aloe vera, *Linn.*, var. officinalis, *sp. Forsk.*, LILIACEÆ.
Foods .
Aura, *Hind.*, Phyllanthus emblica, *Linn.*, EUPHORBIACEÆ.
Foods .
Auri, *N.-W. P.*, Colocasia antiquorum, *Schott.*, AROIDEÆ.
Foods .
Aus, *Pb.*, Ribes rubrum, *Linn*, SAXIFRAGACEÆ.
Foods .
Auza, *Burm.*, Anona squamosa, *Linn.*, ANONACEÆ.
Foods .
Avalo, *Tel.*, Brassica nigra, *Koch.*, CRUCIFERÆ.
Foods .
Avisi, *Tel.*, Sesbania grandiflora, *Pers.*, LEGUMINOSÆ.
Foods .
Awani-buti, *Pb.*, Ballota limbata, *Benth.*, LABIATÆ.
Foods .
Aya, *Tam.*, Ulmus integrifolia, *Roxb.*, URTICACEÆ.
Foods .
Ayeni, *Mal.*, Artocarpus hirsuta, *Lamk.*, URTICACEÆ.
Foods .
Ayma, *Tam*, Careya arborea, *Roxb.*, MYRTACEÆ.
Foods .
Azhinji, *Tam.*, Alangium Lamarckii, *Thwaites*, CORNACEÆ.
Foods .

B

Babassa, *Tel.*, Hydrocotyle asiatica, *Linn.*, UMBELLIFERÆ.
Foods .
Babbil, *Pb.*, Acacia Jacquemontii, *Benth.*, LEGUMINOSÆ.
Foods .

Babboa, *Sind*, Acacia arabica, *Willd.*, LEGUMINOSÆ.
Foods .
Babela, *Pers.*, Terminalia belerica, *Roxb.*, COMBRETACEÆ.
Foods .
Babbúla, *Bom.*, Acacia arabica, *Willd.*, LEGUMINOSÆ.
Foods .
Babla, *Hind.*, *Beng.*, *Dec.*, Acacia arabica, *Willd.*, LEGUMINOSÆ.
Foods .
Babui tulsi, *Beng.*, *Hind.*, Ocimum Basilicum, *Linn.*, LABIATÆ.
Foods .
Bábúl, *Hind.*, *Beng.*, *Dec.*, Acacia arabica, *Willd.*, LEGUMINOSÆ.
Foods .
Babul, *Pb.*, Acacia Jacquemontii, *Benth.*, LEGUMINOSÆ.
Foods .
Babúri, *Pb.*, Ocimum sanctum, *Linn.*, LABIATÆ.
Foods .
Bach, *Beng.*, *Hind.*, Acorus Calamus, *Linn.*, AROIDEÆ.
Foods .
Bacha, *Bom.*, Salix tetrasperma, *Bom.*, SALICINEÆ.
Foods .
Bachang, *Malay.*, Mangifera fœtida, *Lour.*, ANACARDIACEÆ.
Foods .
Badám, , Prunus amygdalus, *Baillon.*, ROSACEÆ.
Foods .
Badam, *Beng.*, Terminalia Catappa, *Linn.*, COMBRETACEÆ.
Foods .
Bádám-chiner, *Beng.*, Arachis hypogæa, *Linn.*, LEGUMINOSÆ.
Foods .
Bádám, Hijli, *Beng.*, Anacardium occidentale, *Linn.*, ANACARDIACEÆ.
Foods .
Badam Jangli, *Hind.*, Canarium commune, *Linn.*, BURSERACEÆ.
Foods .
Badam, Jangli, *Hind.*, Sterculia fœtida, *Linn.*, STERCULIACEÆ.
Foods .
Badam, Jangli, *Hind.*, Terminalia chebula, *Retz.*, COMBRETACEÆ.
Foods .
Bádar, *Kashmir*, *Him. name*, Abies Webbiana, *Lindl.*, CONIFERÆ.
Foods .
Badar, *Pb.*, Picea Webbiana, *Lamb.*, CONIFERÆ.
Foods .
Badar, *Hind.*, Pueraria tuberosa, *DC.*, LEGUMINOSÆ.
Foods .
Badar, *Afg.*, Taxus baccata, *Linn.*, CONIFERÆ.
Foods .
Badha, *Pb.*, Ficus cordifolia, *Roxb.*, URTICACEÆ.
Foods .
Badha, *Pb.*, Salix tetrasperma, *Roxb.*, SALICINEÆ.
Foods .
Bádiánkhatái (fruit), *Bom.*, Illicium anisatum, *Linn.*, MAGNOLIACEÆ.
Foods .
Bádshahi-lac, *Hind.*, Brassica juncea, *H. F & T. T.*, CRUCIFERÆ.
Foods .
Bael Fruit, *Eng.*, Ægle Marmelos, *Correa.*, RUTACEÆ.
Foods .
Bága, *Tam.*, Acacia catechu, *Willd.*, LEGUMINOSÆ.
Foods .
Baghankara, *Beng.*, Alangium Lamarckii, *Thwaites*, CORNACEÆ.
Foods .
Bagri (fruit), *Pb.*, Phœnix dactylifera, *Linn.*, PALMÆ.
Foods .
Bagul, *Nep.*, Holbœllia latifolia, *Wall.*, BERBERIDEÆ.
Foods .

Bahan, *Sind, Pb.*, Populus euphratica, *Olivier*, SALICINEÆ.
Foods .
Bahava, *Bom.*, *Sind*, Casia Fistula, *Linn.*, LEGUMINOSÆ.
Foods .
Baherá, *Hind*, Terminalia belerica, *Roxb.*, COMBRETACEÆ.
Foods .
Bahul, *Hind.*, Grewia oppositifolia, *Roxb.*, TILIACEÆ.
Foods .
Balgun, *Hind.*, Solanum melongena, *Linn.*, SOLANACEÆ.
Foods .
Baikain, *Hind.*, Melia Azedarach, *Linn.*, MELIACEÆ.
Foods .
Baikal gajachinni, *C. P.*, Celastrus senegalensis, *Lam.*, CELASTRINEÆ.
Foods .
Bail, *Simla*, Salix elegans, *Wall.*, *Koch.*, SALICINEÆ.
Foods .
Bains, *N.-W. P. and Oudh*, Salix tetrasperma, *Roxb.*, SALICINEÆ.
Foods .
Bairada, *And.*, Rhizophora mucronata, *Lamk.*, RHIZOPHOREÆ.
Foods .
Baishi, *Hind.*, Salix tetrasperma, *Roxb.*, SALICINEÆ.
Foods .
Bajar-bang, *Pb.*, Physochlaina præalta, *Hook. f.*, SOLANACEÆ.
Foods .
Bajra, *Hind.*, Pennisetum typhoideum, *Rich.*, GRAMINEÆ.
Foods .
Bajra, *Bundelkhand*, Sorghum halepense, *Pers.*, GRAMINEÆ.
Foods .
Bajra-jhupanwa, *N.-W. P. and Oudh*, Sorghum vulgare, *Pers.*, GRAMINEÆ
Foods .
Bájri, *Hind.*, *Deccan*, Pennisetum typhoideum, *Rich.*, GRAMINEÆ.
Foods .
Bajur, *Pb.*, Picea Webbiana, *Lamb.*, CONIFERÆ.
Foods .
Bak, *Beng.*, Sesbania grandiflora, *Pers.*, LEGUMINOSÆ.
Foods .
Bakainu, *Nep.*, Melia Azedarach, *Linn.*, MELIACEÆ.
Foods .
Bakarcha, *Garhwal*, Premna integrifolia, *Linn.*, VERBENACEÆ.
Foods .
Bakas, *Beng.*, Adhatoda Vasica, *Nees.*, ACANTHACEÆ.
Foods .
Bakas-puttah, *Tam.*, Agave americana, *Linn.*, AMARYLLIDEÆ.
Foods .
Bakhra, *Pb.*, Tribulus alatus, *Delile.*, ZYGOPHYLLEÆ.
Foods .
Bakhtmal, *Pb.*, Psoralea plicata, *Delile.*, LEGUMINOSÆ.
Foods .
Bakkiamela, *Nep.*, Rhus semi-alata, *Murray*, ANACARDIACEÆ.
Foods .
Bakru, *Pb.*, Lonicera quinquelocularis, *Hardwicke*, CAPRIFOLIACEÆ.
Foods .
Bakshel, *Pb.*, Salix tetrasperma, *Roxb.*, SALICINEÆ.
Foods .
Bakull, *Bom.*, Mimusops Elengi, *Linn.*, SAPOTACEÆ.
Foods .
Balal, *Kan.*, Diospyros melanoxylon, *Roxb.*, EBENACEÆ.
Foods .
Balanja, *Pb.*, Calligonum polygonoides, *Linn.*, POLYGONACEÆ.
Foods -
Balda, *Dec.*, Terminalia belerica, *Roxb.*, COMBRETACEÆ.
Foods .

Balel, Coriaria nepalensis, *Wall.*, CORIARIEÆ.
Foods .
Balra, *Dec.*, Terminalia belerica, *Roxb.*, COMBRETACEÆ.
Foods .
Balsam, Garden, *Eng.*, Impatiens Balsamina, *Linn.*, GERANIACEÆ.
Foods .
Balút, *Afg.*, Quercus Ilex, *Linn.*, CUPULIFERÆ.
Foods .
Bamboo, *Eng.*, Arundinaria Hookeriana, *Munro*, GRAMINEÆ.
Foods .
Bamboo, *Eng.*, Bambusa arundinacea, *Retz.*, and other species GRAMINEÆ.
Foods .
Bamboo Male, *Eng.*, Dendrocalamus strictus, *Nees*, GRAMINEÆ.
Foods .
Bambway, *Burm.*, Careya arborea, *Roxb.*, MYRTACEÆ.
Foods .
Bammewa, *Pb.*, Elæagnus umbellata, *Thunb.*, ELÆAGNEÆ.
Foods .
Bamsutu, *Kashmir*, Cydonia vulgaris, *Tourn.*, ROSACEÆ.
Foods .
Bamtsunt, *Kashmir*, Cydonia vulgaris, *Tourn.*, ROSACEÆ.
Foods .
Bamul, *Pb.*, Acacia Jacquemontii, *Benth.*, LEGUMINOSÆ.
Foods .
Bamya, *Arab.*, *Pers.*, Hibiscus esculentus, *Linn.*, MALVACEÆ.
Foods .
Ban, *Hind.*, Zizyphus vulgaris, *Lamk.*, RHAMNEÆ.
Foods .
Ban, *Pb.*, Quercus dilitata, *Lindl.*, CUPULIFERÆ.
Foods .
Ban, *Pb.*, Quercus Ilex, *Linn.*, CUPULIFERÆ.
Foods .
Ban, *Pb.*, Quercus incana, *Roxb.*, CUPULIFERÆ.
Foods .
Banakhor, *Pb.*, Aralia achemirica, *Dcne.*, ARALIACEÆ.
Foods .
Banana, *Eng.*, Musa sapientum, *Linn.*, SCITAMMEÆ.
Foods .
Banchir, *Pb.*, Syringa Emodi, *Wall.*, OLEACEÆ.
Foods .
Banchor, *Pb.*, Euonymus fimbriatus, *Wall.*, CELASTRINEÆ.
Foods .
Banda, *Pb.*, Hedera Helix, *Linn.*, ARALIACEÆ.
Foods .
Banda, *N.-W. P.*, Heteropogon contortus, *R. & S.*, GRAMINEÆ.
Foods .
Bandar, *Pb.*, Capparis spinosa, *Linn.*, LEGUMINOSÆ.
Foods .
Bandara, *Tel.*, Hymenodictyon excelsum, *Wall.*, RUBIACEÆ.
Foods .
Bandarlati, *Beng.*, Cassia Fistula, *Linn.*, LEGUMINOSÆ.
Foods .
Bandhenras, *Beng.*, Hibiscus ficulneus, *Linn.*, MALVACEÆ.
Foods .
Bandhona, *Uriya*, Ougeinia dalbergioides, *Benth.*, LEGUMINOSÆ.
Foods .
Bandolat, *Cachar.*, Cassia Fistula, *Linn.*, LEGUMINOSÆ.
Foods .
Bandukel, *Pb.*, Equisetum debile, *Roxb.*, EQUISETACEÆ.
Foods .
Bane, *Trans-Indus*, Periploca aphylla, *Dcne.*, ASCLEPIADEÆ.
Foods

Banga, *Nep.*, Quercus lanuginosa, *Don.*, CUPULIFERÆ.
Foods .
Bang-sarson, *Hind.*, Brassica campestris, *Linn.*, var. Napus, sub-var. glauca, CRUCIFERÆ. Foods .
Ban-gulab, *Hind.*, Rosa macrophylla, *Lindl.*, ROSACEÆ.
Foods .
Bandt, *Surat*, name for a form of Pennisetum typhoideum, *Rich.*, GRAMINEÆ. Foods .
Banj katús, *Nep.*, Caslanopsis indica, *A. DC.*, CUPULIFERÆ.
Foods .
Ban-kagri, *Pb.*, Podophyllum emodi, *Wall.*, BERBERIDÆ.
Foods .
Bankas, *Hind.*, Pollinia eriopoda, *Hance.*, GRAMINEÆ.
Foods .
Bankass, *Eng.*, Pollinia eriopodo, *Hance.*, GRAMINEÆ.
Foods .
Banket, *Garo*, Ficus bengalensis, *Linn.*, URTICACEÆ.
Foods .
Bankhor, *Hind.*, *Pb.*, Æsculus indica, *Colebr.*, SAPINDACEÆ.
Foods .
Bankunch, *Pb.*, Viburnum cotinifolium, *Don.*, CAPRIFOLIACEÆ.
Foods .
Ban-mehal, *Hind.*, Pyrus baccata, *Linn.*. ROSACEÆ.
Foods .
Ban-nimbu, *Hind.*, Glycosmis pentaphylla, *Correa.*, RUTACEÆ.
Foods .
Ban-pala, *Pb.*, Pyrus kumaoni, *Dcne.*, ROSACEÆ.
Foods .
Banpálu, *Him. name*, Corylus colurna, *Linn.*, CUPULIFERÆ.
Foods .
Bán-phúnt, *Pb.*, Syringa emodi, *Wall.*, OLEACEÆ.
Foods .
Ban-potal, *Beng.*, Trichosanthes cucumerina, *Linn.*, CUCURBITACEÆ.
Foods .
Banraj, *Beng.*, Bauhinia racemosa, *Lam.*, LEGUMINOSÆ.
Foods .
Ban-rithá, *Beng.*, Acacia concinna, *DC.*, LEGUMINOSÆ.
Foods .
Bans, *Beng.*, *Hind.*, Bambusa arundinacea, *Retz.*, and other species, GRAMINEÆ. Foods .
Bans, *Hind.*, Dendrocalamus strictus, *Nees*, GRAMINEÆ.
Foods .
Bansa, *Hind.*, Albizezia odoratissima, *Benth.*, LEGUMINOSÆ.
Foods .
Bansl, *N.-W. P.*, Panicum miliaceum, *Linn.*, GRAMINEÆ.
Foods .
Bans kaban, *Hind.*, Dendrocalamus strictus, *Nees*, GRAMINEÆ.
Foods .
Bans keora, *Tam.*, Agave americana, *Linn.*, AMARYLLIDEÆ.
Foods .
Bantil, *Pb.*, Impatiens Balsamina, *Linn.*, MAGNOLIACEÆ.
Foods .
Banyan Tree, *Eng.*, Ficus bengalensis, *Linn.*, URTICACEÆ.
Foods .
Baobab Tree, *Eng.*, Adansonia digitata, *Linn.*, MALVACEÆ.
Foods .
Bar, *Hind.*, Ficus bengalensis, *Linn.*, URTICACEÆ.
Foods .
Bara, *Bundelkhand*, Sorghum halepense, *Pers.*, GRAMINEÆ.
Foods .
Barachar, *Pb.*, Quercus dilitata, *Lindl.*, CUPULIFERÆ.
Foods .

Bara flawar, *Ass.*, Caryota urens, *Willd.*, PALMÆ.
Foods .
Bara gorakuri, *Nep.*, Viburnum coriaceum, *Bl.*, CAPRIFOLIACEÆ.
Foods .
Bara-joman, *Nep.*, Eugenia formosa, *Wall.*, MYRTACEÆ.
Foods .
Bara-juar, *Hind.*, Zea Mays, *Linn.*, GRAMINEÆ.
Foods .
Baran, *Pb.*, Taraxacum officinale, *Wigg.*, COMPOSITÆ.
Foods .
Baranj, *Pers.*, Oryza sativa, *Linn.*, GRAMINEÆ.
Foods .
Bara-salpan, *Beng.*, Elemingia conjesta, *Roxb.*, LEGUMINOSÆ.
Foods .
Barat, *Pb.*, Dolichos biflorus, *Linn.*, LEGUMINOSÆ.
Foods .
Barbara, *Sans.*, Acacia arabica, *Willd.*, LEGUMINOSÆ.
Foods .
Barbati, *Beng.*, Vigna Catiang. *Endl.*, LEGUMINOSÆ.
Foods .
Barberry, *Eng.*, Berberis aristata *DC.*, and B. Lycium, *Royle*, BERBERIDEÆ.
Foods .
Barchar, *Pb.*, Quercus semicarpifolia, *Smith*, CUPULIFERÆ.
Foods .
Barethi, *Beng.*, Panicum paludosum, *Roxb.*, GRAMINEÆ.
Foods .
Bargat, *Hind.*, Ficus bengalensis, *Linn.*, URTICACEÆ.
Foods .
Barhal, *Hind.*, Artocarpas Lakucha, *Roxb.*, URTICACEÆ.
Foods .
Barhingori, *Ass.*, Castanopsis tribuloides, *A. DC.*, CUPULIFERÆ.
Foods .
Bariál, *Hind.*, Bauhinia variegata, *Linn.*, LEGUMINOSÆ.
Foods .
Bari boj, *Pb.*, Acorus Calamus, *Linn.*, AROIDEÆ.
Foods .
Bárik-tél, *Dec.*, Sesamum indicum, *Linn.*, PEDALINEÆ.
Foods .
Bari manhári, *Pb.*, Solanum coagulans, *Forsk.*, SOLANACEÆ.
Foods .
Bari-shopha, *Bom.*, Fœniculum vulgare, *Gærtn.*, UMBELLIFERÆ.
Foods .
Barlái, *Hind.*, Brassica juncea, *H. F. & T. T.*, CRUCIFERÆ.
Foods .
Barli-arisi, *Tam.*, Hordeum vulgare, *Linn.*, GRAMINEÆ.
Foods .
Barma, *Kashmir*, Taxus baccata, *Linn.*, CONIFERÆ.
Foods .
Barokoli, *Uriya*, Zizphus Œnoplia, *Mill.*, RHAMNEÆ.
Foods .
Baroli, *Mahr.*, Indigofera pulchella, *Roxb.*, LEGUMINOSÆ.
Foods .
Barrarra, *Trans-Indus*, Periploca aphylla, *Dcne.*, ASCLEPIADEÆ.
Foods .
Barsanga, *Beng.*, Murraya Kœnigii, *Spr.*, RUTACEÆ.
Foods .
Bartoodi, *Bom.*, Morinda citrifolia, *Linn.*, RUBIACEÆ.
Foods .
Bartu, *Pb.*, Hymenodictyon excelsum, *Wall.*, RUBIACEÆ.
Foods .
Baru, *Pb.*, Skimmia Laureola, *Hook.*, RUTACEÆ.
Foods .

Barua, *Pb.*, Sorghum halepense, *Pers.*, GRAMINEÆ.
Foods
Barumbiss, *Tel.*, Imperata arundinacea, *Cyrill.*, GRAMINEÆ.
Foods .
Bas, *Bom.*, Dendrocalamus strictus, *Nees.*, GRAMINEÆ.
Foods .
Basaunta, *N.-W. P.*, Panicum helopus, *Trin.*, GRAMINEÆ.
Foods .
Bashal, *Pb.*, Salix daphnoides, *Vill.*, SALICINEÆ.
Foods .
Bashang arús, *Him. name*, Adhatoda Vasica, *Nees.*, ACANTHACEÆ.
Foods .
Basil, sweet or common, Ocimum Basilicum, *Linn.*, LABIATÆ.
Foods .
Basla, *Pb.*, Cenchrus echinatus, *Linn.*, GRAMINEÆ.
Foods .
Basna, *Hind.*, Sesbania grandiflora, *Pers.*, LEGUMINOSÆ.
Foods .
Bassar, *Pb.*, Caparis spinosa, *Linn.*, CAPPARIDEÆ.
Foods .
Bastard Cedar, *Eng.*, Melia Azedarach, *Linn.*, MELIACEÆ.
Foods .
Bastard Jute, *Eng.*, Hibiscus cannabinus, *Linn.*, MALVACEÆ.
Foods .
Bastra, *Hind.*, Callicarpa lanata, *Wall.*, VERBENACEÆ.
Foods .
Basúti, *Him. name*, Adhatoda Vasica, *Nees.*, ACANTHACEÆ.
Foods .
Batata, *Bom.*, Solanum tuberosum, *Linn.*, SOLANACEÆ.
Foods .
Batavi nebu, Citrus decumana, *Willd.*, RUTACEÆ.
Foods .
Batkar, *Pb.*, Celtis caucasica, *Willd.*, URTICACEÆ.
Foods .
Batra, *Dec.*, Terminalia belerica, *Roxb.*, COMBRETACEÆ.
Foods .
Batwasi, *Nep.*, Flemingia congesta, *Roxb.*, LEGUMINOSÆ.
Foods .
Bather, *Pb.*, Grewia salvifolia, *Heyne*, TILIACEÆ.
Eoods .
Bathor, *Pb.*, Viburnum cotinifolium, *Don.*, CAPRIFOLIACEÆ.
Foods .
Bathua, *Pb.*, Chenopodium album, *L.*, CHENOPODIACEÆ.
Foods .
Bathia, *Jhelum & Chenab*, Periploca aphylla, *Dcne.*, ASCLEPIADEÆ.
Foods .
Bauri, *Pb.*, Capparis spinosa, *Linn.*, CAPPARIDEÆ.
Foods .
Baus, *Pb.*, Oxybaphus Himalaicus, *Edge.*, NYCTAGINEÆ.
Foods .
Bávache, *Sind*, Flacourtia Ramontchi, *L'Herit.*, BIXINEÆ.
Foods .
Baxthoa, *Pb.*, Hymenodictyon excelsum, *Wall.*, RUBIACEÆ.
Foods .
Bazrul, *Beng.*, *Hind.*, Hyocyamus niger, *Linn.*, SOLANACEÆ.
Foods .
Bead Tree, *Eng.*, Melia Azederach, *Linn.*, MELIACEÆ.
Foods .
Beans, French, *Eng.*, Phaseolus vulgaris, *Linn.*, LEGUMINOSÆ.
Foods .
Bean, Negro, *Eng.*, Mucuna monosperma, *DC.*, LEGUMINOSÆ.
Foods .

Berma, *Hind.*, Albiezzia odoratissima, *Benth.*, LEGUMINOSÆ.
Foods .
Beru, *Hind.*, Ficus virgata, *Roxb.*, URTICACEÆ.
Foods .
Bet, *Beng.*, *Hind.*, Calamus Rotang, *Linn.*, PALMÆ.
Foods .
Betain, *Kumaun*, Melia Azadirachta, *Linn.*, MELIACEÆ.
Foods .
Betain, *Hind.*, Melia Azedarach, *Linn.*, MELIACEÆ.
Foods .
Beta mu, *Tel.*, Calamus Rotang, *Linn.*, PALMÆ.
Foods .
Betar, *Him. name*, Juniferus communis, *Linn.*, CONIFERÆ.
Foods .
Betel Palm, *Eng.*, Areca Catechu, *Linn.*, PALMÆ.
Foods .
Betsa, *Pb.*, Salix daphnoides, *Vall.*, SALICINEÆ.
Foods .
Betu-sag, *Beng.*, Chenopodium album, *L.*, CHENOPODIACEÆ.
Foods .
Beymadá, *And.*, Albizzia Lebbek, *Benth.*, LEGUMINOSÆ.
Foods .
Bhabar, *Hind.*, Pollinia eriopoda, *Hance.*, GRAMINEÆ.
Foods .
Bhádli, *Deccan*, Setaria glauca, *Beauv.*, GRAMINEÆ.
Foods .
Bhadras, *Nep.*, Elæocarpus laneæfolius, *Roxb.*, TILIACEÆ.
Foods .
Bhagmili, *Nep.*, Rhus semi-alata, *Murray*, ANACARDIACEÆ.
Foods .
Bhagur, *Deccan*, Amarantus spicatus, AMARANTACEÆ.
Foods .
Bhains, *Simla*, Salix elegans, *Wall*, *Koch.*, SALICINEÆ.
Foods .
Bhaira, *Hind.*, Terminalia belerica, *Roxb.*, COMBRETACEÆ.
Foods .
Bhalena, *Hind.*, Hymenodictyon excelsum, *Wall.*, RUBIACEÆ.
Foods .
Bhalia, *Beng.*, *Hind.*, Flemingia conjesta, *Roxb.*, LEGUMINOSÆ.
Foods .
Bhamina, *Hind.*, Hymenodictyon excelsum, *Wall.*, RUBIACEÆ.
Foods .
Bhandir, *Hind.*, Albizzia odoratissima, *Benth.*, LEGUMINOSÆ.
Foods .
Bhandra, *N.-W. P. & Pb.*, Setaria glauca, *Beauv.*, GRAMINEÆ.
Foods .
Bhandri, *N.-W. P. & Pb.*, Setaria glauca, *Beauv.*, GRAMINEÆ.
Foods .
Bhang, *Beng.*, Cannabis sativa, *Linn.*, URTICACEÆ.
Foods .
Bhanjra, *Bundelkhand*, Apluda aristata, *Linn.*, GRAMINEÆ.
Foods .
Bhanjuri, *Bundelkhand*, Apluda aristata, *Linn.*, GRAMINEÆ.
Foods .
Bhanjuri, *N.-W. P.*, Eleonurus hirsutus, *Vahl.*, GRAMINEÆ.
Foods .
Bhanwar, *Pb.*, Ipomæa eriocarpa, *Br.*, CONVOLVULACEÆ.
Foods .
Bhara, *Beng.*, Rhizophora mucronata, *Lamk.*, RHIZOPHOREÆ.
Foods .
Bharree, *Aligarh*, Eragrostis Brownei, *Nees.*, GRAMINEÆ.
Foods

P I

Bhuimága, *Bom.*, Arachis hypogæa, *Linn.*, LEGUMINOSÆ.
Foods .
Bhuisenga, *Bom.*, Arachis hypogæa, *Linn.*, LEGUMINOSÆ.
Foods .
Bhuj, *Pb.*, Betula Bhojpattra, *Wall.*, CUPULIFERÆ.
Foods .
Bhujpattra, *Hind.*, Betula Bhojpattra, *Wall.*, CUPULIFERÆ.
Foods .
Bhumphor, *Pb.*, Tulipa stellata, *Hook.*, LILIACEÆ.
Foods .
Bhurbhuri, *N.-W. P.*, Eragrostis plumosa, *Link.*, GRAMINEÆ.
Foods .
Bhúrkúr, *Hind.*, Hymenodictyon excelsum, *Wall.*, RUBIACEÆ.
Foods .
Bhutakesa, *Bom.*, Mussænda frondosa, *Linn.*, RUBIACEÆ.
Foods .
Bhut-bhiravi, *Beng.*, Premna integrifolia, *Linn.*, VERBENACEÆ.
Foods .
Bhutta, *Beng.*, *Hind.*, Zea Mays, *Linn.*, GRAMINEÆ.
Foods .
Bhúttuá, *Hind.*, Benincasa cerifera, *Savi.*, CUCURBITACEÆ.
Foods .
Bidái, *Pb.*, Salix daphnoides, *Vill.*, SALICINEÆ.
Foods .
Bidu, *Pb.*, Salix tetrasperma, *Roxb.*, SALICINEÆ.
Foods .
Bihi, *Hind.*, Cydonia vulgaris, *Tourn.*, ROSACEÆ.
Foods .
Bija, *Hind.*, Pterocarpus Marsupium, *Roxb.*, LEGUMINOSÆ.
Foods .
Bijapúra, *Bom.*, Citrus medica, *Linn.*, RUTACEÆ.
Foods .
Bijasar, *Hind.*, Pterocarpus Marsupium, *Roxb.*, LEGUMINOSÆ.
Foods .
Bijori, *Bom.*, Citrus medica, *Linn.*, RUTACEÆ.
Foods .
Bij-palak, *Pb.*, Spinacia oleracea, *Mill.*, CHINOPODIACEÆ.
Foods .
Bila, *Bom.*, Ægle Marmelos, *Correa.*, RUTACEÆ.
Foods .
Bilga, *Koti*, Rodetia Amherstiana, *Moq.*, AMARANTACEÆ.
Foods .
Bilimbi, *Beng.*, *Hind.*, Averrhoa Bilimbi, *Linn.*, GERANIACEÆ.
Foods .
Bilimbi Tree, *Eng.*, Averrhoa Bilimbi, *Linn.*, GERANIACEÆ.
Foods .
Bilin, *Sans.*, Feronia Elephantum, *Correa.*, RUTACEÆ.
Foods .
Billa, *Sylhet*, Excœcaria baccata, *Müll.*, EUPHORBIACEÆ.
Foods .
Billi, *Hind.*, Pueraria tuberosa, *DC.*, LEGUMINOSÆ.
Foods .
Billi, *Nilgiris*, Rhododendron arboreum, *Sm.*, ERICACEÆ.
Foods .
Bilsa, *N.-W. P. & Oudh.*, Salix tetrasperma, *Roxb.*, SALICINEÆ.
Foods .
Bilva, of the ancients, *Bom.*, Ægle Marmelos, *Correa.*, RUTACEÆ.
Foods .
Bilwara, *Tam.*, Albizzia odoratissima, *Benth.*, LEGUMINOSÆ.
Foods .
Bimla, *Hind.*, Grewia vestita, *Wall.*, TILIACEÆ.
Foods .

Boktok, *Lepcha*, Careya arborea, *Roxb.*, MYRTACEÆ.
Foods .
Bokul, *Beng.*, Mimusops Elengi, *Linn.*, SAPOTACEÆ.
Foods .
Bola, *Ass.*, Morus cuspidata, *Wall.*, URTICACEÆ.
Foods .
Bolchú, *Garo*, Bombax malabaricum, *DC.*, MALVACEÆ.
Foods .
Bole-siyah, *Pers.*, Aloe vera, *Linn.*, LILIACEÆ.
Foods .
Bolkobak, *Garo*, Gmelina arborea, *Roxb.*, VERBENACEÆ.
Foods .
Bolsal, *Garo*, Shorea robusta, *Gærtn.*, DIPTEROCARPEÆ.
Foods .
Bolsobak, *Garo*, Eugenia formosa, *Wall.*, MYRTACEÆ.
Foods .
Bommakachika, *Tel.*, Costus speciosus, *Sm.*, SCITAMINEÆ.
Foods .
Bonam, *Mal.*, Bassia latifolia, *Roxb.*; SAPOTACEÆ.
Foods .
Bonda-janu, (the plant), *Tel.*, Sorghum vulgare, *Pers.*, GRAMINEÆ.
Foods .
Bon-methi, *Beng.*, Melilotus parviflora, *Desf.*, LEGUMINOSÆ.
Foods .
Bon-poi, *Beng.*, *Hind.*, Basella alba, *L.*, CHENOPODIACEÆ.
Foods .
Bonta-shama, *Tel.*, Panicum frumentaceum, *Roxb.*, GRAMINEÆ.
Foods .
Boo-ambilla, *Cingh.*, Antidesma Ghæsembilla, *Gærtn.*, EUPHORBIACEÆ.
Foods .
Booa-sow, *Malay*, Mimusops Kauki, *Linn.*, SAPOTACEÆ.
Foods .
Boomaiza, *Burm.*, Albizzia stipulata, *Boivin.*, LEGUMINOSÆ.
Foods .
Bor, *Hind.*, Ficus bengalensis, *Linn.*, URTICACEÆ.
Foods .
Borar, *Nep.*, Ficus bengalensis, *Linn.*, URTICACEÆ.
Foods .
Borara, *Uriya*, Bauhinia variegata, *Linn.*, LEGUMINOSÆ.
Foods .
Bora singoli, *Nep.*, Cinamomum obtusifolium, *Nees.*, LAURINEÆ.
Foods .
Borboli, *Beng.*, *Hind.*, Dolichos lablab, *Linn.*, LEGUMINOSÆ.
Foods .
Boria, *Kumaun*, Cordia Myxa, *Linn.*, BORAGINEÆ.
Foods .
Borthekra, *Ass.*, Garcinia pedunculata, *Roxb.*, GUTTIFERÆ.
Foods .
Boru, *Uriya*, Ficus bengalensis, *Linn.*, URTICACEÆ.
Foods .
Bosha, *Gond.*, Bauhinia racemosa, *Lam.*, LEGUMINOSÆ.
Foods .
Bot, *Ass.*, Ficus bengalensis, *Linn.*, URTICACEÆ.
Foods .
Bottle Gourd, *Eng.*, Lagenaria vulgaris, *Seringe.*, CUCURBITACEÆ.
Foods .
Bouro, *Uriya*, Bombax malabaricum, *DC.*, MALVACEÆ.
Foods .
Bowchee, *Hind.*, *Dec.*, Flacourtia Ramontchi, *L'Herit.*, BIXINEÆ.
Foods .
Bowla, *Pl.*, Murraya Kœnigii, *Spr.*, RUTACEÆ.
Foods .

Budhal, *N.-W. P.*, Marlea begoniæfolia, *Roxb.*, CORNACEÆ.
Foods .
Budidi gummadi, *Tel.*, Benincasa cerifera, *Savi.*, CUCURBITACEÆ.
Foods .
Búdshúr, *Pb.*, Ephedra Gerardiana, *Wall.*, GNETACEÆ.
Foods .
Bugra, *Pb.*, Gynandropsis pentaphylla, *DC.*, CAPPARIDEÆ.
Foods .
Buhal, *Beng.*, Cordia Myxa, *Linn.*, BORAGINEÆ.
Foods .
Bui, *Pb.*, Ballota limbata, *Benth.*, LABIATÆ.
Foods .
Buka, *Beng.*, Sesbania grandiflora, *Pers.*, LEGUMINOSÆ.
Foods .
Buksha, *Beng.*, Hemarthria compressa, *R. Br.*, GRAMINEÆ.
Foods .
Bullock's Heart, *Eng.*, Anona reticulata, *Linn.*, ANONACEÆ.
Foods .
Bulrush, *Eng.*, Pennisetum typhoideum, *Rich.*, GRAMINEÆ.
Foods .
Bulu, *Cingh.*, Terminalia belerica, *Roxb.*, COMBRETACEÆ.
Foods .
Bulyeltra, *Nep.*, Butea frondosa, *Roxb.*, LEGUMINOSÆ.
Foods .
Bun-am, *Ass.*, Mangifera Sylvatica, *Roxb.*, ANACARDIACEÆ.
Foods .
Bun-chichinga, *Beng.*, Trichosanthes lobata, *Roxb.*, CUCURBITACEÆ.
Foods .
Bunj, *Hind.*, *Dec.*, Flacourtia Ramontchi, *L'Herit.*, BIXINEÆ.
Foods .
Bunkonkri, *Machi*, Eugenia formosa, *Wall.*, MYRTACEÆ.
Foods .
Bun-okra, *Beng.*, Xanthium strumarium, *Linn.*, COMPOSITÆ.
Foods .
Bun-palung, *Beng.*, Rumex Wallichii, *Meisn.*, POLYGONACEÆ.
Foods .
Bun-tepoori, *Beng.*, Physalis minima, *Linn.*, SOLANACEÆ.
Foods .
Bunun, *Pb.*, Fragaria vesca, *Linn.*, ROSACEÆ.
Foods .
Bur (Duthie), Bambusa spinosa, *Roxb.*, GRAMINEÆ.
Foods .
Bur, *Beng.*, Ficus bengalensis, *Linn.*, URTICACEÆ.
Foods .
Buraga, *Tel.*, Bombax malabaricum, *DC.*, MALVACEÆ.
Foods .
Burans, *Pb.*, Rhododendron arboreum, *Sm.*, ERICACEÆ.
Foods .
Buraye, *Sind*, Periploca aphylla, *Dcne.*, ASCLEPIADEÆ.
Foods .
Burdunul, *N.-W. P.*, Setaria verticillata, *Beauv.*, GRAMINEÆ.
Foods .
Búrga, *Tel.*, Bombax malabaricum, *DC.*, MALVACEÆ.
Foods .
Burgee, *Pb.*, Phytolacca acinosa, *Roxb.*, VERBENACEÆ.
Foods .
Búrgú, *Tel.*, Bombax malabaricum, *DC.*, MALVACEÆ.
Foods .
Burj, *Pb.*, Betula Bhojpattra, *Wall.*, CUPULIFERÆ.
Foods .
Burkai, *Tel.*, Luffa acutangula, *Roxb.*, CUCURBITACEÆ.
Foods .

Burmack, *Ladak*, Artemisia sacrorum, *Ledele.*, COMPOSITÆ.
Foods .
Burmar, *Ladak*, Artemisia parviflora, *Roxb.*, COMPOSITÆ.
Foods .
Burr, *Arab.*, Triticum sativum, *Lam*, GRAMINEÆ.
Foods .
Burr-wood, *Eng.*, Withania Somnifera, *Dun.*, SOLANACEÆ.
Foods .
Burun, *Sans.*, Salix tetrasperma, *Roxb.*, SALICINEÆ.
Foods .
Bur-weed, *Eng.*, Xanthium strumarium, *Linn.*, COMPOSITÆ.
Foods .
Burzal, *Pb.*, Betula Bhojpattra, *Wall.*, CUPULIFERÆ.
Foods .
Bush Caper, *Eng.*, Capparis spinosa, *Linn.*, CAPPARIDEÆ.
Foods .
Bút, *Beng.*, Cicer arietinum, *Linn.*, LEGUMINOSÆ.
Foods .
But, *Beng.*, Ficus bengalensis, *Linn.*, URTICACEÆ.
Foods .
Bútshúr, *Pb.*, Ephedra Gerardiana, *Wall.*, GNETACEÆ.
Foods .
Butter Tree, *Eng.*, Bassia latifolia, *Roxb.*, SAPOTACEÆ.
Foods .
Bwaycheng, *Burm.*, Bauhinia variegata, *Linn.*, LEGUMINOSÆ.
Foods .
Bwaygyin, *Burm.*, Bauhinia malabarica, *Roxb*, LEGUMINOSÆ.
Foods .
Byalt-sin, *Burm.*, Antidesma Ghœsembilla, *Gærtn.*, EUPHORBIACEÆ.
Foods .
Byu, *Burm.*, Rhizophora mucronata, *Lamk.*, RHIZOPHOREÆ.
Foods .

C

Caat-kododo, *Mal.*, Gynandropsis pentaplylla, *DC.*, CAPPARIDEÆ.
Foods .
Caat-siragum, *Tam.*, Vernonia anthelmintica, *Willd.*, COMPOSITÆ.
Foods .
Cabbage, *Eng.*, Brassica oleracea, *Linn.*, CRUCIFERÆ.
Foods .
Cabbage, Red or White, *Eng.*, Brassica oleracea capitata, *Linn.*, CRUCIFERÆ. Foods .
Cabbage, Savoy, *Eng.*, Brassica oleracea bulleata, *Linn.*, CRUCIFERÆ.
Foods .
Cabbage, Turnip-stemmed, *Eng.*, Brassica oleracea, caulo-rapa, *Linn.*, CRUCIFERÆ. Foods .
Cabli. *See* Pisum sativum, *Linn.*, LEGUMINOSÆ.
Foods .
Cacao, *Eng.*, Theobroma Cacao, *Linn.*, STERCULIACEÆ.
Foods .
Caden, *Eng.*, Phœnix sylvestris, *Roxb.*, PALMÆ.
Foods .
Camel Thorn, *Eng.*, Alhagi maurorum, *Desb.*, LEGUMINOSÆ.
Foods .
Cane Rattan, *Eng.*, Calamus Rotang, *Linn.*, PALMÆ.
Foods .
Cape Gooseberry, *Eng.*, Physalis peruviana, *Linn.*, SOLANACEÆ.
Foods .

Carachunal, *Tam.*, Tacca pinnatifida, *Forsk.*, TACCACEÆ.
Foods .
Caraway seed, *Eng.*, Carum Carui, *Linn.*, UMBELLIFERÆ.
Foods .
Cardamom, Greater, *Eng.*, Amomum subulatum, *Roxb.*, SCITAMINEÆ.
Foods .
Cardamom, Lesser, *Eng.*, Elettaria Cardamomum, *Maton.*, SCITAMINEÆ.
Foods .
Cardamom plant, *Eng.*, Amomum aromaticum, *Roxb.*, SCITAMINEÆ.
Foods .
Carinsiragum, *Tam.*, Nigella sativa, *Linn.*, RANUNCULACEÆ.
Foods .
Carob Tree, *Eng.*,Ceratonia Siliqua, *L.*, LEGUMINOSÆ.
Foods .
Carrot, *Eng.*, Daucus Carota, *Linn.*, UMBELLIFERÆ.
Foods .
Cashew Nut, *Eng.*, Anacardium occidentale, *Linn.*, ANACARDIACEÆ.
Foods .
Cassava, Bitter, *Eng.*, Manihot utilissima, *Pohl.*, EUPHORBIACEÆ.
Foods .
Cassia Fœtid, *Eng.*, Cassia Tora, *Linn.*, LEGUMINOSÆ.
Foods .
Castor-oil, *Eng.*, Ricinus communis, *Linn.*, EUPHORBIACEÆ.
Foods .
Casua-Chetty, *Tam.*, Memecylon edule, *Roxb.*, MELASTROMACEÆ.
Foods .
Catappa, *Malay.*, Terminalia Catappa, *Linn.*, COMBRETACEÆ.
Foods .
Catechu, *Eng.*, Acacia Catechu, *Willd.*, LEGUMINOSÆ.
Foods .
Catechu, *Germ.*, Acacia Catechu, *Willd.*, LEGUMINOSÆ.
Foods .
Cat's-tail, Grass Meadow, *Eng.*, Pheleum pratense, *Linn.*, GRAMINEÆ.
Foods .
Cat's Tail, Lesser, *Eng.*, Typha angustifolia, *Linn.*, TYPHACEÆ.
Foods .
Cauliflower, *Eng.*, Brassica oleracea botrytis, *Linn.*, CRUCIFERÆ.
Foods .
Cavalum, *Mar.*, Sterculia balanghas, *Linn.*, STERCULIACEÆ.
Foods .
Cavara-fullu, *Mal.*, Eleusine ægyptiaca, *Pers.*, GRAMINEÆ.
Foods .
Cayenne Pepper, *Eng.*, Capsicum frutescens, *Linn.*, SOLANACEÆ.
Foods .
Cedar Himalayan, *Eng.*, Cedrus Deodara, *London*, CONIFERÆ.
Foods .
Cedar Himalayan pencil, *Eng.*, Juniperus excelsa, *M. Bieb.*, CONIFERÆ.
Foods .
Celery, *Eng.*, Apium graveolens, *Linn.*, UMBELLIFERÆ.
Foods .
Cha, *Beng.*, *Hind.*, Camellia theifera, *Griff*, TERNSTRŒMIACEÆ.
Foods .
Chachinda, Jangli, *Hind.*, Trichosanthes cucumerina, *Linn.*, CUCURBITACEÆ. Foods .
Chachinga, *Hind.*, Trichosanthes anguina, *Linn.*, CUCURBITACEÆ.
Foods .
Chaiura, *Kumaun*, Dassia butyracea, *Roxb.*, SAPOTACEÆ.
Foods .
Chakotra, Citrus decumana, *Willd.*, RUTACEÆ.
Foods .
Chakua, *Beng.*, Albizzia stipulata, *Boivin.*, LEGUMINOSÆ.
Foods .

Chakunda, *Hind.*, *Beng.*, Cassia Tora, *Linn.*, LEGUMINOSÆ.
Foods .
Chalai, *Himalayan name*, Juniperus excelsa, *M. Bieb.*, CONIFERÆ.
Foods .
Challa mantu, *C. P.*, Securinega Leucopyrus, *Müll. Arg.*, EUPHORBIACEÆ.
Foods .
Chalmeri, *Hind.*, Phyllanthus distichus, *Müll. Arg.*, EUPHORBIACEÆ.
Foods .
Chalodra, *Pb.*, Eleusine Corocana, *Gærtn.*, GRAMINEÆ.
Foods .
Chalta, *Beng.*, *Hind.*, Dillenia indica, *Linn.*, DILLENIACEÆ.
Foods .
Cham-ari, *Mar.*, Premna integrifolia, *Linn.*, VERBENACEÆ.
Foods .
Chambe, *Garo*, Eugenia Jambolana, *Lam.*, MYRTACEÆ.
Foods .
Chambu, *Garo*, Sizygium jambolanum, *DC.*, MYRTACEÆ.
Foods .
Chambu, *Tam.*, Pennisetum typhoideum, *Rich.*, GRAMINEÆ.
Foods .
Chambun, *Pb.*, Hovenia dulcis, *Thunb.*, RHAMNEÆ.
Foods .
Chanbuli, *Dec.*, Bauhinia Vahlii, *W. & A.*, LEGUMINOSÆ.
Foods .
Chamlári, *Pb.*, Prunus Puddum, *Roxb.*, ROSACEÆ.
Foods .
Chamoti, *Pb.*, Tulipa stellata, *Hook.*, LILIACEÆ.
Foods .
Champ, *Pb.*, Alnus nitada, *Endl.*, CUPULIFERÆ.
Foods .
Champa, *Beng.*, Michelia Champaca, *Linn.*, MAGNOLIACEÆ.
Foods .
Champa, *Hind.*, Michelia Champaca, *Linn.*, MAGNOLIACEÆ.
Foods .
Champaka, *Beng.*, Michelia Champaca, *Linn.*, MAGNOLIACEÆ.
Foods .
Chamrúr, *Hind.*, Ehretia lævis, *Roxb.*, BORAGINEÆ.
Foods .
Chamui, *Pb.*, Tulipa stellata, *Hook.*, LILIACEÆ.
Foods .
Chán, *Pb.*, Rhododendron arboreum, *Sm.*, ERICACEÆ.
Foods .
Chaná, *Hind.*, *Deccan*, Cicer arientinum, *Linn.*, LEGUMINOSÆ.
Foods .
Chanangi, *Hyderabad*, Murraya Kœnigii, *Spr.*, RUTACEÆ.
Foods .
Chánay Kéléngu, *Eng.*, Tacca pinnatifida, *Forsk.*, TACCACEÆ.
Foods .
Changma, *Pb.*, Salix alba, *Linn.*, SALICINEÆ.
Foods .
Changma, *W. Tibet*, Populus balsanifera, *Linn.*, SALICINEÆ.
Foods .
Changma, *W. Tibet*, Salix daphnoides, *Vill.*, SALICINEÆ.
Foods .
Chanu, *Beng.*, Carum Roxburghianum, *Benth.*, UMBELLIFERÆ.
Foods .
Cháphá, *Bom.*, Michelia Champaca, *Linn.*, MAGNOLIACEÆ.
Foods .
Chapkia, *Kumaun*, Orthanthera viminea, *Wight*, ASCLEPIADEÆ.
Foods .
Char, *C. P.*, Buchanania latifolia, *Roxb.*, ANACARDIACEÆ.
Foods .

Chara, *N.-W. P. & Oudh*, Eruca sativa, *Lam.*, CRUCIFERÆ.
Foods .
Chara, *Tel.*, Buchanania latifolia, *Roxb.*, ANACARDIACEÆ.
Foods .
Charachi, *Tel.*, Grewia tiliæfolia, *Vahl.*, TILIACEÆ.
Foods .
Charang, *Garo*, Castanopsis indica, *A. DC.*, CUPULIFERÆ.
Foods .
Chari (stalks), *Beng.*, *Hind.*, Sorghum vulgare, *Pers.*, GRAMINEÆ.
Foods .
Charmaghz, *Pers.*, Juglans regia, *Linn.*, JUGLANDEÆ.
Foods .
Chároli, *Bom.*, Buchanania latifolia, *Roxb.*, ANACARDIACEÆ.
Foods .
Charrel, *Afg.*, Quercus Ilex, *Linn.*, CUPULIFERÆ.
Foods .
Charwa, *N.-W. P.*, Pennisetum conchroides, *Rich.*, GRAMINEÆ.
Foods .
Charwari, *Hyderabad*, Buchanania latifolia, *Roxb.*, ANACARDIACEÆ.
Foods .
Chashme-khuros, *Pers.*, Abrus precatorius, *Linn.*, LEGUMINOSÆ.
Foods . .
Chattri, *Afg.*, *bazar name*, Agaricus campestris, *Linn.*, FUNGIÆ.
Foods .
Chatung, *Kashmir*, Taxus baccata, *Linn.*, CONIFERÆ.
Foods .
Chaulai, *Hind.*, Wendlandia exerta, *DC.*, RUBIACEÆ.
Foods .
Chaulai, *Pb.*, Amarantus Anardana, *Hamilt.*, AMARANTACEÆ.
Foods .
Chaulai, *Upper India*, Amarantus mangostanus, *L.*, AMARANTACEÆ.
Foods .
Chaun, *Beng.*, Apium graveolens, *Linn.*, UMBELLIFERÆ.
Foods .
Chavela, *Mar.*, Sorghum vulgare, *Pers.*, GRAMINEÆ.
Foods .
Chavli, *Deccan*, Vigna Catiang, *Endl.*, LEGUMINOSÆ.
Foods .
Cháwal (husked), *Hind.*, *Beng.*, Oryza sativa, *Linn.*, GRAMINEÆ.
Foods .
Chaya-pula, *Sans.*, Citrullus vulgaris, *Schrad.*, CUCURBITACEÆ.
Foods .
Chechar, *Pb.*, Rhus semi-alata, *Murray*, ANACARDIACEÆ.
Foods .
Cheena, *Hind.*, *Beng.*, Panicum miliaceum, *Linn.*, GRAMINEÆ.
Foods .
Chehna, *N.-W. P.*, Panicum miliaceum, *Linn.*, GRAMINEÆ.
Foods .
Chehur, *Beng.*, Bauhinia Vahlii, *W. & A.*, LEGUMINOSÆ.
Foods .
Chein, *Sutlej*, Melia Azedarach, *Linn.*, MELIACEÆ.
Foods .
Chel (fibre) , Cannabis sativa, *Linn.*, URTICACEÆ.
Foods .
Chelun, *Simla*, Populus ciliata, *Wall.*, SALICINEÆ.
Foods .
Chena, *Eng.*, Panicum miliaceum, *Linn.*, GRAMINEÆ.
Foods .
Chench, *Pb.*, Rubus fruticosus, *Linn.*, ROSACEÆ.
Foods .
Chenjul, *Pb.*, Bœhmeria Salicifolia, *D. Don.*, URTICACEÆ.
Foods .

Chenna, *Hind.*, Cicer arietinum, *Linn.*, LEGUMINOSÆ.
Foods .
Chennka, *Sans.*, Cicer arietinum, *Linn.*, LEGUMINOSÆ.
Foods .
Cheppura, *Kan.*, Bauhinia malabarica, *Roxb.*, LEGUMINOSÆ.
Foods .
Cheroo-pinnay, *Tam.*, Calophyllum Wightianum, *Wall.*, GUTTIFERÆ.
Foods .
Cherry, Bird, *Eng.*, Prunus Padus, *Linn.*, ROSACEÆ.
Foods .
Cherry Sweet, *Eng.*, Prunus Avieum, *Linn.*, ROSACEÆ.
Foods .
Cherry, Wild, *Eng.*, Prunus Cerasus, *Linn.*, ROSACEÆ.
Foods .
Cherukoo-bodi, *Tel.*, Saccharum officinarum, *Linn.*, GRAMINEÆ.
Foods .
Chestnuts, Spanish, *Eng.*, Castanea vulgaris, *Lam.*, CUPULIFERÆ.
Foods .
Chestnut, Sweet, *Eng.*, Castanea vulgaris, *Lam.*, CUPULIFERÆ.
Foods .
Chettipa, *Tel.*, Hymenodictyon excelsum, *Wall.*, RUBIACEÆ.
Foods .
Cheull, *Oudh*, Bassia butyracea, *Roxb.*, SAPOTACEÆ.
Foods .
Chewa, *Pb.*, Ephedra Gerardiana, *Wall.*, GNETACEÆ.
Foods .
Chhágul-bátl, *Beng.*, Dæmia extensa, *R. Br.*, ASCLEPIADEÆ.
Foods .
Chibbur, *Sind.*, Cynodon Dactylon, *Pers.*, GRAMINEÆ.
Foods .
Chibil, *Hind.*, Ulmus integrefolia, *Roxb.*, URTICACEÆ.
Foods .
Chibúda, *Bom.*, Cucumis Melo, *Linn.*, CUCURBITACEÆ.
Foods .
Chichia, *Him. names*, Juniperus communis, *Linn.*, CONIFERÆ.
Foods .
Chichinda, *Pb.*, Trichosanthes anguina, *Linn.*, CUCURBITACEÆ.
Foods .
Chichinga, *Beng.*, Trichosanthes anguina, *Linn.*, CUCURBITACEÆ.
Foods .
Chichra, *Hind.*, Butea frondosa, *Roxb.*, LEGUMINOSÆ.
Foods .
Chicken Pea, *Eng.*, Cicer arietinum, *Linn.*, LEGUMINOSÆ.
Foods .
Chick-lenta, *Tel.*, Setaria verticillata, *Beauv.*, GRAMINEÆ.
Foods .
Chicory, *Eng.* Cichorium Intybus, *Linn.*, COMPOSITÆ.
Foods .
Chijakri, *Pb.*, Podophyllum emodi, *Wall.*, BERBERIDÆ.
Foods .
Chikaya, *Tel.*, Acacia concinna, *DC.*, LEGUMINOSÆ.
Foods .
Chiki, *Ladak*, Arenaria holosteoides, *Edge.*, CARYOPHYLLEÆ.
Foods .
Chikti, *Hind.*, Triumfetta annua, *Linn.*, TILIACEÆ.
Foods .
Chil, *Pb.*, Pinus longifolia, *Roxb.*, CONIFERÆ.
Foods .
Chila, *Hind.* Wendlandia exerta, *DC.*, RUBEACEÆ.
Foods .
Chilagada, *Tel.*, Ipomæa Batatas, *Lamk.*, CONVOLVULACEÆ.
Foods .

Chilghoza, *Afg.*, Pinus Gerardiana, *Wall.*, CONIFERÆ.
Foods .
Chilgoja, *Simla*, Pinus Gerardiana, *Wall.*, CONIFERÆ.
Foods .
Chilkadudu, *Tel.*, Saccopetalum tomentosum, *Hook.*, ANONACEÆ.
Foods .
Chilla, *Tel.*, Strychnos potatorum, *Linn. fil.*, LOGANIACEÆ.
Foods .
Chillies, *Eng.*, Capsicum frutescens, *Linn.*, SOLANACEÆ.
Foods .
Chilta-eita, *Tel.*, Phœnix ferinifera, *Willd.*, PALMÆ.
Foods .
Chilu, *Kan.*, Strychnos potatorum, *Linn. fil.*, LOGANIACEÆ.
Foods .
Chimbari, *Pb.*, Eleusine ægyptiaca, *Pers.*, GRAMINEÆ.
Foods .
Chimman, *Bhil.*, Gmelina arborea, *Roxb.*, VERBENACEÆ.
Foods .
Chimu, *Pb.*, Morus serrata, *Roxb.*, URTICACEÆ.
Foods .
Chin, *Pb.*, Fagopyrum esculentum, *Mænch.*, POLYGONACEÆ.
Foods .
Chinam, *Pb.*, Panicum miliaceum, *Linn.*, GRAMINEÆ.
Foods .
Chindi, *Gond.*, Phœnix acaulis, *Roxb.*, PALMÆ.
Foods .
Chinese Dates, *Eng.*, Zizyphus Jujuba, *Lam.*, RHAMNEÆ.
Foods .
Chinni, *Hind.*, Morus alba, *Linn.*, URTICACEÆ.
Foods .
Chinta, *Tel.*, Tamarindus indica, *Linn.*, LEGUMINOSÆ.
Foods .
Chinwa, *N.-W. P.*, Panicum miliaceum, *Linn.*, GRAMINEÆ.
Foods .
Chir, *Pb.*, Pinus longifolia, *Roxb.*, CONIFERÆ.
Foods .
Chirati, *Sind*, Mukia scabrella, *Arn.*, CUCURBITACEÆ.
Foods .
Chirauli, *Pb.*, Buchanania latifolia, *Roxb.*, ANACARDIACEÆ.
Foods .
Chirchitta, *Pb.*, Lycium europœum, *Linn.*, SOLANACEÆ.
Foods .
Chiri, *Chenab*, Pinus Gerardiana, *Wall.*, CONIFERÆ.
Foods .
Chirkal, *N.-W. P.*, Panicum helopus, *Trin.*, var. hirsutum, sp. *Koen.*, GRAMINEÆ. Foods .
Chirmiti, *Hind.*, Abrus precatorius, *Linn.*, LEGUMINOSÆ.
Foods .
Chironji, *C. P.*, Buchanania latifolia, *Roxb.*, ANACARDIACEÆ.
Foods .
Chirorœ, *Garo*, Terminalia belerica, *Roxb.*, COMBRETACEÆ.
Foods .
Chirru, *Pb.*, Xanthium strumarium, *Linn.*, COMPOSITÆ.
Foods .
Chirua, *N.-W.-P.*, Pod annua, *Linn.*, GRAMINEÆ.
Foods .
Chirwa, *N.-W. P.*, Panicum miliaceum, *Linn.*, GRAMINEÆ.
Foods .
Chirwi (fruit), *Pb.*, Phœnix dactylifera, *Linn.*, PALMÆ.
Foods .
Chitana, *Pb.*, Pyrus kumaoni, *Dcne.*, ROSACEÆ.
Foods .

Chit-batto, *Kashmir,* Trifolium fragiferum, *Linn.,* LEGUMINOSÆ.
Foods .
Chitompa, *Garo,* Garuga pinnata, *Roxb.,* BURSERACEÆ.
Foods .
Chitra, *Hind., Nep., Pers.,* Berberis aristata, *DC.,* and B. Lycium, *Royle,* BERBERIDEÆ. Foods .
Chitra, *Nep.,* Berberis asiatica, *Roxb.,* BERBERIDEÆ.
Foods .
Chittania, *Hind.,* Zizyphus xylopyra, *Will.,* RHAMNEÆ.
Foods .
Chin, *Pb.,* Rhododendron arboream, *Sm.,* ERICACEÆ.
Foods .
Chiura, *Kumaun,* Bassia butyracea, *Roxb.,* SAPOTACEÆ.
Foods .
Chochar, *Pb.,* Berberis vulgaris, *Linn.,* BERBERIDEÆ.
Foods .
Chocolate Plant, *Eng.,* Theobroma Cacao, *Linn.,* STERCULIACEÆ.
Foods .
Choka, *Dec.,* Piper nigrum, *Linn.,* PIPERACEÆ.
Foods .
Cholá, *Beng.,* Cicer arietinum, *Linn.,* LEGUMINOSÆ.
Foods .
Cholam, *Tam.,* Zea Mays, *Linn.,* GRAMINEÆ.
Foods .
Cholum, *Tam.,* Sorghum vulgare, *Pers.,* GRAMINEÆ.
Foods .
Chora, *Pb.,* Quercus dilitata, *Lindl.,* CUPULIFERÆ.
Foods .
Chore-kanta, *Beng.,* Chrysopogon acicularis, *Retz.,* GRAMINEÆ.
Foods .
Chore pushpi, *Sans.,* Chrysopogon acicularis, *Retz.,* GRAMINEÆ.
Foods .
Chota, *Nep.,* Cinnamomum Tamala, *Nees.,* LAURINEÆ.
Foods .
Chota, *Nep.,* Morus indica, *Linn.,* URTICACEÆ.
Foods .
Choti juar, *N.-W. P. & Oudh,* Sorghum vulgare, *Pers.,* GRAMINEÆ.
Foods .
Choti mauhari, *Pb.,* Solanum xanthocarpum, *Schrad. & Wendl.,* SOLANACEÆ. Foods .
Choti van, *Pb.,* Salvadora persica, *Garcin.,* SALVADORACEÆ.
Foods .
Chotra, *Hind.,* Berberis, *DC.,* and B. Lycium, *Royle,* BERBERIDEÆ.
Foods .
Chou deschamps, *Fr.,* Brassica campestris, *Linn.,* var. campestris proper, CRUCIFERÆ. Foods .
Chou-Navet, *Fr.,* Brassica campestris, *Linn.,* var. Napus, CRUCIFERÆ.
Foods ..
Chowlee of India, *Eng.,* Vigna Catiang, *Endl.,* LEGUMINOSÆ.
Foods .
Chua, *Lahoul,* Rosa Webbiana, *Wall.,* ROSACEÆ.
Foods .
Chúari, *Hind.,* Prunus armeniaca, *Linn.,* ROSACEÆ.
Foods .
Chubrei, *Pb.,* Eleusine ægyptiaca, *Pers.,* GRAMINEÆ.
Foods .
Chuchi, *Pb.,* Polygonum polystachyum, *Wall.,* POLYGONACEÆ.
Foods .
Chuchi-am, *Nep.,* Mangifera sylvatica, *Roxb.,* ANACARDIACEÆ.
Foods .
Chuj, *Pb.,* Fraxinus Xanthoxyloides, *Wall.,* OLEACEÆ.
Foods .

Chuka, , Rhododendron Nobile, , ERICACEÆ.
Foods .
Chuka pálak, *N.-W.P.*, Rumex vesicarius, *Linn.*, POLYGONACEÆ.
Foods .
Chuka-palang, *N.-W.P.*, Rumex vesicarius, *Linn.*, POLYGONACEÆ.
Foods .
Chukha, *Pb.*, Oxalis corniculata, *Linn.*, GERANIACEÆ.
Foods .
Chukri, *Pb. Himalaya & Afg.*, Rheum Emodi, *Wall.*, POLYGONACEÆ.
Foods .
Chumlani, *Nep.*, Skimmia Laureola, *Hook.*, RUTACEÆ.
Foods .
Chun, *Hind.*, Morus alba, *Linn.*, URTICACEÆ.
Foods .
Chung, *Pb.*, Caralluma edulis, *Benth.*, ASCLEPIADEÆ.
Foods .
Chun-hatl, *Beng.*, Abrus precatorius, *Linn.*, LEGUMINOSÆ.
Foods .
Chunt, *Pb.*, Pyrus Malus, *Linn.*, ROSACEÆ.
Foods .
Chúr, *Pb.*, Quercus Ilex, *Linn.*, CUPULIFERÆ.
Foods .
Chúra, *Pb.*, Angelica glauca, *Edgw.*, UMBELLIFERÆ.
Foods .
Chura, *Pb.*, Commelina bengalensis, *L.*, COMMELINACEÆ.
Foods .
Churi, *Nep.*, Bassia butyracea, *Roxb.*, SAPOTACEÆ.
Foods .
Churial, *Pb.*, Aralia achemirica, *Dcne.*, ARALIACEÆ.
Foods .
Chúsbal, *Ladak.*, Potamogeton crispus, *Linn.*, NAIADACEÆ.
Foods .
Chutial, *Pb.*, *Himalaya & Afg.*, Rheum Emodi, *Wall.*, POLYGONACEÆ.
Foods .
Chyad-potta, *Tel.*, Trichosanthes cucumerina, *Linn.*, CUCURBITACEÆ.
Foods .
Chyal beng, *Burm.*, Semecarpus Anacardium, *Linn.*, ANACARDIACEÆ.
Foods .
Cinnamon, *Eng.*, Cinnamomum Tamala, *Nees.*, LAURINEÆ.
Foods .
Cinnamon Tree, *Eng.*, Cinnamomum zeylanicum, *Breyn.*, LAURINEÆ.
Foods .
Citron, *Eng.*, Citrus medica, *Linn.*, RUTACEÆ.
Foods .
Civet-Cat fruit tree, *Eng.*, Durio Zibethinus, *DC.*, MALVACEÆ.
Foods .
Clover, red or broad-leaved, *Eng.*, Trifolium fratense, *Linn.*, LEGUMINOSÆ. Foods .
Clover, Strawberry-headed, *Eng.*, Trifolium fragiferum, *Linn.*, LEGUMINOSÆ. Foods .
Clover, White or Dutch, *Eng.*, Trifolium repens, *Linn.*, LEGUMINOSÆ.
Foods .
Cloves, *Eng.*, Caryophyllus aromaticus, *Linn.*, MYRTACEÆ.
Foods .
Coat comul, *Tam.*, Callicarpa lanata, *Wall.*, VERBENACEÆ.
Foods .
Cocoa-nut Tree, *Eng.*, Cocos nucifera, *Linn.*, PALMÆ.
Foods .
Codagam, *Mal.*, Hydrocotyle asiatica, *Linn.*, UMBELLIFERÆ.
Foods .
Coffee, *Eng.*, Coffea, *Linn.*, RUBIACEÆ.
Foods .

Coleseed, *Eng.*, Brassica campestris, *Linn.*, var. Napus, CRUCIFERÆ.
Foods .
Colewort, Wild, *Eng.*, Brassica (oleracea) sylvestris, *Linn.*, CRUCIFERÆ.
Foods .
Colocynth, English, *Eng.*, Citrullus Colocynthis, *Schrad.*, CUCURBITACEÆ.
Foods .
Colza, *Eng.*, Brassica campestris, *Linn.*, var. campestris proper, CRUCIFERÆ. Foods .
Common Wheat, *Eng.*, Triticum sativum, *Lam.*, GRAMINEÆ.
Foods .
Conda-pani, *Tam.*, Corypha umbraculifera, *Linn.*, PALMÆ.
Foods .
Conda-panna, *Tam.*, Caryota urens, *Willd.*, PALMÆ.
Foods .
Cong, *Cingh.*, Schleichera trijuga, *Willd.*, SAPINDACEÆ.
Foods .
Conghas, *Cingh.*, Schleichera trijuga, *Willd.*, SAPINDACEÆ.
Foods .
Congo Pea, *Eng.*, Cajanus indicus, *Spreng.*, LEGUMINOSÆ.
Foods .
Coriander, *Eng.*, Coriandrum sativum, *Linn.*, UMBELLIFERÆ.
Foods .
Corn, Guinea, *Eng.*, Sorghum vulgare, *Pers.*, GRAMINEÆ.
Foods .
Cotton, Common Indian, *Eng.*, Gossypium herbaceum, *Linn.*, MALVACEÆ. Foods .
Cotton Tree Silk, *Eng.*, Eriodendron anfractuosum, *DC.*, MALVACEÆ.
Foods .
Cotton Tree, White, *Eng.*, Eriodenodron anfractuosum, *DC.*, MALVACEÆ.
Foods .
Cowgrass, *Eng.*, Trifolium pratense, *Linn.*, LEGUMINOSÆ.
Foods .
Coya, *Tel.*, Psidium Guyava, *Raddi.*, MYRTACEÆ.
Foods .
Cuchore, *Fr.*, Acacia Catechu, *Willd.*, LEGUMINOSÆ.
Foods .
Cucumber, *Eng.*, Cucumis sativus, *Linn.*, CUCURBITACEÆ.
Foods .
Cumboo, *Eng.*, Pennisetum typhoideum, *Rich.*, GRAMINEÆ.
Foods .
Cumin Seed, Black, *Eng.*, Nigella sativa, *Linn.*, RANUNCULACEÆ.
Foods .
Cummi, *Tam.*, Gmelina arborea, *Roxb.*, VERBENACEÆ.
Foods .
Cummin, *Eng.*, Cuminum Cyminum, *Linn.*, UMBELLIFERÆ.
Foods .
Cunda, *Tel.*, Tacca pinnatifida, *Forsk.*, TACCACEÆ.
Foods .
Currant, Black, *Eng.*, Ribes nigrum, *Linn.*, SAXIFRAGACEÆ.
Foods .
Currant, Red, *Eng.*, Ribes rubrum, *Linn.*, SAXIFRAGACEÆ.
Foods .
Curri, *Nep.*, Corylus colurna, *Linn.*, CUPULIFERÆ.
Foods .
Curri, *Nep.*, Corylus Feron, *Wall.*, CUPULIFERÆ.
Foods .
Curry-leaf Tree, *Eng.*, Murraya Kœnigii, *Spr.*, RUTACEÆ.
Foods .
Cuscus, *Eng.*, Andropogon muricatus, *Retz.*, GRAMINEÆ.
Foods .
Cusunt, *Hind.*, Flemingia nana, LEGUMINOSÆ.
Foods .

D

Dab, *Beng.*, Cocos nucifera, *Linn.*, PALMÆ.
Foods .
Dab, *N.-W. P.*, Eragrostis Brownei, *Nees.*, GRAMINEÆ.
Foods .
Dab, *Pb.*, Viburnum nervosum, *Don.*, CAPRIFOLIACEÆ.
Foods .
Dabdabbi, *Nep.*, Garuga pinnata, *Roxb.*, BURSERACEÆ.
Foods .
Daboi, *N.-W. P.*, Eragrostis cynosuroides, *Retz.*, GRAMINEÆ.
Foods .
Dadár, *Kashmir, Garhwal, Kumaun*, Cedrus Deodara, *Loudon*, CONIFERÆ. Foods .
Dadhuri, *Pb.*, Ficus glomerata, *Roxb.*, URTICACEÆ.
Foods .
Daduri, *Pb.*, Ficus hispida, *Linn f.*, URTICACEÆ.
Foods .
Dahan, *Rajputana*, Toddalia aculeata, *Pers.*, RUTACEÆ.
Foods .
Dalim, *Beng.*, *Kumaun*, Punica Granatum, *Linn.*, LYTHRACEÆ.
Foods .
Dain, *Hind.*, Brassica campestris, *Linn.*, var. Napus, sub-var. Toria, CRUCIFERÆ. Foods .
Dain-lai, *Hind.*, Brassica campestris, *Linn.*, var. Napus, sub-var. Toria, CRUCIEERÆ. Foods .
Daintha, *Burm.*, Moringa pterygosperma, *Gærtn.*, MORINGEÆ.
Foods .
Dajkar, *Pb.*, Celastrus senegalensis, *Lam.*, CELASTRINEÆ.
Foods .
Dajkar, *Pb.*, Flacourtia sepiaria, *Roxb.*, BIXINEÆ.
Foods .
Dak, *Pb.*, Ribes rubrum, *Linn.*, SAXIFRAGACEÆ.
Foods .
Dakari, *Pb.*, Hedera Helix, *Linn.*, ARALIACEÆ.
Foods .
Dakh, *Hind.*, Vitis vinifera, *Linn.*, AMPELIDEÆ.
Foods .
Dakhani-babul, *Hind.*, Pithecolobium dulce, *Benth.*, LEGUMINOSÆ.
Foods .
Dakhmila, *N.-W. P.*, Rhus semi-alata, *Murray*, ANACARDIACEÆ.
Foods .
Dalchini, *Hind.*, Cinnamomum Tamala, *Nees.*, LAURINEÆ.
Foods .
Dalchini, *Hind.*, Cinnamomum zeylanicum, *Breyn.*, LAURINEÆ.
Foods .
Dalkaramcha, *Beng.*, Pongamia glabra, *Vent.*, LEGUMINOSÆ.
Foods .
Dalme, *Hind.*, Securinega obovata, *Müll.*, EUPHORBIACEÆ.
Foods .
Dalné katús, *Nep.*, Castanopsis rufescens, *Hook. S. & Th.*, CUPULIFERÆ.
Foods .
Dama, *Ladak*, Caragana pygmæa, *DC.*, LEGUMINOSÆ.
Foods .
Dam-bel, *Garo*, Careya arborea, *Roxb.*, MYRTACEÆ.
Foods .
Damra-shama, *Beng.*, Panicum frumentaceum, *Roxb.*, GRAMINEÆ.
Foods .
Dana, *Pb.*, Anabasis multiflora, *Moq.*, CHENOPODIACEÆ.
Foods .

Dandarna, *Pb.*, Physochlaina præalta, *Hook. f.*, SOLANACEÆ.
Foods .
Dandelion, *Eng.*, Taraxacum officinale, *Wigg.*, COMPOSITÆ.
Foods .
Dandhal, *Kumaun.*, Luffa ægyptiaca, *Mill. ex Hook. f.*, CUCURBITACEÆ.
Foods .
Dáúdi, *C. P.*, form of Triticum sativum, *Lam.*, GRAMINEÆ.
Foods .
Dandura, *Pb.*, Hyoscyamus niger, *Linn.*, SOLANACEÆ.
Foods .
Da-ne, *Burm.*, Nipa fruticans, *Wurmb.*, PALMÆ.
Foods .
Danimma-chettu, *Tel.*, Punica Granatum, *Linn.*, LYTHRACEÆ.
Foods .
Dan-ky-wai, *Burm.*, Cassia Tora, *Linn.*, LEGUMINOSÆ.
Foods .
Danla, *Hind.*, Phyllanthus Emblica, *Linn.*, EUPHORBIACEÆ.
Foods .
Danti, *Tel.*, Celastrus senegalensis, *Lam.*, CELASTRINEÆ.
Foods .
Darakhte-nar, *Pers.*, Punica Granatum, *Linn.*, LYTHRACEÆ.
Foods .
Daran, *Pb.*, Fagopyrun emarginatum, *Meisn.*, POLYGONACEÆ.
Foods .
Dararhi, *N.-W. P. & Oudh*, Cyamopsis psoralioides, *DC.*, LEGUMINOSÆ.
Foods .
Dargola, *Simla*, Sageretia theezans, *Brongn.*, RHAMNEÆ.
Foods .
Dargu, *Tel.*, Ougeinia dalbergioides, *Benth.*, LEGUMINOSÆ.
Foods .
Dar-haldi, *Hind.*, Berberis aristata, *DC.*, and B. Lycium, *Royle*, BERBERIDEÆ. Foods .
Dari, *Tel.*, Pueraria tuberosa, *DC.*, LEGUMINOSÆ.
Foods .
Darim, *Hind.*, Punica Granatum, *Linn.*, LYTHRACEÆ.
Foods .
Darim, *Hind.*, Securinega obovata, *Müll.*, EUPHORBIACEÆ.
Foods .
Darnel, *Eng.*, Lolium temulentum, *Linn.*, GRAMINEÆ.
Foods .
Darshana, *Tel.*, Albizzia Lebbek, *Benth.*, LEGUMINOSÆ.
Foods .
Daswila, *N.-W. P.*, Rhus semi-alata, *Murray*, ANACARDIACEÆ.
Foods .
Date Palm, *Eng.*, Phœnix dactylifera, *Linn.*, PALMÆ.
Foods .
Date Plum, European, *Eng.*, Diospyros Lotus, *Linn.*, EBENACEÆ.
Foods .
Date, Wild, *Eng.*, Phœnix sylvestris, *Roxb.*, PALMÆ.
Foods .
Datura, *Pb.*, Hyoscyamus niger, *Linn.*, SOLANACEÆ.
Foods .
Daurva, *Pb.*, Cynodon Dactylon, *Pers.*, GRAMINEÆ.
Foods .
Dedhún, *Beng.*, Sorghum bicolor, *Willd.*, GRAMINEÆ.
Foods .
Degar, *Pb.*, Ficus hispida, *Linn f.*, URTICACEÆ.
Foods .
Dekkelé, *Fr.*, Pennisetum typhoideum, *Rich.*, GRAMINEÆ.
Foods .
Del, *Cingh.*, Artocarpus nobilis, *Thw.*, URTICACEÆ.
Foods .

Delha, *Pb.*, Capparis aphylla, *Roth.*, CAPPARIDEÆ.
Foods .
Dendra, *Pb.*, Lonicera quinquelocularis, *Hardwicke*, CAPRIFOLIACEÆ.
Foods .
Deodar, *Eng.*, *Kashmir*, *Garhwal*, *Kumaun.*, Cedrus Deodara, *Loudon*, CONIFERÆ. Foods .
Dephal, *Beng.*, Artocarpus Lakoocha, *Roxb.*, URTICACEÆ.
Foods .
Der Ruben, *Ger.*, Brassica campestris, *Linn.*, var. Napus, CRUCIFERÆ.
Foods .
Dezu, *Naga*, Colocasia antiquorum, *Schott.*, AROIDEÆ.
Foods .
Dhadonjra, *Simla*, Acer cultratum, *Wall.*, syn. of Acer pictum, *Thumb.*, SAPINDACEÆ. Foods .
Dhak, *Hind.*, Butea frondosa, *Roxb.*, LEGUMINOSÆ.
Foods .
Dhal, *Eng.*, Cajanus indicus, *Spreng.*, LEGUMINOSÆ.
Foods .
Dhalákura, *Beng.*, Alangium Lamarckii, *Thwaites*, CORNACEÆ.
Foods .
Dhaman, *N.-W. P.*, Cenchrus echinatus, *Linn.*, GRAMINEÆ.
Foods .
Dhaman, *Pb.*, Pennissetum cenchroides, *Rich.*, GRAMINEÆ.
Foods .
Dhami, *Ajmir*, Grewia asiatica, *Linn.*, TILIACEÆ.
Foods .
Dhamin, *Hind.*, Grewia tiliæfolia *Vahl.*, TILIACEÆ.
Foods .
Dhamman, *Pb.*, Grewia oppositifolia, *Roxb.*, TILIACEÆ.
Foods .
Dhamono, *Uriya*, Grewia tiliæfolia, *Vahl.*, TILIACEÆ.
Foods .
Dhamun, *Hind.*, Grewia vestita, *Wall.*, TILIACEÆ.
Foods .
Dhamna, *Hind.*, Ulmus integrifolia, *Roxb.*, URTICACEÆ.
Foods .
Dhamnak, *Bhil.*, Grewia tiliæfolia, *Vahl.*, TILIACEÆ.
Foods .
Dhan (unhusked), *Hind.*, *Beng.*, Oryza sativa, *Linn.*, GRAMINEÆ.
Foods .
Dhand, *N.-W. P.*, Panicum crus-galli, *Linn.*, GRAMINEÆ.
Foods .
Dhani, *Hind.*, Securinega obovata, *Mull.*, EUPHORBIACEÆ.
Foods .
Dhania, *Beng.*, *Hind.*, Coriandrum sativum, *Linn.*, UMBELLIFERÆ.
Foods .
Dhanyaka, *Sans.*, Coriandrum sativum, *Linn.*, UMBELLIFERÆ.
Foods .
Dhanyalu, *Tel.*, Coriandrum sativum, *Linn.*, UMBELLIFERÆ.
Foods .
Dhár, *Pb.*, Momordica dioica, *Roxb.*, CUCURBITACEÆ.
Foods .
Dhauli, *Hind.*, Hymenodictyon excelsum, *Wall.*, RUBIACEÆ.
Foods .
Dhaura, *Oudh*, Zizyphus rugosa, *Lamk.*, RHAMNEÆ.
Foods .
Dheniani, *Hind.*, Olax scandens, *Roxb.*, OLACINEÆ.
Foods .
Dhenras, *Beng.*, Hibiscus esculentus, *Linn.*, MALVACEÆ.
Foods .
Dher, *Pb.*, Rubus biflorus, *Ham.*, ROSACEÆ.
Foods .

Doodi-palla, *Tel.*, Oxystelma esculentum, *Br.*, ASCLEPIADEÆ.
Foods .
Dooghdika, *Sans.*, Oxystelma esculentum, *Br.*, ASCLEPIADEÆ.
Foods .
Doommaala, *Eng.*, Trichosanthes cucumerina, *Linn.*, CUCURBITACEÆ.
Foods .
Doomoor, *Beng.*, Ficus glomerata, *Roxb.*, URTICACEÆ.
Foods .
Doomoor, *Beng.*, Ficus Roxburghii, *Wall.*, URTICACEÆ.
Foods .
Doorwa, *Eng.*, Cynodon Dactylon, *Pers.*, GRAMINEÆ.
Foods .
Dopatti, *Ass.*, Cinnamomum Tamala, *Nees.*, LAURINEÆ.
Foods .
Dora-byara, *Hind.*, Setaria verticillata, *Beauv.*, GRAMINEÆ.
Foods .
Dorga-kaia, *Tel.*, Cucumis sativus, *Linn.*, CUCURBITACEÆ.
Foods .
Dosray, *Tel.*, Cucumis Melo, *Linn.*, var. utilissimus (*sp.* Roxb.), CUCURBITACEÆ. Foods .
Dotti, *Gond.*, Ehretia lævis, *Roxb.*, BORAGINEÆ.
Foods .
Dráb, *Pb.*, Pinus longifolia, *Roxb.*, CONIFERÆ.
Foods .
Draksha, *Mahr.*, Vitis vinifera, *Linn.*, AMPELIDEÆ.
Foods .
Draksha, *Sans.*, Vitis vinifera, *Linn.*, AMPELIDEÆ.
Foods .
Drakshapondu, *Tel.*, Vitis vinifera, *Linn.*, AMPELIDEÆ.
Foods .
Drange, *Pb.*, Sageretia oppositifolia, *Brongn.*, RHAMNEÆ.
Foods .
Drangie, *Pb.*, Sageretia theezans, *Brongn.*, RHAMNEÆ.
Foods .
Drawi, *Pb.*, Cedrela Toona, *Roxb.*, MELIACEÆ.
Foods .
Drek, *Hind.*, Melia Azedarach, *Linn.*, MELIACEACEÆ.
Foods .
Dú, *Pb.*, Quercus Ilex, *Linn.*, CUPULIFERÆ.
Foods .
Dua, *N.-W. P. & Oudh.*, Eruca sativa, *Lam.*, CRUCIFERÆ.
Foods .
Duan, *N.-W. P. & Oudh*, Eruca sativa, *Lam.*, CRUCIFERÆ.
Foods .
Dúb, *Pb.*, *Beng.*, Cynodon Dactylon, *Pers.*, GRAMINEÆ.
Foods .
Dubha, *Tel.*, Eragrostis cynosuroides, *Retz.*, GRAMINEÆ.
Foods .
Dudal, *Pb.*, Taraxacum officinale, *Wigg.*, COMPOSITÆ.
Foods .
Dudela, *Nep.*, Hedera Helix, *Linn.*, ARALIACEÆ.
Foods .
Dud en, *Pb.*, Syringa Emodi, *Wall.*, OLEACEÆ.
Foods .
Dudh-bathal, *Pb.*, Taraxacum officinale, *Wigg.*, COMPOSITÆ.
Foods .
Dudhi, *Pb. hills*, Ficus virgata, *Roxb.*, URTICACEÆ.
Foods .
Dudhu-ki-lakri, *Hind.*, Holarrhena antidysenterica, *Wall.*, APOCYNACEÆ.
Foods .
Dudippi, *Tel.*, Careya arborea, *Roxb.*, MYRTACEÆ.
Foods .

E

Elandap-pazham, *Tam.*, Ziryphus Jujuba, *Lam.*, RHAMNEÆ.
Foods .
Elava, *Tam.*, Eriodendron anfractuosum, *DC.*, MALVACEÆ.
Foods .
Elengi, *Mal.*, Mimusops Elengi, *Linn.*, SAPOTACEÆ.
Foods .
Elephant-grass, *Eng.*, Typha elephantina, *Roxb.*, TYPHACEÆ.
Foods .
Eliya (resin), *Dec.*, Aloe vera, *Linn.*, LILIACEÆ.
Foods .
Ellakay, *Tam.*, *Tel.*, Elettaria Cardamonum, *Maton.*, SCITAMINEÆ.
Foods .
Ella-kura, *Tel.*, Suœda indica, *Moq.*, CHENOPODIACEÆ.
Foods .
Elm, *Eng.*, Ulmus campestris, *Linn.*, URTICACEÆ.
Foods .
Elumich-cham-pazham, *Tam.*, Citrus medica, *Linn.*, RUTACEÆ.
Foods .
Elupa, *Tam.*, Bassia latifolia, *Roxb.*, SAPOTACEÆ,
Foods .
Elupa, *Tam.*, Bassia longifolia, *Willd.*, SAPOTACEÆ.
Foods .
Elupay, *Tam.*, Terminalia belerica, *Roxb.*, COMBRETACEÆ.
Foods .
Em., *Pb.*, Chenopodium album, *L.*, CHENOPODIACEÆ.
Foods .
Emiga-junum, *Tel.*, Typha elephantina, *Roxb.*, TYPHACEÆ.
Foods .
Era, *Pb.*, Viburnum stellalatum, *Wall.*, CAPRIFOLIACEÆ.
Foods .
Eragu, *Tel.*, Ulmus integrifolia, *Roxb.*, URTICACEÆ.
Foods .
Eranda, *Sans.*, Ricinus communis, *Linn.*, EUPHORBIACEÆ.
Foods .
Eri, *Pb.*, Viburnum stellulatum, *Wall.*, CAPRIFOLIACEÆ.
Foods .
Erra-gom-kaya, *Tel.*, Hibiscus Sabdariffa, *Linn.*, MALVACEÆ.
Foods .
Eruvali, *Tam.*, Maba buxifolia, *Pers.*, EBENACEÆ.
Foods .
Esar, *Kumaun*, Rubus ellipticus, *Smith*, ROSACEÆ.
Foods .
Escali, *Nep.*, Rubus ellipticus, *Smith*, ROSACEÆ.
Foods .
Etok, *Bhutia*, *Lepchn.*, Rhododendron arborium, *Sm.*, ERICACEÆ.
Foods .

F

Fagara, *Pb. plains*, Ficus virgata, *Roxb.*, URTICACEÆ.
Foods .
Fagari, *Pb.*, Ficus Carica, *Linn.*, URTICACEÆ.
Foods .
Fagu, *Pb.*, Ficus Carica, *Linn.*, URTICACEÆ.
Foods .
Fagu, *Pb. hills*, Ficus virgata, *Roxb.*, URTICACEÆ.
Foods .
Faguri, *Pb.* Ficus Carica, *Linn.*, URTICACEÆ.
Foods .

Famsikol, *Lepcha*, Eugenia formosa, *Wall.*, MYRTACEÆ.
Foods .
Farri, *Pb.*, Grewia vestita, *Wall.*, TILIACEÆ.
Foods .
Farsi, *Mar.*, Chrysophyllum Roxburghii, *G. Don.*, SAPOTACEÆ.
Foods .
Farw, *Pb.*, Panicum sanguinale, *Linn.*, GRAMINEÆ.
Foods .
Fennel, *Eng.*, Fœniculum Vulgare, *Gærtn.*, UMBELLIFERÆ.
Foods .
Fenugœc, *Eng.*, Trigonella Fœnum-grœcum, *Linn.*, LEGUMINOSÆ.
Foods .
Fenugreek, *Eng.*, Trigonella Fœnum-grœcum, *Linn.*, LEGUMINOSÆ.
Foods .
Fescue Grass, Hard, *Eng.*, Festuca duriuscula, *Linn.*, GRAMINEÆ.
Foods .
Fescue, Purple, *Eng.*, Festuca rubra, *Linn.*, GRAMINEÆ.
Foods .
Fescue, Sheep's, *Eng.*, Festuca ovina, *Linn.*, GRAMINEÆ.
Foods .
Fibre Rozelle, *Eng.*, Hibiscus Sabdariffa, *Linn.*, MALVACEÆ.
Foods .
Field Bean, *Eng.*, Vicia Faba, *Linn.*, LEGUMINOSÆ.
Foods .
Fig, Common, *Eng.*, Ficus Carica, *Linn.*, URTICACEÆ.
Foods .
Fig, Sacred, *Eng.*, Ficus religiosa, *Linn.*, URTICACEÆ.
Foods .
Filliah, *Mandla*, Wendlandia exserta, *DC.*, RUBIACEÆ.
Foods .
Findák, *Pb.*, Corylus colurna, *Linn.*, CUPILIFERÆ.
Foods .
Florin or White Bent Grass, *Eng.*, Agrostis alba, *Linn.*, GRAMINEÆ.
Foods .
Fir, Himalayan, Silver, *Eng.*, Abies Webbiana, *Lindl.*, CONIFERÆ.
Foods .
Flag, Sweet, *Eng.*, Acorus Calamus, *Linn.*, AROIDEÆ.
Foons .
Forbidden Fruit, *Eng.*, Citrus decumana, *Willd.*, RUTACEÆ.
Foods .
Fox-tail Grass, *Eng.*, Alopecurus geniculatus, *Linn.*, GRAMINEÆ.
Foods .
Fox-tail, Meadow Grass, *Eng.*, Alopecurus pratensis, *Linn.*, GRAMINEÆ.
Foods .
Fox-tail, Slender Grass, *Eng.*, Alopecurus agrestis, *Linn.*, GRAMINEÆ.
Foods .

G.

Gáb, *Eng.*, *Beng.*, *Hind.*, Diospyros Embryopteris, *Pers.*, EBENACEÆ.
Foods .
Gabna, *Beng.*, Nipa fruticans, *Wurmb.*, PALMÆ.
Foods .
Gachoolá, *And.*, Albizzia Lebbek, *Benth.*, LEGUMINOSÆ.
Foods .
Gadda (cabbage of leaves) *Pb.*, Phœnix dactylifera, *Linn.*, PALMÆ.
Foods .
Gaggarwah, *C. P.*, Cassia Fistula, *Linn.*, LEGUMINOSÆ.
Foods .

Gaha, *N.-W. P.*, *C. P.*, Fraxinus xanthoxyloides, *Wall.*, OLEACEÆ.
Foods .
Gahu, *Deccan*, Triticum sativum, *Lam.*, GRAMINEÆ.
Foods .
Gahung, *Mar.*, Triticum sativum, *Lam.*, GRAMINEÆ.
Foods .
Gai aswat, *Beng.*, Ficus cordifolia, *Roxb.*, URTICACEÆ.
Foods .
Gajar, *Beng.*, *Hind.*, Daucus Carota, *Linn.*, UMBELLIFERÆ.
Foods .
Gajir, *Hind.*, Dioscorea versicolor, *Wall.*, DIOSCOREACEÆ.
Foods .
Gajjara, *Tam.*, Daucus Carota, *Linn.*, UMBELLIFERÆ.
Foods .
Gajjara gadda, *Tel.*, Daucus Carota, *Linn.*, UMBELLIFERÆ.
Foods .
Gajna, *Hind.*, Ficus cordifolia, *Roxb.*, URTICACEÆ.
Foods .
Gakró, *Naga Hills*, Hibiscus cannabinus, *Linn.*, MALVACEÆ.
Foods .
Galgala, *N.-W. P.*, Eragrostis plumosa, *Link.*, GRAMINEÆ.
Foods .
Galgoja, *Chenab*, Pinus Gerardiana, *Wall.*, CONIFERÆ.
Foods .
Galion, *Hind.*, Pyrus lanata, *Don.*, ROSACEÆ.
Foods .
Galka, *Pb.*, Rubus lasiocarpus, *Smith*, ROSACEÆ.
Foods .
Galli (cabbage of leaves), *Pb.*, Phœnix dactylifera, *Linn.*, PALMÆ.
Foods .
Gam, *Beng.*, Triticum sativum, *Lam.*, GRAMINEÆ.
Foods .
Gambari, *Nep.*, *Uriya*, Gmelina arborea, *Roxb.*, VERBENACEÆ.
Foods .
Gamboge Tree, *Eng.*, Garcinia Morella, *Desr.*, GUTTIFERÆ.
Foods .
Gamur, *N.-W. P.*, Panicum antidotale, *Retz.*, GRAMINEÆ.
Foods .
Ganaba, *Cingh.*, Brassica nigra, *Koch.*, CRUCIFERÆ.
Foods .
Gandal, *Hind.*, Avena fatua, *Linn.*, GRAMINEÆ.
Foods .
Gandalún, *Pb.*, Daphne mucronata, *Royle*, THYMELÆACEÆ.
Foods .
Gandana, *Afg.*, Allium ascalonicum, *Linn.*, LILIACEÆ.
Foods .
Gandera, *Pb.*, Rhazya stricta, *Dcne.*, APOCYNACEÆ.
Foods .
Gandhan, *Pb.*, Allium ascalonicum, *Linn.*, LILIACEÆ.
Foods .
Gandhat rince, *Bom.*, Andropogon citratus, GRAMINEÆ.
Foods .
Gandhuli, *Pb.*, Gynandropsis pentaphylla, *DC.*, CAPPARIDEÆ.
Foods .
Gandi, *N.-W. P.*, Chloris barbata, *Swartz.*, GRAMINEÆ.
Foods .
Gandi, *Pb.*, Murraya Kœnigii, *Spr.*, RUTACEÆ.
Foods .
Gandial, *Pb.*, Arenaria holosteoides, *Edge.*, CARYOPHYLLEÆ.
Foods .
Gandla, *Pb.*, Murraya Kœnigii, *Spr.*, RUTACEÆ.
Foods .

Gandum, *Pers.*, Triticum sativum, *Lam.*, GRAMINEÆ.
Foods .
Gange, *Sind*, Zizyphus nummularia, *W. & A.*, RHAMNEÆ.
Foods .
Ganger, *Pb.*, Grewia populifolia, *Vahl.*, TILIACEÆ.
Foods .
Ganger, *Pb.*, Lycium europæum, *Linn.*, SOLANACEÆ.
Foods .
Ganger, *Pb.*, Sageretia Brandrethiana, *Aitch.*, RHAMNEÆ.
Foods .
Gangerun, *Rajputana*, Grewia populifolia, *Vahl.*, TILIACEÆ.
Foods .
Gango, *Sind*, Grewa populifolia, *Vahl.*, TILIACEÆ.
Foods .
Ganhar, *Pb.*, Amarantus Anardana, *Hamilt.*, AMARANTACEÆ.
Foods .
Ganhar, *Upper India*, Amarantus mangostanus, *L.*, AMARANTACEÆ.
Foods .
Gani, *Pb.*, Oxystelma esculentum, *Br.*, ASCLEPIADEÆ.
Foods .
Ganiari, *Oudh*, Premna integrifolia, *Linn.*, VERBENACEÆ.
Foods .
Ganjá, *Beng.*, Cannabis sativa, *Linn.*, URTICACEÆ.
Foods .
Ganja-chedi, *Tam.*, Cannabis sativa, *Linn.*, URTICACEÆ.
Foods .
Ganjan, *Burm.*, Mesua ferrea, *Linn.*, GUTTIFERÆ.
Foods .
Gánjari-chettu, *Tel.*, Cannabis sativa, *Linn.*, URTICACEÆ.
Foods .
Gánje-ká-pér, *Hind.*, Cannabis sativa, *Linn.*, URTICACEÆ.
Foods .
Ganjira, *Hind.*, Dioscorea versicolor, *Wall.*, DIOSCOREACEÆ.
Foods .
Ganthiam, *Pb.*, Ipomæa aquatica, *Forsk.*, CONVOLVULACEÆ.
Foods .
Gantiloo (grain), *Tel.*, Pennisetum typhoideum, *Rich.*, GRAMINEÆ.
Foods .
Garar, *Afg.*, Reptonia buxifolia, *A. DC.*, MYRSINEÆ.
Foods .
Gardal, *Bom.*, Entada scandens, *Bth.*, LEGUMINOSÆ.
Foods .
Gardalu, *Pb.*, Prunus armeniaca, *Linn.*, ROSACEÆ.
Foods .
Garden Cress, *Eng.*, Lepidium sativum, *Linn.*, CRUCIFERÆ.
Foods .
Garden Spinach, *Eng.*, Spinacia oleracea, *Mill.*, CHENOPODIACEÆ.
Foods .
Gár-gá, *Tel.*, Garuga pinnata, *Roxb.*, BURSERACEÆ.
Foods .
Gargas, *Pb.*, Grewia salvifolia, *Heyne*, TILIACEÆ.
Foods .
Gargu-naru, *Hind.*, Bryonia lociniosa, *Linn.*, CUCURBITACEÆ.
Foods .
Gari, *Tel.*, Batanites Roxburghii, *Planch.*, SIMARUBEÆ.
Foods .
Gari-kulay, *Beng.*, Glycine soja, *Sieb. & Zucc.*, LEGUMINOSÆ.
Foods .
Garjara, *Sans.*, Daucus Carota, *Linn.*, UMBELLIFERÆ.
Foods .
Garkum, *N.-W. P.*, Marlea begoniæfolia, *Roxb.*, CORNACEÆ.
Foods .

Garlic, *Eng.*, Allium sativum, *Linn.*, LILIACEÆ.
Foods .
Garm, *Pb.*, Panicum antidotale, *Retz.*, GRAMINEÆ.
Foods .
Garnikura, *Sans.*, Hibiscus cannabinus, *Linn.*, MALVACEÆ.
Foods .
Garpipal, *Kumaun*, Populus ciliata, *Wall.*, SALICINEÆ.
Foods .
Garrah, *Gond.*, Balanites Roxburghii, *Planch.*, SIMARUBEÆ.
Foods .
Garso, *Hind.*, Albizzia Lebbek, *Benth.*, LEGUMINOSÆ.
Foods .
Garuga, *Tel.*, Garuga pinnata, *Roxb.*, BURSERACEÆ.
Foods .
Gasa-gasa-tol, *Tam.*, Papaver somniferum, *Linn.*, PAPAVERACEÆ.
Foods .
Gasa-gasa-tolu, *Tel.*, Papaver somniferum, *Linn.*, PAPAVERACEÆ.
Foods .
Gaub, *Eng.*, Diospyros Embryopteris, *Pers.*, EBENACEÆ.
Foods .
Gaunri, *Kashmir*, Trapa bispinosa, *Roxb.*, ONAGRACEÆ.
Foods .
Gaura, *Beng.*, Elæagnus latifolia, *Linn.*, ELÆAGNEÆ.
Foods .
Gausam, *Hind.*, Schleichera trijuga, *Willd.*, SAPINDACEÆ.
Foods .
Gavuldu, *Mysore*, Careya arborea, *Roxb.*, MYRTACEÆ.
Foods .
Gavung, *N.-W. P.*, Chloris barbata, *Swartz.*, GRAMINEÆ.
Foods .
Geang, *Pb.*, Lonicera angustifolia, *Wall.*, CAPRIFOLIACEÆ.
Foods .
Geelabu, *Beng.*, Psidium Guyava, *Raddi.*, MYRTACEÆ.
Foods .
Gela, *Hind.*, Briedelia montana, *Willd.*, EUPHORBIACEÆ.
Foods .
Gelo, *Nep.*, Briedelia montana, *Willd.*, EUPHORBIACEÆ.
Foods .
Geli, *N.-W. P.*, Taxus baccata, *Linn.*, CONIFERÆ.
Foods .
Gempe, *Nep.*, Rubus lineatus, *Reinw.*, ROSACEÆ.
Foods .
Gendeli, *Ass.*, Garuga pinnata, *Roxb.*, BURSERACEÆ.
Foods .
Genhu, *Hind.*, Triticum sativum, *Lam.*, GRAMINEÆ.
Foods .
Genthi, *Hind.*, Dioscorea versicolor, *Wall.*, DIOSCOREACEÆ.
Foods .
Geredi, *Uriya*, Entada scandens, *Bth.*, LEGUMINOSÆ.
Foods .
Gesse, *Eng.*, Lathyrus sativus, *Linn.*, LEGUMINOSÆ.
Foods .
Ghain, *Pb.*, Elæagnus umbellata, *Thunb.*, ELÆAGNEÆ.
Foods .
Ghalme, *Pb.*, Anabasis multiflora, *Moq.*, CHENOPODIACEÆ.
Foods .
Ghamor, *N.-W. P.*, Panicum antidotale, *Retz.*, GRAMINEÆ.
Foods .
Ghari, *Hind.*, Securinega obovata, *Mull.*, EUPHORBIACEÆ.
Foods .
Ghariam, *Ass.*, Mangifera indica, *Linn.*, ANACARDIACEÆ.
Foods .

Gharot, *Pb.*, Oxystelma esculentum, *Br.*, ASCLEPIADEÆ.
Foods .
Ghau, *Gujarát*, Triticum sativum, *Lam.*, GRAMINEÆ.
Foods .
Ghebu-nelli, *Tel.*, Premna integrifolia, *Linn.*, VERBENACEÆ.
Foods .
Ghechu, *Hind.*, Aponogeton monostachyum, *Linn.*, NAIADACEÆ.
Foods .
Gheea-sim, *Beng.*, Dolichos Lablab, *Linn.*, LEGUMINOSÆ.
Foods .
Ghericha, *Tel.*, Cynodon Dactylon, *Pers.*, GRAMINEÆ.
Foods .
Gheal, *Nep.*, Quercus semicarpifolia, *Smith*, CUPULIFERÆ.
Foods .
Ghia, *Kumaun*, Syringa Emodi, *Wall.*, OLEACEÆ.
Foods .
Ghikawár, *N.-W. P.*, Aloe vera, *Linn.*, var., officinalis, *Sp. Forsk.*, LILIACEÆ. Foods .
Ghikuwári, *Hind.*, Aloe vera, *Linn.*, LILIACEÆ.
Foods .
Ghirta-kanvár, *Beng.*, Aloe vera, *Linn.*, var. officinalis, *sp. Forsk.*, LILIACEÆ.
Foods .
Ghirta-kanmári, *Beng.*, *Sans.*, Aloe vera, *Linn.*, LILIACEÆ.
Foods .
Ghiwain, *Kumaun*, Elæagnus latifolia, *Linn.*, ELÆAGNEÆ.
Foods .
Ghiwain, *Pb.*, Elæagnus umbellata, *Thunb.*, ELÆAGNEÆ.
Foods .
Ghogar, *Hind.*, Garuga pinnata, *Roxb.*, BURSERACEÆ.
Foods .
Ghol, *Pb.*, Cephalandra indica, *Naud.*, CUCURBITACEÆ.
Foods .
Ghont, *Hind.*, Zizyphus xylopyra, *Will.*, RHAMNEÆ.
Foods .
Ghora nim, *Beng.*, Melia Azedarach, *Linn.*, MELIACEÆ.
Foods .
Ghorbach, *Hind.*, Acorus Calamus, *Linn.*, AROIDEÆ.
Foods .
Ghosali, *Bom.*, Luffa ægyptiaca, *Mill. ex Hook. f.*, CUCURBITACEÆ.
Foods .
Ghuiya, *N.-W. P.*, Colocasia antiquorum, *Schott.*, AROIDEÆ.
Foods .
Ghungachi, *Bom.*, Abrus precatorius, *Linn.*, LEGUMINOSÆ.
Foods .
Ghurchua, *N. India*, Eleusine ægyptiaca, *Pers.*, GRAMINEÆ.
Foods .
Ghurie-ghénzá, *Tel.*, Abrus precatorius, *Linn.*, LEGUMINOSÆ.
Foods .
Ghwareshtai, *Afg.*, Prunus persica, *Benth. & Hook.*, ROSACEÆ.
Foods .
Ghya-tarol, *Kumaun*, Luffa ægyptiaca, *Mill. ex Hook. f.*, CUCURBITACEÆ.
Foods .
Gia, *Mechi*, Garuga pinnata, *Roxb.*, BURSERACEÆ.
Foods .
Giam, *Tibet*, Cedrus Deodara, *Loudon*, CONIFERÆ.
Foods .
Gidardak, *Pb.*, Sageretia oppositifolia, *Brongn.*, RHAMNEÆ.
Foods .
Gidhro, *Sind*, Cucumis Melo, *Linn.*, CUCURBITACEÆ.
Foods .
Gilás, , Prunus Avium, *Linn.*, ROSACEÆ.
Foods .

Gilla, *Beng.*, Entada scandens, *Bth.*, LEGUMINOSÆ.
Foods .
Gineri, *Nep.*, Premna integrifolia, *Linn.*, VERBENACEÆ.
Foods .
Gineri, *Nep.*, Premna latifolia, *Roxb.*, VERBENACEÆ.
Foods . .
Gingelly oil, *Eng.*, Sesamum indicum, *Linn.*, PEDALINEÆ.
Foods .
Ginger, *Eng.*, Zingiber officinale, *Roscoe*, SCITAMINEÆ.
Foods .
Gingili, *South Ind.*, Sesamum indicum, *Linn.*, PEDALINEÆ.
Foods .
Ginyan, *Hind.*, Odina Wodier, *Roxb.*, ANACARDIACEÆ.
Foods .
Gira, *Pb.*, Alnus nitida, *Endl.*, CUPULIFERÆ.
Foods .
Gira-málá, *Bom.*, *Sind.*, Cassia Fistula, *Linn.*, LEGUMINOSÆ.
Foods .
Girchhatra, *Pb.*, **(hills)**, Morchella semilibera, *L.*, FUNGI.
Foods .
Girdardak, *Pb.*, Cissus carnosa, *Lam.*, AMPELIDEÆ.
Foods .
Girgitti, *Hind.*, Glycosmis pentaphylla, *Correa.*, RUTACEÆ.
Foods .
Girikarnika, *Sans.*, Alhagi maurorum, *Desv.*, LEGUMINOSÆ.
Foods .
Girta kanvár, *Beng.*, Aloe vera, *Linn.*, LILIACEÆ.
Foods .
Girthan, *Pb.*, Sageretia oppositifolia, *Brongn.*, RHAMNEÆ.
Foods .
Girul, *Pb.*, Panicum antidotale, *Retz.*, GRAMINEÆ.
Foods .
Gitoran, *Ajmir*, Capparis Gorrida, *Linn.*, CAPPARIDEÆ.
Foods .
Gnooshway, *Burm.*, Cassia Fistula, *Linn.*, LEGUMINOSÆ.
Foods .
Goa Potatoe, *Eng.*, Dioscorea aculeata, *Roxb.*, DIOSCOREACEÆ.
Foods .
Gobia, *Nepal*, Cephalostaclyon capitatum, *Munro*, GRAMINEÆ.
Foods .
Gobla, *Hind.*, Ficus hispida, *Linn. f.*, URTICACEÆ.
Foods .
Gobli, *Kan.*, Acacia arabica, *Willd.*, LEGUMINOSÆ.
Foods .
Gobria sulah, *Nep.*, Abies Webbiana, *Lindl.*, CONIFERÆ.
Foods .
Goda, *Beng.*, Vitex leucoxylon, *Linn.*, VERBENACEÆ.
Foods .
Godhi, *Kan.*, Triticum sativum, *Lam.*, GRAMINEÆ.
Foods .
Godumai, *Tam.*, Triticum sativum, *Lam.*, GRAMINEÆ.
Foods .
Gódu muhi, *Tel.*, Triticum sativum, *Lam.*, GRAMINEÆ.
Foods .
Gogen, *Nep.*, Saurauja nepaulensis, *DC.*, TERNSTRÆMIACEÆ.
Foods .
Gogina, *Hind.*, Saurauja nepaulensis, *DC.*, TERNSTRÆMIACEÆ.
Foods .
Gogi-sag, *Pb. & Sind*, Malva parviflora, *Linn.*, MALVACEÆ.
Foods .
Gogonda, *Hind.*, Saurauja nepaulensis, *DC.*, TERNSTRÆMIACEÆ.
Foods .

Gogsa, *Hind.*, Mæsa argentea, *Wall.*, MYRSINEÆ.
Foods .
Gogu, *Tel.*, Acacia concinna, *DC.*, LEGUMINOSÆ.
Foods .
Goher, *Pb.*, Sageretia Brandrethiana, *Aitch.*, RHAMNEÆ.
Foods .
Gohun, *Hind.*, Triticum sativum, *Lam.*, GRAMINEÆ.
Foods .
Gokatú, *Cingh.*, Garcinia Morella, *Desr.*, GUTTIFERÆ.
Foods .
Gokhrudesi, *Pb.*, Tribulus alatus, *Delile*, ZYGOPHYLLEÆ.
Foods .
Gol-kadu, *Hind.*, Lagenaria vulgaris, *Seringe*, CUCURBITACEÆ.
Foods .
Golab-Jam, *Beng.*, *Hind.*, Eugenia jambos, *Linn.*, MYRTACEÆ.
Foods .
Gole-marich, *Beng.*, *Hind.*, Piper nigrum, *Linn.*, PIPERACEÆ.
Foods .
Golphal (fruits), *Beng.*, Nipa fruticans, *Wurmb.*, PALMÆ.
Foods .
Gomari, *Ass.*, Gmelina arborea, *Roxb.*, VERBENACEÆ.
Foods .
Gombo, *Fr.*, Hibiscus esculentus, *Linn.*, MALVACEÆ.
Foods .
Gondhona, *Uriya*, Premna latifolia, *Roxb.*, VERBENACEÆ.
Foods .
Gondi, *Hind.*, Cordia Myxa, *Linn.*, BORAGINEÆ.
Foods .
Gondi, *Hind.*, Cordia Rothii, *Rom. & Sch.*, BORAGINEÆ.
Foods .
Gooseberry, Hill, *Eng.*, Rhodomyrtus tomentosa, *Wight*, MYRTACEÆ.
Foods .
Gooseberry, Rough or Hairy, *Eng.*, Ribes Grossularia, *Linn.*, SAXIFRAGACEÆ. Foods .
Gophla, *Kumaun*, Holbællia latifolia, *Wall.*, BERBERIDEÆ.
Foods .
Gopi, *Nep.*, Cephalostachyon capitatum, *Munro*, GRAMINEÆ.
Foods .
Gorakh chintz churi chintz, *Bom.*, Adansonia digitata, *Linn.*, MALVACEÆ.
Foods .
Goraláne, *Pb.*, Anabasis multiflora, *Moq.*, CHENOPODIACEÆ.
Foods .
Gorgon plant, *Eng.*, Euryale ferox, *Salisb.*, NYMPHÆACEÆ.
Foods .
Goroma, *Beng.*, Apluda aristata, *Linn.*, GRAMINEÆ.
Foods .
Gori-kachú, *Hind.*, *Beng.*, Colocasia antiquorum, *Schott.*, AROIDEÆ.
Foods .
Gori nim, *Bom.*, Melia Azedarach, *Linn.*, MELIACEÆ.
Foods .
Goti, *Hind.*, *Tel.*, Zizyphus xylopyra, *Will.*, RHAMNEÆ.
Foods .
Goukura, *Tel.*, Hibiscus cannabinus, *Linn.*, MALVACEÆ.
Foods .
Gourkh amll, *Hind.*, Adansonia digitata, *Linn.*, MALVACEÆ.
Foods .
Grains of Paradise, *Eng.*, Amomum subulatum, *Roxb.*, SCITAMINEÆ.
Foods .
Gram, Common, *Eng.*, Cicer arietinum, *Linn.*, LEGUMINOSÆ.
Foods .
Granata, *Ger.*, Punica Granatum, *Linn.*, LYTHRACEÆ.
Foods .

Grass, Blue Kentucky, *American*, Poa pratensis, *Linn.*, GRAMINEÆ.
Foods .
Grass, Cock's Foot, *Eng.*, Dactylis glomerata, *Linn.*, GRAMINEÆ.
Foods .
Grass, Hill, *Eng.*, Andropogon miliaceus, *Roxb.*, GRAMINEÆ.
Foods .
Grass, Lemon, *Eng.*, Andropogon citratus, GRAMINEÆ.
Foods .
Grass, Lemon, *Eng.*, Andropogon Schœnanthus, *Linn.*, GRAMINEÆ.
Foods .
Grass, Meadow, **Rough,** *Eng.*, Poa trivialis, *Linn.*, GRAMINEÆ.
Foods .
Grass, Meadow, **Smooth-stalked,** *Eng.*, Poa pratensis, *Linn.*, GRAMINEÆ. Foods .
Grass, Prairie, of Australia, *Eng.*, Bromus schaderi, *Kunth.*, GRAMINEÆ.
Foods .
Grenades, *Fr.*, Punica Granatum, *Linn.*, LYTHRACEÆ.
Foods .
Guá, *Beng.*, Areca Catechu, *Linn.*, PALMÆ.
Foods .
Guár, *N.-W. P. & Oudh*, Cyamopsis psoralioides, *DC.*, LEGUMINOSÆ.
Foods .
Guava Tree, *Eng.*, Psidium Guyava, *Raddi.*, MYRTACEÆ.
Foods .
Guback, *Sans.*, Areca Catechu, *Linn.*, PALMÆ.
Foods .
Guch, Coriaria nepalensis, *Wall.*, CORIARIEÆ.
Foods .
Gúch, *Kashmir*, Viburnum cotinifolium, *Don.*, CAPRIFOLIACEÆ.
Foods .
Guch, *Kashmir*, *Pb.*, Viburnum fœtens, *Decaisne*, CAPRIFOLIACEÆ.
Foods .
Gudha, *N.-W. India*, Eleusine indica, *Gærtn.*, GRAMINEÆ.
Foods .
Gudhuma, *Sans.*, Triticum sativum, *Lam.*, GRAMINEÆ.
Foods .
Gudúrichakanda, *Bom.*, Costus speciosus, *Sm.*, SCITAMINEÆ.
Foods .
Gugal, *Tel.*, Shorea robusta, *Gærtn.*, DIPTEROCARPEÆ.
Foods .
Gúhor, *Nep.*, Pyrus vestita, *Wall.*, ROSACEÆ.
Foods .
Gúhú, *Hind.*, Sterculia urens, *Roxb.*, STERCULIACEÆ.
Foods .
Guinea, Grass, *Eng.*, Panicum jumentosum, *Pers.*, GRAMINEÆ.
Foods .
Gujon soba, *Burm.*, Triticum sativum, *Lam.*, GRAMINEÆ.
Foods .
Gul, *Pb.*, Cichorium Intybus, *Linn.*, COMPOSITÆ.
Foods .
Gulab, *Hind.*, Rosa macrophylla, *Lindl.*, ROSACEÆ.
Foods .
Gúlar, *Hind.*, Ficus glomerata, *Roxb.*, URTICACEÆ.
Foods .
Gular, *Hind.*, Ficus virgata, *Roxb.*, URTICACEÆ.
Foods .
Gúlar tabsi, *Hind.*, Sterculia urens, *Roxb.*, STERCULIACEÆ.
Foods .
Gulatti, *Pb.*, Dolichos biflorus, *Linn.*, LEGUMINOSÆ.
Foods .
Gúlgá, *Beng.*, Nipa fruticans, *Wurmb.*, PALMÆ.
Foods .

Gul-kakru, *Pb.*, Podophyllum emodi, *Wall.*, BERBERIDÆ.
Foods .
Gullu, *N.-W. P.*, Taxus baccata, *Linn.*, CONIFERÆ.
Foods .
Gulu (seeds) , Cannabis sativa, *Linn.*, URTICACEÆ.
Foods .
Gum, Arabic, Indian, *Eng.*, Acacia arabica, *Willd.*, LEGUMINOSÆ.
Foods .
Gum, Kino, *Eng.*, Pterocarpus Marsupium, *Roxb.*, LEGUMINOSÆ.
Foods .
Gumar, *Beng.*, *Hind.*, Gmelina arborea, *Roxb.*, VERBENACEÆ.
Foods .
Gumartek, *Tel.*, Gmelina arborea, *Roxb.*, VERBENACEÆ.
Foods .
Gumi, *Garo Hills & Sylhet*, Aglaia edulis, *A. Gray*, MELIACEÆ.
Foods .
Gummaddikaia, *Tel.*, Cucurbita maxima, *Duchesne*, CUCURBITACEÆ.
Foods .
Gummar, *Gond.*, Careya arborea, *Roxb.*, MYRTACEÆ.
Foods .
Gumodi, *Tel.*, Pueraria tuberosa, *DC.*, LEGUMINOSÆ.
Foods .
Gumpini, *Tel.*, Odina Wodier, *Roxb.*, ANACARDIACEÆ.
Foods .
Gún, *Hind.*, *Pb.*, Æsculus indica, *Colebr.*, SAPINDACEÆ.
Foods .
Gun, *Pb.*, Pyrus kumaoni, *Dcne.*, ROSACEÆ.
Foods .
Gunacha, *Pb.*, Rubus lasiocarpus, *Smith*, ROSACEÆ.
Foods .
Gunch, *Beng.*, Abrus precatorius, *Linn.*, LEGUMINOSÆ.
Foods .
Gunchi, *Hind.*, Abrus precatorius, *Linn.*, LEGUMINOSÆ.
Foods .
Gundi, *Hind.*, Cordia Rothii, *Rom. & Sch.*, BORAGINEÆ.
Foods .
Gundra, *Tel.*, *Sans.*, Saccharum Sara, *Roxb.*, GRAMINEÆ.
Foods .
Gundui, *Hind.*, Cordia Rothii, *Rom. & Sch.*, BORAGINEÆ.
Foods .
Gun-dumani, *Tam.*, Abrus precatorius, *Linn.*, LEGUMINOSÆ.
Foods .
Gungru, *Pb.*, Dioscorea deltoides, *Wall.*, DIOSCOREACEÆ.
Foods .
Guniadi, *Tam.*, Gmelina arborea, *Roxb.*, VERBENACEÆ.
Foods .
Gunja, *Bom.*, *Sans.*, Abrus precatorius, *Linn.*, LEGUMINOSÆ.
Foods .
Guracha, *Pb.*, Rubus ellipticus, *Smith*, ROSACEÆ.
Foods .
Gurapu-badam, *Tel.*, Sterculia fœtida, *Linn.*, STERCULIACEÆ.
Foods .
Gur-begun, *Beng.*, *Hind.*, Lycopersicum esculentum, *Miller*, SOLANACEÆ.
Foods .
Gurdub, *N.-W. India*, Eleusine flagellifera, *Nees.*, GRAMINEÆ.
Foods .
Gurgur, *Beng.*, Coix lachryma, *Linn.*, GRAMINEÆ.
Foods .
Gurgura, *Pb.*, Reptonia buxifolia, *A. DC.*, MYRSINEÆ.
Foods .
Gúriál, *Hind.*, Bauhinia racemosa, *Lam.*, LEGUMINOSÆ.
Foods .

Gurinda, *Hazara*, Prinsepia utiles, *Royle*, ROSACEÆ.
Foods .
Gurkhi, *Beng.*, Solanum nigrum, *Linn.*, SOLANACEÆ.
Foods .
Guri pata, *Kumaun*, Skimmia Laureola, *Hook.*, RUTACEÆ.
Foods .
Gurmala, *Gus.*, Cassia Fistula, *Linn.*, LEGUMINOSÆ.
Foods .
Gurti-chettu, *Tel.*, Dæmia extensa, *R. Br.*, ASCLEPIADEÆ.
Foods .
Gutgumma, *Pb.*, Salvia Moorcroftiana, *Wall.*, LABIATÆ.
Foods .
Guya, *Kumaun*, Viburnum fœtens, *Decaisne*, CAPRIFOLIACEÆ.
Foods .
Gwala, *Hind.*, Securinega obovata, *Müll.*, EUPHORBIACEÆ.
Foods .
Gwálam, *Hind.*, Pyrus baccata, *Linn.*, ROSACEÆ.
Foods .
Gwal kakri, *Pb.*, Trichosanthes cucumerina, *Linn.*, CUCURBITACEÆ.
Foods .
Gway, *Burm.*, Spondias mangifera, *Pers.*, ANACARDIACEÆ.
Foods .
Gwia, *Kumaun*, Viburnum cotinifolium, *Don.*, CAPRIFOLIACEÆ.
Foods .
Gyoben, *Burm.*, Schleichera trijuga, *Willd.*, SAPINDACEÆ.
Foods .
Gyootnway, *Burm.*, Gnetum scandens, *Roxb.*, GNETACEÆ.
Foods .

H

Hadar, *Pb.*, Ribes rubrum, *Linn.*, SAXIFRAGACEÆ.
Foods .
Haddú, *Hind.*, *Pb.*, Cornus macrophylla, *Wall.*, CORNACEÆ.
Foods .
Hakna, *Hind.*, Indigofera pulchella, *Roxb.*, LEGUMINOSÆ.
Foods ,
Halada, *Bom.*, Curcuma longa, *Roxb.*, SCITAMINEÆ.
Foods .
Hála-koratige, *Kan.*, Dæmia extensa, *R. Br.*, ASCLEPIADEÆ.
Foods .
Halbambar, *Pb.*, Hedera Helix, *Linn.*, ARALIACEÆ.
Foods .
Haldi, *Hind.*, Curcuma longa, *Roxb.*, SCITAMINEÆ.
Foods .
Haleem, *Dec.*, Lepidium sativum, *Linn.*, CRUCIFERÆ.
Foods .
Haleo, *Hind.*, Cornus macrophylla, *Wall.*, CORNACEÆ.
Foods .
Hali, *Kan.*, Chrysophyllum Roxburghii, *G. Don.*, SAPOTACEÆ.
Foods .
Halim, *Beng.*, *Hind.*, Nasturtium officinale, *Br.*, CRUCIFERÆ.
Foods .
Halu, *Pb.*, Impatiens Balsamina, *Linn.*, GERANIACEÆ.
Foods .
Halu, *Pb.*, Salvia Moorcroftiana, *Wall.*, LABIATÆ.
Foods .
Halud, *Beng.*, Curcuma longa, *Roxb.*, SCITAMINEÆ.
Foods .

Hemp, Indian or Deccani, *Eng.*, Hibiscus cannabinus, *Linn.*, MALVACEÆ. Foods .
Hemp, Rosselle, *Eng.*, Hibiscus cannabinus, *Linn.*, MALVACEÆ. Foods .
Henbane, *Eng.*, Hyoscyamus niger, *Linn.*, SOLANACEÆ. Foods .
Herar (Poisonous forms), Agaricus campestris, *Linn.*, FUNGI. Foods .
Herra, *Hind.*, Terminalia chebula, *Rets.*, COMBRETACEÆ. Foods .
Heru, *Pb.*, Quercus Ilex, *Linn.*, CUPULIFERÆ. Foods .
Hevúr, *Bom.*, Acacia leucophlæa, *Willd.*, LEGUMINOSÆ. Foods .
Hibiscus, Edible, *Eng.*, Hibiscus esculentus, *Linn.*, MALVACEÆ. Foods .
Hibiscus, Hemp-leaved, *Eng.*, Hibiscus cannabinus, *Linn.*, MALVACEÆ. Foods .
Hikpi, *Lepcha*, Indigofera pulchella, *Roxb.*, LEGUMINOSÆ. Foods .
Hilikha, *Ass.*, Terminalia chebula, *Rets.*, COMBRETACEÆ. Foods .
Hillooa, *Hind.*, *Pers.*, Asparagus officinalis, *Willd.*, LILIACEÆ. Foods .
Hilyoon, *Beng.*, Asparagus officinalis, *Willd.*, LILIACEÆ. Foods .
Hims, *Arab.*, Cicer arietinum, *Linn.*, LEGUMINOSÆ. Foods .
Himu, *Hind.*, Morus serrata, *Roxb.*, URTICACEÆ. Foods .
Hindwana, *N.-W. P.*, Citrullus vulgaris, *Schrad.*, CUCURBITACEÆ. Foods .
Hing, *Beng.*, *Hind.*, Ferula Narthex, *Boiss.*, UMBELLIFERÆ. Foods .
Hingan, *Mar.*, Balanites Roxburghii, *Planch.*, SIMARUBEÆ. Foods .
Hingol, *Hind.*, Balanites Roxburghii, *Planch.*, SIMARUBEÆ. Foods .
Hingore, *Ass.*, Castanopsis rufescens, *Hook. f & Th.*, CUPULIFERÆ. Foods .
Hingota, *Hind.*, Balanites Roxburghii, *Planch.*, SIMARUBEÆ. Foods .
Hingu, *Hind.*, Balanites Roxburghii, *Planch.*, SIMARUBEÆ. Foods .
Hingu, *Sans.*, Ferula Narthex, *Boiss.*, UMBELLIFERÆ. Foods .
Hippe, *Kan.*, Bassia longifolia, *Willd.*, SAPOTACEÆ. Foods .
Hisalu, *Kumaun*, Rubus ellipticus, *Smith*, ROSACEÆ. Foods .
Hisalu, *Hind.*, Rubus paniculatus, *Smith*, ROSACEÆ. Foods .
Hittum, *Gond.*, Sterculia urens, *Roxb.*, STERCULIACEÆ. Foods .
Hiun-garna, *Pb.*, Capparis horrida, *Linn.*, CAPPARIDEÆ. Foods .
Hlar, *Pb.*, Cocculus Leæba, *DC.*, MENISPERMACEÆ. Foods .
Hlo sa hlot-kúng, *Lepcha*, Prunus Padus, *Linn.*, ROSACEÆ. Foods .
Hlyanpyoo, *Burm.*, Sterculia fœtida, *Linn.*, STERCULIACEÆ. Foods .

Hman, *Burm.*, Feronia Elephantum, *Correa.*, RUTACEÆ.
Foods .
Hnan, *Burm.*, Sesamum indicum, *Linn.*, PEDALINEÆ.
Foods .
Hodung, *Ladak*, Populus euphratica, *Olivier*, SALICINEÆ.
Foods .
Hogla, *Beng.*, Typha elephantina, *Roxb.*, TYPHACEÆ.
Foods .
Hog-plum, *Eng.*, Spondias mangifera, *Pers.*, ANACARDIACEÆ.
Foods .
Hol, *Afg.*, *Lahoul*, Medicago falcata, *Linn.*, LEGUMINOSÆ.
Foods .
Holma, *Pb.*, Leea aspera, *Wall.*, AMPELIDEÆ.
Foods .
Honge, *Kan.*, Bassia latifolia, *Roxb.*, SAPOTACEÆ.
Foods .
Hoom, *Bom.*, Saccopetalum tomentosum, *Hook.*, ANONACEÆ.
Foods .
Hop, *Eng.*, Medicago lupulina, *Linn.*, LEGUMINOSÆ.
Foods .
Hops, *Eng.*, Humulus Lupulus, *L.*, URTICACEÆ.
Foods .
Horina, *Beng.*, Vitex leucoxylon, *Linn.*, VERBENACEÆ.
Foods .
Hornbean Hop, *Eng.*, Ostrya carpinifolia, *Scop.*, CUPULIFERÆ.
Foods .
Horse Chestnut, Indian, *Eng.*, Æsculus indica, *Colebr.*, SAPINDACEÆ.
Foods .
Horse Gram, *Eng.*, Dolichos biflorus, *Linn.*, LEGUMINOSÆ.
Foods .
Horse Radish or Ben Nut Tree, *Eng.*, Moringap terygosperma, *Gærtn.*, MORINGEÆ. Foods .
Horse Tail, *Eng.*, Equisetum debile, *Roxb.*, EQUISETACEÆ.
Foods .
Howa, *Pb.*, Solanum gracilipes, *Dcne.*, SOLANACEÆ.
Foods .
Hpalan, *Burm.*, Bauhinia racemosa, *Lam.*, LEGUMINOSÆ.
Foods .
Hsaymakyee, *Burm.*, Vangueria spinosa, *Roxb.*, RUBIACEÆ.
Foods .
Hseng neng thayet, *Burm.*, Mangifera sylvatica, *Roxb.*, ANACARDIACEÆ.
Foods .
Hshoo, *Burm.*, Carthamus tinctorius, *Linn.*, COMPOSITÆ.
Foods .
Htan, *Burm.*, Borassus flabelliformis, *Linn.*, PALMÆ.
Foods .
Htouksha, *Burm.*, Vitex leucoxylon, *Linn.*, VERBENACEÆ.
Foods .
Hub-ul-mushk, *Arab.*, Hibiscus Abelmoschus, *Linn.*, MALVACEÆ.
Foods .
Huile de Sesame, *Fr.*, Sesamum indicum, *Linn.*, PEDALINEÆ.
Foods .
Hujed, *Arab.*, Adansonia digitata, *Linn.*, MALVACEÆ.
Foods .
Hula, *Pb.*, Rumex Wallichii, *Meisn.*, POLYGONACEÆ.
Foods .
Hulashing, *Pb.*, Rhus semi-alata, *Murray*, ANACARDIACEÆ.
Foods .
Hulhul, *Pb.*, Gynandropsis pentaphylla, *DC.*, CAPPARIDEÆ.
Foods .
Hulluch, *Ass.*, Terminalia belerica, *Roxb.*, COMBRETACEÆ.
Foods .

Humbili, *Tam.*, Maba buxifolia, *Pers.*, EBENACEÆ.
Foods .
Humbu, *Pb.*, *Ladak*, Myricaria elegans, *Royle*, TAMARISCINEÆ.
Foods .
Husalban-achsir, *Arab.*, Rosmarinus officinalis *Linn.*, LABIATEÆ.
Foods .

I

Ibharankusha, *Beng.*, *Hind.*, Andropogon laniger, *Desf.*, GRAMINEÆ.
Foods .
Ichal, *Kan.*, Phœnix farinifera, *Willd.*, PALMÆ.
Foods .
Ik, *Beng.*, Saccharum officinarum, *Linn.*, GRAMINEÆ.
Foods .
Ikh, *N.-W. P. & Oudh*, Saccharum officinarum, *Linn.*, GRAMINEÆ.
Foods .
Ikhari, *N.-W. P. & Oudh*, Saccharum officinarum, *Linn.*, GRAMINEÆ.
Foods .
Ikshu (pale var.), *Sans.*, Saccharum officinarum, *Linn.*, GRAMINEÆ.
Foods .
Iktibi, *Lepcha*, Securinega obovata, *Müll.*, EUPHORBIACEÆ.
Foods .
Ilavan, *Tam.*, Eriodendron anfractuosum, *DC.*, MALVACEÆ.
Foods .
Illavam, *Tam.*, Bombax malabaricum, *DC.*, MALVACEÆ.
Foods .
Illupi, *Tam.*, Bassia latifolia, *Roxb.*, SAPOTACEÆ.
Foods .
Imbir, *Pb.*, Ulmus campestris, *Linn.*, URTICACEÆ.
Foods .
Imli, *Hind.*, Tamarindus indica, *Linn.*, LEGUMINOSÆ.
Foods .
Inderjau, *Hind.*, Holarrhena antidysenterica, *Wall.*, APOCYNACEÆ.
Foods .
Indian-corn, *Eng.*, Zea Mays, *Linn.*, GRAMINEÆ.
Foods .
Indra-varuni, *Sans.*, Citrullus Colocynthis, *Schrad.*, CUCURBITACEÆ.
Foods .
Indrawan, *Dec.*, Citrullus Colocynthis, *Schrad.*, CUCURBITACEÆ.
Foods .
Indrayan, *Hind.*, Citrullus Colocynthis, *Schrad.*, CUCURBITACEÆ.
Foods .
Induga, *Tel.*, Strychnos potatorum, *Linn. f.*, LOGANIACEÆ.
Foods .
Ingie, *Tam.*, Zingiber officinale, *Roscoe*, SCITAMINEÆ.
Foods .
Ingrach, *Pb.*, Fragaria vesca, *Linn.*, ROSACEÆ.
Foods .
Ingua, *Hind.*, Balanitis Roxburghii, *Planch.*, SIMARUBEÆ.
Foods .
Inguva, *Tel.*, Ferula Narthex, *Boiss.*, UMBELLIFERÆ.
Foods .
Inzarra, *Pb.*, Grewia villosa, *Willd.*, TILIACEÆ.
Foods .
Ippi, *Tel.*, Bassia latifolia, *Roxb.*, SAPOTACEÆ.
Foods .
Ippi, *Tel.*, Bassia longifolia, *Willd.*, SAPOTACEÆ.
Foods .

J

Jalldar, *Salt Range*, Grewia villosa, *Willd.*, TILIACEÆ.
Foods .
Jalldar, *Pb.*, Rhamnus persicus, *Boiss.*, RHAMNEÆ.
Foods .
Jal kukar, *Pb.*, Tulipa stellata, *Hook.*, LILIACEÆ.
Foods .
Jallur, *Hind.*, Bauhinia Vahlii, *W. & A.*, LEGUMINOSÆ.
Foods .
Jalpai, *Beng.*, Elæocarpus serratus, *Linn.*, TILIACEÆ.
Foods .
Jal-sawank, *N.-W. P.*, Panicum crus-galli, *Linn.*, GRAMINEÆ.
Foods .
Jám, *Beng.*, *Hind.*, Eugenia Jambolana, *Lam.*, MYRTACEÆ.
Foods .
Jam, *Hind.*, Sizygium jambolanum, *DC.*, MYRTACEÆ.
Foods .
Jama, *Tel.*, Psidium Guyava, *Radi.*, MYRTACEÆ.
Foods .
Jáman, *Beng.*, *Hind.*, Eugenia jambolana, *Lam.*, MYRTACEÆ.
Foods .
Jaman, *Hind.*, Sizygium Jambolanum, *DC.*, MYRTACEÆ.
Foods .
Jamana, *Hind.*, Prunus Padus, *Linn.*, ROSACEÆ.
Foods .
Jamara, *Kashmir*, Viburnum fœtens, *Decaisne*, CAPRIFOLIACEÆ.
Foods .
Jambira, *Sans.*, Citrus medica, *Linn.*, RUTACEÆ.
Foods .
Jamb khúdi, *Beng.*, Antidesma Ghæsembila, *Gærtn.*, EUPHORBIACEÆ.
Foods .
Jambo-ayer, Eugenia aquea, *Burm.*, MYRTACEÆ.
Foods .
Jambool, *Bom.*, Eugenia Jambolana, *Lam.*, MYRTACEÆ.
Foods .
Jambool, *Bom.* Sizygium jambolanum, *DC.*, MYRTACEÆ.
Foods .
Jambu, *Tam.*, Prosopis spicigera, *Linn.*, LEGUMINOSÆ.
Foods .
Jamoon, *Beng.*, *Hind.*, Eugenia Jambolana, *Lam.*, MYRTACEÆ.
Foods .
Jamrool, *Beng.*, *Hind.*, Eugenia javanica, *Lamk.*, MYRTACEÆ.
Foods .
Jamrool, Malacca, *Beng.*, *Hind.*, Eugenia malaccensis, *Linn.*, MYRTACEÆ.
Foods .
Jamu, *Ass.*, Eugenia Jambolana, *Lam.*, MYRTACEÆ.
Foods .
Jamu, *Ass.*, Sizygium jambolanum, *DC.*, MYRTACEÆ.
Foods .
Jámun, *Hind.*, Sizygium jambolanum, *DC.*, MYRTACEÆ.
Foods .
Janar, *Beng.*, Zea Mays, *Linn.*, GRAMINEÆ.
Foods .
Jandar lamba, *Pb.*, Aristida depressa, *Retz.*, GRAMINEÆ.
Foods .
Jangi, *Him. name*, Corylus Colurna, *Linn.*, CUPULIFERÆ.
Foods .
Jangra, *Sind.*, Zizyphus nummularia, *W. & A.*, RHAMNEÆ.
Foods .
Janjhan, *Hind.*, Sesbania ægyptiaca, *Pers.*, LEGUMINOSÆ.
Foods .
Japhala, *Bom.*, Aleurites moluccana, *Willd.*, EUPHORBIACEÆ.
Foods .

Jara, *Circars,* Grewia salvifolia, *Heyne,* TILIACEÆ.
Foods .
Jard-aru bari, *Pb.,* Prunus armeniaca, *Linn,* ROSACEÆ.
Foods .
Jarila, *Nep.,* Elæagnus latifolia, *Linn.,* ELÆAGNEÆ.
Foods .
Jariya, *Hind.,* Brassica campestris, *Linn.,* var. campestris proper, CRUCIFERÆ. Foods .
Jarlangel, *Pb.,* Lonicera quinquelocularis, *Hardwicke,* CAPRIFOLIACEÆ.
Foods .
Jarosse, *Eng.,* Lathyrus sativus, *Linn.,* LEGUMINOSÆ.
Foods .
Jati, *Hind.,* Myristica moschata, *Willd.,* MYRISTICEÆ.
Foods .
Jati-koroi, *Ass.,* Albizzia odoratissima, *Benth.,* LEGUMINOSÆ.
Foods .
Jatiphala, *Sans.,* Myristica moschata, *Willd.,* MYRISTICEÆ.
Foods .
Jatipullum, *Cingh.,* Myristica moschata, *Willd.,* MYRISTICEÆ.
Foods .
Jauntari (Mace), *Hind.,* Myristica moschata, *Willd,* MYRISTICEÆ.
Foods .
Jav, *Hind.,* Hordeum vulgare, *Linn.,* GRAMINEÆ.
Foods .
Java, *Tel.,* Hordeum vulgare, *Linn.,* GRAMINEÆ.
Foods .
Jawa, *Pb.,* Viburnum cotinifolium, *Don.,* CAPRIFOLIACEÆ.
Foods .
Jawani, *Pb.,* Cicer soongaricum, *Steph.,* LEGUMINOSÆ.
Foods .
Jawári, *C. P.,* Sorghum vulgare, *Pers.,* LEGUMINOSÆ.
Foods .
Jayanti, *Beng.,* Sesbania ægyptiaca, *Pers.* LEGUMINOSÆ.
Foods .
Jazar, *Arab.,* Daucus Carota, *Linn.,* UMBELLIFERÆ.
Foods .
Jei, *Hind.,* Avena fatua, *Linn.,* GRAMINEÆ.
Foods .
Jerimu, *Simla,* Acer cultratum, *Wall.,* syn. of Acer pictum, *Thumb.* SAPINDACEÆ. Foods .
Jewar, *Pb.,* Euryale erox, *Salisb.,* NYMPHÆACEÆ.
Foods .
Jhal, *Hind., Pb., Tam.,* Salvadora oleoides, *Linn.,* SALVADORACEÆ.
Foods .
Jhand, *Pb.,* Prosopis spicigera, *Linn.,* LEGUMINOSÆ.
Foods .
Jhangora, *Kumaun & Garhwal,* Panicum frumentaceum, *Roxb.* GRAMINEÆ. Foods .
Jhar, *Hind., Pb., Tam.,* Salvadora oleoides, *Linn.,* SALVADORACEÆ.
Foods .
Jhari, *N.-W. P.,* Zizyphus nummularia, *W. & A.,* RHAMNEÆ.
Foods .
Jhikrai, *Beng.,* Vigna pilosa, *Baker,* LEGUMINOSÆ.
Foods .
Jhinga, *Beng.,* Luffa acutangula, *Roxb.,* CUCURBITACEÆ.
Foods .
Jhingan, *Hind., N.-W. P.,* Odina Wodier, *Roxb.,* ANACARDIACEÆ.
Foods .
Jhinja, *Ajmir,* Bauhinia racemosa, *Lam.,* LEGUMINOSÆ.
Foods .
Jhinjan, *Hind.,* Sesbania ægyptiaca, *Pers.,* LEGUMINOSÆ.
Foods .

Jhinjhor, *N.-W. India*, Eleusine indica, *Gærtn.*, GRAMINEÆ.
Foods .
Jhunjhuni-ankari, *Hind.*, Vicia hirsuta, *Koch.*, LEGUMINOSÆ.
Foods .
Jhusa, *N.-W. P.*, Eragrostis plumosa, *Link.*, GRAMINEÆ.
Foods .
Jia puta, *Hind*, Putranjiva Roxburghii, *Wall.*, EUPHORBIACEÆ.
Foods .
Jiban, *N.-W. P.*, Odina Wodier, *Roxb.*, ANACARDIACEÆ.
Foods .
Jidimamidi, *Tel.*, Anacardium occidentale, *Linn.*, ANACARDIACEÆ.
Foods .
Jidkar, *Pb.*, Flacourtia sepiaria, *Roxb.*, BIXINEÆ.
Foods .
Jinga, *Hind.*, *Beng.*, Luffa acutangula, *Roxb.*, CUCURBITACEÆ.
Foods .
Jinti, *Chenab*, Prinsepia utiles, *Royle*, ROSACEÆ.
Foods .
Jira, *Beng.*, Carum Carui, *Linn.*, UMBELLIFERÆ.
Foods .
Jira, *Beng.*, Cuminum Cyminum, *Linn.*, UMBELLIFERÆ.
Foods .
Jiraka, *Sans.*, *Tel.*, Cuminum Cyminum, *Linn.*, UMBELLIFERÆ.
Foods .
Jiri, *Tel.*, Semecarpus Anacardium, *Linn.*, ANACARDIACEÆ.
Foods .
Jirka, *Pb.*, Phytolacca acinosa, *Roxb.*, VERBINACEÆ.
Foods .
Jirugu, *Tel.*, Caryota urens, *Willd.*, PALMÆ.
Foods .
Jit, *Pb.*, Salvadora persica, *Garcin*, SALVADORACEÆ.
Foods .
Jittupáku, *Tel.*, Dæmia extensa, *R. Br.*, ASCLEPIADEÆ.
Foods .
Jiyal, *Beng.*, Odina Wodier, *Roxb.*, ANACARDIACEÆ.
Foods .
Job's tears, *Eng.*, Coix lachryma, *Linn.*, GRAMINEÆ.
Foods .
Jondri, *Mar.*, Antidesma Ghæsembilla, *Gærtn.*, EUPHORBIACEÆ.
Foods .
Jonna, *Tel.*, Sorghum vulgare, *Pers.*, GRAMINEÆ.
Foods .
Jool-palum, *Hind.*, Rumex Wallichii, *Meisn.*, POLYGONACEÆ.
Foods .
Joti-juti, *Hind.*, Putranjiva Roxburghii, *Wall.*, EUPHORBIACEÆ.
Foods .
Jowan, *Beng.*, Carum copticum, *Benth.*, UMBELLIFERÆ.
Foods .
Juar, *N.-W. P. & Oudh*, *Beng.*, *Hind.*, Sorghum vulgare, *Pers.*, GRAMINEÆ. Foods .
Jub, *Beng.*, Hordeum vulgare, *Linn.*, GRAMINEÆ.
Foods .
Juephal, *Hind.*, Myristica moschata, *Willd.*, MYRISTICEÆ.
Foods .
Jujube, *Eng.*, Zizyphus Jujuba, *Lam.*, RHAMNEÆ.
Foods .
Jum, *Beng.*, Garuga pinnata, *Roxb.*, BURSERACEÆ.
Foods .
Jong-song, *Lepcha*, Eugenia obovata, *Wall.*, MYRTACEÆ.
Foods .
Juniper, *Eng.*, Juniperus communis, *Linn.*, CONIFERÆ.
Foods .

Junvásá, *Hind.*, *Bom.*, Alhagi maurorum, *Desv.*, LEGUMINOSÆ.
Foods .
Junri, *N.-W. P. & Oudh*, Sorghum vulgare, *Pers.*, GRAMINEÆ.
Foods .
Junri, *Hind.*, Zea Mays, *Linn.*, GRAMINEÆ.
Foods .
Jutuk, *Hind.*, *Dec.*, Dæmia extensa, *R. Br.*, ASCLEPIADEÆ.
Foods .
Juwasa, *Hind.*, *Bom.*, Alhagi maurorum, *Desv.*, LEGUMINOSÆ.
Foods .
Jvári, *Deccan*, Sorghum vulgare, *Pers.*, LEGUMINOSÆ.
Foods .

K

Kabal, *Cingh.*, Albizzia stipulata, *Boivin.*, LEGUMINOSÆ.
Foods .
Kabar, *Hind.*, Ficus cordifolia, *Roxb.*, URTICACEÆ.
Foods .
Kabar, *Sind.*, Salvadora persica, *Garcin.*, SALVADORACEÆ.
Foods .
Kabbar, *Pb.*, Cynodon Dactylon, *Pers.*, GRAMINEÆ.
Foods .
Kabbar, *Hind.*, *Pb.*, *Tam.*, Salvadora oleoides, *Linn.*, SALVADORACEÆ.
Foods .
Kabra, *Ladak*, Capparis spinosa, *Linn.*, CAPPARIDEÆ.
Foods .
Kabuli, *Hind.*, Lagenaria vulgaris, *Seringe.*, CUCURBITACEÆ.
Foods .
Kachará, *Bom.*, Cyperus rotundus, *Linn.*, CYPERACEÆ.
Foods .
Kachein, *Sutlej*, Melia Azedarach, *Linn.*, MELIACEÆ.
Foods .
Kach-hur, *N.-W. P. & Oudh*, Cyamopsis psoralioides, *DC.*, LEGUMINOSÆ.
Foods .
Kachir, *Hind.*, Cornus macrophylla, *Wall.*, CORNACEÆ.
Foods .
Kachmach, *Pb.*, Solanum nigrum, *Linn.*, SOLANACEÆ.
Foods .
Kachnál, *Hind.*, Bauhinia racemosa, *Lam.*, LEGUMINOSÆ.
Foods .
Kachnar, *Pb.*, Bauhinia purpurea, *Linn.*, LEGUMINOSÆ.
Foods .
Kachnár, *Hind.*, Bauhinia variegata, *Linn.*, LEGUMINOSÆ.
Foods .
Kachra (unripe), *Hind.*, Cucumis Melo, *Linn.*, var. Momordica (*sp. Roxb.*), CUCURBITACEÆ. Foods .
Kachú, *Hind.*, *Beng.*, Colocasia antiquorum, *Schott.*, AROIDEÆ.
Foods .
Kachúr, *Hind.*, Cornus macrophylla, *Wall.*, CORNACEÆ.
Foods .
Kadagho, *Tam.*, Brassica nigra, *Koch.*, CRUCIFERÆ.
Foods .
Kadakai, *Tam.*, Terminalia chebula, *Retz.*, COMBRETACEÆ.
Foods .
Kadalay, *Tam.*, Cicer arietinum, *Linn.*, LEGUMINOSÆ.
Foods .
Kadali, *Sans.*, Musa sapientum, *Linn.*, SCITAMINEÆ.
Foods .

Kadam, *Beng.*, *Mar.*, Anthocephalus Cadamba, *Miq.*, RUBIACEÆ.
Foods .
Kadamba, *Sans.*, *Bom.*, *Tam.*, Anthocephalus Cadamba, *Miq.*, RUBIACEÆ.
Foods .
Kadambe, *Tel.*, Anthocephalus Cadamba, *Miq.*, RUBIACEÆ.
Foods .
Kadami, *Tel.*, Eriodendron anfractuosum, *DC.*, MALVACEÆ.
Foods .
Kada-rai, *Beng.*, Brassica campestris, *Linn.*, var. campestris proper, CRUCIFERÆ. Foods .
Kaddam, *Hind.*, Anthocephalus Cadamba, *Miq.*, RUBIACEÆ.
Foods .
Kaddu, *Hind.*, *Pb.*, Lagenaria vulgaris, *Seringe.*, CUCURBITACEÆ.
Foods .
Kaddú, Mitha, *N.-W. P.*, Cucurbita moschata, *Duchesne*, CUCURBITACEÆ.
Foods .
Kaddu, Safed, *Hind.*, *Beng.*, Cucurbita Pepo, *DC.*, CUCURBITACEÆ.
Foods .
Kadera, *Simla*, Ilex dipyrena, *Wall.*, ILICINEÆ.
Foods .
Kadimah, *Beng.*, *Hind.*, Cucurbita Pepo, *DC.*, CUCURBITACEÆ.
Foods .
Kadot, *Burm.*, Ficus hispida, *Linn. f.*, URTICACEÆ.
Foods .
Kadrajuvi, *Tel.*, Putranjiva Roxburghii, *Wall.*, EUPHORBIACEÆ.
Foods .
Kadu, *Hind.*, Cucurbita maxima, *Duchesne*, CUCURBITACEÆ.
Foods .
Kadungbi, *Lepcha*, Clerodendron Colebrookianum, *Walp.*, VERBINACEÆ.
Foods .
Kagara, *Hind.*, Saccharum spontaneum, *Linn.*, GRAMINEÆ.
Foods .
Kagsha, *Hind.*, Ficus hispida, *Linn. f.*, URTICACEÆ.
Foods .
Kahi, *Pb.*, Saccharum spontaneum, *Linn.*, GRAMINEÆ.
Foods .
Kahu, *Hind.*, *Pb.*, Lactuca scariola, *Linn.*, COMPOSITÆ.
Foods .
Kahu, *Sind*, Saccharum spontaneum, *Linn.*, GRAMINEÆ.
Foods .
Kaida, *Mal.*, Pandanus odoratissimus, *Willd.*, PANDANEÆ.
Foods .
Kaikar, *Hind.*, Garuga pinnata, *Roxb.*, BURSERACEÆ.
Foods .
Kaikra, *C. P.*, Garuga pinnata, *Roxb.*, BURSERACEÆ.
Foods .
Kain, *Pb.*, Ulmus campestris, *Linn.*, URTICACEÆ.
Foods .
Kain, *Pb.*, Ulmus Wallichiana, *Planch.*, URTICACEÆ.
Foods .
Kaiphal, *N.-W. P.*, Myrica sapida, *Wall.*, MYRICACEÆ.
Foods .
Kairt, *Tam.*, Feronia Elephantum, *Correa.*, RUTACEÆ.
Foods .
Kaisho, *Ass.*, Briedelia montana, *Willd.*, EUPHORBIACEÆ.
Foods .
Kait, *Beng.*, Feronia Elephantum, *Correa.*, RUTACEÆ.
Foods .
Kaita-chakka, *Mal.*, Ananassa sativa, *Linn.*, BROMELIACEÆ.
Foods .
Kajooli (red var.), *Beng.*, Saccharum officinarum, *Linn.*, GRAMINEÆ.
Foods .

Kala bogotl, *Nep.*, Baccaurea sapida, *Müll.-Arg.*, EUPHORBIACEÆ.
Foods .
Kala-hisalu, *Kumaun*, Rubus lasiocarpus, *Smith*, ROSACEÆ.
Foods .
Kalajam, *Beng.*, Sizygium jambolanum, *DC.*, MYRTACEÆ.
Foods .
Kalajira, *Beng.*, Nigella sativa, *Linn.*, RANUNCULACEÆ.
Foods .
Kalakadu, *Bom.*, Hymenodictyon excelsum, *Wall.*, RUBIACEÆ.
Foods .
Kalakalaya, *Hind.*, Ribes glaciale, *Wall.*, SAXIFRAGACEÆ.
Foods .
Kala kasturi, *Beng.*, Hibiscus Abelmoschus, *Linn.*, MALVACEÆ.
Foods .
Kalakat, *Pb.*, Prunus Padus, *Linn.*, ROSACEÆ.
Foods .
Kalambi, *Sans.*, Ipomæa aquatica, *Forsk.*, CONVOLVULACEÆ.
Foods .
Kala-marich, *Beng.*, *Hind.*, Piper nigrum, *Linn.*, PIPERACEÆ.
Foods .
Kala-mewa, *Pb.*, Solanum verbascifolium, *Linn.*, SOLANACEÆ.
Foods .
Kalasnar, *Beng.*, Panicum paludosum, *Roxb.*, GRAMINEÆ.
Foods .
Kala titmaliya, *Kumaun*, Viburnum coriaceum, *Bl.*, CAPRIFOLIACEÆ.
Foods .
Kala túlsí, *Hind.*, *Beng.*, *Tel.*, Ocimum sanctum, *Linn.*, LABIATÆ.
Foods .
Kalawar, *Kumaun*, Rubus lasiocarpus, *Smith*, ROSACEÆ.
Foods .
Kale, Green, *Eng.*, Brassica (oleracea) acephala, *Linn.*, CRUCIFERÆ.
Foods .
Kalee-jeeree, *Bom.*, Vernonia anthelmintica, *Willd.*, COMPOSITÆ.
Foods .
Kalejira, *Bom.*, *Hind.*, Nigella sativa, *Linn.*, RANUNCULACEÆ.
Foods .
Kalga, *Sutlej*, Rubus niveus, *Wall.*, ROSACEÆ.
Foods .
Kali, *Pb.*, Bupleurum falcatum, *Linn.*, var. marginata, *Wall.*, UMBELLIFERÆ. Foods .
Kaliar, *Hind.*, Bauhinia purpurea, *Linn.*, LEGUMINOSÆ.
Foods .
Kaliezeorie, *Hind.*, Vernonia anthelmintica, *Willd.*, COMPOSITÆ.
Foods .
Kali jarri, *Pb.*, Salvia Moorcroftiana, *Wall.*, LABIATÆ.
Foods .
Kali-kiker, *Bom.*, Acacia arabica, *Wild.*, LEGUMINOSÆ.
Foods .
Kalinda, *N.-W. P.*, Citrullus vulgaris, *Schrad.*, CUCURBITACEÆ.
Foods .
Kali-taroi, *Bundelkhand*, Luffa acutangula, *Roxb.*, CUCURBITACEÆ.
Foods .
Kali-zeerie, *Dec.*, Vernonia anthelmintica, *Willd.*, COMPOSITÆ.
Foods .
Kallal, *C. P.*, Dillenia pentagyna, *Roxb.*, DILLENIACEÆ.
Foods .
Kallat, *Pb.*, Dolichos biflorus, *Linn.*, LEGUMINOSÆ.
Foods .
Kalmi-sak, *Beng.*, Ipomæa aquatica, *Forsk.*, CONVOLVULACEÆ.
Foods .
Kalon, *N.-W. P.*, Pisum arvense, *Linn.*, LEGUMINOSÆ.
Foods .

Kanda, *Pb.*, Sageretia theezans, *Brongn.*, RHAMNEÆ.
Foods .
Kándan, *Hind.*, Bauhinia variegata, *Linn.*, LEGUMINOSÆ.
Foods .
Kandar, *Pb.*, Cornus macrophylla, *Wall.*, CORNACEÆ.
Foods .
Kandei, *Pb.*, Flacourtia Ramontchi, *L'Herit.*, BIXINEÆ.
Foods .
Kandi, *Sind*, Prosopis spicigera, *Linn.*, LEGUMINOSÆ.
Foods .
Kandiara, *Pb.*, Carthamus oxyacantha, *Bieb.*, COMPOSITÆ.
Foods .
Kandiara kandei, *Pb.*, Astragalus multiceps, *Wall.*, LEGUMINOSÆ.
Foods .
Kandiari, *Kashmir*, Rubus lasiocarpus, *Smith*, ROSACEÆ.
Foods .
Kandiari, *Pb.*, Solanum gracilipes, *Dcne.*, SOLANACEÆ.
Foods .
Kandieri, *Pb.*, Cousinia minutu, *Boiss.*, COMPOSITÆ.
Foods .
Kandurí, *Pb.*, Cephalandra indica, *Naud.*, CUCURBITACEÆ.
Foods .
Kanga, *Tel.*, Pongamia glabra, *Vent.*, LEGUMINOSÆ.
Foods .
Kangar, *Pb.*, Pistacia integerrima, *J. L.Stewart*, ANACARDIACEÆ.
Foods .
Kanghol mirch (the fruit), *Pb.*, Celtis caucasica, *Willd.*, URTICACEÆ.
Foods .
Kangi, *Nep.*, Wendlandia exserta, *DC.*, RUBIACEÆ.
Foods .
Kangji, *Lepcha*, Ficus bengalensis, *Linn.*, URTICACEÆ.
Foods .
Kangri, *Indian.* See Phœnix farinifera, *Willd.*, PALMÆ.
Foods .
Kangri, *N.-W.P. & Oudh*, Setaria italica, *Kunth.*, GRAMINEÆ.
Foods .
Kangú, *Pb.*, Flacourtia Ramontchi, *L'Herit.*, BIXINEÆ.
Foods .
Kangu, *Pb.*, Lycium europœum, *Linn.*, SOLANACEÆ.
Foods .
Kanguruku (red var.), *Sans.*, Saccharum officinarum, *Linn.*, GRAMINEÆ.
Foods .
Kanhya, *Nep.*, Ficus Cunia, *Buch.*, URTICACEÆ.
Foods .
Kaniár, *Hind.*, Bauhinia variegata, *Linn.*, LEGUMINOSÆ.
Foods .
Kanj, *Hind.*, Toddalia aculeata, *Pers.*, RUTACEÆ.
Foods .
Kanjar, *Pb.*, Acer cultratum, *Wall.*, syn. of Acer pictum, *Thunb.*, SAPINDACEÆ. Foods .
Kanju, *Kumaun*, Ulmus integrifolia, *Roxb.*, URTICACEÆ.
Foods .
Kanka, *Tel.*, Dendrocalamus strictus, *Nees.*, GRAMINEÆ.
Foods .
Kankóli, *Pb.*, Elæagnus umbellata, *Thunb.*, ELÆAGNEÆ.
Foods .
Kankrei, *Hind.*, Butea frondosa, *Roxb.*, LEGUMINOSÆ.
Foods .
Kankri, *Hind.*, Cucumis Melo, *Linn.*, var. utilissimus (*sp. Roxb*)., CUCURBITACEÆ. Foods .
Kán-kur, *Beng.*, Cucumis Melo, *Linn.*, var. utilissimus (*sp. Roxb.*), CUCURBITACEÆ. Foods .

Kapasi, *Him. name*, Corylus Colurna, *Linn.*, CUPULIFERÆ.
Foods .
Kaphal, *N.-W. P.*, Myrica sapida, *Wall.*, MYRICACEÆ.
Foods .
Kapittha, *Sans.*, Feronia Elephantum, *Correa.*, RUTACEÆ.
Foods .
Karachu, *C. P.*, Cassia Fistula, *Linn.*, LEGUMINOSÆ.
Foods .
Karafsh (roots), *Hind.*, Apium graveolens, *Linn.*, UMBELLIFERÆ.
Foods .
Karafsh, *Arab.*, Apium graveolens, *Linn.*, UMBELLIFERÆ.
Foods .
Karail, *Beng.*, Dendrocalamus strictus, *Nees.*, GRAMINEÆ.
Foods .
Karak, *Tel.*, Terminalia Chebula, *Retz.*, COMBRETACEÆ.
Foods .
Karalá, *Beng.*, Momordica Charantia, *Linn.*, CUCURBITACEÆ.
Foods .
Karamara, *Bom.*, Averrhoa Carambola, *Linn.*, GERANIACEÆ.
Foods .
Kara marda, *Tam.*, Terminalia tomentosa, *W. & A.*, COMBRETACEÆ.
Foods .
Karambru, *Pb.*, Albizzia odoratissima, *Benth.*, LEGUMINOSÆ.
Foods .
Karamm, *N. Pb. & Ladak*, Dracocephalum heterophyllum, *Benth.*, LABIATÆ. Foods .
Karanga, *Hind.*, Prinsepia utilis, *Royle*, ROSACEÆ.
Foods .
Karangal, *Pb.*, Cassia Fistula, *Linn.*, LEGUMINOSÆ.
Foods .
Karangalli, *Tam.*, Acacia Catechu, *Willd.*, LEGUMINOSÆ.
Foods .
Karangi, *Mysore*, Tamarindus indica, *Linn.*, LEGUMINOSÆ.
Foods .
Karanj, *Hind.*, Pongamia glabra, *Vent.*, LEGUMINOSÆ.
Foods .
Karanja, *Beng.*, Pongamia glabra, *Vent.*, LEGUMINOSÆ.
Foods .
Karanji, *Hind.*, Ulmus integrifolia, *Roxb.*, URTICACEÆ.
Foods .
Karaunda, *Hind.*, Carissa Carandas, *Linn.*, APOCYNACEÆ.
Foods .
Karay-paak, *Hind.*, Murraya Kœnigii, *Spr.*, RUTACEÆ.
Foods .
Karbara, *Pb.*, Hedera Helix, *Linn.*, ARALIACEÆ.
Foods .
Karbi (stalks), *Beng.*, *Hind.*, Sorghum vulgare, *Pers.*, GRAMINEÆ.
Foods .
Kare, *Kan.*, Randia dumetorum, *Lam.*, RUBIACEÆ.
Foods .
Karé, *Kan.*, Randia uliginosa, *DC.*, RUBIACEÆ.
Foods .
Karea-pela, *Mal.*, Murraya Kœnigii, *Spr.*, RUTACEÆ.
Foods .
Karea-phul, *Hind.*, *Beng.*, Murraya Kœnigii, *Spr.*, RUTACEÆ.
Foods .
Karela, *Hind.*, Momordica Charantia, *Linn.*, CUCURBITACEÆ.
Foods .
Karela, *Pb.*, Momordica dioica, *Roxb.*, CUCURBITACEÆ.
Foods .
Kareli, *Hind.*, Momordica Charantia, *Linn.*, CUCURBITACEÆ.
Foods .

Karendera, *Simla*, Acer villosum, *Wall.*, SAPINDACEÆ.
Foods .
Karenja, *Beng.*, Carissa Carandas, *Linn.*, APOCYNACEÆ.
Foods .
Karepak, *Tel.*, Murraya Kœnigii, *Spr.*, RUTACEÆ.
Foods .
Karer, *Pb.*, Rubus biflorus, *Ham.*, ROSACEÆ.
Foods .
Kargnalla, *Hind.*, Briedelia montana, *Willd.*, EUPHORBIACEÆ.
Foods .
Karhar, *Hind.*, Randia dumetorum, *Lam.*, RUBIACEÆ.
Foods .
Karial, *Pb.*, Dæmia extensa, *R. Br.*, ASCLEPIADEÆ.
Foods .
Karik, *Pb.*, Cissus carnosa, *Lam.*, AMPELIDEÆ.
Foods .
Karil, *Pb.*, Capparis aphylla, *Roth.*, CAPPARIDEÆ.
Foods .
Kari-mughilan, *Pers.*, Acacia arabica, *Willd.*, LEGUMINOSÆ.
Foods .
Karir, *Hind.*, Acacia leucophlœa, *Willd.*, LEGUMINOSÆ.
Foods .
Karivepa, *Tel.*, Murraya Kœnigii, *Spr.*, RUTACEÆ.
Foods .
Kariya-polam, *Tam.*, Aloe vera, *Linn.*, LILIACEÆ.
Foods .
Karka, *Gond.*, Terminalia Chebula, *Retz.*, COMBRETACEÆ.
Foods .
Karkanna, *Afg.*, Zizyphus nummularia, *W. & A.*, RHAMNEÆ.
Foods .
Karkapili, *Tam.*, Pithecolobium dulce, *Benth.*, LEGUMINOSÆ.
Foods .
Karkar, *Pb.*, Iris kumaonensis, *Wall.*, IRIDEÆ.
Foods .
Karkaya, *Hyderabad*, Terminalia tomentosa, *W. & A.*, COMBRETACEÆ.
Foods .
Karkotta, *Beng.*, Dillenia pentagyna, *Roxb.*, DILLENIACEÆ.
Foods .
Karmai, *Beng.*, Bauhinia malabarica, *Roxb.*, LEGUMINOSÆ.
Foods .
Karmal, *Hind.*, Averrhoa Carambola, *Linn.*, GERANIACEÆ.
Foods .
Karmurunga, *Sans.*, Averrhoa Carambola, *Linn.*, GERANIACEÆ.
Foods .
Karna, *Hind.*, Saccopetalum tomentosum, *Hook.*, ANONACEÆ.
Foods .
Karni, *Kashmir*, Panicum frumentaceum, *Roxb.*, GRAMINEÆ.
Foods .
Karolla, *Pb.*, Capparis horrida, *Linn.*, CAPPARIDEÆ.
Foods .
Karola, *Hind.*, Momordica Charantia, *Linn.*, CUCURBITACEÆ.
Foods .
Karo-monga, *Tel.*, Averrhoa Carambola, *Linn.*, GERANIACEÆ.
Foods .
Karpasi, *Sans.*, Gossypium herbaceum, *Linn.*, MALVACEÆ.
Foods .
Karra, *Tel.*, Dalbergia Sissoo, *Roxb.*, LEGUMINOSÆ.
Foods .
Karrai, *Hind.*, Sterculia urens, *Roxb.*, STERCULIACEÆ.
Foods .
Karralura, *Oudh*, Capparis horrida, *Linn.*, CAPPARIDEÆ.
Foods .

Karre vembu, *Tam.*, Garuga pinnata, *Roxb.*, BURSERACEÆ.
Foods .
Karri, *Hind.*, Saccopetalum tomentosum, *Hook.*, ANONACEÆ.
Foods .
Karruwa, *Tam.*, Cinnamomum zeylanicum, *Breyn.*, LAURINEÆ.
Foods .
Karsh, *Pb.*, Quercus dilatata, *Lindl.*, CUPULIFERÆ.
Foods .
Karshu, *Pb.*, Quercus semicarpifolia, *Smith*, CUPULIFERÆ.
Foods .
Karuk, *Pb.*, Cordia vestita, *H. f. & T.*, BORAGINEÆ.
Foods .
Karukarinda, *Dec.*, Dioscorea bulbifera, *Linn.*, DIOSCOREACEÆ.
Foods .
Karun, *Pb.*, Euonymus fimbriatus, *Wall*, CELASTRINEÆ.
Foods .
Karun, *Pb.*, Morus serrata, *Roxb.*, URTICACEÆ.
Foods .
Karuna, *Tam.*, *Mal.*, Amorphophallus campanulatus, *Blume.*, AROIDEÆ.
Foods .
Karupale, *Tam.*, Putranjiva Roxburghii, *Wall.*, EUPHORBIACEÆ.
Foods .
Karur, *Pb.*, Hedera Helix, *Linn.*, ARALIACEÆ.
Foods .
Karur, *Pb.*, Sageretia theezans, *Brongn.*, RHAMNEÆ.
Foods .
Karúvelum, *Tam.*, Acacia arabica, *Willd.*, LEGUMINOSÆ.
Foods .
Kar vaghe, *Tam.*, Albizzia odoratissima, *Benth.*, LEGUMINOSÆ.
Foods .
Kasári, *N.-W. P.*, Lathyrus sativus, *Linn.*, LEGUMINOSÆ.
Foods .
Kaseru, *Pb.*, Scirpus Kysoor, *Roxb.*, CYPERACEÆ.
Foods .
Kaseruka, *Sans.*, Scirpus Kysoor, *Roxb.*, CYPERACEÆ.
Foods .
Kash, *Beng.*, Saccharum spontaneum, *Linn.*, GRAMINEÆ.
Foods .
Káshá, *Sans.*, Saccharum spontaneum, *Linn.*, GRAMINEÆ.
Foods .
Kashgem, *Lepcha*, Rubus ellipticus, *Smith*, ROSACEÆ.
Foods .
Kashini-viral, *Tam.*, Cichorium Intybus, *Linn.*, COMPOSITÆ.
Foods .
Kashlorón, *Lepcha*, Castanopsis indica, *A. DC.*, CUPULIFERÆ.
Foods .
Kashiphal, *Hind.*, Lagenaria vulgaris, *Seringe*, CUCURBITACEÆ.
Foods .
Kashmal, *Hind.*, Berberis aristata, *DC.*, and B. Lycium, *Royle*, BERBERIDEÆ. Foods .
Kashmal, *Pb.*, Berberis vulgaris, *Linn.*, BERBERIDEÆ.
Foods .
Kashti, *Ravi*, Pinus Gerardiana, *Wall.*, CONIFERÆ.
Foods .
Kashu kutti, *Tam.*, Acacia Catechu, *Willd.*, LEGUMINOSÆ.
Foods .
Kashumba, *Tam.*, Carthamus tinctorius, *Linn.*, COMPOSITÆ.
Foods .
Kasi (white variety), *Naga Hills*, Coix lachryma, *Linn.*, GRAMINEÆ.
Foods .
Kasir, *Hind.*, *Pb.*, Cornus macrophylla, *Wall.*, CORNACEÆ.
Foods .

Kaskei, *Pb.*, Indigofera Dosua, *Ham.*, LEGUMINOSÆ.
Foods .
Kaskúsri, *Salt Range*, Grewia villosa, *Willd.*, TILIACEÆ.
Foods .
Kasmal, *Pb.*, Berberis aristata, *DC.*, and B. Lycium, *Royle*, BERBERIDEÆ.
Foods .
Kasni, *Hind.*, *Pers.*, *Pb.*, Cichorium Intybus, *Linn.*, COMPOSITÆ.
Foods .
Kaspat, *Pb.*, Dioscorea deltoides, *Wall.*, DIOSCOREACEÆ.
Foods .
Kaspat, *Pb.*, Fagopyrum esculentum, *Mœnch.*, POLYGONACEÆ.
Foods .
Kasrekan, *Nep.*, Ficus Roxburghii, *Wall.*, URTICACEÆ.
Foods .
Kasru, *Nep.*, Quercus semicarpifolia, *Smith*, CUPULIFERÆ.
Foods .
Kassaibija, *Bom.*, Coix lachryma, *Linn.*, GRAMINEÆ.
Foods .
Kassar, *N.-W. P.*, Lathyrus sativus, *Linn.*, LEGUMINOSÆ.
Foods .
Kassi, *Hind.*, Briedelia retusa, *Spreng.*, EUPHORBIACEÆ.
Foods .
Kastura benda, *Tam.*, Hibiscus Abelmoschus, *Linn.*, MALVACEÆ.
Foods .
Kasturi, *Hind.*, *Bom.*, Hibiscus Abelmoschus, *Linn.*, MALVACEÆ.
Foods .
Kasturi bendavittulu, *Tel.*, Hibiscus Abelmoschus, *Linn.*, MALVACEÆ.
Foods .
Kasturi, Kalla, *Hind.*, *Bom.*, Hibiscus Abelmoschus, *Linn.*, MALVACEÆ.
Foods .
Kasur, *Lepcha*, Saurauja napaulensis, *DC.*, TERNSTRŒMIACEÆ.
Foods .
Kasurio, *Hind.*, Scirpus Kysoor, *Roxb.*, CYPERACEÆ.
Foods .
Kat ambolam, *Mal.*, Spondias mangifera, *Pers.*, ANACARDIACEÆ.
Foods .
Kat illupi, *Tam.*, Bassia longifolia, *Willd.*, SAPOTACEÆ.
Foods .
Kat maá, *Tam.*, Buchanania latifolia, *Roxb.*, ANACARDIACEÆ.
Foods .
Kat-mara, *Tam.*, Spondias mangifera, *Pers.*, ANACARDIACEÆ.
Foods .
Katai, *Hind.*, Solanum xanthocarpum, *Schrad. & Wendl.*, SOLANACEÆ.
Foods .
Katakamee, *Tel.*, Strychnos potatorum *Linn f.*, LOGANIACEÆ.
Foods .
Kata-kelenga, *Tel.*, Dioscorea aculeata, *Roxb.*, DIOSCOREACEÆ.
Foods .
Kata-mita, *Pb.*, Rumex vesicarius, *Linn.*, POLYGONACEÆ.
Foods .
Katan, *Hind.*, Eriodendron anfractuosum, *DC.*, MALVACEÆ.
Foods .
Katar-kanda, *Pb.*, Astragalus multiceps, *Wall.*, LEGUMINOSÆ.
Foods .
Katbel, *Hind.*, Feronia Elephantum, *Correa.*, RUTACEÆ.
Foods .
Katber, *Hind.*, Zizyphus xylopyra, *Will.*, RHAMNEÆ.
Foods .
Katell, *Hind.*, Solanum xanthocarpum, *Schrad. & Wendl.*, SOLANACEÆ.
Foods .
Katerni, *Gond.*, Capparis horrida, *Linn.*, CAPPARIDEÆ.
Foods .

Katha, *Hind.*, Acacia Catechu, *Willd.*, LEGUMINOSÆ.
Foods .
Kath-bel, *Beng.*, Feronia Elephantum, *Correa.*, RUTACEÆ.
Foods .
Kathe kasturi, *Tam.*, Hibiscus Abelmoschus, *Linn.*, MALVACEÆ.
Foods .
Kathgular, *Pb.*, Ficus glomerata, *Roxb.*, URTICACEÆ.
Foods .
Katil, *Gond.*, Randia uliginosa, *DC.*, RUBIACEÆ.
Foods .
Katillipi, *Tam.*, Bassia latifolia, *Roxb.*, SAPOTACEÆ.
Foods .
Katnim, *Hind.*, Murraya Kœnigii, *Spr.*, RUTACEÆ.
Foods .
Katonda, *Pb.*, Viburnum cotinifolium, *Don.*, CAPRIFOLIACEÆ.
Foods .
Katoo-bala, *Mal.*, Canna indica, *Linn.*, SCITAMINEÆ.
Foods .
Katori, *Sind.*, Feronia Elephantum, *Correa.*, RUTACEÆ.
Foods .
Katrain, *Pb.*, Sageretia theezans, *Brongn.*, RHAMNEÆ.
Foods .
Kattáli, *Tam.*, Aloe vera, *Linn.*, LILIACEÆ.
Foods .
Kattang, *Hind.*, Bambusa arundinacea, *Retz.*, and other species, GRAMINEÆ. Foods .
Katthah, *Dec.*, Acacia Catechu, *Willd.*, LEGUMINOSÆ.
Foods .
Kattra, *Ass.*, Bauhinia malabarica, *Roxb.*, LEGUMINOSÆ.
Foods .
Kattu, *Tam.*, Terminalia belerica, *Roxb.*, COMBRETACEÆ.
Foods .
Kat turanji, *Tam.*, Albizzia stipulata, *Boivin.*, LEGUMINOSÆ.
Foods .
Katu, *Pb.*, Fagopyrum esculentum, *Mœnch.*, POLYGONACEÆ.
Foods .
Katu-imbúl, *Cingh.*, Bombax malabaricum, *DC.*, MALVACEÆ.
Foods .
Katu-katsjil, *Mal.*, Dioscorea bulbifera, *Linn.*, DIOSCOREACEÆ.
Foods .
Katul, *Hind.*, Randia uliginosa, *DC.*, RUBIACEÆ.
Foods .
Katur, *Lepcha*, Mangifera sylvatica, *Roxb.*, ANACARDIACEÆ.
Foods .
Kau, *Pb.*, *Hind.*, Olea cuspidata, *Royle*, OLEACEÆ.
Foods .
Kaula, *Nep.*, Ilex dipyrena, *Wall.*, ILICINEÆ.
Foods .
Kauni, *N.-W. P. & Oudh*, Setaria italica, *Kunth.*, GRAMINEÆ.
Foods .
Kaur, *Pb.*, Capparis spinosa, *Linn.*, CAPARIDEÆ.
Foods .
Kaúra, *Pb.*, Morus serrata, *Roxb.*, URTICACEÆ.
Foods .
Kauri, *N.-W. P. & Oudh*, Cyamopsis psoralioides, *DC.*, LEGUMINOSÆ.
Foods .
Kaurijal, *Pb.*, Salvodora persica, *Garcin.*, SALVADORACEÆ.
Foods .
Kaurio, *Panch Mehals*, Randia uliginosa, *DC.*, RUBIACEÆ.
Foods .
Kauri van, *Pb.*, Salvodora persica, *Garcin.*, SALVADORACEÆ.
Foods .

Kavatha, *Sind*, Feronia Elephantum, *Correa.*, RUTACEÆ.
Foods .
Kavika tree, *Eng.*, Engenia malaccensis, *Linn.*, MYRTACEÆ.
Foods .
Kawat, *Mahr.*, Lemonia acidissima, *Linn.*, RUTACEÆ.
Foods .
Kayaphala, *Bom.*, Myrica sapida, *Wall.*, MYRICACEÆ.
Foods .
Kayoung-wa, *Magh.*, Melocanna bambusoides, *Trin.*, GRAMINEÆ.
Foods .
Kayur, *Tam.*, Eleasine corucana, *Gærtn.*, GRAMINEÆ.
Foods .
Kazwan, *Burm.*, Ipomæa Batatas, *Lamk.*, CONVOLVULACEÆ.
Foods .
Keá, *Beng.*, Pandanus odoratissimus, *Willd.*, PANDANEÆ.
Foods .
Keá kholr, *Beng.*, Pandanus odoratissimus, *Willd.*, PANDANEÆ.
Foods .
Kechu, *Naga*, Dolichos Lablab, *Linn.*, LEGUMINOSÆ.
Foods .
Keharsu, *Pb.*, Quercus Ilex, *Linn.*, CUPULIFERÆ.
Foods .
Keint, *Pb.*, Pyrus Pashia, *Ham.*, ROSACEÆ.
Foods .
Kela, *Hind.*, *Bom.*, Musa sapientum, *Linn.*, SCITAMINEÆ.
Foods .
Kelangu, *Tam.*, Dancus Carota, *Linn.*, UMBELLIFERÆ.
Foods .
Kelu, *Him. name*, Cedrus Deodara, *Loudon*, CONIFERÆ.
Foods .
Kemá, *Naga*, Perilla ocimoide, *Linn.*, LABIATÆ.
Foods .
Kempu girus, *Kan.*, Anacardium occidentale, *Linn.*, ANACARDIACEÆ.
Foods .
Kemuka, *Bom.*, *Sans.*, Costus speciosus, *Sm.*, SCITAMINEÆ.
Foods .
Kenbwon, *Burm.*, Acacia concinna, *DC.*, LEGUMINOSÆ.
Foods .
Kend, *Beng.*, Diospyros melanoxylon, *Roxb.*, EBENACEÆ.
Foods .
Kendu, *Ass.*, Diospyros Embryopteris, *Pers.*, EBENACEÆ.
Foods .
Kendu, *Hind.*, Diospyros melanoxylon, *Roxb.*, EBENACEÆ.
Foods .
Kendu, *Pb.*, Diospyros tomentosa, *Roxb.*, EBENACEÆ.
Foods .
Keoli, *Him. name*, Cedrus Deodara, *Loudon*, CONIFERÆ.
Foods .
Kerasya, *Arab.*, Prunus Cerasus, *Linn.*, ROSACEÆ.
Foods .
Kerin, *Pb.*, Capparis aphylla, *Roth.*, CAPPARIDEÆ.
Foods .
Keshini, *Sans.*, Chrysopogon acicularis, *Retz.*, GRAMINEÆ.
Foods .
Kesun-ni, *Burm.*, Allium Cepa, *Linn.*, LILIACEÆ.
Foods .
Kesún-phiu, *Burm.*, Allium sativum, *Linn.*, LILIACEÆ.
Foods .
Kesur, *Beng.*, Scirpus Kysoor, *Roxb.*, CYPERACEÆ.
Foods .
Kesuri, *Beng.*, Scirpus Kysoor, *Roxb.*, CYPERACEÆ.
Foods .

Ketaki, *Sans.*, Pandanus odoratissimus, *Willd.*, PANDANEÆ.
Foods .
Keú, *Beng.*, *Hind.*, Costus speciosus, *Sm.*, SCITAMINEÆ.
Foods .
Keura, *Hind.*, Pandanus odoratissimus, *Willd.*, PANDANEÆ.
Foods .
Kewal, *N.-W. P.*, Panicum sanguinale, *Linn.*, GRAMINEÆ.
Foods .
Kewal, *N.-W. P.*, Panicum sanguinale, *Linn.*, var. ciliare, *Retz. sp.*, GRAMINEÆ. Foods .
Khabar, *Hind.*, Ficus virgata, *Roxb.*, URTICACEÆ.
Foods .
Khaderi, *Bom.*, Acacia Catechu, *Willd.*, LEGUMINOSÆ.
Foods .
Khadir, *Sans.*, Acacia Catechu, *Willd.*, LEGUMINOSÆ.
Foods .
Khair, *Hind.*, Acacia Catechu, *Willd.*, LEGUMINOSÆ.
Foods .
Khaira, *Bom.*, Acacia Catechu, *Willd.*, LEGUMINOSÆ.
Foods .
Khairwál, *Hind.*, Bauhinia variegata, *Linn.*, LEGUMINOSÆ.
Foods .
Khaja, *Hind.*, Briedelia montana, *Willd.*, EUPHORBIACEÆ.
Foods .
Khaja, *Hind.*, Bredelia retusa, *Spreng.*, EUPHORBIACEÆ.
Foods .
Khaji, *Hind.*, Phœnix dactylifera, *Linn.*, PALMÆ.
Foods .
Khaji, *Hind.*, Phœnix sylvestris, *Roxb.*, PALMÆ.
Foods .
Khajur, *Hind.*, Phœnix dactylifera, *Linn.*, PALMÆ.
Foods .
Khajur, *Hind.*, Phœnix sylvestris, *Roxb.*, PALMÆ.
Foods .
Khajur, Jangli, *Hind.*, Phœnix acaulis, *Roxb.*, PALMÆ.
Foods .
Khajuri, *Hind.*, Phœnix acaulis, *Roxb.*, PALMÆ.
Foods .
Khámbúr, *Afg.*, *Bazar name,* Agaricus campestris, *Linn.*, FUNGI.
Foods .
Khamrak, *Dec.*, Averrhoa Carambola, *Linn.*, GERANIACEÆ.
Foods .
Kha-maraka, *Bom.*, Averrhoa Carambola, *Linn.*, GERANIACEÆ.
Foods .
Khan, *Sind,* Saccharum spontaneum, *Linn.*, GRAMINEÆ.
Foods .
Khanijira, *Pb.*, Withania coagulans, *Dun.*, SOLANACEÆ.
Foods .
Khanna, *Pb.*, Ephedra Gerardiana, *Wall.*, GNETACEÆ.
Foods .
Khar, *Pb.*, Caroxylon Griffithii, *Moq.*, CHENOPODIACEÆ.
Foods .
Khar, *Pb.*, Prosopis spicigera, *Linn.*, LEGUMINOSÆ.
Foods .
Kharabúja, *Bom.*, Cucumis Melo, *Linn.*, CUCURBITACEÆ.
Foods .
Kharál, *Pb.*, Celastrus senegalensis, *Lam.*, CELASTRINEÆ.
Foods .
Kharak, *Simla,* Celtis australis, *Linn.*, URTICACEÆ.
Foods .
Kharawune, *Pb.*, Solanum verbascifolium, *Linn.*, SOLANACEÆ.
Foods .

Kharbúj, *N.-W. P.*, Curcurbita moschata, *Duchesne*, CUCURBITACEÆ.
Foods .
Kharbúja, *Hind.*, Cucumis Melo, *Linn.*, CUCURBITACEÆ.
Foods .
Khareza, *Pb.*, Carthamus oxyacantha, *Bieb.*, COMPOSITÆ.
Foods .
Kharmo, *Pb.*, Lonicera hypoleuca, *Dne.*, CAPRIFOLIACEÆ.
Foods .
Kharmuch, *Kashmir*, Rubus lasiocarpus, *Smith*, ROSACEÆ.
Foods .
Kharmuj, *Beng.*, Cucumis Melo, *Linn.*, CUCURBITACEÆ.
Foods .
Kharnub-nubti, *Pb.*, Ceratonia Siliqua, *L.*, LEGUMINOSÆ.
Foods .
Kharpat, *Beng.*, *Pb.*, Garuga pinnata, *Roxb.*, BURSERACEÆ.
Foods .
Khar-usara-ghas, *N.-W. P.*, Sporobolus tenacissimus, *Beauv.*, GRAMINEÆ.
Foods .
Kharwala, *Pb.*, Salix alba, *Linn.*, SALICINEÆ.
Foods .
Khas-khas (the root), *Beng.*, *Hind.*, Andropogon muricatus, *Retz.*, GRAMINEÆ. Foods .
Khash-khash-ka-post, *Dec.*, Papaver somniferum, *Linn.*, PAPAVRACEÆ.
Foods .
Khatál, *Pb.*, Flacourtia Sepiaria, *Pb.*, BIXINEÆ.
Foods .
Khatta-mitha, *Pb.*, Oxalis corniculata, *Linn.*, GERANIACEÆ.
Foods .
Khau, *Sind*, Olea cuspidata, *Royle*, OLEACEÆ.
Foods .
Khawe, Mulgedium tartaricum, *DC.*, COMPOSITÆ.
Foods .
Khawi, *Pb.*, Andropogon laniger, *Desf.*, GRAMINEÆ.
Foods .
Khaya, *Burm.*, Mimusops Elengi, *Linn.*, SAPOTACEÆ.
Foods .
Khayer, *Beng.*, Acacia Catechu, *Willd.*, LEGUMINOSÆ.
Foods .
Khejjur-rus, *Beng.*, Phœnix sylvestris, *Roxb.*, PALMÆ.
Foods .
Khejoor, *Beng.*, Phœnix sylvestris, *Roxb.*, PALMÆ.
Foods .
Khelaa, *Gond.*, Grewia tiliæfolia, *Vahl.*, TILIACEÆ.
Foods .
Khenti, *Pb.*, Indigofera Dosua, *Ham.*, LEGUMINOSÆ.
Foods .
Khesari, *Beng.*, Lathyrus sativus, *Linn.*, LEGUMINOSÆ.
Foods .
Khetimal, *Pb.*, Rumex hastatus, *Don.*, POLYGONACEÆ.
Foods .
Khetiya, *Hind.*, Brassica campestris, *Linn.*, var. Napus, sub var. toria, CRUCIFERÆ. Foods .
Khewnau, *Hind.*, Ficus Cunia, *Buch.*, URTICACEÆ.
Foods .
Khijra, *Rajputana*, Prosopis spicigera, *Linn.*, LEGUMINOSÆ.
Foods .
Khip, *Delhi*, Orthanthera viminea, *Wight*, ASCLEPIADEÆ.
Foods .
Khir, *Hind.*, Mimusops hexandra, *Roxb.*, SAPOTACEÆ.
Foods .
Khira, *Bom.*, *Hind.*, Cucumis sativus, *Linn.*, CUCURBITACEÆ.
Foods .

Khirdab, *Arab.*, Brassica nigra, *Koch.*, CRUCIFERÆ.
Foods .
Khirni, *Hind.*, Mimusops hexandra, *Roxb.*, SAPOTACEÆ.
Foods .
Khoda Millet, *Eng.*, Paspalum scrobiculatum, *Linn.*, GRAMINEÆ.
Foods .
Khoira, *Ass.*, Acacia Catechu, *Willd.*, LEGUMINOSÆ.
Foods .
Khoridjhar, *Sind*, Salvadora persica, *Garcin.*, SALVADORACEÆ.
Foods .
Khoriru, *Uriya*, Acacia Catechu, *Willd.*, LEGUMINOSÆ.
Foods .
Khoskadu-mar, *Ass.*, Ficus hispida, *Linn. f.*, URTICACEÆ.
Foods .
Khubani, *Hind.*, Prunus armeniaca, *Linn.*, ROSACEÆ.
Foods .
Khulen, *Pb.*, Ulmus integrifolia, *Roxb.*, URTICACEÆ.
Foods .
Khulti, *N.-W. P. & Oudh*, Cyamopsis psoralioides, *DC.*, LEGUMINOSÆ.
Foods .
Rhum, *Pb.*, Lonicera quinquelocularis, *Hardwicke*, CAPRIFOLIACEÆ.
Foods .
Khumb (plains), *Pb.*, Morchella semilibera, *L.*, FUNGI.
Foods .
Khúmbah, *Bom.*, *Afg.*, *Bazar name*, Agaricus campestris, *Linn.*, FUNGI.
Foods .
Khumbi, *Hind.*, Careya arborea, *Roxb.*, MYRTACEÆ.
Foods .
Khurbuj, *Hind.*, Cucumis Melo, *Linn.*, CUCURBITACEÆ.
Foods .
Khurhur, *Hind.*, Ficus Cunia, *Buch.*, URTICACEÆ.
Foods .
Khuri, *Beng.*, Saccharum fuscum, *Roxb.*, GRAMINEÆ.
Foods .
Khurti, *N.-W. P. & Oudh*, Cyamopsis psoralioides, *DC.*, LEGUMINOSÆ.
Foods .
Khus-khus, *Eng.*, Andropogon muricatus, *Retz.*, GRAMINEÆ.
Foods .
Khwan, *Trans-Indus*, Olea cuspidata, *Royle*, OLEACEÆ.
Foods .
Khyar, *Pers.*, Cucumis sativus, *Linn.*, CUCURBITACEÆ.
Foods .
Kiakra, *Gond.*, Odina Wodier, *Roxb.*, ANACARDIACEÆ.
Foods .
Kiamil, *Hind.*, Odina Wodier, *Roxb.*, ANACARDIACEÆ.
Foods .
Kiamoni, *Nep.*, Eugenia obovata, *Wall.*, MYRTACEÆ.
Foods .
Kiár, *Pb.*, Cassia Fistula, *Linn.*, LEGUMINOSÆ.
Foods . .
Kiari, *Pb.*, Capparis spinosa, *Linn.*, CAPPARIDEÆ.
Foods .
Kiditsai, *Chinese*, Brassica nigra, *Koch.*, CRUCIFERÆ.
Foods .
Kidney, *Eng.*, Phaseolus vulgaris, *Linn.*, LEGUMINOSÆ.
Foods .
Kiery, *South India*, Amarantus frumentaceus, *Buch.*, AMARANTACEÆ.
Foods .
Kikar, *Hind.*, *Beng.*, *Dec.*, Acacia arabica, *Willd.*, LEGUMINOSÆ.
Foods .
Kikar, *Pb.*, Acacia Jacquemontii, *Benth.*, LEGUMINOSÆ.
Foods .

Kiker safed, *Hind.*, Acacia leucophlæa, *Willd.*, LEGUMINOSÆ.
Foods .
Kilar, *Him. name*, Cedrus Deodara, *London*, CONIFERÆ.
Foods .
Killo-debdhaor, *Beng.*, Sorghum bicolor, *Willd.*, GRAMINEÆ.
Foods .
Kilmara, *Kumaun*, Berberis asiatica, *Roxb.*, BERBERIDEÆ.
Foods .
Kilmich, *Kashmir*, Viburnum fœtens, *Decaisne*, CAPRIFOLIACEÆ.
Foods .
Kilmira, *Pb.*, Garuga pinnata, *Roxb.*, BURSERACEÆ.
Foods .
Kilonj, *N.-W. P.*, Quercus dilatata, *Lindl.*, CUPULIFERÆ.
Foods .
Kilpattar, *Pb.*, Acer cultratum, *Wall.*, syn. of Acer pictum, *Thunb.*, SAPINDACEÆ. Foods .
Kilu, *Kumaun*, Acer pictum, *Thunb.*, SAPINDACEÆ.
Foods .
Kilut, *Hind.*, Saccharum fuscum, *Roxb.*, GRAMINEÆ.
Foods .
Kimbu, *Nep.*, Morus cuspidata, *Wall.*, URTICACEÆ.
Foods .
Kimbu, *Nep.*, Morus indica, *Linn.*, URTICACEÆ.
Foods .
Kimpa-lin, *Burm.*, Antidesma diandrum, *Tulasn.*, EUPHORBIACEÆ.
Foods .
Kimri, *Pb.*, Ficus Carica, *Linn.*, URTICACEÆ.
Foods .
Kimu, *Hind.*, Morus serrata, *Roxb.*, URTICACEÆ.
Foods .
Kimúl, *Hind.*, Odina Wodier, *Roxb.*, ANACARDIACEÆ.
Foods .
Kindyba, *Arab.*, Cichorium Intybus, *Linn.*, COMPOSITÆ.
Foods .
Kingaro, *Pb.*, Flacourtia sepiaria, *Roxb.*, BIXINEÆ.
Foods .
Kinnee, *Pb.*, Diospyros tomentosa, *Roxb.*, EBENACEÆ.
Foods .
Kin-pa-lin, *Burm.*, Antidesma Menasu, *Müll.-Arg.*, EUPHORBIACEÆ.
Foods .
Kinsuka, *Sans.*, Butea frondosa, *Roxb.*, LEGUMINOSÆ.
Foods .
Kip, *Sind*, Orthanthera viminea, *Wight*, ASCLEPIADEÆ.
Foods .
Kiramber, *Tam.*, Caryophyllus aromaticus, *Linn.*, MYRTACEÆ.
Foods .
Kiran, *Sind*, Securinega Leucopyrus, *Müll.-Arg.*, EUPHORBIACEÆ.
Foods .
Kirara, *Pb.*, Momordica dioica, *Roxb.*, CUCURBITACEÆ.
Foods .
Kirkiria, *Hind.*, Cinnamomum Tamala, *Nees.*, LAURINEÆ.
Foods .
Kirmira, *Bom.*, Glycosmis pentaphylla, *Correa.*, RUTACEÆ.
Foods .
Kirneli, *Mysore*, Phyllanthus distichus, *Müll.-Arg.*, EUPHORBIACEÆ.
Foods .
Kirra, *Pb.*, Capparis aphylla, *Roth.*, CAPPARIDEÆ.
Foods .
Kirui, *Beng.*, Oxystelma esculentum, *Br.*, ASCLEPIADEÆ.
Foods .
Kismis, *Beng.*, Vitis vinifera, *Linn.*, AMPELIDEÆ.
Foods .

Kissl, *Nep.*, Berberis asitica, *Roxb.*, BERBERIDEÆ.
Foods .
Kitchli, *Tam.*, Citrus Aurantium, *Linn.*, RUTACEÆ.
Foods .
Kithi, *Pb.*, Dioscorea deltoides, *Wall.*, DIOSCOREACEÆ.
Foods .
Kitoli, *N.-W. P.*, Cassia Fistula, *Linn.*, LEGUMINOSÆ.
Foods .
Kittali, *Tel.*, Citrus Aurantium, *Linn.*, RUTACEÆ.
Foods .
Kitwali, *N.-W. P.*, Cassia Fistula, *Linn.*, LEGUMINOSÆ.
Foods .
Knlss, *Pb.*, Dioscorea deltoides, *Wall.*, DIOSCOREACEÆ.
Foods .
Ko, *Pb.*, Olea cuspidata, *Royle*, OLEACEÆ.
Foods .
Kobh, **Robi**, *Eng.*, Brassica (oleracea), caulo-rapa, *Linn.*, CRUCIFERÆ.
Foods .
Kobusi, *Nep.*, Myrica sapida, *Wall.*, MYRICACEÆ.
Foods .
Kochi, *Hind.*, Acacia concinna, *DC.*, LEGUMINOSÆ.
Foods .
Koda, *Hind.*, Ehretia lævis, *Roxb.*, BORAGINEÆ.
Foods .
Koda, *Him. name*, Eleusine corocana, *Gærtn.*, GRAMINEÆ.
Foods .
Koda, *N.-W. P. & Oudh*, *Beng.*, Paspalum scrobiculatum, *Linn.*, GRAMINEÆ. Foods .
Koda-ka-choul, *Hind.*, Paspalum scrobiculatum, *Linn.*, GRAMINEÆ.
Foods .
Kodarsi, *Mar.*, Securinega obovata, *Müll.*, EUPHORBIACEÆ.
Foods .
Kodi mun-dirrippa-zham, *Tam.*, Vitis vinifera, *Linn.*, AMPELIDEÆ.
Foods .
Kodoga-pala, *Tel.*, Holarrhena antidysenterica, *Wall.*, APOCYNACEÆ.
Foods .
Kodon, *N.-W. P. & Oudh*, *Pb.*, Pospalum scrobiculatum, *Linn.*, GRAMINEÆ. Foods .
Kodra, *Pb.*, Paspalum scrobiculatum, *Linn.*, GRAMINEÆ.
Foods .
Kodram, *N.-W. P. & Oudh*, Paspalum scrobiculatum, *Linn.*, GRAMINEÆ.
Foods .
Kodruva, *Sans.*, Paspalum scrobiculatum, *Linn.*, GRAMINEÆ.
Foods .
Kodu, *Beng.*, Lagenaria vulgaris, *Seringe.*, CUCURBITACEÆ.
Foods .
Kodu, *Hind.*, Paspalum scrobiculatum, *Linn.*, var. Fluitans, *Duthie*, GRAMINEÆ. Foods .
Kohen, *Pb.*, Edwardsia Hydaspica, *Edge.*, LEGUMINOSÆ.
Foods .
Kohlrapsaat, *Ger.*, Brassica campestris, *Linn.*, var. Napus, CRUCIFERÆ.
Foods .
Kohú, *Pb.*, Olea cuspidata, *Royle*, OLEACEÆ.
Foods .
Kohumba, *Gus.*, Melia Azadirachta, *Linn.*, MELIACEÆ.
Foods .
Koi, *Hind.*, Nymphæa Lotus, *Linn.*, NYMPHÆACEÆ.
Foods .
Koir, *Ass.*, Acacia Catechu, *Willd.*, LEGUMINOSÆ.
Foods .
Koki, *Tam.*, Cassia Fistula, *Linn.*, LEGUMINOSÆ.
Foods .

Koko-aru, *Beng.*, Olax scandens, *Roxb.*, OLACINEÆ.
Foods .
Kokoh, *Burm.*, Albizzia Lebbek, *Benth.*, LEGUMINOSÆ.
Foods .
Koku, *Hind.*, *Pb.*, *Tam.*, Salvadora oleoides, *Linn.*, SALVADORACEÆ.
Foods .
Kokum, *Bom.*, Garcinia indica, *Choisy.*, GUTTIFERÆ.
Foods .
Kokwa, *Beng.*, Dendrocalamus Hamiltonii, *Nees. & Arn*, GRAMINEÆ.
Foods .
Koli, *Kan.*, Baccaurea sapida, *Müll.-Arg.*, EUPHORBIACEÆ.
Foods .
Kollár, *Hind.*, Bauhinia variegata, *Linn.*, LEGUMINOSÆ.
Foods .
Kollu, *Tam.*, Dolichos biflorus, *Linn.*, LEGUMINOSÆ.
Foods .
Kolt, *Pb.*, Dolichos biflorus, *Linn.*, LEGUMINOSÆ.
Foods .
Komári, *Dec.*, Aloe vera, *Linn.*, LILIACEÆ.
Foods .
Konda-cahinda, *Tel.*, Toddalia aculeata, *Pers.*, RUTACEÆ.
Foods .
Kondai, *Hind.*, Flacourtia sepiaria, *Roxb.*, BIXINEÆ.
Foods .
Konda-pulla, *South India*, Chloris barbata, *Swartz.*, GRAMINEÆ.
Foods .
Kone, *Tam.*, Cassia Fistula, *Linn.*, LEGUMINOSÆ.
Foods .
Konea doombur, Ficus hispida, *Linn. f.*, URTICACEÆ.
Foods .
Kongki, *Lepcha*, Prunus Puddum, *Roxb.*, ROSACEÆ.
Foods .
Kongnyin-nway, *Burm.*, Entada scandens, *Bth.*, LEGUMINOSÆ.
Foods .
Kooli-begoon, *Beng.*, Solanum melongena, *Linn.*, SOLANACEÆ.
Foods .
Kooltee, *Eng.*, Dolichos biflorus, *Linn.*, LEGUMINOSÆ.
Foods .
Koolutha, *Sans.*, Dolichos biflorus, *Linn.*, LEGUMINOSÆ.
Foods .
Koosa, *Eng.*, Andropogon muricatus, *Retz.*, GRAMINEÆ.
Foods .
Koosumbia, *Eng.*, Schleichera trijuga, *Willd.*, SAPINDACEÆ.
Foods .
Kootta chirchitta, *N.-W. P.*, Setaria verticillata, *Beauv.*, GRAMINEÆ.
Foods .
Kopar, *Hind.*, Dendrocalamus strictus, *Nees.*, GRAMINEÆ.
Foods .
Kora-kand (the plant), *Dec.*, Aloe vera, *Linn.*, LILIACEÆ.
Foods .
Korakanda, *Sind*, Aloe vera, *Linn.*, LILIACEÆ.
Foods .
Korake, *Pb.*, Atriplex hortensis, *L.*, and A. laciniata, *L.*, CHENOPODIACEÆ
Foods .
Kora-phad, *Sind*, Aloe vera, *Linn.*, LILIACEÆ.
Foods .
Koray, *Tam.*, Cyperus rotundus, *Linn.*, CYPERACEÆ.
Foods .
Korchi, *Gond.*, Securinega obovata, *Müll.*, EUPHORBIACEÆ.
Foods .
Kore-ke-jhár, *Dec.*, Cyperus rotundus, *Linn.*, CYPERACEÆ.
Foods .

Korna-nebu, *Beng.*, Citrus medica, *Linn.*, RUTACEÆ.
Foods .
Koroh, *Oudh*, Shorea robusta, *Gærtn.*, DIPTEROCARPEÆ.
Foods .
Korudoosha, *Sans.*, Paspalum scrobiculatum, *Linn.*, GRAMINEÆ.
Foods .
Kosa, *Hind.*, Saccharum spontaneum, *Linn.*, GRAMINEÆ.
Foods .
Kosi, *Uriya*, Briedelia retusa, *Spreng.*, EUPHORBIACEÆ.
Foods .
Kosum, *Hind.*, Schleichera trijuga, *Willd.*, SAPINDACEÆ.
Foods .
Kosúndra, *Pb.*, Bauhinia racemosa, *Lam.*, LEGUMINOSÆ.
Foods .
Kotaku, *Uriya*, Strychnos potatorum, *Linn. f.*, LOGANIACEÆ.
Foods .
Kotamalli, *Tam.*, Coriandrum sativum, *Linn.*, UMBELLIFERÆ.
Foods .
Kotanpan, *Mal.*, Triticum sativum, *Lam.*, GRAMINEÆ.
Foods .
Kottai, *Tam.*, Anacardium occidentale, *Linn.*, ANACARDIACEÆ.
Foods .
Kottai pakka, *Tam.*, Areca Catechu, *Linn.*, PALMÆ.
Foods .
Kotúr, *Nep.*, Castanopsis tribuloides, *A. DC.*, CUPULIFERÆ.
Foods .
Kovariya, *Bom.*, Cassia Tora, *Linn.*, LEGUMINOSÆ.
Foods .
Kowal, *Lepcha*, Juglans regia, *Linn.*, JUGLANDEÆ.
Foods .
Kraunti, *Pb.*, Lonicera quinquelocularis, *Hardwicke*, CAPRIFOLIACEÆ.
Foods .
Kreu, *Pb.*, Quercus semicarpifolia, *Smith*, CUPULIFERÆ.
Foods .
Krish, Abrus precatorius, *Linn.*, LEGUMINOSÆ.
Foods .
Krishna-tamarah, *Tel.*, Canna indica, *Linn.*, SCITAMINEÆ.
Foods .
Krumbal, *Pb.*, Ficus glomerata, *Roxb.*, URTICACEÆ.
Foods .
Krunda, *Sind*, Tribulus alatus, *Delile.*, ZYGOPHYLLEÆ.
Foods .
Kuchni, *Pb.*, Rhamnus persicus, *Boiss.*, RHAMNEÆ.
Foods .
Kudaka, *Bom.*, Cedrela Toona, *Roxb.*, MELIACEÆ.
Foods .
Kudhá, *Naga Hills*, Coix lachryma, *Linn.*, GRAMINEÆ.
Foods .
Kudira-pullu, *Mal.*, Chrysopogon acicularis, *Retz.*, GRAMINEÆ.
Foods .
Kudoly, *Kan.*, Cicer arietinum, *Linn.*, LEGUMINOSÆ.
Foods .
Kudsumbal Lal, *Hind.*, Canavalia ensiformis, *DC.*, LEGUMINOSÆ.
Foods .
Kudsumbal, Suffed, *Hind.*, Canavalia ensiformis, *DC.*, LEGUMINOSÆ.
Foods .
Kúkadi, *Bom.*, Cucumis Melo, *Linn.*, var. utilissimus. (sp. *Roxb.*)., CUCURBITACEÆ. Foods .
Kúkai, *Pb.*, Flacourtia Ramontchi, *L'Herit.*, BIXINEÆ.
Foods .
Kukai, *Pb.*, Rhamnus persicus, *Boiss.*, RHAMNEÆ.
Foods .

Kaka-pal-kura, *Tel.*, Trianthema crystallina, *Vahl.*, FICOIDEÆ.
Foods .
Kukar, *C. P.*, Garuga pinnata, *Roxb.*, BURSERACEÆ.
Foods .
Kuki, *Kan.*, Baccaurea sapida, *Müll.-Arg.*, EUPHORBIACEÆ.
Foods .
Kukni, *N.-W. P. & Oudh*, Setaria italica, *Kunth.*, GRAMINEÆ.
Foods .
Kukoa, *Pb.*, Flacourtia Ramontchi, *L'Herit.*, BIXINEÆ.
Foods .
Kukri, *Hind.*, Zea Mays, *Linn.*, GRAMINEÆ.
Foods .
Kukuluya, *Hind.*, Ribes glaciale, *Wall.*, SAXIFRAGACEÆ.
Foods .
Kúkúrkat, *Hind.*, Hymenodictyon excelsum, *Wall.*, RUBIACEÆ.
Foods .
Kúl, *Hind.*, *Beng.*, Zizyphus Jujuba, *Lam.*, RHAMNEÆ.
Foods .
Kula-aja, *Beng.*, Ehretia acuminata, *Br.*, BORAGINEÆ.
Foods .
Kulai batana, *N.-W. P.*, Pisum arvense, *Linn.*, LEGUMINOSÆ.
Foods .
Kulara, *Kashmir*, Viburnum fœtens, *Decaisne*, CAPRIFOLIACEÆ.
Foods .
Kúlat, *Pb.*, Dolichos biflorus, *Linn.*, LEGUMINOSÆ.
Foods .
Kulitba gaglip, *Sind*, Dolichos biflorus, *Linn.*, LEGUMINOSÆ
Foods .
Kulith, *Deccan*, Dolichos biflorus, *Linn.*, LEGUMINOSÆ.
Foods .
Kuljud, *Hind.*, Avena fatua, *Linn.*, GRAMINEÆ.
Foods .
Kulla, *Sans.*, Amorphophallus campanulatus, *Blume.*, AROIDEÆ.
Foods .
Kullooa (pale var.), *Beng.*, Saccharum officinarum, *Linn.*, GRAMINEÆ.
Foods .
Kullvalei-mani, *Tam.*, Canna indica, *Linn.*, SCITAMINEÆ,
Foods
Kult, *Pb.*, Dolichos biflorus, *Linn.*, LEGUMINOSÆ.
Foods .
Kulthi gahat, *Hind.*, Dolichos biflorus, *Linn.*, LEGUMINOSÆ.
Foods .
Kúlú, *Hind.*, Sterculia urens, *Roxb.*, STERCULIACEÆ.
Foods .
Kumári, *Hind.* Aloe vera, *Linn.*, LILIACEÆ.
Foods .
Kumari, *Hind.*, Aloe vera, *Linn.*, var. officinalis, sp. *Forsk.*, LILIACEÆ.
Foods .
Kumbal, *Bom.*, Gnetum scandens, *Roxb.*, GNETACEÆ.
Foods .
Kúmbh samarogh (Stewart), Agaricus campestris, *Linn.*, FUNGI.
Foods .
Kumbi, *Hind.*, Careya arborea, *Roxb.*, MYRTACEÆ.
Foods .
Kumbi, *Pb.*, Cordia vestita, *H. f. & T.*, BORAGINEÆ.
Foods .
Kúmbúk, *Cingh.*, Terminalia tomentosa, *W. & A.*, COMBRETACEÆ.
Foods .
Kumbull, *Tam.*, Benincasa cerifera, *Savi*, CUCURBITACEÆ.
Foods .
Kumbyúng, *Lepcha*, Antidesma Menasu, *Müll.-Arg.*, EUPHORBIACEÆ.
Foods .

Kumrá, *Beng.*, Benincasa cerifera, *Savi*, CUCURBITACEÆ.
Foods .
Kumra, *N.-W. P.*, Cucurbita moschata, *Duchesne*, CUCURBITACEÆ.
Foods .
Kumra, *Beng.*, *Hind.*, Cucurbita Pepo, *DC.*, CUCURBITACEÆ.
Foods .
Kúmara konda, *Beng.*, *Hind.*, Cucurbita Pepo, *DC.*, CUCURBITACEÆ.
Foods .
Kumuda, *Sans.*, Nymphæa Lotus, *Linn.*, NYMPHÆACEÆ.
Foods .
Kun, *Pb.*, Edwardsia Hydaspica, *Edge.*, LEGUMINOSÆ.
Foods .
Kunachi, *Pb.*, Rubus ellipticus, *Smith*, ROSACEÆ.
Foods .
Kunch, *Beng.*, Abrus precatorius, *Linn.*, LEGUMINOSÆ.
Foods .
Kunch, *Beng.*, Coix lachryma, *Linn.*, GRAMINEÆ.
Foods .
Kunda, *Sans.*, Amorphophallus campanulatus, *Blume.*, AROIDEÆ.
Foods .
Kundanuga, *Tel.*, Lagenaria vulgaris, *Seringe.*, CUCURBITACEÆ.
Foods .
Kundar, *Pb.*, Typha angustifolia, *Linn.*, TYPHACEÆ.
Foods .
Kundayee, *Hind.*, *Dec.*, Flacourtia Ramontchi, *L'Herit.*, BIXINEÆ.
Foods .
Kundoung, *Lepcha*, Ficus Roxburghii, *Wall.*, URTICACEÆ.
Foods .
Kundru, *Pb.*, Cephalandra indica, *Nand.*, CUCURBITACEÆ.
Foods .
Kungu, *Sans.*, Setaria italica, *Kunth.*, GRAMINEÆ.
Foods .
Kuni, *N.-W. P.*, Panicum helopus, *Trin.*, var. hirsutum, sp. *Koen.*, GRAMINEÆ. Foods .
Kunla, *Kumaun*, Ficus Cunia, *Buch.*, URTICACEÆ.
Foods .
Kúnj, *Hind.*, Ulmus integrifolia, *Roxb.*, URTICACEÆ.
Foods .
Kúnsh, *Pb.*, Alnus nitada, *Endl.*, CUPULIFERÆ.
Foods .
Kunsung, *Lepcha*, Grewia vestita, *Wall.*, TILIACEÆ.
Foods .
Kuntan, *Hind.*, Eriodendron anfractuosum, *DC.*, MALVACEÆ.
Foods .
Kurál, *Hind.*, Bauhinia, variegata, *Linn.*, LEGUMINOSÆ.
Foods .
Kurankusha, *Beng.*, *Hind.*, Andropogon laniger, *Desf.*, GRAMINEÆ.
Foods .
Kurasani-vaman, *Tel.*, Hyoscyamus niger, *Linn.*, SOLANACEÆ.
Foods .
Kurashani-yoman, *Tam.*, Hyoscyamus niger, *Linn.*, SOLANACEÆ.
Foods .
Kurí, *Pb.*, Hedera Helix, *Linn.*, ARALIACEÆ.
Foods .
Kuri, *N-W. P.*, Panicum milliaceum, *Linn.*, GRAMINEÆ.
Foods .
Kurkan, *Pb.*, Pennisetum cenchroides, *Rich.*, GRAMINEÆ.
Foods .
Kurku, *Tam.*, Ficus infectoria, *Wall.*, URTICACEÆ.
Foods .
Kurkul, *Pb.*, Marlea begoniæfolia, *Roxb.*, CORNACEÆ.
Foods .

Karkuna, *Hind.*, Ehretia acuminata, *Br.*, BORAGINEÆ.
Foods .
Kurpa, *Bom.*, Memecylon edule, *Roxb.*, MELASTROMACEÆ.
Foods .
Kurpodur, *Tel.*, Olax scandens, *Roxb.*, OLACINEÆ.
Foods .
Kursah, *Pers.*, Apium graveolens, *Linn.*, UMBELLIFERÆ.
Foods .
Kurse, *Gond.*, Gmelina arborea, *Roxb.*, VERBENACEÆ.
Foods .
Kursl, *Seoni*, Wendlandia exserta, *DC.*, RUBIACEÆ.
Foods .
Kurtam ussul, *Arab.*, Gossypium herbaceum, *Linn.*, MALVACEÆ.
Foods .
Kurti-kalai, *Beng.*, Dolichos biflorus *Linn.*, LEGUMINOSÆ.
Foods .
Kurtoli, *Bom.*, Momordica dioica, *Roxb.*, CUCURBITACEÆ.
Foods .
Kuru, *N.-W. P.*, Panicum helopus, *Trin.*, var. hirsutum, sp. *Koen.*, GRAMINEÆ. Foods .
Kuru, *Kashmir*, Villarsia nymphoides, *Vent.*, GENTIANACEÆ.
Foods .
Kur-undu, *Cingh.*, Cinnamomum zeylanicum, *Breyn.*, LAURINEÆ.
Foods .
Kus, *Hind.*, Saccharum spontaneum, *Linn.*, GRAMINEÆ.
Foods .
Kusa, *Pb.*, Eragrostis cynosuroides, *Retz.*, GRAMINEÆ.
Foods .
Kusa, *N.-W. P.*, Pennisetum cenchroides, *Rich.*, GRAMINEÆ.
Foods .
Kush, *Pb.*, Prunus armeniaca, *Linn*, ROSACEÆ.
Foods .
Kusha, *Beng.*, *Sans.*, Eragrostis cynosuroides, *Retz.*, GRAMINEÆ.
Foods .
Kushiar, *Beng.*, Saccharum officinarum, *Linn.*, GRAMINEÆ.
Foods .
Kushmánda, *Sans.*, Benincasa, cerifera, *Savi*, CUCURBITACEÆ.
Foods .
Kushu, *Ladak*, Pyrus Malus, *Linn.*, ROSACEÆ.
Foods .
Kusi. *Hind.*, Briedelia, montana, *Willd.*, EUPHORBIACEÆ.
Foods .
Kusinb, *Bom.*, Schleichera trijuga, *Willd.*, SAPINDACEÆ.
Foods .
Kust, *Beng.*, *Hind.*, Costus speciosus, *Sm.*, SCITAMINEÆ.
Foods .
Kusum, *Beng.*, *Hind.*, *Dec.*, Carthamus tinctorius, *Linn.*, COMPOSITÆ.
Foods .
Kutha, *Sans.*, Eragrostis cynosuroides, *Retz*, GRAMINEÆ.
Foods .
Kútilál, *Pb.*, Daphne mucronata, *Royle*, THYMELÆACEÆ.
Foods .
Kutki, *Hind.*, Panicum miliare, *Lamb.*, GRAMINEÆ.
Foods .
Kutki, *N.-W. P.*, Panicum psilopodium, *Trin.*, GRAMINEÆ.
Foods .
Kútla, *Hind.*, Citrus medica, *Linn.*, RUTACEÆ.
Foods .
Kutonj, *Kumaun*, Castanopsis tribuloides, *A. DC.*, CUPULIFERÆ.
Foods .
Kuttalay, *Tam.*, Aloe vera, *Linn.*, var. officinalis, sp., *Forsk.*, LILIACEÆ.
Foods .

Kuwára, *N.-W. P. & Oudh*, Cyamopsis psoralioides, *DC.*, LEGUMINOSÆ.
Foods .
Kwam-thee-beng, *Burm.*, Areca Catechu, *Linn.*, PALMÆ.
Foods .
Kwaytanyeng, *Burm.*, Pithecolobium dulce, *Benth.*, LEGUMINOSÆ.
Foods .
Kwyun, *Burm.*, Areca Catechu, *Linn.*, PALMÆ.
Foods .
Kyaka-twa, *Burm.*, Bambusa arundinacea, *Retz.*, and other species, GRAMINEÆ. Foods .
Kyansa, *Burm.*, Castanopsis tribuloides, *A. DC.*, CUPULIFERÆ.
Foods .
Kyetmouk, *Burm.*, Nephelium Longana, *Camb.*, SAPINDACEÆ.
Foods .
Kyetsu, *Burm.*, Ricinus communis, *Linn.*, EUPHORBIACEÆ.
Foods .
Ky-et-thwon-ni, *Burm.*, Allium Cepa, *Linn.*, LILIACEÆ.
Foods .
Kyet-thwonpen, *Burm.*, Allium sativum, *Linn.*, LILIACEÆ.
Foods .
Kyon, *Beng.*, Diospyros Melanoxylon, *Roxb.*, EBENACEÆ.
Foods .
Kyou, *Beng.*, Diospyros tomentosa, *Roxb.*, EBENACEÆ.
Foods .

L

Laburnum, Indian, *Eng.*, Cassia Fistula, *Linn.*, LEGUMINOSÆ.
Foods .
Lac Tree, *Eng.*, Schleichera trijuga, *Willd.*, SAPINDACEÆ.
Foods .
Ladákhi badam, *Almora*, Prunus communis, *Huds.*, var., Domestica, ROSACEÆ. Foods .
Laghme, *Pb.*, Caroxylon Griffithii, *Moq.*, CHENOPODIACEÆ.
Foods .
Laghúne, *Afg.*, Daphne mucronata, *Royle*, THYMELÆACEÆ.
Foods .
Lahan, *Rajputana*, Toddalia aculeata, *Pers.*, RUTACEÆ.
Foods .
Lahi, *Hind.*, Brassica nigra, *Koch.*, CRUCIFERÆ.
Foods .
Lahi-sarson, *Hind.*, Brassica juncea, *H. f. & T. T.*, CRUCIFERÆ.
Foods .
Lahokung, *Lepcha*, Butea frondosa, *Roxb.*, LEGUMINOSÆ.
Foods .
Lahra, *Hind.*, Pennisetum typhoideum, *Rich.*, GRAMINEÆ.
Foods .
Lahsta, *Hind.*, Brassica campestris, *Linn.*, var. campestris proper, CRUCIFERÆ. Foods .
Lahura, *Pb.*, Tecoma undulata, *G. Don.*, BIGNONIACEÆ.
Foods .
Laila, *N.-W. P. & Oudh*, Salix tetrasperma, *Roxb.*, SALICINEÆ.
Foods .
Lailoo, *Burm.*, Olax scandens, *Roxb.*, OLACINEÆ.
Foods .
Laita, *Hind.*, Brassica campestris, *Linn.*, var. campestris proper, CRUCIFERÆ. Foods .
Lakhtel, *Pb.*, Cousinia minutu, *Boiss.*, COMPOSITÆ.
Foods .
Lakshmi-am, *Sylhet*, Mangifera sylvatica, *Roxb.*, ANACARDIACEÆ.
Foods .

Lakucha, *Sans.*, Artocarpus Lakoocha, *Roxb.*, URTICACEÆ.
Foods .
Lala ambadí, *Sind*, Hibiscus Sabdariffa, *Linn.*, MALVACEÆ.
Foods .
Lal-ambari, *Dec.*, *Hind.*, Hibiscus Sabdariffa, *Linn.*, MALVACEÆ.
Foods .
Lal-aloo, *Beng.*, Ipomæa Batatas, *Lamk*, CONVOLVULACEÆ.
Foods .
Lal-guras, *Nep.*, Rhododendron arboreum, *Sm.*, ERICACEÆ.
Foods .
Lal-kainjal, *Nep.*, Excæcaria baccata, *Müll.*, EUPHORBIACEÆ.
Foods .
Lal koi-pura, *Sylhet*, Sapindus attenuatus, *Wall.*, SAPINDACEÆ.
Foods .
Lal-sabuni, *Hind.*, Trianthema monogyna, *Linn.*, FICOIDEÆ.
Foods .
Lal-titmaliya, *Kumaun*, Viburnum stellulatum, *Wall.*, CAPRIFOLIACEÆ.
Foods .
Lamboben, *Burm.*, Buchanania latifolia, *Roxb.*, ANACARDIACEÆ.
Foods .
Lamkana, *Rajputana*, Briedelia retusa, *Spreng.*, EUPHORBIACEÆ.
Foods .
Lamote, *Burm.*, Mangifera fœtida, *Lour.*, ANACARDIACEÆ.
Foods .
Lampourd, *Fr.*, Xanthium strumarium, *Linn.*, COMPOSITÆ.
Foods .
Lana *Pb.*, Ballota limbata, *Benth.*, LABIATÆ.
Foods .
Lanang, *Kanawar*, Vitis vinifera, *Linn.*, AMPELIDEÆ.
Foods .
Lancbar, *Trans-Indus*, Orthanthera viminea, *Wight*, ASCLEPIADEÆ.
Foods .
Landachúta, *Bom.*, Mussænda frondosa, *Linn*, RUBIACEÆ.
Foods .
Lang bang, *Ladak*, Physochlaina præalta, *Hook. f.*, SOLANACEÆ.
Foods .
Lang shúr, *Him. name*, Juniperus Communis, *Linn.*, CONIFERÆ.
Foods .
Langura, *Bhutia*, Corylus Colurna, *Linn.*, CUPULIFERÆ.
Foods .
Langura, *Bhutia*, Corylus Ferox, *Wall.*, CUPULIFERÆ.
Foods .
Lanka, *Beng.*, *Hind.*, Cucurbita Pepo, *DC.*, CUCURBITACEÆ.
Foods .
Lap, *N.-W. P.*, Heteropogon contortus, *R. & S.*, GRAMINEÆ.
Foods .
Laphra, *Pb.*, Salvia Moorcroftiana, *Wall.*, LABIATÆ.
Foods .
Lapta, *Pb.*, Cenchrus echinatus, *Linn.*, GRAMINEÆ.
Foods .
Lasan, *Hind.*, Allium sativum, *Linn.*, LILIACEÆ.
Foods .
Lasora, *Hind.*, Cordia Myxa, *Linn.*, BORAGINEÆ.
Foods .
Lasrin, *Pb.*, Albizzia odoratissima, *Benth.*, LEGUMINOSÆ.
Foods .
Lasuna, *Sans*, Allium sativum, *Linn.*, LILIACEÆ.
Foods .
Laswara, *Pb.*, Cordia Myxa, *Linn.*, BORAGINEÆ.
Foods .
Latechu, *Ass.*, Baccaurea sapida, *Müll.-Arg*, EUPHORBIACEÆ.
Foods .

Late-mahwa, *Nep.*, Aglaia edulis, *A. Gray.*, MELIACEÆ.
Foods .
Latri, *N.-W. P.*, Lathyrus sativus, *Linn.*, LEGUMINOSÆ.
Foods .
Lattia-san, *Hind.*, Hibiscus cannabinus, *Linn.*, MALVACEÆ.
Foods .
Lau, *Beng.*, Lagenaria vulgaris, *Seringe.*, CUCURBITACEÆ.
Foods .
Lauki, *Hind.*, Lagenaria vulgaris, *Seringe.*, CUCURBITACEÆ.
Foods .
Laukl, *Pb.*, Lagenaria vulgaris, *Seringe.*, CUCURBITACEÆ.
Foods .
Laur, *Pb.*, Acer cultratum, *Wall.*, syn. of Acer pictum, *Thumb.*, SAPINDACEÆ. Foods .
Lavanga, *Beng.*, Caryophyllus aromaticus, *Linn.*, MYRTACEÆ.
Foods .
Lavangalu, *Tel.*, Caryophyllus aromaticus, *Linn.*, MYRTACEÆ.
Foods .
Lawúlú, *Cingh.*, Chrysophyllum Roxburghii, *G. Don.*, SAPOTACEÆ.
Foods .
Lea, *Pb.*, Cenchrus echinatus, *Linn.*, GRAMINEÆ.
Foods .
Lee, *Lepcha*, Pyrus Pashia, *Ham.*, ROSACEÆ.
Foods .
Lemon, *Eng.*, Citrus medica, *Linn.*, RUTACEÆ.
Foods .
Lentil, *Eng.*, Ervum Lens, *Linn.*, LEGUMINOSÆ.
Foods .
Lepcha-phal, *Darjeeling*, Phœbe attenuata, *Nees.*, LAURINEÆ.
Foods .
Lesuri, *Sind*, Cordia Myxa, *Linn.*, BORAGINEÆ.
Foods .
Leswa, *Pb.*, Digera arvensis, *Forsk.*, AMARANTACEÆ.
Foods .
Letfan, *Burm.*, Bombax malabaricum, *DC.*, MALVACEÆ.
Foods .
Letkop, *Burm.*, Sterculia fœtida, *Linn.*, STERCULIACEÆ.
Foods .
Lettuce, *Eng.*, Lactuca scariola, *Linn.*, COMPOSITÆ.
Foods .
Lhijo, *Pb. Him. name*, Pyrus baccata, *Linn.*, ROSACEÆ.
Foods .
Liane á reglisse, *Fr.*, Abrus precatorius, *Linn.*, LEGUMINOSÆ.
Foods .
Liar, *Sind*, Cordia Rothii, *Rom. & Sch.*, BORAGINEÆ.
Foods .
Lichi, *Beng.*, *Hind.*, Nephelium Litchi, *Camb.*, SAPINDACEÆ.
Foods .
Lignea Cassia, *Eng.*, Cinnamomum Tamala, *Nees.*, LAURINEÆ.
Foods .
Lilac, Persian, *Eng.*, Melia Azedarach, *Linn.*, MELIACEÆ.
Foods .
Likh-arm, *Nep.*, Prunus Padus, *Linn.*, ROSACEÆ.
Foods .
Likung, *Lepcha*, Docynia indica, *Dene.*, ROSACEÆ.
Foods .
Limblee oil Tree, *Eng.*, Murraya Kœnigii, *Spr.*, RUTACEÆ.
Foods .
Limbu, *Hind.*, Citrus medica, *Linn.*, RUTACEÆ.
Foods .
Lime, *Eng.*, Citrus medica, *Linn.*, RUTACEÆ.
Foods .

Lowl, *Dec.*, Artocarpus Lakoocha, *Roxb.*, URTICACEÆ.
Foods .
Lubar, *Pb.*, Phytolacca acinosa, *Roxb.*, VERBENACEÆ.
Foods .
Lucerne, *Eng.*, Medicago falcata, *Linn.*, LEGUMINOSÆ.
Foods .
Lúdúma, *Bhutia*, Decaisnea insignis, *Hook. f. & Th.*, BERBERIDEÆ.
Foods .
Ludut, *Pb.*, Codonopsis ovata, *Benth.*, CAMPANULACEÆ.
Foods .
Luir, *Him. name*, Juniperus excelsa, *M. Bieb.*, CONIFERÆ.
Foods .
Lukh, *Pb.*, Typha angustifolia, *Linn.*, TYPHACEÆ.
Foods .
Luki, *Tel.*, Vitex leucoxylon, *Linn.*, VERBENACEÆ.
Foods .
Lunak, *Pb.*, Chenopodium album, *L.*, CHENOPODIACEÆ.
Foods .
Lunak-haksha, *Pb.*, Portulaca quadrifida, *Linn.*, PORTULACEÆ.
Foods .
Lungar, *Pb.*, Pteris equilina, *Linn*, GRAMINEÆ.
Foods .
Lust, *N.-W. P.*, Taxus baccata, *Linn.*, CONIFERÆ.
Foods .
Lutco, *Hind.*, Baccaurea sapida, *Müll.-Arg.*, EUPHORBIACEÆ.
Foods .

M

Maá, *Burm.*, Buchanania latifolia, *Roxb.*, ANACARDIACEÆ.
Foods .
Máa, *Tam.*, Mangifera indica, *Linn.*, ANACARDIACEÆ.
Foods .
Maa-seenda, *Cingh.*, Mussœnda frondosa, *Linn.*, RUBIACEÆ.
Foods .
Mabura, of the ancients, Ægle Marmelos, *Correa.*, RUTACEÆ.
Foods .
Mace, *Eng.*, Myristica moschata, *Willd.*, MYRISTICEÆ.
Foods .
Mada, *Tel.*, Avicennia officinalis, *Linn.*, VERBENACEÆ.
Foods .
Mad-alaich-chedi, *Tam.*, Punica Granatum, *Linn.*, LYTHRACEÆ.
Foods .
Madana, *Pb.*, Eleusine ægyptiaca, *Pers.*, GRAMINEÆ.
Foods .
Madat, *Mar.*, Terminalia tomentosa, *W. & A.*, COMBRETACEÆ.
Foods .
Madder, European, *Eng.*, Rubia tinctorum, *Linn.*, RUBIACEÆ.
Foods .
Maddi, *Tel.*, Terminalia tomentosa, *W. & A.*, COMBRETACEÆ.
Foods .
Madhuka, *Sans.*, Bassia latifolia, *Roxb.*, SAPOTACEÆ.
Foods .
Madu-karray, *Tam.*, Randia dumetorum, *Lam.*, RUBIACEÆ.
Foods .
Mag, *Bom.*, Phaseolus Mungo, *Linn.*, var. radiatus, *Linn.*, LEGUMINOSÆ.
Foods .
Magadam, *Tam.*, Mimusops Elengi, *Linn.*, SAPOTACEÆ.
Foods .
Magar bans, *Hind.*, Bambusa arundinacea, *Retz.*, and other species, GRAMINEÆ. Foods .

Magyee, *Burm.*, Tamarindus indica, *Linn.*, LEGUMINOSÆ.
Foods .
Mah, *Sind*, Phaseolus Mungo, *Linn.*, var. radiatus, *Linn.*, LEGUMINOSÆ.
Foods .
Mahalay-kani, *Burm.*, Bauhinia purpurea, *Linn.*, LEGUMINOSÆ.
Foods .
Maha-limbo, Melia Azedarach, *Linn.*, MELIACEÆ.
Foods .
Mahálunga, *Bom.*, Citrus medica, *Linn.*, RUTACEÆ.
Foods .
Mahá nibu, Citrus decumana, *Willd.*, RUTACEÆ.
Foods .
Mahanimba, *Sans.*, Melia Azedarach, *Linn.*, MELIACEÆ.
Foods .
Mahaul, *Pb.*, Pyrus kumaoni, *Dcne.*, ROSACEÆ.
Foods .
Mahaushadha, *Sans.*, Allium sativum, *Linn.*, LILIACEÆ.
Foods .
Mahogany Tree, Indian, *Eng.*, Cedrela Toona, *Roxb.*, MELIACEÆ.
Foods .
Mahúa, *Hind.*, *Bom.*, Bassia latifolia, *Roxb.*, SAPOTACEÆ.
Foods .
Mahúla, *Beng.*, Bassia latifolia, *Roxb.*, SAPOTACEÆ.
Foods .
Mahur, *Hind.*, Orthanthera viminea, *Wight*, ASCLEPIADEÆ.
Foods .
Mahura, *Guj.*, Bassia latifolia, *Roxb.*, SAPOTACEÆ.
Foods .
Mahwa, *Hind.*, *Beng.*, Bassia latifolia, *Roxb.*, SAPOTACEÆ.
Foods .
Mahwa Tree, *Eng.*, Bassia latifolia, *Roxb.*, SAPOTACEÆ.
Foods .
Maidal, *Nep.*, Randia dumetorum, *Lam.*, RUBIACEÆ.
Foods .
Maidal, *Nep.*, Randia uliginosa, *DC.*, RUBIACEÆ.
Foods .
Malla, *Pb.*, Pyrus lanata, *Don.*, ROSACEÆ.
Foods .
Maimuna, *Afg.*, Sageretia Brandrethiana, *Aitch.*, RHAMNEÆ.
Foods .
Maina, *Pb.*, Medicago denticulata, *Willd.*, LEGUMINOSÆ.
Foods .
Mainphal, *Hind.*, Randia dumetorum, *Lam.*, RUBIACEÆ.
Foods .
Maize, *Eng.*, Zea Mays, *Linn.*, GRAMINEÆ.
Foods .
Makai, *Hind.*, Zea Mays, *Linn.*, GRAMINEÆ.
Foods .
Makai, *Hind.*, Zizyphus Œnoplia, *Mill.*, RHAMNEÆ.
Foods .
Makanim, *Tel.*, Melia Azedarach, *Linn.*, MELIACEÆ.
Foods .
Makhai, *Oudh.*, Zea Mays, *Linn.*, GRAMINEÆ.
Foods .
Makha-jowari, *Dec.*, Zea Mays, *Linn.*, GRAMINEÆ.
Foods .
Makhal, *Beng.*, Citrullus Colocynthis, *Schrad.*, CUCURBITACEÆ.
Foods .
Makhana, *Beng.*, *Hind.*, Euryale ferox, *Salisb.*, NYMPHÆACEÆ.
Foods .
Makhan-sim, *Hind.*, *Beng.*, Dolichos Lablab, *Linn.*, LEGUMINOSÆ.
Foods .

Makka, *Hind.*, Zea Mays, *Linn.*, GRAMINEÆ.
Foods .
Makka, *Tam.*, *Tel.*, *Deccan*, Zea Mays, *Linn.*, GRAMINEÆ.
Foods .
Makkajona, *Tel.*, Zea Mays, *Linn.*, GRAMINEÆ.
Foods .
Makkal, *Pb.*, Populus balsamifera, *Linn.*, SALICINEÆ.
Foods .
Makki, *Tam.*, Garcinia Morella, *Desr.*, GUTTIFERÆ.
Foods .
Makkúna, *Hind.*, Bauhinia racemosa, *Lam.*, LEGUMINOSÆ.
Foods .
Mako, *Pb.*, Solanum nigrum, SOLANACEÆ.
Foods .
Makra, *N. India*, Eleusine ægyptiaca, *Pers.*, GRAMINEÆ.
Foods .
Makra, *N.-W. P. & Oudh*, Eleusine corocana, *Gærtn.*, GRAMINEÆ.
Foods .
Makra-jali, *Beng.*, *Hind.*, Eleusine ægyptiaca, *Pers.*, GRAMINEÆ.
Foods .
Makri, *N. India*, Eleusine ægyptiaca, *Pers.*, GRAMINEÆ.
Foods .
Makur-jali, *N.-W. P.*, Panicum sanguinale, *Linn.*, var. ciliare, *Rets.*, sp., GRAMINEÆ. Foods .
Makur-kendi, *Beng.*, *Hind.*, Diospyros Embryopteris, *Pers.*, EBENACEÆ.
Foods .
Mala, *Beng.*, Bryonia laciniosa, *Linn.*, CUCURBITACEÆ.
Foods .
Malaing, *Burm.*, Morus lœvigata, *Wall.*, URTICACEÆ.
Foods .
Malai veppam, *Tam.*, Melia Azedarach, *Linn.*, MELIACEÆ.
Foods .
Malaka beng, *Burm.*, Psidium Guyava, *Raddi.*, MYRTACEÆ.
Foods .
Malan, *Pb.*, Edwardsia Hydaspica, *Edge.*, LEGUMINOSÆ.
Foods .
Malatrinukung, *Sans.*, Andropogon Schœnanthus, *Linn.*, GRAMINEÆ.
Foods .
Malay-kaya-pendalam, *Tel.*, Dioscorea bulbifera, *Linn.*, DIOSCOREACEÆ.
Foods .
Malchang, *Pb.*, Salix alba, *Linn.*, SALICINEÆ.
Foods .
Malé-geru, *Kurg.*, Dillenia pentagyna, *Roxb.*, DILLENIACEÆ.
Foods .
Malghan, *Hind.*, Bauhinia Vahlii, *W. & A.*, LEGUMINOSÆ.
Foods .
Maljan, *Hind.*, Bauhinia Vahlii, *W. & A.*, LEGUMINOSÆ.
Foods .
Mál kangoni, *Bom.*, Celastras senegalensis, *Lam.*, CELASTRINEÆ.
Foods .
Malla, *C. P.*, Melia Azedarach, *Linn.*, MELIACEÆ.
Foods .
Malla, *N.-W. P.*, Zizyphus nummularia, *W. & A.*, RHAMNEÆ.
Foods .
Mallai vembu, *Tam.*, Melia Azedarach, *Linn.*, MELIACEÆ.
Foods .
Mallow, Marsh, *Eng.*, Althœa officinalis, *L.*, MALVACEÆ.
Foods .
Malu, *Hind.*, Bauhinia Vahlii, *W. & A.*, LEGUMINOSÆ.
Foods .
Maluk, *Pb.*, Diospyros Lotus, *Linn.*, EBENACEÆ.
Foods .

Mamadi, *Tel.*, Mangifera indica, *Linn.*, ANACARDIACEÆ.
Foods .
Mamid, *Tel.*, Mangifera indica, *Linn.*, ANACARDIACEÆ.
Foods .
Manakká, *Beng.*, Vitis vinifera, *Linn.*, AMPELIDEÆ.
Foods .
Manchi-núne noovooloo, *Tel.*, Sesamum indicum, *Linn.*, PEDALINEÆ.
Foods .
Manda, *Tel.*, Randia dumetorum, *Lam.*, RUBIACEÆ.
Foods .
Mandal, *Pb.*, Eleusine corocana, *Gærtn.*, GRAMINEÆ
Foods .
Mandal, *Pb.*, Rhododendron arboreum, *Sm.*, ERICACEÆ.
Foods .
Mandar, *Pb.*, Acer pictum, *Thunb.*, SAPINDACEÆ.
Foods .
Mandgay, *Bm.*, Bambusa arundinacea, *Retz.*, and other species, GRAMINEÆ.
Foods .
Mandira, *Kumaun & Garhwal*, Panicum frumentaceum, *Roxb.*, GRAMINEÆ.
Foods .
Mandkolla, *Pb.*, Randia dumetorum, *Lam.*, RUBIACEÆ.
Foods .
Mandri, *Pb.*, Ribes nigrum, *Linn.*, SAXIFRAGACEÆ.
Foods .
Mandua, *N.-W. P. & Oudh*, Eleusine corocana, *Gærtn.*, GRAMINEÆ.
Foods .
Mangas, *Tam.*, Mangifera indica, *Linn.*, ANACARDIACEÆ.
Foods .
Mangil, *Tam.*, Bambusa arundinacea, *Retz.*, and other species, GRAMINEÆ.
Foods .
Mango, *Eng.*, Mangifera indica, *Linn.*, ANACARDIACEÆ.
Foods .
Mangosteen, *Eng.*, Garcinia Mangostana, *Linn.*, GUTTIFERÆ.
Foods .
Mangrove Tree, *Eng.*, Rhizophora mucronata, *Lamk.*, RHIZOPHOREÆ.
Foods .
Mangrove, White, *Eng.*, Avicennia officinalis, *Linn.*, VERBENACEÆ.
Foods .
Mangrur, *Pb.*, Panicum antidotale, *Retz.*, GRAMINEÆ.
Foods .
Manjal, *Tam.*, Curcuma longa, *Roxb.*, SCITAMINEÆ.
Foods .
Manjal-mutlangi, *Tam.*, Daucus Carota, *Linn.*, UMBELLIFERÆ.
Foods .
Man-kochoo, *Beng.*, Colocasia indica, *Schott.*, AROIDEÆ.
Foods .
Manna Grass, *Eng.*, Glyceria fluitans, *R. Br.*, GRAMINEÆ.
Foods .
Manna Plant, Hebrew, *Eng.*, Alhagi maurorum, *Desv.*, LEGUMINOSÆ.
Foods .
Mánskhel, *Kashmir*, Agaricus campestris, *Linn.*, FUNGI.
Foods .
Manyúl, *Hind.*, Randia dumetorum, *Lam.*, RUBIACEÆ.
Foods .
Maoo, *Burm.*, Anthocephalus Cadamba, *Miq.*, RUBIACEÆ.
Foods .
Maookadoom, *Burm.*, Anthocephalus Cadamba, *Miq.*, RUBIACEÆ.
Foods .
Marachini, *Mal.*, Manihot utilissima, *Pohl.*, EUPHORBIACEÆ.
Foods .
Maraghúne, *Pb.*, Solanum coagulans, *Fors.*, SOLANACEÆ.
Foods .

Maral, *Pb.*, Ulmus campestris, *Linn.*, URTICACEÆ.
Foods .
Maram, *Tam.*, Eriodendron anfractuosum, *DC.*, MALVACEÆ.
Foods .
Marari, *Pb.*, Ulmus Wallichiana, *Planch.*, URTICACEÆ.
Foods .
Maravuli, *Tam.*, Manihot utilissima, *Pohl.*, EUPHORBIACEÆ.
Foods .
Marazh, *Pb.*, Ulmus campestris, *Linn.*, URTICACEÆ.
Foods .
Mardakusch, *Arab.*, Origanum Marjorana, *Linn.*, LABIATEÆ.
Foods .
Mared, *Hind.*, Ulmus Wallichiana, *Planch.*, URTICACEÆ.
Foods .
Maredu, *Tel.*, Ægle Marmelos, *Correa.*, RUTACEÆ.
Foods .
Mar-ghalawa, *Pb.*. Viburnum cotinifolium, *Don.*, CAPRIFOLIACEÆ.
Foods .
Marghi-pal, *Pb.*, Solanum gracilipes, *Dcne.*, SOLANACEÆ.
Foods .
Margosa Tree, *Eng.*, Melia Azadirachta, *Linn.*, MELIACEÆ.
Foods .
Mári, *Tel.*, Ficus bengalensis, *Linn.*, URTICACEÆ.
Foods .
Marich, Lal gách, *Beng.*, Capsicum frutescens, *Linn.*, SOLANACEÆ.
Foods .
Marigold, *Eng.*, Calendula officinalis, *Linn.*, COMPOSITÆ.
Foods .
Marjoram, Sweet, *Eng.*, Origanum Marjorana, *Linn.*, LABIATÆ.
Foods .
Marjoram, Winter, *Eng.*, Origanum heracleoticum, LABIATÆ.
Foods .
Mark, *Pb.*, Briedelia retusa, *Spreng.*, EUPHORBIACEÆ.
Foods .
Marking-nut Tree, *Eng.*, Semecarpus Anacardium, *Linn.*, ANACARDIACEÆ. Foods .
Marlea, *Sylhet*, Marlea begoniæfolia, *Roxb.*, CORNACEÆ.
Foods .
Marliza, *Sylhet*, Marlea begoniæfolia, *Roxb.*, CORNACEÆ.
Foods .
Marlumulta, *Tam.*, Xanthium strumarium, *Linn.*, COMPOSITÆ.
Foods .
Marria, *Gond.*, endlandia Wexserta, *DC.*, RUBIACEÆ.
Foods .
Marsi, *N.-W. P. & Oudh*, Paspalum scrobiculatum, *Linn.*, GRAMINEÆ.
Foods .
Maru, *Pb.*, Quercus dilatata, *Lindl.*, CUPULIFERÆ.
Foods .
Marua, *Beng.*, Eleusine corocana, *Gærtn.*, GRAMINEÆ.
Foods .
Marua, *N.-W. P. & Oudh*, Eleusine corocana, *Gærtn.*, GRAMINEÆ.
Foods .
Mash, *Hind.*, *Sind*, Phaselus Mungo, *Linn.*, var. radiatus, *Linn.*, LEGUMINOSÆ. Foods .
Masha, *Sans.*, Phaseolus Mungo, *Linn.*, var. radiatus, *Linn.*, LEGUMINOSÆ. Foods .
Mash-kolai, *Beng.*, Phaseolus Mungo, *Linn.*, var. radiatus. *Linn.*, LEGUMINOSÆ. Foods .
Maspati, *Nep.*, Abrus precatorius, *Linn.*, LEGUMINOSÆ.
Foods .
Mastiara, *Pb.*, Scutellaria linearis, *Benth.*, LABIATÆ.
Foods .

Masur, *Hind.*, *Raj.*, *Deccan*, Ervum Lens, *Linn.*, LEGUMINOSÆ.
Foods .
Masúr bauri, *Gond.*, Antidesma diandrum, *Tulasne.*, EUPHORBIACEÆ.
Foods .
Masuri, *Beng.*, Ervum Lens, *Linn.*, LEGUMINOSÆ.
Foods .
Matar, Jangli, *Beng.*, Lathyrus Aphaca, *Linn.*, LEGUMINOSÆ.
Foods .
Matar, *Sind*, Lathyrus sativus, *Linn.*, LEGUMINOSÆ.
Foods .
Matar, *Sind*, Pisum sativum, *Linn.*, LEGUMINOSÆ.
Foods .
Mate, *Nep.*, Berberis asiatica, *Roxb.*, BERBERIDEÆ.
Foods .
Mát-kalai, *Beng.*, Arachis hypogæa, *Linn.*, LEGUMINOSÆ.
Foods .
Matazor, *Pb.*, Phytolacca acinosa, *Roxb.*, VERBENACEÆ.
Foods .
Math, *Deccan*, Phaseolus aconitifolius, *Jacq.*, LEGUMINOSÆ.
Foods .
Mathá-tél, *Hind.*, Sesamum indicum, *Linn.*, PEDALINEÆ.
Foods .
Matra, *Oudh*, Pisum sativum, *Linn.*, LEGUMINOSÆ.
Foods .
Mattar, *N.-W. P.*, Pisum sativum, *Linn.*, LEGUMINOSÆ.
Foods .
Mattar, Chota, *Hind.*, *Beng.*, Pisum arvense, *Linn.*, LEGUMINOSÆ.
Foods .
Mattar, Desi, *Beng.*, *Hind.*, Pisum arvense, *Linn.*, LEGUMINOSÆ.
Foods .
Mattar, Gol, *N.-W. P.*, Pisum sativum, *Linn.*, LEGUMINOSÆ
Foods .
Matti, *Pb.*, Equisetum debile, *Roxb.*, EQUISETACEÆ.
Foods .
Matti, *Beas*, Orthanthera viminea, *Wight*, ASCLEPIADEÆ.
Foods .
Matto-batsala, *Tel.*, Basella alba, *L.*, CHENOPODIACEÆ.
Foods .
Mattu, *Pb.*, Indigofera Dosua, *Ham.*, LEGUMINOSÆ.
Foods .
Matura, of the ancients, Ægle Marmelos, *Correa.*, RUTACEÆ.
Foods .
Maul, *Beng.*, Bassia latifolia, *Roxb.*, SAPOTACEÆ.
Foods .
Mauli, *Hind.*, Pyrus lanata, *Don.*, ROSACEÆ.
Foods .
Maulser, *Hind.*, Mimusops Elengi, *Linn.*, SAPOTACEÆ.
Foods .
Maurain, *Hind.*, Bauhinia Vahlii, *W. & A.*, LEGUMINOSÆ.
Foods .
Mauri, *Bng.*, Fæniculum vulgare, *Gærtn.*, UMBELLIFERÆ.
Foods .
May, *Tel.*, Schleichera trijuga, *Willd.*, SAPINDACEÆ.
Foods .
Mayan, *Burm.*, Bouea burmanica, *Griff.*, ANACARDIACEÆ.
Foods .
Maylull, *Nep.*, Pyrus vestita, *Wall.*, ROSACEÆ.
Foods .
Medick, Black, *Eng.*, Medicago lupulina, *Linn.*, LEGUMINOSÆ.
Foods .
Medick, Purple, *Eng.*, Medicago falcata, *Linn.*, LEGUMINOSÆ.
Foods .

Medlar, Japan, *Eng.*, Eriobotrya japonica, *Lindl.*, ROSACEÆ.
Foods .
Meeta Aloo, *Hind.*, Ipomœa Batatas, *Lamk.*, CONVOLVULACEÆ.
Foods .
Mehal, *Hind.*, Pyrus Pashia, *Ham.*, ROSACEÆ.
Foods .
Meho, *Sind*, Citrullus vulgaris, *Schrad.*, var. fistulosus, CUCURBITACEÆ.
Foods .
Mehul, *Nep.*, Docynia indica, *Dcne.*, ROSACEÆ.
Foods .
Meiskara, *Nep.*, Toddalia aculeata, *Pers.*, RUTACEÆ.
Foods .
Mekrap, *Lepcha*, Morus indica, *Linn.*, URTICACEÆ.
Foods .
Me-kuri, *Naga*, Lagenaria vulgaris, *Seringe.*, CUCURBITACEÆ.
Foods .
Melon, Sweet, *Eng.*, Cucumis melo, *Linn.*, CUCURBITACEÆ.
Foods .
Melon, White, *Eng.*, Benincasa cerifera, *Savi.*, CUCUBITACEÆ.
Foods .
Men, *Kan.*, Trigonella Fœnum-grœcum, *Linn.*, LEGUMINOSÆ.
Foods .
Menasu, *Kan.*, Piper nigrum, *Linn.*, PIPERACEÆ.
Foods .
Mengkop, *Burm.*, Garcinia Mangostana, *Linn.*, GUTTIFERÆ.
Foods .
Mensina kayl, *Kan.*, Capsicum frutescens, *Linn.*, SOLANACEÆ.
Foods .
Mentulu, *Tel.*, Trigonella Fœnum-grœcum, *Linn.*, LEGUMINOSÆ.
Foods .
Mentyá, *Kan.*, Trigonella Fœnum-grœcum, *Linn.*, LEGUMINOSÆ.
Foods .
Mepyoung, *Burm.*, Maba buxifolia, *Pers.*, EBENACEÆ.
Foods .
Merian, *Burm.*, Bouea burmanica, *Griff.*, ANACARDIACEÆ.
Foods .
Merino, *Pb.*, Potentilla fruticosa, *Linn.*, ROSACEÆ.
Foods .
Mesquit, *Eng.*, Prosopis glandulosa, *Torr.*, LEGUMINOSÆ.
Foods .
Mesta, *Beng.*, Hibiscus Sabdariffa, *Linn.*, MALVACEÆ.
Foods .
Mesta pát, *Beng.*, Hibiscus cannabinus, *Linn.*, MALVACEÆ.
Foods .
Methi, *Hind.*, *Beng.*, Trigonella Fœnum-grœcum, *Linn.*, LEGUMINOSÆ.
Foods .
Méthi, *Mahr.*, *Guz.*, Trigonella Fœnum-grœcum, *Linn.*, LEGUMINOSÆ.
Foods .
Metunga, *Beng.*, Melocanna banbusoides, *Trin.*, GRAMINEÆ.
Foods .
Mhaniben, *Burm.*, Randia uliginosa, *DC.*, RUBIACEÆ.
Foods .
Mhowa, *C. P.*, Bassia latifolia, *Roxb.*, SAPOTACEÆ.
Foods .
Mibe, *Burm.*, Arachis hypogæa, *Linn.*, LEGUMINOSÆ.
Foods .
Michapgong, *Lepcha*, Premna latifolia, *Roxb.*, VERBENACEÆ.
Foods .
Mijhanla, *Kumaun*, Elæagnus latifolia, *Linn.*, ELÆAGNUS.
Foods .
Mijhri, *N.-W. P.*, Panicum psilopodium, *Trin.*, GRAMINEÆ.
Foods .

Milagu, *Tam.*, Piper nigram, *Linn.*, PIPERACEÆ.
Foods .
Milkaranal, *Tam.*, Toddalia aculeata, *Pers.*, RUTACEÆ.
Foods .
Millet, *Eng.*, Eleusine corocana, *Gærtn.*, GRAMINEÆ.
Foods .
Millet, German or Italian, *Eng.*, Setaria italica, *Kunth.*, GRAMINEÆ.
Foods .
Millet, Indian, *Eng.*, Panicum miliaceum, *Linn.*, GRAMINEÆ.
Foods .
Millet, Indian or Great, *Eng.*, Sorghum vulgare, *Pers.*, GRAMINEÆ.
Foods .
Millet, Little, *Eng.*, Panicum frumentaceum, *Roxb.*, GRAMINEÆ.
Food .
Millet, Spiked, *Eng.*, Pennisetum typhoideum, *Rich.*, GRAMINEÆ.
Foods .
Mimu-mulee, *Tel.*, Phaseolus Mungo, *Linn.*, var. radiatus, *Linn.*, LEGUMINOSÆ. Foods .
Minbo, *Burm.*, Caryota urens, *Willd.*, PALMÆ.
Foods .
Mindla, *Pb.*, Randia dumetorum, *Lam.*, RUBIACEÆ.
Foods .
Miniyar, *Pb.*, Andropogon petusus, *Willd.*, GRAMINEÆ.
Foods .
Mint, *Eng.*, Mentha Viridis, *Linn.*, LABIATÆ.
Foods .
Mint Marsh, *Eng.*, Mentha arvensis, *Linn.*, LABIATÆ.
Foods .
Mipitmuk, *Lepcha*, Flemingia congesta, *Roxb.*, LEGUMINOSÆ.
Foods .
Minumulu, *Tel.*, Phaseolus aconitifolius, *Jacq.*, LEGUMINOSÆ.
Foods .
Mirchia-gard, *Siwaliks*, Andropogon Schœnanthus, *Linn.*, GRAMINEÆ.
Foods .
Mirich, Dhan, *Hind.*, Capsicum minimum, *Roxb.*, SOLANACEÆ.
Foods .
Mirich, Lal gách, *Hind.*, Capsicum frutescens, *Linn.*, SOLANACEÆ.
Foods .
Miriyalu, *Tel.*, Piper nigrum, *Linn.*, PIPERACEÆ.
Foods .
Merri, *Chenab*, Pinus Gerardiana, *Wall.*, CONIFERÆ.
Foods .
Mirzanjosh, *Pb.*, Origanum normale, *Don.*, LABIATÆ.
Foods .
Mishmush, *Eng.*, Prunus armeniaca, *Linn.*, ROSACEÆ.
Foods .
Misri, *Pb.*, Eulophia campestris, *Lindl.*, ORCHIDEÆ.
Foods .
Misur-pappu, *Tel.*, Ervum Lens, *Linn.*, LEGUMINOSÆ.
Foods .
Misurpurpur, *Tam.*, Ervum Lens, *Linn.*, LEGUMINOSÆ.
Foods .
Mizunjoosh, *Arab.*, Origanum Marjorana, *Linn.*, LABIATÆ.
Foods .
Modhuriam, *Ass.*, Psidium Guyava, *Raddi.*, MYRTACEÆ.
Foods .
Modugu, *Tel.*, Butea frondosa, *Roxb.*, LEGUMINOSÆ.
Foods .
Mohakri, *Pb.*, Trichosanthes cucumerina, *Linn.*, CUCURBITACEÆ.
Foods .
Mohi, *Uriya*, Garuga pinnata, *Roxb.*, BURSERACEÆ.
Foods .

Mohln, *Hind.*, Odina Wodier, *Roxb.*, ANACARDIACEÆ.
Foods .
Moho, *Mar.*, Bassia latifolia, *Roxb.*, SAPOTACEÆ.
Foods .
Mok, *Burm.*, Aloe vera, *Linn.*, LILIACEÆ.
Foods .
Moksha, *Chamba*, Agaricus campestris, *Linn.*, FUNGI.
Foods .
Mokushtha, *Sans.*, Phaseolus aconitifolius, *Jacq.*, LEGUMINOSÆ.
Foods .
Mol, *Hind.*, Pyrus Pashia, *Ham.*, ROSACEÆ.
Foods .
Momakha, *Burm.*, Salix tetrasperma, *Roxb.*, SALICINEÆ.
Foods .
Mooluka, *Sans.*, Raphanus sativus, *Linn.*, CRUCIFERÆ.
Foods .
Moon of the Faithful, *Eng.*, Prunus armeniaca, *Linn.*, ROSACEÆ.
Foods .
Morell, *Eng.*, Morchella semilibera, *L.*, FUNGI.
Foods .
Morich, Dhan, *Beng.*, Capsicum minimum, *Roxb.*, SOLANACEÆ.
Foods .
Morich, Lal lonka, *Beng.*, Capsicum frutescens, *Linn.*, SOLANACEÆ.
Foods .
Morich, Kafri, *Beng.*, *Hind.*, Capsicum grossum, *Willd.*, SOLANACEÆ.
Foods .
Morinda Bark Tree, *Eng.*, Morinda citrifolia, *Linn.*, RUBIACEÆ.
Foods .
Morli, *Tel.*, Buchanania latifolia, *Roxb.*, ANACARDIACEÆ.
Foods .
Morphal, *Pb.*, Pyrus lanata, *Don.*, ROSACEÆ.
Foods .
Morre, *Cingh.*, Nephelium Longana, *Camb.*, SAPINDACEÆ.
Foods .
Moru, *N.-W. P.*, Quercus dilatata, *Lindl.*, CUPULIFERÆ.
Foods .
Morung, *Beng.*, Amomum aromaticum, *Roxb.*, SCITAMINEÆ.
Foods .
Morunga, *Tam.*, Moringa pterygosperma, *Gærtn.*, MORINGEÆ.
Foods .
Mosonea, *Uriya*, Ehretia lævis, *Roxb.*, BORAGINEÆ.
Foods .
Mostarda, *Por.*, Brassica nigra, *Koch.*, CRUCIFERÆ.
Foods .
Moth, *Hind.*, *Raj.*, Phaseolus aconitifolius, *Jacq.*, LEGUMINOSÆ.
Foods .
Mothi, *Hind.*, Phaseolus aconitifolius, *Jacq.*, LEGUMINOSÆ.
Foods .
Mothi-kabbal, *Pb.*, Panicum sanguinale, *Linn.*, GRAMINEÆ.
Foods .
Motku, *Tel.*, Ougeinia dalbergioides, *Benth.*, LEGUMINOSÆ.
Foods .
Motsj, *Japan*, Oryza sativa, *Linn.*, GRAMINEÆ.
Foods .
Mou-alu, *Beng.*, *Hind.*, Dioscorea aculeata, *Roxb.*, DIOSCOREACEÆ.
Foods .
Moutarde Noire, *Fr.*, Brassica nigra, *Koch.*, CRUCIFERÆ.
Foods .
Mová, *Bom.*, Bassia latifolia, *Roxb.*, SAPOTACEÆ.
Foods .
Mowa, *Hind.*, Bassia latifolia, *Roxb.*, SAPOTACEÆ.
Foods .

Mowa, *Trans-Indus,* Orthanthera viminea, *Wight,* ASCLEPIADEÆ.
Foods .
Mowen, *Hind.,* Odina Wodier, *Roxb.,* ANACARDIACEÆ.
Foods .
Moya, *Bom.,* Odina Wodier, *Roxb.,* ANACARDIACEÆ.
Foods .
Moydi, *Tel.,* Ficus glomerata, *Roxb.,* URTICACEÆ.
Foods .
Mu, *Cingh.,* Bassia longifolia, *Willd.,* SAPOTACEÆ.
Foods .
Mudga, *Sans.,* Phaseolus Mungo, *Linn.,* LEGUMINOSÆ.
Foods .
Mudu-kaiyeya, *Cingh.,* Pandanus odoratissimus, *Willd.,* PANDANEÆ.
Foods .
Mug, *Beng.,* Phaseolus Mungo, *Linn.,* LEGUMINOSÆ.
Foods .
Mugalik, *Tel.,* Pandanus odoratissimus, *Willd.,* PANDANEÆ.
Foods .
Mugani, *Beng.,* Phaseolus trilobus, *Ait.,* LEGUMINOSÆ.
Foods .
Mugurela, *Beng.,* Nigella sativa, *Linn.,* RANUNCULACEÆ.
Foods .
Mugra, *Hind.,* Caudatus, var. of Raphanus sativus, *Linn.,* CRUCIFERÆ.
Foods .
Mula, *Beng.,* Raphanus sativus, *Linn.,* CRUCIFERÆ.
Foods .
Mul ahcotá, *Kan.,* Nephelium Longana, *Camb.,* SAPINDACEÆ.
Foods .
Mulampandu, *Tel.,* Cucumis Melo, *Linn.,* CUCURBITACEÆ.
Foods .
Mulangi, *Kan.,* Raphanus sativus, *Linn.,* CRUCIFERÆ.
Food .
Mulberry, Indian, *Eng.,* Marinda citrifolia, *Linn.,* RUBIACEÆ.
Foods .
Mulberry, White, *Eng.,* Morus alba, *Linn.,* URTICACEÆ.
Foods .
Muli, *Beng.,* Melocanna bambusoides, *Tærin.,* GRAMINEÆ.
Foods .
Mull, *Hind.,* Raphanus sativus, *Linn.,* CRUCIFERÆ.
Foods .
Mulkas, *Tel.,* Bambusa arundinacea, *Retz.,* and other species, GRAMINEÆ.
Foods .
Mulsári, *Hind.,* Mimusops Elengi, *Linn.,* SAPOTACEÆ.
Foods .
Muluvelari, *Tam.,* Cucumis sativus, *Linn.,* CUCURBITACEÆ.
Foods .
Muluvengay, *Tam.,* Briedelia retusa, *Spreng.,* EUPHORBIACEÆ.
Foods .
Munchá kunda, *Tel.,* Amorphophallus campanulatus, *Blume.,* AROIDEÆ.
Foods .
Mundiri, *Tam.,* Anacardium occidentale, *Linn.,* ANACARDIACEÆ.
Foods .
Mung, *Hind.,* Phaseolus Mungo, *Linn.,* LEGUMINOSÆ.
Foods .
Mungphall, *Hind.,* Arachis hypogæa, *Linn.,* LEGUMINOSÆ.
Foods .
Munj, *Hind.,* Saccharum Sara, *Roxb.,* GRAMINEÆ.
Foods .
Munja-pavattary, *Tam.,* Morinda citrifolia, *Linn.,* RUBIACEÆ.
Foods .
Munji, *Hind.,* Pollinia eriopoda, *Hance.,* GRAMINEÆ.
Foods .

Munnay, *Tam.*, Premna integrifolia, *Linn.*, VERBENACEÆ.
Foods .
Muradh, *Pb.*, Ribes nigrum, *Linn.*, SAXIFRAGACEÆ.
Foods .
Murgtu, *Lepcha*, Turpinia pomifera, *DC.*, SAPINDACEÆ.
Foods .
Murroo, *Tam.*, Origanum Marjorana, *Linn.*, LABIATÆ.
Foods .
Murwa, *Dec.*, *Sind*, Origanum Marjorana, *Linn.*, LABIATÆ.
Foods .
Musel, *N.-W. P.*, Heteropogon contortus, *R. & S.*, GRAMINEÆ.
Foods .
Mushakdana, *Beng.*, Hibiscus Abelmoschus, *Linn.*, MALVACEÆ.
Foods .
Mushambáram, *Tel.*, Aloe vera, *Linn.*, LILIACEÆ.
Foods .
Mushk-bhendi-bing, *Dec.*, Hibiscus Abelmoschus, *Linn*, MALVACEÆ.
Foods .
Mushk-dana, *Pers.*, Hibiscus Abelmoschus, *Linn.*, MALVACEÆ.
Foods .
Mushroom, *Eng.*, Agaricus campestris, *Linn.*, FUNGI.
Foods .
Musk Mallow, *Eng.*, Hibiscus Abelmoschus, *Linn.*, MALVACEÆ.
Foods .
Musk Melon, *Eng.*, Cucurbita moschata, *Duchesne*, CUCURBITACEÆ.
Foods .
Musré katús, *Nep.*, Castanopsis tribuloides, *A. DC.*, CUPULIFERÆ.
Foods .
Mustá, *Bom.*, *Sans.*, Cyperus rotundus, *Linn.*, CYPERACEÆ.
Foods .
Mustard, Black, *Eng.*, Brassica nigra, *Koch.*, CRUCIFERÆ.
Foods .
Mustard, Indian, *Eng.*, Brassica juncea, *H. f.*, *& T. T.*, CRUCIFERÆ.
Foods .
Mustard, True, *Eng.*, Brassica nigra, *Koch.*, CRUCIFERÆ.
Foods .
Mustard, White, *Eng.*, Brassica alba, *H. f.*, *& T. T.*, CRUCIFERÆ.
Foods .
Mustert, *Ger.*, Brassica nigra, *Koch.*, CRUCIFERÆ.
Foods .
Muthá, *Beng.*, Cyperus rotundus, *Linn.*, CYPERACEÆ.
Foods .
Mutta, *Beng.*, Antidesma diandrum, *Tulasne*, EUPHORBIACEÆ.
Foods .
Muttugú, *Kan.*, Butea frondosa, *Roxb.*, LEGUMINOSÆ.
Foods .
Mu-yan, *Burm.*, Hordeum vulgare, *Linn.*, GRAMINEÆ.
Foods .
Muyna, *Beng.*, Vangueria spinosa, *Roxb.*, RUBIACEÆ.
Foods.
Myínwa, *Burm.*, Dendrocalamus strictus, *Nees.*, GRAMINEÆ.
Foods .
Myooma, *Bhutia*, Arundinaria racemosa, *Munro*, GRAMINEÆ.
Foods .
Myouklouk, *Burm.*, Artocarpus Lakoocha, *Roxb.*, URTICACEÆ.
Foods .
Myoukseit, *Burm.*, Ulmus integrifolia, *Roxb.*, URTICACEÆ.
Foods .
Myrobalans, *Eng.*, Terminalia belerica, *Roxb.*, COMBRETACEÆ.
Foods .

N

Nabar, *Pb.*, Ribes nigrum, *Linn.*, SAXIFRAGACEÆ.
Foods .
Nabatussibr, *Arab.*, Aloe vera, *Linn.*, var. officinalis, *sp. Forsk.*, LILIACEÆ.
Foods .
Nachni, *Sind.* Eleusine corocana, *Gærtn.*, GRAMINEÆ.
Foods .
Naga, *Tam.*, Eugenia Jambolana, *Lam.*, MYRTACEÆ.
Foods .
Nangal, *Tam.*, Mesua ferrea, *Linn.*, GUTTIFERÆ.
Foods .
Nagavela, *Bom.*, Piper Betle, *Linn.*, PIPERACEÆ.
Foods .
Nagbo, *Pers.*, Mentha viridis, *Linn.*, LABIATÆ.
Foods .
Nagesar, *Hind.*, *Beng.*, Mesua ferrea, *Linn.*, GUTTIFERÆ.
Foods .
Naghas, *Hind.*, *Beng.*, Mesua ferrea, *Linn.*, GUTTIFERÆ.
Foods .
Nagli, *Bom.*, Eleusine corocana, *Gærtn.*, GRAMINEÆ.
Foods .
Nahar, *Ass.*, Mesua ferrea, *Linn.*, GUTTIFERÆ.
Foods .
Nal-kadughu, *Tam.*, Gynandropsis pentaphylla, *DC.*, CAPPARIDEÆ.
Foods .
Nairuri, *Tel.*, Eugenia Jambolana, *Lam.*, MYRTACEÆ.
Foods .
Nairuri, *Tel.*, Sizygium jambolanum, *DC.*, MYRTACEÆ.
Foods .
Nai-shakar, *Pers.*, Saccharum officinarum, *Linn.*, GRAMINEÆ.
Foods .
Nal-valla, *Tam.*, Gynandropsis pentaphylla, *DC.*, CAPPARIDEÆ.
Foods .
Nak, *Pb. Hills*, Pyrus communis, *Linn.*, ROSACEÆ.
Foods .
Nak-doun, *Hind.*, *Pers.*, Asparagus officinalis, *Willd.*, LILIACEÆ.
Foods .
Nakhtar, *Afg.*, Cedrus Deodara, *Loudon*, CONIFERÆ.
Foods .
Nakhtar, *Afg.*, Pinus longifolia, *Roxb.*, CONIFERÆ.
Foods .
Nakhud, *Pers.*, Cicer arietinum, *Linn.*, LEGUMINOSÆ.
Foods .
Nala, *Sans.*, Abrus precatorius, *Linn*, LEGUMINOSÆ.
Foods .
Nalaika, *Tel.*, Randia uliginosa, *DC.*, RUBIACEÆ.
Foods .
Nal bans, *Hind.*, Bambusa arundinacea, *Retz.*, and other species, GRAMINEÆ. Foods .
Nali-putiki, *Tel.*, Aristida depressa, *Retz.*, GRAMINEÆ.
Foods .
Nalki, *Beng.*, Hibiscus cannabinus, *Linn.*, MALVACEÆ.
Foods .
Nalla-mada, *Tel.*, Avicennia officinalis, *Linn.*, VERBENACEÆ.
Foods .
Nal lenney, *Tam.*, Sesamum indicum, *Linn.*, PEDALINEÆ.
Foods .
Nalshuna, *Nep.*, Ehretia acuminata, *Br.*, BORAGINEÆ.
Foods .

Nama, *Tel.*, Aponogeton monostachyum, *Linn.*, NAIADACEÆ.
Foods .
Nambyong, *Lepcha*, Morus cuspidata, *Wall.*, URTICACEÆ.
Foods .
Namli, *Tel.*, Ulmus integrifolia, *Roxb.*, URTICACEÆ.
Foods .
Nandi, *Tel.*, Cedrela Toona, *Roxb.*, MELIACEÆ.
Foods .
Nandru, *Pb.*, Physochlaina præalta, *Hook. f.*, SOLANACEÆ.
Foods .
Nangli, *Sind*, Eleusine corocana, *Gærtn.*, GRAMINEÆ.
Foods .
Nanjunda, *Tam.*, Balanites Roxburghii, *Planch.*, SIMARUBEÆ.
Foods .
Nan nan, *Burm.*, Coriandrum sativum, *Linn.*, UMBELLIFERÆ.
Foods .
Nanna-si, *Burm.*, Ananussa sativa, *Linn.*, BROMELIACEÆ.
Foods .
Nanu-witi, *Sylhet*, Gnetum scandens, *Roxb.*, GNETACEÆ.
Foods .
Narangi, *Hind.*, Citrus Aurantium, *Linn.*, RUTACEÆ.
Foods .
Nari, *Pb.*, Equisetum debile, *Roxb.*, EQUISETACEÆ.
Foods .
Nari, *Pb.*, Ipomæa aquatica, *Forsk.*, CONVOLVULACEÆ.
Foods .
Nariel, *Hind.*, Cocos nucifera, *Linn.*, PALMÆ.
Foods .
Narikadam, *Tel.*, Cocos nucifera, *Linn.*, PALMÆ.
Foods .
Narikel, *Beng.*, Cocos nucifera, *Linn.*, PALMÆ.
Foods .
Naringi, *Hind.*, Citrus Aurantium, *Linn.*, RUTACEÆ.
Foods .
Narkel, Jhoona, *Beng.*, Cocos nucifera, *Linn.*, PALMÆ.
Foods .
Narr, *Pb. & Sind*, Malva parviflora, *Linn.*, MALVACEÆ.
Foods .
Narra, *Garhwal*, Ehretia acuminata, *Br.*, BORAGINEÆ.
Foods .
Narvilli, *Tam.*, Cordia Rothii, *Rom. & Sch.*, BORAGINEÆ.
Foods .
Naryepi, *Tel.*, Hardwickia binata, *Roxb.* LEGUMINOSÆ.
Foods .
Nasedu, *Tel.*, Eugenia Jambolana, *Lam.*, MYRTACEÆ.
Foods .
Nasodu, *Tel.*, Sizygium jambolanum, *DC.*, MYRTACEÆ.
Foods .
Naspate, *Pb. hills*, Pyrus communis, *Linn.*, ROSACEÆ.
Foods .
Naspati, *Pb.*, Pyrus communis, *Linn.*, ROSACEÆ.
Foods .
Natchnee, *Eng.*, Eleusine corocana, *Gærtn*, GRAMINEÆ.
Foods .
Natvadum, *Tam.*, Terminalia Catappa, *Linn.*, COMBRETACEÆ.
Foods .
Naug, *Hind.*, Cornus macrophylla, *Wall.*, CORNACEÆ.
Foods .
Naval, *Tam.*, Eugenia Jambolana, *Lam.*, MYRTACEÆ.
Foods .
Navane, *Kan.*, Setaria italica, *Kunth.*, GRAMINEÆ.
Foods .

Navattee, *Eng., Fr.*, Brassica campestris, *Linn.*, var. campestris proper, CRUCIFERÆ. Foods .
Naya, *Tam.*, Sizygium jambolanum, *DC.*, MYRTACEÆ. Foods .
Na-yuwai, *Burm.*, Flacourtia Ramontchi, *L'Herit.*, BIXINEÆ. Foods .
Neela-vayalie, *Tel.*, Vernonia anthelmintica, *Willd.*, COMPOSITÆ. Foods .
Neem Tree, *Eng.*, Melia Azadirachta, *Linn.*, MELIACEÆ. Foods .
Neer-arnga, *Tel.*, Paspalum scrobiculatum, *Linn.*, var. fluitans, *Duthie*, GRAMINEÆ. Foods .
Neernoochie, *Tam.*, Vernonia anthelmintica, *Willd.*, COMPOSITÆ. Foods .
Nehar, *Kumaun*, Skimmia Laureola, *Hook.*, RUTACEÆ. Foods .
Nehœ-maka, *Mal.*, Bryonia laciniosa, *Linn.*, CUCURBITACEÆ. Foods .
Nela-jedi, *Tel.*, Semecarpus Anacardium, *Linn.*, ANACARDIACEÆ. Foods .
Nela-madi, *Tel.*, Maba buxifolia, *Pers.*, EBENACEÆ. Foods .
Nella-madu, *Tel.*, Terminalia tomentosa, *W. & A.*, COMBRETACEÆ. Foods .
Nella-shama, Panicum Miliare, *Lamb.*, GRAMINEÆ. Foods .
Nella-shamaloo (the grain), Panicum miliare, *Lamb.*, GRAMINEÆ. Foods .
Nella tuma, *Tel.*, Acacia arabica, *Willd.*, LEGUMINOSÆ. Foods .
Nellekai, *Tam.*, Phyllanthus Emblica, *Linn.*, EUPHORBIACEÆ. Foods .
Nelli, *Tam., Kan.*, Phyllanthus Emblica, *Linn.*, EUPHORBIACEÆ. Foods .
Nelmal, *Hind.*, Strychnos potatorum, *Linn. f.*, LOGANIACEÆ. Foods .
Neosa Pine, *Eng.*, Pinus Gerardiana, *Wall.*, CONIFERÆ. Foods .
Ner, *Pb.*, Skimmia Laureola, *Hook.*, RUTACEÆ. Foods .
Neva-ledi, *Tel.*, Vitex leucoxylon, *Linn.*, VERBENACEÆ. Foods .
Nevew, *Eng.*, Brassica campestris, *Linn.*, var. Napus, CRUCIFERÆ. Foods .
Nevew, Wild, *Eng.*, Brassica campestris, *Linn.*, var. campestris proper, CRUCIFERÆ. Foods .
Nhyú, *Bom.*, Anthocephalus Cadamba, *Miq.*, RUBIACEÆ. Foods .
Niangha, *Lahoul*, Ribes rubrum, *Linn.*, SAXIFRAGACEÆ. Foods .
Niechak, *N. Pb.*, *Ladak to Lahoul*, Hippophœ rhamnoides, *Linn.*, ELÆAGNEÆ. Foods .
Nikari, *Sylhet*, Castanopsis indica, *A. DC.*, CUPULIFERÆ. Foods .
Nikki-bekkar, *Pb.*, Grewia salvifolia, *Heyne*, TILIACEÆ. Foods .
Nila, *Nilgiris*, Turpinia pomifera, *DC.*, SAPINDACEÆ. Foods .
Nilofar, *Pb.*, *Kashmir*, Nymphœ alba, *Linn.*, NYMPHŒACEÆ. Foods .
Nilon, *N.-W. P.*, Andropogon Bladhii, *Retz.*, GRAMINEÆ. Foods .

Nilotpala, *Sans.*, Nymphœa stellata, *Willd.*, NYMPHÆACEÆ.
Foods .
Nilaáphalá, *Beng.*, Nymphœa stellata, *Willd.*, NYMPHÆACEÆ.
Foods .
Niluvu-pendalum, *Tel.*, Dioscorea alata, *Linn.*, DIOSCOREACEÆ.
Foods .
Nim, *Hind.*, *Beng.*, Melia Azadirachta, *Linn.*, MELIACEÆ.
Foods .
Nim, *C. P.*, Melia Azedarach, *Linn.*, MELIACEÆ.
Foods .
Nimat, *Lepcha*, Cordia Myxa, *Linn.*, BORAGINEÆ.
Foods .
Nimb, *Hind.*, *Beng.*, Melia Azadirachta, *Linn.*, MELIACEÆ.
Foods .
Nimba, *Sans.*, Melia Azadirachta, *Linn.*, MELIACEÆ.
Foods .
Nimbe hanu, *Kan.*, Citrus medica, *Linn.*, RUTACEÆ.
Foods .
Nimbu, *Hind.*, Citrus medica, *Linn.*, RUTACEÆ.
Foods .
Nimma-pandu, *Tel.*, Citrus medica, *Linn.*, RUTACEÆ.
Foods .
Niral, *Pb.*, Lycium europœum, *Linn.*, SOLANACEÆ.
Foods .
Niranji, *Kan.*, Salix tetrasperma, *Roxb.*, SALICINEÆ.
Foods .
Nirmali, *Hind.*, *Mar.*, Strychnos potatorum, *Linn. f.*, LOGANIACEÆ.
Foods .
Nirelli, *Tel.*, Allium Cepa, *Linn.*, LILIACEÆ.
Foods .
Nirulli, *Kan.*, Allium Cepa, *Linn.*, LILIACEÆ.
Foods .
Nobhay, *Burm.*, Odina Wodier, *Roxb.*, ANACARDIACEÆ.
Foods .
No-eye, *Eng.*, Cajanus indicus, *Spreng.*, LEGUMINOSÆ.
Foods .
Nomorchi, *Lepcha*, Decaisnea insignis, *Hook. f. & Th.*, BERBERIDEÆ.
Foods .
Nona, *Beng.*, Anona reticulata, *Linn.*, ANONACEÆ.
Foods .
Non-such, *Eng.*, Medicago lupulina, *Linn.*, LEGUMINOSÆ.
Foods .
Nooniya, *Beng.*, Portulaca quadrifida, *Linn.*, PORTULACEÆ.
Foods .
Nooniya-shag, *Beng.*, *Hind.*, Portulaca oleracea, *Linn.*, PORTULACEÆ.
Foods .
Nori, *Beng.*, Phyllanthus distichus, *Müll.-Arg.*, EUPHORBIACEÆ.
Foods .
Nuch, *Pb.*, Traxinus Xanthoxyloides, *Wall.*, OLEACEÆ.
Foods .
Nuch, *Him. name*, Juniperus Communis, *Linn.*, CONIFERÆ.
Foods .
Nukku-kattai, *Tam.*, Dalbergia Sissoo, *Roxb.*, LEGUMINOSÆ.
Foods .
Nulla-gilakara, *Tel.*, Nigella sativa, *Linn.*, RANUNCULACEÆ.
Foods .
Numing rik, *Lepcha*, Rubus paniculatus, *Smith*, ROSACEÆ.
Foods .
Nuni, *Ass.*, Morus indica, *Linn.*, URTICACEÆ.
Foods .
Nuni-beerd, *Tel.*, Luffa ægyptiaca, *Mill.*, *ex Hook. f.*, CUCURBITACEÆ.
Foods .

Nureni-kelangu, *Mal.*, Dioscorea pentaphylla, *Willd.*, DIOSCOREACEÆ.
Foods .
Nut, Areca, *Eng.*, Areca Catechu, *Linn.*, PALMÆ.
Foods .
Nut, Earth, *Eng.*, Arachis hypogæa, *Linn.*, LEGUMINOSÆ.
Foods .
Nut, Ground, *Eng.*, Arachis hypogœa, *Linn.*, LEGUMINOSÆ.
Foods .
Nutmeg, *Eng.*, Myristica moschata, *Willd.*, MYRISTICEÆ.
Foods .
Nut, Pistachio, *Eng.*, Pistacia vera, *Linn.*, ANACARDIACEÆ.
Foods .
Nut, Singhara, *Eng.*, Trapa bispinosa, *Roxb.*, ONAGRACEÆ.
Foods .
Nut Tree, Clearing, *Eng.*, Strychnos potatorum, *Linn.*, LOGANIACEÆ.
Foods .
Nuwwulu, *Tel.*, Sesamumindicum, *Linn.*, PEDALINEÆ.
Foods .
Nyoungbandi, *Burm.*, Ficus religiosa, *Linn.*, URTICACEÆ.
Foods .
Nyoungchin, *Burm.*, Ficus infectoria, *Wall.*, URTICACEÆ.
Foods .
Nyoungpyoo, *Burm.*, Ficus cordifolia, Roxb., URTICACEÆ.
Foods .

O

Oak, Evergreen or Holm, *Eng.*, Quercus Ilex, *Linn.*, CUPULIFERÆ.
Foods .
Oak, Holly-leaved, *Eng.*, Quercus Ilex, *Linn.*, CUPULIFERÆ.
Foods .
Oat Grass, Downy, *Eng.*, Avena pubescens, *L.*, GRAMINEÆ.
Foods .
Oat Grass, Meadow, *Eng.*, Avena pratensis, *Linn.*, GRAMINEÆ.
Foods .
Oats, *Eng.*, Avena sativa, *Linn.*, GRAMINEÆ.
Foods .
Oat, Wild, *Eng.*, Avena fatua, *Linn.*, GRAMINEÆ.
Foods .
Obul, *Pb.*, Rumex Wallichii, *Meisn.*, POLYGONACEÆ.
Foods .
Ochro of West Indies, *Eng.*, Hibiscus esculentus, *Linn.*, MALVACEÆ.
Foods .
Oda, *Tel.*, Panicum brizoides, *Linn.*, GRAMINEÆ.
Foods .
Odla, *Ass.*, Sterculia urens, *Roxb.*, STERCULIACEÆ.
Foods .
Oe, *Pb.*, Albizzia stipulata, *Boivin.*, LEGUMINOSÆ.
Foods .
Oepata, *Mal.*, Avicennia officinalis, *Linn.*, VERBENACEÆ.
Foods .
Ognon, *Fr.*, Allium Cepa, *Linn.*, LILIACEÆ.
Foods .
Oi, *Pb.*, Albizzia stipulata, *Boivin.*, LEGUMINOSÆ.
Foods .
Okshit, *Burm.*, Ægle Marmelos, *Correa.*, RUTACEÆ.
Foods .
Ola, *Pb.*, Solanum verbascifolium, *Linn.*, SOLANACEÆ.
Foods .

Olá cháhá, *Bom.*, Andropogon citratus, GRAMINEÆ.
Foods .
Olchi, *Pb.*, Prunus communis, *Huds.*, var. domestica, ROSACEÆ.
Foods .
Ole, *Beng.*, *Hind.*, Amorphophallus campanulatus, *Blume.*, AROIDEÆ.
Foods .
Oleaster, *Eng.*, Elæagnus hortensis, *M. Beib.*, ELÆAGNEÆ.
Foods .
Olive, *Eng.*, Olea europœa, *Linn.*, OLEACEÆ.
Foods .
Omamu, *Tel.*, Carum copticum, *Benth.*, UMBELLIFERÆ.
Foods .
Oman, *Tam.*, Carum copticum, *Benth.*, UMBELLIFERÆ.
Foods .
Ombu, *Lahoul*, Myricaria germanica, *Desv.*, TAMARISCINEÆ.
Foods .
Ong, *Burm.*, Cocos nucifera, *Linn.*, PALMÆ.
Foods .
Onion, *Eng.*, Allium Cepa, *Linn.*, LILIACEÆ.
Foods .
Ootalay gudda, *Tel.*, Solanum tuberosum, *Linn.*, SOLANACEÆ.
Foods .
Opa, *Tam.*, Salvadora persica, *Garcin.*, SALVADORACEÆ.
Foods .
Opium, *Eng.*, Papaver somniferum, *Linn.*, PAPAVERACEÆ.
Foods .
Orange, *Eng.*, Citrus Aurantium, *Linn.*, RUTACEÆ.
Foods .
Orcha, *Beng.*, Sonneratia acida, *Linn.*, LYTHRACEÆ.
Foods .
Oruza, *Greek*, Oryza sativa, *Linn.*, GRAMINEÆ
Foods .
Osirka, *Tel.*, Phyllanthus Emblica, *Linn.*, EUPHORBIACEÆ.
Foods .
Otengah, *Ass.*, Dillenea indica, *Linn.*, DILLENIACEÆ.
Foods .
Ourooha, *Sans*, Cynodon Dactylon, *Pers.*, GRAMINEÆ.
Foods .
Ouru palay, *Tel.*, Oxystelma esculentum, *Br.*, ASCLEPIADEÆ.
Foods .
Ovall, *Bom.*, Mimusops Elengi, *Linn.*, SAPOTACEÆ.
Foods .

P

Pabuna, *Hind.*, Ulmus Willichiana, *Planch.*, URTICACEÆ.
Foods .
Padall, *Pb.*, Heracleum, sp., UMBELLIFERÆ.
Foods .
Padám, *N.-W. P.*, Juniperus excelsa, *M. Beib.*, CONIFERÆ.
Foods .
Padavala kayl, *Kan.*, Trichosanthes anguma, *Linn.*, CUCURBITÁCEÆ.
Foods .
Paddam, *Hind.*, Prunus Puddum, *Roxb.*, ROSACEÆ.
Foods .
Padi, *Malay*, Oryza sativa, *Linn.*, GRAMINEÆ.
Foods .
Padma, *Beng.*, Nelumbium speciosum, *Willd.*, NYMPHŒACEÆ.
Foods .

Palúdar, *Him. name*, Abies Webbiana, *Lindl.*, CONIFERÆ.
Foods .
Paludar, *Pb.*, Picea Webbiana, *Lamb.*, CONIFERÆ.
Foods .
Paluk, *Hind.*, Spinacia oleracea, *Mill.*, CHENOPODIACEÆ.
Foods .
Palung, *Beng.*, Spinacia oleracea. *Mill.*, CHENOPODIACEÆ.
Foods .
Palungú, *Tam.*, Hibiscus cannabinus, *Linn.*, MALVACEÆ.
Foods .
Palúpaghel-kalung, *Tam.*, Momordica dioica, *Roxb.*, CUCURBITACEÆ.
Foods .
Palwal, *Hind.*, Trichosanthes dioica, *Roxb.*, CUCURBITACEÆ.
Foods .
Pambah, *Pers*, Gossypium herbaceum, *Linn.*, MALVACEÆ.
Foods .
Pambash. *Pb. Himalaya & Afg.*, Rheum Emodi, *Wall.*, POLYGONACEÆ.
Foods .
Pamposh, *Pb.*, Nelumbium speciosum, *Willd.*, NYMPHŒACEÆ.
Foods .
Pán, *Hind.*, *Beng.*, Piper Betle, *Linn.*, PIPERACEÆ.
Foods .
Pan, *Pb.*, *Sind*, Typha elephantina, *Roxb.*, TYPHACEÆ.
Foods .
Pána, *Bom.*, Piper Betle, *Linn.*, PIPERACEÆ.
Foods .
Pana, *Sind*, Typha elephantina, *Roxb.*, TYPHACEÆ.
Foods .
Panam, *Tam.*, Borassus flabelliformis, *Linn.*, PALMÆ.
Foods .
Panar, *Hind.*, Randia uliginosa. *DC.*, RUBIACEÆ.
Foods .
Panas, *Hind.*, Artocarpus integrifolia, *Linn.*, URTICACEÆ.
Foods .
Panasa, *Sans.*, Artocarpus integrifolia, *Linn.*, URTICACEÆ.
Foods .
Pándharyú, *Bom.*, Acacia leucophlæa, *Willd.*, LEGUMINOSÆ.
Foods .
Pandúr, *Lepcha*, Anthocephalus Cadamba, *Miq.*, RUBIACEÆ.
Foods .
Panelra, *Mar.*, Randia uliginosa, *DC.*, RUBIACEÆ.
Foods .
Pangah, *Burm.*, Terminalia chebula, *Retz.*, COMBRETACEÆ.
Foods .
Pangra, *Nep.*, Entada scandens, *Bth.*, LEGUMINOSÆ.
Foods .
Paniah, *Hind.*, Randia uliginosa, *DC.*, RUBIACEÆ.
Foods .
Panic Grass, Creeping, *Eng.*, Cynodon Dactylon, *Pers.*, GRAMINEÆ.
Foods .
Panichika, *Tam.*, Diospyros Embryopteris, *Pers.*, EBENACEÆ.
Foods .
Pani-jama, *Beng.*, Salix tetrasperma, *Roxb.*, SALICINEÆ.
Foods .
Pani-phal, *Beng*, Trapa bispinosa, *Roxb.*, ONAGRACEÆ.
Foods .
Panir, *Pb.*, Withania coagulans, *Dun.*, SOLANACEÆ.
Foods .
Panir-bad, *Pers.*, Withania coagulans, *Dun.*, SOLANACEÆ.
Foods .
Panirak, *Pb.*, *& Sind*, Malva parviflora, *Linn.*, MALVACEÆ.
Foods .

Panjl, *Lepcha*, Randia dumetorum, *Lam.*, RUBIACEÆ.
Foods .
Panlat, *Burm.*, Elettaria Cardamomum, *Maton.*, SCITAMINEÆ.
Foods .
Panni, *Pb.*, Andropogon laniger, *Desf.*, GRAMINEÆ.
Foods .
Pannle, *Tam.*, Borassus flabelliformis, *Linn.*, PALMÆ.
Foods .
Pánnan, *Oudh*, Ougeinia dalbergioides, *Benth.*, LEGUMINOSÆ
Foods .
Pao, *Lepcha*, Dendrocalamus Hamiltonii, *Nees. & Arn.*, GRAMINEÆ.
Foods .
Papar, *Hind.*, Pongamia glabra, *Vent.*, LEGUMINOSÆ.
Foods .
Papar, *Kumaun*, Ribes nigrum, *Linn.*, SAXIFRAGACEÆ.
Foods .
Papar, *Kumaun*, Ulmus integrifolia, *Roxb.*, URTICACEÆ.
Foods .
Papat-kalam, *Pb.*, Viburnum cotinifolium, *Don.*, CAPRIFOLIACEÆ.
Foods .
Papaw Tree, *Eng.*, Carica papaya, *L.*, PASSIFLOREÆ.
Foods .
Papaya, *Hind.*, Carica Papaya, *L.*, PASSIFLOREÆ.
Foods .
Papaya Tree, *Eng.*, Carica Papaya, *L.*, PASSIFLOREÆ.
Foods .
Paper Birch, Indian, *Eng.*, Betula Bhojpattra, *Wall.*, CUPULIFERÆ.
Foods .
Papra, *Pb.*, Salvia Moorcroftiana, *Wall.*, LABIATÆ.
Foods .
Papri, *Hind.*, *Pb.*, Ulmus integrifolia, *Roxb.*, URTICACEÆ.
Foods .
Papri, *Pb.*, Podophyllum emodi, *Wall.*, BERBERIDEÆ.
Foods .
Paputa, *Sind*, Carica Papaya, *L.*, PASSIFLORÆ.
Foods .
Parami, *Tel.*, Zizyphus Œnoplia, *Mill.*, RHAMNEÆ.
Foods .
Parás, *Mar.*, Butea frondosa, *Roxb.*, LEGUMINOSÆ.
Foods .
Páras, *Pb.*, Prunus Padus, *Linn.*, ROSACEÆ.
Foods .
Parba, *N.-W. P.*, Heteropogon contortus, *R. & S.*, GRAMINEÆ.
Foods .
Paroa, *Hind.*, Ficus glomerata, *Roxb.*, URTICACEÆ.
Foods .
Parosi, *Bom.*, Luffa ægyptiaca, *Mill. ex. Hook f.*, CUCURBITACEÆ.
Foods .
Parpalli, *Kan.*, Zizyphus nummularia, *W. & A.*, RHAMNEÆ.
Foods .
Parsid, *Singrowli*, Hardwickia binata, *Roxb.*, LEGUMINOSÆ.
Foods .
Parsley, *Eng.*, Petroselinum sativum, *Hoff. & Koch.*, UMBELLIFERÆ.
Foods .
Parungi, *Pb.*, Quercus dilatata, *Lindl.*, CUPULIFERÆ.
Foods .
Parupu benda, *Tam.*, Hibiscus ficulneus, *Linn.*, MALVACEÆ.
Foods .
Parwatti, *Pb.*, Cocculus Leæba, *DC.*, MENISPERMACEÆ.
Foods .
Pas, *Pb.*, Grewia villosa, *Willd.*, TILIACEÆ.
Foods .

Pa-shing, *Bhutia*, Dendrocalamus Hamiltonii, *Nees. & Arn.*, GRAMINEÆ.
Foods .
Passi, *Nep.*, Pyrus Pashia, *Ham.*, ROSACEÆ.
Foods .
Pastuwanne, *Afg.*, Grewia oppositifolia, *Roxb.*, TILIACEÆ.
Foods .
Pasupu, *Tel.*, Curcuma longa, *Roxb.*, SCITAMINEÆ.
Foods .
Pat, *Beng.*, Corchorus olitorius, *Linn.*, TILIACEÆ.
Foods .
Patee-khori, *Beng.*, Saccharum fuscum, *Roxb.*, GRAMINEÆ.
Foods .
Patenga, *Tel.*, Briedelia montana, *Willd.*, EUPHORBIACEÆ.
Foods .
Pathioo, *Nep.*, Arundinaria racemosa, *Munro*, GRAMINEÆ.
Foods .
Pathor, *Pb.*, Briedelia retusa, *Spreng.*, EUPHORBIACEÆ.
Foods .
Patimil, *Nep.*, Antidesma diandrum, *Tulasne*, EUPHORBIACEÆ.
Foods .
Pativa, *Uriya*, Randia dumetorum, *Lam.*, RUBIACEÆ.
Foods .
Patmoro, *Nep.*, Cornus macrophylla, *Wall.*, CORNACEÆ.
Foods .
Patnal. See Pisum sativum, *Linn.*, LEGUMINOSÆ.
Foods .
Patsan, *Hind.*, *Dec.*, Hibiscus cannabinus, *Linn.*, MALVACEÆ.
Foods .
Patur, *Hind.*, Hymenodictyon excelsum, *Wall.*, RUBIACEÆ.
Foods .
Patu-swa, *Nep.*, Polygonum molle, *Don.*, POLYGONACEÆ.
Foods .
Patwa, *Dec. Hind.*, Hibiscus Sabdariffa, *Linn.*, MALVACEÆ.
Foods .
Pauch-sim, *Beng.*, Dolichos Lablab, *Linn.*, LEGUMINOSÆ.
Foods .
Pauttie, *Tel.*, Gossypium herbaceum, *Linn.*, MALVACEÆ.
Foods .
Pává, *Tam.*, Schleichera trijuga, *Willd.*, SAPINDACEÆ.
Foods .
Payála, *Garhwal*, Buchanania latifolia, *Roxb.*, ANACARDIACEÆ.
Foods .
Paycoomutí, *Tam.*, Citrullus Colocynthis, *Schrad.*, CUCURBITACEÆ.
Foods .
Pea, common, *Eng.*, Pisum sativum, *Linn.*, LEGUMINOSÆ.
Foods .
Pea, Field, *Eng.*, Pisum arvense, *Linn.*, LEGUMINOSÆ.
Foods .
Pea, Grey, *Eng.*, Pisum arvense, *Linn.*, LEGUMINOSÆ.
Foods .
Peach, *Eng.*, Prunus persica, *Benth. & Hook.*, ROSACEÆ.
Foods .
Pear, common, *Eng.*, Pyrus communis, *Linn.*, ROSACEÆ.
Foods .
Pebeng, *Burm.*, Corypha umbraculifera, *Linn.*, PALMÆ.
Foods .
Pech, *Sind*, Daphne mucronata, *Royle*, THYMELÆACEÆ.
Foods .
Peda-kanru, *Tel.*, Flacourtia Ramontchi, *L'Herit.*, BIXINEÆ.
Foods .
Pedda, *Tel.*, Eleusine corocana, *Gærtn*, GRAMINEÆ.
Foods .

Pedda-are, *Tam.*, Bauhinia purpurea, *Linn.*, LEGUMINOSÆ. Foods .
Pedda chintu, *Tel.*, Celastrus senegalensis, *Lam.*, CELASTRINEÆ. Foods .
Pedda dosray, *Tel.*, Cucumis Melo, *Linn.*, var. Momordica (*sp. Roxb.*), CUCURBITACEÆ. Foods .
Pedda eita, *Tel.*, Phœnix sylvestris, *Roxb.*, PALMÆ. Foods .
Pedda-ganti (plant), *Tel.*, Pennisetum typhoideum, *Rich.*, GRAMINEÆ. Foods .
Peddagi, *Tel.*, Pterocarpus Marsupium, *Roxb.*, LEGUMINOSÆ. Foods .
Pedda-jila-kurra, *Tel.*, Fœniculum vulgare, *Gærtn.*, UMBELLIFERÆ. Foods .
Pedda-kal, *Tel.*, Cucumis Melo, *Linn.*, var. Momordica (*sp. Roxb.*), CUCURBITACEÆ. Foods .
Pedda-nella-kura, *Tel.*, Premna latifolia, *Roxb.*, VERBENACEÆ. Foods .
Peddanolwli, *Tel.*, Ulmus integrifolia, *Roxb.*, URTICACEÆ. Foods .
Pedda-warago-wenki, *Tel.*, Salvadora persica, *Garcin.*, SALVADORACEÆ. Foods .
Peddi-mari, *Tel.*, Ficus bengalensis, *Linn.*, URTICACEÆ. Foods .
Peechenggah, *Mal.*, Luffa acutangula, *Roxb.*, CUCURBITACEÆ. Foods .
Peekun-kai, *Tam.*, Luffa acutangula, *Roxb.*, CUCURBITACEÆ. Foods .
Peepul, Pahari, *N.-W. Bengal*, Piper sylvaticum, *Roxb.*, PIPERACEÆ. Foods .
Peetha-kalaban-tha, *Tam.*, Agave americana, *Linn.*, AMARYLLIDEÆ. Foods .
Peingnal, *Burm.*, Artocarpus integrifolia, *Linn.*, URTICACEÆ. Foods .
Pelándu, *Sans.*, Allium cepa, *Linn.*, LILIACEÆ. Foods .
Pella-gumudu, *Gond.*, Antidesma diandrum, *Tulasne*, EUPHORBIACEÆ. Foods .
Pender, *Gond.*, Randia uliginosa, *DC.*, RUBIACEÆ. Foods .
Pendra, *Uriya*, Randia uliginosa, *DC.*, RUBIACEÆ. Foods .
Penma, *Ladak*, Potentilla fruticosa, *Linn.*, ROSACEÆ. Foods .
Penti tadi, *Tel.*, Borassus flabelliformis, *Linn.*, PALMÆ. Foods .
Pepper, Bell, *Eng.*, Capsicum grossum, *Willd.*, SOLANACEÆ. Foods .
Peppermint, *Eng.*, Mentha piperita, *Linn.*, LABIATÆ. Foods .
Pepre, *Tam.*, Ficus infectoria, *Wall.*, URTICACEÆ. Foods .
Pepul Tree, *Eng.*, Ficus religiosa, *Linn.*, URTICACEÆ. Foods .
Perambu, *Tam.*, Calamus Rotang, *Linn.*, PALMÆ. Foods .
Pera pastawane, *Afg.*, Securinega Leucopyrus, *Müll.-Arg.*, EUPHORBIACEÆ. Foods .
Periaeetcham, *Tam.*, Phœnix sylvestris, *Roxb.*, PALMÆ. Foods .
Perinkara, *Kan.*, Elæocarpus serratus, *Linn.*, TILIACEÆ. Foods .

Perkhatúna, *Pb.*, Cocculus Leæba, *DC.*, MENISPERMACEÆ.
Foods .
Peru, *Bom.*, Psidium Guyava, *Raddi.*, MYRTACEÆ.
Foods .
Perumbe, *Tam.*, Prosopis spicigera, *Linn.*, LEGUMINOSÆ.
Foods .
Perungayam, *Tam.*, Ferula Narthex, *Boiss.*, UMBELLIFERÆ.
Foods .
Pessaloo, *Tel.*, Phaseolus Mungo, *Linn.*, LEGUMINOSÆ.
Foods .
Petakara, *Beng.*, Chrysophyllum Roxburghii, *G. Don.*, SAPOTACEÆ.
Foods .
Pethá, *Hind.*, Benincasa cerifera, *Savi*, CUCURBITACEÆ.
Foods .
Pethra, *Him. name*, Juniperus communis, *Linn.*, CONIFERÆ.
Foods .
Péyara, *Beng.*, Psidium Guyava, *Raddi.*, MYRTACEÆ.
Foods .
Phair-posh, *Kashmir*, Villarsia nymphoides, *Vent.*, GENTIANACEÆ.
Foods .
Phálase, *Bom.*, Grewia asiatica, *Linn.*, TILIACEÆ.
Foods .
Phaldu, *Hind.*, Hymenodictyon excelsum, *Wall.*, RUBIACEÆ.
Foods .
Phallgawar, *N.-W. P. & Oudh*, Cyamopsis psoralioides, *DC.*, LEGUMINOSÆ. Foods .
Phalja, *Pb.*, Populus ciliata, *Wall.*, SALICINEÆ.
Foods .
Phálsa, *Hind.*, *Sind*, *Pb.*, Grewia asiatica, *Linn.*, TILIACEÆ.
Foods .
Phalsh, *Pb.*, Populus balsamifera, *Linn.*, SALICINEÆ.
Foods .
Phalwa, *Pb.*, Grewia vestita, *Wall.*, TILIACEÆ.
Foods .
Phalwara, *Hind.*, Bassia butyracea, *Roxb.*, SAPOTACEÆ.
Foods .
Phamsikol, *Lepcha*, Dillenia indica, *Linn.*, DILLENIACEÆ.
Foods .
Phanl, *Lepcha*, Phœbe attenuata, *Nees.*, LAURINEÆ.
Foods .
Phapar, *Kumaun*, Fagopyrum emarginatum, *Meisn.*, POLYGONACEÆ.
Foods .
Phaphra, *Pb.*, Fagopyrum esculentum, *Mœnch.*, POLYGONACEÆ.
Foods .
Pharoah, *Hind.*, *Sind*, *Pb.*, Grewia asiatica, *Linn.*, TILIACEÆ.
Foods .
Pharsa, *Hind.*, Grewia tiliæfolia, *Vahl.*, TILIACEÆ.
Foods .
Pharsia, *Hind.*, Grewia vestita, *Wall.*, TILIACEÆ.
Foods .
Pharsia, *Kumaun*, Grewia scabrophylla, *Roxb.*, TILIACEÆ.
Foods .
Pharwa, *Pb.*, Grewia oppositifolia, *Roxb.*, TILIACEÆ.
Foods .
Phatak, *Him. name*, Betula Bhojpattra, *Wall.*, CUPULIFERÆ.
Foods .
Phikar, *N.-W. P.*, Panicum miliaceum, *Linn.*, GRAMINEÆ.
Foods .
Philku, *Pb.*, Lonicera angustifolia, *Wall.*, CAPRIFOLIACEÆ.
Foods .
Phogalli (flowers), *Pb.*, Calligonum polygonoides, *Linn.*, POLYGONACEÆ.
Foods .

Phok, *Pb.*, Calligonum polygonoides, *Linn.*, POLYGONACEÆ.
Foods .
Phomphli, *Pb.*, Sageretia theezans, *Brongn.*, RHAMNEÆ.
Foods .
Phulahi, *Pb.*, Acacia modesta, *Wall.*, LEGUMINOSÆ.
Foods .
Phulan, *Pb.*, Fagopyrum emarginatum, *Meisn.*, POLYGONACEÆ.
Foods .
Phularwa, *N.-W. P.*, Eragrostis flexuosa, *Roxb.*, GRAMINEÆ.
Foods .
Phularwa, *N.-W. P.*, Eragrostis plumosa, *Link.*, GRAMINEÆ.
Foods .
Phulel, *Kumaun*, Bassia butyracea, *Roxb.*, SAPOTACEÆ.
Foods .
Phulsan, *N. Ind.*, Crotalaria juncea, *Linn.*, LEGUMINOSÆ.
Foods .
Phulsel, *Kashmir*, Viburnum stellulatum, *Wall.*, CAPRIFOLIACEÆ.
Foods .
Phul-wara, *Chenab*, Prinsepia utilis, *Royle*, ROSACEÆ.
Foods .
Phus, *Pb.*, *Ladak*, Potamogeton gramineus, *L.*, NAIADACEÆ.
Foods .
Phusera, *Hind.*, Mæsa argentea, *Wall.*, MYRSINEÆ.
Foods .
Phuspat, *Nep.*, Betula Bhojpattra, *Wall.*, CUPULIFERÆ.
Foods .
Phut, *Hind.*, Cucumis Melo, *Linn.*, var. Momordica (*sp. Roxb.*), CUCURBITACEÆ. Foods .
Phut, *Pb.*, Lonicera quinquelocularis, *Hardwicke*, CAPRIFOLIACEÆ.
Foods .
Phuti, *Beng.*, Cucumis Melo, *Linn.*, var., Momordica (*sp. Roxb.*), CUCURBITACEÆ. Foods .
Phutiki, *Tel.*, Grewia asiatica, *Linn.*, TILIACEÆ.
Foods .
Phútkonda, *Pb.*, Ballota limbata, *Benth.*, LABIATÆ.
Foods .
Pi, *Eng.*, Tacca pinnatifida, *Forsk.*, TACCACEÆ.
Foods .
Piál, *Garhwal*, Buchanania latifolia, *Roxb.*, ANACARDIACEÆ.
Foods .
Piár, *Oudh*, Buchanania latifolia, *Roxb.*, ANACARDIACEÆ.
Foods .
Piasal, *Beng.*, Terminalia tomentosa, *W. & A.*, COMBRETACEÆ.
Foods .
Piaz, *Pb.*, Iris kumaonensis, *Wall.*, IRIDEÆ.
Foods .
Piaz barani, *Hind.*, Allium Rubelium, *Bieb.*, LILIACEÆ.
Foods .
Piazi, *Pb.*, Asphodelus fistulosus, *Linn.*, LILIACEÆ.
Foods .
Piazi chiri, *Hind.*, Allium Rubelium, *Bieb.*, LILIACEÆ.
Foods .
Piaz, Jangli, *Hind.*, Allium Rubelium, *Bieb.*, LILIACEÆ.
Foods .
Pigeon, *Eng.*, Cajanus indicus, *Spreng*, LEGUMINOSÆ.
Foods .
Pilak, *Pb.*, Solanum gracilipes, *Dcne.*, SOLANACEÆ.
Foods .
Pila-sarson, *Hind.*, Brassica campestris, *Linn.*, var. Napus, sub-va glauca, CRUCIFERÆ. Foods .
Pilru, *Pb.*, Lonicera angustifolia, *Wall.*, CAPRIFOLIACEÆ.
Foods .

Pilaa, *Lahoul*, Ribes Grossularia, *Linn.*, SAXIFRAGACEÆ.
Foods .
Pilu, *Mar.*, Salvadora oleoides, *Linn.*, SALVADORACEÆ.
Foods .
Pimento Tree, *Eng.*, Eugenia Pimento, *DC.*, MYRTACEÆ.
Foods .
Pin, *Burm.*, Butea frondosa, *Roxb.*, LEGUMINOSÆ.
Foods .
Pinári, *Tam.*, Sterculia fœtida, *Linn.*, STERCULIACEÆ.
Foods .
Pincho, *Pb.*, Boehmeria salicifolia, *D. Don.*, URTICACEÆ.
Foods .
Pind (fruit), *Pb.*, Phœnix dactylifera, *Linn.*, PALMÆ.
Foods .
Pindalu, *Hind.*, Randia uliginosa, *DC.*, RUBIACEÆ.
Foods .
Pind-khajur, *Hind.*, Phœnix acaulis, *Roxb.*, PALMÆ.
Foods .
Pindra, *Mar.*, Randia uliginosa, *DC.*, RUBIACEÆ.
Foods .
Pine-apple, *Eng.*, Ananassa sativa, *Linn.*, BROMELIACEÆ.
Foods .
Pinju, *Pb.*, Capparis aphylla, *Roth.*, CAPPARIDEÆ.
Foods .
Pinjung, *Ladak*, Potentilla fruticosa, *Linn.*, ROSACEÆ.
Foods .
Pinlaytsee, *Burm.*, Ximenia americana, *Willd.*, OLACINEÆ.
Foods .
Pinna, *Tel.*, Bassia longifolia, *Willd.*, SAPOTACEÆ.
Foods .
Pintayan, *Burm.*, Grewia vestita, *Wall.*, TILIACEÆ.
Foods .
Pipal, *Hind.*, Ficus religiosa, *Linn.*, URTICACEÆ.
Foods .
Pipal, Pahari, *Pb.*, Populus ciliata, *Wall.*, SALICINEÆ.
Foods .
Pipli, Jangli, *Pb.*, Ficus infectoria, *Wall.*, URTIACCEÆ.
Foods .
Piplo, *Guz.*, Ficus religiosa, *Linn.*, URTICACEÆ.
Foods .
Pippa, *Pb.*, Caralluma edulis, *Benth.*, ASCLEPIADEÆ.
Foods .
Pipudel, *Tam.*, Trichosanthes cucumerina, *Linn.*, CUCURBITACEÆ.
Foods .
Pipul, *Hind.*, Ficus cordifolia, *Roxb.*, URTICACEÆ.
Foods .
Piralo, *Beng.*, Randia uliginosa, *DC.*, RUBIACEÆ.
Foods .
Pishina, *Tel.*, Maba buxifolia, *Pers.*, EBENACEÆ.
Foods .
Pista, *Beng.*, *Hind.*, *& Bom.*, Pistacia vera, *Linn.*, ANACARDIACEÆ.
Foods .
Pita, *Tam.*, Agave americana, *Linn.*, AMARYLLIDEÆ.
Foods .
Pita-kanda, *Tel.*, Daucus Carota, *Linn.*, UMBELLIFERÆ.
Foods .
Pitar-saleri, *Pb.*, Petroselinum sativum, *Hoff. & Koch.*, UMBELLIFERÆ.
Foods .
Pithogarkh, *Ass.*, Chrysophyllum Roxburghii, *G. Don.*, SAPOTACEÆ.
Foods .
Pitwa, *Hind.*, Hibiscus cannabinus, *Linn.*, MALVACEÆ.
Foods .

Poráśu, *Uriya*, Butea frondosa, *Roxb.*, LEGUMINOSÆ.
Foods .
Poróa, *Kol.*, Artocarpus integrifolia, *Linn.*, URTICACEÆ.
Foods .
Posa, *Burm.*, Morus indica, *Linn.*, URTICACEÆ.
Foods .
Possy, *Nep.*, Docynia indica, *Dcne.*, ROSACEÆ.
Foods .
Post, *Beng.*, *Hind.*, Papaver somniferum, *Linn.*, PAPAVERACEÆ.
Foods .
Potal, *Beng.*, Trichosanthes dioica, *Roxb.*, CUCURBITACEÆ.
Foods .
Potali, *Hind.*, Glycosmis pentaphylla, *Correa.*, RUTACEÆ.
Foods .
Potato, *Eng.*, Solanum tuberosum, *Linn.*, SOLANACEÆ.
Foods .
Potatoe, Sweet, *Lamk.*, Ipomæa Batatas, *Lamk.*, CONVOLVULACEÆ.
Foods .
Poto-dhamun, *Palamow*, Grewia vestita, *Wall.*, TILIACEÆ.
Foods .
Potu tadi, *Tel.*, Borassus flabelliformis, *Linn.*, PALMÆ.
Foods .
Pouk, *Burm.*, Butea frondosa, *Roxb.*, LEGUMINOSÆ.
Foods .
Poukpan, *Burm.*, Sesbania grandiflora, *Pers.*, LEGUMINOSÆ.
Foods .
Poulto, *Eng.* *See* Pisum arvense, *Linn.*, LEGUMINOSÆ.
Foods .
Prab, *Garo*, Ficus cordifolia, *Roxb.*, URTICACEÆ.
Foods .
Prabanatha, *Sans.*, Cassia Tora, *Linn.*, LEGUMINOSÆ.
Foods .
Praong, *Lepcha*, Arundinaria Hookeriana, *Munro*, GRAMINEÆ.
Foods .
Prau, *Pb.*, Eremurus spectabelis, *Bieb.*, LILIACEÆ.
Foods .
Pride of India, *Eng.*, Melia Azedarach, *Linn.*, MELIACEÆ.
Foods .
Pritu, *Chenab*, Pinus Gerardiana, *Wall.*, CONIFERÆ.
Foods .
Pronchadik, *Lepcha*, Holbællia latifolia, *Wall.*, BERBERIDEÆ.
Foods .
Prong, *Lepcha*, Arundinaria Hookeriana, *Munro*, GRAMINEÆ.
Foods .
Pú, *Tam.*, Schleichera trijuga, *Willd.*, SAPINDACEÆ.
Foods .
Puagakara (male plants), *Tel.*, Momordica dioica, *Roxb.*, CUCURBITACEÆ.
Foods .
Pucha-payaroo, *Tam.*, Phaseolus Mungo, *Linn.*, LEGUMINOSÆ.
Foods .
Pudding Pipe, *Eng.*, Cassia Fistula, *Linn.*, LEGUMINOSÆ.
Foods .
Pudel, *Tam.*, Trichosanthes cucumerina, *Linn.*, CUCURBITACEÆ.
Foods .
Pudina, *Beng.*, *Hind.*, *Dec.*, Mentha arvensis, *Linn.*, LABIATÆ.
Foods .
Pudina, Pahari, *Hind.*, Mentha viridis, *Linn.*, LABIATÆ.
Foods .
Pukana, *Pb.*, Rubus ellipticus, *Smith*, ROSACEÆ.
Foods .
Pulá, *Tam.*, Bombax malabaricum, *DC.*, MALVACEÆ,
Foods .

Pulachi, *Tam.*, Schleichera trijuga, *Willd.*, SAPINDACEÆ.
Foods .
Púli, *Tam.*, Tamarindus indica, *Linn.*, LEGUMINOSÆ.
Foods .
Pulichinta, *Tel.*, Oxalis corniculata, *Linn.*, GERANIACEÆ.
Foods .
Pulladondur, *Tel.*, Bauhinia malabarica, *Roxb.*, LEGUMINOSÆ.
Foods .
Pulmu, *Pb.*, Viburnum fœtens, *Decaisne*, CAPRIFOLIACEÆ.
Foods .
Pulooah, *N.-W. P.*, Chloris barbata, *Swartz.*, GRAMINEÆ.
Foods .
Pulréah, *N.-W. P.*, Andropogon pertusus, *Willd.*, GRAMINEÆ.
Foods .
Pulsur, *Tel.*, Antidesma Ghæsembilla, *Gærtn.*, EUPHORBIACEÆ.
Foods .
Pulua, *Beng.*, Hibiscus cannabinus, *Linn.*, MALVACEÆ.
Foods .
Pulu pinan myauk, *Burm.*, Manihot utilissima, *Pohl.*, EUPHORBIACEÆ.
Foods .
Pulwal, *N.-W. P.*, Andropogon pertusus, *Willd.*, GRAMINEÆ.
Foods ,
Pulwan, *Pb.*, Andropogon pertusus, *Willd.*, GRAMINEÆ.
Foods .
Pumæ, *Pb.*, Oxybaphus himalaicus, *Edge.*, NYCTAGINEÆ.
Foods .
Pummoon, *Lepcha*, Arundinaria racemosa, *Munro*, GRAMINEÆ.
Foods .
Pumpkin, *Eng.*, Cucurbita Pepo, *DC.*, CUCURBITACEÆ.
Foods .
Pun, *Him. name*, Abies Webbiana, *Lindl.*, CONIFERÆ.
Foods .
Puná, *Courtallum*, Nephelium Longana, *Camb.*, SAPINDACEÆ.
Foods .
Punanto-si, *Burm.*, Trigonella Fœnum-grœcum, *Linn.*, LEGUMINOSÆ.
Foods .
Punar puli, *Kan.*, Garcinia Morella, *Desr.*, GUTTIFERÆ.
Foods .
Pung-chu, *Ladak*, Taxus baccata, *Linn.*, CONIFERÆ.
Foods .
Púnil, *Kan.*, Odina Wodier, *Roxb.*, ANACARDIACEÆ.
Foods .
Púnirke-bíf, *Hind.*, Withania coagulans, *Don.*, SOLANACEÆ.
Foods .
Púnyan, *Hind.*, Ehretia acuminata, *Br.*, BORAGINEÆ.
Foods .
Pur, *Tel.*, Eriodendron anfractuosum, *DC.*, MALVACEÆ.
Foods ,
Pura-gadi, *Tel.*, Cyperus bulbosus, *Vahl.*, CYPERACEÆ.
Foods .
Purkar, *Ladak*, Tanacetum senecionis, *Gay in DC.*, COMPOSITÆ.
Foods .
Pursan, *Pb.*, Ehretia acuminata, *Br.*, BORAGINEÆ.
Foods .
Purslane, Common, *Eng.*, Portulaca oleracea, *Linn.*, PORTULACEÆ.
Foods .
Pushini-kaia, *Tam.*, Cucurbita maxima, *Duchesne*, CUCURBITACEÆ.
Foods .
Pusku, *Tel.*, Schleichera trijuga, *Willd.*, SAPINDACEÆ.
Foods .
Putájan, *Pb.*, Putranjiva Roxburghii, *Wall*, EUPHORBIACEÆ.
Foods .

Putiki, *Tel.*, Grewia asiatica, *Linn.*, TILIACEÆ.
Foods .
Pútra-jiva, *Hind.*, Putranjiva Roxburghii, *Wall.*, EUPHORBIACEÆ.
Foods .
Putsa-kaya, *Tel.*, Citrullus Colocynthis, *Schrad.*, CUCURBITACEÆ.
Foods .
Put-strangali, *Tel.*, Apluda aristata, *Linn.*, GRAMINEÆ.
Foods .
Putulika, *Sans.*, Trichosanthes dioica, *Roxb.*, CUCURBITACEÆ.
Foods .
Pyal, *Bom.*, Buchanania latifolia, *Roxb.*, ANACARDIACEÆ.
Foods .
Pyeenyoung, *Burm.*, Ficus bengalensis, *Linn.*, URTICACEÆ.
Foods .

Q

Quince, *Eng.*, Cydonia vulgaris, *Tourn.*, ROSACEÆ.
Foods .

R

Radam, *Pb.*, Taraxacum officinale, *Wigg.*, COMPOSITÆ.
Foods .
Rade, *Pb.*, Ribes rubrum, *Linn.*, SAXIFRAGACEÆ.
Foods .
Radish, *Eng.*, Raphonus sativus, *Linn.*, CRUCIFERÆ.
Foods .
Rag, *Pb.*, Picea Webbiana, *Lamb.*, CONIFERÆ.
Foods .
Rag, *Him. name*, Abies Webbiana, *Lindl.*, CONIFERÆ.
Foods .
Ragee, *Eng.*, Eleusine corocana, *Gærtn.*, GRAMINEÆ.
Foods .
Ragha, *Kumaun*, Abies Webbiana, *Lindl.*, CONIFERÆ.
Foods .
Ragi, *Tel.*, Ficus religiosa, *Linn.*, URTICACEÆ.
Foods .
Rahira, *Pb.*, Tecoma undulata, *G. Don.*, BIGNONIACEÆ.
Foods .
Rai, *Eng.*, *Hind.*, Brassica juncea, *H. f.*, *& T. T.*, CRUCIFERÆ.
Foods .
Rai, *Hind.*, Brassica nigra, *Koch.*, CRUCIFERÆ.
Foods .
Rai, *Uriya*, Dillenia indica, *Linn.*, DILLENIACEÆ.
Foods .
Rai, *Uriya*, *Tam.*, Dillenia pentagyna, *Roxb.*, DILLENIACEÆ.
Foods .
Rai, *Tel.*, Ficus religiosa, *Linn.*, URTICACEÆ.
Foods .
Rai-asl, *Hind.*, Brassica nigra, *Koch.*, CRUCIFERÆ.
Foods .
Rai-banj, *Kumaun*, Quercus lanuginosa, *Don.*, CUPULIFERÆ.
Foods .
Rai-bari, *Hind.*, Brassica juncea, *H. f.*, *& T. T.*, CRUCIFERÆ.
Foods .
Rai-ghor, *Hind.*, Brassica nigra, *Koch.*, CRUCIFERÆ.
Foods .

Rai-Jaman, *Hind.*, Eugenia operculata, *Roxb.*, MYRTACEÆ.
Foods .
al-kali, *Hind.*, Brassica nigra, *Koch.*, CRUCIFERÆ.
Foods .
al-khas, *Hind.*, Brassica juncea, *H. f.*, *& T. T.*, CRUCIFERÆ.
Foods .
al-makara, *Hind.*, Brassica nigra, *Koch.*, CRUCIFERÆ.
Foods .
Rain, *Meywar*, Mimusops hexandra, *Roxb.*, SAPOTACEÆ.
Foods .
Rai sarisha, *Beng.*, Brassica nigra, *Koch.*, CRUCIFERÆ.
Foods .
Rai-shahzada, *Hind.*, Brassica juncea, *H. f.*, *& T. T.*, CRUCIFERÆ.
Foods .
Rajáin, *Pb.*, Ulmus integrifolia, *Roxb.*, URTICACEÆ.
Foods .
Rajankhirni, *Guz.*, Mimusops hexandra, *Roxb.*, SAPOTACEÆ.
Foods .
Raj birij, *Nep.*, Cassia Fistula, *Linn.*, LEGUMINOSÆ.
Foods .
Raji, *Dec. & S. India*, Eleusine corocana, *Gærtn.*, GRAMINEÆ.
Foods .
Rajika, *Sans.*, Brassica campestris, *Linn.*, var. Napus, sub-var. glauca, CRUCIFERÆ. Foods .
Rajika, *Sans.*, Brassica juncea, *H. f.*, *& T. T.*, CRUCIFERÆ.
Foods .
Rajika, *Sans.*, Brassica nigra, *Koch.*, CRUCIFERÆ.
Foods .
Rajika, *Sans.*, Eleusine corocana, *Gærtn.*, GRAMINEÆ.
Foods .
Rakta-kanchan, *Beng.*, Bauhinea purpurea, *Linn.*, LEGUMINOSÆ.
Foods .
Rakta-kánchan, *Beng.*, Bauhinea variegata, *Linn.*, LEGUMINOSÆ.
Foods .
Rakt-reora, *Mar.*, Tecoma undulata, *G. Don.*, BIGNONIACEÆ.
Foods .
Rála, *Deccan*, Setaria italica, *Kunth.*, GRAMINEÆ.
Foods .
Rali, *N.-W. P.*, Panicum miliaceum, *Linn.*, GRAMINEÆ.
Foods .
Ráma-káti, *Bom.*, Acacia arabica, *Willd.*, LEGUMINOSÆ.
Foods .
Ramleh, *Eng.*, Baccaurea sapida, *Müll.-Arg.*, EUPHORBIACEÆ.
Foods .
Ranga-aloo, *Beng.*, Ipomæa Batatas, *Lamk.*, CONVOLVULACEÆ.
Foods .
Rangkrum, *Pb.*, Syringa Emodi, *Wall.*, OLEACEÆ.
Foods .
Ranj, *Kumaun*, Quercus lanuginosa, *Don.*, CUPULIFERÆ.
Foods .
Ransheroo, *Beng.*, Hemarthria compressa, *R. Br.*, GRAMINEÆ.
Foods .
Ranturai, *Guz.*, Luffa acutangula, *Roxb.*, var. amara, *Roxb.*, CUCURBITACEÆ.
Foods .
Ranturi, *Hind.*, Hibiscus esculentus, *Linn.*, MALVACEÆ.
Foods .
Rapeseed, *Eng.*, Brassica campestris, *Linn.*, var. Napus, CRUCIFERÆ.
Foods .
Rapesho, *Pb.*, Lonicera hypoleuca, *Dne.*, CAPRIFOLIACEÆ.
Foods .
Raram, *Hind.*, Anthocephalus Cadamba, *Miq.*, RUBIACEÆ.
Foods .

Rara-rada, *Hind.*, Brassica campestris, *Linn.*, var. Napus, sub-var. glauca, CRUCIFERÆ. Foods .
Rara-sarson, *Hind.*, Brassica campestris, *Linn.*, var. Napus, sub-var. glauca. CRUCIFERÆ. Foods .
Rasaut, *Hind.*, Berberis aristata, *DC.*, and B. Lycium, *Royle*, BERBERIDEÆ. Foods .
Rashtu, *Sutlej*, Rhus semi-alata, *Murray*, ANACARDIACEÆ. Foods .
Raspberry, *Eng.*, Rubus Idœns, ROSACEÆ. Foods .
Rassaul, *Oudh*, Acacia concinna, *DC.*, LEGUMINOSÆ. Foods .
Rassu, *Cingh.*, Cinnamomum zeylanicum, *Breyn.*, LAURINEÆ. Foods .
Rasun, *Beng.*, Allium sativum, *Linn.*, LILIACEÆ. Foods .
Ratabaull, *Guz.*, Acacia Jacquemontii, *Benth.*, LEGUMINOSÆ. Foods .
Rata innala, *Cingh.*, Solanum tuberosum, *Linn.*, SOLANACEÆ. Foods .
Rat-kihiri, *Cingh.*, Acacia Catechu, *Willd.*, LEGUMINOSÆ. Foods .
Rátálu, *Hind.*, Dioscorea sativa, *Willd.*, DIOSCOREACEÆ. Foods .
Rati, *Hind.*, Abrus precatorius, *Linn.*, LEGUMINOSÆ. Foods .
Ratrirta, *Tel.*, Sonchus oleraceus, *Linn.*, COMPOSITÆ. Foods .
Raunj, *Hind.*, Acacia leucophlæa, *Willd.*, LEGUMINOSÆ. Foods .
Rausa, *N.-W. P. & Oudh*, Vigna Catiang, *Endl.*, LEGUMINOSÆ. Foods .
Ravi, *Tel.*, Ficus religiosa, *Linn.*, URTICACEÆ. Foods .
Rawadan, *Tel.*, Dilienia pentagyna, *Roxb.*, DILLENIACEÆ. Foods .
Rawan rawari, *Hind.*, *Pb.*, Lathyrus Aphaca, *Linn.*, LEGUMINOSÆ. Foods .
Rawás, *N.-W. P. & Oudh*, Vigna Catiang, *Endl.*, LEGUMINOSÆ. Foods .
Rawásh, *Pb.*, *Himalaya & Afg.*, Rheum Emodi, *Wall.*, POLYGONACEÆ. Foods .
Rawsita, *Tam.*, Anona reticulata, *Linn.*, ANONACEÆ. Foods .
Rayan, *Guz.*, Mimusops hexandra, *Roxb.*, SAPOTACEÆ. Foods .
Ray, Perennial, *Eng.*, Lalium perenne, *Linn.*, GRAMINEÆ. Foods .
Razil, *Pb.*, Syringa Emodi, *Wall.*, OLEACEÆ. Foods .
Re, *Him. name*, Abies Webbiana, *Lindl.*, CONIFERÆ. Foods .
Rebdan, *Pb.*, Tecoma undulata, *G. Don.*, BIGNONIACEÆ. Foods .
Reed, Common, *Eng.*, Phragmites communis, *Trin.*, GRAMINEÆ. Foods .
Reed, Mace, *Eng.*, Typha angustifolia, *Linn.*, TYPHACEÆ. Foods .
Ragi, *Tel.*, Zizyphus Jujuba, *Lam.*, RHAMNEÆ. Foods .
Reiz, *Ger.*, Oryza sativa, *Linn.*, GRAMINEÆ. Foods .

Rellu-gaddi, *Tel.*, Saccharum spontaneum, *Linn.*, GRAMINEÆ.
Foods .
Re-mo, *Naga*, Cucumis Melo, *Linn.*, CUCURBITACEÆ.
Foods .
Rendi, *Hind.*, Ricinus communis, *Linn.*, EUPHORBIACEÆ.
Foods .
Rengha, *Tel.*, Zizyphus Jujuba, *Lam.*, RHAMNEÆ.
Foods .
Reodana, *Pb.*, Tecoma undulata, *G. Don.*, BIGNONIACEÆ.
Foods .
Reri, *Hind.*, Ricinus communis, *Linn.*, EUPHORBIACEÆ.
Foods .
Reri bherenda, *Beng.*, Ricinus communis, *Linn.*, EUPHORBIACEÆ.
Foods .
Rerú, *Hind.*, Acacia leucophlæa, *Willd.*, LEGUMINOSÆ.
Foods .
Re-see (collective name), *Naga Hills*, Coix lachryma, *Linn.*, GRAMINEÆ.
Foods .
Rethei, *Pb.*, Securinega Leucopyrus, *Müll.-Arg.*, EUPHORBIACEÆ.
Foods .
Reuchini, *Beng.*, Rheum Emodi, *Wall.*, POLYGONACEÆ.
Foods .
Rewari, *Him. name*, Abies Webbiana, *Lindl.*, CONIFERÆ.
Foods .
Reylu, *Tel.*, Cassia Fistula, *Linn.*, LEGUMINOSÆ.
Foods .
Rha, *Lepcha*, Bauhinia variegata, *Linn.*, LEGUMINOSÆ.
Foods .
Rhetsa maum, *Tel.*, Zanthoxylum Rhetsa, *DC.*, RUTACEÆ.
Foods .
Rhin, *Pb.*, Quercus incana, *Roxb.*, CUPULIFERÆ.
Foods .
Rhubarb, Turkey, *Eng.*, Rheum Emodi, *Wall.*, POLYGONACEÆ.
Foods .
Rice, *Eng.*, Oryza sativa, *Linn.*, GRAMINEÆ.
Foods .
Richabi, *Kashmir*, Viburnum cotinifolium, *Don.*, CAPRIFOLIACEÆ.
Foods .
Richang, *Lahoul*, Salix daphnoides, *Vill.*, SALICINEÆ.
Foods .
Ringa, *Hind.*, Acacia leucophlæa, *Willd.*, LEGUMINOSÆ.
Foods .
Ringri, *Tel.*, Balanites Roxburghii, *Planch.*, SIMARUBEÆ.
Foods .
Rinj, *Hind.*, Acacia leucophlæa, *Willd.*, LEGUMINOSÆ.
Foods .
Rinj, *Pb.*, Quercus incana, *Roxb.*, CUPULIFERÆ.
Foods .
Rinjal, *C. P.*, Shorea robusta, *Gærtn.*, DIPTEROCARPEÆ.
Foods .
Rinsag, *Pb.*, Phytolacca acinosa, *Roxb.*, VERBENACEÆ.
Foods .
Ris, Viburnum nervosum, *Don.*, CAPRIFOLIACEÆ.
Foods .
Rishka, *Afg.*, *Lahoul*, Medicago falcata, *Linn.*, LEGUMINOSÆ.
Foods .
Ritha, *Beng.*, Sapindus Mukorrossi, *Gærtn.*, SAPINDACEÆ.
Foods .
Rithá, *Hind.*, Acacia concinna, *DC.*, LEGUMINOSÆ.
Foods .
Ritha, *Hind.*, Sapindus Mukorrossi, *Gærtn.*, SAPINDACEÆ.
Foods .

Riz, *Fr.*, Oryza sativa, *Linn.*, GRAMINEÆ.
Foods .
Roatanga, *Tel.*, Schleichera trijuga, *Willd.*, SAPINDACEÆ.
Foods .
Robhay, *Bhutia*, Ribes glaciale, *Wall*, SAXIFRAGACEÆ.
Foods .
Róghané kunjad, *Pers.*, Sesamum indicum, *Linn.*, PEDALINEÆ.
Foods .
Roghu, *Ass.*, Anthocephalus Cadamba, *Miq.*, RUBIACEÆ.
Foods .
Roira, *Mhair.*, Tecoma undulata, *G. Don.*, BIGNONIACEÆ.
Foods .
Rolka, *N.-W. P. & Oudh*, Eleusine crocana, *Gærtn.*, GRAMINEÆ.
Foods .
Ronchiling, *Lepcha*, Spondias mangifera, *Pers.*, ANACARDIACEÆ.
Foods .
Rosemary, *Eng.*, Rosmarinus officinalis, *Linn.*, LABIATEÆ.
Foods .
Ruchia, *Hind.*, Cornus macrophylla, *Wall.*, CORNACEÆ.
Foods .
Rudraksha, *Tel.*, Guazuma tomentosa, *Kunth.*, STERCULIACEÆ.
Foods .
Rui, *Hind.*, *Pb.*, Gossypium herbaceum, *Linn.*, MALVACEÆ.
Foods .
Rukar, *N.-W. P.*, Andropogon pertusus, *Willd.*, GRAMINEÆ.
Foods .
Rukh baer, *Nep.*, Zizyphus rugosa, *Lamk.*, RHAMNEÆ.
Foods .
Rumbal, *Pb.*, Ficus cordifolia, *Roxb.*, URTICACEÆ.
Foods .
Rundhani, *Beng.*, Carum Roxburghianum, *Benth.*, UMBELLIFERÆ.
Foods .
Rungbong, *Lepcha*, Caryota urens, *Willd.*, PALMÆ.
Foods .
Rusala (pale var.), *Sans.*, Saccharum officinarum, *Linn.*, GRAMINEÆ.
Foods .
Rusam, *Uriya*, Schleichera trijuga, *Willd.*, SAPINDACEÆ.
Foods .
Russa-usareki, *Tel.*, Phyllanthus distichus, *Müll.-Arg.*, EUPHORBIACEÆ.
Foods .
Rye-grass, *Eng*, Lolium perenne, *Linn.*, GRAMINEÆ.
Foods .
Ryst, *Dutch*, Oryza sativa, *Linn.*, GRAMINEÆ.
Foods .

S

Sabi-si, *Burm.*, Vitis vinifera, *Linn.*, AMPELIDEÆ.
Foods .
Sacred Pythagorean or Egyptian Bean or Lotus, *Eng.*, Nelumbium speciosum, *Willd.*, NYMPHÆACEÆ Foods .
Sadachu, *Mal.*, Grewia tiliæfolia, *Vahl.*, TILIACEÆ.
Foods .
Sadikka, *Cingh.*, Myristica moschata, *Willd.*, MYRISTICEÆ.
Foods .
Sadora, *Hyderabad*, Terminalia tomentosa, *W. & A.*, COMBRETACEÆ.
Foods .
Sadri, *Hind.*, Terminalia tomentosa, *W. & A.*, COMBRETACEÆ.
Foods .

Salopa, *Uriya*, Caryota urens, *Willd.*, PALMÆ.
Foods .
Salunl, *Pb.*, Rumex vesicarius, *Linn.*, POLYGONACEÆ.
Foods .
Sálwa, *Hind.*, Shorea robusta, *Gærtn.*, DIPTEROCARPEÆ.
Foods .
Salzat, *Dec.*, Ocimum Basilicum, *Linn.*, LABIATÆ.
Foods .
Sama, *N.-W. P. & Oudh.*, Panicum frumentaceum, *Roxb.*, GRAMINEÆ.
Foods .
Samada, *Sind*, Prosopis spicigera, *Linn.*, LEGUMINOSÆ.
Foods .
Sama-kadan, *Lepcha*, Garcinia stipulata, *T. And.*, GUTTIFERÆ.
Foods .
Samanka, *Hind.*, Citrullus vulgaris, *Schrad.*, CUCURBITACEÆ.
Foods .
Samara, *Guz.*, Prosopis spicigera, *Linn.*, LEGUMINOSÆ.
Foods .
Samdl, *Guz.*, Prosopis spicigera, *Linn.*, LEGUMINOSÆ.
Foods .
Same, *Kan.*, Panicum frumentaceum, *Roxb.*, GRAMINEÆ.
Foods .
Samel, *N.-W. P. & Oudh*, Panicum frumentaceum, *Roxb.*. GRAMINEÆ.
Foods .
Saml, *Sind.*, Prosopis spicigera, *Linn.*, LEGUMINOSÆ.
Foods .
Samsundra, *Hind.*, Albizzia stipulata, *Boivin.*, LEGUMINOSÆ.
Foods .
San, *Pb.*, Andropogon laniger, *Desf.*, GRAMINEÆ.
Foods .
San, *Hind.*, Hibiscus cannabinus, *Linn.*, MALVACEÆ.
Foods .
Sanalsan, *N. India*, Crotalaria juncea, *Linn.*, LEGUMINOSÆ.
Foods .
Sanalinga, *Tel.*, Cinnamomum zeylanicum, *Breyn.*, LAURINEÆ.
Foods .
Sanchl, *Beng.*. Brassica campestris, *Linn.*, var. campestris proper, CRUCIFERÆ. Foods .
Sandal Wood, False, *Eng.*, Ximenia americana, *Willd.*, OLACINEÆ.
Foods .
Sandan, *Hind.*, Ougeinia dalbergioides, *Benth.*, LEGUMINOSÆ.
Foods .
Sandarl, *Uriya*, Cassia Fistula, *Linn.*, LEGUMINOSÆ.
Foods .
San hemp, *Eng.*, Crotalaria juncea, *Linn.*, LEGUMINOSÆ.
Foods .
Sanl, *N. India*, Crotalaria juncea, *Linn.*, LEGUMINOSÆ.
Foods .
Sanni-nayan, *Cingh.*, Vernonia anthelmintica, *Willd.*, COMPOSITÆ.
Foods .
Sanjit, *Afg.*, Elæagnus hortensis, *M. Beib.*, ELÆAGNEÆ.
Foods .
Sanjna, *Hind.*, Moringa pterygosperma, *Gærtn.*, MORINGEÆ.
Foods .
Sankokla, *Dec.*, *Hind.*, Hibiscus cannabinus, *Linn.*, MALVACEÆ.
Foods .
Sankroo, *Hind.*, Coix lachryma, *Linn.*, GRAMINEÆ.
Foods .
Sanuagalu, *Hind.*, Cicer arietinum, *Linn.*, LEGUMINOSÆ.
Foods .
Sansaru, *Pb.*, Bœhmeria salicine, *D. Don.*, URTICACEÆ.
Foods .

Sarwali, *Pb.*, Celosia argentea, *Linn.*, AMARANTACEÆ.
Foods .
Sarwar, *N.-W. P.*, Heteropogon contortus, *R. & S.*, GRAMINEÆ.
Foods .
Sasa, *Beng.*, Cucumis sativus, *Linn.*, CUCURBITACEÆ.
Foods .
Sasam, *Arab.*, Dalbergia Sissoo, *Roxb.*, LEGUMINOSÆ.
Foods .
Sasem, *Arab.*, Dalbergia Sissoo, *Roxb.*, LEGUMINOSÆ.
Foods .
Satoo, *Dec.*, Hordeum vulgare, *Linn.*, GRAMINEÆ.
Foods .
Satpatiya, *Bundelkhand*, Luffa acutangula, *Roxb.*, CUCURBITACEÆ.
Foods .
Suaj, *Pb.*, Quercus semicarpifolia, *Smith*, CUPULIFERÆ.
Foods .
Saulkuri, *Ass.*, Elæocarpus Varunua, *Ham.*, TILIACEÆ.
Foods .
Saundad, *Dec.*, Prosopis spicigera, *Linn.*, LEGUMINOSÆ.
Foods .
Saunf, *Hind.*, Fœniculum vulgare, *Gærtn.*, UMBELLIFERÆ.
Foods .
Sáva, *Deccan*, Panicum miliaceum, *Linn.*, GRAMINEÆ.
Foods .
Sawa, *Tel.*, Panicum frumentaceum, *Roxb.*, GRAMINEÆ.
Foods .
Sawál, *Pb.*, Potamogeton crispus, *Linn.*, NIADACEÆ.
Foods .
Sawali, *Pb.*, Alnus nitada, *Endl.*, CUPULIFERÆ.
Foods .
Sawan, *N.-W. P. & Oudh*, Panicum frumentaceum, *Roxb.*, GRAMINEÆ.
Foods .
Sawan-bhadeha, *N.-W. P. & Oudh*, Panicum frumentaceum, *Roxb.*, GRAMINEÆ. Foods .
Sawan-chaitwa, *N.-W. P.*, Panicum miliaceum, *Linn.*, GRAMINEÆ.
Foods .
Sawan-jethwa, *N.-W. P.*, Panicum miliaceum, *Linn.*, GRAMINEÆ.
Foods .
Sawank, Jangli, *N.-W.-P.*, Panicum colonum, *Linn.*, GRAMINEÆ.
Foods .
Schap, *Lepcha*, Phœnix acaulis, *Roxb.*, PALMÆ.
Foods .
Schiap, *Lepcha*, Phœnix rupicola, *T. And.*, PALMÆ.
Foods .
Scratch-coco, *Eng.*, Colocasia antiquorum, *Schott.*, AROIDEÆ.
Foods .
Screw Bean, *Eng.*, Prosopis pubescens, *Bth.*, LEGUMINOSÆ.
Foods .
Screw Mesquit, *Eng.*, Prosopis pubescens, *Bth.*, LEGUMINOSÆ.
Foods .
Sebestens, *Eng.*, Cordia Myxa, *Linn.*, BORAGINEÆ.
Foods .
Segapu, *Tam.*, Canavalia ensiformis, *DC.*, LEGUMINOSÆ.
Foods .
Segapu, *Tam.*, Psidium Guyava, *Raddi.*, MYRTACEÆ.
Foods .
Segapumanthari, *Tam.*, Bauhinia variegata, *Linn.*, LEGUMINOSÆ.
Foods .
Segata, *Bom.*, Moringa pterygosperma, *Gærtn.*, MORINGEÆ.
Foods .
Segava, *Bom.*, Moringa pterygosperma, *Gærtn.*, MORINGEÆ.
Foods .

Shaft álu, *Pb.*, Prunus communis, *Huds.*, var. domestica, ROSACEÆ.
Foods .
Shagall, *Pb.*, Indigofera Dosua, *Ham.*, LEGUMINOSÆ.
Foods .
Shah-sufiam, *Pers.*, Mentha viridis, *Linn.*, LABIATÆ.
Foods .
Shahtut, *Kumaun*, Morus indica, *Linn.*, URTICACEÆ.
Foods .
Shaing, *Tam.*, Semecarpus Anacardium, *Linn.*, ANACARDIACEÆ.
Foods .
Shajratur-rumman, *Arab.*, Punica Granatum, *Linn.*, LYTHRACEÆ.
Foods .
Shakarkand, *Hind.*, *Beng.*, Ipomæa Batatas, *Lamk.*, CONVOLVULACEÆ.
Foods .
Shaka tunga, *Tel.*, Cyperus rotundus, *Linn.*, CYPERACEÆ.
Foods .
Shakel, *Pb.*, Bœhmeria salicifolia, *D. Don.*, URTICACEÆ.
Foods .
Shákpad, *Him. name*, Betula Bhojpattra, *Wall.*, CUPULIFERÆ.
Foods .
Shaktekas, *Pb.*, Ribes nigrum, *Linn.*, SAXIFRAGACEÆ.
Foods .
Shakul, *Nep.*, Cycas pectinata, *Griff.*, CYCADACEÆ.
Foods .
Shalakat kathi, *Pb.*, Myricaria germanica, *Desv.*, TAMARISCINEÆ.
Foods .
Shalgam, *Hind.*, *Beng.*, Brassica alba, *H. f.* & *T. T.*, var. Rapa, CRUCIFERÆ. Foods .
Shallet, *Eng.*, Allium ascalonicum, *Linn.*, LILIACEÆ.
Foods .
Shallot (Stewart), Allium ascalonicum, *Linn.*, LILIACEÆ.
Foods .
Shaluk, *Beng.*, Nymphœa Lotus, *Linn.*, NYMPHÆACEÆ.
Foods .
Shama, *Beng.*, Panicum colonum, *Linn.*, GRAMINEÆ.
Foods .
Shama. *See* Panicum frumentaceum, *Roxb.*, GRAMINEÆ.
Foods .
Shamak, *N.-W. P.*, *C. P.*, Panicum colonum, *Linn.*, GRAMINEÆ.
Foods .
Shamaloo (the seed), *Tel.*, Panicum frumentaceum, *Roxb.*, GRAMINEÆ.
Foods .
Shamay, *Eng.*, Panicum miliare, *Lamb.*, GRAMINEÆ.
Foods .
Shami, *Beng.*, Prosopis spicigera, *Linn.*, LEGUMINOSÆ.
Foods .
Shamoola, *Eng.*, Panicum frumentaceum, *Roxb.*, GRAMINEÆ.
Foods .
Shamrock of Ireland, *Eng.*, Trifolium repens, *Linn.*, LEGUMINOSÆ.
Foods .
Shamukel, *Pb.*, Taraxacum officinale, *Wigg.*, COMPOSITÆ.
Foods .
Shandal-gul, *Pb.*, Tulipa stellata, *Hook.*, LILIACEÆ.
Foods .
Shang, *Afg.*, Fraxinus xanthoxyloides, *Wall.*, OLEACEÆ.
Foods .
Shangal, *Pb.*, Fraxinus xanthoxyloides, *Wall.*, OLEACEÆ.
Foods .
Shangala, *Pb.*, Ilex dipyrena, *Wall.*, ILICINEÆ.
Foods .
Shánjan, *Oudh*, Ougeinia dalbergioides, *Benth.*, LEGUMINOSÆ.
Foods .

Shim, Makham, *Beng.*, Canavalia ensiformis, *DC.*, LEGUMINOSÆ.
Foods .
Shinduga, *Tel.*, Albizzia odoratissima, *Benth.*, LEGUMINOSÆ.
Foods .
Shioli, *Uriya*, Bauhinia Vahlii, *W. & A.*, LEGUMINOSÆ.
Foods .
Shipur-gadi, *Tel.*, Aristida setacea, *Retz.*, GRAMINEÆ.
Foods .
Shirán, *Pb.*, Prunus armeniaca, *Linn.*, ROSACEÆ.
Foods .
Shirsha, *Pb.*, Albizzia stipulata, *Boivin.*, LEGUMINOSÆ.
Foods .
Shisham, *Hind.*, *Pb.*, Dalbergia Sissoo, *Roxb.*, LEGUMINOSÆ.
Foods .
Shiúlik, *N.-W. P.*, Elæagnus hortensis, *M. Beib.*, ELÆAGNEÆ.
Foods .
Sholar, *Pb.*, Physochlaina præalta, *Hook. f.*, SOLANACEÆ.
Foods .
Sholri, *Pb.*, Salvia Moorcoftiana, *Wall.*, LABIATÆ.
Foods .
Shot, Indian, *Eng.*, Canna indica, *Linn.*, SCITAMINEÆ.
Foods .
Shotul, *Pb.*, Trifolium repens, *Linn.*, LEGUMINOSÆ.
Foods .
Shour, *Ladak*, Potentilla salessovii, *Steph.*, ROSACEÆ.
Foods .
Shriphula, *Beng.*, Ægle Marmelos, *Correa.*, RUTACEÆ.
Foods .
Shrol, *Pb.*, Alnus nitada, *Endl.*, CUPULIFERÆ.
Foods .
Shta, *Pb.*, Morus serrata, *Roxb.*, URTICACEÆ.
Foods ,
Shu, *Pb.*, Pyrus Malus, *Linn.*, ROSACEÆ.
Foods .
Shúftalú, *Pers.*, Prunus persica, *Benth. & Hook.*, ROSACEÆ.
Foods .
Shuknl, *Lepcha*, Dillenia pentagyna, *Roxb.*, DILLENIACEÆ.
Foods .
Shúkpa, *Him. name*, Juniperus excelsa, *M. Bieb.*, CONIFERÆ.
Foods .
Shukri, *Beng.*, Grewia asiatica, *Linn.*, TILIACEÆ.
Foods .
Shunkhim, *Sans.*, Chrysopogon acicularis, *Retz.*, GRAMINEÆ.
Foods .
Shur, *Beng.*, *Hind.*, Saccharum Sara, *Roxb.*, GRAMINEÆ.
Foods .
Shura, *Tel. & Sans.*, Saccharum Sara, *Roxb.*, GRAMINEÆ.
Foods .
Shúrbuta, *Him. name*, Juniperus excelsa, *M. Bieb.*, CONIFERÆ.
Foods .
Shúrli, *Him. name*, Corylus Colurna, *Linn.*, CUPULIFERÆ.
Foods .
Shutarkhor, *Pers.*, Alhagi maurorum, *Desv.*, LEGUMINOSÆ.
Foods .
Shwan, *Trans-Indus*, Olea Cuspidata, *Royle*, OLEACEÆ.
Foods .
Shwet huli, *Beng.*, Zeuxine sulcata, *Lindl.*, ORCHIDEÆ.
Foods .
Shwet-rai, *Beng.*, Brassica campestris, *Linn.*, var. Napus, sub-var, glauca, CRUCIFERÆ. Foods .
Shwet-Simúl, *Beng.*, Eriodendron anfractuosum, *DC.*, MALVACEÆ.
Foods .

Shyakul, *Beng.*, Zizyphus Œnoplia, *Mill.*, RHAMNEÆ.
Foods .
Shyamaka, *Sans.*, Panicum frumentaceum, *Roxb.*, GRAMINEÆ.
Foods .
Sia, *Ladak, Spiti*, Rosa Webbiana, *Wall.*, ROSACEÆ.
Foods .
Siali, *Pb.*, Dæmia extensa, *R. Br.*, ASCLEPIADEÆ.
Foods .
Siali, *Hind.*, Pueraria tuberosa, *DC.*, LEGUMINOSÆ.
Foods .
Sialu, *Pb.*, Marlea begoniæfolia, *Roxb.*, CORNACEÆ.
Foods .
Siaru, *Pb.*, Bœhmeria salicifolia, *D. Don.*, URTICACEÆ.
Foods .
Sibr, *Arab.*, *Pers.*, Aloe vera, *Linn.*, LILIACEÆ.
Foods .
Si-dalimbi, *Kan.*, Punica Granatum, *Linn.*, LYTHRACEÆ.
Foods .
Siddartha, *Sans.*, Eruca sativa, *Lam.*, CRUCIFERÆ.
Foods .
Siddhartha, *Sans.*, Brassica alba, *H. f. & T. T.*, CRUCIFERÆ.
Foods .
Sidhera, *Pb.*, Euonymus fimbriatus, *Wall.*, CELASTRINEÆ.
Foods .
Sigé, *Kan.*, Acacia concinna, *DC.*, LEGUMINOSÆ.
Foods .
Sikekai, *Bom.*, *Dec.*, Acacia concinna, *DC.*, LEGUMINOSÆ.
Foods .
Siki, *Pb.*, Euonymus fimbriatus, *Wall.*, CELASTRINEÆ.
Foods .
Sil (seed), *Pb.*, Amarantus Anardana, *Hamilt.*, AMARANTACEÆ.
Foods .
Silang, *Kumaun*, Osmanthus fragrans, *Lour.*, OLEACEÆ.
Foods .
Sill, *Khasia*, Cephalostaclyon capitatum, *Munro*, GRAMINEÆ.
Foods .
Silim, *Lepcha*, Terminalia Chebula, *Retz.*, COMBRETACEÆ.
Foods .
Silk, Vegetable, *Eng.*, Agave americana, *Linn.*, AMARYLLIDEÆ.
Foods .
Sim, *N.-W. P.*, Cassia Fistula, *Linn.*, LEGUMINOSÆ.
Foods .
Sim, *Hind.*, Dolichos Lablab, *Linn.*, LEGUMINOSÆ.
Foods .
Simal, *Lepcha*, Cedrela Toona, *Roxb.*, MELIACEÆ.
Foods .
Simal, *Hind.*, Eriodendron anfractuosum, *DC.*, MALVACEÆ.
Foods .
Simati, *Bom.*, Odina Wodier, *Roxb.*, ANACARDIACEÆ.
Foods .
Simbal, *Him. name*, Bombax malabaricum, *DC.*, MALVACEÆ.
Foods .
Sime hunase, *Kan.*, Pithecolobium dulce, *Benth.*, LEGUMINOSÆ.
Foods .
Simli, *Hind.*, Zizyphus vulgaris, *Lamk.*, RHAMNEÆ.
Foods .
Simlú, *Pb.*, Berberis aristata, *DC.*, and B. Lycium, *Royle*, BERBERIDEÆ.
Foods .
Sin, *Pb.*, Withania somnifera, *Don.*, SOLANACEÆ.
Foods .
Sinakadang, *Lepcha*, Aglaia edulis, *A. Gray*, MELIACEÆ.
Foods .

Sindan, *N.-W. P.*, Odina Wodier, *Roxb.*, ANACARDIACEÆ.
Foods .
Singhani, *Nep.*, Arundinaria Hookeriana, *Munro*, GRAMINEÆ.
Foods .
Singhara, *Hind.*, Trapa bispinosa, *Roxb.*, ONAGRACEÆ.
Foods .
Singka, *Bhutia*, Pyrus vestita, *Wall.*, ROSACEÆ.
Foods .
Singodi, *Guz.*, Trapa bispinosa, *Roxb.*, ONAGRACEÆ.
Food .
Singtok, *Bhutia*, Morus cuspidata, *Wall.*, URTICACEÆ.
Foods .
Sinji, *Pb.*, Melilotus parviflora, *Desf.*, LEGUMINOSÆ.
Foods .
Sinjli, *Hind.*, Zizyphus vulgaris, *Lamk.*, RHAMNEÆ.
Foods .
Sin-tha-hpan, *Burm.*, Ficus Roxburghii, *Wall.*, URTICACEÆ.
Foods .
Sipil, *Pb.*, Bupleurum falcatum, *Linn.*, var. marginata, *Wall.*, UMBELLIFERÆ. Foods .
Sir, *Pers.*, Allium sativum, *Linn.*, LILIACEÆ.
Foods .
Siragam, *Tam.*, Cuminum Cyminum, *Linn.*, UMBELLIFERÆ.
Foods .
Siral, *Hind.*, Albizzia Lebbek, *Benth.*, LEGUMINOSÆ.
Foods .
Siran, *Hind.*, Albizzia stipulata, *Boivin.*, LEGUMINOSÆ.
Foods .
Siras, *Hind.*, Albizzia Lebbek, *Benth.*, LEGUMINOSÆ.
Foods .
Siras, *Bom.*, Albizzia odoratissima, *Benth.*, LEGUMINOSÆ.
Foods .
Sir-hutungchir, *Lepcha*, Sapindus attenuatus, *Wall.*, SAPINDACEÆ.
Foods .
Sirikishu, *Lepcha*, Castanopsis rufescens, *Hook.f. & Th.*, CUPULIFERÆ.
Foods .
Sirikone, *Tam.*, Cassia Fistula, *Linn.*, LEGUMINOSÆ.
Foods .
Sirin, *Hind.*, Albizzia Lebbek, *Benth.*, LEGUMINOSÆ.
Foods .
Siris, *Hind.*, Albizzia odoratissima, *Benth.*, LEGUMINOSÆ.
Foods .
Siris, *Hind.*, *Beng.*, Albizzia Lebbek, *Benth.*, LEGUMINOSÆ.
Foods .
Sirisha, *Beng.*, Albizzia Lebbek, *Benth.*, LEGUMINOSÆ.
Foods .
Sirma, *North Pb.*, *Ladak to Lahoul*, Hippophæ rhamnoides, *Linn.*, ELÆAGNEÆ. Foods .
Sirola, *Bom.*, Luffa acutangula, *Roxb.*, CUCURBITACEÆ.
Foods .
Sirrúghá, *Tam.*, Aloe vera, *Linn.*, var. officinalis, sp. *Forsk.*, LILIACEÆ.
Foods .
Sirshaf, *Pers.*, Brassica nigra, *Koch.*, CRUCIFERÆ.
Foods .
Sirshing, *Tibet*, Elæagnus hortensis, *M. Beib.*, ELÆAGNEÆ.
Foods .
Sir sil, *Upper Ind.*, Imperata arundinacea, *Cyrill*, GRAMINEÆ.
Foods .
Sissai, *Hind.*, *Oudh*, Dalbergia Sissoo, *Roxb.*, LEGUMINOSÆ.
Foods .
Sissoo, *Eng.*, Dalbergia Sissoo, *Roxb.*, LEGUMINOSÆ.
Foods .

Sissu, *Tel., Hind.*, Dalbergia Sissoo, *Roxb.*, LEGUMINOSÆ.
Foods .
Sita, *Tam.*, Anona squamosa, *Linn.*, ANONACEÆ.
Foods .
Sitaber, *Hind.*, Zizyphus xylopyra, *Will.*, RHAMNEÆ.
Foods .
Sitaphal, *Hind., Guz.*, Anona squamosa, *Linn.*, ANONACEÆ.
Foods .
Sitaphal, *N.-W. P.*, Cucurbita moschata, *Duchesne*, CUCURBITACEÆ.
Foods .
Sivappu-kashuruk-kai, *Tam.*, Hibiscus Sabdariffa, *Linn.*, MALVACEÆ.
Foods .
Skinnung, *Pb.*, Equisetum debile, *Roxb.*, EQUISETACEÆ.
Foods .
Snake-gourd, *Eng.*, Trichosanthes anguina, *Linn.*, CUCURBITACEÆ.
Foods .
Soa, *Pb.*, Morus serrata, *Roxb.*, URTICACEÆ.
Foods .
Soanjna, *Hind.*, Moringa pterygosperma, *Gærtn.*, MORINGEÆ.
Foods .
Sohikire, *Tam.*, Fœniculum vulgare, *Gærtn.*, UMBELLIFERÆ.
Foods .
Solára, *Pb.*, Andropogon laniger, *Desf.*, GRAMINEÆ.
Foods .
Somr, *Hind., Beng.*, Bombax malabaricum, *DC.*, MALVACEÆ.
Foods .
Somraj, *Beng.*, Vernonia anthelmintica, *Willd.*, COMPOSITÆ.
Foods .
Sonalú, *Garo*, Cassia Fistula, *Linn.*, LEGUMINOSÆ.
Foods .
Sonchal, *Pb. & Sind*, Malva parviflora, *Linn.*, MALVACEÆ.
Foods .
Sonta, *N.-W. P. & Oudh*, Vigna Catiang, *Endl.*, LEGUMINOSÆ.
Foods .
Soomuna, *Sans.*, Triticum sativum, *Lam.*, GRAMINEÆ.
Foods .
Soopwotnway, *Burm.*, Acacia concinna, *DC.*, LEGUMINOSÆ.
Foods .
Sophee, *Eng.*, Myrica integrifolia, *Roxb.*, MYRICACEÆ.
Foods .
Sopho, *Khasia*, Docynia indica, *Done.*, ROSACEÆ.
Foods .
Sop, Sweet, *Eng.*, Anona squamosa, *Linn.*, ANONACEÆ.
Foods .
Sorakaya, *Tel.*, Lagenaria vulgaris, *Seringe*, CUCURBITACEÆ.
Foods .
Soriai-kai, *Tam.*, Lagenaria vulgaris, *Seringe*, CUCURBITACEÆ.
Foods .
Sorrel, *Eng.*, Rumex vesicarius, *Linn.*, POLYGONACEÆ.
Foods .
Sour Gourd, or Monkey Bread Tree of Africa, *Eng.*, Adansonia digitata, *Linn.*, MALVACEÆ. Foods .
Sowa, *Eng., Hind.*, Peucedanum graveolens, *Benth.*, UMBELLIFERÆ.
Foods .
Soy Bean, *Eng.*, Glycine Soja, *Sieb. & Zucc.*, LEGUMINOSÆ.
Foods .
Spang-jho, *Pb.*, Potentilla fruticosa, *Linn.*, ROSACEÆ.
Foods .
Spear Grass, *Eng.*, Heteropogon contortus, *R. & S.*, GRAMINEÆ.
Foods .
Spearmint, *Eng.*, Mentha viridis, *Linn.*, LABIATÆ.
Foods .

Spinach, Country, *Eng.*, Beta vulgaris, *Moq.*, CHENOPODIACEÆ.
Foods .
Spinach, Indian, *Eng.*, Basella alba, *L.*, CHENOPODIACEÆ.
Foods .
Spin-bajja, *Pb.*, Withania coagulans, *Dun.*, SOLANACEÆ.
Foods .
Spindle Tree, *Eng.*, Euonymus fimbriatus, *Wall.*, CELASTRINEÆ.
Foods .
Spin-khalak, *Pb.*, Aristida depressa, *Retz.*, GRAMINEÆ.
Foods .
Spin-wege, *Pb.*, Aristida depressa, *Retz.*, GRAMINEÆ.
Foods .
Spitzklette, *Ger.*, Xanthium strumarium, *Linn.*, COMPOSITÆ.
Foods .
Spun, *Him. name*, Abies Webbiana, *Lindl.*, CONIFERÆ.
Foods .
Spun, *Pb.*, Picea Webbiana, *Lamb.*, CONIFERÆ.
Foods .
Spurpepper, *Eng.*, Capsicum frutescens, *Linn.*, SOLANACEÆ.
Foods .
Squash Gourd, *Eng.*, Cucurbita maxima, *Duchesne*, CUCURBITACEÆ.
Foods .
Sringata, *Sans.*, Trapa bispinosa, *Roxb.*, ONAGRACEÆ.
Foods .
Sriphal, *Sans.*, Ægle Marmelos, *Correa.*, RUTACEÆ.
Foods .
Star Anise of China and Japan, *Eng.*, Illicium anisatum, *Linn.*, MAGNOLIACEÆ. Foods .
Star Apple, *Eng.*, Chrysophyllum Roxburghii, *G. Don.*, SAPOTACEÆ.
Foods .
Stin, *Pb.*, Rubus lasiocarpus, *Smith*, ROSACEÆ.
Foods .
St. John's Bean, *Eng.*, Ceratonia siliqua, *L.*, LEGUMINOSÆ.
Foods .
Strawberry, *Eng.*, Fragaria vesca, *Linn.*, ROSACEÆ.
Foods .
Strawberry, Indian, *Eng.*, Fragaria indica, *Andr.*, ROSACEÆ.
Foods .
Suadoo-kuntuka, *Sans.*, Flacourtia Ramontchi, *L'Herit.*, BIXINEÆ.
Foods .
Suchal, *Pb.*, Cichorium Intybus, *Linn.*, COMPOSITÆ.
Foods .
Sufed-pai, *Sylhet*, Elæocarpus lanceæfolius, *Roxb.*, TILIACEÆ.
Foods .
Suffed-shorahi, *Beng.*, Eruca sativa, *Lam.*, CRUCIFERÆ.
Foods .
Sufok-ji, *Lepcha*, Rubus moluccanus, *Linn.*, ROSACEÆ.
Foods .
Sugarcane, *Eng.*, Saccharum officinarum, *Linn.*, GRAMINEÆ.
Foods .
Sugarcane, Chinese, *Eng.*, Sorghum saccharatum, *Pers.*, GRAMINEÆ.
Foods .
Suiminta, *Tel.*, Sesbania ægyptiaca, *Pers.*, LEGUMINOSÆ.
Foods .
Sujana, *Beng.*, Moringa pterygosperma, *Gærtn.*, MORINGEÆ.
Foods .
Sukasa, *Sans.*, Cucumis sativus, *Linn.*, CUCURBITACEÆ.
Foods .
Sullea, *Khasia*, Cephalostaclyon capitatum, *Munro*, GRAMINEÆ.
Foods .
Sulpha, *Beng.*, Peucedanum graveolens, *Benth.*, UMBELLIFERÆ.
Foods .

Súmlú, *Pb.*, Berberis aristata, *DC.*, and B. Lycium, *Royle*, BERBERIDEÆ.
Foods .
Sunagalu, *Tel.*, Cicer arietinum, *Linn.*, LEGUMINOSÆ.
Foods .
Sunaru, *Ass.*, Cassia Fistula, *Linn.*, LEGUMINOSÆ.
Foods .
Sundali, *Beng.*, Cassia Fistula, *Linn.*, LEGUMINOSÆ.
Foods .
Sungtu, *Pb.*, Xanthium strumarium, *Linn.*, COMPOSITÆ.
Foods .
Sungungrik, *Lepcha*, Bauhinia Vahlii, *W. & A.*, LEGUMINOSÆ.
Foods .
Suni, *Dec.*, *Hind.*, Hibiscus cannabinus, *Linn.*, MALVACEÆ.
Foods .
Sunkeint, *Pb. Hills*, Pyrus communis, *Linn.*, ROSACEÆ.
Foods .
Suntala, *Nep.*, Citrus Aurantium, *Linn.*, RUTACEÆ.
Foods .
Sunwar, *Hind.*, Rhazya stricta, *Dcne.*, APOCYNACEÆ.
Foods .
Supáré, *Hind.*, *Beng.*, Areca Catechu, *Linn.*, PALMÆ.
Foods .
Supra, *Pb. & Sind*, Malva parviflora, *Linn.*, MALVACEÆ.
Foods .
Supta, *Hind.*, Flemingia nana, LEGUMINOSÆ.
Foods ,
Suraka, *Pb.*, Atriplex hortensis, *L.* and A. laciniata, *L.*, CHENOPODIACEÆ.
Foods .
Suran, *C.P.*, Zizphus rugosa, *Lamk.*, RHAMNEÆ.
Foods .
Suranji, *A trade name*, Morinda citrifolia, *Linn.*, RUBIACEÆ.
Foods .
Surari, *Pb.*, Heteropogon contortus, *R. & S.*, GRAMINEÆ.
Foods .
Surbo-jaya, *Beng.*, Canna indica, *Linn.*, SCITAMINEÆ.
Foods .
Surchi, *Pb.*, Oxalis corniculata, *Linn.*, GERANIACEÆ.
Foods .
Suriala, *Pb.*, Heteropogon contortus, *R. & S.*, GRAMINEÆ.
Foods .
Surshi, *Beng.*, Brassica campestris, *Linn.*, var. campestris proper, CRUCIFERÆ. Foods .
Sursi, *Hind.*, *Beng.*, Brassica campestris, *Linn.*, var. campestris proper, CRUCIFERÆ. Foods .
Suringi, *Mar.*, Ochrocarpus longifolius, *Benth. & Hook.*, GUTTIFERÆ.
Foods .
Susuvi, *Sans.*, Momordica Charantia, *Linn.*, CUCURBITACEÆ.
Foods .
Suvyrnak, *Sans.*, Cassia Fistula, *Linn.*, LEGUMINOSÆ.
Foods .
Sweet-sabuni, *Hind.*, Trianthema monogyna, *Linn.*, FICOIDEÆ.
Foods .
Syalita, *Mal.*, Dillenia indica, *Linn.*, DILLENIACEÆ.
Foods .
Syansundari, *N.-W. P. & Oudh*, Cyamopsis psoralioides, *DC.*, LEGUMINOSÆ. Foods .

T

Tacamhac, *Eng.*, Populus balsamifera, *Linn.*, SALICINEÆ.
Foods .
Tád, *Guz.*, Borassus flabelliformis, *Linn.*, PALMÆ.
Foods .
Tagarisha chettu, *Tel.*, Cassia Tora, *Linn.*, LEGUMINOSÆ.
Foods .
Tagashing, *Bhutia*, Juglans regia, *Linn.*, JUGLANDEÆ.
Foods .
Tag hemp, *Eng.*, Crotalaria juncea, *Linn.*, LEGUMINOSÆ.
Foods .
Tagho, *Afg.*, Celtis australis, *Linn.*, URTICACEÆ.
Foods .
Tagumudu, *Tel.*, Gmelina arborea, *Roxb.*, VERBENACEÆ.
Foods .
Tallo, *Cachar*, Castanopsis indica, *A. DC.*, CUPULIFERÆ.
Foods .
Taki, *Nep.*, Bauhinia variegata, *Linn.*, LEGUMINOSÆ.
Foods .
Takli, *Kurru.*, Sterculia urens, *Roxb.*, STERCULIACEÆ.
Foods .
Takpa, *Him. name*, Betula Bhojpattra, *Wall.*, CUPULIFERÆ.
Foods .
Takri, *Pb.*, Panicum sanguinale, *Linn.*, GRAMINEÆ.
Foods .
Taksor, *Lepcha*, Terminalia tomentosa, *W. & A.*, COMBRETACEÆ.
Foods .
Tál, *Hind.*, *Beng.*, Borassus flabelliformis, *Linn.*, PALMÆ.
Foods .
Tala, *Cingh.*, Corypha umbraculifera, *Linn.*, PALMÆ.
Foods .
Tála, *Hind.*, Borassus flabelliformis, *Linn.*, PALMÆ.
Foods .
Talbsu, *Tel.*, Sterculia urens, *Roxb.*, STERCULIACEÆ.
Foods .
Tali. *Pb.*, Dalbergia Sissoo, *Roxb.*, LEGUMINOSÆ.
Foods .
Talkar, *Pb.*, Celastrus senegalensis, *Lam.*, CELASTRINEÆ.
Foods .
Talla, *Tel.*, Sorghum vulgare, *Pers.*, GRAMINEÆ.
Foods .
Talum, *Tam.*, Pandanus odoratissimus, *Willd.*, PANDANEÆ.
Foods .
Tama, *Ladak*, Caragana pygmæa, *DC.*, LEGUMINOSÆ.
Foods .
Tama, *Nep.*, Dendrocalamus Hamiltonii, *Nees & Arn.*, GRAMINEÆ.
Foods .
Tam-a-kha, *Burm.*, Melia Azedarach, *Linn.*, MELIACEÆ.
Foods .
Tamálá, *Bom.*, Cinnamomum Tamala, *Nees.*, LAURINEÆ.
Foods .
Tamal-pakoo, *Tel.*, Piper Betle, *Linn.*, PIPERACEÆ.
Foods .
Tamarind, *Eng.*, Tamarindus indica, *Linn.*, LEGUMINOSÆ.
Foods .
Tamarinds, *Madras. See* Prosopis dulcis, LEGUMINOSÆ.
Foods .
Tamarinds, Manilla, *Eng.*, Pithecolobium dulce, *Benth.*, LEGUMINOSÆ.
Foods .

Tamarta, *Tam.*, Averrhoa Carambola, *Linn.*, GERANIACEÆ.
Foods .
Tamati, *Beng.*, *Hind.*, Lycopersicum esculentum, *Miller*, SOLANACEÆ.
Foods .
Támbula, *Sans.*, Piper Betle, *Linn.*, PIPERACEÆ.
Foods .
Tamidalu, *Tel.*, Eleusine corocana, *Gærtn.*, GRAMINEÆ.
Foods .
Tamu, *Burm.*, Sonneratia acida, *Linn.*, LYTHRACEÆ.
Foods .
Tan, *Chin.*, Oryza sativa, *Linn.*, GRAMINEÆ.
Foods .
Tandala, *Pb.*, Digera arvensis, *Forsk.*, AMARANTACEÆ.
Foods .
Tandei, *Pb.*, Viburnum fœtens, *Decaisne*, CAPRIFOLIACEÆ.
Foods .
Tandi, *Tel.*, Terminalia belerica, *Roxb.*, COMBRETACEÆ.
Foods .
Tang, *Pb.*, Pirus Pashia, *Ham.*, ROSACEÆ.
Foods .
Tang, *Pb. Hills*, Pyrus communis, *Linn.*, ROSACEÆ.
Foods .
Tangan, *N.-W. P. & Oudh*, Setaria italica, *Kunth.*, GRAMINEÆ.
Foods .
Tani, *Tam.*, Terminalia belerica, *Roxb.*, COMBRETACEÆ.
Foods .
Tani, *Tel.*, Terminalia belerica, *Roxb.*, COMBRETACEÆ.
Foods .
Tankalá, *Bom.*, Cassia Tora, *Linn.*, LEGUMINOSÆ.
Foods .
Tanoung, *Burm.*, Acacia leucophlæa, *Willd.*, LEGUMINOSÆ.
Foods .
Tantal, *Hind.*, Albizzia Lebbek, *Benth.*, LEGUMINOSÆ.
Foods .
Tapioca, *Eng.*, Manihot utilissima, *Pohl.*, EUPHORBIACEÆ.
Foods .
Tapu, *Burm.*, Sonaratia acida, *Linn.*, LYTHRACEÆ.
Foods .
Tapuay, *Burm.*, Marlea begoniæfolia, *Roxb.*, CORNACEÆ.
Foods .
Tar, *Pb.*, Dioscorea deltoides, *Wall.*, DIOSCOREACEÆ.
Foods .
Tár, *Hind.*, Borassus flabelliformis, *Linn.*, PALMÆ.
Foods .
Tara, *N.-W. P. & Oudh*, Eruca sativa, *Lam.*, CRUCIFERÆ.
Foods .
Tara, *Pb.*, Eruca sativa, *Lam.*, CRUCIFERÆ.
Foods .
Taramira, *N.-W. P.*, Eruca sativa, *Lam.*, CRUCIFERÆ.
Foods .
Tarbuza, *N.-W. P.*, Citrullus vulgaris, *Schrad.*, CUCURBITACEÆ.
Foods .
Tardi, *Pb.*, Dioscorea deltoides, *Wall.*, DIOSCOREACEÆ.
Foods .
Tare, Hairy, *Eng.*, Vicia hirsuta, *Koch.*, LEGUMINOSÆ.
Foods .
Tari, *Beng.*, *Hind.*, Phœnix sylvestris, *Roxb.*, PALMÆ.
Foods .
Taro, *Eng.*, Colocasia antiquorum, *Schott.*, AROIDEÆ.
Foods .
Tarod, *Kumaun*, Luffa ægyptiaca, *Miller*, *Hook. f.*, CUCURBITACEÆ.
Foods .

Tarota, *Dec.*, Cassia Tora, *Linn.*, LEGUMINOSÆ.
Foods .
Tarru, *North Pb., Ladak to Lahoul,* Hippophæ rhamnoides, *Linn.*, ELÆAGNEÆ. Foods .
Tartara, *Pb.*, Digera arvensis, *Forsk.*, AMARANTACEÆ.
Foods .
Taru, *Kan.*, Terminalia Catappa, *Linn.*, COMBRETACEÆ.
Foods .
Taruka vepu, *Tel.*, Melia Azedarach, *Linn.*, MELIACEÆ.
Foods .
Tasha, *Burm.*, Phyllanthus Emblica, *Linn.*, EUPHORBIACEÆ.
Foods .
Tatri, *Pb.*, Rhus semi-alata, *Murray*, ANACARDIACEÆ.
Foods .
Tatua, *Chenab*, Prinsepia utilis, *Royle*, ROSACEÆ.
Foods .
Tatwen, *Ladak*, Artemisia sacrorum, *Ledeb.*, COMPOSITÆ.
Foods .
Tau Malyain, *Burm.*, Indigofera pulchella, *Roxb.*, LEGUMINOSÆ.
Foods .
Taur, *Pb.*, Bauhinia racemosa, *Lam.*, LEGUMINOSÆ.
Foods .
Taushouk, *Burm.*, Glycosmis pentaphylla, *Correa.*, RUTACEÆ.
Foods .
Tauzeenway, *Burm.*, Zizyphus Œnoplia, *Mill.*, RHAMNEÆ.
Foods .
Tawal, *Pb.*, Fragaria vesca, *Linn.*, ROSACEÆ.
Foods .
Tawal, *Pb.*, Amarantus Anardana, *Hamilt.*, AMARANTACEÆ.
Foods .
Tay, *Burm.*, Diospyros pyrrhocarpa, *Miq.*, EBENACEÆ.
Foods .
Tea Plant, China, *Eng.*, Camellia theifera, *Griff.*, TERNSTRŒMIACEÆ.
Foods .
Teemoti, *Beng.*, *Hind.*, Lycopersicum esculentum, *Miller*, SOLANACEÆ.
Foods .
Tehongtay, *Lepcha*, Ficus glomerata, *Roxb.*, URTICACEÆ.
Foods .
Teila, *Lahoul*, Ribes Grossularia, *Linn.*, SAXIFRAGACEÆ.
Foods .
Tél, *Beng.*, Sesamum indicum, *Linn.*, PEDALINEÆ.
Foods .
Tél, Krishna, *Hind.*, Sesamum indicum, *Linn.*, PEDALINEÆ.
Foods .
Telhanj, *Pb.*, Viburnum fœtens, *Decaisne*, CAPRIFOLIACEÆ.
Foods .
Tella, *Tel.*, Ougeinia dalbergioides, *Benth.*, LEGUMINOSÆ.
Foods .
Tella-chikurkai, *Tel.*, Dolichos Lablab, *Linn.*, LEGUMINOSÆ.
Foods .
Tella-gadda, *Tel.*, Allium sativum, *Linn.*, LILIACEÆ.
Foods .
Tella-janular (the grain), *Tel.*, Sorghum vulgare, *Pers.*, GRAMINEÆ.
Foods .
Tella-kalwa, *Tel.*, Nymphæa Lotus, *Linn.*, NYMPHÆACEÆ.
Foods .
Tellatúma, *Tel.*, Acacia leucophlæa, *Willd.*, LEGUMINOSÆ.
Foods .
Tellay tumbetten kaza, *Tel.*, Canavalia ensiformis, *DC.*, LEGUMINOSÆ.
Foods .
Telus, *Khandesh*, Ougeinia dalbergioides, *Benth.*, LEGUMINOSÆ.
Foods .

Thankya, *Burm.*, Chrysophyllum Roxburghii, *G. Don.*, SAPOTACEÆ.
Foods .
Thapur, *Pb. plains*, Ficus virgata, *Roxb.*, URTICACEÆ.
Foods .
Thara, *Uriya*, Terminalia belerica, *Roxb.*, COMBRETACEÆ.
Foods .
Tharwar, *Pb.*, Cornus capitata, *Wall.*, CORNACEÆ.
Foods .
Thaur, *Hind.*, Bauhinia racemosa, *Lam.*, LEGUMINOSÆ.
Foods .
Thayet, *Burm.*, Mangifera indica, *Linn.*, ANACARDIACEÆ.
Foods .
Thee-haya-za, *Burm.*, Lemonia acidissima, *Linn.*, RUTACEÆ.
Foods .
Thee-noh thayet, *Burm.*, Anacardium occidentale, *Linn.*, ANACARDIACEÆ.
Foods .
Thenwian, *Burm.*, Pongamia glabra, *Vent.*, LEGUMINOSÆ.
Foods .
Theot, *Simla*, Indigofera Dosua, *Ham.*, LEGUMINOSÆ.
Foods .
Thesi, *Pb.*, Cornus capitata, *Wall.*, CORNACEÆ.
Foods .
Thilkain, *Pb.*, Viburnum fœtens, *Decaisne*, CAPRIFOLIACEÆ.
Foods .
Thilkain, *Pb.*, Viburnum nervosum. *Don.*, CAPRIFOLIACEÆ.
Foods .
Thimbaubhempu, *Burm*, Melia Azadirachta, *Linn.*, MELIACEÆ.
Foods .
Thimbau-ta-ma-kha, *Burm.*, Melia Azadirachta, *Linn.*, MELIACEÆ.
Foods .
Thinboung, *Burm.*, Phœnix acaulis, *Roxb.*, PALMÆ.
Foods .
Thin-bo-zi-pyoo, *Burm.*, Phyllanthus distichus, *Müll.-Arg.*, EUPHORBIACEÆ. Foods .
Thindar, *Pb.*, Pyrus Pashia, *Ham.*, ROSACEÆ.
Foods .
Thistle, *Eng.*, Carduus nutans, *Linn.*, COMPOSITÆ.
Foods .
Thistle, Milk, *Eng.*, Sonchus oleraceus, *Linn.*, COMPOSITÆ.
Foods .
Thitkado, *Burm.*, Cedrela Toona, *Roxb.*, MELIACEÆ.
Foods .
Thitmagyi, *Burm.*, Albizzia odoratissima, *Benth.*, LEGUMINOSÆ.
Foods .
Thitsein, *Burm.*, Terminalia belerica, *Roxb.*, COMBRETACEÆ.
Foods .
Thodapga-pulla, *Tam.*, Aristida setacea, *Retz.*, GRAMINEÆ.
Foods .
Thor, *N.-W. P. & Oudh*, Cajanus indicus, *Spreng.*, LEGUMINOSÆ.
Foods .
Thorás, *Kan.*, Butea frondosa, *Roxb.*, LEGUMINOSÆ.
Foods .
Thorn, Jerusalem, *Eng.*, Parkinsonia aculeata, *Linn.*, LEGUMINOSÆ.
Foods .
Thosk, *Gond.*, Saccopetalum tomentosum, *Hook.*, ANONACEÆ.
Foods .
Thul-kuré, *Beng.*, Hydrocotyle asiatica, *Linn.*, UMBELLIFERÆ.
Foods .
Thum, *Pb.*, Fraxinus xanthoxyloides, *Wall.*, OLEACEÆ.
Foods .
Thum, *Pb.*, Sageretia theezans, *Brongn.*, RHAMNEÆ.
Foods .

Thúner, *N.-W. P.*, Taxus baccata, *Linn.*, CONIFERÆ.
Foods .
Thúnu, *Kashmir*, Taxus baccata, *Linn.*, CONIFERÆ.
Foods .
Thur, *N.-W. P. & Oudh*, Cajanus indicus, *Spreng.*, LEGUMINOSÆ.
Foods .
Thut, *Pb.*, Salvia Moorcroftiana, *Wall.*, LABIATÆ.
Foods .
Thya, *Kan.*, Trigonella Fœnum-grœcum, *Linn.*, LEGUMINOSÆ.
Foods .
Tia of the Chinese, *Eng.*, Sageretia theezans, *Brongn.*, RHAMNEÆ.
Foods .
Ti (black variety), *Naga Hills*, Coix lachryma, *Linn.*, GRAMINEÆ.
Foods .
Tiari, *Pb.*, Solanum verbascifolium, *Linn.*, SOLANACEÆ.
Foods .
Tikhria, *N.-W. P.*, Panicum sanguinale, *Linn.*, var. ciliare, *Retz.* sp., GRAMINEÆ. Foods .
Tikhur, *Hind.*, Curcuma angustifolia, *Roxb.*, SCITAMINEÆ.
Foods .
Tikjik, *Pb.*, Rosa macrophylla, *Lindl.*, ROSACEÆ.
Foods .
Tikul, *Beng.*, Garcinia pedunculata, *Roxb.*, GUTTIFERÆ.
Foods .
Tikur, *Beng.*, Garcinia pedunculata, *Roxb.*, GUTTIFERÆ.
Foods .
Til, *Raj.*, *Deccan*, Sesamum indicum, *Linn.*, PEDALINEÆ.
Foods .
Tila, *Hind.*, Wendlandia exserta, *DC.*, RUBIACEÆ.
Foods .
Tila, *Sans.*, Sesamum indicum, *Linn.*, PEDALINEÆ.
Foods .
Tili, *Beng.*, Sesamum indicum, *Linn.*, PEDALINEÆ.
Foods .
Tilki, *Hind.*, *Nep.*, Wendlandia exserta, *DC.*, RUBIACEÆ.
Foods .
Tilluk, *Hind.*, Saccharum fuscum, *Roxb.*, GRAMINEÆ.
Foods .
Tilpatra, *Pb.*, Marlea begoniæfolia, *Roxb.*, CORNACEÆ.
Foods .
Tilpattar, *Pb.*, Acer pictum, *Thunb.*, SAPINDACEÆ.
Foods .
Timal, *Hind.*, Ficus Roxburghii, *Wall.*, URTICACEÆ.
Foods .
Timboree, *Bom.*, Diospyros Embryopteris, *Pers.*, EBENACEÆ.
Foods .
Timburnyok, *Lepcha*, Skimmia Laureola, *Hook.*, RUTACEÆ.
Foods .
Timil, *Nep.*, Marlea begoniæfolia, *Roxb.*, CORNACEÆ.
Foods .
Timothy, *Eng.*, Phleum pratense, *Linn.*, GRAMINEÆ.
Foods .
Timsha, *N.-W. P.*, Quercus dilatata, *Lindl.*, CUPULIFERÆ.
Foods .
Tinani, *Afg.*, Astragalus multiceps, *Wall.*, LEGUMINOSÆ.
Foods .
Tinda, *Pb.*, Citrullus vulgaris, *Schrad.*, var. fistulosus, CUCURBITACEÆ.
Foods .
Tinda, *Sind*, Citrullus vulgaris, *Schrad.*, var. fistulosus, CUCURBITACEÆ.
Foods .
Tinduka, *Sans.*, Diospyros Embryopteris, *Pers.*, EBENACEÆ.
Foods .

Tingi, *Pb.*, Solanum coagulans, *Forsk.*, SOLANACEÆ.
Foods .
Tinnas, *Hind.*, Ougeinia dalbergioides, *Benth.*, LEGUMINOSÆ.
Foods .
Tintil, *Beng.*, Tamarindus indica, *Linn.*, LEGUMINOSÆ.
Foods .
Tintre, *Beng.*, Tamarindus indica, *Linn.*, LEGUMINOSÆ.
Foods .
Tintuli, *Uriya*, Tamarindus indica, *Linn.*, LEGUMINOSÆ.
Foods .
Tira, *N.-W. P. & Oudh*, Eruca sativa, *Lam.*, CRUCIFERÆ.
Foods .
Tirunitrup-pattri, *Tam.*, Ocimum Basilicum, *Linn.*, LABIATÆ.
Foods .
Tiso, *Pb.*, Carduus nutans, *Linn.*, COMPOSITÆ.
Foods .
Tita-bateri, *Kashmir*, Lonicera quinquelocularis, *Hardwicke*, CAPRIFOLIACEÆ. Foods .
Titri, *Nep.*, Tamarindus indica, *Linn.*, LEGUMINOSÆ.
Foods .
Titri, *Pb.*, Rhus semi-alata, *Murray*, ANACARDIACEÆ.
Foods .
Titsappa, *Ass.*, Michelia Champaca, *Linn.*, MAGNOLIACEÆ.
Foods .
Tiún, *Pb.*, Artocarpus Lakoocha, *Roxb.*, URTICACEÆ.
Foods .
Tiura, *N.-W. P.*, Lathyrus sativus, *Linn.*, LEGUMINOSÆ.
Foods .
Tiuri, *N.-W. P.*, Lathyrus sativus, *Linn.*, LEGUMINOSÆ.
Foods .
Tivara, *Sind*, Avicennia officinalis, *Linn.*, VERBENACEÆ.
Foods .
Tizhu, *Pb.*, Cicer soongaricum, *Steph.*, LEGUMINOSÆ.
Foods .
Todda-maram, *Mal.*, Cycas Rumphii, *Miq.*, CYCADACEÆ.
Foods .
Toddalia, *Eng.*, Toddalia aculeata, *Pers.*, RUTACEÆ.
Foods .
Toddy, *Eng.*, Phœnix sylvestris, *Roxb.*, PALMÆ.
Foods .
Tœma-gerika, *Tel.*, Sporobolus tenacissimus, *Beauv.*, GRAMINEÆ.
Foods .
Togari, *Kan.*, Cajanus indicus, *Spreng.*, LEGUMINOSÆ.
Foods .
Togri, *Bhil.*, Indigofera pulchella, *Roxb.*, LEGUMINOSÆ.
Foods .
Tomato, *Eng.*, Lycopersicum esculentum, *Miller*, SOLANACEÆ.
Foods .
Tomi tomi, *Mal.*, Flacourtia inermis, *Roxb.*, BIXINEÆ.
Foods .
Tondi teregam, *Mal.*, Callicarpa lanata, *Wall.*, VERBENACEÆ.
Foods .
Tongrong, *Garo*, Spondias mangifera, *Pers.*, ANACARDIACEÆ.
Foods .
Toombe, *Hind.*, Lagenaria vulgaris, *Seringe*, CUCURBITACEÆ.
Foods .
Toon, *Eng.*, Cedrela Toona, *Roxb.*, MELIACEÆ.
Foods .
Torabujja, *Him. name*, Adhatoda Vasica, *Nees.*, ACANTHACEÆ.
Foods .
Toran, *Konkan*, Zizyphus rugosa, *Lamk.*, RHAMNEÆ.
Foods .

Tor-elaya, *Tel.*, Lemonia acedissima, *Linn.*, RUTACEÆ. Foods .
Tori, *Hind.*, Brassica campestris, *Linn.*, var. Napus, sub-var. toria, CRUCIFERÆ. Foods .
Toriya, *Hind.*, Brassica campestris, *Linn.*, var. Napus, sub-var. toria, CRUCIFERÆ. Foods .
Tornillo, *Eng.*, Prosopis pubescens, *Bth.*, LEGUMINOSÆ. Foods .
Torooi, *Hind.*, Luffa acutangula, *Roxb.*, CUCURBITACEÆ. Foods .
Tosa, *Nep.*, Hordeum vulgare, *Linn.*, GRAMINEÆ. Foods .
Tosh, *Him. name*, Abies Webbiana, *Lindl.*, CONIFERÆ. Foods .
Totmila, *Hind.*, Ficus hispida, *Linn. f.*, URTICACEÆ. Foods .
Totnye, *Nep.*, Polygonum molle, *Don.*, POLYGONACEÆ. Foods .
Toukkyan, *Burm.*, Terminalia tomentosa, *W. & A.*, COMBRETACEÆ. Foods .
Toukyap, *Burm.*, Putranjiva Roxburghii, *Wall.*, EUPHORBIACEÆ. Foods .
Toung-ong, *Burm.*, Arenga sacchrifera, *Labill.*, PALMÆ. Foods .
Tow Cok of China, *Eng.*, Vigna Catiang, *Endl.*, LEGUMINOSÆ. Foods .
Trekhan, *Pb.*, Acer cultratum, *Wall.*, syn. of Acer pictum, *Thunb.*, SAPINDACEÆ. Foods .
Trekhan, *Pb.*, Acer pictum, *Thunb.*, SAPINDACEÆ. Foods .
Trepatra, *Pb.*, Trifolium pratense, *Linn.*, LEGUMINOSÆ. Foods .
Trindus, *Sind*, Citrullus vulgaris, *Schrad.*, var. fistulosus, CUCURBITACEÆ. Foods .
Tripattra, *Pb.*, Marsilea quadrifolia, *Linn.*, MARSILEACEÆ. Foods .
Triwaka, *Pb.*, Rumex vesicarius, *Linn.*, POLYGONACEÆ. Foods .
Tror, *Pb.*, Polygonum polystachyum, *Wall.*, POLYGONACEÆ. Foods .
Trotak, *Pb.*, Equesetum debile, *Roxb.*, EQUESETACEÆ. Foods .
Trual, *Pb.*, Impatiens Balsamina, *Linn.*, GERANIACEÆ. Foods .
Trumba, *Pb.*, Fagopyrum esculentum, *Mœnch.*, POLYGONACEÆ. Foods .
Tsaga, *Burm.*, Michelia Champaca, *Linn.*, MAGNOLIACEÆ. Foods .
Tsarap, *North Pb.*, *Ladak to Lahoul*, Hippophœ rhamnoides, *Linn.*, ELÆAGNEÆ. Foods .
Tsat-tha-pu, *Burm.*, Pandanus odoratissimus, *Willd.*, PANDANEÆ. Foods .
Tsichyee, *Burm.*, Briedelia retusa, *Spreng.*, EUPHORBIACEÆ. Foods .
Tsiron-panna, *Mal.*, Calophyllum Wightianum, *Wall.*, GUTTIFERÆ. Foods .
Tsjána-kua, *Mal.*, Costus speciosus, *Sm.*, SCITAMINEÆ. Foods .
Tsu dza, *Naga*, Glycine Soja, *Sieb. & Zucc.*, LEGUMINOSÆ. Foods .
Tukhm malanga, *Pb.*, Salvia pumila, *Benth.*, LABIATÆ. Foods .

Tukhril, *Lepcha*, Rhus semi-alata, *Murray*, ANACARDIACEÆ.
Foods .
Tul, *Hind.*, Morus alba, *Linn.*, URTICACEÆ.
Foods .
Túl, *Pb.*, Morus indica, *Linn.*, URTICACEÆ.
Foods .
Tulasa, *Bom.*, Ocimum sanctum, *Linn.*, LABIATÆ.
Foods .
Túlasi, *Hind.*, *Beng.*, Ocimum villosum, sp., *Roxb.*, LABIATÆ.
Foods .
Tulati-pati, *Hind.*, Physalis minima, *Linn.*, SOLANACEÆ.
Foods .
Tulklu, *Hind.*, Morus alba, *Linn.*, URTICACEÆ.
Foods .
Tulouch, *Pb.*, Rubus lasiocarpus, *Smith*, ROSACEÆ.
Foods .
Tulsi, *Hind.*, *Beng.*, Ocimum villosum, sp. *Roxb.*, LABIATÆ.
Foods .
Túlsi, Krishna, *Hind.*, *Beng.*, *Tel.*, Ocimum sanctum, *Linn.*, LABIATÆ.
Foods .
Tulsi, Sacred, or Tulsi of the Hindus, *Eng.*, Ocimum sanctum, *Linn.*, LABIATÆ. Foods .
Tumal, *Hind.*, Diospyros tomentosa, *Roxb.*, EBENACEÆ.
Foods .
Túmari, *Kumaun*, Castanopsis tribuloides, *A. DC.*, CUPULIFERÆ.
Foods .
Tumba, *Hind.*, *Pb.*, Lagenaria vulgaris, *Seringe*, CUCURBITACEÆ.
Foods .
Tumbali, *Tam.*, Diospyros melanoxylon, *Roxb.*, EBENACEÆ.
Foods .
Tumberch, *Lepcha*, Mussænda frondosa, *Linn.*, RUBIACEÆ.
Foods .
Tumbi, *Tam.*, Diospyros melanoxylon, *Roxb.*, EBENACEÆ.
Foods .
Tumbika, *Tam.*, Diospyros Embryopteris, *Pers.*, EBENACEÆ.
Foods .
Tumbri, *N.-W. P.*, Marlea begoniæfolia, *Roxb.*, CORNACEÆ.
Foods .
Tumi, *Tel.*, Diospyros melanoxylon, *Roxb.*, EBENACEÆ.
Foods .
Tumik, *Tel.*, Diospyros Embryopteris, *Pers.*, EBENACEÆ.
Foods .
Tumki, *Gond.*, *Tel.*, Diospyros melanoxylon, *Roxb.*, EBENACEÆ.
Foods .
Tummer, *Gond.*, Diospyros melanoxylon, *Roxb.*, EBENACEÆ.
Foods .
Tumri, *Gond.*, Diospyros melanoxylon, *Roxb.*, EBENACEÆ.
Foods .
Tumri, (a small variety), *Hind.*, Lagenaria vulgaris, *Seringe*, CUCURBITACEÆ. Foods .
Tún, *Beng.*, *Hind.*, Cedrela Toona, *Roxb.*, MELIACEÆ.
Foods .
Tunamarum, *Tam.*, Cedrela Toona, *Roxb.*, MELIACEÆ.
Foods .
Tunani, *Pb.*, Viburnum fœtens. *Decaisne*, CAPRIFOLIACEÆ.
Foods .
Tundú, *Kan.*, Cedrela Toona, *Roxb.*, MELIACEÆ.
Foods .
Túng, *Kashmir*, Taxus baccata, *Linn.*, CONIFERÆ.
Foods .
Tunga, *Pb.*, Pistacia integerrima, *J. L. Stewart*, ANACARDIACEÆ.
Foods .

Tungcher, *Lepcha*, Antidesma Menasu, *Mull.-Arg.*, EUPHORBIACEÆ. Foods .
Tungrung, *Lepcha*, Osomanthus fragrans, *Lour.*, OLEACEÆ. Foods .
Túpa, *Bom.*, Cedrela Toona, *Roxb.*, MELIACEÆ. Foods .
Tur, *C. P.*, *Deccan*, Cajanus indicus, *Spreng.* LEGUMINOSÆ. Foods .
Turai, *Bom.*, Luffa acutangula *Roxb.*, CUCURBITACEÆ. Foods .
Turai, *Kumaun*, Luffa ægyptiaca, *Mill.*, *ex Hook. f.*, CUCURBITACEÆ. Foods .
Turi, *Hind.*, Luffa acutangula, *Roxb.*, CUCURBITACEÆ. Foods .
Turi, *Sind*, Luffa acutangula, *Roxb.*, CUCURBITACEÆ. Foods .
Turmeric, *Eng.*, Curcuma longa, *Roxb.*, SCITAMINEÆ. Foods .
Turnip, *Eng.*, Brassica alba, *H. f. & T. T.*, var. Rapa, CRUCIFERÆ. Foods .
Turnip, Swedish, *Eng.*, Brassica campestris, *Linn.*, var. campestris proper, CRUCIFERÆ. Foods .
Tusk, *North Pb.*, *Ladak to Lahoul*, Hippophæ rhamnoides, *Linn.*, ELÆAGNEÆ. Foods .
Tustus, *Pb.*, Viburnum cotinifolium, *Don.*, CAPRIFOLIACEÆ. Foods .
Tút, *Beng.*, *Hind.*, Morus indica, *Linn.*, URTICACEÆ. Foods .
Tút, *Hind.*, Morus lævigata, *Wall.*, URTICACEÆ. Foods .
Tut, *Pb.*, Morus serrata, *Roxb.*, URTICACEÆ. Foods .
Tuti, *Hind.*, Cucumis Melo, *Linn.*, var. Momordica, sp., *Roxb.*, CUCURBITACEÆ. Foods .
Tutri, *Hind.*, Morus indica, *Linn.*, URTICACEÆ. Foods .
Tuttealy, *Ass.*, Elæocarpus Varunua, *Ham.*, TILIACEÆ. Foods .
Tuver, *Bom.*, Cajanus indicus, *Spreng.*, LEGUMINOSÆ. Foods .
Tuverica, *Sans.*, Brassica campestris, *Linn.*, var. Napus, sub.-var. toria, CRUCIFERÆ. Foods .
Tuwanne, *Pb.*, Grewia villosa, *Willd.*, TILIACEÆ. Foods .

U

Uaval, *Tam.*, Sizygium jambolanum, *DC.*, MYRTACEÆ. Foods .
Ubbolu, *Kan.*, Flacourtia inermis, *Roxb.*, BIXINEÆ. Foods .
Udha, *Bom.*, Dendrocalamus strictus, *Nees.*, GRAMINEÆ. Foods .
Udid, *Deccan* Phaseolus Mungo, *Linn.*, var. Max, LEGUMINOSÆ. Foods .
Udu-gadi, *Tel.*, Penicum brizoides, *Linn.*, GRAMINEÆ. Foods .
Ughal, *Hind.*, *Pb.*, Salvadora oleoides, *Linn.*, SALVADORACEÆ. Foods .

Ughai, *Tam.*, Salvadora persica, *Garcin.*, SALVADORACEÆ.
Foods .
Uk, *Beng.*, Saccharum officinarum, *Linn.*, GRAMINEÆ.
Foods .
Ukh, *N.-W. P. & Oudh*, Saccharum officinarum, *Linn.*, GRAMINEÆ.
Foods .
Ukhari, *N.-W. P. & Oudh*, Saccharum officinarum, *Linn.*, GRAMINEÆ.
Foods .
Ukilbar-ki-munker, *Dec.*, Canna indica, *Linn.*, SCITAMINEÆ.
Foods .
Ukleel-ul-jilbul, *Arab.*, Rosmarinus officinalis, *Linn.*, LABIATEÆ.
Foods .
Uklu, *Pb.*, Viburnum fœtens, *Decaisne*, CAPRIFOLIACEÆ.
Foods .
Ulatkambal, *Beng.*, Abroma augusta, *Linn.*, STERCULIACEÆ.
Foods .
Ulu, *Beng.*, Imperata arundinacea, *Cyrill*, GRAMINEÆ.
Foods .
Umar, *Hind.*, Ficus glomerata, *Roxb.*, URTICACEÆ.
Foods .
Umbar, *C. P.*, Ficus glomerata, *Roxb.*, URTICACEÆ.
Foods .
Umbli, *Bom.*, Gnetum scandens, *Roxb.*, GNETACEÆ.
Foods .
Umbuti, *Duk.*, Oxalis corniculata, *Linn.*, GERANIACEÆ.
Foods .
Unoo, *Sans.*, Panicum miliaceum, *Linn.*, GRAMINEÆ.
Foods .
Upoo-poma, *Tel.*, Rhizophora mucronata, *Lamk.*, RHIZOPHOREÆ.
Foods .
Uppu nérle, *Kan.*, Morinda citrifolia, *Linn.*, RUBIACEÆ.
Foods .
Uppu nerle, *Kan.*, Morus alba, *Linn.*, URTICACEÆ.
Foods .
Urad, *Hind.*, Phaseolus aconitifolius, *Jacq.*, LEGUMINOSÆ.
Foods .
Urad, *Hind.*, Phaseolus Mungo, *Linn.*, var. radiatus, *Linn.*, LEGUMINOSÆ.
Foods .
Uranechra, *Tel.*, Ximenia americana, *Willd.*, OLACINEÆ.
Foods .
Urd, *Hind.*, *Oudh*, Phaseolus Mungo, *Linn.*, var. radiatus, *Linn.*, LEGUMINOSÆ Foods .
Urni, *Him. name*, Corylus Colurna, *Linn.*, CUPULIFERÆ.
Foods .
Usan, *Pb.*, Eruca sativa, *Lam.*, CRUCIFERÆ.
Foods .
Usan, *Beng.*, Terminalia tomentosa, *W. & A.*, COMBRETACEÆ.
Foods .
Usar-ki-ghas, *N.-W. P.*, Sporobolus tenacissimus, *Beauv.*, GRAMINEÆ.
Foods .
Ushit-tagari, *Tam.*, Cassia Tora, *Linn.*, LEGUMINOSÆ.
Foods .
Usirh, *Upper Ind.*, Imperata arundinacea, *Cyrill*, GRAMINEÆ.
Foods .
Usri, *Tel.*, Phyllanthus Emblica, *Linn.*, EUPHORBIACEÆ.
Foods .
Ustumri, *Gond.*, Strychnos potatorum, *Linn. f.*, LOGANIACEÆ.
Foods .
Utrain, *Hind.*, *Dec.*, Dæmia extensa, *R. Br.*, ASCLEPIADEÆ.
Foods .
Uttámani, *Tam.*, Dæmia extensa, *R. Br.*, ASCLEPIADEÆ.
Foods .

Uva, *Tam.*, *Tel.*, Dillenia indica, *Linn.*, DILLENIACEÆ.
Foods .

V

Vabbúla, *Sans.*, Acacia arabica, *Willd.*, LEGUMINOSÆ.
Foods .
Vacha, *Sans.*, Acorus Calamus, *Linn.*, AROIDEÆ.
Foods .
Vada, *Mahr.*, Ficus bengalensis, *Linn.*, URTICACEÆ.
Foods .
Vadaja, *Tel.*, Acorus Calamus, *Linn.*, AROIDEÆ.
Foods .
Vaghe, *Tam.*, Albizzia Lebbek, *Benth.*, LEGUMINOSÆ.
Foods .
Vaj, *Arab.*, Acorus Calamus, *Linn.*, AROIDEÆ.
Foods .
Vakhanda, *Bom.*, Acorus Calamus, *Linn.*, AROIDEÆ.
Foods .
Valur, *Pb.*, Solanum gracilipes, *Dcne*, SOLANACAÆ.
Foods .
Vallai-pandu, *Tam.*, Allum sativum, *Linn.*, LILIACEÆ.
Foods .
Vallanga, *Tam.*, Feronia Elephantum, *Correa.*, RUTACEÆ.
Foods .
Vallúr, *Pb.*, Cocculus Lemba, *DC.*, MENISPERMACEÆ.
Foods .
Vani, *Hind.*, *Pb.*, *Tam.*, Salvadora oleoides, *Linn.*, SALVADORACEÆ.
Foods .
Vansa, *Sans.*, Bambusa arundinacea, *Retz.*, and other species, GRAMINEÆ.
Foods .
Van-veri, *Pb.*, Pentatropis spiralis, *Dcne.*, ASCLEPIADEÆ.
Foods .
Varagu, *S. Ind.*, Panicum miliaceum, *Linn.*, GRAMINEÆ.
Foods .
Vari, *Deccan*, Panicum miliare, *Lamk.*, GRAMINEÆ.
Foods .
Vari, *Pb.*, Quercus incana, *Roxb.*, CUPULIFERÆ.
Foods .
Vasaka, *Sans.*, *Beng.*, Adhatoda Vasica, *Nees.*, ACANTHACEÆ.
Foods .
Vashambu, *Tam.*, Acorus Calamus, *Linn.*, AROIDEÆ.
Foods .
Vátána, *Deccan*, Pisum sativum, *Linn.*, LEGUMINOSÆ.
Foods .
Vavoll, *Mar.*, Mimusops Elengi, *Linn.*, SAPOTACEÆ.
Foods .
Vazhaip pazham, *Tam.*, Musa sapientum, *Linn.*, SCITAMINEÆ.
Foods .
Vedam, *Tel.*, Terminalia Catappa, *Linn.*, COMBRETACEÆ.
Foods .
Vehri, *Pb.*, Cocculus Leæba, *DC.*, MENISPERMACEÆ.
Foods .
Vela, *Tam.*, Feronia Elephantum, *Correa.*, RUTACEÆ.
Foods .
Velagá, *Tel.*, Feronia Elephantum, *Correa.*, RUTACEÆ.
Foods .
Vélip-parutti, *Tam*, Dæmia extensa, *R. Br.*, ASCLEPIADEÆ.
Foods

Vella, *Tam.*, Anthocephalus Cadamba, *Miq.*, RUBIACEÆ.
Foods .
Vellari-veral, *Tam.*, Cucumis Melo, *Linn.*, CUCURBITACEÆ.
Foods .
Vella-vengayan, *Tam.*, Allium Cepa, *Linn.*, LILIACEÆ.
Foods .
Vellay putáll, *Tam.*, Sterculia urens, *Roxb.*, STERCULIACEÆ.
Foods .
Vellulli, *Tel.*, Allium sativum, *Linn.*, LILIACEÆ.
Foods .
Vena. *Pb.*, Rhazya stricta, *Dcne.*, APOCYNACEÆ.
Foods
Vendaik-kay, *Tam.*, Hibiscus esculentus, *Linn.*, MALVACEÆ.
Foods .
Venda-kaya, *Tel.*, Hibiscus esculentus, *Linn.*, MALVACEÆ.
Foods .
Vendayam, *Tam.*, Trigonella Fœnum-grœcum, *Linn.*, LEGUMINOSÆ.
Foods .
Vendi (or Bhendi), *Tam.*, Hibiscus esculentus, *Linn.*, MALVACEÆ.
Foods .
Vengai, *Tam.*, Pterocarpus Marsupium, *Roxb.*, LEGUMINOSÆ.
Foods .
Ventagam, *Mal.*, Trigonella Fœnum-grœcum, *Linn.*, LEGUMINOSÆ.
Foods .
Vepa, *Tel.*, Melia Azadirachta, *Linn.*, MELIACEÆ.
Foods .
Vepali, *Tam.*, Holarrhena antidysenterica, *Wall.*, APOCYNACEÆ.
Foods .
Veppalay, *Tam.*, Holarrhena antidysenterica, *Wall.*, APOCYNACEÆ.
Foods .
Veppaula, *Tam.*, Holarrhena antidysenterica, *Wall.*, APOCYNACEÆ.
Foods .
Veragoo, *Eng.*, Panicum miliaceum, *Linn.*, GRAMINEÆ.
Foods .
Verasu, *Tam.*, Cordia Myxa, *Linn.*, BORAGINEÆ.
Foods .
Veri-tel-nep, *Tel.*, Xanthium strumarium, *Linn.*, COMPOSITÆ.
Foods .
Vérk-kadalal, *Tam.*, Arachis hypogæa, *Linn.*, LEGUMINOSÆ.
Foods .
Verushanaga-káya, *Tel.*, Arachis hypogæa, *Linn.*, LEGUMINOSÆ.
Foods .
Vettilee, *Tam.*, Piper Betle, *Linn.*, PIPERACEÆ.
Foods .
Ve-velam, *Tam.*, Acacia leucophlæa, *Willd.*, LEGUMINOSÆ.
Foods .
Veypale, *Tam.*, Melia Azadirachta, *Linn.*, MELIACEÆ.
Foods .
Veypam, *Tam.*, Melia Azadirachta, *Linn.*, MELIACEÆ.
Foods .
Vi, *Eng.*, Spondias dulas, ANACARDIACEÆ.
Foods .
Vibudi-patri, *Tel.*, Ocimum Basilicum, *Linn.*, LABIATÆ.
Foods .
Vidi, *Tam.*, Cordia Myxa, *Linn.*, BORAGINEÆ.
Foods .
Vilaiati kikkar, *Pb.*, Parkinsonia aculeata, *Linn.*, LEGUMINOSÆ.
Foods .
Viláyatimúga, *Bom.*, Arachis hypogæa, *Linn.*, LEGUMINOSÆ.
Foods .
Viledele, *Kan.*, Piper Betle, *Linn.*, PIPERACEÆ.
Foods .

W

Wara-gudu, *Tel.*, Cycas Ramphii, *Miq.*, CYCADACEÆ.
Foods .
Warga, *N.-W. P. & Oudh*, Cassia Fistula, *Linn.*, LEGUMINOSÆ.
Foods .
Wariaree, *Gus.*, Fœniculum vulgare, *Gærtn.*, UMBELLIFERÆ.
Foods .
Warree, *Eng.*, Panicum miliaceum, *Linn.*, GRAMINEÆ.
Foods .
Warumba, *Pb.*, Solanum xanthocarpum, *Schrad. & Wendl.*, SOLANACEÆ.
Foods .
Watana, *Bom.*, Pisum sativum, *Linn.*, LEGUMINOSÆ.
Foods .
Water-cress, Common, *Eng.*, Nasturtium officinale, *Br.*, CRUCIFERÆ.
Foods .
Water-lily, White, *Eng.*, Nymphæa alba, *Linn.*, NYMPHÆACEÆ.
Foods .
Water-melon, *Eng.*, Citrullus vulgaris, *Schrad.*, CUCURBITACEÆ.
Foods .
Wattal, *Pb.*, Euonymus fimbriatus, *Wall.*, CELASTRINEÆ.
Foods .
Wayaka, *Eng.*, Pachyrhizus angulatus, *Rich.*, LEGUMINOSÆ.
Foods .
Wilaayati-jau, *Hind.*, Avena sativa, *Linn.*, GRAMINEÆ.
Foods .
Willow, Weeping, *Eng.*, Salix elegans, *Wall.*, *Koch.*, SALICINEÆ.
Foods .
Willow, White or Huntingdon, *Eng.*, Salix alba, *Linn.*, SALICINEÆ.
Foods .
Wing-stalked-yam, *Eng.*, Dioscorea alata, *Linn.*, DIOSCOREACEÆ.
Foods .
Winri, *Him. name*, Corylus Colurna, *Linn.*, CUPULIFERÆ.
Foods .
Wodalior, *Tam.*, Acacia Catechu, *Willd.*, LEGUMINOSÆ.
Foods .
Wodier, *Tam.*, Odina Wodier, *Roxb.*, ANACARDIACEÆ.
Foods .
Wominta, *Tel.*, Gynandropsis pentaphlylla, *DC.*, CAPPARIDEÆ.
Foods .
Wood-apple, *Eng.*, Feronia Elephantum, *Correa.*, RUTACEÆ.
Foods .
Worga, *Tel.*, Panicum miliaceum, *Linn.*, GRAMINEÆ.
Foods .
Worglo (the grain), *Tel.*, Panicum miliaceum, *Linn.*, GRAMINEÆ.
Foods .
Wulawalli, *Tel.*, Dolichos biflorus, *Linn.*, LEGUMINOSÆ.
Foods .
Wulwalu, *Tel.*, Dolichos biflorus, *Linn.*, LEGUMINOSÆ.
Foods .
Wumb, *Bom.*, Nephelium longana, *Camb.*, SAPINDACEÆ.
Foods .

Y

Yae-chinya, *Burm.*, Securinega obovata, *Müll.*, EUPHORBIACEÆ.
Foods .
Yal-yæ, *Burm.*, Morinda citrifolia, *Linn.*, RUBIACEÆ.
Foods .
Yajya-domur, *Beng.*, Ficus Cunia, *Buch.*, URTICACEÆ.
Foods .

Yew, *Eng.*, Taxus baccata, *Linn.*, CONIFERÆ.
Foods .
Yira, *Kashmir*, Typha angustifolia, *Linn.*, TYPHACEÆ.
Foods .
Yúr, *Pb.*, Salix alba, *Linn.*, SALICINEÆ.
Foods .
Yúr, *Kashmir*, Salix daphnoides, *Vill.*, SALICINEÆ.
Foods .
Yurra-galjeror, *Tel.*, Trianthema monogyna, *Linn.*, FICOIDEÆ.
Foods .
Yúru, *Pb.*, Quercus Ilex, *Linn*, CUPULIFERÆ.
Foods .
Yuva, *Sans.*, Hordeum vulgare, *Linn.*, GRAMINEÆ.
Foods .

Z

Zagukel, *Pb.*, Rumex Wallichii, *Meisn.*, POLYGONACEÆ.
Foods .
Zaltún, *Afg.*, Olea cuspidata. *Royle*, OLEACEÆ.
Foods .
Zambu, *Pb.*, Prunus Padus, *Linn.*, ROSACEÆ.
Foods .
Zaminkand, *N. India*, Amorphophallus campanulatus, *Blume.*, AROIDEÆ.
Foods .
Zaminkand, *Hind.*, Dioscorea bulbifera, *Linn.*, DIOSCOREACEÆ.
Foods .
Zanda, *N. Pb. & Ladak*, Dracocephalum heterophyllum, *Benth.*, LABIATÆ.
Foods .
Zardak, *Pers.*, Daucus Carota, *Linn.*, UMBELLIFERÆ.
Foods .
Zardálu, *Hind.*, Prunus armeniaca, *Linn.*, ROSACEÆ.
Foods .
Zargal, *Pb.*, Flacourtia sepiaria, *Roxb.*, BIXINEÆ.
Foods .
Zeirishk, *Pb.*, Berberis vulgaris, *Linn.*, BERBERIDEÆ.
Foods .
Zergul, *Trans-Indus Tract. See* Calendula officinalis, *Linn.*, COMPOSITÆ.
Foods .
Zewar, *Pb.*, Bupleurum falcatum, *Linn.*, var. marginata, *Wall.*, UMBELLIFERÆ. Foods.
Zhido, *Pb.*, Lonicera hypoleuca, *Dne.*, CAPRIFOLIACEÆ.
Foods .
Ziben, *Burm.*, Zizyphus Jujuba, *Lam.*, RHAMNEÆ.
Foods .
Zimbil, *Pb.*, *Ladak*, Potamogeton gramineus, *L.*, NAIADACEÆ.
Foods .
Zimbryun, *Burm.*, Dillenia pentagyna, *Roxb.*, DILLENIACEÆ.
Foods .
Zira, *Hind.*, Carum Carui, *Linn.*, UMBELLIFERÆ.
Foods .
Zira, *Hind.*, Cuminum Cyminum, *Linn.*, UMBELLIFERÆ.
Foods .
Zirishk, *Pers.*, Berberis aristata, *DC.*, and B. Lycium, *Royle*, BERBERIDEÆ.
Foods .
Zolim-buriki, *Tam.*, Schleichera trijuga, *Willd.*, SAPINDACEÆ.
Foods .
Zonalu, *Tel.*, Zea Mays, *Linn.*, GRAMINEÆ.
Foods .

www.ingramcontent.com/pod-product-compliance
Lightning Source LLC
Chambersburg PA
CBHW021115270326
41929CB00009B/897

* 9 7 8 3 7 4 1 1 1 8 0 2 9 *